Career, Lifestyle, and Spiritual Development

Bassim Hamadeh, CEO and Publisher
Jennifer Codner, Senior Field Acquisitions Editor
Michelle Piehl, Project Editor
Abbey Hastings, Associate Production Editor
Miguel Macias, Senior Graphic Designer
Stephanie Kohl, Licensing Associate
Don Kesner, Interior Designer
Natalie Piccotti, Senior Marketing Manager
Kassie Graves, Vice President of Editorial
Jamie Giganti, Director of Academic Publishing

Cover image copyright © 2016 iStockphoto LP/guvendemir.

Printed in the United States of America.

ISBN: 978-1-5165-1047-4 (pbk) / 978-1-5165-1048-1 (br)

Career, Lifestyle, and Spiritual Development

WORK, PURPOSE, CALLING, AND GOD

Edited by Cyrus R. Williams III, Ph.D., L.P.C. and Teri Hourihan, M.A., L.P.C., N.C.C.

cognella® | ACADEMIC PUBLISHING

Contents

About the Authors

VICTOR BAEZ is a credentialed multicultural high school intervention counselor in San Diego, California. Baez is currently completing a Master of Arts in Counseling with specializations in School Counseling and Clinical Mental Health from the University of San Diego. He is best known for assisting students in identifying their potential and highlighting their strengths. He has interest in wellness, resiliency, and coping strategies for at-risk students. He also focuses on incorporating technologically driven strategies and practices in his counseling practice.

S. KENT BUTLER JR. holds a PhD in Educational Psychology: Counseling Psychology from the University of Connecticut. Butler is a Licensed Professional Counselor (LPC), Nationally Certified Counselor (NCC), and Nationally Certified School Counselor (NCSC). Faculty advisor to CHI SIGMA IOTA International Honor Society. Principal Investigator for The High-Risk Delinquent and Dependent Child Educational Research Project: Situational Environmental Circumstances Mentoring Program (SEC). President of the Association for Multicultural Counseling and Development (AMCD), 2011–2012. Representative of the American Counseling Association (ACA) Governing Council, 2015–2018. Member of AMCD's Multicultural Counseling Competencies Revisions Committee, 2014–2015, which produced the newly endorsed Multicultural Social Justice Counseling Competencies (MSJCC). Bestowed with an ACA Fellow Award in 2016. Research interests: multicultural counseling, social justice, mentoring, counseling African American males, group and school counseling, and multicultural supervision.

ERIKA R. N. CAMERON is an associate professor in the Department of Counseling and Marital and Family Therapy at the University of San Diego. Cameron has worked as a career counselor for low-income and disabled youth and adults at the City and County of Honolulu and as a professional school counselor for ten years in Hawaii and Missouri. She is an active counselor educator and enjoys learning and teaching in creative and innovative ways. Her scholarly interests include school counselor professional development, qualitative research methods, multicultural issues in counselor preparation, individual psychology, and interventions for children of military families.

HANNAH COGNETTI is a professional school counselor in Upstate New York. Cognetti has an MA in Counseling from the University of San Diego and is a certified professional school counselor in California and New York. She has a background in college admissions and is passionate about career and college selection. Her research interests are focused on multiculturalism and how it affects students' career and college choices.

KATHIE ERWIN is a Licensed Mental Health Counselor, National Certified Counselor, National Certified Gerontological Counselor, Diplomate in Clinical Mental Health, and associate professor at the School of Psychology and Counseling at Regent University. Erwin has an EdD in Counseling Psychology from the University of Sarasota (now Argosy), an MA in Counseling from Liberty University, and a BA from Eckerd College. She is a board member of two major counseling organizations: Florida Mental Health Counselors Association and Green Cross Academy of Traumatology, and a Certified Field Traumatologist and director of Tampa Trauma Education Center. She is the author of six academic books on aging and gerontology and has earned a three-year appointment on the Fulbright Specialist roster for international teaching and research.

JOCELYN FOWLER holds an MS in Marriage and Family Therapy from the University of Alabama. Fowler is a PhD student in Medical Family Therapy at Saint Louis University and an adjunct professor and student supervisor at the University of Alabama. She serves as a therapy consultant for the Capstone Village Assisted Living and Dementia Wing.

SANNYU MCDONALD HARRIS holds a Masters in Counseling from North Carolina A&T State University. She is an Employee Assistance Counseling Program therapist for a local hospital in Greensboro, North Carolina where she is a Licensed Professional Counselor. She is a third-year doctoral student at Regent University in Virginia Beach. Sannyu's research interests include a focus on calling, career development and advocacy. Sannyu also has interests in the intersectionality of gender, race, culture and multigenerational experiences and their impact on communication and relationships.

PRISCILLA MONDT currently serves as Chief, Chaplain service at a Veterans Administration facility. Dually credentialed in mental health (PhD, Counseling Education and Supervision) and spirituality (Master of Divinity), she specializes in the intersection of the two fields. Dr. Mondt answered this chapter's call for a spiritual approach theory to career development that reflects current business practices and embraces religious values with her own theory called SERVICE.

NEVIN J. HEARD is a doctoral candidate in the Counseling Education program at the College of Education and Human Performance, University of Central Florida. Heard holds an MA in Clinical Counseling from the Ohio State University. His primary research focuses on intersectionality while incorporating a social justice lens. Specifically, his research entails investigating concepts such as wellness and equity within populations who are racial and ethnic minorities, LGBTQ+, affected by HIV/AIDS, and of lower socioeconomic status.

TERI HOURIHAN is a Licensed Professional Counselor and Nationally Credentialed Counselor. Hourihan works full time as a clinician in an outpatient behavioral health agency and an inpatient behavioral agency. Her specialties are chemical dependency issues, trauma, and adolescent and adult services. She is passionate about areas of suicide prevention, trauma work using eye movement desensitization and reprocessing (EMDR), addiction treatment in group settings, supervising masters-level interns, and multifamily counseling. She is a native of Arizona and currently the president of the Arizona Association of Counselor Education and Supervision, a division of the Arizona Counseling Association. She is a doctoral student at Regent University in the Counselor Education and Supervision PhD program, and a research and teaching assistant for Dr. Lee Underwood. Teri enjoys advocating for underserved populations, volunteering in her church, spending time with her family, and studying at local coffeehouses.

NICOLE G. JOHNSON has a PhD in Counselor Education and Supervision from Regent University and is a Licensed Professional Counselor, Certified Advanced Alcohol and Drug Counselor, and Certified Co-Occurring Disorder Professional Diplomate. Johnson currently serves as a Visiting Assistant Professor in the Community and Trauma Counseling Program at Thomas Jefferson University in Philadelphia, Pennsylvania. Her primary research interests include addictions treatment effectiveness, behavioral consequences of exposure to sexual imagery, mental health stigma in African American communities, perceptions of mental health disorders and treatment in the Black church, pastoral stress and suicidality, and the impact of trauma on behavior. She is the owner of NGJohnson Counseling & Consulting.

BRENDA KECK is a licensed Marriage and Family Therapist and a third-year student in Regent University's PhD in Counselor Education program. For more than a decade, Keck has practiced as an MFT with a focus on trauma recovery and families that live and work cross-culturally. She is a third culture kid who has served families in over 10 countries by providing brief therapy, debriefings, and training on issues of cross-cultural living, compassion fatigue, and raising resilient families. She has led workshops at national conferences, served as Global Adjunct Faculty at Le Tourneau University, and as a teaching assistant in Regent University's master's and doctoral programs.

JASMINE L. KNIGHT holds a doctorate in Counselor Education and Supervision from Old Dominion University and is a licensed School Counselor in the state of Virginia. Knight currently works as an assistant professor in the counseling program at Regent University in Virginia Beach, Virginia, with both masters and doctoral students. Prior to Regent, she taught in the counseling and human services program at Roosevelt University in Chicago and worked for several years as a professional school counselor with Newport News Public Schools in Virginia. She has a passion for the field of school counseling and her research interest includes school counselor preparation, specifically college and career readiness; relational aggression; and how school counselors develop and implement multicultural competence. She has published and presented regionally and nationally on various topics such as child and adolescent spirituality, relational aggression, career development, multicultural competence, and working with African American families.

MAYRA MASSEY holds an MA in Marriage and Family Therapy from Abilene Christian University and is currently a doctoral student in the Medical Family Therapy program at

Saint Louis University. Massey is a Medical Family Therapy Research Fellow working in the area of research and providing medical family therapy and behavioral medicine services at SLUCare family medicine clinics. Her research interests include children and families, caregivers, chronic illness, romantic relationship quality, cultural competency, cultural diversity in therapy, and play therapy. Mayra enjoys spending time with her husband and two dogs, Gracie and Zeke; traveling; volunteering at her church; and listening to and playing music.

MICHELLE D. MITCHELL is a doctoral candidate in the Counseling Education and Supervision Department at the University of Central Florida. Mitchell holds an MS.Ed in Mental Health Counseling from Duquesne University and is a Licensed Professional Counselor. Her primary research interests include multiculturalism, advocacy counseling, assessment, and scale development.

DIXIE MEYER holds an M.Ed and PhD in Counseling from University of Missouri-Saint Louis State University. She works at Saint Louis University in the Department of Family and Community Medicine. She is a faculty member in the Behavioral Health Division, and teaches in the master's in Marriage and Family Therapy and Medical Family Therapy programs and in the doctorate in Medical Family Therapy Program. She is a licensed professional counselor and a nationally certified counselor. Her research interests include neurobiological applications in counseling, couples counseling, drama therapy, trauma, and attachment.

YASHIKA D. NEAVES holds an M.Ed in Counseling from Northwestern State University and is a PhD student in Counselor Education and Supervision at Regent University. Neaves works for the U.S. Department of Defense (DoD) on interagency policy and congressional issues related to military pre-separation counseling, psychosocial interventions, transition, and reintegration. She is an adjunct professor at the University of Valley Forge and serves as Education Director on the Northern Virginia Licensed Professional Counselors (NVLPC) Board. Yashika is an Armed Forces veteran, a military spouse, and the daughter of a retired Army officer.

KAITLYN C. STAFFORD holds a BS in psychology from Louisiana State University and an MSW from Florida State University and is currently pursuing her PhD in Counselor Education and Supervision at Regent University. Stafford is independently licensed to practice clinical social work in Alabama and Florida. She is an EMDR-trained clinician and her clinical specialties include treating trauma and addiction in adults, service members, and veterans. Her current research interests include military spouses' career and life satisfaction, professional identity, and the treatment of trauma and addiction. Kaitlyn is proudly married to a Reconnaissance Marine.

TAYLOR WAGONSELLER is a professional school counselor in San Diego, California. Wagonseller's interest in counseling focuses on equity and successful pathways for all students. She has a passion in career technical education and helping to further develop this program within California. Working within the high school setting, she continually sees the need for college and career counseling to evolve with the ever-evolving workplace demands. She believes showing students how to navigate their interests, skills, and futures is one of the best parts of being a counselor.

CYRUS R. WILLIAMS III has a PhD in Counselor Education and Supervision from the University of Florida and is a Licensed Professional Mental Health Counselor in both Florida and Virginia. Williams is an Associate Professor and the director of the CES PhD program at Regent University and teaches in both the master's and doctoral counseling programs. His overall research interest centers on career development and the intersection of ethnicity and social economic status as it pertains to mental health. Additional research interests include multiculturalism, advocacy, and addictions counseling. He has worked for more than twenty years in various administrative positions in higher education at the University of Connecticut, the University of Florida, and Regent University, helping students find their purpose in life through essential mental health counseling and mentorship. His focus centers on career, spirituality, calling, and meaning. He is the owner of Impact Counseling, Coaching and Consulting, LLC, a private mental health counseling practice.

Foreword

Cyrus R. Williams III, PhD, LPC

> *And they heard the sound of the LORD God walking in the garden in the cool of the day, and the man and his wife hid themselves from the presence of the LORD God among the trees of the garden.*
>
> Genesis 3:8 English Standard Version

I grew up in an urban area in a single-parent family with two sisters. We were very low income, we lived in an undereducated community, and I had few resources and mentors. Work, for people like me, was clearly defined: it was something to endure. For me, work had nothing to do with calling, purpose, or meaning. I didn't even know such concepts existed. We worked to eat; nothing more, nothing less. Work allowed us to pay our bills, buy food, and survive. At the time, this perspective served me well.

We worked to eat; nothing more, nothing less.

From early childhood, I absorbed the attitudes of my mother and the other women in the community. They often talked about how they hated work and frequently proclaimed that no matter how hard they labored, they still could not pay their bills. I remember my mother coming home daily and complaining about her two jobs; she would instruct me, "When you get a job, make sure you do the least work and get paid the most you can." She would tell me, "Your boss doesn't care about you. The company only wants to get as much work out of you as possible. They'll fire you whenever they feel like it." At the time, my mother had a ninth-grade education and was working in food service, so I completely understood her perspective.

When the adults in my community complained about their jobs, they were teaching me that work was in no way enjoyable and was to be avoided at all costs. That was my impression of work for most of my early life. I admit it was jaded, but this perspective served me well as I progressed through school, college, and beyond. It simplified my life; I did not have to deal with the pressures of listening for a calling, trying to find my purpose, or finding meaning in work.

My mother was right; work was torture, drudgery to be endured.

Meanwhile, after barely squeaking through high school (and I mean barely), I got my first real job at a film-processing kiosk (that is a real thing; Google it ☺). It was not nearly as strenuous as my mother's job; all I did was take orders, give people their pictures, and cash them out. My mother's words seemed strange in this context, because I loved working. I felt like a traitor telling her that I was avoiding hard work, while I was being considered for a management position.

I eventually realized that my work was meaningless; the pay was terrible; and at 18 years of age, I had no future. My whole life lay before me but I had no marketable skills. So, what could I do? I did what many low-income minority kids did in the 1980s; I went to community college.

My entire goal was to put off working as long as I could and then try to get a better job than my mother. I hoped my work experience would be better than hers. But no, all my negative attitudes were only reinforced by what followed.

After my first year in college I went to work at a chemical plant. My dad, a custodian at the plant, was able to get me a job "pulling pans" on rotating shifts throughout the summer. For two long summers I worked seven days a week, alternating weekly between first, second, and third shifts. My work consisted of draining pans full of extremely volatile chemicals while dressed in a full HAZMAT suit equipped with an oxygen tank. The work was hot, physical, and dangerous.

My mother was right; work was torture, drudgery to be endured. I hated the job. The only advantages were that it did not require any thought and although it did not pay nearly as much as I liked, I still earned more than my peers. At least the job motivated me to keep studying; I dreamed of one day working in middle management so I could supervise the people who pulled the pans.

After a couple years, I graduated from a community college and then transferred to a state university, furthering my objective to be the first person in my family to graduate from college. By that time, my goal was to get a job running a hotel in Atlantic City. I was aiming for something that would set me apart from my mother and our community. Little did I know that I was in for a major mental adjustment.

The summer prior to my senior year in college, I had the opportunity to work as a peer advisor to low-income, first-generation college students. I discovered that I truly enjoyed teaching, mentoring, and helping others. For the first time, I had work that was meaningful to me. I had discovered my calling and purpose.

I discovered that almost without trying I had developed
a career, a passion, a purpose, and a calling.

That fall I swiftly shifted my academic focus from finance and economics to the helping professions. This rocked my world; I could not understand this concept of loving your work.

I knew I wanted to counsel college students; I desired to teach, mentor and advocate. This was something I loved and it quickly became my passion.

Here was another shock to my system. Remember, I had been taught to view work as a necessary evil. Passion for work was a totally new concept. It was a major milestone in my own career development when I could accept that it was okay to have work I actually enjoyed.

As I continued my education, pursuing a master's degree in counseling, I discovered that almost without trying I had developed a career, a passion, a purpose, and a calling. I was blessed to be able to work my dream job at my dream school after I earned my degree. My work was gratifying and meaningful. I was even happy.

Work and worship are not separate entities; God is involved in every aspect of my life.

At the same time, I became committed to my faith. As a young Christian, I became keenly aware that my God was ordering my steps. This only added to my hope for great things in the future. Five years into my dream job, I was offered a position at a major university hundreds of miles and a 22-hour drive away from my friends and family. Confident of God's provision, I accepted the position.

I enjoyed my work and was happy with the way my life was turning out. Then I accomplished my next career milestone: I was fired!

Fired! Why? I was a hard worker, loved by all, and I got along with most everybody. After recovering from the shock, I was able to evaluate the experience. It seemed like God was giving me a wake-up call. I had strayed off course. I had become so focused on my goal of becoming the vice president of Student Services that I had lost track of why I was really there: to serve. I was starting to worship my career; that's why God stopped me cold.

Soon thereafter, God provided me an entry-level job at an entry-level salary, way below what my experience and skills warranted. It was humbling but necessary. I needed some time to reorient myself along the lines of God's calling. His message came loud and clear: "You work for me. I did not call you to just a job; I called you to listen and wait and move where I want you to move."

That sobered me up. For the first time, I understood that:

- my work is only a part of my ministry and calling;
- vocation is not just about my work;
- anything that becomes bigger than my relationship with God is not good; and
- work and worship are not separate entities—God is involved in every aspect of my life.

I then set out to realign my focus upon God and to walk with Him throughout the day.

Amazingly, after God had humbled and humiliated me for a short time, He restored me tenfold! In addition to finding a great job—a job I was not qualified for, by the way—I also found my wife and before long had two delightful babies in tow. What a crazy couple of years! I was back on track to become vice president of Student Services, but this time I did not get caught up in the goal. I had learned my lesson.

I submitted my desires to God and asked what He wanted me to do. God's cryptic reply was that he wanted me to increase my territory. As a new Christian, I had no idea what that phrase meant. I had never come across what is popularly termed "The Prayer of Jabez," but eventually I was directed to the book of First Chronicles in the Bible and read "Now Jabez called on the God of Israel, saying, 'Oh that You would bless me indeed and enlarge my border, and that Your hand might be with me, and that You would keep me from harm that it may not pain me!' And God granted him what he requested" (I Chronicles 4:10) New American Standard Bible (NASB).

> *If your intention is to honor God and build his Kingdom, then God will gladly expand your territory. He will increase your influence and provide the resources necessary for this work.*

Upon reflection, I realized I had been praying my entire life for God to enlarge my territory so that I could help others. An immature Christian like me would normally never pray like this, because it seems selfish. I can only say that God placed this desire in my spirit even before I was a Christian. I learned that if your intention is to honor God and build his Kingdom, then God will gladly expand your territory. He will increase your influence and provide the resources necessary for this work.

After much prayer and listening, it became clear this meant I should quit my job, forego my dream of becoming VP of Student Services, go back to college, and become a professor in clinical mental health. As I look back now, I can see how my life experiences prepared me for this work: as a child learning common work attitudes from my community, my own work experiences, working as a mentor and counselor in undergraduate school, obtaining a master's degree in counseling, and being viewed as a counselor by peers and instructors. Today, some twenty years after I started, I am still here, still listening and growing and making mistakes, still connected and listening to God, still trying to get it right the first time to avoid the necessity of being humbled again.

You would think that with all these years and advantages I would become more confident as I grew older and wiser, but the opposite is actually true. I have spent years untangling my own view of work only to encounter my former misconceptions in my clients. Words like work, career, purpose, meaning, vocation, and calling are often used interchangeably and inconsistently, only adding to the confusion.

At the same time, I discovered that often what presents itself as a work issue has its roots in relational and identity issues and a deep, often unacknowledged, hunger of spirit. At first, I didn't see the connection between what my clients thought about work and the struggles they experienced in their personal lives.

The key to this problem became clear in an unusual place: church. One Sunday I had basically tuned the minister out because I knew the story of Adam and Eve and the Garden of Eden. Sure, sure, blah, blah, blah, I thought; it's all about sin and how we all are sinners like the First Couple. Prepared to be bored, I proceeded to let my mind wander.

I was yanked back into the present by the pastor crying out "Adam, where are you?" In that moment, I heard not just the pastor's voice but my God's voice searching and filled with longing to be with his children, Adam and Eve. For the first time, I got it! Yes, God gave Adam and Eve work to do, but more important than the work was walking with God himself. In the same paragraph, it says "And they heard the sound of the LORD God walking in the garden in the cool of the day… ." The revelation that I received was that God did not separate work from fellowship. God is with us all the time, not just when we are at church or Bible study. He is with us when we work and when we rest. In fact, He walks and talks with us while we work. All we need to do is listen.

It became clear to me that my clients were suffering because they did not look at work as co-laboring with God; without God in the picture, work was just that: work.

God wants a relationship with us that is unbroken and continuous.

We may put God in a box and feel we cannot bring him into our work, but God wants to be with us no matter where we are. Since we spend so much time at work, of course He would want to walk with us as He did with Adam and Eve in the Garden. It came to me so clearly that morning at church. God wants a relationship with us that is continuous. Unbroken fellowship is what He desires. He wants not only to provide us with a purpose and a calling for our lives but He also wants to walk with us, to guide us and talk to us while we work at what He has given us to do.

God longs for our presence, for our questions, for our listening, for us to understand His deepest desires. Work has less to do with the labor, our identity, or our status than with deep fellowship. Labor was intended as an opportunity for us to walk with our God; it serves as a symbol of how we can walk alongside God in every area of life.

Since that day, I have continued my work on the inter- and intrarelationships between work and the inner workings of humans: self-identity and spiritual health. Currently, I work as a full-time faculty member at a Christian-based university. I also work as a licensed mental health counselor.

My research focus remains the same as my undergraduate passion: working with college students around career and life issues. I also conduct research on career development, addictions, and marital counseling. In my clinical work I focus on the influence of spirituality, mental health, and calling upon our work, life, and relationships.

Because I teach career development and counseling to master's and PhD students, I can see the clear need for a holistic and spiritually focused textbook for students to use in their graduate work.

Labor was intended as an opportunity for us to walk with our God.

This book shares the fruit of decades of personal growth and clinical experience in helping others as well as ongoing study of the latest research literature on the subjects of career development and career counseling. It includes the results of my wrestling to understand how work and spirituality interrelate. It also contains the results of research based on the convergence of my dual focus on career counseling and career development.

I created this book because I see in my counseling practice, in my work as a professor, and in life in general that many people, like me, inherited a twisted perspective on work. Some view it with distaste, as something to endure. Others attach their worth and identity to their work. A third group of people takes it further: they love work and identify with it so thoroughly that self gets lost. This group becomes their work. They eventually discover that although they may love their job, their job cannot love them back.

Each of these work perspectives, if persisted in, may manifest over time in the form of feelings of futility and insignificance, mental health distress, physical ailments, family tensions, or distress across an entire community.

This book is designed to help the reader address these issues by

- clarifying what work is and, of equal importance, what it is not;
- accurately defining terms that are used to describe work;
- portraying the mental health issues that can result from a twisted perception of work;
- explaining how our perspective on work can affect our happiness;
- providing activities and strategies for discovering one's own purpose and calling;
- detailing exercises and approaches to use to uncover jobs, careers, and occupations in line with one's purpose and calling;
- outlining strategies to help one live a life that is holistic and spiritually based; and
- providing the reader with activities to grow—personally and spirituality—as well as help others to grow and change.

This book is intended to help you first unlearn misconceptions about work, purpose, and calling and then assist as you rebuild. The objective is to establish a fresh, personal understanding of the 21st century workforce and how it relates to your calling. The spiritual aspect of this book will invite you to explore this facet of yourself as deeply as you wish. Overall, my hope is that you will be able to live a balanced life as you care for body, mind, and spirit and walk in the purpose God has provided you.

It is my desire that no matter your education, abilities, life stage, or the job that you currently have or aspire to have, you will understand that defining yourself by your job is not healthy. Such absorption will eventually cause mental health issues such as anxiety, depression, and general unhappiness. A healthier perspective is to understand that

- you work for God (Colossians 3:23–24);
- you have other callings and life roles and work is just one of them; and
- God designed work so that we can fellowship with him and receive guidance, direction, and purpose from Him (James 4:8).

RATIONALE FOR THE BOOK

This book is a much-needed text for a graduate-level career and lifestyle development class or a human services class at the undergraduate level. It can also be used in divinity or other faith-based programs. The main focus of the book is to aid faculty in faith-based colleges and universities who teach in counseling/helping professionals-in-training programs. This book was created as a primary text for faculty to use to empower students who are preparing to work with clients who desire to understand their life, work, and vocational calling in a therapeutic setting. Specifically, this book includes mainstream theories and theorists, counseling practices and standards, and scriptures that reinforce these concepts. This book will also include spirituality-focused case studies, interventions, and activities for faculty to use to challenge students and for students to implement with their clients. Finally, this text is designed to be easy to read and in line with the counseling standards put forth by CAREPP, NCDA, ASERVIC, and other counseling standards and competencies. Biblical and spiritual references are integrated for further growth and examination. Stated plainly, this text will provide faculty with all of the content needed to satisfy the requirements for a secular class as well as the information, activities, and case studies to transform teaching career development into a spiritual quest to discover calling as opposed to just a secular quest to find meaningful work.

PURPOSE OF THE BOOK

This book provides comprehensive details regarding the process of career counseling and career development. Additionally, it is intended to aid faculty who desire to integrate spirituality into career counseling and development and expand students' idea of what calling and purpose are in regards to work. The motivation of this book is to provide a spiritual perspective and overlay to career counseling, lifestyle, and theories, and to amplify content that is missing from secular textbooks—for instance, calling, meaning, purpose, and God. In other words, this book will provide the reader with essential information about the career counseling process and specific career theories and theorists, all from a spiritual perspective. It will also provide a foundation for helping professionals-in-training to understand and implement spiritually focused career counseling when working with clients. Finally, the book is designed to be easy to read, be faith focused, and provide useful case studies, activities, and interventions that can be implemented when working with clients who are interested in exploring God's calling in their lives, both spiritually and vocationally.

TARGET AUDIENCE

This book is targeted to college and university professors and teachers who teach in counselor/helping professionals-in-training programs. Specifically, this book can be used as a main text for graduate and undergraduate training programs. Ultimately, the book was created to aid faculty seeking to teach, empower, and provide opportunities for helping professionals grow and learn about spirituality, calling, purpose, and vocation from a faith-based viewpoint.

USE OF CASE SCENARIOS AND INTERVENTION

This text will offer up case studies, interventions, and activities that are designed to help counselors-in-training to learn, expand, and explore their understanding of work, spirituality, and meaning. The case studies, activities, and interventions can also be used when counseling clients.

SECTIONAL DIVISIONS OF BOOK

Section I: Foundations of Career Development, Counseling, and Spirituality

The first section of the book will address the history of work and what work was originally intended to accomplish from a scriptural and secular perspective. It untangles the terms, myths, history, and philosophy of work.

Chapter 1: Introduction—History of Calling and Career Counseling

Chapter 1 will begin with an articulation of the current state of work within American culture as opposed to God's original design and intention of work. The tone of this chapter will be a serious, but optimistic, description of work in the 21st century. There are serious threats that affect the workforce, such as decreased loyalty of both the employee and the employers as well as layoffs, lower pay, and other negative aspects. However, the workforce remains one of the most important institutions in our society and the one place of interface between religious and secular values. Work is also the place where God speaks to us, provides for us, and offers us an opportunity to take care of our family and our community and to worship Him. As such, the focus will be on changing our understanding of work and its relationship to our relationship to God.

This chapter addresses many of the distractions, stressors, and anxieties that affect individuals' abilities to determine their call and purpose as well as how society has elevated work to a level of idolatry. Specific topics that affect the workforce such as social media, workaholism, and stress and anxiety related to work will be discussed. Focus will be placed on the juxtaposition between the secular and biblical perspective of work. Also, the numerous, confusing terms that are used when discussing labor, including work, vocation, avocation, meaning, purpose, and calling will be outlined. From a secular standpoint, this chapter will provide the reader with the history of career development. Definitions of terms and information concerning the differences in perception and philosophy regarding career development and counseling from a spiritual versus a secular standpoint will be outlined.

Chapter 2: An Ethical (Wonderful) Counselor

This chapter will continue focus on the many factors in society that affect individuals in the workplace, however from a helping professional standpoint. Literature concerning the differences between religion and spirituality will be discussed. The focus will be to explain the expectations and standards of an ethical counselor. Specific counseling standards and competencies that focus on spirituality, career counseling in general, multicultural competency, and, most importantly, the CACREP Standards will be illustrated.

This chapter will define the role, responsibility, and boundaries for therapists, pastors, and lay counselors working with clients. A most difficult challenge for helping professionals and counselors is to not be overly enmeshed with the clients. The professional is seeking to provide insight, understanding, growth, and resources. Helping professionals are particularly vulnerable to this enmeshment because of the importance that is placed on "saving the client." Professional boundaries in counseling are clear, but that boundary is often blurred. The desire to help may look more like telling, and there may be an over reliance on assessments or a focus on finding jobs for clients as opposed to challenging clients to focus on understanding the why as opposed to the what. This chapter seeks to aid helping professionals focus on calling rather than vocation, gifts over talents, and waiting (serving) over waiting (not moving). To help protect counselors, instruction is offered for how they are to think of themselves in relation to the needs of their clients. Finally, it is vital for the counselor-in-training to have a well-defined definition and level of comfort regarding calling and purpose. Additionally, they must understand their ethical limits and the extent of their responsibility as they provide career counseling. The objective is for the counselor to be close to the client's struggle but separated from the client.

Chapter 3: Career Counseling, Mental Health, and Assessment

Prior to facilitating growth, the helping professional must be able to engage with the client and facilitate an intake as well as discuss how they can be of help to the client. Chapter 3 will focus on how to conduct an intake specifically for career counseling as well as the key elements of a treatment plan. This chapter discusses the intersection between mental health and career counseling. These two aspects of life cannot be separated; however, this is a very delicate balance that the career counselor has to navigate. Details regarding understanding the difficulty of being lost and without a purpose will be provided. The chapter will also discuss what it is like to be floundering at different stages of life. The goal is to label these feelings and be able to normalize thoughts, feelings, and behaviors as we pass through these seasons of our growth and development.

Section II: Overview of Career Development Theory

Section II constitutes the biggest portion of the book. These chapters will discuss the major career counseling theories and theorists. It will include a review of the various stages of career development, the issues that occur in each of the stages and, most importantly, how to help clients develop, grow, and discover their purpose and calling at different stages of their life. Specifically, these chapters will offer greater detail as to how to recognize, aid, and guide individuals at different ages and stages of life. Also, the chapters will include additional resources for the readers as well as a Christian perspective to the theories where appropriate. The following theories will be discussed in each chapter.

Chapter 4: Modern Career Counseling Theory

This chapter will begin with a summary of the guidance movement, as this is the beginning point of the counseling field. This will lead into the work of Parsons and Williamson as the first persons to make significant headway in the counseling field regarding career counseling. Nonetheless, it is noted that the career counseling movement started much earlier than the movement begun by these famous early theorists. The trait and factor theory is described in detail along with the work adjustment theory and Holland's type theory. Several occupational tools are described that today give direction for career counselors to follow.

Chapter 5: Postmodern Career Counseling

The postmodern career counseling approaches are the theories most current in the field today. This chapter will provide a critique of Krumboltz's social learning theory, the social cognitive career theories, and the constructivistic and narrative approaches to career counseling. The author of Chapter 5 will also speak to the role of professional career counselors and the responsibilities they take in their approach to counseling using these theories.

Chapter 6: Spiritual Approaches to Career Theory

This chapter highlights the specific nature of spirituality in career counseling with clients through theory. The author will speak about how to engage clients in career counseling despite varied belief systems of client and counselor. How to integrate spirituality ethically and responsibly with clients will also be summarized in addition to how to think about spirituality in light of client care within a career counseling domain.

Section III: Facilitating Clients' Call

The chapters in Section III will focus on equipping helping professionals and counselors-in-training to aid clients to discover their vocational strengths, understand how to set their path, and how to reach their career goals. Furthermore, these chapters will discuss these issues from a traditional perspective. Facilitating and discovering what God wants us to accomplish both vocationally and in life in general will be discussed in each chapter.

Chapter 7: Career Development in Elementary and Middle School

Our calling from God comes early in our lives. This is an important time to begin the career development process. Chapter 7 will focus on helping youth to focus on making a life instead of making a living. This chapter will talk about how a helping professional can help this population pay attention to what is going on in their lives and how God is speaking to them. Details concerning helping youth as they explore vocations and understanding purpose and calling will be discussed in this chapter.

Chapter 8: Career Development in High School

This chapter will discuss this generally awkward period when it comes to purpose and calling. Adolescents are reviewing pressure internally and externally, they are trying to decide if they should go to college, and where they should go. Parents are heavy influences on these individuals, which can be good or bad. Additionally, adolescents are at an age where they are coming to grips with their desires, aptitudes, values, and personality. This chapter also provides instruction in what to do with the assessment tools that are popular among helping professionals, particularly in career counseling. Instruments such as the Holland Self-Directed Search and the Myers-Briggs as well as spiritually focused gifting assessments are frequently used in initial sessions with the client and are often the focus of the treatment plan. It is suggested that counselors decrease the use of these instruments and increase the use of nonconventional assessments that require clients to rely on their spirituality.

Chapter 9: The Quarter-Life Crisis

This chapter will focus on emerging adults, those twenty somethings who, although they went to school and fulfilled all of the academic, social, and political tasks necessary to be successful, now realize that their life is not going as planned. As such, this population is frustrated, unemployed, anxious, depressed, and angry. Their future does not look promising, their relationships with their parents and peers are fractured, they are confused, and some are paralyzed when they think about the future. This is a new and popular area of research that focuses on the generational work, life, and culture of millennials.

Chapter 10: Job Loss and Transitions

This chapter will focus on the uniqueness of the 21st century workforce, where many adults have had to transition to other positions because of downsizing or and because they were fired later in their career. The focus of the chapter will be on helping this population evaluate their skills, knowledge, and abilities and to understand and address the mental health and personal issues associated with having to change career at a later age in life.

Section IV: Counseling Multicultural and Distinctive Populations

Section IV focuses on chapters that highlight distinct groups in the field that career counselors will at some point likely come across in the counseling session. Knowing how to provide all clients with ethical career counseling focus is a must in the field of career counseling.

Chapter 11: The Purpose of Multiculturalism and Social Justice in Holistic Career Development

This chapter presents literature, examples, and practical interventions for conducting career counseling to specific populations, such as ethnic and cultural minorities.

Chapter 12: Career Counseling and Gender Issues

Gender roles in the workplace have radically changed since the 1970s largely due to social and political forces. As new career opportunities opened for women and the economy hit several downturns, the dual career couple became the norm rather than the exception in both Christian and secular households. The dual career couple faces both challenges and benefits in blending their work demands with their priorities for the relationship, parenting, job advancement, and role satisfaction in both personal and work life. This chapter looks at career counseling theories and practical realities for dual career couples who seek to find satisfaction in both career and spiritual life.

Chapter 13: Counseling LGBTQ Groups

This chapter focuses on clients from lesbian, gay, bisexual, transgender, and queer (LGBTQ) populations and career counseling specific with this group. The author of the LGBTQ chapter served as president for the Association for Lesbian, Gay, Bisexual, and Transgender Issues in Counseling (ALGBTIC) division of the Arizona Counseling Association during the writing of this chapter. Therefore, this chapter highlights this population in general as well the specific discrimination issues presenting in career roles for LGBTQ people. The author's inside experience with advocating for this group is enhanced through current research regarding ways to work competently with the LGBTQ community. In career placement, for instance, LGBTQ people in certain states can be fired or discriminated against without any repercussions for their employer. When career counselors begin to work with this group, they need to realize that there is more at stake for the client who is fearful of coming out to their employer as transgender, for example. This chapter will help career counselors and students realize the circumstances across the nation regarding LGBTQ persons and the need for competent counselors to be prepared to work with them.

Chapter 14: Career Counseling and Individuals with Disabilities

Career counselors need to have a general understanding of some of the issues they can run into when working with persons with disabilities concerning job placement and counseling services. This is a population that should not go unnoticed, as counselors are also expected to advocate for their clients when they enter their counseling rooms. By realizing that not everyone has the same benefits in life and that hardships are experienced by all people differently, counselors can provide a standard of care that is empathic and genuine.

Section V: Career Counseling with Special Populations

This last section of chapters is based on the special populations not already considered in the previous section. These populations include military personnel, third culture kids, and people in religious vocations. This is an opportunity for the reader to engage in learning about what special considerations to take when working with people from these backgrounds. It also is to be noted that it is important for the career counselor to realize that all clients enter with unique backgrounds; therefore, continued learning is necessary throughout a career as a counselor. These chapters highlight the basics of working with these groups, but further reading and education is needed if counselors plan to work exclusively with individuals from these groups.

Chapter 15: Career Counseling and the Military
The authors of Chapter 15 are well informed regarding counseling military personnel. Each of them is a military spouse and one has served in the military. Therefore, each has an inside perspective regarding this population. This chapter aims to provide an understanding of the military and how treatment through counseling this population is utilized. The various service branches, rank structures, and language in the military is summarized along with some history of American wars. An outline of not only the challenges faced by service persons but also the challenges that befall their families is provided. Career counseling challenges are described as well.

Chapter 16: Career Counseling and Third Culture Kids
This chapter is unique because there is not much literature regarding the impact third culture kids experience when they develop in a world unlike themselves. Like other chapter authors who have personal closeness to the subject, the authors of Chapter 16 are each third culture kids: one is an American who lives in Germany and the other is an American who was raised in East Africa and lives in California. They start off this chapter with common third culture kids' characteristics, continue with discussion about the population's lifetime development in this unique setting, and end with how to apply career counseling interventions to clients from these backgrounds. Career development and life challenges for third culture kids are also described.

Chapter 17: Career Counseling and Religious Vocations
This chapter will further discuss life roles and responsibilities of life and how to balance them. Details concerning how to help clients focus on all of their life roles and responsibilities with the goal of integrating them instead of compartmentalizing them will be discussed. Finally, this chapter focuses on the exploration and meaning of vocational interests related to careers in ministry, career development for people in religious vocations, and career development considerations for career counselors working with individuals in these vocations.

Foundations of Career Development, Counseling, and Spirituality

1

Introduction – History of Calling and Career Counseling

Cyrus R. Williams III, PhD, LPC

> *8 Then the man and his wife heard the sound of the Lord God as he was walking in the garden in the cool of the day, and they hid from the Lord God among the trees of the garden. 9 But the Lord God called to the man, "Where are you?"*

> Genesis 3: 8–9 New International Version

CHAPTER HIGHLIGHTS

- Definitions, Calling, Vocation, Purpose, Meaningful Work
- The Birth of the Career-Guidance Movement
- Growth of the Career-Guidance Movement
- A Glance into the Past and a Look into the Future
- The Rise of Industrialism
- Frank Parson's Early Contributions
- First National Conference on Vocational Guidance
- Labor Market Statistics
- Career Counseling and Career Development

If you are a reader of the Bible, you are familiar with this passage of scripture. It is located in the beginning of Genesis where it speaks about the Fall. When Adam and Eve ate from the Tree of Knowledge, the world was changed from that day forward. For many, the focus of this scripture is on the introduction of sin into the world, but for me this particular verse also illustrates that (a) God would walk and fellowship with Adam and Eve as they worked and (b) work is very important to God, so much so that when Adam and Eve disobeyed God,

He redefined work and turned it into labor. See the changes from work to labor illustrated below Genesis 3:17–19, New International Version (NIV).

> 17 To Adam he said, "Because you listened to your wife and ate Fruit from the tree about which I commanded you, 'You must not eat from it,' Cursed is the ground because of you; through painful toil you will eat food from it all the days of your life." 18 It will produce thorns and thistles for you, and you will eat the plants of the field. 19 By the sweat of your brow you will eat your food until you return to the ground, since from it you were taken; for dust you are and to dust you will return."

There are some misconceptions considering this particular scripture as it pertains to work. Often people think that God cursed work; however, if you read carefully, it was the ground that was cursed, not work. God loves to work; it is the first thing that we learn about God in the Bible. Work is also one of the first tasks God commands Adam to do. When Adam and Eve disobey God, it affects the manner in which they work.

Specifically after the Fall, work turned into labor. Today we use the words work and labor synonymously; however, prior to the Fall, Adam never had to labor in the Garden. His job was to tend the Garden, not work it, nor was the work laborious. In fact, the verse shows us that it was a time for Adam and Eve to fellowship with God; He walked, conversed, and met with them as they worked. It is my contention that work was always designed as a time when God and man could talk, and man could receive guidance and direction. This concept is the foundation of this book. It is important that we take our direction from God as we seek to discover our talents and interests. When we receive our vocational calling, it is important to use our time at work to communicate with God and get further guidance and direction.

Today the word **work** has an entirely different meaning, such as place of employment or one's livelihood. Work is associated with terms such as **successful**, **efficient**, and **performance**. In terms of our relationship with work, work has become vital to our being; work not only sustains but also defines us. Regarding our mental health and overall well-being, work provides us with a sense of purpose; it affects positively and negatively our self-identity and self-esteem. Finally, our society sees work as one of the most important status symbols in our communities. For many of us, work is no longer about communing with God. It is about finding work that will make us feel better. Work is something that is completed without our knowledge of the presence of God, and in some cases, work replaces God and becomes an idol. Stated plainly, we no longer realize God as our provider and we do not experience work as a time to communicate with God. Examining this new relationship with work will be discussed at length in this book. Additionally, key elements of this book include gaining insight, skills, abilities, and knowledge to help clients understand their relationship with work and determine if that relationship is healthy; guiding helping professionals understand work; and integrating spiritual and secular perspectives when conducting career counseling.

SPIRITUALITY

So why is spirituality a part of this book? That is a really easy question. Americans are very spiritual people. Many Americans consider themselves religious or spiritual (Richards & Bergin, 1997). Data cited in a year 2000 research study by Cashwell and Young (2005) found that 96% of Americans believe in God, more than 90% pray, 69% are members of a house of worship, and 43% have attended services in a mosque, church, or synagogue weekly. Additionally, Americans believe that their spirituality or religious beliefs can provide answers to their problems. They also report that spirituality and career are connected (Hansen, 2001).

What the research findings tell us is that as a group, particularly for younger millennials, we are significantly less religious than previous generations (Pew Center, 2009). Therefore, it is important to know and be able to discuss the difference between spirituality and religion because often these terms are used interchangeably.

Spirituality is distinctly different than religion. Religion is a set of beliefs, practices, and doctrines that explain creation and authority of the universe (Asher, 2001). Typically, members of a specific religion worship together in a location such as a church, mosque, or synagogue; they follow structured rituals; and generally have a well-defined dogma (Ellwood & McGraw, 2014). Religion also tends to be more social in nature than spirituality, which is often an individual and a personal practice (Miller, 1998) that does not subscribe to traditions and is often unstructured (Ellwood & McGraw, 2014).

Palmer et al. (2010) offers a religion-neutral perspective on spirituality: "Spirituality is the eternal yearning to be connected to something larger than one's ego" (p. 48). Spirituality is a personal commitment, a way of life, and the search for meaning. Ultimately, spirituality is a mechanism for individuals to find the answers to the larger, existential questions of life. One of those existential questions has to do with **calling**, another term that is often used in society. It has very different meanings in secular, religious, and spiritual contexts.

CALLING

There are many definitions of calling, both sacred and religious. From a Christian perspective, God's call can be described as containing two aspects. Our primary calling is to Christ and our secondary calling is to everyone, everywhere, acting as God's hands and feet in this world (Whelchel, 2012). In other words, our primary calling is to be like Christ, whereas the secondary calling is to do, which leads Christians to find their unique purpose in life (Whelchel). From a secular and spiritual standpoint, calling is (a) a transcendent summons originating beyond oneself for a particular type of work, (b) the work allows for individuals to live out a broader life purpose or derive life purpose from the work, and (c) the work is "other oriented" (Dik & Duffy, 2009).

Although the secular and the Christian definitions of calling are different, their commonality is that a calling is not just about vocation. Dik and Duffy (2009) write that calling is focused on the manner in which one approaches work and not on the work itself. They go on to say calling has neither a secular nor a religious component and neither an occupational nor a nonoccupational aspect (Elangovan et al., 2010). Lastly, they contend that an individual's mental and emotional state impacts their discovery of meaning and purpose in all aspects of life (Dik & Duffy, 2009).

From a Christian perspective, the concept of work had to be adjusted after the Fall. The same is true for the secular definition of work. The concept of work has changed over the years from a secular perspective. With this being said, there still is a very different definition of work from a Christian perspective as opposed to a secular perspective. Sherman and Hendricks (1987), the authors of "Your Work Matters to God," define work, but their definition does not focus on job titles nor do they mention types of work. Sherman and Hendricks's definition focuses on the blessing of work; it is more focused on defining work as a gift and blessing and how work is supposed to help us to accomplish our life goals.

They write that through work we

1. serve people,
2. meet our own needs,
3. meet our family's needs, and
4. earn money to give to others.

(Sherman & Hendricks, 1999).

THE 21ST CENTURY AND WORK

From a secular perspective, work has a different meaning and connection to society. In a survey conducted by Good Technology, 1,000 people were polled and it was discovered that 80% of people continue to work after leaving the office, and doing so not because they have to but in order to keep up and survive. Additionally, 68% check email before 8 a.m. This study also revealed that the amount of extra time these individuals spend working outside of office hours amounts to approximately seven extra hours of work per week. That amounts to 30 hours a month, or another work week.

In relationship to our family and leisure time, the survey also found that 57% of respondents checked email on family outings; 38% at the dinner table; 69% can't go to sleep without checking email; and 40% check email after 10 p.m. A quarter of respondents from this study indicated that the extra work caused occasional disagreements with their partner. What this study does not reveal but what we can ascertain is that all of these extra work hours affect people's ability to be the best fathers, mothers, brothers and sisters, and husbands and wives that they can be. Additionally, spending more time working means more stress and anxiety and less time for self-care, including health and spirituality. The bottom line, for the purposes of this text, is that work takes away from your fellowship with God. The more time you are working means less time spent with God. The more one works, the less time one can spend waiting and being still so God can lead, guide, and direct them. With all the work, noise, and technology, it is easy to understand why our society is anxious, depressed, overweight, and tired.

This is not a 21st-century phenomena. Given that technology provides us with the ability to connect and work from anywhere coupled with the fact that our relationship with work is much more intimate and self-defining, the idea of work has changed to an entirely different social entity. Today, work has taken such a prominent role in our lives that often our other life roles (leisure, social, family, spiritual) suffer because of the prominent role that work plays in our lives.

If you track the history of work in American society from a secular and spiritual perspective, it has evolved over the generations. Work grew from being a task-oriented activity meant to offer basic necessities such as food and clothing to a task that consumes us. Today, work is where we find meaning and purpose. It defines us as individuals and is closely associated with our self-worth and self-esteem, and we experience consternation when we cannot find our specific purpose, a meaningful job, or the career track that will satisfy our purpose for which God created us. Additionally, work establishes our standing in life and our social economic status. The type of work that is performed is also critical. Working with our hands is perceived very differently than working as professionals or white-collar workers. Status, titles, and time spent working is important to our society. We experience significant stress, anxiety, and time trying to figure out what is the best career track for us—one that will fit our personality, talents, and goals and add meaning to our lives. Work is not intended to be the goal of our life; it is designed to be a job that helps us accomplish the goals of our lives. Unfortunately, work has become the goal in our lives. As a result, we experience significant stress and anxiety and, for many, this activity not only consumes our time but it keeps us from building a relationship with God, who thus becomes a "small g" god or an idol. The roots of how this transformation of work is discussed below.

Protestant Work Ethic

The Calvinist focuses on embracing hard work as a way to portray one's faith and to transform the world. Their emphasis was upon working hard to provide for one's immediate family. This became what Max Weber labeled "the protestant work ethic" (Furnham, 1990). Beginning with the Puritans, the traits of self-discipline, deferral of gratification, thrift, determination, and hard work became an indication of a true Christian and a model citizen. The objective of the protestant work ethic was the transformation of society through the dedicated efforts of Christians. According to Yankelovich (1981, p. 247), the protestant work ethic gave "moral sanction to profit making through hard work, organization, and rational calculation." When these traits were blended with the acceptance of profit making as a righteous activity, the protestant work ethic became a force in the world (1981, p. 247).

Work in the New World

The American experience had a profound effect on European thought. Before that time, it was understood that grinding, degrading poverty was the inescapable destination of certain classes of people (Yankelovich, 1981). In prerevolutionary America, even though life consisted of hard work, there was not the state of abject poverty that existed in much of the "civilized" world. Yankelovich is quick to point out, however, that the American experience did include poverty of a much more degrading sort than seen in Europe; this was experienced by the 20% of the population who were black slaves, their lives largely invisible to the eye of outsiders (1981). While European visitors came expecting to find another Eden, the Puritans arrived with no such illusions. They understood that their lives would be full of hard work and danger.

Revised Work Ethic

In the past century, our understanding of work has, of necessity, changed to keep pace with the changing workplace. The new work ethic does not just consist of supporting self and family. Rather, shortly after the conclusion of World War II a new value emerged. Home ownership became important. The prominent image was one of a simple clapboard house with a white picket fence.

This image was soon subsumed by an image of what was coined the American Dream. In this great land of ours we believed that anybody who was willing to work hard could rise to success. Success was redefined to include not only a good name and character but also wealth and material things. In time, the fruits of a sound work ethic became more important than the ethic itself. Our identity became linked to the material things that indicated our level of financial success. You can see the progression of change from the Garden of Eden to today. Work is no longer merely something one does; it is now who you are. It defines you and determines your place in society. For many of us, work dominates our thoughts and actions. Work is instrumental in one's day-to-day thoughts, actions, and decisions.

WORK NEVER ENDS

Up until the last century, work and life were less segregated. A farmer would live surrounded by his work 24/7. Cows demand regular milking, the harvest did not respect an eight-hour workday, and animals were rarely born between eight and five. In the town, artisans would often live with their family above the shop where they performed their work. "Bankers' hours" were experienced by few professionals other than bankers themselves. However, something allowed us space in which to breathe. There was time for family, time for worship, even time for recreation and leisure. At its best, life followed a rhythm of work and rest, of highly focused activity and relaxed meandering. If our values have changed and we demand more from ourselves, wouldn't that increase the pace of life? Because our attitudes toward work have changed, don't we typically burn the candle at both ends, thus increasing our activity?

It's not so much that the pace of life has increased today, although in places that is definitely the case. No, something has changed within us, a value or a source of identity. Something drives us to demand more and more of ourselves, often pushing ourselves to the point that we break. Something became twisted inside us so that we slight the things that are most important: relationships, rest, and time for reflection, time for being.

With the advent of the Internet, email, text messaging, tweeting, and smartphones, the workday seems to never end. At one time it was a treat to be able to respond to requests instantly, no matter where we were. However, the joy of being able to work from anywhere has lost its luster. With the blurring of boundaries between work and private life, work has a tendency to invade even our leisure. Unless zealously guarded, relationships with family and close friends will be eroded by the pressure to be constantly connected to the job.

This is a new and frankly dangerous perspective, relationship, and narrative that has developed regarding work. For example, the new norm might be an interruption to one's workout to respond to an email or a text sent during one's daughter's birthday party. On vacation, it is accepted and maybe encouraged to bring one's laptop and try to carve out one or two hours a day for work. This new behavior has led to a new narrative or perspective of the time spent working. In one sense, the ability to respond quickly and easily to work requests is a blessing. It means that we are able to get in our workout instead of being tied to the office while we wait for an email. Furthermore, rather than missing one's daughter's birthday party entirely, the two-minute phone call interruption is considered quite worthwhile. And, even if we have to miss a couple hours of playing with the kids and engaging with our family and spouse, it's still better than missing the whole week of vacation in order to catch a couple hours of work in the office. This is my opinion, because I have witnessed too many individuals spinning out of control, with relationships ending in divorce and major portions of children's lives being missed. My clients invariably regret the hours they sacrificed in the name of work; they frequently report feeling empty and question their own identity and life purpose.

The pressures of this 21st-century culture of work has contributed to a huge rise in mental health issues including anxiety, depression, narcissism, and stress among a host of other ailments. In our era, the complexities of living in this society place unprecedented pressure on our psyche, our souls, and our bodies.

All of these interpersonal, relational issues illustrate the importance of recognizing the importance for mental health therapists to be versed in all aspects of their client's world and work. The pursuit and understanding of his or her purpose is critical to his or her well-being and happiness. In a nutshell, career counseling is mental health counseling and vice versa. As such, when clients present with a career-focused issue, mental health professionals should first and foremost focus on potential mental health aspects rather than solely on job search, traits, and factor aspects of career counseling. There are trained individuals as well as computer resources and career coaches that can help clients find jobs. Our priority as trained mental health counselors focused on career counseling issues is to apply all one's skills and knowledge during the career counseling sessions and not respond solely as a resource focused on resumes, cover letters, job search strategies, and assessment instruments. Now that work and spirituality have been defined and a brief history established, it is important to understand career counseling and career development and to learn the abilities, skills, knowledge, and ethics that are required to be a competent career counselor in the 21st century.

CAREER COUNSELING

Career counseling has an interesting history in the United States. The one person who is celebrated as the foundation of American guidance and career counseling is Frank Parsons. Born in 1854, Parsons is widely known as the founding father of vocational psychology and guidance. Interestingly, he has a very remarkable career path. Parsons was admitted to Cornell University at age 15 and graduated with a degree in mathematics and engineering. He worked as an engineer and then as a teacher in Massachusetts. He later passed the bar and practiced as a lawyer. Parsons also worked as a college professor before landing in Boston, where he opened the first career-counseling center. Parsons served as the director of the Vocation Bureau of Boston along with Ralph Albertson, Philip Davis, and Lucinda Price. Together they primarily worked with immigrants, assisting them in finding jobs and making good career decisions. Parsons died before the bureau completed its first year of practice. In 1909, a seminal book on career counseling titled Choosing a Vocation put forth three main principles for career choice:

1. A clear understanding of yourself, your aptitudes, interests, ambitions, resources, limitations, and their causes

2. Acknowledgement of the requirements and conditions of success, and the advantages and disadvantages, compensation, opportunities, and prospects of different lines of work

3. True reasoning on the relation of the first two principles (Parsons, 1909)

Parsons established the role of counseling individuals; however, operationalizing this role has grown and transformed over the years. There is now no one way to conduct career counseling; however, there are elements that professional counselors must adhere to.

YOUR ROLE AS A MENTAL HEALTH COUNSELOR/CAREER COUNSELOR

This book was not written for community resource individuals or career coaches who are not formally trained. Rather, it was written for individuals who identify as mental health counselors. As such, it is very important for the readers of this book to first identify as a professional mental health or other trained, helping professional assisting others with work-related issues. There are many individuals who are trained to help clients find jobs, write resumes, and facilitate conversations about traits and interests. As a mental health counselor, you certainly should be versed in and knowledgeable about these important skills. The job of the career counselor today is exponentially more complex. No longer do they simply determine skills and locate jobs. Career counselors not only assist with resumes and help clients identify how to find a job, they also integrate all of these issues. They identify a career development theory that fits that client and their needs and integrate essential issues that come with discovering their calling. This may seem like a daunting task, but I view it as a tremendous opportunity to be impactful in the lives of our clients.

Helping professionals should spend an enormous amount of time helping clients grapple with existential questions: "Why was I born?" What do I want my legacy to look like?" "What should I be doing while I am on this earth?" Since work is what one does eight to twelve hours a day and work has been elevated in our society, it is critical to be informed, ethical, confident, skilled, and competent when counseling clients regarding work. Like any other counseling area, there are specific ethics and competencies that the helping professional must be familiar with. A discussion of the competencies and ethics is presented below.

Goals of Career Counseling

There are two very clear goals of career counseling: the selection of a career and adjusting to the selected career. As stated above, those two very basic goals have evolved over the years and have become so layered that career counselors have to understand the spiritual, interpersonal, and psychological process of selecting a career and be cognizant that career choice is developmental in its nature. In other words, today's decisions, satisfaction, commitment, and passion for a career may be entirely different in three, five, or twenty years. Additionally, because of changes in the world of work, clients may be forced to make changes in their careers without advanced notice or without the desire to do so. These new and different dynamics make career counseling an exciting aspect of mental health counseling. As such, counselors-in-training must view career counseling as an important aspect of counseling and not just an opportunity to assist clients to find a job. In fact, mental health counselors should not be focusing on helping a client locate a job at all nor should they be critiquing resumes and spending a lot of time discussing types of jobs. That is only a small part of the job of a mental health counselor who is focusing on career counseling. The focus of a career counselor who is helping a client with career counseling issues is to concentrate on the psychological, spiritual, relational, and personal issues that the client is presenting with as they attempt to make these important life decisions. The truth is your clients do not need you in order to find a job or complete a resume; there are plenty of qualified individuals, online resources, and private entities that can help them with the logistical parts of finding a job. The mental health counselor's job is to help clients understand their relationship to work, the psychological and mental aspects of work, and how they are currently relating to work.

Career Development Theories

Like other presenting issues, in order to effectively address issues regarding work, a counselor must be knowledgeable about the theories that could be used to aid the client to achieve his or her goals. Personality and counseling theories represent the umbrella from which career development theories are acquired. The difference is that career developmental theories focus specifically on individuals in relation to work and career issues. However, it would be a mistake for counselors-in-training to view career development theories as completely separate from counseling theories. Readers will notice that this text will acknowledge and put forth career theory, which has been gleaned from counseling theory.

It has always been the author's opinion that a counselor-in-training selects a theory that best fits the particular style, worldview, and values that are comfortable for him or her to implement. I do not recommend that counselors-in-training utilize an eclectic orientation to mental health counseling. The true definition of eclectic would indicate that one would have mastery over many theories, pull from each one, and utilize it appropriately in session (Corey, 2013). Therefore, in my opinion, the practice of using an eclectic approach to counseling is not developmentally appropriate for counselors-in-training.

Counseling Ethics

Now that we have established that career counseling is a discipline within the realm of mental health counseling, there are ethics to which one must adhere. Ethics guide mental health counseling in general; in addition, there are specific ethics that are geared toward career counseling. The two ethical standards for this textbook originate from the American Counseling Association (ACA) and the National Career Development Association (NCDA).

The foundation of all mental health counseling consists of anatomy, nonmaleficence, beneficence, justice, and fidelity. As mental health counselors, these foundational standards should guide all of our interactions and expectations with clients. When mental health counselors are facilitating career counseling sessions, these five moral principles must be paramount.

The NCDA is a great resource for students and practitioners as well as educators. NCDA provides professional development, publications, standards, and advocacy to practitioners and educators who inspire and empower individuals to achieve their career and life goals.

The ethical standards created especially for career counselors are outlined by the NCDA Code of Ethics (2015). These standards are grouped in nine sections and were created specifically for career counseling practitioners. The standards are designed to protect the profession and the client and to serve as a guide for career practitioners. These standards focus on the professional relationship; confidentiality, privileged communications, and privacy; professional responsibility; relationships with other professionals; evaluation, assessment, and interpretation; use of the Internet in career services supervision; training and teaching; research and publication; and resolving ethical issues. These standards are explained in detail at NCDA.org.

Of course, you can be a wonderful counselor and knowledgeable of all the ethics associated with both ACA and NCDA; however, there are very specific competencies that are required to be an effective professional career counselor/practitioner. It is recommended that professional counselors who are focusing on career counseling be competent in these eleven areas: "Career Development Theory, Individual and Group Counseling Skills, Individual/Group Assessment, Information/Resources, Program Management and Implementation,

Consultation, Diverse Populations, Supervision, Ethical/Legal Issues, Research/Evaluation, and Technology" (NCDA.org).

What makes this book different than other career textbooks is that it is intended to address all the needs of a secular course while infusing spirituality into the existing content regarding career development and the practice of career counseling. As such, this textbook also subscribes to principles of the Association of Spiritual, Ethical and Religious Values in Counseling (ASERVIC). This organization acknowledges and purports the importance of understanding the clients' and the practitioners' spiritual and religious foundations and provides resources and competencies for practitioners to become proficient in addressing spirituality, religion, and values in a professional counseling relationship.

ASERVIC does not affiliate or promote any specific religion. Its intended purpose is to provide practitioners and scholars with resources and literature that enable the counselor to use spirituality and religion in the counseling relationship. This is the result of the importance American society places upon spirituality and religion.

This textbook will focus on helping counselors-in-training to actively engage clients in the areas of spirituality and religious beliefs. Like the NCDA competencies, the ASERVIC competencies are designed to complement the ACA Code of Ethics (2014).

Consistent with the ACA Code of Ethics, the purpose of the ASERVIC competencies is to "recognize diversity and embrace a cross-cultural approach in support of the worth, dignity, potential, and uniqueness of people within their social and cultural contexts" (p. 3).

The ASERVIC competencies address the following areas (for more details, go to http://www.ASERVIC.org.):

- Culture and Worldview
- Counselor Self-Awareness
- Human and Spiritual Development
- Communication
- Assessment
- Diagnosis and Treatment

Counselors have to take into account the human and developmental part of work and career. This is such an important service that you can provide to your client. However, it would be a disservice if you do not talk about career, purpose, work, and calling without talking about spirituality. It is all so connected, even if one's client does not see it. It is up to the counselor to discuss it in the manner, stage, and developmentally (spiritual or secular) appropriate way that enables the client to accept this connection. Career counselors should not underestimate this. Work is such a big part of who we are as individuals; it is also a confusing and frustrating but necessary part of life.

Assessments

Career counseling is unique from other counseling areas in that it relies upon assessments, inventory, occupational information, and educational information. As such, it is incumbent on the counselor to have an understanding of career-focused assessments and be able to administer and read the results. Additionally, career counselors should be aware of various occupations and how to properly use all of this data in a counseling session. Career counselors should be prepared to locate jobs in the local area as well as across the country. They should be familiar with the various job search resources and databases, such as INDEED and ONET, and online computerized products, such as career tests and inventories that have been a mainstay in career counseling since the 1930s and 1940s. They were first developed to assess the skills of men and women entering the armed services. These inventories were used to gauge skills and interests and place military personnel into the appropriate jobs. Today, there are many assessments and inventories available to use in career counseling. Some of these assessments are proprietary and others are free resources. As a mental health counselor, it is very important to be competent and understand the measurement concepts normative information, reliability, and validity. These skills are covered in assessment courses in counseling programs; however, it is important in test selection, implementation, and appropriateness for the client.

SUMMARY

This chapter is a brief introduction to the importance of understanding how spirituality is critical to our understanding of career, calling, and purposeful working. An overview of many of the topics and issues that will be discussed in detail in this book are presented. The reader can expect a similar format in the chapters that follow.

WHAT TO EXPECT

The reader can expect this book to address in detail all of the issues briefly mentioned in this chapter. In addition, the reader will gain knowledge and skills regarding how to conduct specific career counseling sessions with specific populations. All of the skills and knowledge will be informed by the literature and utilize best practices. The focus, and uniqueness, of this book is its focus on the integration of the secular and spiritual as it pertains to God, work, purpose, and calling. Students can expect discussion questions that are designed to challenge their understanding of work and God. Additionally, scripturally influenced activities and interventions will be put forth by the authors as well as resources that can aid in developing additional career counseling skills.

FIGURE 1.1 Work Place Definitions

Definitions Secular	Definitions Faith Based
Vocation	
"vocation which is comprised of the consolidation of personality inclinations, abilities, professional interests and demands of the world of work occurring in the God's and man's love dialogue" (Danilevicius, 2010, p. 108).	Luther believed that "people could serve God through their work" (Furnham, 1990). He defined vocation as "the specific call to love one's neighbor" (Whelchel, 2012, p. 64). Luther repeatedly taught that all work was holy and equated one's vocation with the calling of God.
Avocation	
"An avocation or hobby by definition is something one does for pleasure, though it shares characteristics of both work and leisure."	
Calling	
Dik and Duffy (2009) define *calling* as an orientation toward a particular life domain such as work. A calling has three dimensions: it is a transcendent summons originating beyond the self, a pursuit of activity within the work role as a source or extension of an individual's overall sense of purpose and meaningfulness in life, and a source of motivation that is directed toward viewing others' values and goals. A secondary definition of calling according to Dik and Duffy is that calling is a sense of purpose or meaning that leads to personally fulfilling and socially significant work (Adams, 2012).	
Career	
Time extended working out of a purposeful life pattern through work undertaken by the person (Zunker, 2016, p. 7). A collection of jobs over time in a specific field.	
Career Counseling	
"Career counseling includes all activities associated with career chosen over a life span. In the career counseling process, all aspects of individual needs (including family, work, personal concerns and leisure) are recognized as integral parts of career decision making and planning" (Zunker, 2016, p. 7).	

Career Development

"The total constellation of psychological, sociological, educational, physical, economic and chance factors that combine to influence the nature and significance of work in the total life span of any given individual" (American Counseling Association, 2014).

Work

Work is an activity that produces something of value for oneself or others. Work refers to the specific tasks you perform as part of your employment." (Reardon et al., 2000, p.7).

DISCUSSION QUESTIONS

You can love your job, but your job can't love you back.

REFLECTION/DISCUSSION EXERCISES

- One of my favorite existential questions to ask is, Why were you born? Please take some time to reflect and answer this question. Your answer should not solely focus on work but on all aspects of your life.
- Use a faith-based scripture or inspirational quote to describe your developmental stage in terms of career development.
- Debate the pros and cons of separating career and mental health counseling.
- Share examples of when you were 100% sure God had spoken to you.
- Which of the basic issues discussed in this chapter was most impactful to you? Discuss why that issue is important to you and add your personal connection to the subject area.

SPIRITUAL ACTIVITY

Find your calling and your Eli

Please read the following scripture about Samuel and Eli and discuss the questions below.

> 1 Samuel 3 New International Version (NIV)
>
> [2] One night Eli, whose eyes were becoming so weak that he could barely see, was lying down in his usual place. [3] The lamp of God had not yet gone out, and Samuel was lying down in the house of the LORD, where the ark of God was. [4] Then the LORD called Samuel.
>
> Samuel answered, "Here I am." [5] And he ran to Eli and said, "Here I am; you called me."
>
> But Eli said, "I did not call; go back and lie down." So he went and lay down. [6] Again the LORD called, "Samuel!" And Samuel got up and went to Eli and said, "Here I am; you called me."
>
> "My son," Eli said, "I did not call; go back and lie down." [7] Now Samuel did not yet know the LORD: The word of the LORD had not yet been revealed to him.
>
> [8] A third time the LORD called, "Samuel!" And Samuel got up and went to Eli and said, "Here I am; you called me."
>
> Then Eli realized that the LORD was calling the boy. [9] So Eli told Samuel, "Go and lie down, and if he calls you, say, 'Speak, LORD, for your servant is listening.'" So Samuel went and lay down in his place.
>
> [10] The LORD came and stood there, calling as at the other times, "Samuel! Samuel!" Then Samuel said, "Speak, for your servant is listening."

This is a great scripture to use when you are looking for a word from God. Often, we are waiting for a word but we don't know He has been calling us all along. Sometimes you need some good, Godly counsel like Eli was for Samuel. Other times you need to listen more closely and be able to discern God's voice. What is important to know is that God will continue to call you. He wants to reveal to you what He wants you to do for Him vocationally, personally, and in the community. What is important is for you to have an attitude like Samuel, to "Speak, for your servant is listening."

Here are exercises for you to ponder:

- Name a time when you were sure God spoke to you. How are you sure it was Him?
- Name a time when you thought you heard from God but it wasn't Him.
- Share who your Eli is (a person who helps you to hear, discern, and understand when God calls you).
- Consider who and how you would find your Eli if you were looking for one outside of your family and circle of friends.
- Discuss your thoughts regarding your calling.

REFERENCES

Adams, C. M. (2012). Calling and career counseling with college students: Finding meaning in work and life. Journal of College Counseling, 15, 65–80, http://dx.doi.org/10.1002/j.2161-1882.2012.00006.x.

Asher, M. (2001). Spirituality and religion in social work practice. Social Work Today, 29, 15–18.

Cashwell, C. S., & Young, J. S. (Eds.). (2005). Integrating spirituality and religion into counseling: A guide to competent practice. Alexandria, VA: American Counseling Association.

Corey, Gerald (2013). Belmont, CA: Brooks/Cole. Theory and practice of counseling and psychotherapy (9th edition).

Danilevičius, E. (2010). "The assumptions of professional vocation discovery from the perspective of personality education", Tiltai, 3(52), 105–113.

Dik, B. J., & Duffy, R. D. (2009). Calling and vocation at work: Definitions and prospects for research and practice. The Counseling Psychologist, 37, 424–450. doi:10.1177/0011000008316430

Dik, B. J., Duffy, R. D., & Eldridge, B. (2009). Calling and vocation in career counseling: Recommendations for promoting meaningful work. Professional Psychology: Research and Practice, 40, 625–632. doi:10.1037/a0015547

Dik, B. J., Eldridge, B. M., & Steger, M. F. (2008, August). Development of the Calling and Vocation Questionnaire (CVQ). Paper presented at the annual convention of the American Psychological Association, Boston, MA.

Dik, B. J., Sargent, A. M., & Steger, M. F. (2008). Career development strivings: Assessing goals and motivation in career decision-making and planning. Journal of Career Development, 35, 23–41. doi:10.1177/0894845308317934

Dik, B. J., & Steger, M. F. (2008). Randomized trial of a calling-infused career workshop incorporating counselor self-disclosure. Journal of Vocational Behavior, 73, 203–211. doi:10.1016/j.jvb.2008.04.001

Duffy, R. D., & Autin, K. L. (2013). Disentangling the link between perceiving a calling and living a calling. Journal of Counseling Psychology, 60, 219–227. doi:10.1037/a0031934

Elangovan, A. R., Pinder, C. C., & McLean, M. (2010). Callings and organizational behavior. Journal of Vocational Behavior, 76, 428–440, http://dx.doi.org/10.1016/j.jvb.2009.10.009.

Ellwood, R. S., & McGraw, B. A. (2014). Many peoples, many faiths: Women and men in the world religions (10th ed.). Upper Saddle River, NJ: Pearson.

Furnham, A. (1990). A content, correlational, and factor analytic study of seven questionnaire measures of the Protestant Work Ethic. Human Relations, 43(4), 383–399.

Gelber, S. M. (1999). Hobbies: Leisure and the culture of work in America. New York: Columbia University Press.

Hernandez, E. F., Foley, P. F., & Beitin, B. K. (2011). Hearing the call: A phenomenological study of religion in career choice. Journal of Career Development, 38, 62–88, Retrieved from http://dx.doi.org/10.1177/0894845309358889.

Miller, W.R. (1998). Researching the spiritual dimensions of alcohol and other drug problems. Addiction, 93(7), 979–990.

National Career Development Association Ethical Standards. Retrieved from http://www.ncda.org

Palmer, P. J., Zajonc, A., & Scribner, M. (2010). The heart of higher education: a call to renewal. San Francisco, CA: Jossey-Bass.

Pan, J., & Zhou, W. (2015). How do employees construe their career success: An improved measure of subjective career success. International Journal of Selection and Assessment, 23, 45–58.

Pew Research Center. (2009). MILLENNIALS Confident. Connected. Open to Change. Retrieved from http://pewresearch.org/pubs/1501/millennials-new-survey-generational-personality-upbeat-open-new-ideas-technology-bound

Pratt, Richard J. (1993). Designed for Dignity: What God Has Made IT Possible for You to Be. N. J.: P & R Publishing.

Richards, P. S., & Bergin, A. E. (1997). A spiritual strategy for counseling and psychotherapy. Washington, DC: American Psychological Association.

Sears, S.J. (1982). A definition of career guidance terms: A national vocational guidance association perspective. Vocational Guidance Quarterly, 31(2), 137–143.

Sharf, R. S. (2013). Applying career development theory to counseling (6th ed.). Belmont, CA: Brooks/Cole.

Sherman, D., & Hendricks, W. (1987). Your work matters to God. Colorado Springs, CO: Navpress.

Toryough, G. (2010). The biblical ethics of work: A model for African nations. Verbum et Ecclesia. Retrieved from http://verbumetecclesia.org.za/index.php/VE/article/view/363/479

Treadgold, R. (1999). Transcendent vocations: Their relationship to stress, depression, and clarity of self-concept. Journal Of Humanistic Psychology, 39(1), 81–105.

Whelchel, H. (2012). How then should we work? Rediscovering the Biblical doctrine of work. Bloomington, IN: West Bow Press.

Whiteley, J.M. (1984). Counseling psychology: A historical perspective. Schenectady, NY: Character Research Press.

Williams, C., & Nelson, M. (in press). The Quarter Life Crisis: Career and Psychological Distress in Young Adulthood.

Yankelovich, D. (1981). New rules: Searching for self-fulfillment in a world turned upside down. New York, NY: Random House.

Zunker, V.G. (2016). Career Counseling: a holistic approach. 9th Edition. Boston, MA: Cengage Learning

2

An Ethical (Wonderful) Counselor

Brenda Stewart, MA, NCC

For a child is born to us, a son is given to us.
The government will rest on his shoulders. And he
will be called: Wonderful Counselor, Mighty God,
Everlasting Father, Prince of Peace.

Isaiah 9:6, New Living Translation

LEARNING OBJECTIVES

In this chapter, students will learn about

- The code of ethics as it pertains to career counseling based on the principles set forth by the Association for Spiritual, Ethical, and Religious Values in Counseling (ASER-VIC), the National Career Development Association (NCDA), the Association for Multicultural Counseling and Development (AMCD), and the Counsel for Accreditation of Counseling and Educational Related Programs (CACREP)
- How to practice within one's realm of ethical competency
- How to implement ethical career counseling via the Christian faith
- How to provide ethically sound, multicultural career counseling

LEARNING OUTCOMES

At the end of this chapter, students will be able to

- Identify ethical versus unethical counseling practice
- Implement processes of decision-making aligning with the code of ethics when faced with gray areas
- Identify the responsibilities of a faith-based career counselor

- Understand how their personhood as a counselor of faith directly impacts their counseling practice
- Detect ethical conflicts with which they struggle

CHAPTER HIGHLIGHTS

- Jesus as the Wonderful (Ethical) Counselor
- Codes of ethics and their importance
- Client confidentiality
- Client documentation
- Counselor professional responsibility
- Intersection of career counseling and mental health issues
- Tests and assessments in ethical career counseling
- Multicultural competence
- Use of technology

INTRODUCTION TO CONCEPT

Well-established graduate counseling programs integrate the concept of ethics within their program objectives. There are specific courses on ethics in counseling as well as class discussions and assignments that focus on ethical decision-making. Understanding the crucial nature of ethics is foundational to counseling, as clients trust counselors to assist them on their journey of growth and healing. Ethics has two very distinct purposes: first, to protect the counselor against lawsuits, and secondly, ethics as foundational to being an effective and competent counselor. When ethics in counseling are not upheld, there exists increased risk for client injury and further harm. For example, consider these scenarios:

1. A client takes a risk and shares dynamics of her partner abuse in an individual counseling session. The counselor automatically reacts in frustration and is unable to remain objective. Countertransference is taking place and this leaves the client vulnerable and potentially reinjured.

2. A counselor believes he is acting competently by coordinating care with his client's medical provider. However, after speaking to the provider he realizes there is no documentation of a release of information.

3. The counselor and client have different religious beliefs. During their third session, the counselor asks if she can pray for the client and provides information on churches within the counselor's denominational preference.

4. A counselor terminates counseling prematurely, without proper notice given to the client, and provides no referrals. When questioned, the counselor states he felt the client was finished and needed to move on.

5. A client of a different ethnicity than the counselor comes in for assistance with career choice. There is an internal conflict in the client based on family expectations, values, and what the client desires. The counselor tells the client to follow his or her dreams and reminds the client that he or she is an adult and can make independent choices without considering the cultural values.

Following these scenarios through helps one see some of the potential impacts ethical violations can have on clients and counselors.

Clients are in vulnerable positions in counseling settings.

As faith-based counselors, not only do we agree to uphold the counseling profession in adherence to ethical guidelines, but we are also working for Jesus, the King of Kings, the Creator of the Universe, and the all-powerful, all-knowing, ever-present Savior of the world. This is our highest calling. Colossians 3:23 (New Living Translation) states "work willingly at whatever you do as though you were working for the Lord rather than for people." There is a horizontal responsibility and calling to people for whom we work, but more importantly there is a vertical responsibility and calling that is foundational to our investment as career counselors.

Herr reports that data from Gallup polls show nearly two in 10 working Americans change jobs each year and one in 10 need career assistance (Sterner, 2016). Having competent, ethical career counselors is necessary in today's changing society.

JESUS, THE WONDERFUL (ETHICAL) COUNSELOR

Adhering to the counseling code of ethics is critical. It is not only crucial to understand and abide by the codes of ethics established but also to be ethical in character. One's behaviors and choices stem from what one values and believes. In order for ethical behavior to occur, one must be ethical in his or her core personhood. Jesus is the perfect example of what it means to be an ethical, wonderful counselor. Isaiah 9:6 is a familiar passage. It describes four names of God—Wonderful Counselor, Mighty God, Everlasting Father, Prince of Peace. The Hebrew word used for wonderful counselor is Ya'as or Yoes. It is used 23 times in the Old Testament and the term is most often translated to mean one who will advise, plan, decide, counsel, purpose, or devise (Smith & Clendenen, 2007). We first see Ya'as used in Exodus 18:19 as it states "now listen to me and let me give you a word of advice…." The names of God represented in Isaiah 9:6 are descriptive of his roles and character. Smith (2007) states that "wonderful counselor combines the idea of doing something wonderful, extraordinary, miraculous with the skill of giving wise advice, making plan, counsel" (p. 3).

It is important to look at what qualities are involved in Jesus as the wonderful counselor, the ideal model for Christian counselors to imitate. Since Jesus is the Wonderful Counselor, how does he interact with people? What does it look like to be living in relationship with Jesus? The book of John, most likely written by the Apostle John, gives an eyewitness account of the life of Jesus (Wenham, Motyer, Carson, & France, 2002). It is through entering into relationship with Him, understanding His nature, how He acts in various situations, and seeing His heart toward people that we become more attuned to how He lives out His calling in an ethical manner.

Five themes emerge from the book of John giving direction to counselors in how to imitate Jesus, the Wonderful Counselor. These include communication, empathy and compassion, consistency, self-care, and trust.

Effective communication is core to the counseling process. Jesus exhibits various communication styles as He relates to people. In the first seven chapters of the gospel of John, Jesus uses open-ended questions, assertiveness skills, direct communication, and confrontation and reflects understanding. Jesus does not show fear in how he communicates with people but rather speaks truth in love. At times he took drastic measures, for example, when he chases moneychangers out of the temple. He is clear in his communication. The more effectively we can communicate with clients, the better the opportunity clients have to heal as they feel understood, seen, and respected.

Empathy and compassion flows from the very nature of Jesus. He does not condemn the woman at the well but rather invites her to drink from the living water he offers. He comforts those after the death of Lazarus. He heals the sick and wounded. He offers hope to people who are hurting. He is nonjudgmental, even when people are skeptical or refusing his help. He accepts people for who they are and invites them to change. Clients who may not be entering into the counseling process voluntarily or who are mandated by the courts to be in counseling may challenge our ability to consistently show compassion. Yet, as we look at how Jesus relates to people, he speaks truth, reflects what he sees, and continues to offer compassion. Clients are each on a journey. Consistent compassion and genuine empathy can sometimes speak louder than words.

Throughout the book of John, notice that Jesus is consistent with his own character and grounded in truth. As counselors, we can provide consistency, safety, and security in the therapeutic environment but there will still be people who do not trust or choose not to accept the help. It is important that we do not take it personally or we will become burned out quickly. We are responsible to fulfill the calling God has placed on our life, to do it ethically, with integrity, and to continue to reflect on how we are conducting counseling, but what the client chooses to do or not do is not our responsibility. As we are secure in our identity, secure in what God has called us to do and in our belief system, we will be able to engage with clients who are resistant or threatening or hard to love and allow space for them to wrestle and experience while keeping a calm, grounded sense of self.

Jesus continually practices self-care as he deals with people. Self-care is a crucial aspect of counselor wellness. Jesus, being fully God and fully man, demonstrates self-care in the book of John. Jesus, the perfect one, still took time to go away and be by himself or be with his friends or with the Father. As we pour into the lives of people, it is crucial that we take time to care for our own soul. If we do not, it is more likely that we will experience burnout and be an impaired counselor. Clients have heavy stories. It is normal to be impacted emotionally by our clients' stories. If nothing ever impacted us, then our hearts would be hard. How we handle the impact is the important piece. Feelings allow us to better show empathy for clients. As we tend to our own emotional state, process appropriately, and practice self-care, we can better engage with our clients.

Without trust in the therapeutic relationship, client change is unlikely. Jesus exemplified relationships based on trust, as he trusted God the Father's plan. Jesus also showed himself trustworthy, as he stayed grounded in his truth, displayed a secure identity, lovingly shepherded people, and nonjudgmentally pursued people with unconditional, positive regard. As Holeman (2002) states, "Just as the triune God invites us to trust him, counselors invite clients to trust them by relating to clients respectfully and graciously" (p. 75). As we counsel a variety of clients, each with different personalities, experiences, and struggles, we need to consistently treat them with respect and value. Ethical, wonderful counselors extend grace and mercy while at the same time staying consistent with truth and setting appropriate boundaries. As the trust in the relationship develops, therapeutic change can occur.

Do you desire to be a wonderful counselor? Have it be your goal, your prayer, and your desire to continually grow in the grace and knowledge of Jesus so that you can effectively counsel others and be a reflection of His love to those with whom you interact.

CODES OF ETHICS

Now that we have looked at a few examples of Jesus interaction with people and how this applies to being an ethical counselor, let's turn to the code of ethics given to us as counselors. A code of ethics is a guide for behavior. It is a set of principles by which practitioners abide in order to protect the safety and well-being of clients (Welfel, 2010). Codes of ethics create a value system to which practitioners are to adhere. A code of ethics puts a group value forward that each member of the profession must uphold rather than relying on each individual set of morals and values for decision-making (Francis & Dugger, 2014). They are not just to be used in times of ethical dilemmas; clinicians are to treat each interaction as an ethical moment in how we care for clients (Birrell & Freyd, 2006). Ethical competence is not only about avoiding the risk of a lawsuit or information on how to use risk management techniques. It is about consistently thinking of the best interest of the clients, seeing the totality of the therapeutic relationship, and creatively and efficiently handling a variety of situations (Birrell & Bruns, 2016). Whereas state laws provide the minimum standard of care for which one is responsible, codes of ethics go above and beyond the minimum and serve as guidelines for optimum care (Francis & Dugger, 2014). In order to assimilate ethical principles into one's behavior, each aspect of ethical behavior needs to be addressed. (Kress, Hoffman, Adamson, & Eriksen, 2013) Not only are specific codes of ethics to be observed but clinicians need to remember the ethical principles of nonmaleficence, beneficence, autonomy, fidelity, and justice when working through an ethical dilemma (Jungers & Gregoire, 2016).

Although codes of ethics are crucial, as Christians, the utmost standard is that of Jesus Christ. The NCDA (2015) code of ethics describes ethical behavior as integrating the concepts of an ethical code into one's personal and professional life which then impacts decision-making processes. When values and morals are internalized, counselors face ethical dilemmas with authenticity. Authenticity in ethical decision-making is a topic of discussion found mostly among existentialists such as Kierkegaard, Heidegger, and Sartre (Jungers & Gregoire, 2016). In order to be authentic, one must have a deep understanding of who he or she is created to be and live out of the passion that ensues. It is a continual process of becoming. If ethical counselors are to be authentic, they need to go beyond simply adhering to specific codes and guidelines set forth by the profession. They must internalize the values and morals set forth by the profession alongside their own value systems, wrestle with their authentic counselor identity, and actually live out the principles within the ethical codes. Authenticity invites counselors to reach a higher level of both personal and professional development. Let's refer back to the life of Jesus. He is the model for authentic living. He was congruent in who he was, both alone and with other people. His value system, beliefs, and view of people serve as the foundation for how he interacted with others. This is the example to follow. Ethically competent counseling requires one not only to adhere to a code set forth by the profession but to adopt it, internalize it, and be changed on the inside so as to congruently and authentically live out the values and morals to which one chooses to adhere.

As career counselors, it is crucial to read, understand, and apply the code of ethics from American Counseling Association (ACA), NCDA, as well as standards of conduct from the ASERVIC, the CACREP, and the AMCD. The ACA serves as the umbrella agency for ethical codes. Counselors are upheld to these codes in courts of law. Underneath the ACA are various divisions or branches that clinicians join by areas of specialty. These divisions have their own code of ethics, such as the NCDA, but these codes are not to surmount the ACA code of ethics (2014). Rather, they are to serve in conjunction with them (Francis & Dugger, 2014).

At the basis of the ACA code of ethics (2014) is the inherent worth of people. Counselors are to treat clients with respect and see the value in each person (Francis & Dugger, 2014; ACA, 2014,). As Christians, this aligns with scripture, as it states people are created in the image of God (Genesis 1:26). Ethical counselors are not to impose their own value system on clients. Due to the given power differential between counselor and client, any verbal or nonverbal communication of the counselor's value system can be taken as an imposition by a client who is in the space of vulnerability. Counselors need to be critically aware of their own value systems and understand how this may influence the counseling process. In so doing, counselors will be better able to assist the client in making decisions that are consistent with the client's belief systems and set of values.

Because the focus of this text is on career counseling, the NCDA code of ethics is one to visit often and to where we will turn our attention in the following pages. It was developed in 1952 and is a division of ACA (NCDA, 2015). It is important to note that a single, specific code of ethics is not all-conclusive and needs to be read in light of the population for which is has been developed and as advice sought for any situation in question (NCDA, 2015). There are nine sections in the NCDA Code of Ethics (2015): "(1) professional relationship, (2) confidentiality, privileged communication and privacy, (3) professional responsibility, (4) relationships with other professionals, (5) evaluation, assessment and interpretation, (6) providing career services online, technology, and social media, (7) supervision, training, and teaching, (8) research and publication, and (9) resolving ethical issues."

CONFIDENTIALITY, PRIVILEGED COMMUNICATION, AND PRIVACY

Counseling relationships are built on trust, and part of the process of building that trust includes client confidentiality (ACA, 2014, Standard B). At the onset of counseling as well as throughout the process, career counselors have the ethical obligation to discuss with the client if information will be shared, with whom, and in what manner (NCDA, 2015, Standard B.1.a.). It is important to note cultural differences and sensitivities when discussing client confidentiality and the sharing of information (ACA, 2014, Standard B.1.a.). Counselors are to do everything possible to maintain confidentiality of the client and his or her process. While confidentiality and client privacy is a right of clients, counselors have the responsibility to ensure clients fully understand the limitations (AMHCA, 2010). The three main areas to discuss with clients regarding when confidentiality is broken are if clients are a danger to themselves or others, if counselors are required by a court of law to release information, or if there is elder or child abuse occurring (ACA, 2014). Outside of these times, counselors should not disclose any information without "client consent or without sound legal or ethical justification (NCDA, 2015, Standard B.1.c.).

CLIENT DOCUMENTATION

Documentation of client sessions and interactions is an ethical responsibility. In terms of confidentiality, records are to be kept private and in a secured location, and only authorized people should able to access client files (ACA, 2014, Standard B.6.d.). At times, clients may request access to their records. Counselors who are ethically competent discuss the request with the client, provide copies of information necessary for the client, and above all, ensure that no harm is done to the client if records are provided (ACA, 2014, Standard B.6.e.). An understanding of state and federal laws regarding the specifics of how documentation is to be stored and how long client files must be retained is required. Brennan (2013) encourages counselors to adhere to a specific and consistent form of client documentation. There are several models from which to choose.

What information and how much information is a critical balance to find when documenting client sessions. Records need to be enough to withstand in a court of law for both client and counselor protection as well as provide a summary of the client session (Brennan, 2013). Information such as client name, date of service, and counselor signature must be included in the documentation for each session.

CONSULTATION AND SUPERVISION

Consultation and supervision are regular aspects of counselor responsibility. To keep confidentiality when clients seek consultation or supervision, or work within a treatment team, counselors are to keep specific information that could disclose client identity confidential (ACA, 2014, Standard B.7.b.; NCDA, 2015, Standard, B.7.d.). If clients are using insurance, third-party payors may request information. It is necessary to have client consent and authorization to disclose information, including what information is allowed to be shared by the client before releasing any information (ACA, 2015, Standard, B.2.d.).

INFORMED CONSENT

Informed consent is an ongoing process and needs to be continually revisited (AMHCA, 2010, Standard B.2.d.). Lehr, Lehr, and Sumarah (2007) define informed consent as "the right to freely agree to counseling, to understand what is involved in the process, and to comprehend the possible and probable consequences of involvement" (p. 17). The NCDA code of ethics (2015) discusses the ethical obligation for counselors, in the informed consent process, to let clients know they can freely choose whether they want to engage in a professional relationship. Clients are to know they have the ability to terminate at their own choosing and the ability to make informed choices. In order for clients to make informed choices, they must have the knowledge and understanding to do so (Standard A.2.a.).

Counselors must obtain informed consent from clients at the beginning of the counseling process both verbally and in writing (NCDA, 2015, Standard A.2.a). As part of the informed consent process, clients are to be made aware of the counselor's qualifications, the therapeutic approach utilized, and potential tests or assessments used including the risks and benefits of each, and be given an explanation of confidentiality and its limitations, the use of technology, any payment or billing procedures, the benefits and risks of counseling, emergency protocol, and any other information the clinician deems necessary for the client to understand (NCDA, 2015, Standard A.2.b.). In order for clients to give informed consent, the information provided needs to be given at a developmentally and culturally appropriate level (Brennan, 2013). While informed consent regularly happens at the beginning of the counseling process, the NCDA code of ethics (2015) states that it needs to be a continual process throughout the counseling relationship and counselors are to document when clients give informed consent (Standard A.2.a).

In addition to the items discussed above, part of the informed consent process needs to be around diagnosis. This is an area that many clinicians do not include in their informed consent process. However, at the very least, clients need to be made aware that they may be given a diagnosis and told what the diagnosis is (Kress et al., 2013). Many insurance companies require diagnosis in order to reimburse payment, and clients need to understand the benefits and risks of obtaining a diagnosis. Most times, as clients enter counseling, they are not knowledgeable about the risks associated with diagnosis (Kress et al., 2013). If counselors do not explain the risks of diagnosis to a client, they are being unethical as the values of beneficence and autonomy are at risk (Kress et al., 2013).

Some of the benefits of diagnosis include third-party reimbursement, availability of services to populations where there is specific government funding if they have a certain diagnosis, and the fact that some clients feel a sense of relief that what they are experiencing makes sense and there is a label to describe it (Kress et al., 2013). While there are benefits, there are also several risks that have been researched and documented. These include stigmatization, negative self-worth, and living according to a diagnosis and identifying as mentally ill or sick; additionally, the financial reimbursement benefit may not happen because not all diagnoses are required to be covered by insurance (Kress et al., 2013). Counselors are to ensure clients understand these dynamics.

Knowing how much to share is a delicate balance for counselors to obtain. Some counselors may feel uncomfortable and desire the client to get the needed help in the short-term without thinking through long-term consequences and what is actually in the best interest of the client. Veracity, the commitment to be open and honest, is a core value in counseling and therefore an aspect of ethical competence (Kress et al., 2013). Counselors need to be willing to step outside their comfort zone when discussing difficult topics with clients around diagnosis. Because most insurance companies require a diagnosis at the first session, this needs to be a part of the initial informed consent process. Kress et al. (2013) describe four areas to discuss when communicating information about diagnosis in the informed consent process. These include "(a) whether the client's third-party payer or a prospective and desired program will require a diagnosis; (b) the most common problems associated with a diagnosis; (c) the benefits of a diagnosis; and (d) what the options are should the client choose not to receive a diagnosis or not to have a third-party payer involved" (p. 18).

Taking the necessary time to discuss the informed consent process and ensure clients understand it thoroughly is an ethical obligation. It is not something to rush through in order to get to the agenda the client may have for the first session, or continuing sessions, as the informed consent is an ongoing process to be revisited. Obtaining written and verbal consent benefits both the counselor and the client.

PROFESSIONAL RESPONSIBILITY

Self-Awareness
Self-awareness is a key responsibility of counselors. The ACA code of ethics (2014) speaks of counselor self-reflection in several of its sections. Ethically speaking, "self-awareness serves as a foundation for thoughtfully rendering decisions and taking actions" (Pompeo & Levitt, 2014, p. 81). One primary way to become more self-aware is through self-reflection, which leads to greater self-awareness. As counselors, we consistently hear other people's stories about traumas, losses, difficulties, addictions, and other painful life circumstances. If we are not self-aware and practicing effective self-care, we will become crippled in our ability to help

other people, potentially engage in countertransference, experience compassion fatigue, and not have the ability to care well for our clients, and in so doing be unethical as counselors. It is a professional duty of counselors to continually engage in regular self-reflection (Schmidt & Adkins, 2012). In counseling programs, self-care and self-awareness are concepts that are spoken of frequently, yet there are various definitions by which these terms are discussed. Some see it as a process that lasts a lifetime while others see it as a state of being (Pompeo & Levitt, 2014). Increased self-awareness leads to deeper clarity and understanding of personal values which in turn culminates into stronger adherence to best practices in client care (Pompeo and Levitt, 2014). As counselors understand their value systems and the lens through which they practice, self-awareness heightens and the ability to engage in self-reflection increases. Self-reflection involves observing, evaluating, and interpreting counselors' thoughts, emotions, and behaviors (Pompeo & Levitt, 2014). It is understood that when facing an ethical dilemma, the counselors' personal values and viewpoints directly impact the decision process (Pompeo & Levitt, 2014).

There will be times both personally and professionally that provide opportunity for growth. Whether it is a trigger of something internal based on client sessions and issues or conditions in one's personal life that are opportunities for growth and change as we notice reactions, thoughts, or behaviors that render a warning signal. If we take the opportunity to self-reflect, growth occurs, and this impacts ethical decision-making and professional practice as the person of the counselor is enhanced. If we ignore it or are disconnected from our own experience, "stagnation" can occur (Pompeo & Levitt, 2014). Ethical decision-making; consistent reflection; and experience, both personally and professionally, alongside supportive relationships, all are indicative of counselors being in a place of self-awareness (Pompeo & Levitt, 2014). When we as counselors are in a state of humility and regularly practice self-care and mindfulness, and are open to feedback from others, self-reflection increases, which breeds ground for deeper self-awareness.

Boundaries of Competence

Practicing within one's area of expertise, training, and competence is an ethical obligation. According to the ACA code of ethics (2014), boundaries of competence means that counselors only implement the skills, tests, assessments, theoretical approaches, and techniques that they have been fully educated, trained, and supervised in and that are in line with their scope of practice (Standard C.2.a). Supervision, consultation, and continual training assist counselors in ensuring they practice only within areas in which they are competent. Part of practicing within one's area of competence includes recognizing potential counselor impairment. We need to be aware of any physical, emotional, or mental issues that could interfere with providing utmost care for clients (ACA, 2014, Standard, C.2.g.). Engaging in self-reflection and having accountability with friends, colleagues, and supervisors are all ways to safeguard against counselor impairment. If you are experiencing concerns in any level of functioning, engaging in your own counseling process becomes priority and, if needed, counselors ethically need to step aside from engaging in client sessions until they are back to an appropriate level of health.

Counselor Representation

Part of counselor responsibility according to the ACA code of ethics (2014) and the NCDA code of ethics (2015) is to ensure they represent themselves accurately by stating the highest level of degree obtained, differentiating between an earned or honorary doctorate, accurately representing certifications and areas of specialty, displaying only active professional memberships with which one is involved, and with integrity and honesty only promoting events or services accurately so as not to deceive clients in vulnerable situations (ACA, 2014, Standard C.; NCDA, 2015, Standard C). In professional disclosure statements, which are to be given to clients and available in the office, counselors provide information on their qualifications, experience, where to go if clients have complaints about care, licensing board information, cost of sessions, and practice policies and regulations (Brennan, 2013). Because counselors obtain continuing education credits by going to a workshop or attending a seminar does not equal competence in dealing with a population (Brennan, 2013). In order to claim an area of expertise, counselors need to complete any additional courses required as well as obtain appropriate supervision (Brennan, 2013). Supervision is a great opportunity to increase one's competence in career counseling. Because the link between mental health and career counseling is now a greater consideration than in the past, supervisors need to adequately assist supervisees in learning how to competently integrate the two (Luke & Redekop, 2016).

MENTAL HEALTH AND CAREER COUNSELING

There is an interrelationship between career satisfaction and mental health (Sterner, 2016). Sterner identifies that incorporating career planning and assistance into mental health counseling benefits and strengthens the mental health outcome for clients (2016). In the United States, work is an integral part of one's daily life. The US Department of Labor and Statistics estimates that people spend more time working than engaging in any other activity, including sleep (Zunker, 2008).

Evidence continues to display that people's degree of functioning is impacted by levels of stress regarding career issues (Zunker, 2008). If people are satisfied in their career, feel a sense of accomplishment and purpose, are increasing their confidence in skills, and have a work environment that is safe and positive, they are more likely to experience joy and happiness in their external life (Zalaquett, 2009). On the other hand, if people are in negative work environments, feel unsafe, are not satisfied, and do not see that they are utilizing their skills or passions, it directly impacts one's mood, state of well-being, and overall outlook on life. Research suggests that long-term unemployment increases risk for depression and anxiety. Also, dysfunctional cognitive beliefs are linked to career indecision (Osborn, Belle, Gonzalez, & McCain, 2016). Mental health concerns impact career counseling and, vice versa, career concerns impact one's state of mental health (Luke & Redekop, 2016; Sangganjanavanich & Headley, 2015; Zalaquett, 2009).

Counselors need to look at career counseling and mental health as a "both and" rather than an "either or" (Luke & Redekop, 2016, p. 130). Luke and Redekop (2016) discuss that practitioners are increasingly aware of the complementary nature of career and mental health. It is a two-way street, each impacting the other and reciprocal in nature. Clients may have career concerns as a presenting issue, which actually stem from another mental health concerns such as personality disorders, depressive disorders, anxiety disorders, substance use disorders, or other emotional issues. They may also on the other hand present with the symptoms of anxiety, depression, lack of concentration, cognitive impairment, or behavioral issues, not realizing that career dissatisfaction can be the underlying cause of the symptoms. It is the counselors' responsibility to holistically assess the situation and help clients understand the underlying issues as well as offer tools to help decrease the symptoms experienced (Zalaquett, 2009).

Mental health issues in the workplace are directly related to the increased rate of job turnover, inflated amount of absences, and decreased level of production (Zalaquett, 2009). People with mental health issues are statistically absent from work more, have a higher likelihood of utilizing medical and disability benefits, have higher rates of turnover, exhibit less productivity on the job, and impact the atmosphere of the work environment (Zalaquett, 2009). Not only do career counselors need to be skilled to specifically counsel clients in regards to career, but because there is a strong link between career issues and mental health, they need to be competent in providing mental health counseling. It is important to note that while the interaction of mental health and career issues many times interrelate, this is not always the case. Some people will have dissatisfaction in their career but not necessarily need to address deep counseling issues. Skillful clinicians will do a thorough assessment and look at the overall picture of clients' experiences to determine the best course of action and develop a collaborative treatment plan together with their clients.

Stoltz and Haas (2016) believe that because career counseling and mental health counseling are so interrelated, it is crucial to include biopsychosocialspiritual aspects of human behavior into holistic counseling practice. Topics to be reviewed include cultural and social variables, mental health diagnosis, core belief systems, barriers to career satisfaction, and specific stressors based on individual experiences (Zunker, 2008). One way Stoltz and Haas suggest for providing holistic counseling is for career counselors to counsel from a strengths-based, wellness approach. In so doing, a goal is to obtain optimal functioning across all spans of life roles and responsibilities. Three variables shown to increase the level of functioning in people are positive outlook, contentment in life, and a secure view of self (Seligman, 2011).

In order to ethically and competently counsel, practitioners must recognize the relationship between career and mental health issues, assess clients holistically for accuracy as to the issue at hand, and balance client concerns of career as well as their physical, mental, and emotional health.

EVALUATION, ASSESSMENT, AND INTERPRETATION

One activity in which career counselors will frequently be involved is testing and assessments. The reason for assessments is to get valid and reliable data by which to compare to norms (NCDA, 2015, Standard E.1.). Career tests and assessments are used in a variety of settings including schools, private practice, rehabilitation centers, military settings, and community workforce and job placement settings. Completing a career counseling course in graduate school does not properly train counselors to be competent in providing tests and assessments; however, these courses do provide an overview of crucial material and an opportunity for the counselor to continue self-motivated learning and training.

Career assessments assist counselors with identifying attributes of the client, and as a result, the counselors can offer career choices that align with those characteristics (Osborn & Zunker, 2012) One challenge, even for the most seasoned professionals, is to not fall into the trap of giving a test, explaining the results, and expecting that to be ethical practice in career counseling. Career counseling is not just about taking a test in hopes of determining what path someone should move toward in their quest for finding a fulfilling career (Anderson, Peila-Shuster, Carlson, & Szamos, 2014). Tests and assessments are created as helpful tools in the process of a holistic, comprehensive assessment and evaluation process. They are not stand-alone items for determination of a career but rather they are one tool in the midst of a complete assessment process. Assessments take into account the client's life experiences, clinical observation, test scores, and any additional data that leads to a comprehensive review of the person's situation (Hunsley, 2002). There is a difference between tests and assessments. As one scholar notes, testing is what the client desires to complete whereas the counselor seeks to complete a thorough assessment, which includes various tests as one part of the process (Anderson et al., 2014).

Ethical counselors understand the purpose, role, and appropriateness for each client within the context of the comprehensive assessment including written information, verbal interaction, and direct observation. Informed consent should also be obtained before the assessment instrument is given (NCDA, 2015, Standard E.3.a.). This includes explaining to the client the purpose of the assessment, how it will be used, and potential ramifications of assessment results. Before assuming a certain test is beneficial to the client, counselors need to understand the purpose for which the test was originally created, if it is multiculturally sensitive, how utilizing the test will help the specific client, what the client is seeking through desiring a test, and how to properly interpret the test results within the accurate context. Before utilizing an assessment with clients, clinicians need to read the manual to ensure the assessment chosen is research based, provides valid and reliable data, and offers a guideline for proper use by professionals. This is consistent with guidelines for ethical practice (Osborn & Zunker, 2012).

Since ethical use of tests and assessments requires knowledge of the purpose, population, and interpretation of results, how do counselors become competent if there is typically only one course on career counseling in graduate school? Hayden and Kronholz (2014) suggest that supervision is one of the best ways to increase one's skills. Other ways to increase competency include continuing education and further coursework, specifically in testing assessments, procedures, and interpretation. If a test is used improperly or interpreted inaccurately, it can cause harm to the client, which is unethical practice. The welfare of the client needs to always be of primary concern.

With the use of tests being frequent for career counselors, it is necessary to know the required level of training for various tools. According to Hayden and Kronholz (2014) there are three levels of assessment. Level 1 only requires counselors to have obtained a master's degree in order to use the tests with clients. There is no additional training or certification required. However, note that it is still ethical practice for the clinician to understand the purpose of the test and assessment, know how to administer the test, and how to interpret test results properly. Hayden and Kronholz (2014) indicate that Level 1 assessments include the Career Attitudes and Strategies Inventory (CASI), Career Decision-Making System, the Mental Status Checklist, and the Self-Directed Search (SDS). Level 2 assessments require clinicians to have a master's degree as well as obtain specific certification, training, and supervision in order to purchase and use the test. Level 2 assessments include the Myers-Briggs Type Indicator (MBTI), Strong Interest Inventory (SII), the NEO, and the Career Thoughts Inventory (CTI) (Hayden & Kronholz). Finally, Level 3 assessments require clinicians to have a doctoral degree and approval from a governing agency. They include the Wechsler Adult Intelligence Scale (WAIS), the Millon Clinical Multiaxial Inventory (MCMI), and the Minnesota Multiphasic Personality Inventory (MMPI-2).

USE OF TECHNOLOGY IN CAREER SERVICES

Use of technology, online resources, and social media is utilized frequently in career counseling (Harris & Bernbaum, 2015). Counselors need to be certain they are using these resources in an ethical manner and protecting the confidentiality of the client. The NCDA code of ethics (2015) discusses the importance of career counselors obtaining continual training on available online resources to increase competency as well as to know the various laws and ethical guidelines surrounding Internet-based services. Online counseling is on the rise and ethical codes are increasing practice guidelines for such services (Haberstroh, Barney, Foster, & Duffey, 2014).

Both the benefits and limitations of the use of technology are to be discussed with clients during the informed consent process (ACA, 2014). Harris and Bernbaum (2015) note that obtaining informed consent can be more difficult with online services because the capacity to ask and answer questions is more limited and the ability to assess whether clients have a thorough understanding of the process is more difficult. While counselors have the ethical responsibility to use encrypted email services and HIPPA-compliant online software for electronic record keeping and to take every precaution possible to secure client information, there is the risk that information can be hacked and exposed.

Email

Email is one of the most widely used means of communication. While it may have benefits such as being able to communicate regardless of location, despite the time of day, and some clients may feel they can share more openly through email versus speaking face to face, there are also many risks (Klaus & Hartshorne, 2015). First, there is no way to be certain client confidentiality is maintained, as one is not able to verify who is reading the email (Harris & Bernbaum, 2015). This could potentially put the client in harm's way, which is an ethical violation. It is important to have password-protected emails if a counselor chooses to communicate in this fashion (Klaus & Hartshorne, 2015). Second, although counselors may delete the email communication, Internet service providers are able to pull deleted emails and gain access to confidential information. Third, while some clients may be more apt to share openly through email, there is much that is missed. Tone, intentionality, emotion, verbal and nonverbal communication cues, and being able to relate to another in person are missed. This can cause misunderstanding, miscommunication, and potentially risk the therapeutic alliance (Harris & Bernbaum, 2015; Klaus & Hartshorne, 2015). It is important to be clear about email policies in the informed consent process of the counseling relationship.

Texting and Telephone

Texting and telephone use are other means by which technology can enhance therapeutic work or pose potentially ethical downfalls. One of the biggest concerns is boundary violation. There are many benefits to technology, yet it can also be used as a shield to hide behind. People do not have to be as vulnerable as they may be in person, and difficult topics of conversation or confrontations can be sent through text, which clients or counselors may use as an escape. This presents ethical dilemmas. With phone calls, confidentiality is critical, as counselors need to be in a private area without the possibility of anyone overhearing a confidential conversation. The same is true of text messaging. Clinicians need to ensure the screen is blocked from others being able to view it and privacy filters need to be in place so that text messages cannot be read by another person who may use the phone (Klaus & Hartshorne, 2015). The ACA code of ethics (2014) specifies ethical considerations to adhere to when using technology in counseling (Section H).

Videoconferencing and Social Media

Videoconferencing and social media are two more technological advances that impact career counselors. Videoconferencing sessions can be an advantage for those who do not have access to an office, for those who do not have the time to drive to and from session as well as attend session, and for those who are physically unable to attend session in an office (Klaus & Hartshorne, 2015; Harris & Bernbaum, 2015). Videoconferencing enables clients in remote areas to see clinicians who specialize in issues they struggle with and opens the possibilities to greater healing. As with other technological advances, videoconferencing poses ethical concerns. As with the means previously mentioned, confidentiality is an issue that needs to be identified and discussed with the client. State licensure boards also vary in their videoconferencing laws, so counselors need to be aware of the laws in their own state and the state in which the client resides to ensure legal and ethical counseling (Klaus & Hartshorne, 2015; Harris & Bernbaum, 2015). Competence in the area of providing videoconferencing sessions is crucial. There are technology issues that may arise, being able to assess the body language and nonverbal communication of clients may be reduced, and the handling of crisis situations are just a few of the things that will be in question (Harris & Bernbaum, 2015). Training and supervision is necessary when offering videoconferencing sessions to ensure the utmost care for clients and doing what is in their best interest as well as ensuring counselors abide by ethical guidelines.

Social media, such as Facebook, is a way counselors can make their presence known, market their services, and provide information to a large number of people. However, risks occur with the use of social media. Boundary issues abound as clients may try to friend counselors, clients may be able to look up or find personal information about counselors, and counselors may try to search information on a client (Klaus & Hartshorne, 2015). All of these are ethical concerns. Discussing specific boundaries around social media is necessary. This will help ward off potential misunderstandings that could impede the therapeutic relationship. Counselors need to be accountable to not search for information about a client on social media, as this puts them in a dangerous place regarding what they may find and what is being said in sessions. With the use of technology in counseling continuing to increase, it is wise to have liability insurance which covers social media (Klaus & Hartshorne, 2015).

When considering technology in the use of counseling, there are three main areas to address in regards to ethical behavior. These are confidentiality, boundaries, and areas of competence (Klaus & Hartshorne, 2015; Harris & Bernbaum, 2015). Counselors must refer to their ethical codes and state laws, and seek supervision and consultation before beginning the journey of utilizing technological advances in the scope of counseling practice.

MULTICULTURAL COMPETENCE

From the beginning of the career counseling movement, there have been ethical concerns. Frank Parsons, also known as the father of career guidance counseling, initiated his movement in the workforce to bring about social justice and keep children and immigrants from entering the workforce inappropriately (Anderson, Peila-Shuster, & Aragon, 2012). Career counseling needs to be culturally sensitive and applicable. CACREP standards (2016) define multicultural as a word that signifies differences in age, race, ethnicity, cultural background, sexual orientation, beliefs, socioeconomic status, or abilities, including physical, mental, and emotional aptness.

Career counseling was initially built upon a dominant culture—that of Western European values, founded by Caucasian people and the specific values of individuality, work as central to our identity, autonomy, and a linear career process (Vespia et al., 2010). This fails to account for the various cultural and contextual backgrounds of clients. The way career concerns are processed in counseling sessions is directly impacted by both the counselor's and the client's cultural backgrounds and experiences (Anderson, Peila-Shuster & Aragon, 2012). It is crucial for clinicians to understand one's own cultural history and biases and how these impact one's outlook on situations as well as understand the cultural context of the client and their experiences, values, and beliefs. Multiple factors influence one's multicultural competence. These include the amount of training received, quality of the training, one's own self-awareness, experience in multi-cultural settings, and level of multicultural counseling experience (Vespia et al., 2010). It is important to note the way in which counselors' rate themselves as culturally competent and how the ways they actually practice in a culturally sensitive manner could differ (Vespia, et al., 2010).

One research study conducted reported that counselors feel less competent to work with the lesbian, gay, bisexual, and transgender population (LGBT), Asians, Native Americans, and older adult clients due to what they considered their lack of training in cultural differences (Vespia, et al., 2010). Multicultural competence also takes into account the role work plays in the life of the client, pressures and expectations from family units versus individualism, whether the client has the financial means to seek out career counseling, and the availability of various opportunities through the lens of discrimination at hand. One's employment and financial stability have a direct correlation on one's mental health status (Mainzer & Dipeolu, 2015). In order to treat clients holistically, counselors need to understand the components that form one's career beliefs and experiences including personal history, political factors, and social experiences (Anderson, Peila-Shuster & Aragon, 2012).

Disabilities

Within the context of career counseling, laws and ethics regarding people with disabilities must be seen as an area of multicultural competence. Since the 1970s, three laws passed including the Individuals with Disabilities Education Act, the Americans with Disabilities Act, and Section 504 of the Rehabilitation Act (Mainzer & Dipeolu, 2015). Knowing these laws and how to apply them in career counseling is pertinent to being an ethical career counselor.

Section 504 of the Rehabilitation Act protects those with disabilities and agencies that receive federal funding to assist those with disabilities. This law assists in providing training and direct assistance to people so that they can be qualified for employment. It also prohibits employers from discrimination against people with disabilities in the hiring or termination process. As career counselors, this is an important law to understand. In order to accurately apply it, we need to know how the Rehabilitation Act defines disability. According to the Rehabilitation Act, people with disabilities include those with a history of or current mental or physical impairment that significantly impacts a person's life (Mainzer & Dipeolu, 2015).

Because Section 504 of the Rehabilitation Act is limited and failed to end discrimination, the Americans with Disabilities Act (ADA) was formed in 1990. This broadens the scope of protection for people with disabilities and rather than only protecting agencies receiving federal funding, it protects programs that are operated by state and local governments as well as nonprofit organizations who have 15 or more employees (Mainzer & Dipeolu, 2015).

The Individuals with Disabilities Education Act is the third law pertaining to ethical counseling that career counselors need to know. This was put into place in 1975 and amended in 2004. It ensures students have access to education in the least restrictive environment and it offers a transition program for students in high school. They are provided vocational training, social skill straining, employment preparation, family involvement, and collaboration with local entities.

Spirituality and Religion

Spirituality and religious practices is another aspect of multicultural competence. Clients' spirituality can be used as a positive coping mechanism as it is a source of hope for clients and it increases resiliency (Elkonin, Brown, & Naicker, 2014). During the assessment process, a thorough biopsychosocialspiritual assessment will give the clinician an idea about clients' spiritual and religious practices and how they utilize them, and whether clients want their practices integrated into the therapy process. This needs to be a focus of discussion so there is clarity between the client and the counselor (Leighton, 2016). Many practitioners shy away from discussing spirituality and religion in the counseling process as it is not a value-free subject and the counselor or client may be uncomfortable with such topics (Elkonin, Brown, & Naicker, 2014). However, if we are to be ethical counselors (which includes multicultural competence, and within multicultural competence is spirituality) it is our obligation as counselors to incorporate this aspect of one's personhood into the process as the client desires and provides informed consent.

We are created as physical, psychological (mental and emotional), and spiritual beings. To disregard or ignore one of these aspects of a person in the counseling process is unethical. According to Vader (2006), clinicians who do not incorporate spirituality into the counseling process are ignoring a powerful resource that can be utilized to enhance the client's process of achieving mental health. As ethical counselors, it is imperative that we do not impose our own value or belief system onto the client yet at the same time utilize the client's spirituality for positive growth.

Lesbian, Gay, Bisexual, and Transgender

Becoming multiculturally competent with LGBT clients in career counseling is not an easy task, but it is one that needs attention. There are approximately four million people who consider themselves lesbian, gay, bisexual, or transgender in society today (Gates, 2012). As society becomes more accepting of the LGBT community, the need for culturally competent career counselors rises. In the past, many stereotypes around LGBT employees in the workplace created an environment where this community felt the need to hide their sexual orientation, keep things secret for fear of not obtaining a promotion, and maintain a sense of safety if they did decide to let their sexual orientation be known (Pope et al., 2004). While the stereotype of gay men being feminine in nature and lesbian women being masculine in nature is changing, it is crucial that counselors assess their own biases or beliefs in this realm.

Within the last ten years, research has increased around the specific needs and stressors of gay and lesbian clients in the workplace. Counselors need to be educated and informed about the specific struggles LGBT clients face in career development and the workplace in order to competently offer them career counseling. Clients who consider themselves LGBT are aware of counselor bias, lack of knowledge, and misunderstanding (Pope et al., 2004). Issues such as oppression, privilege, and intersectionality are areas to specifically address when working with LGBT clients (Troutman & Packer-Williams, 2014).

One particular issue career counselors need to be competent in is LGBT clients' sexual identity formation as it relates to their career development (Pope et al., 2004). People identify with a particular sexual orientation at different times, which directly impacts their career development process. As counselors gain an understanding of each client, it is necessary to assess how many multicultural factors are at play. For example, if someone is of ethnic minority and gay, they face two potential areas of discrimination. If there is a female who is lesbian in the workplace, she faces potential discrimination because of her gender and sexual orientation. This multilevel potential for discrimination is crucial to address (Troutman & Packer-Williams, 2014). Many LGBT clients coming for career counseling may desire help in knowing how and when to come out in their work environment. This is seen as an important process in their sexual identity development and acceptance. Counselors need to be prepared to assist clients based on what is best for the client.

Literature on this topic recommends counselors provide LGBT clients with educational information on how to speak about their sexual preference in the workplace and how to respond to questions in a professional manner as well as resources specific to their career concerns (Pope et al., 2004). Other important areas to understand in order to provide ethical career counseling to LGBT clients are internalized homophobia or shame clients may have about their sexual orientation, the impact of potential moves and child-care on dual-career couples in a same sex relationship, the relational dynamic for people who have changed orientation and have children from a previous marriage, and how available assessments are or are not appropriate to use with this population (Pope et al., 2004). Allowing the client to come to their own decision on the how and when to come out in the workplace empowers them, yet counselors need to adequately assist in helping them understand the purpose of coming out, what they hope to gain, and how to cope with potential responses and reactions.

To continue developing competence in counseling the LGBT population, seek out information and understanding through trainings, spend time with this community, ask questions, and read published literature (Pope et al., 2004).

RESOLVING ETHICAL DILEMMAS

There is no doubt that career counselors will experience ethical dilemmas. There will be situations that fall into the "gray" areas of ethical codes. There will be times when the legal and ethical guidelines apparently contradict and there will be circumstances where one's personal value system is in conflict with ethically appropriate behavior. The NCDA code of ethics (2015) states that when working toward a decision in an ethical dilemma, counselors need to communicate openly and clearly to all people involved as well as seek consultation and supervision when appropriate (Standard I).

When ethical dilemmas arise, first and foremost counselors have the obligation to know the applicable codes of ethics and state laws and to abide by them. If there is a conflict between a governing body and the code of ethics, counselors need to communicate and seek to help the other party understand that they are obligated to adhere to the specified code of ethics for their profession. If agreement cannot be obtained, the NCDA code of ethics (2015) states that counselors are to adhere to the federal, state, and local laws (Standard I.1.b.).

When an ethical dilemma is still unclear after applying laws and ethical codes, counselors have the responsibility to seek consultation (NCDA, Standard, I.2.d.). People who are sought out for consultation should be knowledgeable, experienced in the field, and ethical in their personhood and behavior.

Various ethical decision-making models have been proposed for counselors to use when they are in the midst of an ethical dilemma. These models provide an organized and calculated method of tackling ethical decisions when there are differing components (Evans, Levitt, & Burkholder, 2012). Regardless of which decision-making model is chosen, ethical decisions are made through the lens of the practitioner's experience and perspective; therefore, self-reflection and self-exploration are crucial.

Kocet and Herlihy (2014) discuss a decision-making model for when counselors face ethical dilemmas, particularly when there is value-based conflict. They encourage counselors to engage in "ethical bracketing" (p. 182). This occurs when counselors set their personal values and beliefs apart from their professional values and responsibilities. In so doing, Kocet and Herlihy believe that this will assist counselors in avoiding value imposition as well as empowering clients toward their therapeutic goals. These scholars state that engaging in ethical bracketing involves several steps: immersion, education, consultation, supervision, and personal counseling (Kocet & Herlihy, 2014). This process aligns with various codes of ethics as it requires counselors to immerse themselves in self-reflection, educate themselves on the type of ethical dilemma they are facing, consult the code of ethics and legal requirements, seek consultation and supervision from other professionals in the field, and engage in personal counseling to resolve any internal issues that may be triggered through a client's process.

As the overarching agency for counselors, the ACA published a guide for practitioners to use when facing an ethical dilemma and trying to make a decision. Forester-Miller and Davis propose a seven-step process by which to adhere when determining the course of action in an ethical dilemma. While engaging this model, it is crucial to think about the client's belief system and how it may impact the use of the model (Forester-Miller & Davis, 2016).

The first step is to identify the issue or dilemma. This brings clarity into the situation in order to guide the next steps of the decision-making process. When identifying the problem, it is important to look at the situation objectively and write down observations. When it is put on paper or on the computer and not kept in our own minds, the situation is apt to be seen more clearly (Forester-Miller & Davis, 2016). As the identification process continues, it is important to separate out any assumptions, suspicions, and hypothesis and adhere to the facts. Forester-Miller and Davis (2016) provide questions for counselors to ask during the identification process. These include "Is it an ethical, legal, professional, or clinical problem? Is it a combination of more than one of these? Is the issue related to me and what I am or am not doing? Is it related to a client and/or the client's significant others and what they are or are not doing? Is it related to technology in the provision of services or of storing" (p. 2–3)?

Forester-Miller and Davis (2016) discuss the second step of the process, which is to apply the ACA code of ethics and any other state laws, agency guidelines, and codes of ethics applicable pertaining to the practitioner and the dilemma at hand. In order to apply the code properly, counselors need to know and understand how to implement the various codes. If there is clarity in the first two steps of the decision-making process, the ethical dilemma is resolved. However, most ethical dilemmas are complex situations and require further steps in the process in order to come to an ethical course of action.

The third step dictates that counselors are to be specific regarding the actual dilemma and surrounding variables at hand (Forester-Miller & Davis, 2016). This step includes consulting with other professionals, contacting professional associations to see if they can be of assistance, reading current literature on the topic at hand, and spending time evaluating what principle in the ACA code of ethics (2014) is in question: autonomy, justice, beneficence, maleficence, or fidelity.

Once the first three steps of the decision-making process are complete, counselors need to develop a plan of action, which is the fourth step in the process (Forester-Miller & Davis, 2016). This is where your decision-making skills come into hand. Brainstorm as many possible ways to move forward in resolving the ethical dilemma. Try to do this without judgment, but rather externalize every idea that comes to mind and then discuss this with a trusted colleague who adheres to the same code of ethics to see if you have overlooked a potential course of action.

The fifth step is to reflect on all possible outcomes and then decide on an implementation process (Forester-Miller & Davis, 2016). Address each of the options that you brainstormed in light of what consequences there could be on the client, the affected parties, and on you as the counselor if that course of action is taken. This begins the process of elimination. Once you have narrowed down the viable courses of action, discuss this with your supervisor or consultation colleague and look at these alongside the priorities you have determined previously.

Once the course of action is chosen, steps six and seven include evaluating and implementing the chosen course (Forester-Miller & Davis, 2016). Think through whether the course of action is appropriate and if it poses any new ethical dilemmas. Another way to evaluate the decision is to consider whether the same conclusion would be made regardless of the client. Finally, consider how it would feel if the ethical decision is made public. If your answers to these questions are all positive, then implementation of the plan is ready to happen. Note that just because the course of action has been decided, carrying out the decision may not be easy. Prepare yourself for roadblocks you may face and seek encouragement from others in the field who are walking through this process with you.

The final recommendation for ethical decision-making processes when faced with a dilemma is outlined by Anderson et al. (2012). These are designed specifically for career counselors, although the principles are applicable and pertinent to all counselors. The 11 ethical considerations include:

1. Counselors own their response to what the client is saying
2. Respect clients cultural and family values
3. Counselors understand their own cultural identity, any biases present, and their career values to be aware of how this may impact the therapeutic relationship
4. Identify the purpose of assessments as well as which ones are appropriate for the particular client
5. Client and counselor jointly agree on a career service plan that aligns with the client's abilities and current situations in accordance with the NCDA code of ethics
6. Determine if standardized assessment is needed
7. Clinicians take into account the specific assessment's validity and reliability
8. Instrument selection and multicultural issues
   o Check that the specific culture of the client is represented in the assessment data
   o Place test results in perspective with client's culture, SES, gender, ethnic group, age, disability, race, sexual orientation, and spirituality
9. Clinicians only use the tests and assessments within their realm of competency
10. Explain the assessment appropriately to the client before administering a test
11. The interpretive session goes over the test results in light of the client's culture, values, and goals

When ethical dilemmas are complex, there is not usually one right decision. Counselors may vary in their approach and course of action. Having a decision-making model and process to adhere to is important and assists counselors in working through the various dilemmas encountered. It is crucial to accurately document the decision and course of action in the client file (Forester-Miller & Davis, 2016). Keeping a record of steps taken and the reasoning in the decision-making process is crucial.

CONCLUSION

Ethical counseling is more than adhering to a code of ethics and abiding by state laws. It penetrates to the core of the person of the counselor, where the counselor lives out his or her values and morals along with adhering to a professional code of ethics set forth. An ethical counselor incorporates both the person and the profession of the counselor. As counselors continue to grow, it is like Christians seeking to know Jesus on a deeper level. It is through Jesus that the inner person is changed into His likeness, which then transforms actions and behaviors. Being an ethical Christian counselor is a high calling. There is continual learning, seeking of knowledge, consulting with colleagues and supervisors, and growing in order to fulfill the calling Jesus has placed on a Christian counselor's life.

KEY TERMS

Beneficence: working for the good of the client and society by promoting mental health and well-being (ACA, 2014, p. 2).

Boundaries of competence: working within one's area of education, skill, and expertise

Career Counselor: "a student or professional with an advanced degree in counselor education, counseling psychology or closely related counseling degree, engaged in a career counseling practice or other career counseling related services. Career counselors fulfill many roles and responsibilities such as career counselor educators, researchers, supervisors, practitioners, and consultants" (NCDA, 2015, p. 26).

Code of ethics: a collective group of values and morals to which members of a profession adhere

Confidentiality: "the ethical duty of counselors to protect a client's identity, identifying characteristics, and private communications" (NCDA, 2015, p. 26).

Ethics: values and morals that oversee a person's behavior

Fidelity: faithful in honoring commitments and keeping promises (ACA, 2014, p. 2).

Informed consent: "a process of information sharing associated with possible actions clients may choose to take, aimed at assisting clients in acquiring a full appreciation and understanding of the facts and implications of a given action or actions" (NCDA, 2015, p. 26).

Justice: fairness, treating people equally and without discrimination (ACA, 2014, p. 2).

Multicultural competency: "cultural and diversity awareness and knowledge about self and others, and how this awareness and knowledge is applied effectively in practice with clients and client groups" (NCDA, 2015, p. 26).

Nonmaleficence: avoid actions that cause harm (ACA, 2014, p. 2).

Veracity: dealing truthfully with people (ACA, 2014, p. 2).

REFLECTION AND DISCUSSION

1. What are your values, both personally and professionally?

2. What will you do when there is a value conflict in counseling? What will you do when your belief system is different than what the code of ethics requires?

3. Which of the five areas given around Jesus as the wonderful, ethical, counselor do you struggle with and how do you plan to change?

4. To provide ethical service, what areas of competency are specific to career counselors?

5. Explain the integration of career counseling and mental health concerns.

ADDITIONAL READINGS, RESOURCES, AND WEBSITES

www.aacc.net

www.amhca.org

www.cacrep.org

www.caps.net

www.counseling.org

www.ncda.org

TRADITIONAL ACTIVITY

Case Study

Leo is an international student from Hong Kong studying at a university in New York. This is his sophomore year as a business major. His family wants him to major in business in the United States so he can go back to Hong Kong and take over the family company once his father retires. He adheres to strong cultural values and is close with his family. After all, he is an only child. He comes to the university counseling center stating that he has been feeling stressed and unhappy and wants to quit school because his grades are dropping and he lacks motivation. Following his biopsychosocialspiritual assessment, you find he does not like the classes in the business degree program; however, he wants to please his family and uphold their value system. He also has come to realize that he is interested in dating other males and is secretly in a relationship.

Respond

As a career counselor, what are the areas of concern? How are his career processing and mental health concerns related? As a competent, multicultural counselor, how would you go about creating a treatment plan for this client? How do you ensure that you are culturally competent as well as not placing any bias or personal beliefs and value systems on the client?

SPIRITUAL ACTIVITY

Situation

Let's reflect back to the beginning of the chapter and the book of John. Jesus is the ultimate example and role model we, as Christians, are to follow. In John 4, we find the story of the Samaritan woman. She was of a different ethnic background, there was racial tension (Jesus was a Jew and she was a Samaritan), there were gender differences (Jewish rabbis would not speak with women in public) she lived a different lifestyle (she had multiple husbands), and she lied to Jesus ("I do not have a husband"). Yet, Jesus defied all expectations and spoke to the woman, cared for her, showed genuine kindness, confronted her with truth, and met her need. Now, let's take this example and bring it to the modern day. You are a male career counselor at a community counseling agency. A female client, of a different ethnic background, enters your office in ragged clothes and smells as though she has not showered in days. She asks for help finding a job. As you provide an assessment, you find out that she works as a prostitute to provide food for her five children, all of whom are from different men. She also tells you that she met a street evangelist and recently gave her life to Christ.

Respond

What are your initial thoughts and feelings about the situation? What is your value system and belief system around work and personal responsibility? Of which ethical considerations do you need to be aware? In what way can this situation be an opportunity for you to grow personally and professionally, to become more like Jesus, and be a more competent, ethical counselor?

REFERENCES

American Counseling Association (2014). ACA code of ethics: as approved by the ACA governing council. Retrieved from http://acaa.informz.net/ACAA/archives/archive_3163716.html

American Mental Health Counselors Association (2015). AMHCA code of ethics. Retrieved from http://connections.amhca.org/viewdocument/amhca-code-of-ethics

Anderson, S. K., Peila-Shuster, J. J., & Aragon, A. (2012). Cross cultural career counseling: ethical issues to consider. Career Planning & Adult Development Journal, 28(1), 127–139.

Anderson, S. K., Peila-Shuster, J. J., Carlson, L., & Szamos, A. (2014). Testing or assessment: choosing the ethical ideal. Career Planning & Adult Development Journal, 30(4), 185–197.

Birrell, P. J., & Bruns, C. M. (2016). Ethics and relationship: from risk management to relational engagement. Journal of Counseling & Development, 94(4), 391–397. doi:10.1002/jcad.12097

Birrell, P. J., & Freyd, J. J. (2006). Betrayal trauma: Relational models of harm and healing. Journal of Trauma Practice, 5(1), 49–63

Brennan, C. (2013). Ensuring ethical practice: Guidelines for mental health counselors in private practice. Journal of Mental Health Counseling, 35(3), 245–261.

Counsel for Accreditation of Counseling and Related Educational Programs (2016). 2016 CACREP standards. Retrieved from http://www.cacrep.org/for-programs/2016-cacrep-standards/

Elkonin, D., Brown, O., & Naicker, S. (2014). Religion, spirituality and therapy: Implications for training. Journal of Religion & Health, 53(1), 119–134. doi:10.1007/s10943-012-9607-8

Evans, A. M., Levitt, D. H., Henning, S., & Burkholder, D. (2012). The application of ethical decision-making and self-awareness in the counselor education classroom. Journal of Counselor Preparation & Supervision, 4(2), 41–52. doi:10.7729/42.0029

Forester-Miller, H. & Davis, T. E. (2016). Practitioner's guide to ethical decision making. American Counseling Association. The Center for Counseling Practice, Policy and Research, 1–6. Retrieved from www.counseling.org/docs/default-source/ethics/practitioner's-guide-to-ethical-decision-making

Francis, P. C., & Dugger, S. M. (2014). Professionalism, ethics, and value-based conflicts in counseling: An introduction to the special section. Journal of Counseling & Development, 92(2), 131–134. doi:10.1002/j.1556-6676.2014.00138.x

Gates, G. J. (2012). LGBT identity: A demographer's perspective. Loyola of Los Angeles Law. Retrieved from http://digitalcommons.lmu.edu/llr/vol45/iss3/2

Goldingay, J. (1999). The compound name in Isaiah 9:5(6). The Catholic Biblical Quarterly, 61(2), 239–244.

Haberstroh, S., Barney, L., Foster, N., & Duffey, T. (2014). The ethical and legal practice of online counseling and psychotherapy: A review of mental health professions. Journal of Technology In Human Services, 32(3), 149–157. doi:10.1080/15228835.2013.872074

Harris, B., & Birnbaum, R. (2015). Ethical and legal implications on the use of technology in counselling. Clinical Social Work Journal, 43(2), 133–141. doi:10.1007/s10615-014-0515-0

Hayden, S., & Kronholz, J. (2014). Integration of assessments in counseling: Developing competence within clinical supervision. Career Planning & Adult Development Journal, 30(4), 156–169.

Holeman, V. T. (2002). Theology for better counseling: Trinitarian reflections for healing and formation. Downers Grove, IL: IVP Academic

Hunsley, J. (2002). Psychological testing and psychological assessment: A closer examination. American Psychologist, 33(2), 139–140. doi: 10.1037/0003-066X.57.2.139

Jungers, C. M., & Gregoire, J. (2016). Authenticity in ethical decision making: Reflections for professional counselors. Journal of Humanistic Counseling, 55(2), 99–110. doi:10.1002/johc.12027

Klaus, C. L., & Hartshorne, T. S. (2015). Ethical implications of trends in technology. The Journal of Individual Psychology, 71(2), 195–204.

Kocet, M. M., & Herlihy, B. J. (2014). Addressing value-based conflicts within the counseling relationship: A decision-making model. Journal of Counseling & Development, 92(2), 180–186. doi:10.1002/j.1556-6676.2014.00146.

Kress, V. E., Hoffman, R. M., Adamson, N., Eriksen, K. (2013). Informed consent, confidentiality, and diagnosing: Ethical guidelines for counselor practice. Journal of Mental Health Counseling, 35 (1), 15–28.

Lehr, R., Lehr, A., & Sumarah, J. (2007). Confidentiality and informed consent: School counsellors' perceptions of ethical practices. Canadian Journal of Counselling, 41(1), 16–30.

Leighton, T. (2016). Faith as a therapeutic companion: Instructing counselling students on the import of religion. Canadian Journal of Counselling & Psychotherapy/Revue Canadienne De Counseling Et De Psychothérapie, 50(3), 348–364.

Levitt, D. H., Farry, T. J., & Mazzarella, J. R. (2015). Counselor ethical reasoning: Decision-making practice versus theory. Counseling & Values, 60(1), 84–99. doi:10.1002/j.2161-007X.2015.00062.x

Luke, C., & Redekop, F. (2016). Supervision of co-occurring career and mental health concerns: Application of an integrated approach. Career Planning & Adult Development Journal, 32(1), 130–136

Mainzer, E. A., & Dipeolu, A. (2015). Doing right by those we serve: Law, ethics and career services for individuals with disabilities. Career Planning & Adult Development Journal, 31(4), 131–141.

National Career Development Association (2015). NCDA Code of Ethics. Retrieved from www.ncda.org/aws/NCDA/asset.../3395

Osborn, D. S., Belle, J., Gonzalez, A., & McCain, S. C. (2016). Linking career and mental health concerns through technology. Career Planning & Adult Development Journal, 32(1), 151–160.

Osborn, D. S., & Zunker, V. G. (2012). Using assessment results for career development (5th ed.). Belmont, CA: Brooks/Cole

Pompeo, A. M., & Levitt, D. H. (2014). A path of counselor self-awareness. Counseling & Values, 59(1), 80–94.

Pope, M., Barret, B., Szymanski, D. M., Chung, Y. B., Singaravelu, H., McLean, R., & Sanabria, S. (2004). Culturally appropriate career counseling with gay and lesbian clients. Career Development Quarterly, 53(2), 157–177.

Sangganjanavanich, V. F., & Headley, J. (2015). Addressing the connection between career and mental health concerns: The utilization of career assessments. Career Planning and Adult Development Journal, 30(4), 198–208. Retrieved from http://0-search.proquest.com.library.regent.edu/docview/1845685112?accountid=13479

Seligman, M. E. P. (2011). Flourish: A visionary new understanding of happiness and wellbeing. New York, NY: Free Press

Schmidt, C. D., & Adkins, C. P. (2012). Understanding, valuing, and teaching reflection in counselor education: A phenomenological inquiry. Reflective Practice: International & Multi-disciplinary Perspectives, 13, 77–96.

Smith, G. V. & Clendenen, E. R. (2007). Isaiah 1–39. Nashville, TN: B&H Publishing Group. Retrieved from LOGOS Bible Software, www.logos.com

Sterner, W. R. (2016). Integrating career planning in community and agency settings: Issues, factors, and considerations. Career Planning & Adult Development Journal, 32(1), 73–85.

Stewart, J. (1999). Ethical issues in career counselling. Guidance & Counseling, 14(2), 18–22.

Stoltz, K. B., & Haas, K. J. (2016). Mental health or career counseling: A forced choice? no need! Career Planning & Adult Development Journal, 32(1), 43–53.

Troutman, O., & Packer-Williams, C. (2014). Moving beyond CACREP standards: Training counselors to work competently with LGBT clients. Journal of Counselor Preparation & Supervision, 6(1), 1–19. doi:10.7729/51.1088

Vader, J. P. (2006). Spiritual health: The next frontier. European Journal of Public Health, 16(5), 457.

Vespia, K. M., Fitzpatrick, M. E., Fouad, N. A., Kantamneni, N., & Chen, Y. (2010). Multicultural career counseling: A national survey of competencies and practices. Career Development Quarterly, 59(1), 54–71.

Welfel, E. R. (2010). Ethics in counseling and psychotherapy: Standards, research, and emerging issues (4th ed.). Belmont, CA: Brooks/Cole

Wenham, G. J., Motyer, J. A., Carson, D. D., & France, R. T. (2002). New bible commentary (21st century ed.). Downers Grove, IL: IVP Academic

Zalaquett, C. P. (2009). Career and mental health. Career Planning & Adult Development Journal, 25(1), 119–133.

Zunker, V. G. (2008). Career, work, and mental health: Integrating career and personal counseling. Thousand Oaks, CA: Sage

3

Career Counseling, Mental Health, and Assessment

Dixie Meyer, PhD, Jocelyn Fowler, MS, MFT, and Mayra Massey, MA

For we are his workmanship, created in Christ Jesus
for good works, which God prepared beforehand,
that we should walk in them.

Ephesians 2:10, English Standard Version

LEARNING OBJECTIVES

In this chapter, students will learn about

- The assessment process
- Information to gather during the initial intake interview
- How mental health diagnoses impact career counseling
- Psychometric concerns and important instruments in career counseling
- Uses of technology in career counseling

LEARNING OUTCOMES

At the end of this chapter, students will be able to

- Successfully conduct an intake interview
- Identify important information to observe in career counseling
- Identify types of instruments utilized in career counseling
- Understand special considerations when counseling clients with mental health diagnoses about their career
- Select reliable and valid instruments to use in career counseling

CHAPTER HIGHLIGHTS

- Assessment
- Intake interview
- Diagnosis
- Career counseling process
- Psychometric concepts
- Equity in testing
- Career inventories
- Technology in career counseling

CAREER COUNSELING, MENTAL HEALTH, AND ASSESSMENT

We all have great plans, hopes, and dreams about our ideal career. However, for most people it takes time and effort to make those dreams come true. There are times when people want to pursue many fields of career interest but cannot decide which life course is best for them. There are other times when people may wonder if there is anything that they can do to succeed. However, life and career are never perfect; there are always ups and downs. The great part to realize is there are ways to cope with the ups and downs in healthy and functional ways. Individuals who need vocational resources and help can find that help through professional guidance. Today, individuals are increasingly referred to, or are encouraged to pursue, career services (Metz & Jones, 2013; Neukrug & Fawcett, 2015). The referral may involve a trip to a career counselor who specializes in helping individuals find their dream career according to their skills, strengths, challenges, values, interests, and goals (Dagley & Salter, 2004).

Career counselors help clients search for the ideal career (Guidon & Richmond, 2004). Career counselors provide information about educational degrees, resources to internships, and interviewing techniques, and provide support to clients experiencing work adjustments and clients in different life stages. Most career services offer help with resume and cover-letter writing as well as host career fairs. Career counselors are available to bridge the gap from trying to figure out life's purpose to embarking on a journey to obtain valuable work experience and knowledge. One of the main goals in career counseling is to aid in the process of finding a job that matches the client's talents, abilities, values, skills and interests.

The next section will provide a general framework for understanding the process following the initial appointment with a career counselor. This framework introduces the assessment process, diagnostic concerns, psychometric concepts, and technology uses.

ASSESSMENT PROCEDURES FOR CAREER COUNSELING

Assessment is comprehensive, dynamic, and a core component of the career counseling process. The Standards for Educational and Psychological Testing (2014) describes assessment as a systematic method that gathers information from multiple resources (e.g., tests) to generate inferences about individual characteristics. Moreover, the assessment process is a multilevel process including informal and formal assessment and guidance from a career counselor (Groth-Marnat, 2009). Informal assessment includes information gathered from client interviews and counselor observations of the client. Formal assessment includes information gathered from standardized tests taken by the client. Informal and formal assessment will be described in more depth later in this chapter. The purpose of assessment is to gather information about the client's concerns, personal attributes, and goals to evaluate and address the issues in counseling (Hood & Johnson, 2007). Engaging in assessment helps the client and counselor make informed decisions. Throughout the assessment process, issues will be identified and plans will be devised to resolve the identified concerns.

Wood and Hays (2012) offer guidelines for the assessment process in counseling. They note that assessment should be a conjoint process with the client. All findings from the assessment process are owned by the client. Tests given to identify aptitudes, achievement, values, interests, personality factors, and career guidance should support client education and development. All components of the assessment process should enhance the client's education and development. Furthermore, the materials used to form the assessment process should be complementary or add something new to the process. In addition, the assessment process should create client self-awareness. Assessments should, therefore, be used for educational and developmental purposes. Finally, the information gathered throughout the assessment process should inform future decisions (Wood & Hays, 2012).

Often clients cannot provide all the information needed in career counseling, so specialized career testing may be necessary. The term **assessment** is often used interchangeably with testing, yet these concepts are not synonymous (Anastasi & Urbina, 1997). Testing is a static representation of an identified construct whereas assessment is a dynamic process (Anastasi & Urbina, 1997). Assessment is evaluated throughout counseling and testing provides a snapshot of the current state of the client (Hood & Johnson, 2007). The client state may include current moods, personality features, and abilities. At each session, the counselor should make a current client assessment (Cameron & Turtle-Song, 2002). The process of assessment will include both formal, standardized evaluations and informal data gathering such as client-shared information, hunches based on clinical experiences, and clinical observations (Anastasi & Urbina, 1997).

INFORMAL ASSESSMENT

Intake Interview

To informally assess the client, it is necessary for the counselor to begin with a clinical interview. Depending on the level of structure of the interview, this interview could be considered formal or informal. However, because the information suggested here includes a broader understanding of the client, it is recommended to not limit the information gathering to only the traditional intake interview methods (Groth-Marnet, 2009). The intake interview presented here is included as an informal assessment (Meyer et al., 2001). Core information to acquire during an initial intake with a client includes the essentials, social information, mental and physical health information, and client resources. The essentials, titled this due to their importance for the entire counseling process, include presenting issues, history of the presenting issues, referral information, any client-driven abusive behaviors, client suicidal and homicidal ideation, and emergency contacts (Mears, 2016). Some of the aforementioned information may seem irrelevant for career counseling. However, as counselors are mandatory reporters, once a client presents in counseling, that counselor is responsible for adverse client behaviors like danger to self or others (ACA, 2014).

Humans are social beings and need others for healthy functioning (Cohn & Meyer, 2014). Understanding client social relationships gives the counselor insight into client functioning. Social information to gather at intake includes family history, other social relationship history such romantic relationships, interpersonal dynamics, current social support, cultural background and cultural identity, and religious and spiritual beliefs and influences (Mears, 2016). Culture, religion, and spirituality are core components of client identity and most clients use their cultural, religious, and spiritual framework to inform important decisions.

Careers are important to most individuals. For example, in the United States, many full time working individuals spend over 40 hours a week performing at their place of employment. Not only do individuals spend much of their time working, but a career can provide financial stability and help build personal identity (Fryers, 2006). Individuals often define themselves through their careers (Fryers, 2006). Consequently, loss of a career can have serious mental health consequences. The relationship between mental and physical health is circular with mutual influences. Assessment is key to uncovering potential, significant mental health concerns. The mental and physical health information to uncover at intake includes history of counseling experiences, achievement on developmental tasks, recent and historical medical concerns, current and historical medication information, current mental health symptoms, current and historical substance usage, history of and recent traumatic events, and any chronic stressors currently faced by the client.

Finally, time should be set aside at intake to gather information concerning the status of resources the client has for gaining employment. Client resources to assess at intake include educational history, employment history, parental employment history, special abilities, additional client resources, and client coping skills. Some additional information may include access to transportation, ability to increase education and training, or any client networking relationships. It is also beneficial to know the client personally and discover what the client enjoys such as leisure activities. This may be a good opportunity to ask about dream jobs or what work would they love to do so much that they would be willing to work for free. Clients will enjoy sharing these aspects of themselves and it will help inform the career counseling process. To prepare for a career, both the counselor and the client need to know where they are beginning to accurately plan for end goals.

Observations

Other informal methods of assessment include client observations (Groth-Marnat, 2009). The counselor will look for objective observations such as how the client is presenting in counseling such as client appearance (does their appearance fit the context, does the client appear disheveled), alertness, level of cooperation, physical behaviors (motor behaviors), speech (rate, flow of language), thought process and content, and level of cognitive functioning (Mears, 2016). The counselor will note if the client is behaving within normal limits or if there is something abnormal about their behaviors. Counselors should take note if any objective observations signal a potential clinical, diagnosable condition. Counselors often use clinical experiences to form hunches concerning how the client is functioning. If clinical observations dictate, counselors may refer clients to a mental health counselor for more serious conditions if the career counselor is unable to perform these mental health services. Clinical observations should be assessed at every session and will be an ongoing evaluation of the status of the client.

Aside from clinical observations, counselors may also encourage clients to make personal observations. The purpose is to help clients gain insight into their personality such as their likes and dislikes or to evaluate previous work experiences. If the client currently has a job, this may be a great opportunity to evaluate enjoyable versus nonenjoyable work conditions. Potential questions for clients to ask themselves include: How is their time scheduled? What is it like to work with their boss? What components of the tasks required do they like and dislike? Maybe they do not like the job but realize they like working with their hands. Maybe they can see they want to be their own boss. Maybe they really like working with people but not in the fashion they currently do. Clients can observe what they enjoy at work and what also makes them want to seek alternative employment. This insight is critical to guiding the career counseling process.

Encourage clients to think outside of themselves as they evaluate current and previous jobs. The client will want to assess how the job affects their familial and spiritual relationships. A career and a job may be enjoyable but the person feels it conflicts with family or spiritual life. For example, does the job require them to work on holy days? Are they working nights and weekends and missing precious time with their family? Encourage the client throughout their personal observations to consider how the job meets personal and familial needs. Many clients will also want to determine if they feel they are being called by God into a certain profession or job.

Formal or Standardized Assessments

As the purpose of assessment is to gather information, it may be necessary to use formal sources. Many objective or standardized tests are available to clients in career counseling. This is often in the form of a quantitative assessment. Testing helps clients assess their qualities and characteristics and determine career maturity, among other constructs. The testing process follows the exploration of new perspectives, asks the difficult questions, and challenges clients to self-exploration. The counselor selects the tests that are right for the client and later helps the client form strategies and plans to move forward with finding the ideal career path (Gunz & Peiperl, 2007; O'Brien, Heppner, Flores, & Bikos, 1997; Savickas, 2003).

Individuals play an enormous role in the process of discovering their ideal career path (Brott, 2004). Individuals may know their values, strengths, interests, and weaknesses; however, they may not know the best way to apply this information to a career choice. Not everyone is attuned to themselves or have gone through a self-exploration journey to discover who they are. We all know we are on this earth for some specific reason. We know God has equipped us with gifts and talents, but we may not know how to put those into practice. Formal assessment tools help clients gain a better understanding of themselves, expand their career options, and find a good match with employers. Selecting a psychometric tool can help in the process of uncovering themes, strengths, and areas of growth in the client's personal life so the client can begin to take steps toward a preferred future career.

Some psychometric tests include personality profiles, motivation questionnaires, and ability assessments. In general, psychometric testing helps clients by providing an objective measure of abilities, highlighting strengths and weaknesses, helping to identify interests, and describing personality traits. Formal assessments used in career counseling are often standardized. Standardized tests provide objective scores on subjective constructs (Carmines & Zeller, 1991; Lambert, 2010). A few of these assessments include but are not limited to the NEO Personality Inventory-3, the Career Commitment Measure, the MAPP career test, and the Hall Occupational Orientation Inventory (Woods & Hayes, 2013). Career instruments give individuals valuable information to help find the right career that matches their unique assessment profile. Furthermore, these tests have been used for many years and have helped numerous individuals. More information about common tests used in career counseling will be presented later in this chapter.

Qualitative assessments are equally valid in career counseling. Some researchers believe that the use of quantitative measures solely may leave out important information that may help the individual to find the ideal career (McMahon & Patton, 2002). Qualitative assessments consider the subjective nature of the client and ensure the counselor can take a personalized approach to career counseling. Qualitative assessments can help the counselor identify client work categories by uncovering career themes such as active, analytical, caring/social, or artistic/creative (Savickas, 2003; Gunz & Peiperl, 2007; Sperry, 2011). Common qualitative assessments include card sorts, genograms, creating career lifelines, examining childhood memories, and identifying life patterns (McMahon & Patton, 2002).

GOALS IN CAREER COUNSELING

At the initial session, the counselor should set aside time to focus on goal setting (Mears, 2016). When a counselor asks a client about goals for counseling, the client often does not have a clear goal in mind. The client is often aware that change needs to happen, yet what change looks like is undecided. Yes, the client may want to find a job, but finding a job and finding a career are very different. Finding someplace to work to meet immediate needs, like paying bills, may not be the place the client wants to be long term. The counselor needs to work with the client to set clear goals with specific objectives in mind. Goals should be measurable outcomes. For example, a goal of being happy at one's work is not a goal because it is difficult to tangibly measure happiness. However, setting a goal to find a job in a designated field is measurable.

While relevant mental health or relationship issues may be addressed in career counseling, goals in career counseling should be centralized on occupational development. To execute career counseling, clients first need to gain self-awareness. Many individuals do not have a clear understanding of which careers many be enjoyable for them. Self-awareness is often accomplished through clinical interviews and personality assessments. Instruments like the Clifton Strengths Finder or Self-Directed Search help individuals learn more about their gifts and identify careers that need individuals with those gifts (Wood & Hayes, 2013). The process of self-exploration helps clients identify career options. With this valuable information, the client may select a field or occupation. Before spending time locating or training for an occupation, it is important to determine if preparing for that field is a worthwhile investment. The Bureau of Labor Statistics (https://www.bls.gov) has information about career outlook such as projected job growth and earnings information.

After clients are knowledgeable about career options, it is time to determine the direction to go with those options. First, establishing a clear understanding of what needs the career or job should meet is important. Clients need to evaluate their personal, situational, and family needs. Many individuals select jobs based on temporary needs. This may happen because they are not sure what jobs are available and appealing to them. They may need financial resources to pay bills or they may be restricted by timing and apply for jobs that fit logistical concerns. Yet, many individuals feel unfulfilled when their job is only convenient and provides financial stability. Prioritizing client needs should take center stage as long as it does not limit the client in choosing viable options. Activities like the Knowdell Career Values Card Sort (Knowdell, 2004) may help clients identify their values. Next, activities like reviewing the tasks and logistics of a position will be helpful for the client to assess if the career aligns with situational and familial needs. For example, a client may be interested in the social dynamics of being a bartender, but it may be difficult to find opportunities to have a career in bartending without working nights. Clients with young children may find it difficult to work those hours away from their little ones.

After the client has decided on a career, career counseling goals focus on helping the client prepare for that career. Aptitude and abilities testing may be necessary to determine if the client has the skills and cognitive abilities to be successful in that career. For example, tests like the Armed Services Vocational Aptitude Battery or the O*NET Ability Profiler may be helpful to confirm the career is a good fit for the client (Wood & Hayes, 2013). The client may need additional education. Deciding on a major in undergraduate education may be harder than expected as many careers do not neatly fall under a certain category. For example, someone interested in theatre management may need both theatre and business courses. Many careers need advanced degrees. When compounding education, the counselor needs to ensure the client has the financial resources and time available to devote to preparing for that career.

After appropriate training and abilities are established, clients at this stage of career counseling need to find the job. Inventories like the Job Search Knowledge Scale (Liptak, 2015) may help identify how savvy clients are about the process of obtaining a job (e.g., identifying job leads, employment interviews). Career counselors should have access to large databases for searching careers. Counselors may want to initially search with the client, but after the client is familiar with how to navigate databases, this activity can be done independently. Clients may choose to search databases like Indeed, LinkUp, or SimplyHired on their own. Clients who are unsuccessful at searching for positions could benefit from instruments like the Job Search Attitude Inventory (Liptak, 2010), which identifies thoughts and feelings about the job search. Helping clients to create generic cover letters and resumes will help them be ready to apply for jobs. Certain fields may request interviewees bring additional material or a portfolio to a job interview. For example, clients interested in advertising may want to create a binder of print ads they created or add a website of their work on their resume.

DIAGNOSIS

Let's explore the concept of diagnosis when it comes to career counseling. Diagnosis is the analysis of facts to gain an understanding or reach a conclusion to aid in future planning (APA, 2013). Therapeutic plans are developed around diagnosis. Diagnosis influences career counseling. A career counselor begins by building a relationship with the client to establish a working partnership. Once a relationship is developed, the counselor moves toward helping clients assess their qualities and characteristics and evaluate current quality of life. During this period, the counselor begins to explore the client's history of past jobs and experiences, and any physical or mental health problems.

Few individuals who seek career assistance have the same characteristics and concerns. Career counseling looks different from one client to another. While the goal of career counseling may not initially be to diagnose, if the client presents with a diagnosis or the counselor recognizes clinical concerns, it is within the best practices of the counselor to concurrently work with the client's present conditions. Various diagnoses in the Diagnostic Statistical Manual of Mental Disorders published by the American Psychiatric Association (APA) specifically state occupational difficulties or impairment in occupational functioning are expected (APA, 2013). These include personality disorder such as borderline personality disorder, obsessive-compulsive personality disorder, avoidant personality disorder, schizotypal personality disorder, antisocial personality disorder, and narcissistic personality disorder. Other diagnosis with affective conditions that may influence career issues include depression, generalized anxiety, attention deficit hyperactivity disorder (ADHD), and learning disabilities among many others.

Mental health concerns may be a limitation for individuals trying to find a career. Mental health problems can affect work performance, confidence in decision-making skills, occupational success, and occupational functioning (Dipeolu, Reardon, Sampson, &

Burkhead, 2002). However, because there might be limitations present, counselors should counter limitations by highlighting the client's relative strengths that can influence individual career development, job competencies, employment success, and job satisfaction (Sperry, 2011).

Individuals diagnosed with mental health disorders may have work-related difficulties (Holland, Daiger, & Power, 1980). Discussion surrounding how the diagnoses may limit the client is a topic that should be covered in the sessions along with other topics. It is important to know how the client's diagnosis has interfered with work-related activities in the past and in the present. The key is not to marginalize clients because they have a history of mental health conditions but rather to be sensitive to their unique needs in a career. Once a counselor learns of a mental health condition, asking follow up questions creates a path for the counselor to discover who the client is. Here the counselor wants to assess what happens to the client when the client is actively experiencing mental health symptoms, what the client's current situation is, how the client copes with their mental health issues, what life events have impacted the client, and what has inhibited the client in finding a career.

Each unique diagnosis may need specific consideration. For example, if the client is prone to depression, do they have a history of missing work? Are they able to hold down a job? If this is the case, answering these questions can give the counselor an idea of what types of positions may or may not be appropriate for the client. If the client does have a history of missing work, it is good to know what the reasons are for the absence. If a client has a history of anxiety disorders, the client may have difficulty working in high-stress situations. Clients with ADHD may struggle with focusing or complete accuracy in tasks. When working with clients with psychotic disorders, the counselor should assess level of lucidity or frequency of positive symptoms. If a client as a learning disability, examining what the areas of disabilities are is necessary. For example, if there is a math disability, handling money may not be the best field for the client.

The counselor continues the diagnostic process by exploring new perspectives and helping choose the assessments that are right for the client and later helping them form strategies and plans to move forward with finding the ideal career path (Savickas, 2003; Hood & Johnson, 2007). During this process, counselors should take into consideration cognitive, affective, and physical components when working with clients. Depending on the severity of the diagnosis, a client's ability to keep a job or perform well at a job could potentially be limited. The counselor should also determine what resources are available for the client including family relationships and those around them on a regular basis (Hood & Johnson, 2007). Career instruments can be used to pinpoint client strengths, needs, and areas for improvement and provide a foundation for individualized intervention (Holland, Daiger, & Power, 1980; Gunz & Peiperl, 2007). Discussing the client's potential areas of growth and strengths with the client can start the process of bridging the gap of uncertainty or fear and getting to the desired future.

THE COUNSELING PROCESS

The practice of career counseling was derived from specific principles of counseling theory and career theory (Patton & McMahon, 2006). Due to radical changes in career planning and lifestyle, unpredictable economic development, and the technological advancement of the 21st century, career counseling is shifting to a postmodern approach of counseling (Maree, 2010). While there are multiple theories and frameworks that can be used when conducting career counseling, the microskills associated with the counseling process remain the same.

Microskills are the building blocks of competency in counselor development (Ridley, Mollen, & Kelly, 2011). Microskills are the basic tools that facilitate therapeutic change and help create the therapeutic relationship (Ridley et al., 2011). Microskills are the underpinnings of the counseling process and are often described in a hierarchy where the most essential skills create the foundation (Ivey, Ivey, & Zalaquett, 2014). The bottom of the microskills pyramid ensures the counselor is ethical and multiculturally sensitive. The attending behaviors are next and communicate to the client that the counselor is present. The basic listening skills follow and include paraphrasing and asking questions. From there, skills become more narrowly focused on specific stages or interventions to frequently use in counseling such as confronting, focusing, and making meaning with the client. It is beyond the scope of this text to review and describe the extensive list of microskills here (see Ivey et al., 2014, for more information).

In order for the counseling process to be beneficial for the client, the counselor and client must have a strong working alliance. A working alliance is formed by having an agreement of goals for treatment and an agreement of the tasks associated with meeting these goals, and by developing a personal bond between the client and clinician (Hepner & Hepner, 2003). Although counseling process research has found that the working alliance accounts for 40%–60% of change in the therapeutic outcome, little is known about the importance of a strong working alliance in career counseling (Hepner & Hepner, 2003).

The career counseling process addresses the covert and overt thoughts, behaviors, and feelings of the client (Hepner & Hepner, 2003). The process of career counseling helps clients uncover meanings and themes in their personal life stories so they can actively decide on which path they want to embark (Brott, 2004). Creating goals for therapy can be beneficial for the counselor in order to assess and create a treatment plan. A relatively new concept in career counseling is to use a systems theory perspective when conducting counseling. Systems theory assesses clients from a systemic perspective; the counselor assesses how clients connect with other systems, such as the individual's social system (e.g., family) and environmental/societal system, and how this influences career development (Patton & McMahon, 2006). Systems theory encourages counselors to use interventions at different levels of the system instead of simply at the individual level (Patton & McMahon, 2006). For a career counselor, this may look like working with an organization or a family in the hopes that interventions anywhere in the system will connect with other elements of the system and bring change (Patton & McMahon, 2006).

In this ever-changing world, career counseling is progressively viewed as vital to the future well-being of not only individuals but nations (Patton & McMahon, 2006). Through the career counseling process, clients can regain control over their personal and career development. Upon the completion of career counseling, clients should be better equipped to confront the complexities of determining a career path and be motivated to implement the skills acquired in career counseling (Maree, 2010).

STANDARDIZED TESTING CONCEPTS

Standardized testing analyzes data from an objective perspective. Standardization generates norms for instruments often based on a large representative sample of the population and creates directions for how to use the test that should be implemented in the same manner each time it is given. A standardized test is administered the same way every time to help reduce any test bias. Since objectivity is key to using tests, a good psychometric test provides fair and accurate results each time it is given. In the standardization process, tests will be evaluated for reliability and validity. There will be more on these concepts later.

Before using an assessment, a counselor should know that these assessments are partialities not absolutes and there are no right or wrong answers (Holland, Daiger, & Power, 1980). All career counselors know that the environment or circumstances under which clients take a test may influence the test results (Sampson, Peterson, Lenz, Reardon, & Saunders, 1996; Kirk & Miller, 1986; Maxwell, 1982; Salkind, 2012), so career counselors understand the findings are not absolute. Results from standardized tests should be used to stimulate the client's possibilities rather than lock them into a particular label.

Reliability and Validity

Reliability and validity are two essential concepts valuable in the process of selecting, administering, and interpreting a test (Hood & Johnson, 2007). Reliability is the ability for a test to produce the same or similar results overtime. Reliability measures test consistency. In this case, if the individual takes the same test twice or one hundred times, the scores should be similar. In other words, reliability is how consistent, stable, and trustworthy the results are over time.

There are different ways that reliability can be measured: Test-retest reliability, alternate-form reliability, and internal consistency. Test-retest reliability is the most common measure of reliability (Hood & Johnson, 2007). Test-retest reliability correlates scores across test administration. This type of reliability looks at how consistent the test is and whether it produces the same results each time it is used. An example of this would be to give your client the same test on two different occasions to measure how the scores are similar across administration. The more similar the test scores are, the more reliable the test. Another method to examine correlations between scores involves changing the test format while still measuring the same construct. Alternate-form reliability, also known as parallel or equivalent forms reliability, is used to determine if several different forms of the same test are reliable or alike (Hood & Johnson, 2007). Alternative forms of tests are necessary to prevent individuals from using previous information gained from the first test when answering questions during the second test. Each test form has different items from a pool of questions that covers the same concepts. Both versions of the tests must measure the same concepts and have equitable scores.

Repeating tests, regardless of version, may not be the best measure of reliability in cases where the test may produce a learning effect. For example, simply repeating the test enables the individual to practice and may increase scores (e.g., aptitude tests). Internal consistency reliability examines if the items on a test assess one, and only one, dimension. This type of analysis measures the relationship between the items on the test and the total score of those dimensions (Neukrug & Fawcett, 2015). In other words, internal consistency measures whether the questions on the test are related to each other and related to the overall construct. Types of internal consistency include Cronbach's coefficient alpha, split-half (odd-even), and Kuder-Richardson. Cronbach's and Kuder-Richardson coefficient alphas both correlate all the items with total test score (Salkind, 2012). Cornbach's coefficient alpha can be used across all types of tests whereas Kuder-Richardson coefficient alpha can only be applied to tests that have a correct answer (e.g., achievement tests; Neukrug & Fawcett, 2015). Split-half (odd-even) reliability measures reliability across one test administration. This type of reliability divides the test in half to correlate scores between the two (Neukrug & Fawcett, 2015). An easy method is to divide the test by odd or even numbers.

For a test to have evidence of validity, it must first be reliable. Validity is an examination of the evidence to support that the test accurately measures what it claims to measure. Validity in an instrument varies along a continuum from low to high (Kirk & Miller, 1986). Validity is defined as "the degree to which accumulated evidence supports the proposed interpretation of test scores for the purpose for which they will be used" (Hood & Johnson, 2007, p. 38). In other words, is there support to use the test to measure the intended construct?

There are different ways to test for validity: content validity, criterion-related validity, and construct validity. Content validity determines if the content of the test is reflective of the construct (Neukrug & Fawcett, 2015). Content validity assesses whether the test items are comprehensive enough to capture the full construct. An example would be seeing if the test does a good job at measuring achievement. Criterion-related validity examines if test scores are related to performance or other criteria (Neukrug & Fawcett, 2015). Criterion-related validity can measure both present and future performance. Concurrent validity is a type of criterion-related validity that compares test scores with current abilities. For example, is there a correlation between test performance and job performance? Predictive validity is a type of criterion-related validity that compares test scores against future performance. For example, is there a relationship between GRE scores and performance in graduate school?

Construct validity compiles the evidence that one identified construct is being measured by the test (Neukrug & Fawcett, 2015). There are three traditional methods of measuring construct validity: convergent validity, discriminant validity, and factor analysis (Neukrug

& Fawcett, 2015). Convergent validity measures if the test correlates with other tests measuring the same construct. For example, a test measuring romantic relationship satisfaction is shown to have evidence of convergent validity if scores on the identified instrument are highly correlated with scores on other well-known tests of romantic relationship satisfaction. Discriminant validity is the opposite of convergent validity. Discriminant validity measures that a test is distinct from unrelated constructs. For example, a depression inventory would have evidence of discriminant validity if correlations would show no relationship to tests measuring happiness. Factor analysis is a statistical method of measuring construct validity that measures the relationship between items and total test scores. Factor analysis examines that test items load or are assigned to subscales or total tests measuring the identified construct. When all test items load on the construct, this demonstrates the test is measuring one construct.

Issues in Achieving Equity in Assessment

Counselors see a diverse range of clients of all backgrounds and individuals in different stages of their career. All clients bring a unique system of influences and set ideals that shape who they are. Not every assessment used in the counseling process is considered appropriate for all clients. Equity across tests needs to be thoroughly evaluated with each client. This is important for counselors to consider when selecting tests to administer, interpreting test scores, applying test results, and devising future plans. For years, fields such as psychology, sociology, biology, and anthropology have studied how cultural differences affect assessment, yielding that no global measurement tool can be created to be used cross-culturally (Metz & Jones, 2013). Career inventories can help the counselor address the needs of the client if the inventories take gender, age, ethnicity, sexual orientation, culture, mental health, and physical health into consideration. Due to inequity in assessments, it can be difficult to find measurements that consider the aforementioned cultural variations while standardizing tests.

Career instruments used in professional practice have often been criticized for perpetuation of economic, social, and political barriers affecting individuals such as women, racial and ethnic minorities, low socioeconomic status (SES), language minorities, and individuals with disabilities (Suzuki & Ponterotto, 2007). When looking for appropriate tests for clients, counselors should first consider if the test is a valid measure for the client. Counselor should evaluate whether the client fits the normative sample. Assessment instruments that are normed on majority group populations should not be used with individuals who would be considered nonnormative populations (Suzuki & Ponterotto, 2007). Results may not be accurate for individuals who differ even ever so slightly from the normative sample. Normative samples are often not representative of all populations and careful attention needs to be paid to selecting instruments to ensure the client fits the normative sample.

If normed tests without a reflective sample must be used, special consideration of such factors as age, race, SES, and language should be considered when interpreting test outcomes. Counselors should be aware that how test results are used can harm a client if cultural factors are not evaluated. A test may be capturing a cultural dimension rather than the intended construct. For example, aptitude tests may use descriptive stories in questions to test reading comprehension, but if the story is about an unfamiliar topic, individuals not previously exposed to that topic may perform poorly on that test. In return, the test results may suggest deficiency in the area. Let's say an aptitude test describes sailing. As many individuals have never gone sailing, the novelty of the situation detracts from the cognitive resources available to accurately respond to reading comprehension questions. Until test makers consider cultural bias, many individuals will continue to be adversely affected by test results. Counselors need to ensure any test results are valid before using the information for client treatment.

There are other contextual factors that career counselors should take into consideration when trying to achieve equity in assessments. Religion and spirituality are two important cultural aspects that play a vital role in the development of an individual. Clients who present with career-related concerns are often seeking a greater sense of purpose from their work (Dik, Duffy, & Eldridge, 2009). Career counselors should take this into consideration when determining how to best assess and treat clients. A vital first step is to evaluate the importance and relevance of the spiritual journey for the client (Dik et al., 2009). The client's spiritual journey may determine how the client finds meaning in career choices. Spirituality and religion can be a powerful and motivating role in career development and decision-making, and the counselor would be wise to capitalize on it (Dik et al., 2009). Certain clients may be looking to connect meaning in work to meaning in life. When this is the case, counselors are encouraged to approach these issues through the specific cultural lens of the client (Dik et al., 2009). By doing this, the counselors will be able to take the client's cultural beliefs into account when interpreting results.

Multiple instruments can be used in career counseling. Each instrument will measure different constructs and each instrument will have strengths and weaknesses (Wood & Hayes, 2013). Career counselors should take precaution in picking culturally sensitive, nonbiased assessments for each individual client (Groth-Marnat, 2009).

Information about Assessment Instruments

Assessment instruments are key to facilitating the career counseling process (Wood & Hayes, 2013). Many individuals present in career counseling with no preconceptions of what the best type of position or career is for them. Aside from lack of guidance on career paths, many individuals are not aware how their personalities and values shape their career choices. Individuals also may not know how their personal strengths or abilities will assist them in pursuing a specific career. A variety of instruments are available to test factors important in career counseling. Please note the words test, instrument, inventory, and scale may be used interchangeably to denote a specific method of formal assessment designed to measure specific construct (Anastasi & Urbina, 1997).

Choosing the correct instruments or tests to guide the career counseling process is essential (Groth-Marnat, 2009). Many clients may present for counseling having already taken some widely used inventories. High schools commonly give the Myers-Briggs Type Indicator to help students understand more about their personality (MacLellan, 2011). The Internet has a wide array of inventories available; however, the quality of instruments available online may be called into question. Instruments available freely for use have often not gone through a rigorous standardization process or have not had the reliability and validity tested. Unfortunately, many individuals use Internet tests to make important life decisions. Even if a client has access to a reliable measure with evidence of validity, if clients know little about standardization they may not understand the meaning behind the scores. Without trained counselors available to interpret test scores in the correct context to help the client understand how to use the information, much of the information gleaned from an online test may not be helpful (Hood & Johnson, 2007). For example, someone may score in the 50th percentile on an aptitude test indicating they have average abilities (Groth-Marnat, 2009). However, the client without knowledge of testing may interpret the finding as failing because they are using the traditional grading system as a frame of reference.

Key types of standardized measures used in career counseling include personality inventories, aptitude or achievement tests, interest inventories, values tests, career development measures, and comprehensive career measures (Wood & Hayes, 2013). Most clients enjoy personality tests. Many common personality tests used in career counseling such as the Sixteen Personality Factor Questionnaire, the Career Development Report, or the Career Key provide useful information about personality attributes and translate personality features to what careers the client may be well suited (Wood & Hayes, 2013). Interest inventories are similar to personality tests as they help link client factors to potential careers. Common interest inventories useful in career counseling include the Campbell Interest and Skill Survey and the Career Directions Inventory (Wood & Hayes, 2013). Like many tests, both instruments have multiple scales to provide a more accurate understanding of who the client is. Values inventories help to incorporate what the client views as most important into selecting a career. Tests like the Career and Life Explorer or the Values Preference Indicator assess for factors outside of interests to help clients determine the optimal career (Wood & Hayes, 2013).

Sometimes clients are intimidated by achievement and aptitude tests. Achievement tests measure what skills and knowledge the client has acquired. Aptitude tests measure the ability to develop or master skills. When clients think of these types of tests, they often associate them with the Scholastic Aptitude Test (SAT) or the Graduate Record Examination (GRE), but there are many more tests available that are directly applicable to a work setting such as the Highlands Ability Battery or the Workplace Skills Survey (Wood & Hayes, 2013). Knowing where clients are in terms of their progress for career development needs to be determined. Scales like the Career Development Inventory or the Career Factors Inventory measure readiness for a career whereas tests like Barriers to Employment Success Inventory measure what may hinder the career progress (Wood & Hayes, 2013).

Finally, there are a wide variety of tests designed to assess career suitability from a more comprehensive background. Comprehensive career instruments may provide the client with data on interests, strengths, career alignment, abilities, and achievements in one test. These types of tests tend to take more time to complete (approximately two hours) but they provide the clients with more information than instruments designed to examine only one construct. These instruments may be particularly useful in school settings where students lack career direction. The Differential Aptitude Tests for Personnel and Career Assessment (Bennett, Seashore, & Wesmen, 1996) tests cognitive, perceptual, language, and clerical skills to help students select courses and help guide their career paths. There are other tests that include a battery of inventories that may put numerous types of inventories into one collection such as the Kuder Career Planning System: Kuder Career Interest Assessment, Kuder Skills Confidence Assessment, and Kuder Work Values Assessment (Kuder, 1999).

Remember to keep psychometric testing in perspective as well as provide follow up questions. These tests are only one of many different types of assessments that you can use in career development. No single instrument can provide the right and complete answers. There is no perfect assessment that helps clients determine what career to pursue or their purpose in life. These assessments can assist in providing insights about what areas of work to pursue. Keep in mind that at the end of the day, clients decide what they want to be and do. Tests supply ideas of how to put individual gifts and talents to practice, whether that means working in the ministry or working somewhere else.

USING TECHNOLOGY IN CAREER COUNSELING

Computers have helped change the path of the career counseling process. Technology has changed the way clinicians navigate the counseling process. Using computers before, during, and following counseling sessions has become commonplace in many settings. Standardized assessments are no longer taken with a pencil and paper; instead, clients use computer programs to assess for different career development abilities. With the Internet so widely accessible, computers have become an essential tool for career counselors. Technology has changed how individuals search for positions. Clients can use search engines to help find jobs and make contacts. Materials fundamental to acquiring jobs are all created on computers. Career counselors can help clients create cover letters, resumes, and even execute mock interviews with the use of computer software.

Throughout the years, research regarding the use of information and communication technology in the counseling process has found both potential benefits and multiple limitations (Sampson & Makela, 2014). The Internet provides access to a variety of career resources and services that enable counseling and guidance to extend beyond geographical and physical boundaries (Sampson & Makela, 2014). Even though technology offers countless resources, there are many ethical and legal considerations that must be considered when using computers for career counseling. Two main concerns for counselors are confidentiality and user privacy. Using the Internet to create, store, and retrieve client case notes and assessments increases the opportunities for access to records, which in turn, exacerbates the confidentiality problem (Sampson & Makela, 2014). To decrease violations of confidentiality, career counselors should take appropriate security measures such as periodically changing passwords and using data encryption for Internet communication (Sampson & Makela, 2014). Counselors should also make sure that all computers used are located where others cannot read or see what is on the screen. These simple solutions will help decrease ethical and legal violations when working with clients.

Career counselors must also consider the limitations that may arise when using technology with clients. It is important to first consider client skill ability and comfort regarding computer processes (Osborn et al., 2014). People with certain disabilities may not be capable of working at a computer to perform a test, assessment, or instrument without proper supervision or assistance. Career counselors must evaluate the level of comfort and skill ability prior to sending a client to work at a computer. If a client presents with a low level of comfort or skill, explore different ways a client can build computer and technological skills such as training courses (Osborn et al., 2014).

Technology such as social media, websites, and applications has broadened the resources available for counselors today (Osborn et al., 2014). When used properly, technology can be an asset in the counseling process and can assist clients in meeting their goals. Yet, career counselors must be vigilant to continuously assess for ethical and legal issues that may arise when using computers in their practice.

CONCLUSION

The career counseling process requires a depth of knowledge to meet client needs. Many incorrectly assume career counselors help students select majors and clients locate jobs. The work of the career counselor extends exponentially beyond these tasks. A career counselor knows the importance of a holistic assessment to execute effective career counseling. To begin career counseling, gathering information via a comprehensive intake interview helps the career counselor identify client needs and resources. From there, other methods of informal assessment such as clinical and personal observations are necessary; formal assessments using quality psychometric instruments contribute to career counseling as well. As career counseling progresses, emerging mental health concerns may sway career counseling to pay special attention to the unique needs of clients with clinical diagnoses. Additionally, as career counseling progresses, using more standardized instruments may be necessary to help clients increase self-awareness, assess special abilities, highlight values and interests, guide career options, and evaluate career development and maturity. Selecting tests to use in career counseling should always be a rigorous method to ensure all tests used are reliable, have evidence of validity, have been standardized with a sample that matches the clientele, and considers the findings not as absolutes but as one piece of the puzzle that may or may not accurately represent the client. A good career counselor knows to always seek out feedback from the client because no matter how rigorous the measure, nothing can replace direct client feedback. Career counselors may want to enhance the counseling process with technology, although, technology should only be used in counseling after ethical and confidentiality concerns have been fully evaluated.

KEY TERMS

Assessment: a systematic method that gathers information from multiple resources (e.g., intake interview, tests) to generate inferences about individual characteristics

Concurrent validity: a type of criterion-related validity that compares tests scores to current external performance

Construct validity: evaluates if a test measures a designated construct

Content validity: determines if the content of a test is reflective of the entire construct

Convergent validity: a type of construct validity that measures if the test correlates with other tests measuring the same construct

Criterion-related validity: examines the relationship between test outcome and an external source that measures the same construct

Cronbach's coefficient alpha: measures internal consistency reliability across all types of tests

Diagnosis: the analysis of information to gain an understanding or reach a conclusion to aid in future planning

Discriminant validity: a type of construct validity that measures that a test is distinct from unrelated constructs

Factor analysis: a statistical method of measuring construct validity that measures the relationship between items and total test scores

Formal assessment: standardized or widely used tests designed to gain insight into client personality, attributes, abilities, values, or interests

Informal assessment: nonstandardized methods of gathering client information

Internal consistency: a within-test method of measuring reliability that measures how individual items correlate with total test scores

Kuder-Richardson coefficient alpha: measures internal consistency reliability only with tests where answers must have a correct answer

Predictive validity: a type of criterion-related validity that compares test scores to future external performance

Reliability: the ability for a test to produce the same or similar results overtime

Split-half (odd-even) reliability: measures reliability across one test administration by dividing the test in half to correlate scores between the two

Test-retest reliability: the ability for a test to produce the same or similar results across test administrations

Validity: examining if the test measures the construct it intends to measure

REFLECTION AND DISCUSSION

1. What information should be gathered during an intake interview?
2. How frequently should assessments happen?
3. What types of tests can be used in career counseling?
4. What is the difference between reliability and validity? What are the different types of reliability and validity?
5. What are the ethical concerns when selecting instruments and using technology in career counseling?

ADDITIONAL READINGS, RESOURCES, AND WEBSITES

Helpful career websites:

https://www.bls.gov

https://www.indeed.com

https://linkup.com

https://www.simplyhired.com

For a comprehensive review of assessments, see:

Wood, C., & Hays, D. (2013). A counselor's guide to career assessment instruments (6th ed.) Broken Arrow, OK: National Career Development Association.

Helpful places to search for tests and evaluate their psychometrics:

Mental Measurement Yearbook

Tests in Print

TRADITIONAL ACTIVITY

Read the following case study and discuss how you would work with this client in career counseling.

Case Study

Anna is a single, 36-year-old, Latina woman with two children (a son aged eight and daughter aged six). She presents in career counseling searching for a new career path. She has worked retail for the past twenty years. She is currently a manager of a clothing shop. She has a high school diploma and would like to go to college. Her work will pay for her degree, and she would like to utilize this work benefit. She has no idea what she would like to study but has always imagined herself as a high-powered career woman. She has a history of depression and her current depressive episode was the impetus for her pursuing career counseling. She views her depression as rooted in her career not turning out as she had planned.

Respond

What components of the assessment process would you include in counseling Anna? How would you approach Anna's history of depression in counseling? What questions would be important to ask?

SPIRITUAL ACTIVITY

Read the following Biblical quote and discuss how to use this quote in career counseling.

> The Lord will fulfill his purpose for me; your steadfast love, O Lord, endures forever. Do not forsake the work of your hands.
>
> Psalm 138:8 English Standard Version (ESV)

Respond

How does your choice of career fulfill God's purpose for you? What is the meaning behind the phrase "do not forsake the work of your hands"? How does this apply to career counseling?

REFERENCES

American Counseling Association. (2014). Code of ethics. Retrieved from https://www.counseling.org/Resources/aca-code-of-ethics.pdf

American Psychiatric Association. (2013). Diagnostic and statistical manual of mental disorders (5th ed.). Washington, DC: American Psychiatric Association.

Anastasi, A., & Urbina, S. (1997). Psychological testing. Upper Saddle River, N.J: Prentice Hall.

Anderson, W. P., & Niles, S. G. (2000). Important events in career counseling: Client and counselor descriptions. The Career Development Quarterly, 48, 251–263

Bennett, G., Seashore, H., & Wesmen, A. (1996). Differential aptitude tests for personnel and career assessment. San Antonio, TX: Pearson.

Brott, P. E. (2004). Constructivist Assessment in Career counseling. Journal of Career Development, 30(3), 189–200. doi:10.1023/B:JOCD.0000015539.21158.53

Cameron, S. and Turtle-Song, I. (2002), Learning to write case notes using the SOAP format. Journal of Counseling & Development, 80, 286–292. doi:10.1002/j.1556-6678.2002.tb00193.x

Carmines, E. G., & Zeller, R. A. (1979). Reliability and validity assessment. Thousand Oaks, CA: SAGE Publications Ltd.

Cohn, A., & Meyer, D. (2014). Families and Health. In M. Coleman & L. Ganong. The Social History of the American Family: An Encyclopedia. Thousand Oaks, CA: SAGE Publishing. doi: 10.4135/9781452286143.n205

Dagley, J. C., & Salter, S. K. (2004). Practice and research in career counseling and development. The Career Development Quarterly, 53, 98–156. doi:10.1002/j.2161-0045.2005.tb00145.x

Dik, B. J., Duffy, R. D., & Eldridge, B. M. (2009). Calling and vocation in career counseling: Recommendations for promoting meaningful work. Professional Psychology: Research and Practice, 40(6), 625–632. doi:10.1037/a0015547

Dipeolu, A. O., Hargrave, S., & Storlie, C. A. (2015). Enhancing ADHD and LD diagnostic accuracy using career instruments. Journal of Career Development, 42(1), 19–32.

Dipeolu, A. O., Reardon, R., Sampson, J., & Burkhead, E. J. (2002). The relationship between dysfunctional career thoughts and adjustment to disability in college student with learning disabilities. Journal of Career Assessment, 10, 413–427.

Fryers, T. (2006). Work, identity and health. Clinical Practice and Epidemiology in Mental Health, 2, 12–18. doi: 10.1186/1745-0179-2-12

Groth-Marnat, G. (2009). Handbook of Psychological Assessment 5th Ed. Hoboken, NJ: John Wiley & Sons, Inc.

Gunz, H. & Peiperl, M. (2007). Handbook of career studies. Thousand Oaks, CA: SAGE Publications Ltd.

Heppner, M. J., & Heppner, P. P. (2003). Identifying process variables in career counseling: A research agenda. Journal of Vocational Behavior, 62(3), 429–452.

Heppner, P., Wampold, B., & Kivlighan, D. (2008). Research design in counseling (3rd ed). Belmont, CA: Brooks/Cole.

Holland, J. L., Daiger, D., & Power, P. (1980). My vocational situation. Palo Alto, CA: Consulting Psychologists Press.

Hood, A. B., & Johnson, R. W. (2007). Assessment in counseling: A guide to the use of psychological assessment procedures. Alexandria, VA: American Counseling Association.

Knowdell, R. L. (2004). Career values card sort. San Jose, CA: Career Research & Testing, Inc.

Ivey, A., Ivey, M., & Zalaquett, C. (2014). Intentional interviewing and counseling: Facilitating client development in multicultural society (8th ed). Belmont, CA: Brooks/Cole.

Kirk, J., & Miller, M. L. (1986). Reliability and validity in qualitative research. Beverly Hills: Sage Publications.

Kuder, F. (1999). Kuder Career Planning Services. Adel, IA: Kuder, Inc.

Lambert, M. (2010). Prevention of treatment failure: The use of measuring, monitoring, and feedback in clinical practice. Washington, DC: American Psychological Association.

Liptak, J. (2015). Job search knowledge scale (3rd ed). Indianapolis, IN: JIST Publishing

Liptak, J. (2010). Job search attitude inventory (4th ed). Indianapolis, IN: JIST Publishing

MacLellan, C.R. (2011). Differences in Myers-Briggs personality types among high school band, orchestra, and choir members. Journal of Research in Music Education, 59(1), 85–100. doi:10.1177/0022429410395579

Maree, J. G. (2010). Brief overview of the advancement of postmodern approaches to career counseling. Journal of Psychology in Africa, 20(3), 361–367.

Maxwell, J. A. (1992). Understanding and validity in qualitative research. Harvard Educational Review, 62(3), 279–300.

McMahon, M., & Patton, W. (2002). Using qualitative assessment in Career Counseling. International Journal for Educational and Vocational Guidance, 2, 56–66. doi: 10.1023/A:1014283407496

Mears, G. (2016). Conducting an intake interview. In I. Marini & M. Stebnick. The Professional counselor desk reference 2nd ed. (pp 83–87). New York, NY: Springer Publishing.

Metz, A. J., & Jones, J. E. (2013). Ability and Aptitude Assessment in Career Counseling (2nd ed). Hoboken, NJ: John Wiley & Sons.

Meyer, G. J., Finn, S. E., Eyde, L. D., Kay, G. G., Moreland, K. L., Dies, R. R., Eisman, E.J., Kubiszyn, T.W., & Reed, G. M. (2001). Psychological testing and psychological assessment: A review of evidence and issues. American Psychologist, 56, 128–165.

Neukrug, E. & Fawcett, R. C. (2015). Essentials of Testing & Assessment: A practical guide for counselors, social workers, and psychologists (3rd ed). Stamford, CT: Cengage Learning.

O'Brien, K. M., Heppner, M. J., Flores, L. Y., & Bikos, L. H. (1997). The Career Counseling Self-Efficiency Scale: Instrument development and training applications. Journal of Counseling Psychology, 44(1), 20–31. doi: 10.1037/0022-0167.44.1.20

Osborn, D. S., Kronholz, J. F., Finklea, J. T., & Cantonis, A. M. (2014). Technology-savvy career counselling. Canadian Psychology/Psychologie Canadienne, 55(4), 258. doi:10.1037/a0038160

Patton, W., & McMahon, M. (2006). The systems theory framework of career development and counseling: Connecting theory and practice. International Journal for the Advancement of Counselling, 28(2), 153–166. doi: 10.1007/s10447-005-9010-1

Ridley, C. R., Mollen, D., & Kelly, S. M. (2011). Beyond Microskills Toward a Model of Counseling Competence. The Counseling Psychologist, 39(6), 825–864. doi: 10.1177/0011000010378440

Salkind, N. J. (2012). Tests & measurement for people who (think they) hate tests & measurement. Thousand Oaks, CA: Sage.

Sampson, J. P., & Makela, J. P. (2014). Ethical issues associated with information and communication technology in counseling and guidance. International Journal for Educational and Vocational Guidance, 14(1), 135–148.

Sampson Jr, J. P., Peterson, G. W., Lenz, J. G., Reardon, R. C., & Saunders, D. E. (1996). Improving your career thoughts: A workbook for the Career Thoughts Inventory. Odessa, FL: Psychological Assessment Resources.

Savickas, M. L. (2003). Advancing the career counseling profession: Objectives and strategies for the next decade. The Career Development Quarterly, 52, 87 - 96. doi: 10.1002/j.2161-0045.2003.tb00631.x

Standards for educational and psychological testing (2014). Washington, DC: American Educational Research Association.

Sperry, L. (2011). Family Assessment: Contemporary and Cutting-Edge Strategies. New York, NY:Routledge.

Suzuki, L. A., & Ponterotto, J. G. (Eds.). (2007). Handbook of multicultural assessment: Clinical, psychological, and educational applications, 3rd edition. San Francisco, CA: John Wiley & Sons.

Wood, C., & Hays, D. (2013). A counselor's guide to career assessment instruments (6th Ed.) Broken Arrow, OK: National Career Development Association.

SECTION II

Overview of Career Development Theory

4

Modern Career Counseling Theory

Teri Hourihan, MA, LPC and Cyrus R. Williams III, PhD, LPC

In the beginning there was the Word, and the Word was with God, and the Word was God.

John 1:1, New International Version

LEARNING OBJECTIVES

In this chapter, students will learn about

- The guidance movement
- How the counseling field developed out of the guidance movement
- Trait and factor theory
- The integration of work and personal traits toward longevity in work-related roles
- Work adjustment theory
- Holland's type theory
- Myers-Briggs type theory
- Occupational information systems

LEARNING OUTCOMES

At the end of this chapter, students will be able to

- Summarize the beginning stages of the guidance movement
- Describe the theory behind the trait and factor theory
- Critique what it means to match a work setting to a person
- Intervene to help clients adjust to their work settings
- Provide examples for how abilities, values, and reinforcers work together
- Describe assessment instruments and occupational systems

CHAPTER HIGHLIGHTS

- The beginning of the guidance movement
- Vocational guidance centers
- The trait and factor theory
- Myers-Briggs type theory
- Work adjustment and career matching
- Assessment instruments
- Occupational information systems

INTRODUCTION

Vocational guidance counseling traces its origins back to the Renaissance era (Carson & Altai, 1994). From the very beginning, people were interested in helping others to fit into career placements. The scripture for this chapter is a great title for the purpose running through each section. This is a chapter covering the roots of career counseling, the very beginning points. Around the time of World War I, guidance counseling centers were springing up around the United States to assist returning veterans with vocational guidance (Leong, 2008). Funding was granted for universities to house complete guidance centers connected to the university itself. This was a mile marker for counseling.

Frank Parsons is the one of the most cited individuals for the guidance counseling theory. However, there were several before and after Parsons who began the movement in career counseling. For instance, John Dewey in the 1920s proposed a developmental stage approach to help kids navigate adolescence. His approach supported the idea that schools need to develop steps toward career placement from a cognitive developmental standpoint. John Dewey's developmental model was integrated into career guidance centers in schools to match the student's developmental level (Lambie & Williamson, 2004). In 1930, Williamson built on Parsons' trait and factor theory. Williamson was the first to develop a guidance counseling theory (Lambie & Williamson, 2004). Up until 1942, Williamson's and Freud's approaches—vastly different but both directive—were the only two approaches in the field making an impact on counseling theory in general. This changed, however, when in 1942 Carl Rogers entered the scene with his publication of Counseling and Psychotherapy: New Concepts in Practice. Rogers took a very different approach to counseling, one that would change the field of counseling as it was known during that time (Lambie & Williamson, 2004).

This chapter works like a grounding piece for all other material in the book. Without understanding the beginning, it will be difficult to understand how far the field of counseling has come. The beginning of this chapter will provide information on how the counseling movement began and the direction it has taken throughout the years by various theorists. Several theoretical orientations in career counseling will be reviewed, including the trait and factor theory, the work adjustment theory, and Holland's type theory. These are all early theories that give rise to later theories highlighted throughout the rest of this book.

VOCATIONAL GUIDANCE MOVEMENT

Frank Parsons is known in the field of counseling as the "Father of Guidance" (Lambie & Williamson, 2004). He essentially was the founder of the official guidance movement. However, there is evidence that vocational counseling had been around for many centuries prior to Parsons (Carson & Altai, 1994). The vocational guidance movement began because there was a need to bridge the gap between students and career placement (Briddick, 2009; Kantor, 1986). It is important to note that in the early 1900s, the term for the role of guidance counseling as it is known today was vocational guidance (Lambie & Williamson, 2004). Prior to 1900, Parsons worked in various careers, from railroad worker to educator, and he wrote about the poverty of many people living in the United States. Moreover, he was vocal about the divide between rich and poor and found it troubling that youth were developing in a world of work with no formal direction for how to do so (Zytowski, 2001). Consequently, in 1906 Parsons suggested in a speech that children and adolescents need vocational guidance so they can leave school with some direction along with feeling prepared (Zytowski). Parsons was so motivating that he won the interest of administrators of local high schools, who invited him to come speak at their schools and devise a proposal for financial support for guidance counseling within school districts (Zytowski, 2001). He was given the funding to begin a vocational guidance center where he served both as director and counselor to students (Zytowski, 2001).

Vocational Guidance Centers in Schools

Helping youth find jobs and career placement was at first solely the educator's responsibility (Kantor, 1986). Parties agreeing to this objective wanted to create a way for youth to leave school and begin work, work that they would enjoy and stay in. The first guidance centers developed were in California high schools (Kantor, 1986). It is necessary here to realize there was some fear related to this call for schools to have the responsibility of providing guidance to students for career placement (Kantor, 1986). The fear was that students were aimlessly leaving school without any direction because their career focus was not in reality aligned with their interest or abilities (Kantor, 1986). At first, the drive was to focus on bridging this gap but later it became just a way for guidance counselors to work with teens in the school settings alone. In addition, because the first people to offer guidance counseling were not counselors but teachers (Kantor, 1986), each teacher was given up to 25 students and expected to provide each student with guidance counseling throughout their schooling. However, teachers were not only unequipped to take on this role but they also did not have enough time. Consequently, principals, vice principals, and other administrative staff helped in the process of counseling students into career placement. At the end of school, each student was matched to a job simply through career placement.

Because guidance counseling began in secondary school systems, it was students who began to understand themselves in terms of their preferences for certain careers over others (Kantor, 1986). In fact, there was such a boom throughout the United States, beginning first in California, for guidance counseling that high schools established programs in their schools and required students to take a course on vocational interest. Parsons believed that the interest of students was developed through individual impressions regarding working orientation and roles (Briddick, 2009). These impressions, furthermore, were interests that developed with time and became more focused. However, Parsons' thoughts on interests and careers were not the first to be proposed in the field (Carson & Altai, 1994) and he is mentioned by some to not have developed his theory into a working model (Briddick, 2009). Nonetheless, it is clear that Parsons' contributions to the field are tremendous (Kantor, 1986).

One of the main products of Parsons' work was his suggestion of six steps for matching interests with career placement. McDaniels (1994) summarizes these steps from the work of Parsons (1909) as (1) knowledge about self (areas of strength and weakness), (2) knowledge about the world of work (expectations and roles), and (3) integration of knowledge of self and the world of work. Parsons' view was that the placement came as a product of time spent in life working toward goals and taking in new knowledge (McDaniels, 1994). His role as a counselor and educator was to work alongside students to help them obtain the career placement of their choice. This is much different today in the world of career assessment and match—same day assessment and match. These steps will be defined in the next section.

TRAIT AND FACTOR THEORY

One of the earliest career counseling theories to hit the counseling landscape was the trait and factor theory developed by E. G. Williamson (Chartrand, 1991; Geist, 1990; Lambie & Williamson, 2004; Leong, 2008). This theory sought to give meaning to personality by labeling traits. This was an approach to match prospective career persons with the job placement they fit best. Just like Parsons' matching theory, this too is a matching approach (Chartrand, 1991). Williamson in 1939 (Chartrand & Bertok, 1993) was the contributor most responsible for building the approach from Parsons and implementing it within the counseling field. Williamson expanded the model to represent a career counseling model that helped people to work through change by prescribing a problem-solving agenda (Chartrand & Bertok, 1993). As it remains to this day, there are six proposed steps in Williamson's model: analysis, synthesis, diagnosis, prognosis, counseling, and follow-up. The first four steps are assessment driven, and the last two are psychoeducational- and problem-focused (Chartrand & Bertok, 1993). This is still the current trait and factor approach. There are, however, integrating features in the approach as years continue, such as cognitive behavioral theory (Chartrand & Bertok, 1993).

The trait and factor theory set the stage for later career counseling development (Lambie & Williamson, 2004). This model is driven by its tenet that people naturally aim to work and live in environments that create comfort (Chartrand & Bertok, 1993). Essentially, the proponents of this theory propose that people be matched to their environment to suggest work-setting preferences. Counselors using this model, furthermore, will help their clients gain insight into their preferred environments, setting the stage for clients to understand congruence. As clients and counselors are beginning to understand the areas of congruence of environment and personality trait of clients, they begin to work on matching each of them together. Traits are considered linked to personality and factors that relate to areas of work. Additionally, work settings and individuals are in relationship with one another (Zhang & Au Yeung, 2003). This simply means that these certain parts of human personality are an asset to some particular career role. Zhang and Au Yeung developed a trait and factor approach with prospective college and university students in Hong Kong that matches student interest to academic programming. It was one of the earliest academic online tools to provide pro-gram matching to student interest. One of the key findings in their study is that Hong Kong students' personal attribute characteristics are significantly different than that of students from Western countries. This is important to know as career counselors begin to use certain assessment tools with different client populations.

Trait and Factor Theory Parts

Knowledge about self, knowledge about the world of work, and the integration of knowledge of self and the world of work are related to the work by Parsons. These areas show up in trait and factor theory as signifying how personal traits are matched to career placement. Much like a developmental progression of understanding, it is proposed that people develop interest starting first with self, then work, and then how they two integrate.

Knowledge about self. Self-knowledge develops as a result of a person taking time to explore different areas of one's life to see what they enjoy and do not enjoy. Parsons proposed this is a process and develops over time and cannot be explained solely through assessment alone (McDaniels, 1994). Each person is a participant in their development and their interests can change over time as they change.

Knowledge about the world of work. Work context is labeled "work understanding" (Chartrand, 1991). Parsons suggested here that people need to get out and experience the world of work in its various aspects, to fully explore the options available for career roles (McDaniels, 1994). There is a need for people to explore all possibilities through various sources including education, occupation, and leisure (McDaniels, 1994). In the early part of the twentieth century, people utilized print sources (newspaper and books); in the twenty-first century, digital sources (computer) are used.

Integration of knowledge of self and the world of work. McDaniels (1994) notes that Parsons was a proponent of cognitive use and action-oriented focus on developing interests and knowledge in both self and work. In other words, people should not only read about occupations and interests but should go see these areas in real life. For example, a student who wants to work as a crime scene analyzer should attend a field trip to explore the local crime lab in the city they want to work in to see if their vision is a reality. Some of the most well-known opportunities students have to explore their interests are field trips, academic programs (high school and college), volunteering, and practicum and internship courses. These are real-life settings where students have the opportunity to put their interests into action with less risk involved.

WORK ADJUSTMENT THEORY

The theory of work adjustment (TWA) (Melchiori & Church, 1997) is also derived from Williamson and Parsons model of matching (Dawis, 1980; Dawis & Lofquist, 1984). Developed by Minnesota psychologists Dawis and Lofquist (1984), this model focuses not only on matching but also on adjusting a person to match their environment once in the work role (Renfro-Michel, Burlew, & Robert, 2009). To predict longevity, Dawis and Lofquist wanted to understand how people adjust to their work environment. The work environment, Dawis states, includes the interpersonal, social, physical, and organizational parts. In response to the environment, a person adjusts; in response to a person, an environment adjusts. Furthermore, when differences occur in any setting, there are adjustments that automatically need to be made. In the theory of work adjustment, the environment and the person naturally adjust to one another. Dawis (1980) calls these adjustments needs.

For example, consider what happens when a person is no longer allowed to come into work within a two- to three-hour window because she now has to start clocking in at a certain time every day. Her work employers adjusted the payment scale—from salary to hourly—and in response, she will have to adjust either by coming in on time or finding a new job. The work adjustment theory is based on needs (Dawis, 1980). The needs represent the needs of the industry and of individuals entering the workforce. Each entity must decide what their needs are prior to entering a work relationship with the another. Then, keeping people in a work role once they are fitted to a career requires there to be reinforcers (Dawis, 1980). Reinforcers describes that which works as an attribute of the work role or the person to keep the person in the job. In other words, these are incentives to keep people in the job, such as a pay check and work schedule (for the worker) or flexibility and working weekends (for the employer). Additionally, these reinforcers are satisfiers of the needs of both the work environment (satisfactoriness) and the person working (Dawis, 1980). Evidence that the work environment and the individual adjusted to one another is satisfaction and length of time in the job (Dawis). Essentially, if a person works in a job for several years, for example, it is likely that the adjustment needs have been satisfied for each. The term correspondence is used to describe the match between job and person and the interaction itself (Dawis, 1980). For people entering work, there are workshops to teach them how to fulfill their work role before actually entering the work setting (Wainwright & Couch, 1978). These are called work adjustment programs and they promote the lowering of work adjustment issues including integrating the person with handicaps into a job that does not require handicap assistance (Wainwright & Couch, 1978). More common today, however, are internships, practicums, apprenticeships, and volunteer work. There are several factors that go into the theory of work adjustment. These include abilities, assessment, and personality.

Abilities

The importance of recognizing if a person has the ability to complete a job is critical. Ability is that which recognizes not all people have equal ability—strength, skills, training, education, focus, and age, among other things—to fulfill work requirements (Harper & Shoffner, 2004). Harper and Shoffner's article describes the use of TWA with retirees. One of the few models to work with retirees, TWA helps those who want to continue working although they are officially out of their professional job prior to retirement. This is a good example of how abilities can change over time. A person retiring at age 65, for instance, will likely change in strength, agility, and flexibility compared to when they first entered the workforce at age 22. In addition, a person's memory changes over time (Henry, MacLeod, Phillips, & Crawford, 2004). Therefore, the same environment–person match present before retiring will change (Harper & Shoffner, 2004). For this reason, counselors will help guide clients toward understanding what their current interests, values, and abilities are and match these with work environment. The retiree needs to realize that the same environment that satisfied them before—high correspondence— may not bring the same level of satisfaction following retirement. This model does not hinge on creating a complete fit but rather helping people adjust according to the work setting. There are two dimensions: individual dimension and environmental dimension (Harper & Shoffner, 2004). The individual dimension describes the abilities and skills a person has to offer a work setting. The environmental dimension, similarly, encompasses required skills and abilities a person must have when they enter any particular work setting (Harper & Shoffner, 2004). A high level of correspondence is recommended for both dimensions to survive.

The Ackerman (1988) model of skill acquisition states that through time and experience in a work setting, skill and ability increase in speed and efficiency (Farrell & McDaniel, 2001). Also involved in the development of this type of thinking is Schneider and Shiffrin (1977) who state specifically that speed efficiency changes as time on the job continues (Farrell & McDaniel, 2001). They discovered that not only is the skill and ability composition changing as a result of time on the job but the actual processing that occurs in the brain for these tasks changes as well. To begin a job, the ability to think about and function in the role at a very minimal level is needed. Once a person starts to learn the skills, these areas of ability increase and the job is done with more ease and fluidity (Farrell & McDaniel, 2001). There are three phases in Ackerman's model, named by Anderson (1983): (1) declarative, (2) knowledge compilation, and (3) procedural (Farrell & McDaniel, 2001). In the declarative phase, a person is focusing on learning the tasks and understanding the work to be completing in their new work role. The knowledge phase is one where a person can remember the tasks to do but is now improving in speed and efficiency to complete the tasks. The final phase *procedural!* is one where action is automatic. A person completes the task without having to put much thought into what to do; the actions and job become more rote (Farrell & McDaniel, 2001). The greatest abilities a company can check on regarding a person's functioning ability in the work setting are spatial and content (Farrell & McDaniel, 2001). This means that employers should be asking questions about the person's knowledge of tasks and the job in general. Someone with more experience, in other words, is likely going to stay in the job longer and fit the role better than someone without a lot of experience. Once in the work role, it is speed ability in the procedural phase that predicts tenure of the employee and overall satisfaction (Farrell & McDaniel, 2001). As experience increases, ability changes too; in fact, there are curves in learning that occur over time when a person continues in their work role (Farrell & McDaniel, 2001).

Assessment

Assessment of TWA includes understanding the work environment needs and the needs of individuals entering work (Dawis & Lofquist, 1976). In the counseling room, this means assessing a client's work needs (income, style, and focus needs) and whether the work environment they are wanting to enter satisfies these needs. If the work environment does not satisfy client needs, then counselors can encourage them to change careers or learn to adjust.

Personality

The personality construct of TWA describes the personality of employees (Dawis & Lofquist, 1976). Some people are more flexible to change in response to their environment—including to change in response to the personality of others—and some are not. Dawis and Lofquist (1976) give the example of the flexibility of an employee who is willing to adjust despite their coworker changing the heat to 80 degrees from 70 degrees. Other coworkers may not be willing to be flexible in this situation. There are four personality traits that describe each person: flexibility, activeness, reactiveness, and celerity (Dawis & Lofquist, 1976). Because personality style is an important construct, the work adjustment theory is ever changing. The four personality traits just stated and summarized next are also areas of assessment (Dawis & Lofquist, 1976).

Flexibility. This describes a person who has both work and personal experiences, is gregarious about meeting new people, focuses on exploring new dynamics, and is motivated for change (Dawis & Lofquist, 1976). Flexibility also describes the polarity between perfect correspondence and perfect discorrespondence (Eggerth, 2008). Furthermore, flexibility explains how likely either (work or person) is going to adjust once discorrespondence between the two occurs. For example, if a person's hours are reduced, they may need to adjust their spending habits or acquire a second job in order to keep the existing one and the lifestyle they currently have. If they are not willing to adjust to the change (i.e., flexibility) then they will likely quit for another form of employment.

Activeness. This is a trait that identifies a person who is extroverted, focused, has leadership qualities, and is dedicated to change and movement in all systems (Dawis & Lofquist, 1976). They are also active in their environment and able and willing to adjust to needs. There is also the active mode, which describes the person trying to manipulate their work environment to come back to correspondence (Eggerth, 2008). In this regard, this person feels a need to adjust their current work role to create satisfaction. Essentially, the person in the work role wants to stay in their work position, so they aim to make changes in the work setting rather than directly to self.

Reactiveness. Reactiveness is a trait that describes the responsibility of a person to follow rules, respect boundaries, and have a willingness to be a follower or member (as opposed to leadership). This person is team oriented (Dawis & Lofquist, 1976). Moreover, in this mode, a person will change to meet the needs of the work environment—the person is making changes to self, not the environment (the opposite of activeness) (Eggerth, 2008).

Celerity. A person who works fast and excels in their commitment to completing a job well describes the trait of celerity. This person tries very hard to be thorough in their work responsibilities (Dawis & Lofquist, 1976).

Matching and Combining Abilities, Values, and Reinforcers

Matching is the primary goal of the TWA model. It works to match person to work environment based on their abilities, values, and reinforcers (Eggerth, 2008). The critical aim is to focus on the needs that are going to keep people in their work role. Two terms which describes what occurs when combining the above traits include intrinsic job satisfaction and external job satisfaction (Eggerth, 2008). A person feels joy either from within or from without but either way, they earn these types of satisfactions following the match to environmental work setting. Eggerth states the correspondence between the environment and person match is called person-environment correspondence (PEC), a term to explain this dynamic resulting in adjustment in work roles.

As abilities, values, and reinforcers combine, there is a shift that occurs between environment and person. In effect, at any given time one or both are attempting to correspond with the other to match values, abilities, and reinforcers. In other words, within work environments either the work environment and job role are changing to match the person or the person is changing to match the environment (Eggerth, 2008). Those persons who excel in any job do so because they are able to match and correspond well with their environment (Eggerth, 2008). As a counselor, it is important to note if the change resides in the person or in the environment. The term for this is locus of initiative (Eggerth, 2008). If a match occurs, a person needs to continuously be willing to adjust to work demands and changes in order to stay within their work role (Melchiori & Church, 1997). Once the environment and the worker have achieved high correspondence, neither is in need of adjusting. However, when discorrespondence begins to occur, adjustment from one or both sides must begin in order to meet equilibrium (Melchiori & Church, 1997). At times, this means a person finds a new job when discorrespondence is high and adjustment is not wanted or if a person loses their job.

Job Adjustment and Counseling

Counseling is imbedded into TWA and PEC (Eggerth, 2008). The process of counseling occurs as the client and counselor are working together to match the client to the career setting most appropriate to their interests and abilities. Eggerth states one of the primary functions of counseling using the PEC model is to assess and understand the interaction effect between person and environment regarding the issue presenting in counseling. With this, the counselor needs to engage the client in a conversation about the role of work and interest to pinpoint areas of interests and to formulate a treatment plan accordingly. There are then several battery tests counselors generally choose from that are used to help decide the next steps in counseling. The goal here is to identify discorrespondence occurring and begin to problem solve to arrive at a solution. From this point, Eggerth suggests starting with any change the client can make in themselves versus change to their environment, as people have more control over self. However, it is to be recognized that the client oftentimes wants to start by changing the environment and deflects off self-change (Eggerth, 2008). Changes to the environment sometimes can come at a cost when the client continues to struggle to maintain a position in a career. Obviously, counselors need to use wisdom as they manage this part of counseling clients toward work adjustment changes. Eggerth describes TWA and PEC as working hand in hand with positive psychology. The well-being that describes positive psychology fits into the model of helping people adjust to work environment.

When counselors are working with retirees, they should be assessing their client's past satisfaction in career roles (Harper & Shoffner, 2004). If, for instance, a client was dissatisfied with their work setting, then the likelihood problems will continue to persist is high. Proceeding to job placement is not the first route to go, therefore. Rather, they should begin to assess what went wrong and how to help their client adjust to a new setting.

The Role of Assessment Instruments

The TWA model is one that utilizes several assessment tools to complete work environment and person match. One tool involves 20 dimensions measuring work environment (Eggerth, 2008; Melchiori & Church, 1997). It is named the Minnesota Satisfaction Questionnaire (MSQ) (Weiss, Dawis, England, & Lofquist, 1967). Work settings are characterized by their reinforcers. The importance of satisfaction occurs both for the worker and the environmental setting. The MSQ is a tool designed to provide a general satisfaction score (Melchiori & Church, 1997). It can also provide the intrinsic and extrinsic satisfaction levels people experience in work environments (Melchiori & Church, 1997). The 20 dimensions are within six different values: achievement (putting abilities to use), comfort (absence of stress), status (authority over others), altruism (showing care), safety (structure and organizational qualities), and autonomy (independence and control) (Eggerth, 2008). Other assessment tools include the General Aptitude Test Battery and the Minnesota Importance Questionnaire (Harper & Shoffner, 2004).

General Aptitude Test Battery (GATB). Developed by the U.S. Department of Labor (1970), the GATB consists of nine aptitude variables: intelligence, verbal, numerical, spatial, form perception, clerical perception, motor coordination, finger dexterity, and manual dexterity (Farrell & McDaniel, 2001). Farrell and McDaniel utilized the GATB database to complete a study to determine which ability effects longevity in a career position over time and discovered that ability changes with experience. It was discovered that the ability that determines productivity in a job overtime changes as time and skills change.

Minnesota Importance Questionnaire (MIQ). Developed by Rounds, Henly, Dawis, Lofquist, and Weiss (1981), the MIQ is utilized to measure values and needs: six values—labeled a–f—imbedded in 20 vocational needs—labeled 1–20 (University of Minnesota, 2017a). These include (a) achievement [(1) ability utilization and (2) achievement)], (b) altruism [(3) co-workers, (4) social service, and (5) moral values], (c) comfort [(6) activity, (7) independence, (8) variety, (9) compensation, (10) security, (11) working conditions], (d) safety [(12) company policies and practices, (13) supervision—human relations, (14) supervision—technical], (e) status [(15) advancement, (16) recognition, (17) authority, (18) social status), and (f) autonomy [(19) creativity (20) responsibility] (University of Minnesota, 2017a). Each of the values and dimensions are applied to 185 different occupations that are most commonly searched for in the career field. The greatest predictor of successful match equals occupation reinforcers to person needs. The MIQ is a paper format test, can be given to an individual or in groups, and is in ranked or paired form. Paired form is when the person will pair needs and choose the most important out of the two; ranked form is five needs grouped together and the person chooses the group most fitting to them (University of Minnesota, 2017a).

Minnesota Occupational Classification System I, II, III. The first edition developed by Dawis and Lofquist (2001) was created because of the perceived need for an assessment tool that would match interest to ability. The second edition, by Dawis, Lofquist, Henly and Rounds (1982), utilized the Dictionary of Occupational Titles (DOT) (U. S. Department of Labor, 1965, 1977) to place reinforcer categories into clusters; these all aligned with 1161 occupations and ran along a taxon system of 78 (Dawis et al., 1982). Finally, Dawis, Dohm, Lofquist, Chartrand, and Due (1987) developed the third edition of this instrument. Dawis and associates returned to the propositions of the original version of the first edition to focus on the abilities more than the functions of the individual. The third edition is the most recent. In this edition, there is a focus on finding appropriate work environments with personality factors of the person. Abilities are defined by cognitive, perceptual, and motor classes; reinforcers are defined by internal, social, and environmental classes (Dawis et al., 1987). Then levels are applied: high, average, or not significant. Once a six-digit code is configured, one can locate it through the taxon system.

Minnesota Job Description Questionnaire (MJDQ). The University of Minnesota provides a summary of this assessment tool (2017b) and the MIQ plus links to the instruments on their website. The MJDQ is a 21-item instrument intended to measure reinforcers or needs. Raters, generally supervisors, employees, or analyzers, will rate jobs based on the 21 items for patterns. Patterns developed are then linked to two forms: supervisor form and employee form. The 21 reinforcers are ability utilization, achievement, activity, advancement, authority, autonomy, company policies, compensation, coworkers, creativity, independence, moral values, recognition, responsibility, security, social service, social status, supervision—human relations, supervision—technical, variety, and working conditions. The MJDQ was developed by Borgen, Weiss, Tinsley, Dawis, and Lofquist (1968).

The Role of Occupational Information

The TWA is integrated and partly responsible for the development of Occupational Information Network (O*NET) (Eggerth, 2008). Understanding the significance of occupational information available to all people has been valuable for many years (Rusalem, 1954); Rusalem mentions that the number of choices alone which people have in the area of work setting is substantial. No doubt, people have the flexibility to change their career roles at any time. Careers, therefore, are not concrete. However, career counselors can utilize occupational books such as the O*NET to provide direction in counseling. The O*NET can be used to assist in career counseling in several settings (Tippins & Hilton, 2010). One of the most valid and reliable approaches linked to the O*NET is the content model (Tippins & Hilton, 2010). The content model is descriptors and variables used to describe the process of occupational work roles. The developers of the O*NET utilized the content model to provide descriptors to the occupations (Tippins & Hilton, 2010). Therefore, because the O*NET uses the content model in its own development of theory, it is especially important that the content model stay valid and up to date with the O*NET (Tippins & Hilton, 2010). In 1991, the second edition to the DOT contained 12,000 occupational titles. These were referred to as DOT codes. The DOT codes were systematically induced by the developers going into actual work settings and personally interviewing the people working in the roles (Tippins & Hilton, 2010). The developer asked workers to provide a written description of their work setting, including an aptitude rating, temperament requirements, work interests, physical demands of the job, work environment, work preparation received, general educational development, and complexity of the job (Tippins & Hilton, 2010). Overtime, the O*NET developed out of the DOT because of the need to simplify the intrinsic and thorough nature of the DOT (Tippins & Hilton, 2010).

The purpose of occupational products such as the DOT and the O*NET is to encourage workforce development (Tippins & Hilton, 2010). The O*NET defines occupations, helps persons transfer skills from one work role to the next, identifies areas of education needed for clients, and assists in job placement efforts by counselors (Tippins & Hilton, 2010). The O*NET in particular is used as a supplement to other occupational guides. Tippins and Hilton state the O*NET linked to the Standard Occupational Classification (SOC) is one of the most important linkages between the O*NET and other taxonomy systems. Derived from the link between the O*NET and the SOC are the federal employment statistics. The O*NET and the SOC also inform an occupational assessment tool used by U.S. Marines and Army personnel called the military occupational classification (MOC). Therefore, the O*NET is a tool used in the development of other tools that are focused on specific populations. The SOC and O*NET linked together are used in several other forms of assessment across occupations, including education, the U.S. Census Bureau, and classification systems. The Bureau of Labor and Statistics (2015) is one of many sources providing information on occupational classification systems

(Industry Sectoring Plan, Industry Employment Directory, and Occupational Employment Directory) and Crosswalks (2014 National Employment Matrix/SOC to ACS Crosswalk, 2014 National Employment Matrix/SOC to CPS, and O*NET-SOC to Occupational Outlook Handbook). For further review, please see the book by Tippins and Hilton in its entirety. We will now change focus to summarize in detail Holland's theory of types.

HOLLAND THEORY OF TYPES

Almost 60 years ago John Holland penned the article "A Theory of Vocational Choices" in the John of Counseling Psychology (Holland, 1959). This was the beginning of the creation and development of John Holland's (1959, 1966, 1973, 1985, 1997) theory of types, which relates to how a person interacts with their environment. Still today, this is one of the most influential career counseling theories. As it remains, Holland's theory builds upon the trait and factor theories and includes the individuals' personality and how it best fits the job and the work environment. Stated plainly, Holland's theory melds together personality, work environment, and occupations.

Holland's theory is based on four basic assumptions (Holland, 1973):

1. People can be classified by six personality types: realistic, investigative, artistic, social, enterprising, and conventional.
2. There are six categories of work environments: realistic, investigative, artistic, social, enterprising, and conventional.
3. People search to find the work environment and job tasks that match their personality, values, and attitudes.
4. A person's behavior is determined by the interaction between personality and the characteristics of the environment.

Holland contends that career interests are an expression of an individual's personality (1959, 1966, 1973, 1985, 1997). Individual preferences for leisure activities, school subjects, avocational interests, and work are the foundation for developing these preferences and one's personality. The more an individual aligns with an identified personality type, the more likely that person will manifest the behaviors and traits associated with that work type (Weinrach, 1984). With this in mind, the key to understanding Holland's career typology theory is to understand the six personality types Holland puts forth and which serve as the foundation of his theory. The six personality and environmental types—realistic, investigative, artistic, social, enterprising, and conventional—are commonly referred to as the RIASC. Below is a discussion of the six personality types (Holland, 1973).

The Realistic Type

The realistic personality type prefers activities that entail the explicit, ordered, or systematic manipulation of objects, tools, machines, and animals. These persons have an aversion to educational or therapeutic activities. The realistic person has mechanical abilities but may lack social skills. Realistic personality types prefer jobs such as automobile mechanic, aircraft controller, surveyor, farmer, or electrician. Realistic types are often described as conforming, humble, normal, frank, materialistic, persistent, genuine, modest, and practical hardheaded, natural, shy, honest, and thrifty.

The Investigating Type

The investigative personality type prefers activities that entail the observational, symbolic, systematic, and creative investigation of physical, biological, and cultural phenomena. Investigative types have a dislike of persuasive, social, and repetitive activities; they desire science and mathematical skills. Investigative types prefer jobs such as biologist, chemist, physicist, anthropologist, geologist, or medical technologist. These individuals are described as analytical, independent, modest, cautious, intellectual, pessimistic, complex, introverted, precise, critical, methodical, rational, curious, and reserved.

The Artistic Type

The artistic personality type prefers ambiguous, free activities that entail the manipulation of physical, verbal, or human materials to create art forms. Artistic persons do not care for systematic and ordered activities. They endeavor to acquire artistic competencies in language, art, music, drama, and writing. They are not concerned with clerical or business-system competencies. Artistic types like jobs such as composer, musician, stage director, writer, interior decorator, or actor. Artistic persons are described as complicated, imaginative, introspective, disorderly, impractical, intuitive, emotional, impulsive, nonconforming, expressive, independence, open, idealistic, and original.

The Social Type

The social personality type prefers activities that include the manipulation of others to inform, train, develop, cure, or enlighten. They do not desire to work in environments that include ordered and systematic activities involving materials, tools, or machines. They want to acquire interpersonal, educational, and human relational competences. They do not want to work in environments that require mechanical and scientific ability. Social types like jobs such as teacher, religious worker, counselor, clinical psychologist, psychiatrist, caseworker, or speech therapist. Social persons are often described as convincing, idealistic, social, cooperative, kind, sympathetic, friendly, patient, tactful, generous, responsible, understanding, helpful, and warm.

The Enterprising Type

The enterprising personality prefers activities that entail influencing others to attain organizational or economic gain. They have a dislike of observational, symbolic, and systemic activities. Enterprising types like to be in leadership; they want to acquire interpersonal and persuasive proficiencies. Enterprising types desire jobs such as salesperson, manager, business executive, television production, sports promoter, or buyer. They are often described as acquisitive, domineering, optimistic, adventurous, energetic, pleasure seeking, agreeable, extroverted, attention getting, ambitious, impulsive, self-confident, sociable, and popular.

The Conventional Type

The conventional personality type prefers activities that entail the explicit, ordered, and systematic manipulation of data such as keeping records, filing materials, reproducing materials, organizing written and numerical data according to a prescribed plan, and operating computers to attain organizational or economic goals. Conventional types dislike ambiguous, free, exploratory, or unsystematized activities. They endeavor to acquire skills such as clerical, computational, and business systems competencies. Conventional types enjoy jobs such as bookkeeping, stenographer, financial analyst, banker, cost estimator, or tax expert. Conventional persons are often described as conforming, inhibited, persistent, conscience, obedient, practical, careful, orderly, thrifty, efficient, and unimaginative.

As mentioned, the uniqueness of Holland's theory is that the RIASEC applies to both the individual and the work environment. As such, Holland applied the personal traits on the RIASEC to occupational environments as well as individuals (Holland, 1973).

The realistic environment requires people to see themselves as having mechanical ability and being comfortable with systematic manipulation of objects and working with tools, machines, and animals. The investigative environment encourages scientific competency. The artistic environment is ambitious and free; this environment requires the individual to see him or herself as expressive, independent, and intuitive. The social environment places value on the understanding of others. In the enterprising environment, the focus is on personal interaction, business, and organization. The final environment is conventional; this environment is ordered and systematic.

An important aspect to ensure a good individual and environmental typology match is to check congruence, differentiation, and consistency when interpreting the client's assessment results.

Consistency

The degree of relatedness within types is referred to as consistency. Based on the assessment, people are given their three top personality types. The three personalities should be consistent and complimentary as opposed to personalities that are opposites.

Congruence

Congruence is the degree of fit between an individual's personality type and the work environment type (Nauta, 2010). The object is to have a strong connection or fit between the individual and the environment. The stronger the degree of congruence, the better the fit and the better off the individual and the environment. When there is incongruence with their personality and the occupational environment, there will be unhappiness for both the employer and the employee.

Differentiation

Holland (1959) referred to the degree of distinctness among personality types representing a person's personality profile as "differential." People who are undifferential can have difficulty making career decisions. Career interventions are often directed toward helping clients achieve greater differentiation among Holland types. The career counselor wants the individual to have less differentiation, as less differentiation means greater clarity of vocational choices. It is critical that the individual have stability in vocational choices.

Holland uses a hexagon model to illustrate consistency, congruence, and differential among personality types. Undeniably, the Holland hexagon model is not intuitive at first glance; however, if you start on the outside of the model, the personality types that are closest to each other indicate that the personalities are much more consistent. The personalities that are next to each other are congruent. The personality that are across from each other represent differential (see Figure 4.1).

FIGURE 4.1 The Holland Occupational Themes (RIASEC) refers to a theory of careers and vocational choice. Developed by American psychologist John L. Holland.

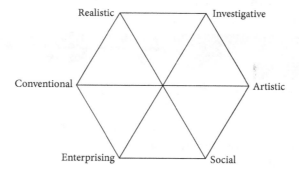

Holland Hexagon

The second major contribution that Holland has given to the field of career counseling is his assessment tools. Holland and his colleagues authored multiple assessments that utilize the RIASEC typology theory. Examples of assessments include the Vocational Preference Inventory (Holland, 1985; Holland et at.,1994) and the Self-Directed Search (Holland, Fritzsche, & Powell, 1994); both of these assessments use the RIASEC personality types. Additionally, the Position Classification Inventory (Gottfredson & Holland, 1991) categorizes work environments using the RIASEC types and the Environmental Assessment Technique (Astin & Holland, 1961) classifies educational environments. There are many other assessments that measure personality and occupational environments.

The third major contribution from Holland was is the creation of comprehensive resources that match personalities with work environments and specific occupations. The most well-known of these resources is the **Dictionary of Holland Occupational Codes** (Gottfredson & Holland, 1996). Today there are many resources that use Holland's RIASEC as it foundation, and many of these resources have now been modernized and are currently available online. One such resource is the very popular occupational resource called O*NET.

MYERS BRIGGS TYPE INDICATOR

The Myers-Briggs type theory (MBTI) is the only theory in this book that was not designed to be used in career development. Nevertheless, it is very popular among career counselors because it allows the client to further understand their personality and have more information to consider when deciding their career path. Developed by Katherine Briggs in the 1920s, the MBTI is based on the work of noted psychologist Carl Jung. Similar to Holland's theory, the MBTI is a typology assessment. Briggs was not a psychologist; she was fan of Jung's work that focused on categories of human behavior. In the 1940s, Briggs' daughter, Isabel Myers, joined her and together they created the Myers Briggs Type Indicator. The focus of this type indicator is based on Jung's 1921 book titled **Psychological Types** (Jung, 1971). Jung wrote about the manner in which individuals use perception and judgment. The focus of Jung's book was to explain what people pay attention to and how they make decisions. Jung described two types of people: those who are primarily concerned with what is happening in the world outside of them and those who are more concerned with their own views and ideas.

To be clear, the MBTI should not be viewed as a career development theory nor as a psychological assessment; rather, it should be regarded as a trait and factor assessment. The goal of the MBTI in career counseling is to gain a clearer understanding of self in order to inform the client and counselor regarding career possibilities and choices.

The MBTI has four dimensions: extraversion and introversion, sensation and intuition, thinking and feeling and judgment and perception. It is important for the counselor to understand all of the dimensions and combinations of the MBTI. This can be overwhelming for both the client and the counselor because of the many combinations that an individual can be assessed as possessing (see Figure 4.2). There is formal and rigorous training to fully understand the MBTI; this chapter is designed to provide the reader with enough basic information to discuss the interrelated combinations and to be able to discuss individual results in the context of selecting an occupation and exploring possibilities and environments as well as aid in the career decision-making needs of the client. The basic concepts of the MBTI is discussed below.

Perceiving and Judging

The focus of this MBTI is to determine how people see their world and make decisions based on that viewpoint (McCauley & Moody, 2008; Myers, 1993). As such, the first portion of

MBTI is perception. People spend much of their time taking in information and perceiving and judging the information that they see (Sharf, 2016). We are consistently perceiving and judging what we see. There are two kinds of perceiving and two styles of judging. The two contrasting styles of perceiving are sensing and intuition. People who use sensing take in information by using visual and auditory processes. They prefer to observe using hearing, touch, and vision. They make clear observations and have a keen sense for details. On the other hand, people who are intuitive use the unconscious. They generally go beyond the visual and audio cues of life and uses insight to go beyond what they see. They are often looking at the events playing out presently and connecting them to future events. When you have intuition as your typology you are much more abstract and creative.

Judging

There are two ways of judging thinking and feeling. Thinking is the manner in which one analyzes an event they have perceived. Thinking people rely on logic and are objective when attempting to interpret what they have perceived. Feeling is the personal response one has to an event that is perceptive. A feeling person focuses on their values and how an event will be judged when interpreting events, thoughts, and ideas that they come into contact with.

With these two combinations of types there are four combinations of perceiving and judging. Myers, McCaulley, Quenk, & Hammer (1998) explain these combinations as sensing and thinking, sensing and feeling, intuition and feeling, and intuition and thinking. Myers (1993) states that an individual will prefer and/or choose one of these four categories.

Sensing and Thinking

People who use sensing for perceiving and thinking for judging will be more prone to accumulating facts that solidify what they have observed. These individuals are practical and pragmatic; they make decisions based on information they have researched and confirmed with others. The career fields that they are most likely drawn to focus on analyzing facts such as accounting, purchasing, and law.

Sensing and Feeling

Individuals who fall in this category make decisions based on feelings. The occupations they are most likely to enter are counseling, social work, medical profession, and teaching.

Intuition and Feeling

These individuals are concerned about how their decisions are based on the future. When making decisions, they are creative and their focus is on humans. Occupations that draw these individuals include the clergy, teaching at the college or high school level, and social services. They are less likely to use facts, and instead they will use instincts.

Intuition and Thinking

These individuals use their instincts, analysis of information, and projections about the future to make decisions. They like theoretical conversations and enjoy solving problems. The occupations that call this population are scientific researchers, and computer work and jobs that allow them to use problem solving skills.

Introversion and Extraversion

Introversion and extraversion is another dimension of the MBTI. Jung (1971) and Meyers (1993) define these terms in reference to how a person relates to the world. For the authors of MBTI, introversion has nothing to do with being shy or quiet nor does extraversion have anything to do with being loud or outgoing, as these two terms are typically understood in society (Sharf 2013). These terms are grounded in perception and judgment. A person who is considered an introvert is generally looking inward into their feelings and thoughts when perceiving and judging the world. Conversely, an extravert's attention is directed toward other people and the outside world when perceiving and judging. Both of these personality types use both the outside and the inside world to perceive and judge. The MBTI provides information that illustrates the individual's disposition.

Extraverts are proactive, they want to work and interact with others, and they like to talk their thoughts through. Introverts enjoy reflecting and processing information, and they may take a lot of time before making a decision. They may be quieter because they are processing and reflecting, not because they are shy. The MBTI uses introversion and extraversion along with judgment and perception. The four combinations of perceiving and judging discussed earlier may perceive or judge preferably in the outside or the inner world. From a career perspective, extraverts may prefer jobs such as in sales and business management where they can use their skills more freely. Introverts may flourish in occupations such as science and accounting where they can focus on processing and problem solving. Adding introversion and extraversion to the MBTI allows the assessment to capture more personalities and offers the client and the counselor with more in-depth results and various dimensions of personality.

In ending, with the inclusion of all the variables discussed (judging and perceiving, preference for judging and perceiving, and extraversion and introversion), there are 16 possible personality types measured by the MBTI. See Figure 4.2 to view the various typologies as well as key terms that describe individuals who generally test with the particular typology.

"In the Myer-Briggs typology, the different ways of judging and perceiving, the preference for judgment or perception, and the preference for introversion or extraversion act in concert with each other to yield 16 different types" (Sharf, 2010, p. 162). See Figure 4.2 to view the various typologies as well as key terms that describe individuals who generally test with the particular typology

FIGURE 4.2 The Myers-Briggs Type Indicator® (MBTI®) and/or 16 personality types overview

Myers-Briggs Type Inventory Personality Test

ISTJ	ISFJ	INFJ	INTJ
"Doing What Should Be Done"	"A High Sense of Duty"	"An Inspiration to Others"	"Everything Has Room for Improvement"
Organizer • Compulsive Private • Trustworthy Rules 'n Regs • Practical	Amiable • Works Behind the Scenes Ready to Sacrifice • Accountable Prefers "Doing"	Reflective/Introspective Quietly Caring • Creative Linguistically Gifted • Psychic	Theory Based • Skeptical • "My Way" High Need for Competency Sees World as Chessboard
Most Responsible	Most Loyal	Most Contemplative	Most Independent
ISTP	ISFP	INFP	INTP
"Ready to Try Anything Once"	"Sees Much But Shares Little"	"Performing Noble Service to Aid Society"	"A Love of Problem Solving"
Very Observant • Cool and Aloof Hands-on Practicality • Unpretentious Ready for what Happens	Warm and Sensitive • Unassuming Short Range Planner • Good Team Member In Touch with Self and Nature	Strict Personal Values Seeks Inner Order/Peace Creative • Non-Directive • Reserved	Challenges others to Think Absent- minded Professor Competency Needs • Socially Cautious
Most Pragmatic	Most Artistic	Most Idealistic	Most Conceptual
ESTP	ESFP	ENFP	ENTP
"The Ultimate Realist"	"You Only Go Around Once in Life"	"Giving Life an Extra Squeeze"	"One Exciting Challenge After Another"
Unconventional Approach • Fun Gregarious • Lives for Here and Now Good at Problem Solving	Sociable • Spontaneous Loves Surprises • Cuts Red Tape Juggles Multiple Projects/Events Quip Master	People Oriented • Creative Seeks Harmony • Life of Party More Starts than Finishes	Argues Both Sides of a Point to Learn Brinksmanship • Tests the Limits Enthusiastic • New Ideas
Most Spontaneous	Most Generous	Most Optimistic	Most Inventive
ESTJ	ESFJ	ENFJ	ENTJ
"Life's Administrators"	"Host and Hostesses of The World"	"Smooth Talking Persuader"	"Life's Natural Leaders"
Order and Structure • Sociable Opinionated • Results Driven Producer • Traditional	Gracious • Good Interpersonal Skills Thoughtful • Appropriate Eager to Please	Charismatic • Compassionate Possibilities for People Ignores the Unpleasant • Idealistic	Visionary • Gregarious • Argumentative Systems Planners • Take Charge Low Tolerance for Incompetency
Most Hard Charging	Most Harmonizing	Most Persuasive	Most Commanding

©Otto and Kroeger Associates, 1997

CONCLUSION

This chapter focuses on early career theories. Summarized throughout is the work by theorists Parsons, Williamson, Ackerman, Dawis, Lofquist, and Holland among others. At the start, the guidance movement is summarized to help readers understand how and where the field of counseling developed. It started in educational systems, specifically high schools, to help students transition out of school and into work. The start of this development was not smooth, however. Part of the problem was that the role of helping students navigate the transition rested almost solely on teachers. Fortunately, out of this sprang the need to develop career counseling positions in schools. Developments from this grassroot beginning include the trait and factor theory, the work adjustment theory, and Holland's type theory. Each of these theories provide a detailed outline for how to match work environment with personal traits. The goal is to help people enter work with more ease and to stay within their career position for longer durations. These theories also benefit the employer, who is better assisted to match their work position to the right candidate. Also useful in career matching are assessment tools, taxonomies, and occupational handbooks. These offer a systematic matching system that can be manipulated depending on the setting.

KEY TERMS

Ability: includes strength, skills, training, education, focus, and age among other areas; not equal among all people for all work roles

Activeness: person who is extroverted, focused, has leadership qualities, and is dedicated to change and movement in all systems

Celerity: person who works fast and excels in their commitment to completing a job well

Discorrespondence: a mismatch between work setting and person

Flexibility: a person who has both work and personal experiences

Locus of initiative: wherever the change resides

Needs: the fit between the person and their environment

Reactiveness: person who is prone to follow rules, respect boundaries, and have a willingness to be a follower or a member

Satisfactoriness: reinforcers are satisfiers of both the work environment and the person

Traits: links to personality and factors related to areas of work

REFLECTION AND DISCUSSION

1. Name the main contributors of the guidance movement.
2. Describe the beginning era of career counseling.
3. What is the trait and factor theory for matching a person to a work setting?
4. Who were the contributors of the work adjustment theory?
5. Describe the six types of career traits in Holland's theory.

ADDITIONAL READINGS, RESOURCES, AND WEBSITES

Brown, S. D., & Lent, R. W. (Eds.). (2013). Career development and counseling: Putting theory and research to work. US: Wiley.

National Center for Educational Statistics; https://nces.ed.gov

O*NET Online; https://www.onetonline.org

Sharf, R. S. (1992). Applying career development theory to counseling. Pacific Grove, CA: Brooks/Cole.

U.S. Bureau of Labor and Statistics; https://www.bls.gov

U.S. Census Bureau; https://census.gov

U.S. Equal Employment Opportunity Commission; https://www.eeoc.gov

TRADITIONAL ACTIVITY

The Eclectic Career Counselor

1. Define eclecticism. Talk about being an eclectic counselor. What are the pros and cons of being eclectic? If you had to pick one career counseling and one noncareer-specific counseling theory, which two counseling theories would you select and how would you integrate them in a session?
2. Compare and contrast a traditional counseling theory with a career-specific counseling theory.

SPIRITUAL ACTIVITY

Gifts from God

God gave us gifts to use to build His Kingdom at work as well as in the community. Read the scripture below and answer the questions.

Romans 12:6–8 New International Version (NIV)

> *⁶We have different gifts, according to the grace given to each of us. If your gift is <u>prophesying</u>, then prophesy in accordance with your[a] faith; ⁷if it is <u>serving</u>, then serve; if it is <u>teaching</u>, then teach; ⁸if it is to <u>encourage</u>, then give encouragement; if it is giving, then give generously; if it is to lead,[b] do it diligently; if it is to show <u>mercy</u>, do it cheerfully.*

1. Identify and discuss the one gift listed above that you identify with the most. How have you used this gift in your work?
2. Identify and discuss the one gift that you least identify with, and why. Explain safe ways you can grow and use the least identified gift in your work and in your community.
3. Often times, your clients will talk about their God-given gifts and talents and how they struggle to use them at work. Taking into account all of the gifts above, discuss how your client can use their gifts appropriately at a secular job.

REFERENCES

Ackerman, P. L. (1988). Determinants of individual differences during skill acquisition: Cognitive abilities and information processing. Journal of Experimental Psychology: General, 117, 288–313.

Anderson, J. R. (1983). The architecture of cognition. Cambridge, MA: Harvard University Press.

Astin, A. W., & Holland, J. L. (1961). The Environmental assessment technique: A way to measure college environments. Journal of Educational Psychology, 52(6), 308–316.

Borgen, Weiss, Tinsley, Dawis, and Lofquist. (1968). The Measurement of Occupational Reinforcer Patterns. Minneapolis, MN: University of Minnesota. Retrieved from http://vpr.psych.umn.edu/sites/g/files/pua2236/f/monograph_xxv_-_the_measurement_of_occupational_reinforcer_patterns.pdf

Briddick, W. C. (2009). Frank parsons on interests. Journal of Vocational Behavior, 74(2), 230–233. doi:10.1016/j.jvb.2008.12.003

Brammer, L. M. (1986). Needed: A paradigm shift in counseling theory. The Counseling Psychologist, 14(3), 443–447. doi:10.1177/0011000086143002

Bureau of Labor and Statistics. (2015). Employment projections: Classifications and crosswalks. Retrieved from https://www.bls.gov/emp/ep_crosswalks.htm

Geist, C. S. (1990). Vocational Counseling for Special Populations. Springfield, IL: Charles C Thomas Pub Ltd.

Carson, A. D., & Altai, N. M. (1994). 1000 years before Parsons: Vocational psychology in classical Islam. The Career Development Quarterly, 43(2), 197. Retrieved from http://0-search.proquest.com.library.regent.edu/docview/219439216?accountid=13479

Chartrand, J. M. (1991). The evolution of Trait-and-Factor career counseling: A person × environment fit approach. Journal of Counseling & Development, 69(6), 518–524. doi:10.1002/j.1556–6676.1991.tb02635.x

Chartrand, J. M., & Bertok, R. L. (1993). Current trait factor career assessment: A cognitive-interactional perspective. Journal of Career Assessment, 1(4), 323–340. doi:10.1177/106907279300100401

Dawis, R. V. (1980). Personnel Assessment from the Perspective of the Theory of Work Adjustment. Public Personnel Management, 9(4), 268.

Dawis, R. V. (2004). The Minnesota theory of work adjustment. In S. D. Brown & R. W. Lent (Eds.), Career development: Putting theory and research into practice (pp. 3–23). Hoboken, NJ: John Wiley.

Dawis, R. V., Dohm, T. E., Lofquist, L. H., Chartrand, J. M., & Due, A. M. (1987). Minnesota Occupational Classification System III. Minneapolis, MN: University of Minnesota.

Dawis, R. V., Lofquist, L. R., Henly, G. A., & Rounds, J.B., Jr. (1979/1982). The Minnesota occupational classification system II. Minneapolis, MN: Work Adjustment Project, Department of Psychology, University of Minnesota.

Dawis, R. V., & Lofquist, L. H. (1976). Personality style and the process of work adjustment. Journal of Counseling Psychology, 23(1), 55–59. doi:10.1037/0022-0167.23.1.55

Dawis, R. V., & Lofquist, L. H. (1984). A psychological theory of work adjustment: An individual-differences model and its applications. Minneapolis, MN: University of Minnesota Press.

Eggerth, D. E. (2008). From theory of work adjustment to person–environment correspondence counseling: Vocational psychology as positive psychology. Journal of Career Assessment, 16(1), 60–74. doi:10.1177/1069072707305771

Farrell, J. N., & McDaniel, M. A. (2001). The stability of validity coefficients over time: Ackerman's (1988) model and the general aptitude test battery. Journal of Applied Psychology, 86(1), 60–79. doi:10.1037/0021-9010.86.1.60

Gottfredson, G. D., & Holland, J. L. (1991). The Position Classification Inventory: Professional manual. Odessa, FL: Psychological Assessment Resources.

Gottfredson, G. D., & Holland, J. L. (1996). The dictionary of Holland occupational codes. Odessa, FL: Psychological Assessment Resources.

Harper, M. C., & Shoffner, M. F. (2004). Counseling for continued career development after retirement: An application of the theory of work adjustment. The Career Development Quarterly, 52(3), 272–284. doi:10.1002/j.2161-0045.2004.tb00648.x

Henry, J. D., MacLeod, M. S., Phillips, L. H., & Crawford, J. R. (2004). A meta-analytic review of prospective memory and aging. Psychology and Aging, 19(1), 27–39. doi:10.1037/0882-7974.19.1.27

Holland, J. L. (1958). A personality inventory employing occupational titles. Journal of Applied Psychology, 42, 336 –342.

Holland, J. L. (1959). A theory of vocational choice. Journal of Counseling Psychology, 6, 35–45.

Holland, J. L. (1966). A psychological classification scheme for vocations and major fields. Journal of Counseling Psychology, 13, 278–288.

Holland, J. L. (1973). Making vocational choices. Englewood Cliffs, NJ: Prentice-Hall.

Holland, J. L. (1985). Making vocational choices: A theory of vocational personalities and work environments. Englewood Cliffs, NJ: Prentice Hall.

Holland, J. L. (1997). Educational Opportunities Finder. Odessa, FL: Psychological Assessment Resources.

Holland, J.L., Fritzsche, B.A., & Powell, A.B. (1994). SDS technical manual. Odessa, FL: Psychological Assessment Resources.

Jung, C. (1971). Psychological types: The collected works of C.G. Jung. Princeton, NJ: Princeton University Press.

Kantor, H. (1986). Choosing a Vocation: The Origins and Transformation of Vocational Guidance in California, 1910–1930. History of Education Quarterly, 26(3), 351–375. doi:10.2307/368243

Lambie, G. W., & Williamson, L. L. (2004). The challenge to change from guidance counseling to professional school counseling: A historical proposition. Professional School Counseling, 8(2), 124–131.

Leong, F. T. (2008). Encyclopedia of Counseling. Los Angeles, CA: SAGE Publications, Inc.

McCaulley, M. H., & Moody, R. A. (2008). Multicultural applications of the Myers-Briggs Type Indicator, In L.A. Suzuki, & J. G. Ponterootto (Eds.), Handbook of multicultural assessment: Clinical, psychological, and educational applications 2nd ed. (pp. 402–424). San Francisco, CA: Jossey-Bass.

McDaniels, C. (1994). Frank parsons: His heritage leads us into the 21st century. Journal of Career Development, 20(4), 327–332. doi:10.1007/BF02106306

Melchiori, L. G., & Church, A. T. (1997). Vocational needs and satisfaction of supported employees: The applicability of the theory of work adjustment. Journal of Vocational Behavior, 50(3), 401–417. doi:10.1006/jvbe.1996.1543

Meyers, I. B. (1993). Gifts differing. Palo Alto, CA: Consulting Psychologists Press.

Myers, I. B., McCaulley, M. H., Quenk, N. L., & Hammer, A. L. (1998). MBTI Manual: A guide to the development and use of the Myers-Briggs Type Indicator (3rd ed.). Palo Alto, CA: Consulting Psychologists Press.

Nauta, M. M. (2010). The development, evolution, and status of Holland's theory of vocational personalities: Reflections and future directions for counseling psychology. Journal of Counseling Psychology, 57(1), 11–22. doi:10.1037/a0018213

Parsons, F. (1909). Choosing a vocation. Boston, MA: Houghton, Mifflin.

Renfro-Michel, E. L., Burlew, L. D., & Robert, T. (2009). The interaction of work adjustment and attachment theory: Employment counseling implications. Journal of Employment Counseling, 46(1), 18–26. doi:10.1002/j.2161-1920.2009.tb00062.x

Rounds, J. B., Henly, G. A., Dawis, R. V., Lofquist, L. H., & Weiss, D. J. (1981). Manual for the Minnesota Importance Questionnaire. St. Paul, MN: Vocational Psychology Research Work Adjustment Project, Department of Psychology, University of Minnesota.

Rusalem, H. (1954). New insights on the role of occupational information in counseling. Journal of Counseling Psychology, 1(2), 84–88. doi:10.1037/h0061789

Sharf, R. S. (2013). Applying career development theory to counseling (6th ed). Belmont, CA: Brooks/Cole.

Schneider, W., & Shiffrin, R. M. (1977). Controlled and automatic human information processing: I. Detection, search, and attention. Psychological Review, 84, 1–66.

Tippins, N. T., & Hilton, M. L. (2010). Database for a changing economy: Review of the occupational information network (ONET). Washington, DC: National Academies Press.

University of Minnesota. (2017). Minnesota Importance Questionnaire (MIQ). Retrieved from http://vpr.psych.umn.edu/instruments/miq-minnesota-importance-questionnaire

University of Minnesota (2017). Minnesota Job Description Questionnaire (MJDQ). Retrieved from http://vpr.psych.umn.edu/instruments/mjdq-minnesota-job-description-questionnaire

United States Department of Labor. (1965). Dictionary of occupational titles (3rd ed.). Washington, D.C.: United States Government Printing Office.

U.S. Department of Labor. (1970). Manual for the USES General Aptitude Test Battery, Section III: Development. Washington, DC: U.S. Government Printing Office.

United States Department of Labor. (1977). Dictionary of occupational titles (4th ed.). Washington, D.C.: United States Government Printing Office.

U.S. Department of Labor. (1980). Manual for the USES General Aptitude Test Battery (Section II-A). Washington, DC: U.S. Employment Service, Employment and Training Administration, U.S. Department of Labor.

Wainwright, C. O., & Couch, R. (1978). Work adjustment: Potential and practice. Journal of Rehabilitation, 44(1), 39.

Weinrach, S.G. (1984). Determinants of vocational choice: Holland's theory. In D. Brown & L. Brooks (Eds.), Career choice and development 1st ed. (pp. 61–93). San Francisco: Jossey-Bass.

Weiss, D. J., Dawis, R. V., England, G. W., & Lofquist, L. H. (1967). Manual for the Minnesota satisfaction questionnaire. Minnesota studies in vocational rehabilitation: XXII. Minneapolis, MN: University of Minnesota.

Zhang, W., & Au Yeung, L. (2003). Online measurement of academic programme preferences for distance learners in Hong Kong. Distance Education, 24(2), 213–226. doi:10.1080/0158791032000127482

Zytowski, D. G. (2001). Frank Parsons and the progressive movement. The Career Development Quarterly, 50(1), 57–65. doi:10.1002/j.2161-0045.2001.tb00890.

Credits

Figure 4.1: Source: https://www.careerkey.org/Images/CK_holland-hex.jpg

Figure 4.2: Source: http://www.svj1.com/res/mbti/MBTItypeChartSmall.jpg

5

Postmodern Career Counseling

Ann Shillingford, PhD, NCC, Seungbin Oh, MS, LPC, NCC,
and Michelle Mitchell, MS.Ed, LPC, NCC

> *Go to the ant, O sluggard, Observe her ways, and*
> *be wise.*
>
> Proverbs 6:6, New American Standard Bible

LEARNING OBJECTIVES

In this chapter, students will learn about

- Krumboltz's social learning theories
- Social cognitive career theories
- Constructivistic and narrative approach to career counseling
- The role and responsibilities of professional career counselors using these approaches

LEARNING OUTCOMES

At the end of this chapter, students will be able to

- Successfully understand the differences between Krumboltz social learning theory of career decision-making, learning theory of career counseling, and happenstance theory
- Understand how to apply the constructs of social cognitive career in practice
- Develop career counseling strategies for working with diverse populations
- Understand the usefulness and application of storytelling in narrative career counseling
- Identify the responsibilities of a career counselor in each of the theories listed
- Be knowledgeable to the benefits of history of post-modern theories in career counseling

CHAPTER HIGHLIGHTS

- Social-cognitive career theory
- Krumboltz learning theory
- Happenstance theory
- Narrative counseling
- Cochran's narrative career theory
- Savicka's career construction theory

As social beings, we are often drawn toward attachments that we have developed with others within our social circles. These attachments may often influence our life choices and decision-making. Career choice is one area where social relationships may play a significant role in influencing one's occupational goals. However, mere social interactions play a minimal role in the determination of career position and direction. Career maturity includes a broader view of who we are as social beings. In this chapter, we will take a critical look at a few postmodern theories with the hopes of expanding the awareness and knowledge of individuals developing career focus for the first time or seeking career change. Whether you are a counselor, educator, parent, or student, read through this chapter with an open mind. Understand that career theories and career counseling can serve as road maps to future outcomes but certainly do not on their own result in determining one's career satisfaction.

INTRODUCTION TO CONCEPT

Postmodern theories of learning focus on new information; they challenge old truths and introduce new ways of thinking. Postmodern career theories extrapolate from previous designs to enlighten clients about new ways of looking at career options. The approaches recognize the client as the author of each chapter of their life and encourages broader methods of thinking and, ultimately, decision-making. The postmodern theories mentioned here encourage exploration of learning experiences as stepping stones to future opportunities and certainly note that there is no one way of learning or doing. This chapter highlights a few of these approaches—namely, the social-cognitive learning theory, Krumboltz's social learning theory, the happenstance theory, and the narrative career theory—and presents each in a format that counselors can find beneficial in promoting positive yet independent thinking for their clients.

Krumboltz's Social Learning Theories: Krumboltz (1996) believed that the career counseling can assist clients with career decision-making by guiding clients through learning exploration and use of assessments. To help clients with career decisions, Krumboltz and Mitchell (1996) emphasize the principle of the social learning theory, including (a) expanding clients' capabilities and interests, (b) preparing them for constant changes in occupations, and (c) empowering them to take action.

Social Cognitive Career Theories: Hackett and Betz (1981) initiated the development of social cognitive career theories by exploring a concept of self-efficacy coined by Bandura (1986). Bandura (1986) believes that self-efficacy is developed through a reciprocal interaction among actual behaviors, personal factors, and environmental factors. His emphasis on the importance of the reciprocal interaction plays a significant role in shaping the principle of social cognitive career theories. As a result, integrating the principles of his self-efficacy and social cognitive theory, Lent, Brown, and Hackett (1994) presented the social cognitive career theory (SCCT) that highlights a triadic relationship among people, their behaviors, and their environment to understand academic and career interest, choice, and performance.

Happenstance Learning Theory: Krumboltz (2009) develops the happenstance learning theory that emphasizes individuals' willingness to take chances in the inevitable uncertainty of our life. To help clients with career decision, Krumboltz (2009) suggests planned happenstance skills that include five components: curiosity, persistence, flexibility, optimism, and risk taking. Recent studies indicate that advanced identity statues are related to the five components of planned happenstance (Sungsik et al., 2015; Eunjeong et al., 2015).

Cochran's Narrative Career Counseling: Cochran (1997) develops narrative career counseling that underscores subjective meanings that individuals make out of their life stories as they reflect back on the personal meanings that have been essential far. The narrative career counseling warrants further studies on its application to practice (Hou, Hou, & Yang, 2014). However, a recent study (Mohamadi et al., 2015) reports that Cochran's narrative career counseling has positive influence on the blind college student's career adaptability.

Savickas's Career Construction Theory: Savickas (2011) develops a career construction theory that highlights the semantic and interpersonal process through which individuals construct themselves. His approach (Savickas, 2011; 2012) pays attention to the interpretive and interpersonal process through which individuals construct a sense of career self and stories about their career life. Within a paradigm of life designing, Savickas (2011; 2012) develops stages of his career construction counseling: construction, deconstruction, reconstruction, and co-construction.

SOCIAL COGNITIVE CAREER THEORY

Originally discussed in a 1994 article by Lent, Brown, and Hackett, the SCCT was presented as a new, innovative learning theory within the field of career development (Duggar, 2015; Lent et al., 1994). The concepts utilized in the SCCT were constructed upon principles found within the social cognitive theory outlined by Bandura (Lent et al., 1994). Originally derived from research exploring self-efficacy research as it relates to career development (Hackett & Betz, 1981), SCCT has become a notable theory that takes multiple variables into consideration when making career decisions.

SCCT emphasizes self-referent thinking in guiding human motivation and behavior (Lent et al., 1994). Moreover, the SCCT framework highlights a triadic relationship among people, their behaviors, and their environment to understand academic and career interest, choice, and performance (Duggar, 2015; Lent & Brown, 1996). When SCCT was originally constructed, the exploration was focused primarily on content discussed as an individual began to consider career choices. However, in more recent years, SCCT has evolved to underscore the importance of process-focused material to explore the methods in which people assist in affect regulation, how changing circumstances cause adaptation, and how people direct their own goal-related behavior in various settings (Lent, Ezeofor, Morrison, Penn, & Ireland, 2016). Despite whether it is more content or process focused, SCCT accentuates personal variables (e.g., self-efficacy, outcome expectations, goals) as well as contextual factors, both early in life and present-day (e.g., distal, proximal). In the following section, a brief overview of SCCT will be outlined; it is not to be mistaken for a more thorough explanation of SCCT and its tenets. We hope to address three primary elements of SCCT: person variables, contextual factors, and triadic reciprocity.

Person Variables

Self-Efficacy Beliefs. Within literature, self-efficacy can be defined in several ways; however, within social cognitive theory, self-efficacy has been defined as "people's judgements of their capabilities to organize and excite courses of action required to attain designated types of performances" (Bandura, 1986, p. 391). Self-efficacy, however, involves judgements about an individual's personal abilities; self-efficacy beliefs are not to be confused with objectively evaluated skills. In fact, self-efficacy often produces only a moderate relationship with an individuals' objective ability (Lent et al., 1994). For example, hundreds of potential contestants audition for American Idol each season and confidently sing for celebrity judges without an awareness that their efficacy in the area of singing isn't nearly as high to onlookers as it is to them as individuals.

Furthermore, social cognitive theory assumes that human ability is a dynamic (not static) attribute. In fact, it is assumed that self-efficacy beliefs are developed and modified through four informational sources: (a) performance accomplishments, (b) vicarious learning, (c) social persuasion, and (d) physiological states and reactions (Lent & Brown, 1996). For this reason, competent performance at complex or challenging tasks generally requires a proficient skillset and a strong sense of efficacy to effectively implement one's resources (Lent et al., 1994). Thus, self-efficacy is predictive of indicators related to academic and career choice and performance (Lent et al., 1994).

Outcome Expectations. Although closely related to self-efficacy, outcome expectations according to SCCT are suggested to focus primarily on the fact that "people act on their judgments of what they can do, as well as on their beliefs about the likely effects of various actions" (Bandura, 1986, p. 231). This means personal beliefs about response outcomes and outcome expectations are another imperative component of SCCT (Lent et al., 1994). While self-efficacy beliefs focus on one's thoughts concerning their own ability (e.g., "Am I able to complete this task?"), more practically, outcome expectations refer to the imagined results of particular behaviors (e.g., "If I complete this task, I believe this will happen.") (Lent et al., 1994).

In literature it has been debated as to which is more important, self-efficacy or outcome expectations; however, despite limitations on which is more imperative, it has been concluded that self-efficacy and outcome expectations both uniquely impact behavior and are dependent upon the nature of the task (Lent et al., 1994). In other words, when quality of performance assures outcomes, self-efficacy is seen as the predominant casual factor and as a partial determinant of outcome expectations. In contrast, when outcomes are only slightly connected to the quality of performance, outcome expectations may have an independent contribution to motivation and behavior (Lent et al., 1994).

The dynamics between self-efficacy and outcome expectations are particularly relevant for counselors exploring career development with their clients because academic and career environments often don't adequately illustrate the connection between quality of performance and outcomes. For instance, it is not difficult to imagine a person with high self-efficacy in interpersonal skills choosing to avoid a human services-related career if the individual anticipates negative outcomes associated to such a decision (e.g., lack of family or social support) (Lent et al., 1994).

Goal Representations. Lastly, social cognitive theory maintains that goals play an important role in the self-regulation of behavior. The third-person variable discussed by Lent and colleagues (2002) explained that

> Goal representations are defined as the determination to engage in a particular activity or to impact a particular future outcome (Bandura, 1986). By setting personal goals, people help to organize, guide, and sustain their own behavior, even through overly long intervals, without external reinforcement. Thus, goals constitute a critical mechanism through which people exercise personal agency or self-empowerment (p. 263).

Within SCCT, goal representations operate principally through the capacity of a person to symbolically represent desired future outcomes (e.g., forethought) and to react in an evaluative manner to their own behavior based on internal standards for performance (Duggar, 2015). Consequently, SCCT postulates important reciprocal interactions among self-efficacy, outcome expectations, and goal representations (Bandura, 1986).

Contextual Factors — environmental factors

Although understanding the influence of person variables is important within SCCT, environmental variables are also considered imperative upon the influence of career behavior (Duggar, 2015). Within the literature, environmental variables are termed contextual factors, which are explored through two subsets. The first explores how the context of learning experiences earlier in life influence personal variables (e.g., self-efficacy, outcomes, goals). These are termed distal contextual factors within SCCT, while career-related behaviors and current environmental factors are termed proximal contextual factors (Duggar, 2015; Lent, Brown, & Hackett, 2000).

Past learning / environment

Distal Contextual Factors. By definition, distal contextual factors refer to relevant variables that are more distant from career decision-making (Duggar, 2015). As a person considers their career choice, earlier factors (e.g., support, self-established goals) are applicable in how choices are made in the present. They've also been mentioned within literature as background contextual affordances because they affect learning experiences through which career-relevant self-efficacy and outcome expectations develop (Lent et al., 2000). This means the cultural context in which people are raised directly influences their career-related exposure and access to quality education, and informs who they recognize as authority figures as well as which socially accepted behaviors were affirmed during rearing years (Dugger, 2015).

Current environment

Proximal Contextual Factors. In addition, SCCT acknowledges the influence of an individual's current environment as a factor in career decisions. Serving as a moderate role, SCCT maintains that proximal contextual factors can either encourage or impede one's ability to transfer career interests into goals and career goals into actions (Dugger, 2015). For instance, a student may develop an interest in being an educator; however, if their environment does not provide adequate resources, the student may never establish career goals or actions in this area. In this scenario, the student's contextual factors involved barriers in the formation of previously desired career aspirations.

Triadic Reciprocity

The interaction between SCCT elements in career decision-making is termed triadic reciprocity in literature (Dugger, 2015; Lent, Brown, & Hackett, 1994). This term was originally coined within Bandura's social cognitive theory, which was later adapted for use with SCCT. The interactive relationship between a person, their environment, and their behavior is an imperative aspect in career decision-making. While the previously explored variables are important, they all work in tandem in the formulation of academic and career interests, goals, and actions. In this way, each element of SCCT has an impact in one's overall conceptualization of career decision-making (Dugger, 2015; Lent et al., 1994).

Ultimately, the social cognitive framework conceptualizes career-related interest, choice, and performance processes as three interlocking segmental models (Lent et al., 1994). This section has provided a brief overview of these basic models, focusing on the interchange among the social cognitive variables (e.g., self-efficacy, outcomes, goals) in guiding career development (Lent & Brown, 1996). Moreover, it is important as counselors to consider how the social cognitive variables function in tandem with other important aspects of persons' identity (e.g., gender, ethnicity), environment, and learning experiences (Lent & Brown, 1996).

KRUMBOLTZ LEARNING THEORY OF CAREER DECISION-MAKING AND CAREER COUNSELING

First developed in 1975, Krumboltz's social learning theory served as a guide to career selection (Krumboltz, Mitchell, & Gelatt, 1975; Mitchell & Krumboltz, 1990). Over time, however, with new discoveries, Krumboltz revised the approach to reflect the importance of clients' career decision-making. Thus, the name of the approach was revised to the social learning theory of career decision-making (SLTCDM) (Mitchell & Krumboltz, 1996). Over the next few paragraphs, we will explain the tenets of Krumboltz's (1979) with illustrations for counselors and educators. We begin with describing the four factors that influence career development and serve as the overarching theme of Krumboltz's learning theories.

Genetic Endowment

Krumboltz and colleagues believed that examining an individual's genetic composition is vital to the career decision-making process. One's genetic endowments include such factors as sex, race, and disabilities. These factors, inherited and uncontrollable—that is, we are who we are—may potentially set limitations on career opportunities for certain individuals. One example might be the female student who decides that she wants to become a computer engineer. These professions have sometimes been highlighted as male dominated, and so a female seeking to pursue this career may very well encounter barriers to obtaining this job or maintaining job satisfaction. Another interesting genetic factor that is talked about in the literature is sexual orientation. Datti (2009) surmised that individuals from the LGBTQ community might have the inert capacity to view the world through both a masculine and a feminine lens, therefore suggesting predisposed genetic endowments that may add to potential career challenges.

Environmental Conditions and Events

Imagine that your client wants to explore career opportunities in a particular field—let's say education. She holds strong beliefs and values related to education and envisions herself becoming a teacher to fix all unsupported children. The career counselor utilizing SLTCDM understands that there may be environmental factors that could possibly impede the client's view of what a successful teaching experience looks like. Educational policies, school support systems, and parental engagement are just a few environmental factors that may be outside of the client's control and may influence development, teaching activities, and career preference.

Instrumental and Associative Learning Experiences

Now suppose the same client decides that she still wants to become a teacher despite potential environmental issues. She may be encouraged to draw from experiences learned that highlighted connections between her actions and ultimate consequences. The counselor helps this client to reflect on a time when she wanted to do something but was told that it was not possible, but she in which she was successful. Her perseverance prevails; she learned that she could move forward in spite of systemic challenges. On the other hand, clients can be made to understand that people learn by observing the experiences of others in our societal circles. For example, the female client who believes that she is destined to be a computer engineer can draw from the inspirational stories of other women who appear to be successful in this same career. The notion here is that the client is allowed to vicariously explore the possibilities through the knowledge of others like her. Instrumental and associative learning can either positively or negatively impact the client. The career counselor plays a significant role in guiding the client to an understanding of the social roles that are at play, both genetically and environmentally.

Task-Approach Skills

Task-approach skills include skill sets that are part of the client's repertoire; they are abilities that we all possess that foster our success or lack thereof. Skills such as problem-solving, emotional responsiveness, cognitive responses, and even work habits assist individuals toward career outcomes. One can imagine that clients with poor problem-solving skills may need to be supported in making greater efforts toward decision-making. Krumboltz recognized the four factors—genetic endowments, environmental conditions, learning experience, and task skills—as the basis for individuals making career decisions. The emphasis remained on the importance of learning as the platform for future endeavors.

Learning Theory of Career Counseling

Upon further insights into social learning theory of career decision-making, Mitchell and Krumboltz (1996) expressed that career counseling can play a significant role in career decision-making of clients by guiding them through learning exploration and use of assessments. Still maintaining the four factors identified as key to career exploration, Mitchell and Krumboltz (1996) developed the learning theory of career counseling (LTCC) and surmised that counselors can serve as facilitators in assisting clients in exploring learning experiences, both past and present. New data also indicated that clients might not always recognize the importance of their experiences and how they shape their career future. Counselors are in a unique position to work with clients in understanding how environmental conditions as well as task skills can be influential as learning experiences. Career counselors may need to work with clients to develop more practical task skills, particularly in areas where they may be deficient. For example, one client may not be skilled in problem solving, so career counseling sessions may be centered around problem-solving skill development. According to Krumboltz and Mitchell (1996), career counselors also are in a position to assist clients in recognizing that we are in a changing world and that their skills and learning experiences can be tailored to adjust to societal changes; that is, instead of focusing career counseling sessions on identifying careers that best suit the client's learning experiences, the sessions may be best spent helping the client understand that they possess skills and experiences that can be regulated successfully regardless of the client's profession of choice.

From a holistic view of LTCC, lifetime experiences influence career choice and decision-making. Clients are given the opportunity to learn new information and skills. Benjamin Franklin once said, "Tell me and I forget, teach me and I may remember, involve me and I learn." Counselors using Krumboltz's LTCC lead clients in exploring who they are as individuals, allowing them the opportunity to understand their life influencers and develop new skills to cope with environmental challenges. Counselors using an LTCC approach understand that genetic endowments as well as environmental conditions affect clients' view of their career possibilities and also recognize that clients' learning experiences, both instrumental and associative, can be efficacious when making career choices. Experience that the client deems as negative can create psychological barriers in pursuing particular career options, thus limiting the client's view of career possibilities. In fact, Dugger (2015) suggested that clients' "faulty thinking" can be and should be reframed in counseling sessions so that clients are able to capture strengths and new insight about their learning experiences (p. 62).

In the traditional sense, career assessments have been used as tools to help clients identify career paths. The career counselor using LTCC understands that career assessments should be used to help clients recognize areas of strengths that they do not know they possess, areas of opportunities that they may never have been exposed to, and areas of interests that might be aligned with their values of which they were never aware. LTCC career counselors are indeed in a unique position to help clients reexamine their positionality in relation to the world of careers, reframe negative learning experiences, and challenge faulty thinking so as to promote healthier views of career opportunities.

HAPPENSTANCE LEARNING THEORY

Children are raised to believe that they need to identify a particular profession so that they can be nurtured toward it by parents and teachers. In fact, in today's society, the question "What do you want to be when you grow up?" is asked across cultures from the youngest age. This notion of prescribed career direction is expected to set the tone for career focus. However, this myopic view of career development can lead children to feel a sense of frustration and self-doubt, especially when they are unable to answer the above question. Krumboltz (2009) posits that as individuals we have no way of knowing how our life's journey is going to proceed, no matter how well planned that journey may be. Learning experiences that we may not even be aware of play a vital role in life outcomes. Krumboltz further suggested that both planned and unplanned experiences shape who we are and who we become. The concept of happenstance then surmises that things happen whether we have control over them or not, and these things are what make up our learning experiences.

Upon exploration and further insights into the learning theory of career counseling (Mitchell & Krumboltz, 1996) and the social learning theory of career decision-making, Krumboltz developed a new version called happenstance theory (Krumboltz, 2009). Maintaining the tenets of his previous learning theories, Krumboltz also emphasized four fundamental propositions:

1. Career counseling should be focused on clients' life satisfaction goals rather than identifying a single career. Counseling sessions should be focused on understanding and appreciating transitions in life, exploring what brings satisfaction to the client as well as taking action and getting involved with different activities for greater self-discovery.

2. Career assessments such as interest assessments, personality assessments, and career briefs assessments should be used as a way of stimulating learning rather than as

career identifiers. Krumboltz (2009) suggested that these assessments be utilized to promote interests and personality traits that the client can use as strongholds for risk taking and self-exploration.

3. Benefits to unplanned events can be found by taking action. Actions could include spontaneously going out and meeting new people, taking up a new hobby, or encouraging the client to do something that they would not have thought to do in the past.

4. Real progress is made by what the client is able to accomplish outside of counseling. Career counseling sets the stage for empowerment and exploration; it is then the client's responsibility to utilize discovered knowledge about self to now take action.

Most salient in happenstance theory is that things happen, sometimes outside of our readiness, and we must be willing to take chances. There are no guarantees that the path a person sets on is going to be a straight one. Life happens along the way and more often than not we have to adjust and keep moving forward, utilizing our interests, values, beliefs, and experiences as learning tools. Happenstance theory promotes the concept and importance of learning as a constant way of being. People behave based on what they know and what they have observed, and with career guidance they can learn to navigate and build new experiences by taking action. Finally, happenstance theory recommends that rather than looking at a client who is undecided about his or her career as lacking in direction, this individual should be considered as being open-minded. Indeed, open-mindedness is considered an asset that can be used as a means of exploring all career possibilities without limitation of time or expectation.

CONSTRUCTIVIST AND NARRATIVE APPROACHES TO CAREER DEVELOPMENT

Narrative Counseling

Michael White (2007), the founder of narrative counseling, believes that therapeutic experience and change can occur through the telling of stories. Philosophically, narrative counseling is premised in the postmodern belief that individuals construct their identity, truths of experiences, and their worldviews through internal and interpersonal interactions (Corey, 2012; Murdock, 2009). Consequently, counselors who espouse narrative counseling believe that truly understanding clients involves seeing how clients perceive themselves and their life.

Narrative counselors also believe that individuals interpret and understand their everyday lives through narratives (Rosen & Kuehlwein, 1996). These stories include more than a list of events that happen in their everyday lives. Indeed, stories reveal what people want, how they perceive themselves, what is important to them, and what they would like to change. Therefore, narrative counselors emphasize the importance of the stories people share because people will act on the stories they develop about themselves (Nichols & Schwartz, 2001).

The goal of narrative counseling is to change the client's way of perceiving themselves and their lives by empowering the clients to develop a better narrative about themselves (Nichols & Schwartz, 2001). Stories people share indicate how they have perceived themselves and their everyday lives. For example, if a person tells you who they are by sharing stories of failure, they may define themselves as unconfident. Within the narrative counseling approach, narrative counselors need to help clients reshape and tell stories in a way that is fulfilling and satisfying (Halbur & Halbur, 2011).

Storytelling

Narrative counseling includes two very importants. Externalization is one of these techniques (Rosen & Kuehlwein, 1996). Narrative counselors help clients to step out from their problems and reflect on the problem from an outside view. This practice of externalizing allows clients to detach themselves from any current life scripts that are self-defeating and unproductive. Exception is another technique of narrative counseling (Halbur & Halbur, 2011). Narrative counselors identify exceptions that are incongruent with how clients perceive their stories. For example, if a client perceives that they are a failure but share a story in which they achieved or succeeded in something, the narrative counselor has the opportunity to reveal the exception. Storytelling is also a significant technique used by narrative counselors (Halbur & Halbur, 2011). Narrative counselors hold to the premise that clients experience healing and therapeutic change through their own sharing (Rosen & Kuehlwein, 1996). Also, storytelling serves as a therapeutic tool that helps clients initiate their own therapeutic work and included the use of metaphors. Consequently, at the end of the counseling session, clients must reconstruct and tell a new story that includes positive and fulfilling themes of themselves and their life.

Cochran's Narrative Career Counseling

Cochran's (1997) narrative career counseling is a postmodern approach that underscores subjective meaning and meaning-making. It is designed to position clients as both the main character and the storyteller in their life stories that are meaningful and fulfilling. Cochran believes that the task of career counseling is to help clients construct their future career trajectory by empowering them to assess their life stories, reflect on the personal meanings that have been fundamental thus far, and compose the future narrative of their lives (Dugger, 2015). Cochran's approach is premised in the belief that narrative is a person's primary way of exploring and making meanings in the world. Rather than emphasizing the counselor's role as expert, his approach focuses on empowering clients to actively explore, design, and implement their career narrative. Cochran suggests that counselors enable clients to self-enhance through narrative counseling their own "practical wisdom, the capacity to narrate one's life story through changing circumstance of life" (1997, p. 24). He indicates that although narrative counseling serves as a tool for the exercise of practical wisdom in a way that bridges a gap between ideals of the person and actual features of situation, a story can be narrated better than others (Dugger, 2015). For example, some people struggle with their career problem because their stories are discontinuous, unachievable, impractical, or self-defeating. Therefore, Cochran believes that clients must be assisted with narrating continuous, fulfilling, plausible, and productive stories. In the course of striving to tell well-formed and productive stories, a client's life story becomes filled with the theme of a "sense of agency, a person's sensed capacity to bring about desirable outcomes or carry out a task" (p. 29).

To help clients author and implement their productive career narrative, Cochran (1997) proposes seven "episodes" (p. 42) in the description of his narrative approach: ① elaborating a career problem, ② composing a life story, ③ founding a future narrative, ④ constructing reality, ⑤ changing a life structure, ⑥ enacting a role, and ⑦ crystallizing a decision. Cochran provides a detailed description of seven episodes from which a counselor can select to meet various clients' needs. These episodes are not meant to be followed in a step-by-step, rigid manner. He emphasizes that "different clients require different episodes and/or a different coordination and ordering of episodes" (p. 42).

1) **Elaborating a Career Problem.** The cornerstone of any career counseling is to form a working alliance with clients to establish a mutual understanding of the career problem. Cochran (1997) perceives a career problem as a gap between a client's desire (e.g., wanting a job) and their anticipation from their actual circumstances (e.g., not anticipating a job). He suggests that counselors pay attention to various themes in a client's life story in order to better elaborate the career problem (Dugger, 2015). For example, a client wants a job but does not have one, whereas another client wants a satisfying job rather than "a job" but cannot anticipate it soon because of their current circumstance. The elaboration of the career problem can be prompted through a variety of narrative-based techniques, including vocational card sorts, exploring anecdotes, storytelling, and drawing.

2) **Composing a Life History.** To understand one's life story from narrative perspective, it is essential to realize that one's life story is filled with more than a list of events. Indeed, a life story includes various subjective meanings associated with those events and the stories behind them. Therefore, career counselors who espouse narrative perspective pay careful attention to the way clients experience and describe their life stories (Dugger, 2015). Within his narrative approach, Cochran (1997) perceives the assessment of subjective meaning and the rewriting of life history as two key components of composing a life story to establish a "unifying plot" (p. 60). In other words, Cochran (1997) recommends that counselors need to allow clients to develop a better understanding of the personal meanings associated with their life stories. Once clients gain insights into the meanings, they should be assisted with rewriting their life stories to reflect themes of fulfilling, self-efficacy, and continuity (Dugger, 2015). Cochran suggests six assessment techniques that help broach the process of gathering information about a client's life history and subjective meanings: lifeline, life chapters, success experiences, family constellation, role models, and early recollections (1997).

3) **Funding a Future Narrative.** Cochran (1997) perceives a career decision as an evaluation of various future career scenarios that will not meet all of client's desire, values, and interests. Consequently, counselors and clients encounter the challenges of making a wise decision among various rival scenarios in order to reflect their fundamental desires, most important values, and remarkable strengths (Dugger, 2015). In his description of this episode, Cochran (1997) suggests that counselors and clients need to differentiate and evaluate

possible future career narratives, while expanding the new themes of fulfilling and self-efficacy into the next chapters of a client's life. In this regard, Cochran recommends the use of two collaboration-based approaches for counselors and clients: "eliciting a future narrative" (p. 85) and "portraying a future narrative" (p. 91). Eliciting a future narrative involves the counselor's collection of information on a future narrative that a client envisions for their future. Cochran (1997) recommends the use of the lifeline technique for counselors to address the client's life history and facilitate them to envision a future that would be most fulfilling and productive. The second step in finding a future narrative is portraying a future narrative. Cochran (1997) perceives this portrayal as the process of coauthoring the next chapter of the client's life story. He suggests that counselors should initially develop a written report that captures key themes and meanings shared by the client, ask for the client's feedback on the written report, and then guide the collaboration with the client to create a viable and satisfying career narrative for the client's future (Dugger, 2015). However, Cochran also cautions against assuming the future narrative portrayed in this episode is a final choice. Instead, he considers it a draft of the future narrative that requires the client's active reevaluation and confirmation in the following three episodes: constructing reality, changing a life structure, and enacting a role.

Constructing Reality. Cochran (1997) considers these three episodes (constructing reality, changing a life structure, and enacting a role) the action-focused episodes that involve a client's active engagement in their future narratives envisioned. The action episode of constructing reality requires clients to actively test the realities of a career that satisfies their values and interests. In this episode, counselors should empower clients to actively explore the feasibility of the career path, experience challenges and actual features of the career path, and incorporate the realities of the career path into their future career narrative (Dugger, 2015). Cochran (1997) emphasizes the active engagement of clients with a desired career, such as job shadowing and volunteering. He believes that this active involvement allows clients to have a taste of what the desired career actually looks like so that they can truly visualize themselves employed and feeling satisfied in the career.

Changing a Life Structure. Life structures consist of two layers: internal and external life structures. Once clients choose their future career narrative, they need to be ready to bring the new narrative to their life by changing these life structures that have been dominant in their life thus far (Dugger, 2015). Clients may need to change some of their internal life structures, such as their unhealthy behaviors and belief systems. On the other hand, the external life structures involve a situation or context in which a client lives. For example, clients can change the external life structures by adjusting daily schedules or negotiating arrangements of childcare.

Enacting a Role. Cochran (1997) believes that clients are encouraged to actualize the future narrative they choose through the active involvement in "activities that are meaningful and enjoyable" (p. 113). Cochran relates active engagement in these activities to enacting a role. He believes that the engagement creates a virtuous circle where the clients have an opportunity to be involved in other enjoyable activities and refine the future narrative (Dugger, 2015).

Crystallizing a Decision. The final episode involves the stabilization of the future narrative the clients constructed and chose. Cochran (1997) emphasizes the counselor's role in facilitating this episode by empowering clients to identify obstacles, actualize their ultimate narrative, and reflect on their choice.

SAVICKAS CAREER CONSTRUCTION THEORY

Savickas's (2011; 2012) career construction counseling is a social constructive, postmodern approach that underscores semantic and interpersonal process through which individuals construct themselves. He disagrees with the modern belief of self and identity in which a person has a preexisting, essential self waiting to be actualized. Instead, he espouses the postmodern idea that an essential self is constructed through internal and interpersonal experience, subjective self-reflection and meaning making, and personal stories that a person develops and narrates about themselves. In other words, a self is a constructed story that a person develops as reflecting back on their subjective experiences rather than as a priori essence existing within a person (Savickas, 2012). In the context of career, therefore, Savickas's approach pays attention to the interpretive and interpersonal process through which an individual constructs a sense of career self and stories about their career life. He believes that clients should be assisted in the interpretive process of constructing their career stories. In particular, counselors need to encourage clients to revisit their past career stories and reconstruct new stories, especially when they encounter an occupational transition or developmental tasks. Savickas (2011; 2012) proposes four stages of career construction counseling: construction, deconstruction, reconstruction, and conconstruction. Following is a summary of each stage.

Construction. When individuals step back from their current situations, they begin an introspection process of their life and construct a story to develop a better understanding of it. Savickas (2011; 2012) perceives this stage of construction as the process of identifying events that dislocate individuals from their current stories, constructing a new story to organize those events into sequence, and then finding a new goal for a new story. He suggests that counselors help clients narrate their small stories that include critical clues to their ways of having constructed their self, identity, and a sense of career self thus far. Narrating their stories, clients develop a better understanding of their belief about themselves, their identity, and their career. Savickas (2011) suggests five topics that counselors need to address in order to understand the client narrative career identity: role models, magazines, favorite story, mottos, and early recollections.

Deconstruction. Forming identity is influenced by the intersecting aspects of various cultures. Indeed, we all live in a certain cultural context that influences how we perceive ourselves and experience our worlds. Thus, counselors need to be attentive of how a client's story is influenced by their respective cultures. In some cases, counselors may realize that clients often embed cultural scripts in their stories that serve as deterrents to their personal and professional growth. In particular, counselors should be sensitive to problematic cultural scripts embedded within the client's stories that reinforce internalized biases against gender, race, and socioeconomic status. Savickas believes that these problematic cultural scripts may limit "the range of possible selves and styles of living that individual may adopt" (2011, p. 110).

Savickas (2011; 2012) refers to deconstruction as a process by which counselors engage clients in exploring, and even questioning, the possible cultural barriers and self-limiting ideas and roles embedded within their stories. The purpose of deconstruction is to invite clients to consider different worldviews that open up various possibilities rather than to destroy their current stories. When counselors need to deconstruct some of the client's stories, they may broach a discussion with clients about what a story "overlooks, omits, forgets, or inadequately address[s]" (Savicaks, 2011. p. 111).

3) **Reconstruction.** Reconstruction involves the counselor's assessment process of information gathered during previous stages (Savickas, 2011; 2012). This assessment process largely consists of two components: ① eliciting thematic meanings from the client's micronarratives or small stories about important events, significant figures, and momentous experiences in their life and ② integrating the thematic meanings into a macronarrative or large story, that is, an identity narrative that address the career concerns. The macronarrative reconstructs fragmented and sporadic experiences, values, and attitudes into a unified story about an individual's life. The individual becomes the main character in the life story and understands their past, gains insight into their present, and navigates their future through the macronarrative of identity (identity narrative). Savickas (2011; 2012) suggests that counselors actively elicit career themes and meanings from the sequence of a client's micronarratives and integrate them into a meaningful macronarrative of the client's work life, which is called a life portrait. He suggests counselors compose a life portrait by assessing the client's macronarrative in order to accurately capture the career themes and meanings shared by the client.

thematic = theme, belonging to, relating to

4) **Conconstruction.** Conconstruction refers to a collaboration process of revising and clarifying a life portrait (Savickas, 2011). A life portrait (the macronarrative) developed by the counselor may not resonate with the client. Thus, it is essential for counselors and clients to work together to clarify and revise the life portrait. First, counselors present to the client a draft of the life portrait so that the client can identify the macronarrative reconstructed by the counselor. Then, counselors invite clients to revise the life portrait, including correction of mistakes and adding new themes and meanings. This collaboration process not only allows for clarification and accuracy of the client's life portrait but also helps clients claim authorship of their macronarrative.

CONCLUSION

The purpose of this chapter is to give the reader an overview of postmodern career theories; in particular, social learning theory, Krumboltz social learning theories, happenstance theory, and narrative career theories. The hope is that counselors understand the importance of clients' internal and external factors that play salient roles in their career decision-making processes. Postmodern theories promote a new vision of reflecting on the needs of clients by infusing clients' historical context and learning experiences into their everyday living in order to bring them to a place of self-understanding. It is then that the counselor can move the client toward believing and understanding that they have the power to make their own career choices. Like Krumboltz mentioned, sometimes we plan and sometimes life happens. We explore, we learn, we accept, and we move forward. What we have attempted to do in this chapter is give the reader an overview of postmodern career theories; in particular, social learning theory, Krumboltz social learning theories, happenstance theory, and narrative career theories. Our hope is that counselors understand the importance of clients' internal and external factors that play salient roles in their career decision-making processes. Postmodern theories promote a new vision of reflecting on the needs of clients by infusing clients' historical context and learning experiences into their everyday living in order to bring them to a place of self-understanding. It is then that the counselor can move the client toward believing and understanding that they have the power to make their own career choices. Like Krumboltz mentioned, sometimes we plan and sometime life happens. We explore, we learn, we accept, and we move forward.

KEY TERMS

Cochran's narrative career counseling: a postmodern approach that underscores the importance of exploring subjective meaning in making career decisions; designed to position clients as both the main character and storyteller in their career life stories that are meaningful and fulfilling

Constructivism: a philosophical paradigm that focus on the subjective meaning and knowledge which individuals attribute to their experience

Goal representations: the determination to engage in a particular activity or to impact a particular future outcome

Happenstance theory: a career theory that emphasizes the importance of taking chances and learning as a constant way of being; happenstance theory perceives indecision about career choice as desirable and open-minded rather than lacking in direction

Krumboltz learning theory of career counseling: an approach to career counseling that embraces Krumboltz's learning theory to reflect the importance of behavior and cognition in making career decisions

Narrative therapy: a postmodern approach that underlines the telling of stories as the cornerstone of therapeutic experience and change

Savickas career construction theory: a postmodern career theory that emphasizes semantic and interpersonal process through which individuals construct themselves to make career decisions

Self-efficacy: an individual's belief in their capabilities to take a course of action necessary to obtain desired goals and designated types of performances

Social cognitive career theory (SCCT): a career theory that integrates the foundation of social cognitive theory to explain an intersecting aspects of career development, including knowledge, behavior, and environments

Social cognitive theory: a theory that emphasizes a triadic relationship among behavior, the cognitive, and the environment to understand how humans' knowledge and behavior patterns can be obtained

Storytelling: a therapeutic tool that allows clients to experience healing through their own sharing and helps clients initiate their own therapeutic work that includes the use of metaphors.

Triadic Reciprocity: interaction among a person, their environment, and their behavior that influence one's career development and experience

REFLECTION AND DISCUSSION

1. How might a counselor using happenstance theory work with parents who are insisting on a career choice for their child?
2. Explain the cultural implications of using postmodern theories.
3. Describe the tenets of self-efficacy. What might be the challenges of working with children exploring self-efficacy?
4. What are noted benefits to storytelling in career counseling?
5. Explore the advantages and disadvantages of postmodern approaches in spiritual counseling.

ADDITIONAL READINGS, RESOURCES, AND WEBSITES

Anderson, P., & Vandehey, M. (2006). Career counseling and development in a global economy. Boston: Hougton Mifflin/Lahaska.

Amundson, N.E., Harris-Bowlsbey, J.H., & Niles, S.G. (2005). Essential elements of career counseling: Processes and techniques. Upper Saddle River, NJ: Pearson Prentice-Hall.

Brown, D. (2007). Career information, career counseling, and career development (9th ed.). Boston: Allyn and Bacon.

College Navigator: http://nces.ed.gov/collegenavigator/

Eight Components of College and Career Readiness Counseling https://www.counseling. org/docs/default-source/library-archives/school-counselor-connection/8-components-of-college-and-career-readiness-counseling.pdf?sfvrsn=2

Liptak, J.J. (2001). Treatment planning in career counseling. Belmont, CA: Wadsworth.

Niles, S.G., & Harris-Bowlsbey, J. (2005). Career development interventions in the 21st century (2nd ed.). Upper Saddle River, NJ: Merrill/Prentice Hall.

Osborn, D.S., & Zunker, V.G. (2006). Using assessment results for career development (7th ed.). Pacific Grove, CA: Brooks/Cole.

Peterson, N., & Gonzalez, R.C. (2000). Career counseling models for diverse populations. Belmont, CA: Wadsworth/Thompson Learning.

Sharf, R.S. (2006). Applying career development theory to counseling (4th ed.). Pacific Grove, CA: Brooks/Cole.

State Academic Performance and Improvement Tool: https://edtrust.org/our-resources/data-tools/state-academic-performance-tool/

Zunker, V.G. (2006). Career counseling: A holistic approach (7th ed.). Pacific Grove, CA: Brooks/Cole.

TRADITIONAL ACTIVITY

Taylor is a 16-year-old high school student. Her family has been inquiring of Taylor about her future plans for college. Taylor is unsure about what she wants to pursue. The question "What do you want to be when you grow up?" has been engraved in her mind, as its been asked ever since she could remember. Taylor has no idea what she wants to do or be. A career counselor working with Taylor could explore her career choices in several different ways. Let's take the social learning approach. Taylor would be encouraged to focus on what she can do. What are her interests, abilities, and strengths? Career inventories would be introduced to enhance Taylor's knowledge and understanding of what will work best for her based on her abilities. Using the happenstance approach, the career counselor would then explore Taylor's strengths, but most importantly help to relieve Taylor's anxieties by encouraging her to embrace all opportunities afforded her (e.g., school clubs, family activities). The thought that these learning opportunities could be the stepping stone of her future, whatever that may be.

Question to consider:

1. Using narrative therapy, how would you support Taylor?
2. Using Krumboltz's learning theory and career decision-making, how would you include Taylor's family in the therapeutic resources to support Taylor?

SPIRITUAL ACTIVITY

David is a 30-year-old magazine editor who is beginning to consider a career change. A counselor instructs an activity that involves David drawing a line on a piece of paper to represent his life up until now. Afterward, David marks various points of career decisions and interests and writes an identification for each decision. Then, David is instructed to think about his spiritual development throughout his life and identify significant moments of his journey. Once the graph has these two developmental markers (i.e., career decisions and interests and spiritual development), how can David's counselor explore his career and spiritual development while incorporating a narrative approach?

Question to consider:

1. Utilizing a Krumboltz learning theory, how would an approach toward David differ if he was 50 years old?
2. While integrating social cognitive learning theory, how can you assist David in exploring his career interests?

REFERENCES

Ann, S., Jung, S.H., Jang, S.H., Du, X., Lee, B.H., Rhee, E., Gysbers, N., & Lee. S.M. (2015). Planned happenstance skills and occupational identity statues in high school students. Journal of Career Development, 64(1), 31–43.

Bandura, A. (1986). Social foundations of thought and action: A social cognitive theory. Englewood Cliffs, NJ: Prentice-Hall.

Cochran, L. (1997). Career counseling: A narrative approach. Thousand Oaks, CA: SAGE Publications.

Corey, G. (2012). Theory and practice of counseling and psychotherapy (9th ed.). Pacific Grove, CA: Wadsworth.

Datti, P. A. (2011). Applying social learning theory of career decision making to gay, lesbian, bisexual, transgender, and questioning young adults. The Career Development Quarterly, 58, 54–64.

Dugger, S. (2016). Foundations of Career Counseling: A Case-Based Approach. New York, NY: Pearson Education.

Hackett, G. & Betz, N. E. (1981). A self-efficacy approach to the career development of women. Journal of Vocational Behavior, 18, 326–336.

Halbur, D. A., & Halbur, K. V. (2011). Developing your theoretical orientation in counseling and psychotherapy (2nd ed.). Boston, MA: Pearson.

Krumboltz, J. D., Mitchell, A. M., & Jones, G. B. (1976). A social learning theory of career selection. The Counseling Psychologist, 6, 71–81.

Krumboltz, J. D. (2009). The Happenstance Learning Theory. Journal of Career Assessment, 17, 135–154.

Krumboltz, J. D. (1996). A learning theory of career counseling. In M. L. Savickas & W. B. Walsh, Handbook of career counseling theory and practice. Palo Alto, CA: Consulting Psychologist.

Lent, R. W., Brown, S. D., & Hackett, G. (2000). Contextual supports and barriers to career choice: A social cognitive analysis. Journal of Counseling Psychology, 49, 36–49.

Lent, R. W. & Brown, S. D. (1996). Social cognitive approach to career development: An overview. The Career Development Quarterly, 44, 310–321.

Lent, R. W., Brown, S. D., & Hackett, G. (1994). Toward a unifying social cognitive theory of career and academic interest, choice, and performance. Journal of Vocational Behavior, 45, 79–122.

Lent, R. W., Brown, S. D., Talleyrand, R., McPartland, E. B., Davis, T., Chopra, S. B., Alexander, M. S., Suthakaran, V., & Chai, C. (2002). Career choice barriers, supports, and coping strategies: College students' experiences. Journal of Vocational Behavior, 60, 61–72.

Lent, R. W., Ezeofor, I., Morrison, A., Penn, L. T., & Ireland, G. W. (2016). Applying the social cognitive model of career self-management to career exploration and decision-making. Journal of Vocational Behavior, 93, 47–57.

Mitchell, L.K. & Krumboltz, J. D. (1996). Krumboltz's learning theory of career choice and counseling. In D. Brown, L. Brook, & Associates, Career Choice and Development. San Francisco, CA: Jossey-Bass.

Mohamadi, E., Nilforooshan, P., & Salimi, S. (2015). The effect of career counseling based on narrative approach on the blind college students' career adaptability. Knowledge & Research in Applied Psychology, 17(1), 80–89.

Murdock, N. (2009). Theories of counseling and psychotherapy: A case approach (2nd ed.). Columbus, OH: Pearson.

Nichols, M. P., & Schwartz, R. C. (2011). Family therapy: Concept and method (5th ed.). Boston, MA: Allyn & Bacon.

Rhee, E., Lee, B.H., Kim, B., Ha., G., & Lee, S.M. (2015). The relationship among the six vocational identity statues and five dimensions of planned happenstance career skills. Journal of Career Development, 43(4). 368–378.

Rosen, H., & Kuehlwein, K. T. (1996). Constructing realities: Meaning-making perspectives for psychotherapists. San Francisco, CA: Jossey-Bass.

Savickas, M. L. (2011). Career counseling. Washington, DC: American Psychological Association.

Savickas, M. L. (2012). Life design: A paradigm for career intervention in the 21st country. Journal of Counseling and Development, 90, 13–19.

White, M. (2007). Maps of narrative practice. New York, NY: WW Norton & Company.

Spiritual Approaches to Career Theory

Priscilla Mondt, PhD, M.Div

For we are his handiwork, created in Christ Jesus to do good works, which God prepared in advance for us to do.

Ephesians 2:10, New International Version

LEARNING OBJECTIVES

In this chapter, students will learn about

- Theories comprising spiritual approaches to career theory: religious and existential
- The emergence of business schools and nonprofits that integrate spirituality with work
- How to address clients as spiritual beings regardless of belief system, including atheists and agnostics
- Ethical boundaries for spiritual approaches to career theory
- Religious biases and social values impacting spiritual approaches to career theory

LEARNING OUTCOMES

At the end of this chapter, students will be able to

- Apply spiritual approaches to career counseling by matching clients to appropriate theory
- Share how they would ethically engage a client with differing belief systems
- Identify potential religious biases or values
- Demonstrate integration of spiritual concepts with career counseling
- Conceptualize a personal theology of work as a framework for career counseling

CHAPTER HIGHLIGHTS

- Definition of spirituality: Religion + Existentialism
- Spiritual approaches
- Religious approaches
- Existential approaches
- Considerations for counseling spiritual clients

With the integration of spirituality gaining emphasis across disciplines, it is natural for career development theories to follow. As humans are multifaceted beings, spirituality must be considered in career counseling. Yet spirituality is discussed less in career development literature than in management, leadership, and religious literature. This is evidenced by the dearth of career development literature versus the explosion of business and management books dedicated to spirituality in the workforce. A growing body of career literature calls for integration of spirituality into career development (Bloch, 2004; Constantine, Miville, Warren, Gainor & Lewis-Coles, 2006; Duffy, 2006; Duffy, Reid & Dik, 2010) while acknowledging that the business world surpassed career literature (Gockel, 2004; Roof, 2015; Smith, Arendt, Lahman, Settle, & Duff, 2006).

Spirituality is defined broadly, and often with individual interpretation. Nascent counseling literature and research agree that spirituality includes two major areas: religion and existentialism (Paloutzian, Bufford, & Wildman, 2012). This chapter will provide an overview of emerging spiritual approaches to career development and address issues specific to this approach with special attention to counseling the client as a spiritual being. This chapter seeks to empower the counselor with theories based on the broad definition of spirituality with emphasis on belief systems. The counselor will become knowledgeable of spiritual approaches that will enable career counseling to embrace all clients, regardless of belief system, including atheists and agnostics.

The reader will note that there is no clear spiritual career counseling approach that integrates religious values, such as belief in a transcendent God that interacts in our lives. Specifically, there is no Christian spiritual career counseling approach, leaving this author to focus on what is called "a theology of work" to set a framework for spiritual discussion (Lewis & Hardin, 2002) and, perhaps, future development of a clear Christian spiritual approach to career development. This chapter seeks to answer the question, "How do we integrate spirituality with work?"

Evaluation of employment is not limited to the choice of career; it also takes into account employment with a company that would fulfill spiritual concerns and not violate a person's closely held ethical or religious principle (Duffy, Reid & Dik, 2010; Gockel, 2004). Career conversations shifted from skill sets and interests to matters of principles sacred to the client (Duffy et al., 2010; Smith, Arendt, Lahman, Settle & Duff, 2006) and reflect the business practice of human flourishing (Guillen, Ferrero & Hoffman, 2015). Contribution to society, a Jewish principle (Fine, 2006), is considered a spiritual decision in selection of careers and employment.

The integration of spirituality into career counseling requires awareness of one's religious framework. If the counselor believes that their role is to assist the client in discovery of God's plan for their life, the career counselor participates in a sacred act of ministry (Nelson, 2011). The counselor must have strong boundaries to ensure personal belief systems do not interfere with the client's belief system. Ethics require that the client's belief system is honored.

DEFINING SPIRITUALITY: RELIGION + EXISTENTIALISM

A postmodern world demanded a new definition of spirituality that was inclusive of everyone to include atheists and agnostics. This is based on the concept that we are multidimensional. It is best reflected in the shift of well-known twelve step program from the word "God" to "higher power" and seeker-sensitive churches that sought to assist nonbelievers in acknowledgement that the core of a person is spiritual. The expansion of the definition of spirituality is built on a holistic concept of health: being physically, mentally and spiritually healthy.

The counseling field generally accepts spirituality as consisting of two prongs: religion and existentialism. This definition emerged across disciplines and allows common language. Career counseling literature does not yet reflect this definition. Rather, career counseling literature addresses spirituality as equal to existentialism, often referring to "spirituality and religion" (Hernandez, Foley, & Beitin, 2011). However, anyone with religious belief systems would balk at the exclusion of spirituality based on religion. People with religious values do not consider themselves limited to religion but consider themselves as spiritual beings (Constantine et al., 2006; Hernandez et al., 2011). Research outside the counseling field explicitly includes the presence of God, an overtly religious theme, as integral to spirituality (Guillen et al., 2015). The current career counseling definition of spirituality refers to the search of the sacred (Constantine et al., 2006; Duffy et al., 2010) while defining religion as adhering to practices and tenets of faith organizations (Miller, 2007).

Duffy et al. (2010) assert that the core of our identity is comprises spirituality (existentialism), religion, and work, yet empirical research in the area of spiritual approaches to career development is limited. The current spiritual approaches to career development are outdated and ill researched. This chapter will address spiritual approaches from two aspects: the current movement toward a popular but unspecified model represented in business and management fields, and the limited and somewhat outdated spiritual approaches in the career development field. Together, these comprise spiritual approaches and point to a need for a well-developed spiritual approach model, especially one that integrates, rather than tolerates, faith.

Religion: Vocation and Calling

Qualitative research reveals that some clients have a belief that God has a plan for their life that guides career choice (Constantine et al., 2006; Hernandez et al., 2011). Vocation is defined as responding to God by engaging the talents, skills, and gifts endowed (Sellers, Thomas, Batts & Ostman, 2005). A calling is defined as a special summons to pursue a life role or task

(Dalton, 2001). Many people regard vocation as the work (Nelson, 2011) and calling as the pull toward the work (Dalton, 2001) while others consider the terms synonymous (Hernandez et al., 2011). Belief that one's work and spirituality should be integrated is central to Miller's (2007) seminal work that outlines the faith at work movement.

To honor a client's belief systems, a fully developed theory is needed but does not yet exist (Lewis & Hardin, 2002). With the gap in literature, a theology of work is necessary. What emerges in Christian literature is tension around work as a curse or as a sacred act of worship (Nelson, 2011). The faith-based counselor must find the client's theological frame of reference and know their own theological frame of reference. If finding one's calling or vocation is a sacred act of worship, then the counselor serves in a role that is highly sacred and acts as God's instrument to assist the client in discovery of God's intention and purpose for their life (Nelson, 2011). Clients with strong religious values and who seek to respond to a calling are often ambivalent and need this normalized (Hernandez et al., 2011).

Existentialism: Meaning and Purpose

Existentialism emphasizes autonomy and all that makes an individual human. Existential philosophy focuses on what gives individuals meaning and purpose. Although religion does give meaning and purpose, existentialism generally does not address religion (Paloutzian et al., 2012). It includes a sense of calling that excludes religion (Duffy et al., 2010; Smith et al., 2006). Considering the amount of time spent at work versus with family, work grants meaning and purpose and, therefore, is existential in nature. Existential approaches are holistic. These approaches are inclusive of atheists and agnostics in addition to those who are religious.

Religion + Existentialism = Spiritual: Lifestyle

The integration of religion and existential concerns creates spirituality (Paloutzian et al., 2012). Together these make up who we are as multifaceted human beings. The combination captures who we are as individuals. What we think about these two areas is reflected in our lifestyle. We invest our time, energy, and money in what matters most to us, in our values. The intent of spiritual approaches is to capture the lifestyle of the client and match it to vocation (Smith et al., 2006).

WORK SELECTION BASED ON SPIRITUALITY

Duffy (2006) identified a significant gap in career development research and literature that called for integration of spirituality into the field. Equal to the seminal career development work launched by efficient business needs of the military rather than the counseling field, the business world filled a void for career development with the evolution of spiritual considerations in the workforce. Business schools incorporated spiritual values in the wake of ethical malfeasance leading to niches that promote a positive workplace, personal well-being, and work that contributes to society in a positive manner (Roof, 2015). Business and management research found that shared values and positive professional practices increased productivity

(Carroll, Stewart-Sicking & Thompson, 2014). Career selections moved from skill sets and interests to consideration of the type of work based on what is sacred to the individual (Duffy et al., 2010) or how one wants to live (Smith et al., 2006).

Business and Management Influences

Service Master is a pioneer in the positive work environment movement. Established in 1929 by a man with strong personal faith who believed every employee and customer is worthy of dignity and respect, it is a forerunner of the movement. Gil Strickland founded Marketplace Ministries in 1984, seizing on the concept that taking care of people makes for productive employees. This ministry has 2,870 chaplains with 630 client companies and is now international. These companies were foundational for the rise of career choices based on the value system of the business rather than skill sets and interests, a key element of spiritual approaches to career development theory.

Tyson Center for Faith and Spirituality in the Workplace was established in 2007 at the University of Arkansas as part of the Sam M. Walton College of Business. Its unique concept includes embedding research and practice into a publicly funded business school to transform personal leadership, organizations, communities, and global markets through integration of faith and spirituality in the workplace. Built on the military model of ministry, Tyson Foods began modeling integration of spirituality into the marketplace in 2007 through integration of chaplains. Tyson currently employs over 100 chaplains globally and actively supports all faith groups. Although the military has long integrated spirituality into the workforce, Tyson currently serves as the civilian model for integration of spirituality into the workforce as a successful business management model.

A WAY TO SERVE THE WORLD

Spiritual values are often reflected in nonprofit work as a way to serve the world. Those who make career decisions based on calling rather than material goods find nonprofits attractive (Smith et al., 2006). These clients value service, sacrifice, calling, and personal reward. These are both religious and existential values.

Issues such as ecology and making the world a better place are viewed as spiritual values. Clients may view stewardship of God's creation, such as reducing the environmental footprint, as extremely important. Serving humanity, such as digging wells in remote locations, may fulfill a sense of higher calling that is spiritual in nature but not rooted in religious values.

Community and Connectedness

Clients may make decisions about career and place of employment based on spiritual issues to include religious values (Gaffen, 2006). Spirituality is viewed as community and connectedness (Gaffin, 2006). Spirituality in the workplace addresses the personal side of the employee in the belief that positive people are more efficient. This includes community among employees. These organizations believe in participatory management. Spiritually infused organizations use training and development focused on character, ethics, values, and creativity (Gockel, 2004).

Another aspect of a spiritually healthy organization is community service. Tyson Foods models integration of spiritual health through a community service program called Meals that Matter, which utilizes semitrucks outfitted with kitchens to feed hot meals in the midst of disasters. Service Master employees throughout the United States are encouraged to serve the community at multiple sites with We Serve Day events to support multiple nonprofits.

Some clients may look for social justice issues in the workplace (Gockel, 2004). Both the treatment of employees and social responsibility are important to these clients. Non-profit work is attractive and viable for this group. Equal treatment and opportunity falls into this category, addressing issues such as oppression both in the work environment and in society.

Faith at Work Movement

Capturing the movement toward integrating one's faith at work, Miller (2007) categorizes people attracted to faith issues into four types: ethics, evangelism, experience, and enrichment. The ethics type are those whose attention is given to social and economic justice, and business and personal ethics. The evangelism type are missional at work; work is an avenue to evangelize the world. The experience type are those who use work to serve people. The enrichment type use work as a form of expression of faith and to focus on inner awareness.

Organizations such as Work Matters (established 2002) emphasize Christian leadership in the marketplace. Work Matters originated as a ministry of a United Methodist church and became a nondenominational nonprofit. The Center for Faith and Work (Duffy et al., 2010) is a ministry of Redeemer Presbyterian Church in New York City that seeks to integrate the concepts. Both of these ministries hold annual conferences highlighting various aspects of how one's faith impacts one's work. Nascent career development literature reflects the growing workplace movement toward spirituality. However, career development literature has not yet integrated these movements into a cogent spiritual approach theory.

SPIRITUAL APPROACHES

Spirituality in career theory is less about religion and more about addressing the whole person (Gockel, 2004). Religion brings an outside focus based on response to a transcendent being. Existentialism focuses on the individual. Both concepts are important in career counseling. Incorporating existentialism allows atheists and agnostics to identify as spiritual. Spiritual approaches focus on the client's belief system and do not attempt to persuade otherwise.

Miller-Tiedeman is the first career theorist to mention spirituality. Bloch built on her theory for a merger of thought with influence from Buddhism. Hansen was the first theorist to name existentialist approach. These approaches allow for religion as an external influence. Religious theories, especially Christian, are underrepresented, if at all.

Life Career Theory

The first career model to address a spiritual approach was the life career theory developed by a couple, Tiedeman and Miller-Tiedeman (1984). The model allows for religion, in somewhat of a tolerance, but does not directly incorporate it. Unlike the emerging definition of spirituality that incorporates both religion and existentialism to constitute spirituality, this approach highlights existentialism but grants religion as an external influence. Tiedeman was a fan of quantum physics and invokes science as his impetus but eventually asserted that "statistics and guidance are logically incompatible" (Miller-Tiedeman, 2008, p. 244). His early writings are very difficult to follow as he invokes science and Newtonian principles (Tiedeman & Miller-Tiedeman, 1984). Nevertheless, the ability to consider religion that evolved with the influence of Miller-Tiedeman allows life career theory to be placed first in this overview of spiritual approaches.

Life career approach is process oriented with autonomy as the highest principle. Because career is considered over lifetime, this approach has close ties to development theories. All of life is considered a process toward career discovery—"life is career," whether hobby, religious belief systems, serendipitous, or intentional influences (Sharf, 2010). In this approach, the individual knows the path to follow and the counselor encourages the client to follow terms considered synonymous: their love, instincts, intuition, and inner self. Contrary to traditional career counseling, life career theory rejects external forces that are prescriptive. Since the theorists view religion as prescriptive, this may be the reason for a weak connection. The counselor assists the client to view life as their career incorporating every experience as cues for career development (Sharf, 2010). The narrative of one's life leads to conclusions about career.

The client has two stages: anticipation and adjusting (Sharf, 2010). In the stage of anticipation, there are four substages: exploration (unsystematic leads), crystallization (definition of thought), choice (unconscious or conscious awareness), and clarification (time to reassess). The adjustment stages include induction (implements choice), reformation (belonging vs. rejection), and integration (normalcy sets in).

Bloch's Model of Spirituality and Career Counseling

Bloch (2004) is the first to call on career counseling to integrate spirituality with a definition of two components: a sense of connection to something beyond the individual and as a search for meaning and purpose. This model was developed in the late 1990s as part of complexity theory (Bloch, 2004) with the belief that work has a purpose beyond money, that it includes calling (Duffy, 2006). This model asks counselors to assist clients in preparation for their life journey considering that life has major changes (Duffy, 2006). Counselors should address what clients feel drawn to and the reasons behind those feelings in order to discover their calling (Duffy, 2006).

Much like mindfulness therapy, Bloch's model focuses on the present and requires clients not to dwell on the past or speculate on the future. Bloch and Richmond (Sharf, 2010) contribute the seven principles that guide this theory (change, balance, energy, community, calling, harmony, and unity). These principles reveal strong influence from Buddhism (harmony and unity) and Hinduism (energy), although Bloch (2004) tones this down in some writings. Some may refer to the concepts as new age. These seven concepts are an attempt to connect spirituality to work:

- **Change.** Everyone experiences change. It occurs at many times throughout one's life career. This may come as roles change from single to couple to parent. Change may happen through transitions in geographic location, employers, or professions.
- **Balance.** The client seeks balance among the many life roles played. This includes balance between work and play and between personal and professional roles.
- **Energy.** Energy is drawn from the universe and channeled through others in order to bring about change and balance.
- **Community.** Individuals make decisions based on three types of communities: community of companionship (immediate and extended family, close friends), community of culture (neighbors, classmates, coworkers), and cosmic community (those which concern large areas such as environment, helping the poor).
- **Calling.** The definition of calling for this model refers to finding one's ideal work. When one feels complete as a result of work, or "at one" with their work, then the calling is identified. Others might call it a compulsion, or a drawing, toward a particular field.
- **Harmony.** Harmony is finding the work that will bring about a true sense of appreciation and understanding.
- **Unity.** Unity refers to trusting the universe and career refers to feeling a sense of flow, a oneness, of being totally involved in one's work. (Bloch, 2004; Sharf, 2010).

This model works well for those who do not like inventory assessments. It works well for nontraditional, independent clients who do not like being defined. The model is flexible and easily adaptable to culture and gender. The negative side of this model is that linear-thinking clients may not embrace the flexibility. There is little literature on this model, especially by the authors, and no definite proof of success through research. The theory is vague and may seem hard to follow. The spirituality represented, such as the Buddhist focus on the here and now, may be uncomfortable for Christians who view life in terms of eternity but it is easily adaptable to Christian principles.

RELIGIOUS APPROACHES

Jewish Approach: R.O.P.E.S.

Rabbi Moshe Fine (2006) attempted to provide a framework that would allow counselors comfort in addressing the integration of spiritual values with career. The R.O.P.E.S. stands for Real, Omni, Paths, Elevation, Self-Actualization. It is a five-step process, beginning with becoming real with the acceptance of spirituality as central to who we are and not living a life that attempts to separate our work from our personal life. The second step is omni a step that requires one to acknowledge that which transcends the borders of time and space draws us toward meaning and purpose in fulfillment of our destiny. Paths is the third step, in which one explores career through luck, grandeur, elevation, and self-actualization. These paths allow one to recognize a personal role in relationship to spirituality, community, and nature. The fourth step is elevating our careers, the transforming daily routines into spiritual endeavors. The fifth step is self-actualization through one's career. The first self-actualization listed in the third step allows the person to see oneself as part of a whole in society. This last step allows the person to see intentionality in creation of personal characteristics and the fulfillment of what God planned for one's life. This is referred to as "spiritual fulfillment."

Christian Approach: Theology of Work

As cited earlier, Christian career approaches are not yet formed (Lewis & Hardin, 2002). Literature on Christian career development is located in theology rather than in career counseling. For Christians, one must begin with development of a theology of work. Christian theologies have evolved from work as a curse to work as a sacred act of worship (Nelson, 2011). Yet, Christians have difficulty developing a spiritual framework that is comfortable across faith lines. One must evaluate whether work is simply for provision or as fulfillment of God's intention in one's life (Hernandez et al., 2011; Nelson, 2011).

Faith at Work: Lifestyle Evangelism or Act of Worship. The faith at work movement is anchored in religion. It asserts that one's faith is expressed through work without necessitation to verbalize an association to a religion (Miller, 2007). Princeton University has an initiative with courses in religion and ethics (Duffy et al., 2010). Similar to the University of Arkansas business school, the Princeton initiative researches the intersection of work and faith but it is housed in the theological, rather than business, department. The faith at work movement attempts to address the bifurcation of work and faith (Miller, 2007). The movement challenges the Christian culture to live out faith at work. For some, when one lives out their faith at work, others notice and inquire about the difference. This is called life-style evangelism. In this form of evangelism, the observer is taught how to live a life of faith simply by watching the person of faith.

Pauline Approach: Varying Gifts. Scripture is replete with instances of God's calling on one's life, with no one reference more career oriented than the apostle Paul. Romans 12:3–8 outlines varying gifts while Corinthians 12 teaches that every role is necessary. Paul appears to celebrate differences rather than have an expectation that humanity is the same or limited. Paul was dual career and often referred to as a "tentmaker," a reference to funding one's calling through secular roles. Romans 12 is a wonderful outline of spiritual approaches to career counseling, instructing Christians to embrace love, justice, service, and hospitality, and to act in an ethical manner in all of their deeds.

EXISTENTIALIST APPROACH

Existential approaches, such as holistic, focus on meaning and purpose, on the search for significance (Sterner, 2012) as opposed to a response to calling. Holistic approaches are process oriented and attempt to match the client's values to career.

Holistic Approach: Integrative Life Planning

Holistic approaches include mental, physical, and spiritual health. It is a reaction to the rise of technology and works to incorporate the human side of career such as relationships, balance, and a concern for community (Hansen, 2001). It bases vocational choice on a holistic view of life, seeing work in relation to other life roles. Hansen (2001) boils this down to "work within a life" and asks career counselors to assist clients with viewing life as interconnected with work as one aspect. This means taking into consideration other areas such as social, cultural, and religious factors.

Integrative life planning (ILP) is a holistic approach emphasizing meaning and purpose and addressing spirituality as a holistic factor. ILP considers counselors as change agents and advocates (Hansen, 2001). Career counselors have six critical life tasks to address with clients: (1) finding work in changing global contexts, (2) attending to their physical, mental, and emotional health, (3) understanding the family and work balance, (4) appreciating diversity and inclusivity, (5) exploring the relationship between spirituality and life purpose, and (6) adjusting to personal and organizational change (Hansen, 2011). Spirituality is recognized as important for self-actualization and wholeness (Hansen, 2011).

Hansen (2001) gives ten kinds of work that need to be done for the first critical task: advocating for human rights, reducing violence, reducing poverty and hunger, using technology constructively, preserving the environment, adapting and understanding changes in the workplace and families, accepting changes in gender roles, understanding and celebrating diversity, discovering new ways of understanding, and exploring spirituality and purpose. For the second critical task, Hansen (2011) emphasizes that family be intentionally put before work. The fifth critical task requires the counselor to explore what the client defines as spiritual and to assist in finding purpose and meaning (Hansen, 2001). The sixth critical task addresses a shift from materialism to simplicity in a redefinition of success (Hansen, 2001).

The holistic career counselor addresses more than selection of a career path; the roles one functions in (parent, community member, employee) and the events that impact the client's life (marriage, illness, first job, retirement, divorce) are addressed as well (Lee & Johnston, 2001). The counselor helps the client build interpersonal resources necessary for workplace success. This includes teaching life skills for the workplace, encouraging mentoring relationships, and facilitating exploration and discovery. This also may mean removing legal or social barriers (Hansen, 2001).

The holistic approach works well for diversity issues, easily incorporating life's concerns such as gender, ethnicity, religion, social economic status, and disability. This is a strength-based counseling approach that seeks to empower the client. It is especially beneficial for clients in crisis or who have significant concerns or challenges needing to be addressed. The client with linear thinking may have great difficulty with the lack of prescription. This approach is comfortable for the Christian who views God's interaction in all of life.

CONSIDERATIONS FOR COUNSELING SPIRITUAL CLIENTS

The American Counseling Association embraces spiritual competencies outlined by the Association for Spiritual, Ethical and Religious Values in Counseling (2016; see Appendix). Competencies are comprehensive and require counselors to recognize both their own worldview and that of the client (competencies two and three). The counselor is expected to understand limitations of training and consult with clergy of the client's faith group.

Ethics: Limitations and Boundaries

The guiding principle for counselors who integrate spirituality is to focus on the client's belief system and not one's own belief system (competencies seven, eight, and nine). For those who believe it is God's, rather than the counselor's, responsibility to change the client, this will be an easy task. For others, this task may be challenging, especially if the client's beliefs are diametrically opposed to the counselor's beliefs. As an example, no one issue has polarized secular and faith-based communities than tensions between lesbian, gay, bisexual, and transgender (LGBT) communities and faith-based communities. The counselor is not required to have the same beliefs as the client, but the counselor must uphold the client's belief system. Some counselors will view interactions as an opportunity to engage in healthy dialogue while other counselors may experience great anxiety.

Counselors are expected to evaluate whether their own belief systems are influencing a client's belief system (competency four). It is important that counselors know the limits of their understanding of a client's belief system and are able to refer to appropriate spiritual resources and leaders (competency five).

The counselor is expected to set goals with the client that are consistent with the client's belief system (competency 12). Regardless of what approach is used, counselors are expected to apply theory and current research (competency 14) and modify therapeutic techniques to include the client's spiritual and religious perspective and practices (competency 13).

Religious Biases

The career counselor using spiritual approaches must suspend religious belief systems to ensure full support of the client's goals and belief systems (Duffy et al., 2010). This may include selection of career or employer, the role of women in the workplace (or home), lifestyle, or other factors. Clients who select careers or employers differing from the counselor may bring strain. Other considerations may include a client who desires to participate in an industry that deviates from the counselor's religious or ethical viewpoint. These could include industries that manufacture alcohol or cigarettes, condone pornography, or exploit oppressed groups.

Investigation of Christian values in careers found that women prioritize work differently (Lewis & Hardin, 2002). Duffy (2010) found that women with religious values do not seek leadership but tend to focus on service. Sellers et al. (2005) found that women often struggle with the dual callings of motherhood and career. Cultural and religious messages may conflict. This requires the career counselor to understand and guide the client through decision-making that best reflects the client's desires without injecting personal religious or cultural bias.

A religiously conservative career counselor could have a lesbian client who wants to pursue nonprofit work advocating for LGBT rights. Furthermore, that client could feel rejected by their religious group requiring the counselor to assist in resolution of dissonance (Duffy, 2006). The counselor may advocate for a particular career for the client but discover that there are strongly held religious beliefs that prohibit the client from pursuit of that path.

Values: Social Justice, Calling, Service, Community

Integrating one's values into work is considered the ultimate spirituality whether the client is religious or atheist. Gockel (2004) recognized the infusion of values into society has had a large impact on business and social issues and calls for career counselors to proactively address these issues as spiritual competence. Justice and stewardship are hallmarks of this movement (Gockel, 2004; Hernandez et al., 2011). This may manifest as ecological stewardship, social justice advocacy, responsible utilization of resources that ensure sustainability, and a general emphasis on social mission considerations over profitability. The counselor must be able to identify corporations, businesses, nonprofits, and career fields that support the spiritually motivated client.

CONCLUSION

Spirituality is central to our lives whether considered existential or religious. As the core of who we are (Duffy et al., 2010) these approaches incorporate all aspects of our lives (Hansen, 2001). As a result, spiritual approaches are flexible and easily adapt to any faith-based principles. These approaches are best for those with narratives, with life experiences to interpret for career development. Those who are linear thinkers, who are less verbal, or who have little life experience may not benefit from this approach.

There is little research for spiritual approach theories (Duffy, 2006). For those whose life rotates around religious aspects, around a transcendent God that interacts in daily life, there is not a solid theory to embrace. Counselors are encouraged to adapt career development theories to incorporate religious values.

If work is an act of worship (Nelson, 2011), a calling, then the career counselor has the highest honor to assist the client to discover what God intends for their life (Hernandez et al., 2011). The decision regarding one's work will impact every aspect of the client's life and is the biggest decision outside of spirituality and family.

REFLECTION AND DISCUSSION

We are not human beings having a spiritual experience, we are spiritual beings having a human experience.

(Pierre Teilhard de Chardin, Jesuit priest and French idealist philosopher)

1. Imagine a client with a belief system you are uncomfortable with or find diametrically opposed to your belief system. How would you ethically conduct career counseling with that client?

2. Discuss the pros and cons of integrating existentialism, inspiration, and motivation as spiritual concepts.

3. Share an example of how either your belief system, your religion, or God guided you toward discovering you should pursue counseling as a career.

4. Discuss career choices of a Biblical character in the context of one of the spiritual approach theories.

5. Explain how your definition of calling either matches or differs from life career theory.

ADDITIONAL READINGS, RESOURCES, AND WEBSITES

Bill Pollard (retired CEO, Service Master), interview at Gordon Conwell Seminary. www.gordonconwell.edu/ockenga/faith-work/documents/MooreM.CapitalismALoveStory.pdf

Faith and Work Initiative, Princeton University. http://www.princeton.edu/faithandwork/research/

Faith in the Workplace, Tyson Foods. http://www.tysonfoods.com/we-care/faith-in-the-workplace

God and Business, Fortune Magazine. http://www.marcgunther.com/god-and-business/

Legatus: Ambassadors for Christ in the Marketplace. http://legatus.org/

Marketplace Ministries. http://www.marketplaceministries.com/

Tyson Center for Faith and Spirituality in the Workplace, Sam M. Walton College of Business, University of Arkansas. http://tfsw.uark.edu/

We Serve Day, Service Master. https://www.servicemaster.com/company/community

Work Matters. http://workmatters.org/

TRADITIONAL ACTIVITY

Envision

1. Consider developing a career theory guided by religion or theology. What would need to be included?
2. Consider how to address those that believe differently from you while maintaining your integrity.

Case Study/Intervention

Annie is a physician who was caught diverting prescription drugs for her personal use. She entered a substance abuse treatment facility and is clean from narcotics. Her medical license was reinstated, but soon afterward she received a DWI, which required entry into another a rehab center. Being a former military surgeon, she was able to enter the Veterans Administration program. Annie was raised Catholic, but her perception of the church's limitations on women and birth control led her away from the church. She considers herself to be an atheist but does not push her personal perspective on others.

Now, Annie's career options are limited and she is without an income, and she does not want to begin all over again with new education. She is 40-years-old, married, and has three teenage children. She is concerned how the transition will impact her children since the family's income level will significantly decline. When the medical license was reinstated, Annie's family moved from the city to a small rural community where everyone knows each other. The children are embarrassed at the legal problems.

As a former military officer, Annie has experience as a leader. She has veteran benefits that will fund four years of school. Her hobbies include reading, poetry, philanthropic work, and painting. She enjoys history and her travelling. The military exposed her to many historical landmarks and current events. She is fluent in the French language.

Respond

1. What strengths and experiences does Annie have that are cues for a new career?
2. Since Annie defines her spirituality as atheist, how would you address her concerns?

SPIRITUAL ACTIVITY

Envision

1. Consider your life story and how God has led you to career choices.
2. Consider how God can turn negative life experiences into positive career opportunities.

Storytelling

A male lawyer was born into an influential family that guaranteed him social and economic privileges. He enjoyed his position in life. A persuasive litigator, he was skilled at convincing national leaders to support his causes. His oratory skills persuaded legislators that certain people groups were intolerable with the current political structure and should be addressed in very direct terms to ensure constraint. He believed that their influence would undermine the national interest. Additionally, he was devout in his faith and he believed the groups would undermine, if not destroy, the beliefs he held dearly. The legislative body protected themselves by enacting laws to ensure those groups were handled legally and swiftly but not necessarily morally. The lawyer was appointed commissioner of this effort.

As the new commissioner traveled to carry out his assignment, there was an extraordinary event that resulted in maiming him. This caused a spiritual crisis that led to reevaluation of his long-held belief system and ultimate conversion. Of course, this lawyer is known as the Apostle Paul, whose life had more impact post-conversion than prior. God's selection of Paul was strategic.

Respond

1. How did Paul's qualifications and characteristics weave together to make him God's perfect candidate for the mission?
2. Paul wrote that "all things work together for good to them that love God, to them who are the called according to his purpose" (Romans 8:28, KJV). Explain how this concept supports spiritual approaches.

REFERENCES

Association for Spiritual, Ethical and Religious Values in Counseling. (2016). Code of Ethics. Retrieved from http://www.aservic.org/resources/spiritual-competencies/

Bloch, D.P. (2004). Spirituality, complexity, and career counseling. Professional School Counseling, 7(5), 343–350.

Carroll, S.T., Stewart-Sicking, J.A., & Thompson, B. (2014). Sanctification of work: Assessing the role of spirituality in employment attitudes. Mental Health, Religion & Culture, 17(6), 545–556. doi:10.1080/13674676.2013.860519

Constantine, M.G., Miville, M.L., Warren, A.K., Gainor, K.A., & Lewis-Coles, M.E.L. (2006). Religion, spirituality, and career development in African American college students: A qualitative inquiry. The Career Development Quarterly, 54, 227–241.

Dalton, J.C. (2001). Career and calling: Finding a place for the spirit in work and community. New Directions for Student Services, 95, 17–25.

Duffy, R.D. (2006). Spirituality, religion, and career development: Current status and future directions. Career Development Quarterly, 55(1), 52–63.

Duffy, R.D. (2010). Spirituality, religion, and work values. Journal of Psychology & Theology, 38(1), 52–61.

Duffy, R.D., Reid, L., & Dik, B.J. (2010). Spirituality, religion, and career development: Implications for the workplace. Journal of Management, Spirituality & Religion, 7(3), 209–221. doi:10.1080/14766086.2010.500004

Fine, M. (2006). Career Spirituality: Learning the R.O.P.E.S. Career Planning and Adult Development Journal, Spring, 10–19.

Gaffen, L. (2006). Spirituality that works: One career counselor's perspective. Career Planning and Adult Development Journal, 22(1), 23–25.

Gockel, A. (2004). The trend toward spirituality in the workplace: Overview and implications for career counseling. Journal of Employment Counseling, 41, 156–167.

Guillen, M., Ferrero, I., & Hoffman, W.M. (2015). The neglected ethical and spiritual motivations in the workplace. Journal of Business Ethics, 28, 803–816. doi:10.107/s10551-013-1985-7

Guindon, M. H., & Richmond, L. J. (2011, December 23). Practice and research in career counseling and development-2004. Retrieved from http://onlinelibrary.wiley.com/doi/10.1002/j.2161-0045.2005.tb00145.x/full

Hansen, L.S. (2001). Integrating work, family, and community through holistic life planning. The Career Development Quarterly, 49, 261–274.

Hansen, S.S. (2011). Integrative Life Planning: A holistic approach. Journal of Employment Counseling, 48(4), 167–169.

Hernandez, E.F., Foley, P.F., & Beitin, B.K. (2011). Hearing the call: A phenomenological study of religion in career choice. Journal of Career Development, 38(1), 62–88. doi: 10.1177/0894845309358889

Lee, F.K., & Johnston, J.A. (2001). Innovations in career counseling. Journal of Career Development, 27(3), 177–185.

Lewis, M.M., & Hardin, S.I. (2002). Relations among and between career values and Christian religious values. Counseling and Values, 46(2), 96–106.

Miller, D. W. (2007). God at work: The history and promise of the Faith at Work movement. Oxford, UK: University Press, Inc.

Miller-Tiedeman, A. (2008). Essential Tiedeman: Anchoring the North Star for human development. The Career Development Quarterly, 56(3), 242–245.

Nelson, T. (2011). Work matters: Connecting Sunday worship to Monday work. Wheaton, IL: Crossway.

Paloutzian, R.F., Bufford, R.K., & Wildman, A.J. (2012). Spiritual well-being scale: Mental and physical health relationships. In M. Cobb, C.M. Puchalski, & B. Rumbold (Eds), Oxford Textbook of Spirituality in Healthcare (pp. 353–358). Oxford, UK: Oxford University Press.

Roof, R.A. (2015). The association of individual spirituality on employee engagement: The spirit at work. Journal of Business Ethics, 130, 585–599. doi: 10.1007/s10551-014-2246-0

Sellers, T.S., Thomas, K., Batts, J., & Ostman, C. (2005). Women called: A qualitative study of Christian women dually called to motherhood and career. Journal of Psychology and Theology, 33(3), 198–209.

Sharf, R.S. (2010). Applying career development theory to counseling (5th ed.). Belmont, CA: Brooks/Cole.

Smith, J.M., Arendt, C., Lahman, J.B., Settle, G.N., & Duff, A. (2006). Framing the work of art: Spirituality and career discourse in the nonprofit arts sector. Communication Studies, 57(1), 25–46.

Sterner, W.R. (2012). Integrating existentialism and Super's Life-Span, Life-Space approach. Career Development Quarterly, 60, 152–162.

Tiedeman, D.V., & Miller-Tiedeman, A. (1984). The trend of life in the human career. Journal of Career Development, March, 221–250.

SECTION III

Facilitating Clients' Call

7

Career Development in Elementary and Middle School

Jasmine L. Knight, PhD and Helen Runyan, PhD

But Jesus said, "Let the children come to me. Don't stop them! For the Kingdom of heaven belongs to those who are like these children."

Matthew 19:14, New Living Translation

LEARNING OBJECTIVES

In this chapter, students will learn about

- How the journey toward discovering what God has purposed one to do begins in childhood
- The importance of beginning career development in childhood
- The role and responsibilities of professional school counselors in promoting career development in elementary and middle schools
- Career and college readiness guidelines, standards, and initiatives that impact youth in schools

LEARNING OUTCOMES

At the end of this chapter, students will be able to

- Identify the career development needs of elementary and middle school students
- Apply career development theories to career counseling with children and adolescents in schools
- Identify how career development can positively impact student development
- Explain how to address career and college readiness with students in elementary and middle schools

CHAPTER HIGHLIGHTS

- Career and college readiness
- Professional school counselor
- ASCA Mindsets & Behaviors for Student Success: K–12 College- and Career-Readiness Standards for Every Student
- Common Core state standards
- National Career Development Guidelines
- Own the Turf campaign

INTRODUCTION TO CONCEPT

While driving down the road one day, I received the following question from my five-year-old niece: "Do you like your job?" I was instantly surprised for two reasons. One, it came out of the blue and left me wondering what she learned about at school that day. Two, she didn't ask the question you would expect to hear: "What is your job?" I immediately realized that how I answered was very important. I wanted to be truthful (and fortunately, I do like my job). Yet, this was also a perfect opportunity for me to discuss with her why I like my job, why I have the opportunity to do a job I like, and how someone selects a job they like. I could have simply told her that yes, I like my job. Instead, I spent the next 15 minutes discussing career choice and satisfaction with a five-year-old. Was this a developmentally appropriate response? Are these the types of discussions we should be having with children around careers as early as kindergarten? The answer to both of these questions is yes. In fact, many counselors, educators, career development theorists, and policy makers have called for career exploration to begin with children as early as the preschool years.

This chapter will explore the call, purpose, and need to implement career development in elementary and middle schools. It will also examine how counselors who work in elementary and middle school settings address career development needs and integrate career counseling into their work.

IMPORTANCE OF CAREER DEVELOPMENT

"I know that nothing is better for them than to rejoice, and to do good in their lives, and also that every man should eat and drink and enjoy the good of all his labor—it is the gift of God" (Ecclesiastes 3:12–13, NKJ). In this verse of the Bible, labor, or work, is seen as a gift from God. The opportunity to enjoy one's work and to perform it for His glory is something God greatly desires for all of His children. Still, the path toward that enjoyment is a long one. The question then becomes: Where does this process begin? Where does one begin to make sense of the spiritual gifts, talents, interest, skills, and abilities with which they have been blessed and how do those traits formulate into a career path? Discovering one's calling does not begin in adulthood. Many childhood career development theorists have posited that information learned early in life has an impact on decisions in adolescence and young adulthood (Palladino Schultheiss, 2008). Therefore, counselors who work with elementary and middle school students have a responsibility to address their career development needs and equip them with the tools they need to discover their calling.

"But Jesus said, 'Let the children come to me. Don't stop them! For the Kingdom of heaven belongs to those who are like these children'" (Matthew 19:14, NLT). Career development gives children the opportunity to understand their place in God's Kingdom, tools that will eventually help them find their calling and purpose here on earth, and directions to the path where they will receive God's gift of enjoyment in their work. Counselors who work with young people are, then, tasked to help them understand and learn what God has purposed them to do.

BEGINNING THE CAREER DEVELOPMENT JOURNEY

Beginning career development in elementary and middle school is important. Childhood is often seen as a time of play and fantasy as well as receiving an education. Critics of early career development interventions are often concerned about forcing choices on children before they are developmentally capable of making important decisions. While proponents have argued that career development interventions at this age better prepare children with the tools they need for future career planning, they also allow children to make the important connection between education, future success, and lifelong learning (Knight, 2015: Palladino Schultheiss, 2005). Consequently, little attention has been given in the research and literature to children's career development. Nonetheless, we do have evidence that childhood is a key time for career exploration. A study by Kenny, Blustein, Haase, Jackson, and Perry (2006) found that ninth grade students with higher levels of career planfulness and positive expectations were more likely to be engaged in school. This finding demonstrates that students need to develop a positive attitude toward career planning during the middle and elementary years. Furthermore, choosing not to implement career interventions in the primary grades does not mean that students will refrain from decision-making around careers. Counselors serve a key role in ensuring that children have accurate career knowledge as they sift through choices and explore the world of work.

Career development in the elementary and middle school grades also assists students in making the key connection between education and future success. Students become more engaged in school when they understand how what they are learning is important for future dreams, aspirations, and endeavors. Without this connection, a student can lack motivation or be academically unsuccessful. The foundation for this connection begins in elementary schools. In a study examining college aspirations of students 9–17 years old, Paulson, Coombs, and Richardson (1990) found that aspirations declined between the ages of 11 and 12. Kao and Tienda (1998) stated that eighth-grade students with low aspirations to go to college were more likely to drop out of high school, while Herr and Cramer (1988) asserted that a 16-year-old high school dropout actually dropped out of school psychologically by the third grade. Conversely, Auger, Blackhurst, and Wahl (2005) found that only a limited number of upper-aged elementary students had not engaged in significant thinking about their future career options. If students are considering their career choices, weighing important options, it is essential that counselors be a part of guiding them through this process.

THE ELEMENTARY AND MIDDLE SCHOOL STUDENT

Developmentally, elementary and middle school students are going through many transitions in their life which can impact their self-esteem, self-efficacy, and their career development. Jean Piaget, a historic and leading developmental theorist, described four main stages of cognitive development: sensorimotor, preoperational, concrete operational, and formal operational (Craig & Dunn, 2010). Children begin elementary school in the preoperational period. During this time, thinking is rigid, irreversible, and very here-and-now centered. Between the ages of five and seven, they transition into the concrete operational stage which ranges from ages five to 12. This period is marked by more logical, reversible, and flexible thinking. Children in this stage are able to perform more mental observations and no longer have to see an object in order to imagine manipulating it. They are also in Erik Erickson's fourth stage of psychosocial development: industry versus inferiority. During this period, students strive to develop a sense of confidence and competence through the successful completion of tasks and the mastery of new skills. Failure to do so can lead to feelings of inferiority. It is helpful for young people to receive encouragement from key figures in their life (e.g., parents, teachers, peers, and school counselors) to help them develop a sense of accomplishment.

Career development activities occur during an exciting yet tumultuous time for young people. As children and adolescents enter school, peers become more important. Students become increasingly aware of how others view them and begin comparing themselves to those around them. Their social interactions are central and can have a huge impact on their self-worth. As students progress into adolescence, they must also contend with physical changes, hormonal developments, and identity and role confusion. While focusing on career development may not always feel like a priority to student and counselors, it is an important aspect of student development.

CAREER COUNSELING IN THE SCHOOL SETTING

While all counselors who work with children should be knowledgeable about their career development needs, professional school counselors primarily work with students in schools. Therefore, the remainder of this chapter will focus on how school counselors work with students in elementary and middle schools. According to the American School Counselor Association (ASCA, n.d.), professional school counselors hold a master's degree in school counseling, are licensed or certified in their state, and are key members of the educational team. School counselors are uniquely trained to facilitate comprehensive school counseling programs and address the academic, social-emotional, and career needs of students. Indeed, ASCA views the role of the school counselor as encompassing the three latter domains (ASCA) Therefore, career development falls clearly within the role of the elementary and middle school counselor.

In the past several decades, the field of school counseling has gone through many shifts and changes. In 2003, ASCA introduced the first edition of the ASCA National Mode: A Framework for School Counseling Programs (ASCA, 2012). The model, a comprehensive program, provided a standardized framework for school counseling programs across the field. It also "reinforced the idea that school counselors help every student improve academic achievement, navigate personal and social development and plan for successful careers after graduation" (ASCA, 2012, p. x). The model was preceded by the ASCA National Standards for Students, which was introduced in 1997 (ASCA, 2004). These standards included competencies and indicators for each of the three domains: academic, social-emotional, and career. These standards provided some guidance to school counselors as to what minimum career development competencies students should attain. However, as the standards were the same for all grade levels, school counselors still needed to interpret how best to apply them to students in their school. This was further complicated by the dearth of research and evidenced-based practices on this topic for the elementary and middle grades.

The ASCA National Standards for Students has recently been replaced by the ASCA Mindsets & Behaviors for Student Success: K–12 College- and Career Readiness for Every Student. The ASCA mindsets and behaviors were developed following a review of research and college and career readiness documents that identified methods that positively impact student performance and academic achievement (ASCA, 2014). These mindsets and behaviors include 35 attitudes, knowledge standards, and skills that students should demonstrate as a result of a school counseling program. Examples of the standards include: apply self-motivation and self-direction to learning, exhibit positive attitude toward work and learning, and identify long- and short-term academic, career, and social-emotional goals. The ASCA mindsets and behaviors are intended to address all three domains of academic, career, and social-emotional concerns for students; however, they are rooted in ensuring all students graduate from high school ready for college and career. As it has become a critical aspect in the field of school counseling, the college and career readiness concept is an important one to explore.

COLLEGE AND CAREER READINESS

Consider for a moment how you would define college and career readiness. Perhaps it means being prepared for college following high school or a readiness to enter the workforce. Is completion of a high school diploma or GED enough to consider one as college and career ready? While the terms college ready and career ready are becoming more widely used, there is not one agreement as to their definitions. The ACT (2008) offers the following definition for college and career readiness: "the acquisition of the knowledge and skills a student needs to enroll in and succeed in credit bearing first-year courses at a postsecondary institution (e.g., a two or four-year college, trade school, or technical school) without the need for remediation." Other definitions of college and career readiness are similar but account for the allowance that not all students will desire to seek out postsecondary education following high school; some students may instead feel led toward the workforce. Conley (2012) defined the college- and career-ready student as "a student who is ready for college and career, can qualify for and succeed in entry-level, credit-bearing college courses leading to a baccalaureate or certificate, or career pathway-oriented training programs without the need for remedial or developmental coursework" (p. 1).

Regardless of the definition, the terms college ready and career ready have made their way into many educational and policy statements. ASCA's position statement on academic, college, and career planning (2013) asserts that the role of the school counselor includes facilitating programs that promote college and career readiness at all levels. This means that career development activities are as much the responsibility of the elementary and middle school counselor as they are the high school counselor.

We see further evidence of this in the Common Core state standards. The Common Core state standards were sponsored by the National Governors Association Center for Best Practice and the Council of Chief State School Officers. The intent was to create a set of academic standards that would enable all students across the United States to graduate high school college and career ready (Common Core, 2016). College and career readiness have continued to be a key focus of this initiative, and the majority of all states have adopted the Common Core state standards.

The above definitions speak to the following student outcomes after high school: a readiness to begin postsecondary study or enter the workforce. With this in mind, what college and career competencies should elementary and middle school counselors promote to achieve this end result? While ASCA (2014) provides some insights with its Mindsets & Behaviors for Student Success, other organizations have also offered guidelines in this area. The National Occupational Information Coordinating Committee (U.S. Department of Education, Office of Vocational and Adult Education, 2004) created the National Career Development Guidelines. Additionally, the National Office for School Counselor Advocacy (NOSCA) has launched the Own the Turf campaign (College Board Advocacy and Policy Center [CBAPC], 2010). As part of this campaign, they call for school counselors to be leaders and advocates in their schools around career and college readiness initiatives. They "identify eight components of college and career readiness counseling. These eight components include:

1. College Aspirations
2. Academic Planning for College and Career Readiness
3. Enrichment and Extracurricular Engagement
4. College and Career Exploration and Selection Processes
5. College and Career Assessments

6. College Affordability Planning
7. College and Career Admission Processes
8. Transition from High School to College Enrollment (CBAPC, n.d., p. 4).

These components are important to a systemic approach to college and career readiness across the K–12 years; however, components seven and eight are the only ones that elementary and middle school counselors do not need to focus on. In action, the NOSCA competencies would resemble a school counselor promoting college aspirations by creating a college-going culture in their school. A middle school counselor may demonstrate academic planning for college and career readiness by helping students select courses that relate to future career goals. Elementary school students participating in an afterschool music club can learn about careers in music, thereby reinforcing the third component of engaging in enriching and extracurricular activities. The fourth component, the college and career exploration and selection process, can be implemented when an elementary school counselor takes a group of fourth-grade students on a field trip to a local university, giving them the opportunity to learn about college life. A middle school counselor including a career assessment as part of a classroom guidance teaching session with sixth graders is engaging in the fifth component, college and career assessments. Additionally, a middle school counselor giving a workshop to parents about planning and paying for college is meeting component six, college affordability planning.

APPLYING CAREER DEVELOPMENT THEORIES

There are a variety of career development theories a counselor can select; however, not all theories have direct application to the elementary or middle school environment. In this section we will review five theories that can be used in this context: two are developmental theories, two are trait and factor theories, and one is a social learning theory.

Developmental Theory

Developmental theories of career development explore how one's career identity is formed across the lifespan (Zunker, 2016). Developmental theorists prescribe to the notion that career development begins in childhood. This makes their theories particularly useful to the work of the elementary and middle school counselor as it informs the needs of preschool through eighth-grade students.

Gottfredson's theory of self-creation, circumscription, and compromise is a developmental theory that seeks to explain both how and why one makes decisions about occupations (Gottfredson, 1981). Gottfredson asserted that career choice is a person's attempt to implement one's self-concept, and that as children develop, they consider careers based on the views they have of themselves and the world around them. According to Gottfredson, individuals pass through key stages, and in each stage, they engage in a process of circumscription and compromise. The first stage, orientation to size and power, corresponds with ages three to five, or the preschool and kindergarten grades. This is when students gain an understanding of what it means to be an adult. They being to view adults as bigger and more powerful in contrast to their own view of themselves as being little and weak. Adults oversee making and enforcing family rules and have certain responsibilities. For example, these children begin to understand that occupations are adult roles. The next stage, orientation to sex roles, spans the first through third grades, or children six to eight years old. During this stage, students begin to assign gender to careers, possibly based on stereotypical thinking. This is a critical time, when students might begin to circumscribe careers from considerations based on beliefs about what careers are acceptable for different genders. This can be a concern, because once careers have been eliminated from consideration, they are unlikely to be considered again. Imagine the young kindergarten boy who has a calling on his life to help others through teaching but now believes this to be an unacceptable occupational choice for a boy. The third stage, orientation to social valuation, occurs during the fourth through eighth grades, or the nine to 13-year-old age range. It is during this time that students evaluate careers based on their perceived prestige. By the eighth grade, students are more aware of their peers and how they are viewed by others. Additionally, they can make connections between income, education, and careers. Furthermore, they are aware of which occupations are considered "acceptable" by family and peers alike. Those that are not viewed as prestigious enough will often not be considered.

Consequently, students may also view a career as unattainable, thereby compromising, or letting go of, a desired occupational choice because it seems out of reach. Students pass through these first three stages, circumscribing careers throughout the elementary and middle school years. It is not until high school, or age 14, that they engage in the final stage, orientation to the internal, unique self. It is only during this final stage that adolescents consider their individual interests, values, preferences, abilities, and knowledge about the world of work. Therefore, school counselors applying Gottfredson's theory would seek to implement career development interventions at the various stages to prevent students from eliminating career options before having an opportunity to fully explore their interests. For example, introducing career role models that contradict the gender stereotypes (e.g., encouraging female students' involvement in math and science activities or providing culturally relevant career role models for children living in low-income communities).

Donald Super's Career Theory of Development

Donald Super, another career theorist, believed that career development is an ongoing process that unfolds throughout the life span (Zunker, 2016). His life span development theory offered an explanation for how children integrate career planning, decision-making, and time perspective into their self-concept. According to Super, individuals pass through stages of career development and must accomplish key tasks in each stage. These stages include growth, exploration, establishment, maintenance, and decline. Elementary and middle school students would be in Super's growth stage, a time in life characterized by the development of attitude, interests, and needs associated with the self-concept (Mau, 2008).

As children progress through the growth stage, they must successfully navigate through nine different conceptual dimensions. Super identified these dimensions as being critical in helping children develop a positive self-concept around good problem solving and decision-making. The first of these dimensions is curiosity. Curiosity is considered a basic need or drive that results in children desiring to seek out or try out new information (Knight, 2015; Zunker, 2016). Children enter school at an age when they are naturally curious. School counselors can encourage this curiosity around career exploration by making career development a part of their school counseling curriculum. Curiosity naturally leads to the next dimension, exploration. Exploration happens when children are involved in seeking new information about themselves and the world of work. Depending on the age of the student, exploratory behaviors can range in type from wanting to know how a computer works to what different types of careers exist for people who like public speaking. Students benefit when school counselors, parents, and teachers encourage these behaviors, as exploration inevitably leads to more exploration. The third dimension, information, involves gaining knowledge about careers, the world of work, and how to access additional information on these topics. As students implement their curiosity through exploration, they will need information about careers. More importantly, they will need to understand how to research careers and college information for future exploration. School counselors can teach these skills to upper-grade elementary and middle school students. Once learned, students will be able to apply them in high school and beyond. Key figures, the fourth dimension, pertains to the role models in a child's life that she or he observe and imitate. Children's first understanding of the world of work is often influenced by the occupations of their parents. It is not uncommon for an elementary student to say they want to be a lawyer because a parent is one. Key figures can have a large impact on children and at times their perceptions of their role models are incorrect. As children enter school, their world expands as does the circle of their role models. School counselors can address this dimension by engaging in conversations with children about their role models and observation. They can also bring career representatives or mentors who represent different genders, cultures, and career fields. The fifth dimension, locus of control, involves children's feelings of control over their environment. When students are able to complete tasks, this has a positive impact on their self-concept, leading to more autonomy and feelings of having more control over future actions. School counselors will need to connect these feelings of control to career planning and help students see how it can empower them. The sixth dimension, development of interest, is reached by students around the age of eight and marks a movement from fantasies around occupations to interests. It is during this time that children become more aware of their likes and dislikes and how they are unique from others. School counselors can attend to this dimension by encouraging students to discover and explore their interests, skills, and abilities but also to understand how those traits connect to different career paths. Time perspective is the seventh dimension children and adolescents must accomplish. This is when students gain an understanding of the impact of past and present and a sense of future orientation (Knight, 2015). Developmentally, students are not ready to engage in this process until at least the age of nine. This leads to the next dimension, planfulness. Planfulness is the recognition that one needs to have a plan in order to meet future goals. School counselors help students with goal setting around career and college planning to keep them motivated as they complete their education. The final dimension, self-concept, is at the heart of Super's theory. Super (1953) viewed career development as the way one develops and implements his or her self-concept. Essentially, self-concept is how one perceives herself or himself and her or his situation. As school counselors help students successfully navigate along these nine dimensions, they will be assisting them in implementing a positive self-concept and gaining in career maturity.

Trait and Factor Theory

Frank Parsons is known as the father of vocational guidance. He introduced his beliefs in his 1909 book Choosing a Vocation. Parsons stated that in order for an individual to make a career decision, the following conditions should occur:

1. An awareness of interests, skills, abilities, likes, dislikes, limitations, and desires (Traits)
2. An understanding of the world of work and the requirements for success (Factors)
3. An ability to comprehend the relationship between the two

This theory has simple application to the work of the elementary and middle school counselor. School counselors can encourage students to learn more about their skills, interests and abilities and connect those traits to world or work (e.g., explaining to students who like math how that translates to different careers).

Another trait and factor theory which school counselors may find helpful, specifically for the middle school years, is Holland's theory of vocational choice and adjustment. The central focus of Holland's theory is that there are six personality types: realistic, investigative, artistic, social, enterprising, and conventional. These personality types match corresponding occupational environments (Holland, 1962). The relationship between the types provides information and predictions around career satisfaction, choice, performance, and decision-making (Nauta, 2007). Ideally, career satisfaction would be achieved by finding congruence between the personality type of the individual and the environment type of the occupation. While students in elementary and middle schools are not going to be making decisions about careers, they do need to learn the tools to help them begin their career development journey. Holland's theory provides a method that school counselors can use to assist students in conceptualizing the connection between their personalities and world of work.

Social Learning Theory

The final theory, social cognitive career theory (SCCT), is based on Albert Bandura's social cognitive theory (Lent & Brown, 1996) and authored by Lent, Brown, and Hackett (1994; 1996). The outcomes of career development are viewed as a result of the interaction between self-efficacy, outcome expectations, and personal goals (Lent & Brown, 1996). Self-efficacy is defined as an individual's belief about his or her own capabilities. Outcome expectations are seen as personal predictions about future activities and personal goals are how behaviors are organized. In other words, individuals will engage in a behavior they feel capable of doing and believe will result in a desirable outcome. According to this theory, students during the elementary and middle school years acquire self-efficacy and outcome expectations around a range of activities, career interests, and aspirations (Lent, 2013). With this in mind, a student may have been blessed with a gift from God that would eventually lead to a fruitful career. However, due to an inaccurate self-efficacy this gift may never get nurtured or promoted. Therefore, the student never has the opportunity to explore this particular path and is possibly precluded from entering this career. Therefore, school counselors can take steps to prevent students from narrowing their career choices before they have a better view of their capabilities.

CAREER DEVELOPMENT ACTIVITIES IN ELEMENTARY SCHOOL

When students enter elementary school they often think of careers in terms of fantasy. If you enter a kindergarten class and ask the children there what they would like to be when they grow up, you are likely to get answers ranging from princess to superhero to teacher. However, as they advance through elementary school, children's career aspirations become more realistic (Gottfredson, 1981; Super, 1990). Career development in elementary school is characterized by curiosity. Young students are deeply interested in the world around them. This curiosity is a benefit that school counselors can nurture and encourage students around career exploration. However, it also makes elementary students susceptible to inaccurate information about careers. In a study examining the career aspirations of 123 first, third, and fifth graders, Auger, Blackhurst, and Wahl (2005) found evidence that by fifth grade, participants had circumscribed certain careers based on perceived gender and social prestige appropriateness. This finding illuminated the role that school counselors play in preventing elementary students from prematurely narrowing their career choices.

Classroom guidance is an important function of the elementary school counselor (Mau, 2008) and a key method for implementing career development in schools (Knight, 2015). School counselors can utilize classroom guidance to teach lessons on career awareness, career exploration, and the world of work. They can also focus on building self-esteem, understanding interest and values, and learning effective communication, social, and conflict resolution skills. Students need to understand how many of the good character or good citizenship traits they learn about in school relate to the world of work. Other ideas of implementing career development at the elementary school level include

- Inviting parents or community members to make presentations about their careers
- Collaborating with school administration and teachers to integrate career development into all aspects of the educational curriculum

- Small-group counseling on career exploration with high-risk or first-generation students
- Teaching upper-elementary students how to set short- and long-terms goals
- Classroom guidance lesson where students learn how school subjects relate to various careers
- Having students research a career, create a media presentation about it, and present it during a PTA night
- Elementary school career day highlighting nontraditional careers and including diverse career representatives

CAREER DEVELOPMENT ACTIVITIES IN MIDDLE SCHOOL

Middle school students are in a period of their life in which they are beginning to better understand their unique self and how they relate to the world around them. Super identified this as development of interest and Gottfredson viewed it as orienting to social valuation and the unique self. This period is marked by exploration for adolescents, and there are various methods that school counselors can implement in career development. Students need opportunities to explore by learning about the career world and learning about themselves (Mau, 2008). Additionally, school counselors need to help students gain an understanding of how school relates to future success.

Career assessments are one method that school counselors can use to help students learn about their traits, skills, interests, and abilities. Both formal and informal assessments can be utilized. For example, Osborn and Reardon (2006) utilized the Self-Directed Search (SDS) in structured career groups with high-risk middle school students. Once students completed the SDS, they were able to use the results to locate careers they were interested in exploring on the online Occupational Outlook Handbook. Pairing an assessment tool with a career exploration tool allows students to immediately connect their interest to occupations. Other ideas for implementing career development at the middle school level include

- Middle school career day highlighting nontraditional careers and including diverse career representatives.
- Career portfolios that tracks students' educational progress, extracurricular activities, and vocational interests
- Classroom guidance lessons teaching students how transferable skills are demonstrated in school, at home, and in future careers
- Participating in extracurricular activities that give students opportunities to experience different career paths (e.g., school newspaper, photography, engineering club, Science Technology, Engineering and Math (STEM).
- Field trips to local colleges and universities

CONCLUSION

God tells us in Matthew 19:14 that even children should seek Him. Counselors who work with young people can attend to this by equipping children and adolescents with the tools that will eventually lead them to discover the calling that God has placed on their lives. This work is essential to the function of the school counselor in elementary and middle schools. Students who have positive expectations around future career success are more likely to complete high school. College and career readiness has become a critical component of educational programs. The ASCA mindsets and behaviors and the National Career Development Guidelines offer additional career competencies that school counselors should address. Additionally, career development theories provide insight into how elementary and middle school students conceptualize careers, engage in career decision-making, and participate in career planning. When given the opportunity to explore the world of work and how it relates to their own skills, abilities, interest, values, and likes and dislikes, elementary and middle school students are handed the keys for future success in career and college engagement.

KEY TERMS

ASCA mindsets and behaviors: thirty-five attitudes, knowledge, and skills that students should demonstrate as a result of a school counseling program

Career and college readiness: the attainment of knowledge and skills one needs in order to be ready to enter a two- or four-year college or attend a technical school, or to be workforce ready

Common Core State Standards: a set of academic standards sponsored by the National Governors Association Center for Best Practice and the Council of Chief State School Officers that enables all students across the United States to graduates college and career ready

National Career Development Guidelines: a set of career development guidelines developed by the National Occupational Information Coordinating Committee

Own the Turf campaign: a college and career readiness campaign launched by the National Office of School Counselor Advocacy which encourages school counselors to implement eight components of college and career readiness counseling

Professional school counselor: an individual who holds a master's degree in school counseling, is licensed or certified in their state, and addresses the social-emotional, career, and academic needs of all students

REFLECTION AND DISCUSSION

1. Why is it important to begin career development in elementary school?
2. Based on Gottfredon's theory, what are primary career development concerns for elementary and middle school students?

3. Identify one strategy for each component of NOSCA's eight components.
4. How can the elementary school counselor promote career development?
5. How can the middle school counselor promote career development?

ADDITIONAL READINGS, RESOURCES, AND WEBSITES

ASCA Mindsets & Behaviors for Student Success: http://www.schoolcounselor.org/school-counselors-members/about-asca/mindsets-behaviors

Common Core State Standards Initiative: http://www.corestandards.org/about-the-standards/development-process

National Career Development Guidelines: http://www.ncda.org/aws/NCDA/asset_manager/get_file/3384?ver=80500

National Office for School Counselor Advocacy's Eight Components of College and Career Readiness Counseling: https://securemedia.collegeboard.org/digitalServices/pdf/nosca/11b_4416_8_Components_WEB_111107.pdf

TRADITIONAL ACTIVITY

Part of the role of the professional school counselor is to ensure all students graduate college career ready. As the primary counselor attending to the career counseling needs of elementary and middle school students, this is an important function.

Imagine that you are a school counselor in an urban elementary school. Your population of students is mostly African American and Hispanic, and largely students of poverty. In your district, a large number of students have been dropping out of high school in the 10th grade. There are not a lot of financial resources in your school, but you believe a good career development program can help build a strong foundation for your students. What are some career development interventions and activities you would institute in this school to meet the needs of all students? Consider the following questions as you make your plans:

1. Which career development theory would you embrace and why?
2. What goals would you have for your students and why?
3. How would you involve parents and teachers in career development?
4. How can you use career development to keep students motivated about education?

SPIRITUAL ACTIVITY

God gives spiritual gifts to each of us. Consider the spiritual gifts in the following list. Identify the spiritual gifts that you feel God has blessed you with.

Administration	Apostleship	Discernment
Evangelism	Exhortation	Faith
Giving	Healing	Interpretation of Tongues
Knowledge	Leadership	Mercy
Miracles	Pastor/Shepherd	Prophecy
Serving/Ministering	Teaching	Tongues
Wisdom		

For additional information about the spiritual gifts, see Romans 12:6–8; I Corinthians 12:8–10, 28–30; and Ephesians 4:11.

If you think back over the course of your life, you can see evidence of your interests and likes throughout childhood. For example, if you enjoy baking now, you may have always been the child who wanted to be in the kitchen helping out. Well, God formed us and knew us before we were born; therefore, our spiritual gifts were always a part of our lives even when we weren't aware of them. Think back to your elementary and middle school years as you answer the following questions:

1. What evidence of your spiritual gifts do you see in your childhood?
2. How were your spiritual gifts encouraged, or discouraged, by the adults in your life?
3. How did those gifts influence the education or career choices you have made?
4. What career development around your spiritual gifts would have been helpful to you as an elementary or middle school student?

REFERENCES

ACT (2008). The forgotten middle: Ensuring that students are on target for college and career readiness before high school. Iowa City, IA: ACT, INC.

American School Counselor Association (2004). ASCA National Standards for Students. Retrieved from http://static.pdesas.org/content/documents/asca_national_standards_for_students.pdf

American School Counselor Association. (2012). The ASCA national model: A framework for school counseling programs (2nd ed.). Alexandria, VA.

American School Counselor Association. (2013). ASCA position statement: The professional school counselor and academic and college/career planning. Retrieved from https://www.schoolcounselor.org/asca/media/asca/PositionStatements/PositionStatements.pdf

American School Counselor Association (2014). Mindsets and Behaviors for Student Success: K-12 College- and Career-Readiness Standards for Every Student. Retrieved from https://www.schoolcounselor.org/asca/media/asca/home/MindsetsBehaviors.pdf

American School Counselor Association (n.d.). The role of the school counselor. Alexandria, VA: Author.

Auger, R., Blackhurst, A., & Wahl, K. (2005). The development of elementary-aged children's career aspirations and expectations. Professional school counseling, 8(4), 322–329.

Bowers, J. & Hatch, T. (2005). The ASCA national model: A framework for school counseling programs (2nd ed.). Alexandria, VA: American School Counselor Association.

College Board Advocacy and Policy Center. (2010). Own the turf: College and career readiness counseling. Retrieved from http://media.collegeboard.com/digitalServices/pdf/advocacy/own-the-turf-faq-010713.pdf

Common Core State Standards Initiative. (2016). Development Process. Common Core State Standards Initiative. Retrieved from http://www.corestandards.org/about-the-standards/development-process/

Conley, D.T. (2012). A complete definition of college and career readiness. Education Policy Improvement Center. Retrieved from http://www.epiconline.org/ccr-definition/

Craig, G.J., & Dunn, W.L. (2010). Understanding Human Development (2nd ed.). Upper Saddle River, NJ: Pearson

Gottfredson, L.S. (1981). Circumscription and compromise: A developmental theory of occupational aspirations. Journal of Counseling Psychology Monograph, 28(6), 545–579. doi: 0022-0167/81/2806-0545

Herr, E.L., & Cramer, S.H. (1988). Career guidance and counseling through the life span (3rd ed.). Glenview, IL: Scott, Foresman & CO.

Holland, J.L. (1962). Some explorations of a theory of vocational choice: One-and-two year longitudinal studies. Psychological monographs: General and Applied, 76(26), 1–49. doi: 10.1037/h0093823

Kao, G., & Tienda, M. (1998). Educational aspirations of minority youth. American Journal of Education, 106(3), 349–384. doi: 10.1086/444188

Kenny, M., Blustein, D., Haase, R., Jackson, J., & Perry, J. (2006). Setting the stage: Career development and the student engagement process. Journal of Counseling Psychology, 53(2), 272–279. doi:10/1037/0022-0167.53.2.272

Knight, J. (2015). Preparing elementary school counselors to promote career development: Recommendations for school counselor education programs. Journal of Career Development, 42(2), 75–85. doi: 10.1177/0894845314533745

Lent, R.W. (2013). Social cognitive career theory. In S.D. Brown, R.W. Lent (Eds.), Career development and counseling: Putting theory and research to work 2nd ed. (pp. 115–146). San Francisco, CA: Jossey-Bass.

Lent, R.W., & Brown, S.D. (1996). Social cognitive approach to career development: An overview. The Career Development Quarterly, 44, 310–321. doi; 10.1002/j.2161-0045

Lent, R.W., Brown, S.D., & Hackett, G. (1994). Toward a unifying social cognitive theory of career and academic interest, choice, and performance (Monograph). Journal of vocational behavior, 45, 79–122. doi: 0001-8791/94

Lent, R.W., Brown, S.D., & Hackett, G. (1996). Career development from a social cognitive perspective. In D. Brown, L. Brooks, & Associates, (Eds.), Career choice and development 3rd ed. (pp. 373–421). San Francisco, CA: Jossey-Bass.

Mau, W.J. (2008). Career development intervention in schools. In H.L.K Coleman, & C. Yeh (Eds), Handbook of school counseling (pp. 497–515). New York, NY: Routledge, Taylor & Francis Group.

Nauta, M. M. (2007). Career interests, self-efficacy, and personality as antecedents of career exploration. Journal of Career Assessment, 15, 162–180.

Osborn, D.S., & Reardon, R.C. (2006). Using the self-directed search: Career explorer with high-risk middle school students. The Career Development Quarterly, 54, 269–273. doi: 10.1002/j.2161-0045.2006.tb00158.x

Palladino Schultheiss, D. E. (2005a). Elementary career intervention programs: Social action initiatives. Journal of Career Development, 31(3), 185–194. doi: 10.1007/s10871-004-2226-1

Palladino Schultheiss, D. E. (2008). Current status and future agenda for the theory, research, and practice of childhood career development. Career Development Quarterly, 57(1), 7–24. Retrieved from http://associationdatabase.com/aws/NCDA/pt/sp/cdquarterly

Paulson, M.J., Coombs, R.H., & Richardson, M.A. (1990). School performance, academic aspirations, and drug use among children and adolescents. Journal of Drug Education, 20(4), 289–303. doi:10.2190/8J0X-LY6D-PL7W-42FA

Super, D.E. (1953). A theory of vocational development. American Psychologist, 8, 185–190. doi: 10.1037/h0056046

Super, D.E. (1990). A life-space approach to career development. In D. Brown, L. Brooks, & Associates, (Eds.), Career choice and development: Applying contemporary theories to practice, 2nd ed. (pp. 197–261). San Francisco, CA: Jossey-Bass.

Seligman, L., Weinstock, L., & Heflin, E.N. (1991). The career development of 10 year olds. Elementary School Guidance & Counseling, 25, 172–181.

U.S. Department of Education, Office of Vocational and Adult Education. (2004). National career development guidelines. Washington, DC: Author. Retrieved from http://associationdatabase.com/aws/NCDA/asset_manager/get_file/3384/ncdguidelines2007.pdf

Zunker, V.G. (2016). Career counseling: A holistic approach 9th ed. Boston, MA: Cengage.

Career Development in High School

Erika R. N. Cameron, PhD, Taylor Wagonseller, MA, Victor Baez, BS, and Hannah Cognetti, MA

Also it is not good for a person to be without knowledge, and he who makes haste with his feet errs.

Proverbs 19:2, New American Standard

LEARNING OBJECTIVES

In this chapter, students will learn about

- The development of career exploration among high school students
- Career development theories applicable to high school students
- The role and responsibilities of professional school counselors

LEARNING OUTCOMES

At the end of this chapter, students will be able to

- Discuss career development theories applicable to the career development of high school students
- Repeat how these principles can be employed in real-world practice
- Interpret the responsibilities of a high school counselor
- Judge how spirituality can be integrated when counseling adolescents in a school setting

CHAPTER HIGHLIGHTS

- Bandura's social cognitive theory
- Social cognitive career theory
- Integrative contextual model of career development
- Career maturity
- National Career Development Guidelines
- American School Counseling Association's National Model Career Domain
- Comprehensive school counseling programs
- School-to-work programs

ADOLESCENT CAREER DEVELOPMENT

It is clear that in our modern world, making a vocational choice is not a single decision made at one point in time but a process involving many decisions, great and small, that combine to set one on an individualized trajectory of career development. The process of vocational decision-making begins from an early age; it is evident in the young child who has a ready answer to the question "What do you want to be when you grow up?" and continues in some developmentally appropriate form throughout the lifespan. The many career decisions that a person makes, beginning with one's first career fantasy and continuing through the adolescent and adult years, involve a complex synthesis of personal, social, and environmental components (Emmerling & Cherniss, 2003).

While it is recognized that deciding on a potential vocational direction is difficult enough, the world of today offers additional complexities in regard to the career decision-making process. The advent of the Information Age has quickly incurred a period of rapid growth, instability, and change, such that the development of one set of roles or responsibilities, or one vocational identity, probably will not take an individual through his or her entire career. The days of a lifetime career, a pension, and a gold watch at retirement are long gone. The 21st century has ushered in a world of work where workers' roles have become more fluid and the concept of "career" is constantly in a state of flux. Changes in the economy, such as recessions, downsizing, an increased exportation of jobs, and layoffs, require that today's youth prepare for the new realities of the 21st-century labor market by building strong foundations for career decision-making across the lifespan.

Proverbs 19:2 tells us that careful, diligent planning is necessary for success and that to not plan and think things through leads to failure. Typically, adolescents have lots of enthusiasm, zeal, and ambition. However, they often lack the knowledge, hands-on experience, and support, which could result in rash decision-making that could have detrimental implications and repercussions (e.g. career choice, college selection) on their futures. The high school years are a time for adolescents to learn and prepare for the future. At this point in their development, adolescents have a greater sense of awareness and knowledge of the world of work, which allows them to make educated decisions when determining their next steps toward their careers (Zunker, 2002). For even the most prepared, motivated, and educated young person, developing the efficacy and maturity necessary to make informed career decisions in this complex and constantly demanding world of work is challenging. However, for those adolescents who lack the necessary preparation, resources, training, or access to the opportunity structure, the process of decision-making (e.g., prescreening, in-depth exploration, and choice; Gati & Asher, 2001) may be even less viable.

The Importance of Career Decision-Making for Adolescents

Typically in high school, adolescents begin to make significant decisions about their future educational and career paths as well as how to identify their aspirations and set their educational and career goals. Therefore, it is imperative that adolescents develop the efficacy, skills, and readiness to make adaptive career decisions and set viable career choice goals. Viable career choice goals can be defined as career goals to which one is committed, goals for which one is actively preparing (including taking advantage of opportunities to achieve), and goals that are measurable, specific, and can be reached through a series of well-defined steps (Lapan, 2004). Setting viable goals does not mean that in the process of career decision-making, adolescents should be dissuaded from considering any career option that might interest them. Adolescents' career decision-making self-efficacy beliefs (i.e., their ability to successfully engage in the tasks involved in making career decisions; Hackett & Betz, 1981) are key components in this decision-making process (Betz & Hackett, 1983; Luzzo, 1993; Taylor & Popma, 1990). Difficulty making a career choice is associated with the concept of career maturity (i.e., the extent to which an adolescent is able to make independent and realistic career-related choices; Super, 1990). Developmentally, career maturity and career decision-making self-efficacy are important concepts for understanding adolescents' career behaviors as well as assessing their progress toward achieving viable career choice goals. There are four career development theories that counselors can utilize when assisting high school students make choices about career development. They are (1) Bandura's social cognitive theory, (2) social cognitive career theory, (3) the integrative contextual model of career development, and (4) career maturity. In the following section, a brief overview of the theories and the salient areas that apply to working with adolescents will be provided.

Bandura's Social Cognitive Theory. Bandura (1977; 1997) proposed a theoretical framework that helps to explain and predict human behavior and decision-making. Self-efficacy, defined as a person's belief in his or her capabilities to perform a particular activity (Bandura, 1977; 1997), varies from individual to individual. Self-efficacy, for the purpose of this chapter, can be delineated via three specific terms: self-efficacy, career decision-making self-efficacy, and career self-efficacy. While self-efficacy is defined as people's beliefs about their capabilities to exercise influence over the events that affect their lives (Bandura, 1997), career decision-making self-efficacy refers specifically to people's beliefs regarding their ability to successfully accomplish tasks related to the career decision-making process (Betz & Hackett, 1983). Career decision-making self-efficacy also differs from career self-efficacy in that career decision-making self-efficacy is efficacy to accomplish the tasks related to making career decisions (i.e., accurate self-appraisal, goal selections, developing plans for the future, gathering occupational information, and problem solving; Betz & Hackett, 1983), while career self-efficacy is defined as a content or task-specific self-efficacy (i.e., efficacy for performing the tasks related to a particular career, such as a science or engineering career; Lent & Brown, 2006).

According to social cognitive theory (SCT), self-efficacy is achieved through one's personal motivation and through one's beliefs regarding his or her capability or competence in performing domain-specific tasks (Bandura, 1997; Betz & Hackett, 1983; Lent, Brown, & Hackett, 1994). Motivation and beliefs together influence one's perceptions of his or her abilities such that an individual's perceived abilities may vary from his or her actual performance. Thus, when an individual's self-efficacy increases regarding his or her personal abilities to perform well on a particular task, levels of persistence and motivation will also increase, with the end result being even greater self-efficacy for completing a specific activity (Bandura, 1997). Indeed, numerous studies have suggested that greater self-efficacy in such domains as academic performance (Lent, Brown, & Larkin, 1986), interests in academic subjects, including math, English, and science (Smith & Fouad, 1999), and career interests and goal setting (Bandura, Barbaranelli, Vittorio-Caprara, & Pastorelli, 2001) is related to increases in desired outcomes such as higher grades, greater interests in core academic subjects, and greater career interests and increased goal-setting activity (Bandura et al., 2001; Lent et al., Smith & Fouad, 1999).

According to SCT, efficacy beliefs regulate human functioning through cognitive processes, motivational processes, affective processes, and selection processes (Bandura, 1995). These processes typically exert a multivariate influence on human functioning. Cognitive processes involve forethought and self-appraisal of capabilities in setting and attaining one's personal goals. In this regard, the stronger one's perceived self-efficacy, the stronger the commitment to one's personal goals (Locke & Latham, 1990). Motivational processes involve forming beliefs about what one can do, anticipating likely outcomes of actions, and setting goals and planning courses of actions to fulfill preset goals. Affective processes involve one's ability to cope with anxiety, stress, or other emotions that may be present in challenging situations. Finally, selection processes involve one's ability to select environments that cultivate certain potentials and lifestyles while avoiding activities and environments that one believes will exceed his or her coping strategies. It can be helpful for counselors to understand a high school student's belief systems and ways in which they find support to overcome challenges (e.g., parents, friends, prayer, church) in order to support their self-efficacy. Thus, when cognitive processes, motivational processes, affective processes, and selection processes are positive and goal directed, those with stronger efficacy beliefs are more likely to persist in the face of perceived and actual barriers than those with weaker efficacy beliefs (Bandura, 1995).

Bandura's (1977; 1997) model also details four types of learning experiences through which self-efficacy beliefs are developed: past performance accomplishments, vicarious (or observational) learning, somatic and emotional states (e.g., anxiety), and verbal persuasion (e.g., encouragement). According to Bandura, the most effective of these forms is performance accomplishments, or obtaining mastery experiences. Here, the experience of personal success builds efficacy. In the classroom, for example, high grades that adolescents attribute to their own efforts can strengthen their self-efficacy beliefs in the academic domain. Bandura (1995) maintains that obtaining mastery experiences is less about developing a habitual way of responding to challenges and more about understanding and acquiring a variety of cognitive, behavioral, and self-regulatory tools that allow one to evaluate and respond to changing life circumstances successfully.

A second influential form of developing self-efficacy is through vicarious learning, or the vicarious experiences provided by those role models to whom we attend. For an adolescent, observing someone who is believed to be similar to himself or herself persist and succeed in tasks provides positive modeling and raises his or her own efficacy to complete a task or master an activity. Alternatively, observing someone deemed to be similar fail, despite persistent efforts, can decrease his or her own efficacy to complete this task. Bandura (1995) asserted that the impact of modeling on self-efficacy beliefs is greatly influenced by perceptions of similarity of the role model to the observer. The greater the perceived similarity, the more influential the model's successes and failures will be on one's own self-efficacy. More than just finding models against whom to compare one's own abilities, people are developing their skills in specific domains and seeking out models with whom they feel are proficient in the competencies they wish to develop. To this end, Bandura noted that observing others demonstrating perseverant attitudes (e.g., when they persist and cope with specific, identified obstacles) could be more beneficial to the development of self-efficacy beliefs than observing others demonstrating particular skills. This does not negate, however, that among adolescents, role models tend to be those in their environments with whom they have social bonds, such as peers or parents, and that role models are not consciously sought out.

People also develop efficacy beliefs, in part, through somatic and emotional states. For instance, stress reactions, tension, anxiety, or physical symptoms such as fatigue are often interpreted as signs of poor performance (Ewart, 1992). Moreover, mood also has a significant effect on perceived judgments of self-efficacy. Whereas a positive mood can enhance perceptions of self-efficacy, a negative mood can greatly dampen perceptions of efficacy (Kavanagh & Bower, 1985).

The fourth and final way people develop efficacy beliefs is through verbal persuasion (i.e., encouragement). With verbal persuasion from others, adolescents can cultivate beliefs in their own capabilities and make strides to ensure that success is attainable. However, just as positive persuasion may be empowering, negative persuasion can serve to weaken self-efficacy beliefs. Although each of the above processes serves to influence the development of self-efficacy beliefs, behavior can best be predicted not by self-efficacy beliefs alone but by the combined effects of self-efficacy, outcome expectations, and personal goals (Bandura, 1997). Therefore, in addition to perceived self-efficacy for tasks, SCT also takes into account outcome expectations for given events. While self-efficacy is generally concerned with an individual's view of his or her own capabilities, outcome expectations are focused on the perceived consequences of a particular action (Bandura, 1997). In other words, self-efficacy is concerned with the question, "Can I do this?" while outcome expectations involve the question, "If I do this, what will happen?" (Lent, Brown, & Hackett, 2000, p. 38). For instance, while adolescents may understand that a college degree can lead to higher pay and more job security (i.e., outcome expectations), they may doubt their ability to achieve this goal (i.e., low self-efficacy beliefs). Conversely, students may perceive themselves as highly capable in fields such as art or dance (i.e., high self-efficacy beliefs), but if their parents expect them to go into the math or science field, it could result in parents displaying outward disappointment or anger toward the student (i.e., outcome expectations).

SCT also considers personal goals in the relationship of self-efficacy beliefs to outcome expectations. Personal goals can be defined as one's intent to take part in a particular activity or to produce a given result (Bandura, 1997). SCT considers two dimensions of goals: choice-content goals (i.e., the type of career one is interested in pursuing) and performance goals (i.e., the level of performance or attainment one is interested in achieving). For example, two adolescents may have the same choice-content goal (e.g., a career in mathematics); however, they may differ in their performance goals (e.g., teaching high school math or obtaining a PhD in statistics). It is through setting and pursuing personal goals that adolescents can build and exercise personal agency in their educational and career pursuits. For instance, high self-efficacy and positive outcome expectations for mathematics will likely enhance the pursuit of math-related educational and career goals, such as continued practice in doing math problems, seeking opportunities to excel in their math performance (e.g., participating in math teams or in advanced math classes), and exploring math-related career pursuits. As expected, progress toward personal goals strengthens adolescents' self-efficacy and outcome expectations, thus continuing this positive cycle. In contrast, low self-efficacy or negative outcome expectations may interfere with performance via negative self-talk or experiences of anxiety, thus perpetuating a negative cycle and leading to less persistence in attaining personal goals. Counselors can support adolescents by empowering them to discuss their interests and goals with parents or guardians and by mediating family discussions.

Throughout the description of SCT, Bandura highlighted the transactional relationships among (a) internal, personal factors, (b) behaviors, and (c) environmental factors through the triadic reciprocal model (see Figure 8.1). According to Bandura (1997), the triadic reciprocal model is defined as a bidirectional model that posits that personal characteristics (e.g., cognitive processes, emotions), contextual variables, and behaviors interact and jointly impact one's perceived self-efficacy. In accordance with SCT, these elements influence each other in a reciprocal manner, where given variables may have different weights at different times (Lent et al., 1994).

FIGURE 8.1 Social Cultural Theory Model. This is a depiction of the model created by the author.

Social Cultural Theory Model

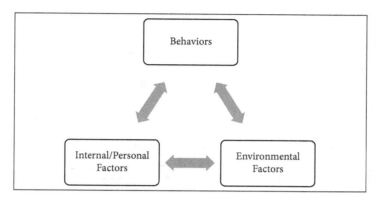

Therefore, according to SCT, behavior can be predicted by one's perceived self-efficacy rather than solely from actual accomplishments (1997). In this sense, Bandura connects self-efficacy with people's motivations and actions, arguing that what people believe influences motivation, actions, and, ultimately, the decision-making process. This is regardless of whether the beliefs are actually true. Bandura's theory underscores the importance of personal, contextual, and environmental factors in understanding adolescents' perceptions regarding their abilities and confidence to perform the actions necessary in making specific career decisions. While these factors do not fully determine adolescents' goal activities, they are influential in the career decision-making process. SCT highlights the integral role of perceived self-efficacy, outcome expectations, and personal goals in the career decision-making process, as well as the sources of influence that can build or detract from adolescents' self-efficacy. Indeed, research conducted with young adults indicates that SCT is predictive of career development trajectories and career choice goals in these adolescents (Bandura, 1997; Lent et al., 1986).

Social Cognitive Career Theory. Based in part on Bandura's social cognitive theory (1977; 1997), social cognitive career theory (SCCT) was developed by Lent et al. (1994; 2000) as a framework for academic and career development. The intent of SCCT is to highlight the dynamic relationships among social cognitive variables (e.g., self-efficacy, outcome expectations, goals) and their relationship with personal and environmental influences (e.g., gender, ethnicity, family, social supports) in order to better understand how people develop vocational interests, make vocational choices, and achieve career success (Brown & Lent, 2005).

In SCCT, Lent et al. (1994; 2000) highlighted the four primary learning experiences postulated by Bandura: performance accomplishments, vicarious learning, social persuasion, and physiological and affective states. These theorists also highlighted the three variables that Bandura identified—self-efficacy beliefs, outcome expectations, and career goals—as they predict the career behaviors of forming interests, setting career goals, and making career choices (Brown & Lent, 2005). In SCCT, Lent et al. (1994, 2000) expanded on Bandura's theory by considering a broader social-cognitive context in the development of individual interests. Moreover, contextual influences on career choice, such as barriers and supports, have been identified within the SCCT model as they interact with cognitive variables to influence career development outcomes (Lent et al., 2000). In this way, SCCT considers the interaction of environmental variables, personal variables, self-efficacy, outcome expectations, performance attainments, choices, goals, and interests in a complex and dynamic fashion.

The model of triadic reciprocally, which was developed for use in SCT, is also utilized within SCCT in order to provide a framework for the relationships among people, their behaviors, and the environment in which they function (Brown & Lent, 1996). In SCCT, the concept of triadic reciprocally is further expanded to describe three distinct yet overlapping models: the interest model, the performance model, and the choice model (Lent et al., 1994). The interest model depicts the avenues through which career interests develop. According to this model, career interests are derived from experiential and cognitive variables that work to influence career choice behaviors as well as skill development. Self-efficacy, goal construction, and outcome expectations interact to foster and focus career interests. In line with Bandura's theory, the interest model proposes that interests are likely to develop when people see themselves as capable (i.e., self-efficacious) and see the tasks they are or will be performing as valuable (i.e., positive outcome expectations; Lent et al., 1994). Again, following SCT, the interest model highlights the relationships among emergent interests, self-efficacy, and outcome expectations and their collective effects on the development and sustainment of personal goals. Personal goals are increased through engagement in particular activities, with the result that young people experience an increase or decrease of their self-efficacy and outcome expectations as they experience success or failure. This feedback loop is seen as ongoing and constantly recycling, particularly during adolescence, as young people define their interests, self-efficacy, outcome expectations, and personal goals.

SCCT also examines the factors that affect academic performance as well as career performance and attainment. In the performance model, SCCT theorists again examine the relationships among self-efficacy, outcome expectations, and personal goals; however, a fourth element is added, namely, young people's levels of ability. Specifically, this model posits that self-efficacy and outcome expectations are, in part, influenced by people's perceptions of their abilities and past performances (Lent et al., 1994). Young people's self-efficacy and outcome expectations then influence the performance attainments they set (e.g., an adolescent's attempt to earn an A in a challenging academic course). Finally, in accordance with SCCT, it should be noted that people's personal and contextual factors influence the perceptions of their abilities, self-efficacy, outcome expectations, and goal setting, and these factors in turn influence their learning experiences.

The choice model is also relevant to the construct of career decision-making self-efficacy in adolescents. This sophisticated and complex model accounts for the numerous factors that influence career choices over time, including self-efficacy, outcome expectations, interests, learning experiences, and past performance accomplishments. In the choice model, personal, contextual, and environmental factors are seen as predicting the formation of career interests (Lent et al., 1994). For instance, gender and ethnicity are viewed as primary factors in one's socially constructed worldview and highly influential in the career development process. In adolescents, these contextual factors may foster or, conversely, inhibit their self-efficacy, outcome expectations, and goal construction in regard to specific career interests. In addition, contextual factors may enhance or detract from young people's access to the opportunity structure in which many career goals are formed (Lent et al., 2000). For instance, while an adolescent may be interested in pursuing a career in theater, he or she may be constrained by economic realities, such as the need for an immediate income or a lack of resources, including funding, training, or parent support. As such, the choice model does not assume that adolescents' career choices are primarily an outcome of their career interests, or an expression of their person-environment fit or self-actualization efforts. Instead, in the choice model, SCCT theorists highlighted the many real-world instances in which adolescents are not free to pursue their principal career interests (Brown & Lent, 2005).

FIGURE 8.2 Social Cognitive Career Theory. This is a depiction of the model created by the author. Adapted from "Contextual Supports and Barriers to Career Choice: A Social Cognitive Analysis" by R. W. Lent, S. D. Brown, and G. Hackett, 2000, *Journal of Counseling Psychology, 47*(1). Copyright 2000 by the American Psychological Association.

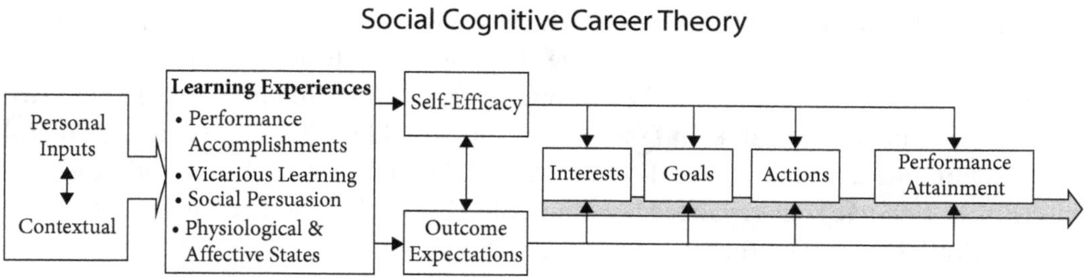

Social Cognitive Career Theory

In a static world, individuals would make career choices based solely on their career interests. However, people's choices are dynamic and involve personal, contextual, and environmental factors that interact with interests to influence their career decision-making processes. To address these dynamic constructs, the concepts of person inputs and contextual affordances (Vondracek, Lerner, & Schulenberg, 1986) are made use of within SCCT (Lent et al., 1994; 2000). Person inputs can be defined as individual factors (e.g., gender, ethnicity, interests, religion, values, abilities) that people bring to the career development process. Contextual affordances refer to those environmental factors that either support (e.g., supports such as access to resources, role models) or hinder (e.g., barriers such as single-parent families, poverty) young people's career development processes. In particular, these constructs highlight the perceived internal or external resources that people feel are available to them.

According to Lent et al. (1994; 2000) contextual affordances can be divided into two categories: distal and proximal factors. Distal factors are background influences (e.g., culture, gender role socialization, skill development opportunities, and available learning models) that influence people's self-efficacy, outcome expectations, and interests. Proximal factors exert their influence during the critical or active phases of young people's choice process (e.g., in certain cultures, adolescents' career decisions may be influenced by family supports; Lent et al., 1994). Proximal influences may include social, familial, emotional, or financial support for the chosen occupation, job availability, and sociocultural barriers such as discrimination.

As noted above, Lent and colleagues' (1994) SCCT model can be used to understand the personal, social, and contextual factors involved in career and educational development. The application of the model to adolescent career decision-making self-efficacy fits well as it provides a useful framework for understanding adolescent career development and decision-making from sociocultural and cognitive contexts, where individual and contextual factors such as gender, ethnicity, race, class, self-efficacy, outcome expectations, personal goals, environmental supports, and opportunity structure are examined. Understanding the personal factors and contextual variables in the career decision-making process of adolescents is paramount, as their career choice processes are greatly influenced by these factors.

The Integrative Contextual Model of Career Development. According to Lapan's (2004) integrative contextual model (ICM) of career development, in order for adolescents to set and reach viable career goals (i.e., goals to which one is committed; goals for which one is actively preparing, including taking advantage of opportunities to achieve; and goals that are measurable, specific, and can be reached through a series of well-defined steps), they must develop six specific vocational skills: (a) career exploration skills (Flum & Blustein, 2000); (b) person-environment fit skills; (c) goal-setting skills; (d) social, prosocial, and work readiness skills (Bloch, 1996); (e) self-regulated learning skills (Lapan, Kardash, & Turner, 2002); and (f) the utilization of social (Turner & Lapan, 2002).

Adolescents are much more likely to approach career decision-making with an adaptive and proactive approach if they can achieve six separate but interrelated vocational outcomes (Turner & Ziebel, 2011). Those vocational outcomes include (a) academic achievement; (b) positive self-efficacy expectations (Bandura, 1997); (c) positive self-attributional styles (i.e., confidence that one's own skills, abilities, and efforts will determine the bulk of one's life experiences; Bandura, 1997); (d) vocational identity (i.e., a clear, stable picture of one's interests, personality, and talents; Flum & Blustein, 2000); (e) the crystallization of personally valued vocational interests (Strong, 1927); and (f) the proactive pursuit of one's life goals (Markus & Nurius, 1986).

Research indicates that these skills and outcomes are integratively and contextually related to one another such that they exert multivariate effects on adolescents' vocational development (Turner, Conkel, Reich, Trotter, & Siewert, 2006; Turner, Trotter, et al., 2006). From an SCCT perspective, these skills and outcomes can be conceptualized as person inputs (e.g., academic achievement) and environmental factors (e.g., career exploration skills, person environment fit skills, goal-setting skills, work readiness skills, and instrumental and emotional support) that interact with each other to influence the career decision-making process, (i.e., an adolescent's confidence in making career decisions, the perceived outcome of a given decision, and an adolescent's ability to set viable and realistic career goals). Specifically, these person and environment factors, according to SCCT theory, affect efficacy and outcome expectations, which affect viable career choice goals. In line with ICM theory (Lapan, 2004), young people who have developed these adaptive career skills and have more positive contextual affordances (e.g., parent support) are more likely to set viable choice goals, whereas those adolescents who lack these skills and supports are less likely to set viable career choice goals.

Career Maturity. Today's emphasis on building the career maturity of adolescents as a way to assist them to make more aware, informed, and realistic career choices began with the work of Donald Super (1957) on the concept of vocational maturity. Super's concept of vocational maturity was based on the idea that vocational development could follow a stage process similar to other life tasks. Super postulated that in each vocational life stage, young people are presented with at least one developmental life task that they must successfully complete before they can move to the next stage in the development process. For instance, during ages 14 through 18, adolescents are typically in Super's exploration stage. During this stage, tasks such as crystallization (i.e., forming a general vocational goal through knowledge of individual characteristics and beginning the process of planning to move in that direction), specification (committing to an occupation), and implementation (obtaining the education or training necessary for one's chosen occupation) must be met before young people can move to the next stage of career development, establishing oneself in a career (1990). According to Super (1957), vocational maturity can be defined via five dimensions: (a) orientation to vocational choice (i.e., concern regarding career choice); (b) information and planning about one's preferred occupation; (c) consistency of vocational preferences (i.e., consistency over time and across occupational fields); (d) crystallization of traits (i.e., realistic attitudes toward work, stability of work interests); and (e) wisdom of vocational preferences (which Super likened to the "fit" between person and vocation).

In 1971, Crites built on Super's concept of vocational maturity and expanded it to include two major factors: career choice content and career choice process. These factors were further broken down into subparts. Crites defined career choice content in terms of the consistency of a choice and realism of choice (i.e., are choices similar over time and are they realistic for this individual). He then defined the second major factor, career choice process, in two parts: competencies (i.e., cognitive factors, such as career decision-making skills) and affective factors (i.e., attitudes toward career). Crites postulated that those with high levels of career maturity were more likely to obtain successful and personally satisfying careers due in part to their greater understanding of the career decision-making processes, their understanding of the links between their present actions and future career goals, the wide variety of career decision-making skills they possess, and their ability to understand the benefits of considering a number of potential careers. In addition, those with high levels of career maturity, according to Crites, also temper their career aspirations with the demands of reality (Savickas, 1990).

In the current literature, career maturity is most often defined as individuals' readiness to make age-appropriate and informed career choices (Savickas, 1984); however, other authors have defined career maturity in terms of understanding the steps necessary to make career decisions, the consistency of career choices, and making realistic career choices (Levinson, Ohler, Caswell, & Kiewra, 1998; Patton & Creed, 2001). The importance of building career maturity through affective interventions and the development of career decision-making skills is reflected in the high number of research studies involving career maturity. According to Powell and Luzzo (1998), it has become one of the most ubiquitous variables examined in adolescent career development research. Therefore, like career decision-making self-efficacy, career maturity is now understood to be an important component to the career development process. Counselors can help students explore their interests and abilities while comparing those to their capacities and work values. It is important to encourage the student to keep exploring interests to figure out their likes and dislikes within their proposed career fields. The student can gain great insight by shadowing a career interest for a day. Here is an example:

Counselor: What do you like spending your time doing?

Student: I spend most of my weekends with animals at the shelter and at home. I've always loved animals and I've been told I have a natural ability to connect with them.

Counselor: How long have you been working with animals?

Student: As long as I can remember. I've always liked being around animals.

Counselor: Wow! It sounds like you have a passion, interest, and ability to care for animals. What's the possibility that your life's work could be working with animals?

Student: I've thought of being a vet and also owning my own ranch for rescues…maybe even researching the biology of cells to help save animals in hospitals.

Counselor: Those are all great ideas and career paths to explore. In thinking about your passion, interest, beliefs, and values, what do you think you could do to learn more about one of these career paths?

Student: Umm…my uncle works at a pet hospital. I could talk to him about what he does and maybe shadow him for the day.

Counselor: That is a great idea! This would be a great opportunity to begin thinking about whether you like to work alone or on a team, have a set schedule or one that constantly changes, and if you prefer to work outdoors, indoors, or both.

Career Counseling in Schools areas of desirable competencies within high school students are outlined in the National Career Development Guidelines. These guidelines are separated into three domains: personal social development, educational achievement and lifelong learning, and career management (see Figure 8.3). Within these domains are specific goals high school counselors and teachers use to drive student success.

FIGURE 8.3 Abbreviation of example by authors from source (National Occupational Information Coordinating Committee, 2004).

National Career Development Guidelines for High School Students

Domain	Competencies
Personal Social Development	• Understanding the influence of a positive self-concept • Skills to interact positively with others • Understanding the impact of growth and development
Education Achievement and Lifelong Learning	• Understanding the relationship between educational achievement and career planning • Understanding the need for positive attitudes toward work and learning • Skills to locate, evaluate, and interpret career information • Skills to prepare to seek, obtain, maintain, and change jobs
Career Management	• Skills to make decisions • Understanding of the interrelationship of life roles • Understanding the continuous changes in male and female roles • Skills in career planning

Personal social development focuses on students obtaining an understanding of self and maintaining a positive self-concept. Another goal within personal social development is for students to develop positive interpersonal skills such as respect for diversity. The National Career Development Guidelines highlight the importance of students finding a balance between their personal, leisure, community, learning, family, and work roles. It is common for high school students to feel stressed balancing all of these roles. Counselors play a critical role in helping students identify each of their roles and manage their time around these responsibilities.

The second domain, educational achievement and lifelong learning, concentrates on encouraging students to attain academic success and to reach education levels that line up with their personal and career goals. Counselors should highlight the correlation between a student's grades and their future while meeting regularly to discuss progress reports and transcripts.

Lastly, the domain of career management focuses on how students design and execute career plans while using a decision-making process to meet their career goals. Students and counselors should seek out accurate and unbiased information during the career-planning stage. Sites such as Naviance, Myfuture.com, and Educationplanner.org can assist students with detailed job searches. Learning about job requirements, desired knowledge, example tasks, and wage information from these sources helps narrow searches and manage goals.

American School Counselors Association (ASCA) National Model. ASCA's National Model (ASCA, 2004) provides career development standards (see Appendix) to assist students in the acquisition of skills, knowledge, and attitudes that enable students to attain career goals. These standards highlight the need for students to have knowledge of self while investigating the working world in order to make informed career decisions. The standards are broken down into the following sections: developing career awareness and employment readiness, acquiring career information, identifying career goals, and applying skills to achieve career goals.

In 2014, ASCA published the ASCA Mindsets & Behaviors for Student Success: K–12 College- and Career Readiness for Every Student (ASCA, 2014). The standards in this document describe the "knowledge, skills and attitudes students need to achieve academic success, college and career readiness and social/emotional development (p. 1)." Based on research and best practices in student achievement, ASCA developed 35 standards that a school counselor can select that align with the specific standards and become the foundation for classroom lessons, small groups and activities addressing student developmental needs. These competencies comprised noncognitive factors (persistence, resilience, grit, goal setting, help seeking, cooperation, conscientiousness, self-efficacy, self-regulation, self-control, self-discipline, motivation, etc.) that support school and future success of the student (ASCA, 2014).

As noted above, the National Career Development Guidelines and the ASCA standards for career counseling emphasize that students need to have an understanding of self throughout the process. School counselors can assist students with a variety of personality inventories and activities that help them better understand their personal preferences. Once a student has completed these, a counselor can meet with the student and translate this information into their personal career goals. School counselors should also provide students with practical skills such as writing a resume, teamwork, and time management.

High School Career Development Goals

Adolescents are at a pivotal moment in their lives. They have to make big decisions about their future and their brain is rapidly changing and developing while they are making decisions about their future. Counselors have to take student's cognitive development into consideration when helping them discover possible career paths and make future-orientated decisions.

For freshmen, this is the first time that their grades will impact their future plans and students may need help through the transition to high school. Students will start to understand the importance of setting goals and how to maintain their academics as well as cocurricular activities outside of school. It is important to note that freshmen are at a unique developmental point where they want to be seen as unique individuals, yet they also want to maintain friends and fit into a group (Curry & Milsom, 2014). This is important for counselors to keep in mind because freshmen are still forming their identity and figuring out who they are, which in turn makes their career decisions inconsistent and subject to change.

Sophomores move a year closer to making decisions about their future. Piaget (1969) notes that at this age, most sophomore students are capable of thinking abstractly, which enables them to start seriously thinking about their future and what they would like to pursue. However, it is important to note that the prefrontal cortex of the brain, which controls teenager's thought process, is still developing, thus students may be more likely to have unrealistic expectations about the future or may be very indecisive about what their future plans entail. Counselors need to be prepared for students to change their minds, and they also need to fully question students about their decisions to ensure that students are not making impulsive decisions.

Junior year is when counselors have to be most cognizant of the influence of peers on decisions that can impact the rest of a student's life. Because students still want to fit in with everyone and are aware of the choices their friends are making, they may be persuaded to make decisions about the college they would like to attend, their major, or future occupation based on what their friends are doing. Students may also face pressures from family members to attend a specific university or pursue a specific career because it has been a family tradition or a student's parents may have very strong feelings about a particular occupation. Student's still have a desire to fit in with everyone else, so their friend's decisions and sometimes their parent's desires may have a more significant impact on a student's future decisions.

As seniors, students realize that their time in high school is limited and they need to make big decisions by the end of the year. Because seniors recognize they do not have ample time, some students may make decisions quickly without fully thinking through what they are committing to. Students may choose a major that is not right for them or choose a school based on other friends that are attending or because they love that school's football team. Seniors want to be independent yet they still feel a connection to those around them, which makes the decision process more difficult for some students (Curry & Milsom, 2014).

Counselors should provide learning opportunities throughout high school for adolescents to develop knowledge and practice in the following areas:

- Have the ability to modify career and educational plans
- Know how to select a program of studies based upon current career information
- Understand how personal preferences and interests will influence career choices and success
- Learn to get along with others
- Understand the employment application and interviewing process and develop effective interviewing techniques
- Know how to dress appropriately
- Develop a personal resume and letter of application
- Know how to conduct a job search
- Identify available employment opportunities
- Understand how to network
- Understand the importance of working hard and being productive
- Understand male and female roles and how this relates to career choice
- Understand how current decisions and choices affect the future
- Understand how to manage change

- Be aware of the relationship of employer and employee in the workplace
- Understand that work demands lifelong learning and training
- Understand the importance of a drug-free workplace
- Know what to look for when choosing a job (e.g., type of work, benefits, location, opportunities for advancement)
- Know how to budget

Self-Knowledge Strategies

High school is characterized by transition. Within this transition, a student's identity can shift. In the early stages, students are transitioning from middle school, forming their identity as a novice high school student. During the next four years, students will be tasked with making important decisions that will potentially impact the rest of their life. Then finally, during their senior year, a student will be transitioning into their postsecondary path. During these transitions, it is vital that school counselors emphasize a student's reflective skills. Students' knowledge about themselves is one of the most important parts of a career conversation (ACRN, 2016). National Career Development Guidelines and ASCA standards consistently stress the importance of a student's self-knowledge and self-concept during this process.

A school counselor can implement interventions geared toward self-knowledge at every grade level. Working together with teachers, a counselor may ask for certain assignments to focus on an individual's self-knowledge. A school counselor can use assignments to steer conversations with individual students (Curry & Milsom, 2013). As mentioned before, personality and interest inventories can be utilized as a starting point for many career conversations with students. Counselors can provide students with free websites such as www.onetonline.org that allow them to explore careers based on their personality type and skills. It is important to remember that, at this age, familiarity and peer influence can direct a student's college and career choice. Knowing this, school counselors should look for creative ways to emphasize the importance of the student's personal preference when developing a postsecondary plan. Exploring individual preferences in addition to a student's strengths can create a productive career conversation. Once a student has a few choices to explore, it is important to provide job-shadowing opportunities where a student will observe their personal environmental preferences. A school counselor can use community resources to gather opportunities, or they may look online for virtual job-shadowing opportunities.

School counselors should incorporate multiculturalism into their individual career conversations. Knowing that all students belong to different cultures, school counselors can ask in-depth questions regarding culture that may influence a student's career path. Additionally, counselors should be cognizant of students' self-efficacy during conversations about careers. It is important school counselors are aware of first-generation students in regards to self-efficacy. Knowing the student's postsecondary confidence level, family history, and peer influence can provide information as to why a student may be playing it safe when choosing their future plans.

Group Strategies for Career Counseling

Group work provides counselors with efficient, effective, and inclusive strategies for career counseling. In a high school setting, a counselor may find it difficult to meet with each student individually to create career plans. Organizing students by classes unique to their grade, such as sophomore English, can help school counselors disseminate career related information to a large group at once. During high school, students explore new identities, interests, and friend groups. This constant flux within individual students has influenced the push for group strategies within career counseling. Group work addresses an adolescent's social needs while providing opportunities for peer acceptance within the group. (Perusse, Goodnough, & Lee, 2009) Students learning alongside their peers benefits student engagement while maximizing the efficiency of school counselors.

During group sessions, a school counselor can guide students with researching careers, writing resumes, finding internships, and gaining access to career resources. Given the current state of technology, school counselors can easily utilize cell phones and laptops to provide tutorials in large groups. A counselor can facilitate activities where students collaborate in small groups to research career fields and follow by having the students report their findings to the larger group. While in the group sessions, school counselors can invite the students to actively participate by completing a career search alongside their peers. This engagement allows the school counselor to answer any questions that arise while the students are using the search tools.

By junior year, postsecondary plans become a significant conversation within career counseling. School counselors can help groups of students link their prospective colleges or vocational training programs to a career path. Activities that focus on current and future goals can be useful tools to help students envision steps they need to take to start their career.

It is important for school counselors to provide instruction to at-risk populations that may have less access to career information. A school counselor can track data on first-generation students, students within low SES, and other marginalized populations that may need extra support. While working in these groups, school counselors should emphasize empowerment. Research suggests that giving these students exposure to empowered leaders in the community can motivate students to participate in social action and play an active role in their education (Hippolito-Delgado & Lee, 2007). A school counselor can facilitate workshops for these students focusing on additional education opportunities, interview skills, and how to acquire jobs in the community.

College Awareness and Readiness Programs for Low-Income Students

As students transition from middle school to high school, school counselors should be assisting students in developing four-year academic and career plans. These four-year plans should not only focus on the student's high school academic achievement but also on what will come after high school. That preparation should include college awareness (e.g., majors, college selection, financial aid) and career readiness skills (e.g., resume development, job related skills, internships) Some students may receive this college readiness from family members who have attended and graduated from college. Yet, this is not the reality for many students, specifically students from low-income households who will be the first in their family to attend college. This creates a gap between those who have access to postsecondary education and those students who do not (Cates & Schaefle, 2011).

The college gap shows a percentage discrepancy between students of different ethnic groups applying and enrolling in colleges and universities. Students from low-income families are less likely to apply to colleges and universities compared to their higher-income peers. The disparity in enrollment rates is shown by ethnic group, with Caucasian students having the highest enrollment percentage (46%) followed by African Americans (33%) and Latinos (24%) (Cates & Schaefle, 2011).

After analyzing the enrollment data, we find different reasons for the disparities. Some of those reasons are course selection, social and cultural capital, standardized test preparation, college plans, and expectations (Cates & Schaefle, 2011). The purpose of programs like GEAR UP and AVID is to educate and prepare students and parents about college. It is to also close the achievement gap by preparing all students for college readiness and success (Smith, Elder, & Stevens, 2014). By educating groups of students through these two programs, entire communities are taught how to navigate the path to higher education. Students and their families witness the successes and triumphs that higher education brings.

The positive impact that these programs make in students' lives leaves a lasting impression on school communities. Both programs were created to help students gain college awareness through self-empowerment. Students in these programs attend college fairs, partake in college campus tours, create plans for college, select rigorous courses in high school, and have active parental involvement. By immersing students in higher education behaviors, it not only serves the students but the community at large. As students gain more college readiness, they can assist other low-income families in their community by disseminating financial aid (grants, scholarships, work study, loans) information they have gained.

GEAR UP and AVID advocate for and work with low-income and first-generation college-bound students. Students with a postsecondary education can take advantage of many opportunities. The opportunities include the ability to enter jobs that value higher skills, the prospect of increased wages and lifetime earning capacities, the improvement of working conditions, increased savings, personal and professional mobility, improved quality of life for their children, and better consumer decision-making (Mudge & Higgins, 2011). These are only some of the benefits of GEAR UP and AVID.

SPIRITUALITY IN SCHOOL COUNSELING CAREER EXPLORATION

Thinking developmentally is essential for school counselors because of the formative developmental stages of children and adolescents, as previously discussed (Sink, 2004). Numerous researchers advocated for the use of spirituality in school counseling (Dobmeier; 2011; Ingersoll & Bauer, 2004; Sink, 2004; Sink &

Richmond, 2004; Ruddock & Cameron, 2010; Wolf, 2004). Ingersol and Bauer (2004) argued that spirituality should naturally be a part of schools because optimum integration, attending to all aspects of an individual's development, leads to optimum functioning, which is the goal of public education. Chin (2006) further advocated for spirituality in schools by suggesting that a relationship between spirituality and formal education creates a global perspective that aids society, rather than an egocentric social outlook. As one of the major components of value-formation in our students, it is essential that school counselors assess and attend to the religious and spiritual dimensions of their students (Richards et al., 2009). (Clark, 2012, p. 22)

Although it is difficult to concretely define spirituality, it can be understood as an animating life force that can be seen in people and expressed by people in a variety of ways (ASERVIC, 2005). As a central component of a person, spirituality is a tool that counselors can use when working with clients (Gold, 2010). Spirituality is particularly salient in the work of school counselors because of the formative developmental stages of their students (Sink, 2004). There are numerous methods suggested for fostering, encouraging, and attending to the spiritual needs of students (Ruddock & Cameron, 2010).

CONCLUSION

High school is the final transition into adulthood and the world of work as students begin separating from parents and exploring and defining their independence. Students are deciding who they are, what they do well and what they will do when they graduate. During these adolescent years, students are evaluating their strengths, skills and abilities.[…] They need guidance in making concrete and compounded career decisions. (Duncan et al., 2006)

Counselors understanding developmental changes, national guidelines and standards in career development for adolescents, career development theories, and strategies to develop career readiness is essential to developing future work satisfaction

REFLECTION AND DISCUSSION

1. What developmental factors do you need to consider when working with high school students?

2. What are potential resources you can use as a provider to assist adolescents and their families?

3. How comfortable are you talking about spirituality with adolescents?

4. How will your knowledge of adolescent career development affect your future work with adults?

5. How would you incorporate parents and guardians into the career exploration discussion?

ADDITIONAL READINGS, RESOURCES, AND WEBSITES

ASCA National Model: https://www.schoolcounselor.org/

AVID: http://www.avid.org/

Education Planner: http://wwweducationplanner.org

Gear UP: http://www.edpartnerships.org/gear-up

My Future: http://www.myfuture.com

Naviance: https://www.naviance.com/

O*Net: http://www.onetonline.org

TRADITIONAL ACTIVITY

Maribel's case illustrates many of the themes we observe in counseling high school students who are unsure of what career they would like to pursue. Her case also highlights the impact of family influence and exposure on career decisions.

Case Study: Maribel

Maribel is a 16-year-old Mexican American female student at Edison High School. She and her family immigrated to America when she was in elementary school. She loves learning and cares deeply about her performance in classes. Despite working at her family's restaurant 30 hours per week, Maribel has a 3.5 GPA. Mrs. Bates, Maribel's school counselor, came to Maribel's class and did a presentation on applying to college and choosing a major. Prior to this presentation, Maribel had not considered college as an option. Maribel's parents expect Maribel to continue working full time in the family restaurant upon graduating from high school. While Maribel feels a responsibility to help her family, she knows that she does not want to work in the restaurant forever but is unsure of her options.

1. What career exploration tasks and activities should have been completed in during Maribel's 9th- and 10th-grade years to help Maribel be exposed to possible options?
2. What multicultural considerations need to be considered by a counselor working with Maribel and her family?

SPIRITUAL ACTIVITY

As you read through the following scenario, consider how career development theories explain how adolescents determine career interests. Keep in mind the following scripture as you read through the case.

> [23]And Jesus looked around and said to his disciples, "How difficult it will be for those who have wealth to enter the kingdom of God!" [24]And the disciples were amazed at his words. But Jesus said to them again, "Children, how difficult it is to enter the kingdom of God! [25]It is easier for a camel to go through the eye of a needle than for a rich person to enter the kingdom of God." [26]And they were exceedingly astonished, and said to him, "Then who can be saved?" [27]Jesus looked at them and said, "With man it is impossible, but not with God. For all things are possible with God.
>
> Mark 10:23–27 English Standard Version (ESV)

Case Study: Nicholas

Nicholas is ninth grader at Springfield High School. He met with his school counselor, Mr. Thomas, to talk about making a change to his class schedule. While working on his schedule, Mr. Thomas inquires, "Are you considering going to college?" Nicholas responds, "Yes, I want to become a doctor." Mr. Thomas says, "What a noble career. It is great that you are wanting to help people." "I don't really care about helping people. I just want to make a lot of money," responds Nicholas.

1. Is it wrong to for adolescents to select careers solely based on having lots of money?

2. How might you help Nicholas in exploring his career interests deeper and connecting to his interests and values?

REFERENCES

America's Career Resource Network (ACRN). (2016). National Career Development Guidelines. Retrieved from http://acrn.ovae.org/ncdg/.

American School Counselor Association (2004). ASCA National Standards for Students. Alexandria, VA: Author.

American School Counselor Association (ASCA). (2014). Mindsets and behaviors for student success: K-12 college- and career- readiness standards for every student. Alexandria, VA: Author.

Association for Spiritual, Ethical, and Religious Values in Counseling (ASERVIC). (2005). Spirituality: A white paper. Retrieved from www.pacounseling.org/whitepaper.rtf

Bandura, A. (1977). Self-efficacy: Toward a unifying theory of behavioral change. Psychological Review, 84, 191–215.

Bandura, A. (1995). Self-efficacy in changing societies. New York, NY: Cambridge University Press.

Bandura, A. (1997). Self-efficacy: The exercise of control. New York, NY : W.H. Freeman.

Bandura, A., Barbaranelli, C., Caprara, G. V., & Pastorelli, C. (2001). Self-efficacy beliefs as shapers of children's aspirations and career trajectories. Child Development, 72, 187–206.

Betz, N., & Hackett, G. (1983). The relationship of mathematics self-efficacy expectations to the selection of science-based college majors. Journal of Vocational Behavior, 23, 329–345.

Bloch, D. T. (1996). Career development and workforce preparation: Educational policy versus school practice. Career Development Quarterly, 45, 20–40.

Brown, S. D., & Lent, R. W. (1996). A social cognitive framework for career choice counseling. Career Development Quarterly, 44, 355–367.

Brown, S. D., & Lent, R. W. (Eds). (2005). Career development and counseling: Putting research and theory to work. Hoboken, NJ: John Wiley & Sons, Inc.

Cates, J. J., & Schaefle, S. E. (2011). The relationship between a college preparation program and at-risk students' college readiness. Journal of Latinos & Education, 10(4), 320–334. doi:10.1080/15348431.2011.605683

Chin, S.S. (2006). "I am a human being and I belong to the world": Narrating the intersection between spirituality and social identity. Journal of Transformative Education, 4(1), 27–42.

Clark, A. M. (2012). Spirituality: a tool for professional school counselors working in an urban secondary setting. Counselor Education Master's Theses, Spring. Retrieved from http://digitalcommons.brockport.edu/edc_theses/124

Curry, J., & Milsom, A. (2014). Career counseling in P-12 schools. New York, NY: Springer Publishing Company, LLC.

Curry, J., & Milsom, A. (2013). Career Counseling in P-12 Schools. Secaucus, NJ: Springer Publishing Company.

Dobmeier, R. (2011). School counselors support student spirituality through developmental assets, character education, and ASCA competency indicators. Professional School Counseling, 14(5), 317–327.

Duncan, K., Dafler, B., Doss, D., Fischer, A., Johnson, T., & Kucker, M....Womeldorf. (2006). South Dakota Comprehensive School Counceling Program Model. Retrieved from https://web.archive.org/web/20090109050141/http:/doe.sd.gov/octe/careerguidance/SD%20Guidance%20Counseling%20Model%20Updated%20Fall%202006.pdf

Emmerling, R. J., & Cherniss, C. (2003). Emotional intelligence and the career choice process. Journal of Career Assessment, 11, 153–167.

Ewart, C. K. (1992). The role of physical self-efficacy in recovery from heart attack. In R. Schwarzer (Ed.), Self-efficacy: Thought control of action (pp. 287–304). Washington, DC: Hemisphere.

Flum, H., & Blustein, D. L. (2000). Reinvigorating the study of vocational exploration: A framework for research. Journal of Vocational Behavior, 56, 380–404.

Gati, I., & Asher, I. (2001). The PIC model for career decision making: Prescreening, indepth exploration, and choice. In F. Leong, & A. Barak (Eds.), Contemporary models of vocational psychology (pp. 7–54). Routledge, USA.

Gold, J. (2010). Counseling and spirituality: Integrating spiritual and clinical orientation. Columbus, OH: Merrill.

Hackett, G., & Betz, N. (1981). A self-efficacy approach to the career development of women. Journal of Vocational Behavior, 18, 326–393.

Hackett, G., & Betz, N. E. (1989). An exploration of the mathematics selfefficacy/mathematics performance correspondence. Journal for Research in Mathematics Education, 20, 261–273.

Hipolito-Delgado, C., & Lee, C. (2007). Empowerment theory for the professional school counselor: A manifesto for what really matters. Professional School Counseling, 10(4), 327–332.

Ingersol, E. & Bauer, A. (2004). An integral approach to spiritual wellness in school counseling settings. Professional School Counseling, 7(5), 301–308.

Lapan, R. (2004). Career development across the K-12 years: Bridging the present to satisfying and successful futures. Alexandria, VA: American Counseling Association.

Lapan, R. T., Kardash, C. A. M., & Turner, S. (2002). Empowering students to become self-regulated learners. Professional School Counseling, 5, 257–265.

Lent, R. W., & Brown, S. D. (2006). On conceptualizing and assessing social cognitive constructs in career research: A measurement guide. Journal of Career Assessment, 14, 12–35.

Lent, R. W., Brown, S. D., & Hackett, G. (2000). Contextual supports and barriers to career choice: A social cognitive analysis. Journal of Counseling Psychology, 47, 36–49.

Lent, R. W., Brown, S. D., & Hackett, G. (1994). Toward a unified social cognitive theory of career/academic interest, choice, and performance. Journal of Vocational Behavior, 45, 79–122.

Lent, R. W., Brown, S. D., & Larkin K. C. (1986). Self efficacy in the prediction of academic performance and perceived career options. Journal of Counseling Psychology, 33, 265–269.

Levinson, E. M., & Ohler, D. L. (2006). Career development. In G. Bear & K. Minke (Eds.), Children's needs III: Development, prevention, and intervention (pp. 515–524). Washington, DC: National Association of School Psychologists.

Levinson, E. M., Ohler, D. L., Caswell, S., & Kiewra, K. (1998). Six approaches to the assessment of career maturity. Journal of Counseling and Development, 76, 475–482.

Locke, E. A., & Latham, G. P. (1990). A theory of goal setting and task performance. Englewood Cliffs, NJ: Prentice Hall.

Luzzo, D. (1993a). Value of career decision-making self-efficacy in predicting career decision-making attitudes and skills. Journal of Counseling Psychology, 40, 194–199.

Markus, H., & Nurius, P. (1986). Possible selves. American Psychologist, 41, 954–969.

Mudge, S., & Higgins, D. J. (2011). College access programming: Removing higher education barriers for underrepresented student populations. International Journal of Learning, 17(11), 123–139.

Myers, J. E., Sweeney, T. J., & Witmer, J. M. (2000). The Wheel of Wellness counseling for wellness: A holistic model for treatment planning. Journal of Counseling and Development, 78(3), 251–266.

National Occupational Information Coordinating Committee. (2004). National Career Development Guidelines. Washington, DC: Author.

Patton, W., & Creed, P. (2001). Developmental issues in career maturity and career decision status. The Career Development Quarterly, 49, 336–351.

Pauly, E., Kopp, H., & Haimson, J. (1995). Homegrown lessons: Innovative programs that link school and work. Jossey-Bass: San Francisco.

Perusse, R., Goodnough, G. E., & Lee, V. V. (2009). Group counseling in the schools. Psychology in Schools, 46(3), 225–231.

Piaget, J. (1969). The intellectual development of the adolescent. In G. Caplan & S. Lebovici (Eds.). Adolescence: Psychosocial perspectives (pp. 22–26). New York, NY: Basic Books, Inc.

Powell, D. F., & Luzzo, D. A. (1998). Evaluating factors associated with the career maturity of high school students. Career Development Quarterly, 47, 145–158.

Richards, S., Bartz, J., & O'Grady, K. (2009). Assessing religion and spirituality in counseling: Some reflections and recommendations. Counseling and Values, 54, 65–79.

Ruddock, B. & Cameron, R. (2010). Spirituality in children and young people: a suitable topic for educational and child psychologists? Educational Psychology in Practice, 26(1), 25–34.

Savickas, M. L. (1984). Career maturity: The construct and its measurement. Vocational Guidance Quarterly, 32, 222–231.

Savickas, M. L. (1990). The use of career choice measures in counseling practice. In E. Watkins & V. Cambell (Eds.), Testing in counseling practice (pp. 373–417). Hillsdale, NJ: Lawrence Erlbaum Associates.

Sink, C. (2004). Spirituality and comprehensive school counseling programs. Professional School Counseling, 7(5), 309–315.

Sink, C. & Richard, L. (2004). Introducing spirituality to professional school counseling. Professional School Counseling, 7(5), 291–292.

Smith, J. B., Elder, E. C., & Stevens, K. (2014). Evaluation of a college readiness program: Advancement Via Individual Determination (AVID). Review of Higher Education & Self-Learning, 7(25), 23–60.

Smith, P., & Fouad, N. A. (1999). Subject-matter specificity of self-efficacy, outcome expectations, interests, and goals: Implications for the social-cognitive model. Journal of Counseling Psychology, 46, 461–471.

Strong, E. J., Jr. (1927). Vocational interests blank. Palo Alto, CA: Stanford University Press.

Super, D. E., (1957). The psychology of careers. New York, NY: Harper and Bros.

Super, D. E. (1990). A life-span, life-space approach to career development. In D. Brown & L. Brooks (Eds.), Career choice and development: Applying contemporary theories to practice 2nd ed. (pp. 197–261). San Francisco, CA: Jossey-Bass.

Taylor, K., & Popma, J. (1990). An examination of the relationships among career decision-making self-efficacy, career salience, locus of control, and vocational indecision. Journal of Vocational Behavior, 37, 17–31.

Tiedeman, D. V., & O'Hara, R. P. (1963). Career development: Choice and adjustment. Princeton, NJ: College Entrance Examination Board.

Turner, S. L., Conkel, J. L., Reich, A. N., Trotter, M. J., & Siewert, J. J. (2006). Social skills efficacy and pro-activity among Native American adolescents. Professional School Counseling, 10, 189–194.

Turner, S. L., & Lapan, R. T. (2002). Career self-efficacy and perceptions of parent support in adolescent career development. Career Development Quarterly, 51, 44–55.

Turner, S. L., & Ziebell, J. (2011). The career beliefs of inner-city adolescents. Professional School Counseling, 15(1), 1–14.

Turner, S. L., Trotter, M. J., Lapan, R. T., Czajka, K. A., Yang, P., Brissett, A. E. (2006). Vocational skills and outcomes among Native American adolescents: A test of the Integrative Contextual Model of Career Development. Career Development Quarterly, 54, 216–226.

U.S. Department of Education (1995) School to Work Opportunities: An Owner's Guide. Retrieved from gopher://.ed.gov.10001/00/OVAE/School2Work/brochure

Vondracek, F. W., Lerner, R. M. & Schulenberg, J. E. (1986). Career Development: A Life-Span Development Approach. Hillsdale, NJ: Lawrence Erlbaum Associates.

Zunker, V. (2002). Career counseling: Applied concepts of life planning (6th Edition). Pacific Grove, CA: Brooks/Cole.

Credits
Figure 8.2: Adapted from Robert W. Lent, Steven D. Brown, and Gail Hackett, "Contextual Supports and Barriers to Career Choice: A Social Cognitive Analysis," Journal of Counseling Psychology, vol. 47, no. 1. Copyright © 2000 by American Psychological Association.

Table 8.1: D. E. Super, from "A Life-Span, Life-Space Approach to Career Development," Career Choice and Development: Applying Contemporary Theories to Practice, ed. Duane Brown and Linda Brooks. Copyright © 1990 by Jossey-Bass. As interpreted by http://career.iresearchnet.com/career-development/supers-career-development-theory/.

Figure 8.3: Source: America's Career Resource Network (ACRN), 2016

9

The Quarter-Life Crisis

Teri Hourihan, LPC, NCC and Sannyu McDonald Harris, MS, LPC

> *As a discipline of engagement, therefore, confession can connect emerging adults to the reality of kingdom life. It opens them to the beauty and joy of forgiveness, something often doubted in the absence of verbal proclamation.*
>
> (Setran & Kiesling, 2013, p. 52)

LEARNING OBJECTIVES

In this chapter, students will learn about

- The emerging adult stage as distinct and specific developmental marks
- The concerns of transitioning from adolescence to adulthood; areas such as moving out of a parent's home, education, and career transition are described
- The role of the career counselor who is working with the emerging adult population

LEARNING OUTCOMES

At the end of this chapter, students will be able to

- Successfully apply Erik Erikson's developmental theory to emerging adulthood and its stages
- Suggest how these principles can be employed in real-world practice
- Identify the responsibilities of a career counselor who is working with emerging adults
- Describe how spirituality is integrated among the emerging adult population
- Suggest resources to help emerging adults through their quarter-life crisis

CHAPTER HIGHLIGHTS

- Stages of adolescent development and early adult development
- What the emerging adult stage is and how people develop through the stages
- Several terms are defined regarding emerging adulthood
- Cultural diversity and emerging adulthood
- Theories of development and career counseling for emerging adults
- The emerging adult stage as a crisis

INTRODUCTION TO CONCEPT

Exactly what is the emerging adult stage? What are the sequences of events during this life stage, which is identified as a life marker that is separate from other life stages?

Millennials are the current generation in the workforce creating a lot of interest. This generation is changing the landscape of politics, academia, marketing, family structure, lifestyles, and motivations surrounding career choice. As the world continues to be transformed by the immediacy of technology and social media, this chapter takes a look at several areas within a multigenerational context to propose directions for career counseling.

The first section of this chapter takes a brief look at the adolescent years and how this developmental stage impacts an emerging adult's experience. Adolescents are in a time of autonomy and self-exploration that marks a person's ability to develop in their adult lives. Brain development, parental support, family context, and leaving home are a few areas highlighted in this section. Following the adolescent years is the emerging adulthood stage. It is during this stage that these authors place a great deal of focus because of its distinction among the stages. It is marked by specific milestones and developmental growing curves unlike other developmental stages. Emerging adults have to consider a wide range of new options and choices, such as whether to attend college after high school. For some, it is a generational legacy expectation that they are going to college. For others, however, the choice is not so clear. Family context and socioeconomic status (SES) are just a few factors that can serve as a promotion of one choice over another.

Through the lens of self-exploration, emerging adults are developing in their relationships, choosing the best time to leave home, getting ready to shift from college to career, and learning how to utilize technology as a useful career developmental tool. Vocational pursuit stress and the quarter-life crisis is highlighted in this section. This is the moment in life when an emerging adult may experience life as stressful and struggle to maintain focus on their career goals. Erik Erikson's theory of development is used to describe this crisis.

The meaning of spirituality and the importance of religion are integrated throughout this chapter. Emerging adults are not all the same. Some believe spirituality is important while others find it meaningless. Each person is unique, and from a career counseling perspective, each person can work toward career fulfillment regardless of beliefs and values. The three theories summarized are NEEDS theory, Schlossberg theory, and happenstance theory. The outcome of career counseling ends the literature review of this chapter.

In the last part of this chapter, a case study of King David is provided to process a Biblical parallel to the emerging adult stage, as his story spans from his youth through adulthood. Reflections, discussion questions, and activities are included.

THE STAGE OF ADOLESCENCE

The U.S. Department of Human Health and Services defines the time span of adolescence from 10 to 19 years of age (HHS, 2018). Adolescents represent 13% of the U.S. population, and in 2050 that number is likely to decrease to somewhere around 11% (HHS, 2016). This percentage, however, represents the overall population rate compared to ages younger and older. While the percentage of adolescents will decline, the number will continue to increase. Accounting for the difference, the aging of adults will outnumber children transitioning to adolescence (HHS, 2016). There are multiple changes that occur internally that manifest externally for adolescents. One such change includes the neurological changes that effect adolescents (Spear, 2000).

Impulsivity, risk taking, and insubordination are a few negative behaviors that can occur as a result of the neurological changes. Many of the changes are the result of the maturation of the adolescent brain (Blakemore, 2012). This is especially true in the areas of the forebrain responsible for stress reactions, the prefrontal cortex responsible for executive functioning, and the increase in total dopamine (Spear, 2000). Also true is that neurological changes are made even before birth (Liu et al., 2013). Impacted by its mother's use of drugs and tobacco, a child's brain can be at risk before conception. Liu et al. provide a glimpse into the effects on the brain development of children overtime after they were exposed to cocaine and tobacco before conception. Highlighted in their study was the finding that impulsivity was more likely to occur in adolescents ages 13–15 years old who were exposed to cocaine or tobacco as an embryo.

Most of the research on adolescent brain development has been completed through the study of animals (Blakemore, 2012). Rats in particular are used to pinpoint the neural development that occurs from early to late adolescence by seeing how certain chemicals motivate behavior (Dwyer & Leslie, 2016). When brain mapping and neurological changes are studied in humans, a magnetic resonance imaging (MRI) can be used (Talbot, 2015). Brain growth is shown to peak in adolescence (Blakemore, 2012) and during certain developmental periods—early to late adolescence—brain response varies depending on the age of the adolescent. The point to make: Emerging adults are emerging from a period of life where just as much is happening on the inside as there is on the outside.

EMERGING FROM ADOLESCENCE AND ENTERING ADULTHOOD

Neurological and internal changes occur from the stage of adolescence to adulthood. Cohen-Gilbert et al. (2014) pinpoint the changes, moving in the direction of emerging adulthood, that occur from adolescence (ages 12–15) to emerging adult (ages 18–25) to adult (ages 26–44) in the brain. Their focus was on the ability of people in these three age brackets to plan and develop strategies for life circumstances. Their research showed that inhibition of impulses begins to peak at about 22 years of age and the response to threat becomes more accurate from adolescence to adulthood. Environmental changes are happening too. For example, emerging adults are beginning to think about moving out on their own, seeking fulltime employment, and attending college.

According to the Center for Generational Kinetics (2016), the three main trends that contribute to the shaping of a generation are parenting, technology, and economics. Demographers add that in addition to politics, having similar values and outlooks are points of interest when shaping a generation (Kotler & Keller, 2006). For millennials or Generation Y (born 1977–2000), this includes being raised by the baby boomers (born 1946–1964), who experienced both the Korean and Vietnam wars; experiencing hard economic times; and desiring to minimize the effect of hardship on their children. iGen (centennials) or Generation Z (born 1996–current) are the new faces in the workplace. They are the children of Generation X (born 1965–1980), who were considered members of the "counterculture"; they attended Woodstock, spoke out against the Vietnam war and the abuse of civil rights, and advocated for equal rights of women.

As there is minimal consensus as to the exact birth years of these generations, there is a considerable amount of overlap in the age range. The persons born in the years that overlap are considered "cuspers" in that they were born in between the generations and share characteristics and experiences of both (Center For Generational Kinectics, 2016). These generational, shared experiences have shaped the perceptions, ideologies, and approaches to success and achievement for both Generation Y and Generation Z (Center for Generational Kinetics, 2016).

As the most globally consistent generation (Center For Generational Kinectics, 2016), millennials are often targeted as being self-absorbed, having a lack of awareness, and being unwilling to pay their dues (Payment, 2008). Although these perceptions may be true, millennials also demonstrate inclusivity, are more racially and ethnically diverse, and are more willing to challenge the old ways of thinking in the workplace (Payment, 2008). The challenge for millennials to find work in the aftermath of the Great Recession (2007–2009) is arguably one of the most trying times in the U.S. labor market (Greenleaf, 2014). With severe job loss as a result of the housing crisis and the sluggish recovery of job creation (National Bureau of Economic Research (NBER), 2010), the increased job uncertainty can be discouraging for the four-year college-educated professional looking for work.

In the United States, it is assumed that age alone determines adulthood. While it is true that at age 18, full adult privileges are granted in most areas, many of these newly granted adults are not ready for this period of newly granted rights (Talbot, 2015). They lack the full understanding of what these rights mean and how to navigate through life successfully while respecting them (Talbot, 2015). The idea that emerging adults navigate this journey with some difficulty supports the notion that the emerging adult stage is relevant.

EMERGING ADULTHOOD: A STAGE OF LIFE

The emerging adult stage is a distinct period of life (Arnett, 2000, 2006). A young person turns 18 and suddenly enters a new way of life and expectations. Within these new adult expectations, there can be much angst experienced and trepidation as they begin to journey down this new path. Arnett (2000) argues that the emerging adult stage is unlike any other stage of human development. He provides three theories that, he believes, lay the foundation for the evidence of the emerging adult stage: Erik Erikson's developmental model, Daniel Levinson's (Atku, 2016) model, and Kenneth Keniston's theory of youth (Arnett, 2000). Erikson's theory will be detailed further into this chapter. For review of Levinson's and Kenistons' theories, please see the resources listed. There are several topics that will be covered under this section on emerging adulthood. These include education development, labor market, living conditions, relationships, the process of splitting away from parental control, pursuing a higher education, shifting from college to career, and the use of the Internet and technology to explore career transitions.

Education Development

The choice to attend college is a major decision for the emerging adult. Parents can help prompt the decision in their emerging adult child to go to college. Waldron, Kloeber, Goman, Piemonte, and Danaher (2014) state that parents send indirect and direct messages that provide the direction children take in life. Very simply, parents actually have more power in their child's future then they may think. Just stating their own important agenda regarding education can provide adequate direction (Waldron et al., 2014). However, for emerging adults who decide to attend college, the financial burden can be a deterrent that contributes to the child staying dependent on their parents longer (Bertogg & Szydlik. 2016). The idea is that when emerging adults attend college, their ability to stay financially independent is reduced.

Nonetheless, when emerging adults do not attend college they are more likely to be still living at home with their parents at the age of 27 than those who have attained a college degree by age 27 (Newman, Wagner, Cameto, & Knokey, 2009). Higher-income families tend to have the resources to allow for adult children to move back home. And, because of this, these adult children are most likely to move back home after attempting to live on their own (Dey & Pierret, 2014). Therefore, it is common for young adults who move out on their own as independent adults to return to their parents' home within a few years.

The United States had an estimated 42 million adults ranging from ages 20 to 29 years old in 2010 (Howden & Meyer, 2011; cited from the U.S. Census Bureau). These authors further report that around age 27, roughly 55% of emerging adults move back home (Howden & Meyer, 2011). Most often, they move back home due to the inability to stay financially independent. Again, this is not uncommon among this age group (Howden & Meyer, 2011), as an increasing number of millennials are struggling with poverty and homelessness (U.S. Census Bureau, 2013). As it stands, upwards of about 20% of adults 18 to 34 years old live in poverty or are homeless. They earn less income then the lowest income rate by persons in 1980. These statistics are in place, despite the fact that more people are earning bachelor's degrees (U.S. Census Bureau, 2013).

Labor market. The current challenges in the labor market include the lack of jobs that require a four-year degree and the increased availability of trade and or skilled jobs that only require a two-year degree or certificate (Greenleaf, 2014). This structural change is a stark difference from the distinction of the college degree in the 1930s following the Great Depression (Greenleaf, 2014; NBER, 2010). During these times, the four-year degree set you apart in the labor force and could almost guarantee you placement. Currently, that is not the case. The current professional labor market offers minimal variances as all of the employees have a four-year degree (Greenleaf, 2014). Without the advanced degree or job experience, there is increased competition for the available jobs. This also means that college graduates are emerging into a workforce that does not need them (Greenleaf, 2014; Payment, 2008; Queenan, 2010).

With the increasingly unstable labor force, many millennials and centennials do not stay in a position with the expectation to work their way up (Maree & Twigge, 2016). Maree and Twigge (2016) report that, historically, the loyalty of employees obtaining work experience and using it to make themselves more marketable in a singular company is considered abnormal, as promotion is no longer guaranteed. In this regard, it makes it easier for millennials and centennials to move on. Yet these constant transitions and possible episodes of unemployment can be a significant contributor to psychological distress.

Living conditions. Emerging adults who are unable to find employment are more likely to represent those living in lower economic standards. Unfortunately, low socioeconomic status (SES) is often coupled with the risk for the onset of depression. As SES decreases, the risk for depression increases (Ferro, Gorter, & Boyle, 2015). Ferro et al.'s study states the risk for depression in emerging adulthood peaks between the ages of 15 and 17 as these adolescents are beginning to transition into the adult stage. This suggests that adolescents are becoming more concerned about graduation, career opportunities, and family lifestyles. There are a number of empirical studies that support the reality of mental health effects on emerging adults as a result of unemployment (Konsram, Celen-Demirtas, Tomek, & Sweeney, 2015; McGee & Thompson, 2015).

McGee and Thompson (2015) researched depression among emerging adults related to unemployment status. Their data was generated from the 2010 Behavior Risk Factor Surveillance System (Smith, 2014). Findings from this data determined that depression ranked higher in those without employment.

Therefore, unemployment among emerging adults is not uncommon and interventions with emerging adults should focus on mental health and employment issues (McGee & Thompson, 2015). According to Paul, Geithner, and Moser (2009), employment establishes purpose, social status, and structure. In the face of unemployment, those same constructs are considered a loss and the level of happiness and overall life satisfaction faces compromise (Konstram et al., 2015).

In response to a number of economic and demographic changes, millennials have shifted away from relationship norms. More than ever, current-day emerging adults are delaying transition steps of moving out of their parents' homes, looking for employment, and starting a family (Piumattis & Rabaglietti, 2015). As a result, the preset social steps have diminished in expectation as the inclination to move toward adulthood is ambiguous. Many emerging adults are choosing to delay getting married and choose cohabitate instead (Taylor, Rappleyea, Fang, & Cannon, 2013).

Relationships

Relationships are a relevant topic to consider when looking at a person's path into adulthood. To begin with, connecting socially and emotionally is easier for those who are religious (Semplonius, Good, & Willoughby, 2015). Semplonius et al. state it is easier for someone who is religious to make friends because religion increases a person's ability to regulate their emotions, thus suggesting that the emotional state of being calm is a precursor to building friendships. As it remains, friendships support overall growth and development (Barry, Chiravalloti, & May, 2013). Additionally, literature indicates that the availability of social support is associated with a positive transition from college to career (Murphy, Blustein, Bohlig, & Platt, 2010; Nichols & Islas, 2016).

Social support, moreover, among emerging adults is linked to an increased sense of well-being, self-esteem, and adjustment (Bland, Melton, & Bigham, 2012; Konstam et al., 2015). Conversely, lack of support contributes to feelings of isolation, confusion, and low self-efficacy. These feelings have a high potential of exacerbation among millennials and centennials, as these generations are considered the most stressed and structured generations (Nichols & Islas, 2016). Related to family, a decrease in family and social support is common when emerging adults enter the workforce. Workman (2015) stated social support is a needed commodity when laying the groundwork for establishing a career choice. Workman focused on undecided students and the process of assisting them in their career exploration. With Workman's work, it was discovered that an emerging adult's degree major and career choice are influenced mostly by their family.

Social capital is another factor worth mentioning. Social capital assists students as they navigate the transition from college to career through network ties (Nichols & Islas, 2016). Lin (2002) stated emerging adults who utilize parental resources for job searching are better prepared for job placement. This is an example of how social capital in a person's family can positively influence later opportunity for self and others. Even when adult children no longer live in their parents' home, they can still profit from the social capital of their family.

Dating relationships. Aligning with Erikson's developmental model, detailed later in the chapter, emerging adults are engaging in romantic, meaningful relationships (Erikson, 1968). Coined the "hook-up" generation (Twenge, Sherman, & Wells, 2016), millennials and iGen have notoriously been identified as oversexed. It is important to note that hooking up can include a number of sexual activities, with intercourse being less frequent (Fielder & Carey, 2010). Rather than focusing on conventional intentions of dating that will lead to marriage, emerging adults spend more time "hanging out" (Banker, Kaestle, & Allen, 2010). This nonthreatening way of getting acquainted is a significant shift and challenges the view on when committed relationship begins or is established (Taylor et al., 2013).

With the increase in freedom of sexual expression, emerging adults are facing difficulty when navigating the uncertainty of uncommitted sex and the rules associated with such vagueness (Waits & Pruitt, 2009). In a recent study on sexual encounters between the generations, the research indicates that millennials and iGen were likely not to have any sexual partners compared to those of Generation X born in the early 60s (Twenge et al., 2016). This data may suggest that between these two cohorts, the propensity to have limited, committed relationships or sexual encounters from their teenage years through to adulthood supports the forgoing of marriage, leaving the home, and establishing careers earlier than previous generations (Twenge et al., 2016).

Millennials and iGen has been identified as the most culturally, ethnically, and racially diverse generation (Blandet al., 2012; Payment, 2008; Johnson & Johnson, 2015; Nichols & Islas, 2016). The increase in acceptance and attitude changes in racial climate lend to an increase in interracial dating and marriages (Tsunokai, Kposowa, & Adams, 2009). However, it is important to note that an increase in tolerance and change in attitude and behavior does not predict actual behavior. Tsunokai et al. (2009) caution against overgeneralization, as the willingness to date outside of a person's racial identity does not equate to actual dating.

Considerations also need to be made in respect to the availability of technology related to dating opportunity. Current generations of emerging adults have the ability to utilize social networks and dating sites to access information about potential partners. With the surge of sites such as eHarmony and Match.com, the market has opened dating in the virtual context without the traditional courting (Tsunokai et al., 2009) and modernized the dating market. The availability of information of the Internet can serve as an obstacle for individuals when considering their actual life and the life they want to live. Viewing the online profile of their peers can cause a shift toward cognitive dissonance and drive perfectionism and poor decision-making (Leonard & Harvey, 2008). In other words, the individuals' online persona and reality may not align with who they see themselves as or who they can see themselves with. As a result, the demonstrated online presentation of perfection is in direct conflict with their reality and unconsciously causes distress (Lehmann & Konstam, 2011).

Splitting Away from Parental Control

The splitting away from parents is a time of excitement for some and a time of dread for others. The types of relationships that are built between an adolescent and their parent(s) is one of the first indicators for how this duo, or trio, will cope with the moving-out process (Kins, Soenens, & Beyers, 2011). Kins et al. (2011) found in their study that a strong predictor of emerging adults' separation anxiety is the attachment style of their parents. In effect, they found there is likely a generational trend that occurs—parents have attachment anxiety in their childhood related to their parental relationships and they transcend this into the separation process of their children when it comes time for their children to become independent. When the attachment style of each parent is insecure, this can prompt parents to use tactics to keep emerging adults from moving out, such as pulling away any financial support (Kins et al., 2011).

Millennials are largely the product of older parents and structured environments like daycare and afterschool programs. These parents, often labeled as "helicopter parents" who are seemingly ready to be involved in the mentoring, advocating, and troubleshooting for their children, may simultaneously disable their child from the ability to problem solve and be patient (Brunner, Wallace, Reymann, Sellers, & McCabe, 2014). As a result, these highly structured and scheduled individuals can experience conflict in the first years when navigating through their college experience, as lack of supervision and structure can produce stress (Bland et al., 2012).

Then there is the factor of a parent having a mental illness and the impact this can have on the adult child. In particular, a parent with a mental illness can prompt difficulty in the moving-out stage. Emerging adults whose mothers have a mental illness are, for instance, more likely to experience role reversal and psychopathology during this stage compared to those whose mothers do not have a mental illness (Abraham & Stein, 2013). The role reversal occurs because the adult child becomes the parent and feels the obligation to stay in the home to provide support and care to the parent. There are some multicultural differences as well. Korean emerging adults, for one, experience leaving home as stressful (Kang & Larson, 2014). This is because they have a sense of commitment to their parents that jolts separation guilt. One of the norms of Korean culture states children of native Korean parents are obligated to take care of their parents as they age. Therefore, while Korean adults still part ways from their parents to prompt self-growth in areas of career, family, and roles in society, those who have a parent native to Korea are more likely to feel a sense of indebtedness to their parents following the moving out process (Kang & Larson, 2014).

On the other hand, emerging adults native to Belgium have a harder time leaving their parents' home altogether (Kins, De Mol, & Beyers, 2014). Kins et al. focused their research in Belgium on emerging adults ages 24 to 25. These emerging adults were struck with a sense of separation fear. Apparently, for these emerging adults, growing up is scary. Then, in southern Europe it is common for emerging adults to not leave their parent's home until around age 30 (Kins et al., 2011). This is much different compared to the United States where most emerging adults are out of their parent's home by 25 or 26 years old (Kins et al., 2011).

Aligning with cultural influences on career choice is the inclusion of career calling and the significance of spirituality and religion on career development (Gibbons, Hughes, & Woodside, 2015). The concept of career calling centers around the religious or secular domains that focus on the drive to engage in interests that are meaningful and fulfil purpose (Praskova, Creed, & Hood, 2015). When examining career calling as an integral part of planning, Praskova et al. note that adults with a spiritual calling have a sense of meaning that is stronger than those without such a calling. They also have a propensity toward community involvement. This motivation can be considered internal as the continuous pursuit for fulfilment can aid in adaptability, thus providing a protective factor in the form of intrinsic inspiration.

Pursuing Higher Education

In 2015, 69.2% of high school graduates enrolled into college. Also in 2015, over 500,000 high school students dropped out of school; out of this group, less than half were working. This was less than those who graduated high school (Bureau of Labor and Statistics, 2016). The Bureau of Labor Statistics reported that 72.7% of high school graduates who did not enroll into college began to work, a percentage much higher than those who did enroll into college. Those who work while attending college is only 36% (Bureau of Labor and Statistics, 2016).

The dream of going to college is not a vision shared by all emerging adults, especially when these young people view student loans as a never-ending hardship (Houle, 2014). From a biblical perspective, "All things are possible" (Matthew 19:26 New International Version). However, there is evidence to suggest that sometimes there are greater odds of one person making it versus another person; pursuing a higher education is just one of those odds. Houle's (2014) study, for instance, found that those who were born into and raised in a higher SES and whose parents were college educated incurred less debt over the course of their college careers. They were also more likely to attend prestigious universities (Grodsky & Jackson, 2009). Unfortunately, Houle's study also discovered that those who came from homes with a stepparent, were middle class, or whose parents have little to no college education incur the most dept. In fact, those who are middle class versus those who are lower class incur the most debt because the opportunity for state funding is reduced.

An emerging adult's success in college likely results from the earlier years in middle school and high school. Not only is motivation required to develop their higher education goals, but how involved their teachers were in high school largely projects their success in college and career (Holwerda, Brouwer, Boer, Groothoff, & Klink, 2015). Holwerda et al. discovered that above all other influences, a high school teacher's expectation of their student was the number one predictor of their student's employment as an adult. Student and parent expectations coupled with the teacher's expectations was the key. Nonetheless, above all else the teacher's expectation was the highest predictor of student employment success (Holwerda et al., 2015).

The journey for some is not as promising. Emerging adults with disabilities, for instance, desire to enter college but are less likely than students without disabilities to finish a four-year degree (Newman et al., 2009). And once in college, they are less likely to graduate (Newman et al.). Lack of support for college and career attainment might be the caveat. Students with disabilities have an easier time requesting formal support for their disability if they feel the university or college supports their needs (O'Shea & Meyer, 2016). There is no question that students entering college should feel support from students, faculty, and support services, yet at times this is not the case, as many faculty and students lack insight about the disadvantages of having a disability (Sniatecki, Perry, & Snell, 2015)

Shifting from College to Career

How does the work ethic or mindset of the millennial transfer to the workplace?

Many students and parents of students have expectations that obtaining a college degree has prepared the student to enter the workforce and increased their employability. There is no question that earning a college degree has the potential for opportunity. For instance, those who attain a bachelor's degree make an average of $49,900 annually. According to the National Center for Education Statistics (NCES), this is almost $20,000 more than if that same person attained only a high school diploma (NCES, 2016). Without a high school diploma, a person's averaged income per year is $25,000 (NCES, 2016).

During the college years, students have an opportunity to explore various interests and redefine what is important to them, and complete college with a degree that will allow them to contribute to the world of work. There is a greater demand and expectation that career services will be an integral part of the process of career success and placement (Brunner et al., 2014).

Career assistance. Career fantasy employs thinking that allows for brainstorming without the boundaries of abilities or circumstances in an effort to establish awareness of other opportunities (Crabbs, 1979). A way to assist students progress from career fantasy to a realistic occupation is through career planning.

The challenge for many college students who did not have the opportunity to explore these fantasies in high school is that they assume earning a college degree is a guarantee to the career of their choosing (Payment, 2008). Many millennials do not research their career of choice to find out what degree path they have to follow to get there. As such, at times they are receiving too much education for the career desire. Obviously, this wastes both time and money. Many skilled jobs, for example, do not require that a person with a four-year degree be hired for the work. Instead, many times these jobs only require a certificate that can be completed in two years. According to Carol Christen, the coauthor of What Color is Your Parachute?, many young adults have not verified the particulars of a job before beginning to train for it (Christen, Bolles, & Bloomquist, 2010). With the increasing cost of education, it would be wise to make an assessment based on realistic interests and abilities through career planning.

Moreover, during this school-to-career transition there should be a considerable amount of energy directed toward maturing students in the area of work readiness. This includes preparing them to deal with workforce perplexities that might spring up during their early career development stages (Greenleaf, 2014; Murphy et al., 2010). Gibbons et al. (2015) state that the exposure to available careers can negatively affect the perception of career choices for students. Counselors can be the bridge that engages students in participating in career planning activities such as career counseling, job shadowing, and internships (Payment, 2008). These opportunities provide students with real life experiences where they can learn to adapt to the adjustments of career development and demonstrate resilience and adaptive attitudes (Brunner et al., 2014). As millennials are the first generation to be in competition for jobs with baby boomers, increasing their awareness of market trends and teaching them how to leverage their employability through adapting and flexibility can improve their chances of successful job placement and job satisfaction (Murphy et al., 2010).

According to Savickas (2012), the ability for an individual to adapt in their career demonstrates a level of maturity that is flexible in the face of unpredictable work conditions and tasks. Within today's global market place, it is increasingly relevant for the next generation of employees to embody these skills to survive and be successful. (Murphy et al., 2010). In reflection, the current generation of workers has blurred the lines between work and life, and career calling supports the focus that career goals should be relevant and meaningful to life as much as one's life is involved in some nature of work (Johnson & Johnson, 2015; Murphy et al., 2010).

Results gathered from the Career Calling Scale for Emerging Adults (Praskova et al., 2015) developed in response to a lack of assessments specifically for this population found three central themes: personal meaning (meaning congruent with self-identity), other-oriented (meaning socially prescribed and action toward the betterment of others), and active engagement (meaning behind the motivation to strive for bettering self and others). By assessing these three domains, the researchers were able to determine that the career calling approach is synonomous with satisfaction and a protensity toward a career relevant to a person's goals and overall development (Duffy, Allan, & Bott, 2012; Praskova et al., 2015). Not every student has a strong career calling; therefore, particpating in career assessments that incorporate calling can be useful in clarifying goals and interests that are congruent to one's identity and values. These planning behaviors can assist those intersted in exploring their calling through examining their personal values, their willinginess to help each other, and their motivation to participate in a rewarding career (Praskova et al., 2015). One of the means to entering a fulfilling career is through the Internet and online access.

Internet, Technology, and Career Exploration

Technology and the Internet have impacted every facet of our lives, from the way we communicate to the way we shop and look for a job (Lehmann & Konstam, 2011). Communication through email, text messaging, social media, and cell phones are primary resources for today's emerging adults (Papp, 2010). According to a report by Experian Marketing Services (2014), millennials spend an average of nine and a half hours a day using media. Of those 67 hours in the week, millennials spend almost half of that time using digital media including computers, tablets, game consoles, and cell phones.

The Internet provides an enhanced opportunity for job seekers to learn about careers, job openings, and market trends. However, this information can be overwhelming and difficult to navigate for many users (Lehmann & Konstam, 2011). This difficulty can be spawned by the conflicting information encountered with the wealth of information found on the Internet. These contradictions can create challenges for the emerging millennial and centennial adults as their search for identity, autonomy, and purpose is coupled with the pressure to find the perfect job, the perfect mate, and build the perfect life (Bland et al., 2012).

These afflictions caused by Internet use during this life stage can create an increased sense of disconnect as the continual impression to keep up with the images and perceptions of success in social media can cause a person to feel as though they lack purpose and direction in the pursuit of perfection (Bland et al., 2012; Lehman & Konstam, 2011). This supports the concept of career indecision as too much information or inadequate information can create allowances for procrastination and fear in light of not making the "right choice" (Lehmann & Konstam, 2011). When considering perfectionism, Leonard and Harvey (2008) assert that the internal and external conflicts regarding career indecision may also be influenced by dysfunctional beliefs of oneself and irrational beliefs of others. As the dependence on technology and the Internet continue to increase, this disparity can create cognitive dissonance, thus fueling perfection and career indecision.

CAREER EXPLORATION

One of the top stressors for emerging adults is the thought of future career and work acquisition (North et al., 2016). Surpassing topics of family and sex, emerging adults are more worried about what they are going to do for work once they graduate (North et al., 2016). There is some truth in this fear. In 2007 during the recession, college graduates had a difficult time entering the mortgage industry workforce, in particular, and holding on to their self-motivation to find work once the recession passed (Greenleaf, 2014). Many of these college graduates entered careers that make no use of their college degrees. In fact, many jobs do not require a college degree at all (Vedder, Denhart, & Robe, 2013). Consequently, the potential of earning the amount of revenue that can be obtained from a college education is less likely to be earned when one works outside of their degree umbrella (Vedder et al., 2013).

People with developmental disabilities many times struggle to enter the workforce at the same rate as people without developmental disabilities. Frustration concerning their perceived or real ability to successfully enter the workforce is a true reality for many people with developmental disabilities (Holwerda et al., 2015). Lindstrom, Kahn, and Lindsey (2013) conducted a literature review on the difficulties related to young adults with a disability entering the workforce. Their review of the literature marks very clearly that there is indeed discrimination happening in communities that limit the entry of persons with disabilities into well-paying jobs. There is also a significant amount of discrimination that happens within the work setting once a person with a disability begins to work (National Organization on Disability, 2010). One issue occurring with emerging adults with disabilities entering the workforce is the hardship they face trying to enter the workforce once they finish school. Here, they graduate and are ready to work but are denied access into the well-paying salary positions (Briel & Getzel, 2014; Murray, 2010).

Emerging adults with a disability and who identify as religious have a different experience in college than those who have no religion (Feldman, Davidson, Ben-Naim, Maza, & Margalit, 2016). Feldman et al. focused their research on two constructs: hope and optimism. Their research looked at how these two constructs linked to the experience of being a college student. Their study revealed that students entering college with a sense of hope were less likely one month later to report feeling lonely and distressed, feelings often felt by students with disabilities (Feldman et al., 2016). It is full circle—religion increases the likelihood of students having hope and optimism (Feldman et al.) and their sense of hope and optimism is evidence that they are religious (Knabb & Grigorian-Routon, 2014).

Knabb and Grigorian-Routon (2014) provide evidence that religious maturity (maturity meaning the behaviors stemming from beliefs) is correlated with lower depression and greater coping ability among college-age students. This also holds true for students with disabilities who are geared toward religious beliefs (Chen, Brown, & Kotbungkair, 2015). Chen et al. conducted research with students with disabilities who identified as Christian or Buddhist and found that these students experienced less depression and more hope. Somewhere in the midst of these findings is the process of self-exploration.

Self-Exploration in the Emerging Adult

The exploration of self-identity is paramount in the lives of most people. Arguably, each person at some point in their life brings self into existence. This can be an identity which one likes or dislikes but either way this process of exploring an identity is a process most human beings go through. Self-exploration occurs when people construct meaning through their experiences. These experiences prompt a person's thoughts, feelings, perceptions, and interpretations (Popa & Kordes, 2014). Self-growth is related to life course development. For the college-age student, it is also an important part of life (Lekes, Houlfort, Milyavskaya, Hope, & Koestner, 2016).

A person exploring their own concept of personal self is related to their vocational interest (Ouyang, Jin, & Tien, 2016). Exploring self is also a growth factor for transitioning into independent life. Ouyang et al. focused their research specifically on Chinese emerging adult culture. As it remains, Chinese culture is known for its high standards across school systems, excellent training models in universities, and student outcome levels exceeding other countries (Zhao, Selman, & Haste, 2015). However, there is a cost that comes with rigorous training models. In 2013 there was a campaign in China to reduce students' academic stress because the stress was taking a toll on emerging adults' mental health (Zhao et al., 2015). Emerging adults from both American and Chinese cultures aim toward having the career with the highest income and the career that is mainstream and widely accepted, and they often have student loans that surpass their earned income after graduation (Ouyang et al., 2016).

Vocational pursuit stress. The stress of academic and vocational pursuit endures among college students in the United States (Dill, 2014). As it remains, the United States is known for its individualistic culture that breeds perfectionism and independence. Much of the resources from the United States are dedicated to the development of its economic structure and standards (Chang, Chang, & Sanna, 2012). However, state-level funding for K–12 education in the United States has decreased over the years (Leachman & Mai, 2014). Unfortunately, with reduced funding, preventative actions to protect against risk factors such as depression, anxiety, and suicide are not available (Rasminsky & Chan, 2015). With suicide being the second to third leading cause of death of college age students in the United States and globally (Center for Disease Control and Prevention, 2011, 2015], understanding the risk factors precipitating such an event is critical.

QUARTER-LIFE CRISIS

The emerging adult experience, for some, equates to a quarter-life crisis (Atwood & Scholtz, 2008). Cyrus Williams, a professor of Regent University School of Psychology and Counseling and an author of this textbook, stated in an interview with Lynne Shallcross that the quarter-life crisis describes the period of life that is marked with transitions and struggles in people 22 to 30 years old (Shallcross, 2016). These years can include college graduation, career changes, and family transitions. Williams stated that people tend to underestimate these years as stressful and difficult. Atwood and Scholtz state that increase in technology use is just one culprit for why the adolescent time span has expanded, from the time between adolescence and adulthood.

From a Christian perspective, the quarter-life crisis is a time when emerging adults begin to formulate faith stories and identities (Kimball, Cook, Boyatzis, & Leonard, 2013). There is a rendering of focus on the experience of identity formation regarding a person's beliefs and values in relationship to their faith. Whereas in the adolescent years a person spends more time searching for the meaning of faith as their beliefs begin to take hold (Inskip, 2013), the emerging adults' beliefs are much more concrete (Inskip, 2013). There is evidence to suggest that adolescents who have a Christian foundation in life experience this stage of life differently (Byrd, 2011; Inskip, 2013, Kimball et al., 2013).

Religions are a protective factor during the stages of adulthood where substance abuse and risky behavior are more likely (Berry, Bass, Shimp-Fassler, & Succop, 2013). First-year college students were less likely to engage in binge drinking if they identified as Christian, Jewish, or Muslim, for instance (Berry et al., 2013). There is a correlation effect that happens between a person practicing religion and their choices and behaviors. Speaking to this emerging adult stage, there is a need to seek ways to integrate spirituality into secular universities, workforces, and organizations (Crossman, 2015). Of course, completing this goal is difficult. Berry et al. state that integrating spiritual and religious dimensions into secular settings is most difficult because of ethical stipulations and standards. Crossman (2015) wrote an article that supports "workplace spirituality" development. Seemingly, according to Crossman, workplace spirituality is impacting the workforce in this period of time. In fact, companies are finding ways to increase and support spirituality in the workforce because of the positive effects it tends to have for employees and the organization (van der Walt & de Klerk, 2014). Therefore, millennials notably have the greatest opportunity to enter the workforce with a spiritual emphasis already implemented. Nonetheless, the millennial period of life from 18 to about 30 years of age represents a specific stage of development, as mentioned already. One of the most widely known developmental models still current today that speaks of this stage of development is, again, Erik Erikson's model (Weiland, 1993).

Erik Erikson

Erik Erikson is a well-known theorist who developed an eight-stage model of human development. Around the year 1950, Erikson's theory began to take root (Weiland, 1993). His theory emerged from theories present at his time. This stage model of development expands over the whole life course, from childhood to later adulthood. Also integrated within Erikson's model is a spiritual and holistic component (Slater, 2003). A person strolling through the developmental stages of Erikson's model passes through transition points from one stage to the next. There are no stopping points (Slater, 2003; Weiland, 1993). Erikson's model is also a foundation for many churches to build on when developing adolescent faith curriculum (Going, 2011). Subsequently, faith is a growth point for many emerging adults moving into adulthood. When young adults have parents who have inculcated them over the years with the importance of faith, for instance, children are more likely to continue their faith development throughout their later adult years (Briggs, 2014).

The fifth and sixth stage of Erikson's model represent the emerging adult years (Weiland, 1993). Each stage is a psychosocial crisis (Sneed, Whitbourne, & Culang, 2006), making this the perfect model when talking about the quarter-life crisis of emerging adulthood. The fifth stage of development is the stage of identity versus role confusion. At this stage, the crisis is the experience of trying to find self (Sneed et al., 2006). The fifth stage starts in early adolescence and goes into early adulthood. A person, subsequently, can cycle through the stages at later or earlier times, essentially revisiting the stage as the crisis of identity achievement exists (Jones, Valerlaus, Jackson, & Morrill, 2014). The sixth stage, intimacy versus isolation, concerns a person who is trying to enter into an intimate relationship. This is the stage when finding love becomes a search for meaning (Orlofsky, Marcia, & Lesser, 1973). Unfortunately, when a person does not successfully pass through the fifth stage of identity formation, there is a lower likelihood they will find satisfaction at the sixth stage. As a result, those persons who have trouble forming intimate relationships are really experiencing the crisis of stage five, identity achievement (Orlofsky et al., 1973).

The stage cycle is a sequential event. When a child is born, their first experiences in life consist of their family, home environment, and religion (Jones et al., 2014). As children develop, these same influences are presenting as potential risk or protective factors in the first four stages of Erikson's model: (1) trust versus mistrust, (2) autonomy versus shame and doubt, (3) initiative versus guilt, and (4) industry versus inferiority (Jones et al., 2014). When children pass through life to reach adolescence—and thus, reach the fifth stage of development where they begin to build self-identity—their ability to pass through the first four stages in a positive sequence effects their identity formation. In other words, to build a healthy self-identity at stage five, a person must first pass through the first four stages of Erikson's model within the healthy sequences. Therefore, the adolescent who passes through the healthy sequence (trust, autonomy, initiative, and industry) will develop trust, autonomy, initiative, and industry. There is hope, however, for those who do not pass through the healthy sequences to reach the identity stage. Their hope rests in cycling back through the stages to rectify and move on. Chiefly, a person can achieve identity and move on to find intimacy (Orlofsky et al., 1973).

Protective and Risk Factors

Protective and risk factors are those factors which make a positive versus negative outcome more likely. As related to entering adulthood, it is important to consider the factors that undermine a person's experience of transitioning through stages. Already stated, religion is a protective factor. It is not that religion itself is the protective factor as much as it is the person's belief and behavior related to their religion that are protective (Berry et al., 2013;

Feldman et al., 2016). For instance, just because someone goes to church every Sunday and is a Christian does not mean their transition from adolescence to adulthood will be a less difficult experience then it would be for a person who is not Christian. Instead, it is their core belief related to Christianity that makes the change less diffiuclt (Berry et al., 2013). This is not the only factor related to adult trajectory. Growing up in an impoverished, low-income neighborhood, for instance, promotes medical concern (Lippert, 2016).

Lippert (2016) found that when adolescents grow up within a low SES, they are more likely to become obese in adulthood. Of course, causation effect cannot be shown but Lippert's study does point out a correlation between living in a low-income neighborhood and young adult obesity. Sirniö, Martikainen, and Kauppinen (2016) also provided evidence that family of origin income level is a factor in adulthood transitions. When adolescents come from homes that are middle to high income, the resources available to them are greater so their support for independent living and transitions is also greater (Sirniö et al., 2016). Parents are in a better position to provide longer-term care for their adult children in the event independent life for the emerging adult does not work out initially (Bertogg & Szydlik. 2016). On the other hand, when adult children who were raised in impoverished living conditions struggle to maintain independence, moving back home is not always an option.

Yet another factor related to adult trajectory, living with a hearing disability is a risk factor for not attaining a college education (Chute, 2012). Children and adolescents who have hearing loss experience fewer opportunities to engage in everyday activities with the general public. Their ability to be successful is limited because higher education institutions are not always equipped to provide education aligned with their needs. Fortunately, with the advent of the cochlear implant the risk related to hearing disability and higher education attainment decreased. Currently, emerging adults with cochlear implants experience more success in higher education (Chute, 2012).

Family context. There is also a need to consider the family context regarding risk and protective factors. First, consider the idea that all children are reared differently despite the similarity of context they might live in (Siennick, 2013). Even if there are two to five children in the same home with the same caregivers, each child is raised in their own unique way. Even if everything was held the same, the children would not share the same perspective; thus, their experience becomes different. Siennick (2013) discovered that when there are two or more children in the home, the one with the closest bond with either or both of the parents are provided more financial support in emerging adulthood. This study by Siennick suggests that it is the early developmental years prior to emerging adulthood that matter most for how the emerging adult will experience support from their parents.

Family context is also considered in respect to how parents deal with their children moving out of their home. It may be interesting to know that parents, too, can struggle emotionally when their adult children decide to move out. However, autonomy is important to the emerging adult stage (Barry et al., 2013). Emerging adults need autonomy to develop self apart from parent. This is a natural transition. Moving away from a parent is not usually a sudden movement. Instead, it happens over a period of time. Adolescents begin to part ways with their parents years before the emerging adult stage arrives (this is the stage of autonomy in Erikson's stage model). Yet, some parents resist their adolescent transitioning out of their home. In fact, some parents experience the onset of depression and psychological issues as their child transitions out of the home (Hellwig, 2015). Other parents keep their adult children in the home only to experience frustration and a feeling of being burdened due to the financial stress that can come as a result of adult children prolonging their stay (Kadlec & Renzulli, 2014). In retrospect, it is the parent, not the adult child, who is prolonging the stay by enabling the decision of the adult child to stay at home.

THE MEANING OF SPIRITUALITY

The type of home a child is raised in impacts their adult experience. Spirituality in the home of a child is more likely to be in that child's home when they are an adult, for example. And, how an emerging adult experiences spirituality depends on their experience of spirituality as an adolescent (DeAngelis, Acevedo, & Xu, 2016; Yonker, Schnabelrauch, & DeHaan, 2012). Being raised in a religious home also decreases future risky behavior such as binge drinking, substance use, and premarital sex (Yonker et al., 2012). In addition, children who are religious are more likely to be involved in volunteer work as an emerging adult (DeAngelis et al., 2016). Religion also increases self-forgiveness following mistakes (Yonker et al., 2012).

Additionally, parental modeling of values and beliefs leads to emerging adults' values and beliefs (Waldron et al., 2014). Waldron et al. studied "moral messages" told by parents to adolescents. They were interested to find out from the emerging adults' perspectives what moral messages were told to them as adolescents. As they suspected, the moral messages told by parents to adolescents were the same messages these now-emerging adults were living by (Walden et al., 2014).

With about 40% of college-age students believing religious values are important to follow in everyday life (Astin & Astin, 2010), Christianity is just one of many faiths that can provide a foundation for morality to develop. Higher moral development, interestingly enough, is more likely to occur in college-age emerging adults who deny religious involvement (Tatum, Fuqua, Foubert, & Ray, 2013). This is likely the result of their less-liberal views on moral development; religious people tend to have a set belief of right and wrong (Tatum et al., 2013).

Importance of Religion

Religion, God, and prayer is important to a large percentage of emerging adults. According to Astin and Astin (2010), 40% of first-year college students believe in God, most engage in daily prayer, and four out of five are interested in spiritual topics. Interested in the inner spiritual development of college students, Astin and Astin underwent a three-year, longitudinal study where they followed over 14,000 first-year college students from 136 universities for three years. Their discovery was that spiritual matters are important to most students; yet, few outlets in secular universities are provided for them to engage with and grow in their spirituality, such as in their engagement with faculty or peers to learn about such topics (Astin & Astin, 2010).

Spirituality and religion, although meaningful to many emerging adults, is certainly not meaningful to all. A study conducted by researchers Gunnarsson et al. (2016) in Iceland found that 58.4% of emerging adults enrolled in college denied religious beliefs were critical to life and 75.1% disagreed that prayer was important. However, out of this group, 59.4% stated it is important for people to believe in something and 81.2% stated it is important to live by your personal beliefs. It seems the issue is really how to define spiritually and religion, not whether these topics are important. Regardless, emerging adults are all individuals living different life courses. Nonetheless, there are theories that describe the emerging adult stage.

THEORIES GUIDING EMERGING ADULTHOOD

Theories guide progress in client care. Moreover, theories of emerging adult development are in place, at least partly, to guide professionals as they work with the emerging adult population. Especially in today's world, theories are in place to guide ethical practice within an evidenced-based framework. There are several theories we could review in this chapter; however, for purposes of space only three theories of development will be described. These include the needs approach, Schlossberg theory, and happenstance theory.

The NEEDS Approach

Introduced in 1943 was Abraham Maslow's hierarchy of needs approach (Mennella, 2016). Maslow's theory premises that human needs fall along a five-tier paradigm, depicted as a pyramid in most theory books. From the bottom moving up, the first level is a person's basic needs or psychological needs (food, water, shelter); the second level is safety needs (shelter and employment); the third level is belongingness and love; the fourth level is esteem needs and psychological needs (feeling a sense of appreciation from others); and the fifth level is self-actualization (autonomy and self-fulfillment) (Mennella, 2016). As it remains, those who make it to the fifth level do so only after they have passed successfully through the first four stages. Furthermore, Maslow's model is a model representing a stage sequence so that healthcare professionals, for instance, can understand how to formulate goals for treatment (Mannella, 2016).

Outside of the career counseling field there are needs approaches to work in negotiation (Needs Theory of Negotiation, 2002). The idea behind such theories, however, are the same: People seek out options, or negotiate options, with people, places, and events to acquire their needs. Therefore, counselors can utilize even these theories when working with clients (Davis & Leggate, 1997). Davis and Leggate, for instance, provide research on counselors using negotiation in counseling to help clients develop goals, to structure their therapeutic approach, and to develop the therapeutic relationship with their clients as they go on to achieve these goals.

Williams and Nelson (in press) propose a new type of needs theory for counseling with millennials. Their NEEDS theory was produced to work with millennials experiencing the quarter-life crisis. NEEDS means Normalizing the crisis, Empowering the individual, offering Existential counseling, Developmental perspective to career counseling, and Screening and assessment (Williams & Nelson, in press). The NEEDS approach is derived from several other theories. These include crisis intervention theories; existential approaches; and developmental theories including Erik Erikson's (1959) model of development, Donald Super's (1975, 1980) life-span approach, Savickas' (2002, 2005) career construction theory, Marcia's career identity theory (Schwartz, 2002), and solution-focused theory (deShazer, 1991).

The NEEDS approach is one of the newer approaches to counseling millennials. Essentially, the NEEDS approach is useful for counselors to help normalize the quarter-life crisis for millennials, help empower this generation toward solutions, use as a brief therapeutic approach to reduce dropout in counseling (e.g., solution-focused techniques), help millennials find hope in the future (e.g., existential techniques), and help millennial clients understand how their development is curved by biology and natural life progressions (Williams & Nelson, in press).

The Schlossberg Theory

The Schlossberg theory (Schlossberg, Waters, & Goodman, 1995) is a transition theory that places emphasis on the changes required as life transitions occur. It is a framework for counselors to utilize with clients as they move them through these transitions (Winter, 2014). The framework itself takes into consideration the client's perspective as it builds a direct approach to provide treatment for each client. There are four points of transition: the four S's. These transitions are situation, self, support, and strategies (Griffin & Gilbert, 2015).

Griffin and Gilbert (2015) used Schlossberg's theory to frame the transitions veterans make as they leave military service and enter into higher education. This study provides a good example of this theory being used in real life. Their article provides support to counselors working with veterans and also with adults transitioning through the stages of career and life changes. The four S's provide support for a counseling framework. They are reviewed next.

S1: Situation. Counselors first need to recognize the **situation** that their client is in. This can be a transition from their parent's home, a transition out of the military, or a transition into a new job. Whatever situation the client is in is the setting in which the person is placed. This is their context and the impact the context has imprinted upon them (Griffin & Gilbert, 2015).

S2: Self. The transition of **self** details what happens in a person internally during the time of transition (Griffin & Gilbert, 2015). This is where a person who has had prior trauma in their life could be more at risk during these transition points if they have low minimal psychological support to help manage their trauma. For emerging adults, this is a transition where support needs to be in place to help them move in a direction of positive change. Their support could include providers, family members, or friends.

S3: Support. Support is the transition point that provides direct or indirect support to the emerging adult. This point is aligned as an important piece to moving forward in the process of transitioning into any given lifestyle, time period, or change. When there is low social support, there is risk for complication during the transitioning into the final point of strategies. Essentially, the idea is that if there is not enough social support present, the strategies to move forward may suffer. Support is crucial for emerging adults as they move toward change (Griffin & Gilbert, 2015).

S4: Strategies. Strategies reflects the transition where all of the transitions prior to this transition are combined to suggest strategies to move forward (Griffin & Gilbert, 2015). Anderson, Goodman, and Schlossberg (2012) state strategies is the transition that provides the direction to the approach. In fact, there is oftentimes a motive here for persons to reflect on the prior transition points and gain momentum to move forward. Subsequently, this is the point in which emerging adults begin to make plans and design a course of action.

Happenstance Theory

The happenstance theory is summarized in Chapter 5 but will be briefly summarized in this chapter as well. The focus on the opportutnities that can occur from the culmination of planned and unplanned events is the central tenet of the happenstance learning theory (HLT). The creator of HLT, John D. Krumboltz (2009), considers learning to be constant and that rigid focus on any one thing goes against how all experiences can work together. Instead, the focus of HLT is to encourage creativity, maximize the possibilities of interactions, and turn events into opportunities that enhance a person's life.

When considering the college student, Krumboltz (2009) stated that if students are not ready to commit to a career, they should not focus on a specific career goal. The premise for this thought is based upon the uncertainty of existing positions in the future (Krumboltz, 2011). The HLT encourages those who are not ready to commit to be openminded. Semantics does not change the meaning. Krumboltz posits that the position of openess creates an opportunity for creativity and planning, not the position of indecision.

The goal of the HLT is to assist people in creating a more satisfying life by developing life skills. The benefit to inlisting these skills is the improvement in feelings regarding life and work cirucmstances (Krumboltz, 2011). The first proposition of HLT considers clients, learning, actions, and satisfaction to be integral to personal and professional lives (Krumboltz, 2009). The goal of this plan for counselors is to consider their engaged audience.

The HLT has several components. These components include the client, learning, action, satisfaction, career, and personal. To start, the client involves a person seeking counseling. This type of counseling is either individual or group and focuses on career interests or career development. Learning occurs multidirectionally; students and counselors are involved in this process. Each is provided the opportunity to learn from the other. Overall, the goal of counseling is to move students from obtaining information to applying information. This is the action component. It can come in the form of volunteering, joining organizations, or exploring careers through internships or part-time jobs. The next component is satisfaction. Satisfication represents the changing of interests over time. This can be a powerful concept because it motivates clients toward change. Satisfaction, furthermore, undermines a person's denial; denial states that an unsatisfied career is normal. The purpose is to prompt each client to consider change when change is needed.

Career and personal are two components that are meant to complement each other. When either component is considered in isolation, the caution is that one will be neglected. Mediating the multiple aspects of each can help to organize thoughts and ensure greater satisfaction.

The second part of HLT is career assessments. There are three: interest assessments, personality assessments, and career beliefs assessments.

- Interest assessments can be used to encourage conversation about possible career interests. As interests change over time, clients can understand and appreciate that they do not have to stay with one career for the rest of their life.
- Personality assessments can be used to explore self-efficacy and discuss values and assumptions about careers and how they fit. These assessments can also be used to engage in conversation regarding personality influences in the work place.
- Career beliefs assessments are used to challenge schemas that may cause difficulty. If the belief is irrational, then the counseling session can be used to challenge this belief in an effort to bring about dialogue that invokes congruence.

The third component of HLT concerns exploratory actions as a means of benefiting from unplanned events. According to HLT, unplanned events happen everyday. Nonetheless, despite these unplanned events, clients can learn to be attentive and senstive to potential opportunties. The more conscious a client becomes the more assertive they become in recognizing maxmimizing chance encounters.

Finally, the fourth component of HLT is the activation of the clients to implement what they learned in counseling in their real world. The activation of applying what the client has learned during sessions into real life activiities is the means by which satisfaction can be understood and experienced. Action steps are the result of collaborative conversations between the counselor and the client. Although counseling follow through is ultimately up to the client, counselors can help build client motivation to stay in counseling (Krumboltz, 2009, 2011).

In today's global economy, the challenge to remain relevant and flexible is what makes HLT applicable to the career development process. Emphasis on taking action and exploring new opportunites from diverse opportunities requires skill and some risk taking (Kim, Rhee, Ha, Joonyoung, & Lee, 2016). In today's rapidly changing, technologically advanced world and uncertain environments, learning the skills necessary to be satisfied with one's career development is applicable in any generation (Krumboltz, 2011).

PUTTING THEORY INTO PRACTICE

This final section looks at the outcome of counseling. Considering the outcome of counseling should be one of the guiding principles behind why counselors choose one theory over another theory. During the treatment planning stages, counselors should engage clients in goal development. The goals and outcomes of the client are the most important. Verbrugeen, Dries, and Van Laer (2016) found in their research that the outcome of counseling closely resembled the client's initial goals for counseling, suggesting it is important that counselors begin to encourage clients from the very start to explore what they want out of counseling. The implications for counselors is mentioned next.

Counselor implications. The integration of career theories to facilitate student transitions into the workforce is the overall focus of this chapter. The focus of a career counseling center in higher education is to provide students the opportunity to learn or build upon the skills that will increase employability, increase their self-confidence, and enhance their lives by presenting them with options toward building a satisfying life (Maree & Twigge, 2016). Becoming more resilient and open minded gives students the tools to adapt to the rapidly changing workforce. Student services should be as dynamic as the ever-changing world. Therefore, engaging students in a dialogue about how to be flexible and adapt to work-life transitions empowers them to take control of offered career services.

When it comes to working with multiple generations, career centers have the opportunity to identify the characteristics of the cohorts and assess what will work in their favor toward career development. The millennial generation has already been identified as a highly structured generation that has been supported by parents, teachers, and coaches (Brunner et al., 2014; Payment, 2008). Millennials often consider the influence of these authority figures to have substantial influence on their decisions as these individuals have been key problem solvers throughout their lives (Much, Wagener, Breitkreutz, & Hellenbrand, 2014). Their packed schedules may reduce their willingness to take ownership of their choices to engage in life and work opportunities to prepare for their future (Brunner et al., 2014; Workman, 2015).

Because millennials have great reliance on and are significantly influenced by their parents, they are cautious when it comes to making career choices (Brunner et al., 2014; Nichols & Islas, 2016; Workman, 2015). Although the phenomenon of the "helicopter parent" is not specific to this generation, the increase in parental involvement in the life of the millennial is consistent through the college years (Brunner et al., 2014; Workman, 2015).

Schiffrin et al. (2014) considered parental involvement to be "unprecedented" in these emerging adults. As competition for solid jobs after college continues to rise (Nichols & Islas, 2016), emerging adults are willing to use all resources available to them. These resources include the influence and persistance of their parents. Through the exploration of the students' cultural background and the affect that parental involvement has on student success (Gibbons et al., 2015), university counselors can ultimately utilize these relationships to their advantage as a means to mobilize students in their career development. Career counselors can also offer support and assistance to students to prompt them to be responsible for their growth and independence (Maree & Twigge, 2016; Much et al., 2014).

In the same manner that students are encouraged to participate in real-life experiences to diversify their experiences, career counselors are expected to do the same. As career changes take effect, so too should the reach and availability of career services. This results in a strengthening of the opportunity for career services to be rendered to students and emerging adults. Furthermore, learning about students' basic understanding and knowledge will allow career counselors to fill in the gaps in order to provide real-world context and clarity (Gibbons et al., 2015). Counseling centers are structured mostly by their mission, size, and availability of expertise. To fill in the gaps, college counseling professionals spend a significant amount of time providing education and support through workshops and seminars that focus on a variety of concerns including mental health and college-to-career transition. Twenge et al. (2016) report that a strong predictor of graduation is emotional support. As we have established that parents can prove to be a natural support to students, this demonstrates a need for counseling centers to provide assistance in this area.

CONCLUSION

This chapter speaks to the developmental time period of emerging adulthood. Each section relates to the focus of career counseling with the inclusion of spiritual and religious integration. A chapter focused on these areas is critical for professionals and students in the counseling field, especially because this stage is different from other developmental stages. To lump adults together because they are all over the age of 18 is not a recommendation from the research, noted throughout this chapter.

This chapter begins by summarizing adolescent development, how this developmental stage seeps into the developmental years of the emerging adult, and how they influence each other. Paramount, of course, is the adolescent stage impacting the emerging adult stage because of their sequence. However, it is noted in Erikson's model, for example, that although someone is in the emerging adult stage, it does not mean they will stay at that stage of development throughout their development. Yes, they do stay the same age; however, their developmental cycle can change as a result of social learning, family context, SES, friendships, school attainment, and career goals. Each stage of this period is summarized as it relates to either development, career, or spirituality.

Theories and outcomes of career counseling are detailed last. These two areas are critical components to consider in career counseling with emerging adults. Counselors need to understand that theory drives the use of counseling with this population. Counselors can utilize theory to guide their practice. They can also know which theories provide successful outcomes for the majority. Not using theory to guide practice is loose therapy, at most. Finally, in the last part of this chapter the case of King David is explored. Specific attention to his period of adolescence and early adulthood as portrayed in the Bible is detailed. Discussion questions and reflections are also provided.

KEY TERMS

Generation X The major experiences that have shaped the lives of Generation X was the Spaceship Challenger, AIDS, the Great Recession, and the rise of the computer (Payment, 2008). Generation X also became latch-key kids, largely as result of increased divorce among their parents (Wiedmer, 2015; Payment, 2008). As adults, this generation experienced hard economic times, reflected by the impact of both the Korean and Vietnam wars and the fall of the Berlin Wall (Wiedmer, 2015). Out of these experiences, it is not surprising that this generation has become synonymous with identifiers such as resilient, independent, balanced, and active (Wiedmer, 2015). As employees, they expect to have a good balance between work and family life. As opposed to the boomer generation, whose members worked long hours for money and titles, Generation Xers are extremely vigilant about not having that experience, as they have watched their parents get laid off regardless of loyalty to the company. (Wiedmer, 2015; Payment, 2008). As a result, they are flexible, willing to reinvent themselves as they operate in social protest by deferring marriage and moving back home (Weidmer, 2015) as they consider the impact of working in between baby boomers, who are not retiring due to inadequate retirement income, and millennials who are ascending on the workforce in great numbers with innovative skills and ideas. (Payment, 2008; Wiedmer, 2015).

Generation Y Millennials or Generation Y were born to baby boomers who experienced hard economic times and coincidently were motivated to minimize the effect of hardship on their children. As a result, utilization of daycare, afterschool care, and extra-curricular activities increased (Bland et al., 2012). This highly structured model supported by increasingly involved parents led to this generation being labeled as impatient, entitled, team oriented and optimistic (DeVaney, 2015; Nichols & Islas, 2016). Some of the historical events that have shaped millennials are the release of Nelson Mandela, the death of Princess Diana, the 9/11 attacks, Columbine High School shootings, and Hurricane Katrina (Wiedmer, 2015). The single-most influential entity that has impacted these generations is the invention of the Internet in the 1990s (Haigh, Russell, & Dutton, 2015). Millennials are considered to be "digital natives," which is in contrast to baby boomers and some of Generation X, who are considered to be "digital immigrants" in that they have spent a considerable amount of time of their life offline (Presnsky, 2001). According to a report by Experian Marketing Services (2014), millennials spend an average of nine and a half hours a day using media. Millennials spend almost half of those 67 hours in the week using digital media including computers, tablets, game consoles, and cell phones. As a technologically advanced generation, many of the social media platforms that are utilized today such as Facebook, Twitter, Instagram, and Groupon were developed and founded by millennials (Burstein, 2013).

Generation Z iGen—Centennials or Generation Z—are the new faces in the workplace. They are the children of Generation X (born 1965–1976) who attended Woodstock and were considered members of the counterculture who spoke out against the Vietnam war and the abuse of civil rights and advocated for equal rights of women. Most of the characteristics of this generation are still being formed, as their strong technological connections will continue to allow them greater access to information across their lifespan than the generations before them (Wiedmer, 2015). The author also notes that iGen are self-starters who are not interested in traditional learning through lectures, as they are the most home-schooled generation. As result, they prefer a customizable learning experience that is flexible and supports the use of advanced technology. (Wiedmer, 2015)

REFLECTION AND DISCUSSION

1. What is the emerging adult stage?
2. Why do emerging adults move out on their own only to likely return a few years later? What would mark their departure with greater promise?
3. What is the role of the career counselor when working with a new client in counseling?
4. How can a career counselor build a treatment plan around the client's needs?
5. How is spirituality reflected in the emerging adult population?

TRADITIONAL ACTIVITY

Case Study/Intervention

The Case of Emily

Emily is a junior in college and is on a pre-med track at her parents' alma mater. Emily's parents have been instrumental to her success as a student and have connected her to various key individuals who have access to opportunities for internships and job placements after graduation. She is a member of several social and academic clubs, has a solid group of friends, and considers herself to be a well-rounded student. Recently, Emily has been having concern about her readiness to enter the workforce despite her connections and support from her parents.

This semester, Emily took an elective that focused on arts as a way to engage students in artistic expression and integrate the arts into everyday life. Emily enjoyed the class immensely and was surprised at her growing curiosity. She began to question her scholastic choices and weigh the parental expectations of continuing the family legacy of medicine. Emily's processing became intense as she considered switching her major and doubted her decision to enter medicine.

When discussing her interest with friends, she discovered that many, if not all, of them were confident in their choice for pre-med. She could not understand why she would consider changing her major and giving up on what she is working toward. Emily often found herself deep in thought and coincidentally started retreating from her social circles, pondering her decisions regarding her life including school choice and her future if she is not in medicine. The increased relay of thoughts about the life she was supposed to live created increased stress and anxiety, which further cemented her isolation and increased feelings of depression. At the recommendation of a friend, Emily eventually connects with a university counselor who engages her in a conversation about life satisfaction. They focus on how being open to the possibilities of our life experiences positively shapes our decisions versus derails them. This is active participation in career development.

Emily continues to meet with the counselor to process goals of both her personal and her professional life. She soon finds that increasing her knowledge about other careers and being self-aware regarding her anxieties about life transitions allows her to feel less isolated and normalizes her career confusion.

When considering next steps for someone like Emily, it may be helpful to put yourself in her place to assist in processing what it is like to consider the legacy and expectation of her parents, the expected responsibility that she has to the established network of support, and the apprehensions that may exist around leaving something behind to explore new opportunities.

Searching for independence in the search for congruence does not equate to complete abandonment and neglect. Utilizing the support and influence of supportive family and friends can be an integral source of strength as clients continue to develop in their career.

Respond

1. How can each of the career theories in this chapter be used to assist Emily in her career development? Examine the strengths and weakness in devising a treatment plan.
2. Consider the multigenerational landscape and global reach of the workforce. Where can Emily fit? How can she capitalize on social influence and familial support to navigate this stage in her life?

SPIRITUAL ACTIVITY

Case Study: King David

David was between 10 and 13 years of age when he was first mentioned in the Bible (Gross, 2005). The Bible states he was "ruddy" yet handsome (1 Samuel 16:3, New International Version [NIV]). The youngest of his seven brothers, David was the last to be summoned. Samuel was unsure of God's choice to anoint David as king due to his appearance and his age. At first, David was not concerned with the kingdom call; he was in the field tending to sheep when he was asked to join his brothers for the call of anointing. It was years later before he would fulfill his unknown purpose.

David was laughed at when he went before the war to fight Goliath. Yet, David knew the strength in his God and understood that the Lord had called him to do great things when he was young. He knew God was with him, and victory was his that day as he won the fight with one sling shot of a stone (1 Samuel 17, NIV). As he grew out of adolescence and into adulthood, he was sequestered by kings and princes to serve and lead in their armies (1 Samuel 16–18, NIV). He followed the rules but had an ego—knowing his strength, he wrestled with lions and conquered whole cities. With all of his success, he also would know loss and hurt as he struggled to maintain peace despite the surrounding frustrations. Over the span of his life, David continued to experience the favor of God through covenant friendships and marriage. He found a strong friendship with the Kings' son, Jonathan (1 Samuel

18:1, NIV), and could marry any woman he chose. However, conflicts with his flesh would cause him to take another man's wife and have him murdered. He experiences repercussions because of his choices and learns to work through them with God. Overtime he comes to the end of warring and settles down to enjoy the last years of his life in peace.

David is the only person in the Bible who is followed from early life to death with much detail (Gross, 2005). He was a man of great influence and strength, yet his relationship with God allowed him to experience humility. David revered God as his Father, and his connection with him proves to be paramount when you reflect over his life. When God is considered in the journey of adolescence to young adulthood, an easy transition is expected. The adverse of this statement is also true; denying the reliance on God can create rough experiences in life. This is parallel to what happens for emerging adults. As was detailed in the chapter, the emerging adult stage is about self-exploration, making education and career decisions, following rules and obligations, deciding on what is desired for the future, and family building.

When considering the story of David, it is important to recognize the importance of timing. Although David was anointed and called to be King at a young age, he did not become King until much later in life. This is a strong indication of how your calling in life can be fulfilled across your lifespan.

Another point to consider is that of appearance. David did not appear to be the obvious choice for a king. However, his perseverance, humility, love for God, and faith created opportunities for him to be successful despite adversity.

When considering the pursuit of your calling, discuss the implications of the following:

1. Unknown calling (next steps after graduating high school or college)
2. Delay in your calling (e.g., lack of faith, obstacles)
3. Threats to your calling (e.g., mindset, relationships)

Respond

1. When considering 1 Timothy 4:12, what are your thoughts regarding your age and your ability to pursue your calling? How do the tenets of this scripture align with the positive and negative transitions experienced in David's life?
2. There is significant loss and triumph experienced in David's life? In what ways can support affect this?

REFERENCES

Abraham, K. M., & Stein, C. H. (2013). When mom has a mental illness: Role reversal and psychosocial adjustment among emerging adults. Journal of Clinical Psychology, 69(6), 600–615.

Aktu, Y. (2016). Life structure of early adulthood period in levinson's theory. Psikiyatride Guncel Yaklasimlar, 8(2), 162–177. doi:10.18863/pgy.12690

Anderson, M. Goodman, J., & Schlossberg, N. (2012). Counseling adults in transition: Linking Schlossberg's theory with practice in a diverse world. New York: Springer.

Arnett, J. J. (2000). Emerging adulthood: A theory of development from the late teens through the twenties. American Psychological Association, Inc, 55(5), 469–480. Retrieved from http://jeffreyarnett.com/articles/ARNETT_Emerging_Adulthood_theory.pdf

Arnett, J. J. (2006). Emerging adulthood: The winding road from the late teens through the twenties. New York, NY: Oxford University Press.

Astin, A. W., & Astin, H. S. (2010). Exploring and nurturing the spiritual life of college students. Journal of College and Character, 11(3), 1–9. Retrieved from http://www.campusministry.net/wp-content/uploads/2015/02/Exploring-and-Nurturing-the-Spiritual-Life-of-College-Students.pdf

Atwood, J., & Scholtz, C. (2008). The quarter-life time period: an age of indulgence, crisis or both?. Contemporary Family Therapy: An International Journal, 30(4), 233–250.

Banker, J. E., Kaestle, C. E., & Allen, K. R. (2010). Dating is hard work: A narrative approach to understanding sexual and romantic relationships in young adulthood. Contemporary Family Therapy, 32(2), 173–191. doi:10.1007/s10591-009-9111-9

Barry, C. M., Chiravalloti, L., & May, E. (2013). Emerging Adults' Psychosocial Adjustment: Does a Best Friend's Gender Matter?. Psi Chi Journal of Psychological Research, 18(3), 94–102.

Berry, D., Bass, C. P., Shimp-Fassler, C., & Succop, P. (2013). Risk, religiosity, and emerging adulthood: Description of Christian, Jewish, and Muslim university students at entering the freshman year. Mental Health, Religion & Culture, 16(7), 695–710.

Bertogg, A., & Szydlik, M. (2016). The closeness of young adults' relationships with their parents. Swiss Journal of Sociology, 42(1), 41–59.

Blakemore, S. (2012). Imaging brain development: The adolescent brain. NeuroImage, 61(2), 397–406. doi: 10.1016/j.neuroimage.2011.11.080

Bland, H., Melton, B., & Bigham, L. (2012). Stress tolerance: New challenges for millenial college students. College Student Journal, 362–375.

Briel, L. W., & Getzel, E. E. (2014). In their own words: The career planning experiences of college students with ASD. Journal of Vocational Rehabilitation, 40(3), 195–202. doi:10.3233/JVR-140684

Briggs, D. (2014). Parents are top influence in teens remaining active in religion as young adults. The Christian Century. Retrieved from http://www.christiancentury.org/article/2014-11/parents-no-1- influence-teens-remaining-religiously-active-young-adults

Brunner, J., Wallace, D., Reymann, L., Sellers, J., & McCabe, A. (2014). College counseling today: Contemporary students and how counseling centers meet their needs. Journal of College Student Psychotherapy, 28(4), 257–324. doi.org/10.1080/87568225.2014.948770

Bureau of Labor and Statistics. (2016). College enrollment and work activity of 2015 high school graduates. Retrieved from http://www.bls.gov/news.release/hsgec.nr0.htm

Burstein, B. (2013). "It's all the women's fault...". The Journal of Psychohistory, 41(1), 52–54. Retrieved from http://eres.regent.edu:2048/login?url=https://search-proquest- com.ezproxy.regent.edu/docview/1412594681?accountid=13479

Byrd, N. C. (2011). Narrative discipleship: Guiding emerging adults to "connect the dots" of life and faith. Christian Education Journal, 8(2), 244–262. Retrieved from http://0- search.proquest.com.library.regent.edu/docview/896481205?accountid=13479

Center for Disease Control and Prevention (CDC). (2011). Suicide among youth. Retrieved from http://www.cdc.gov/healthcommunication/ToolsTemplates/EntertainmentEd/Tips/SuicideYouth.ht ml

Center for Disease Control and Prevention (CDC). (2015). Years of potential life lost. Retrieved from http://www.cdc.gov/injury/wisqars/years_potential.html

Chang, E., Chang, R., & Sanna, L. (2012). A Test of the usefulness of Perfectionism Theory across cultures: Does perfectionism in the US and Japan predict depressive symptoms across time?. Cognitive Therapy & Research, 36(1), 1–14.

Chen, R. K., Brown, A. D., & Kotbungkair, W. (2015). A comparison of self-acceptance of disability between Thai Buddhists and American Christians. Journal of Rehabilitation, 81(1), 52–62.

Chute, P. M. (2012). College experience for young adults with hearing loss. Deafness & Education International, 14(1), 60–65. doi:10.1179/1557069X12Y.0000000002

Cohen-Gilbert, J., Killgore, W., White, C., Schwab, Z., Crowley, D., Covell, M., & … Silveri, M. (2014). Differential influence of safe versus threatening facial expressions on decision-making during an inhibitory control task in adolescence and adulthood. Developmental Science, 17(2), 212–223. doi:10.1111/desc.12123

Christen, C., Bolles, R., & Bloomquist, J. (2010). What color is you parachute? For teens: Discovering yourself, defining your future. Berkeley, CA: Ten Speed Press.

Crabbs, M. (1979). Fantasy in career development. Personnel and Guidance Journal, 57(6), 292–295.

Crossman, J. (2015). Manager perspectives on embedding workplace spirituality into the business curriculum: Bridging the gap. Thunderbird International Business Review, 57(5), 367–378. doi:10.1002/tie.21674

Davis, A., & Leggate, C. (1997). Negotiation: A critical competency for rehabilitation counselors. Retrieved from http://eric.ed.gov/?id=ED413563

DeAngelis, R. T., Acevedo, G. A., & Xu, X. (2016). Secular volunteerism among Texan emerging adults: Exploring pathways of childhood and adulthood religiosity. Religions, 7(6), 74. doi: 10.3390/rel7060074

deShazer, S. (1991). Putting difference to work. New York, NY: Norton.

Dey, J. G., & Pierret, C. R. (2014). Independence for young millennials: Moving out and boomeranging back. Monthly Labor Review, 137(12), 1A.

Dill, D. D. (2014). Ensuring academic standards in US higher education change. The Magazine of Higher Learning, 46(3), 53–59.

Duffy, R., Allan, B., & Bott, E. (2012). Calling and life satisfaction amoung undergraduate students: Investigating mediators and moderators. Journal of Happiness Studies, 13, 469–479. doi:10.1007/s10902-011-9274-6

Experian Marketing Services. (2014, June). Experian information solutions. Retrieved from https://www.experian.com/assets/marketing-services/reports/ems-ci-millennials-come-of-age- wp.pdf

Dwyer, J., & Leslie, F. (2016). Adolescent maturation of dopamine D1 and D2 receptor function and interactions in rodents. Plos ONE, 11(1), 1–21. doi:10.1371/journal.pone.0146966

Erikson, E. (1968). Identity: Youth and crisis. New York, NY: Norton.

Feldman, D. B., Davidson, O. B., Ben-Naim, S., Maza, E., & Margalit, M. (2016). Hope as a mediator of loneliness and academic self-efficacy among students with and without learning disabilities during the transition to college. Learning Disabilities Research & Practice (Lawrence Erlbaum), 31(2), 63–74. doi:10.1111/ldrp.12094

Ferro, M. A., Gorter, J. W., & Boyle, M. H. (2015). Trajectories of depressive symptoms in Canadian emerging adults. American Journal of Public Health, 105(11), 2322–2327. doi:10.2105/AJPH.2015.302817

Fielder, R. L., & Carey, M. P. (2010). Predictors and consequences of sexual "hookups" among college students: A short-term prospective study. Archives of Sexual Behavior, 39(5), 1105. doi:10.1007/s10508-008-9448-4

Gibbons, M., Hughes, A., & Woodside, M. (2015). Exploring the influence of culture on career through the career-in-culture interview. Adulstpan Journal, 14(2), 77–89.Going, N. (2011). The way of Jesus: adolescent development as theological process. The Journal of Youth Ministry, 9(2), 49–66.

Greenleaf, A. T. (2014). Making the best of a bad situation: Career counseling young adults in the aftermath of the great recession. Journal of Employment Counseling, 51(4), 158–169. doi:10.1002/j.2161- 1920.2014.00049.x

Griffin, K. A., & Gilbert, C. K. (2015). Better transitions for troops: An application of Schlossberg's transition framework to analyses of barriers and institutional support structures for student veterans. Journal of Higher Education, 86(1), 71–97.

Grodsky, E., & Jackson, E. (2009). Social stratification in higher education. Teachers College Record, 111(10), 2347–2384.

Gross, W. (2005). The chronology of king David's life. Retrieved from http://livingstonesclass.org/Archive/ DavidChronologyGross.pdf

Gunnarsson, G. J., Ragnarsdóttir, H., Finnbogason, G., & Jónsdóttir, H. (2016). Young people's views on religions in a multicultural society. Theological Journal/Usuteaduslik Ajakiri, 69(1), 93–109.

Haigh, T., Russell, A. L., & Dutton, W. H. (2015). Histories of the internet: Introducing a special issue of info romation & culture, 50(2), 143.

Hellwig, J. (2015). Empty nest syndrome: How to cope when the kids leave home. Health Library: Evidence-BasedInformation.Retrievedfrom http://healthlibrary.epnet.com/GetContent.aspx? token=83f7f9e3- fb2d-41e8-b5cac08ef7b70677&chunkiid=13475

Holwerda, A., Brouwer, S., Boer, M., Groothoff, J., & Klink, J. (2015). Expectations from different perspectives on future work outcome of young adults with intellectual and developmental disabilities. Journal of Occupational Rehabilitation, 25(1), 96–104. doi:10.1007/s10926-014-9528-3

Houle, J. N. (2014). Disparities in debt: Parents' socioeconomic resources and young adult student loan debt. Sociology of Education, 87(1), 53–69. doi:10.1177/0038040713512213

Howden, L., & Meyer, J. (2011). Age and sex composition: 2010. Retrieved from http://www.census.gov/ prod/cen2010/briefs/c2010br-03.pdf

Inskip, Y. C. (2013). My journey in adult faith formation. Journal of adult theological education, 10(2), 162–173. doi:10.1179/1740714114Z.00000000021

Johnson, L., & Johnson, M. (2015, March). Stop talking work life balance!: TEQ and the millennial generation. Retrieved from http://www.ihrimpublications.com/WSR_Online_Archives /Meagan%20Johnson-WSR_ MAR2015web.pdf

Jones, R., Vaterlaus, M., Jackson, A., & Morrill, B. (2014). Friendship characteristics, psychosocial development, and adolescent identity formation. Personal Relationships, 21(1), 51–67. doi:10.1111/pere.1201

Kadlec, D., & Renzulli, K. A. (2014). Paying for your kids … forever? Money, 43(8), 60.

Kang, H., & Larson, R. W. (2014). Sense of indebtedness toward parents: Korean American emerging adults' narratives of parental sacrifice. Journal of Adolescent Research, 29(4), 561–581.

Katz, E. & DeRose, R. (2010). The ADA 20 years later: the 2010 survey of Americans with disabilities. New York, NY: American Paralegia Society. Retrieved from https://www.ncbi.nlm.nih.gov/pmc/articles/ PMC2964021/

Kim, B., Rhee, E., Ha, G., Joonyoung, Y., & Lee, S. (2016). Tolerance of uncertainty: Links to happenstance, career decision self efficacy, and career satsifaction. The Career and Development Quarterly, 64(2), 140–152.

Kimball, C. N., Cook, K. V., Boyatzis, C. J., & Leonard, K. C. (2013). Meaning making in emerging adults' faith narratives: Identity, attachment, and religious orientation. Journal of Psychology and Christianity, 32(3), 221–233.Retrievedfromhttp://0- search.proquest.com.library.regent.edu/ docview/1462485007?accountid=13479

Kins, E., De Mol, J., & Beyers, W. (2014). "Why should I leave?" Belgian emerging adults' departure from home. Journal of Adolescent Research, 29(1), 89–119. doi:10.1177/0743558413508201

Kins, E., Soenens, B., & Beyers, W. (2011). "Why do they have to grow up so fast?" Parental separation anxiety and emerging adults' pathology of separation-individuation. Journal of Clinical Psychology, 67(7), 647–664. doi:10.1002/jclp.20786

Knabb, J. J., & Grigorian-Routon, A. (2014). The role of experiential avoidance in the relationship between faith maturity, religious coping, and psychological adjustment among Christian university students. Mental Health, Religion & Culture, 17(5), 458–469. doi:10.1080/13674676.2013.846310

Konstram, V., Celen-Demirtas, S., Tomek, S., & Sweeney, K. (2015). Career adaptability and subjective well-being in umployed emerging adults: A promising and cautionary tale. Journal of Career Development, 42(6), 463–477. doi: 10.1177/0894845315575151

Kotler, Ph., Keller K. L. (2006) Marketing Management 12th ed. New Jersey: Pearson Ed.

Krumboltz, J. (2009). The Happenstance Learning Theory. Journal of Career Assessment, 17(2), 135–154.

Krumboltz, J. (2011). Capitalizing on happenstance. Journal of Employment Counseling, 48, 156–158. doi:10.1002/j.2161-1920.2011.tb01101.x

Leachman, M., & Mai, C. (2014). Most states funding schools less than before the recession. Center on Budget and Policy Priorities. Retrieved from http://www.cbpp.org/research/most-states-funding- schools-less-than-before-the-recession

Lehmann, I., & Konstam, V. (2011). Growing up perfect: Perfectionism, problematic internet use and career indecision in emerging adults. Journal of Counseling and Development, 89(2), 155–162.

Lekes, N. n., Houlfort, N., Milyavskaya, M., Hope, N. H., & Koestner, R. (2016). The role of intrinsic values for self-growth and community contribution at different life stages: Differentially predicting the vitality of university students and teachers over one year. Personality & Individual Differences, 98, 48–52. doi:10.1016/j.paid.2016.03.093

Leonard, N. H., & Harvey, M. (2008). Negative perfectionism: Examining negative excessive behavrios in the workplace. Journal of Applied Social Psychology, 38(3), 585–610. Retrieved from http://onlinelibrary.wiley.com/wol1/doi/10.1111/j.1559-1816.2007.00318.x/full

Lin, N. (2002). Social capital: A theory of social structure and action. Cambridge, UK: Cambridge University Press.

Lindstrom, L., Kahn, L. G., & Lindsey, H. (2013). Navigating the early career years: Barriers and strategies for young adults with disabilities. Journal of Vocational Rehabilitation, 39(1), 1–12. doi:10.3233/JVR- 130637

Lippert, A. M. (2016). Stuck in unhealthy places: how entering, exiting, and remaining in poor and nonpoor neighborhoods is associated with obesity during the transition to adulthood. The Journal of Health and Social Behavior, 57(1), 1–21. doi:10.1177/0022146515627682

Liu, J., Lester, B. M., Neyzi, N., Sheinkopf, S. J., Gracia, L., Kekatpure, M., & Kosofsky, B. E. (2013). Regional brain morphometry and impulsivity in adolescents following prenatal exposure to cocaine and tobacco. JAMA Pediatrics, 167(4), 348.

Maree, J. G., & Twigge, A. (2016, January). Career and self construction of emerging adults: The value of life designing. Frontiers in Psychology, 6(2041), 1–12.

McGee, R. E., & Thompson, N. J. (2015). Unemployment and depression among emerging adults in 12 states, behavioral risk factor surveillance system, 2010. Preventing Chronic Disease, 12, E38.

Mennella, H. A. (2016). Maslow's Hierarchy of Needs. CINAHL Nursing Guide.

Morsünbül, Ü. M. (2016). The relations between personal growth initiative and identity styles among youth. Online Journal of Counseling & Education, 5(3), 31–38.

Much, K., Wagener, A. M., Breitkreutz, H. L., & Hellenbrand, M. (2014). Working with the millennial generation: Challenges facing 21st-Century students from the perspective of university staff. Journal of College Counseling, 17(1), 37–47. doi:10.1002/j.2161-1882.2014.00046.x

Murphy, K., Blustien, D., Bohlig, A., & Platt, M. (2010). The college-to-career transition. An exploration of emerging adulthood. Journal of Counseling & Developmet, 88(2), 174–181.

Murray, S. (2010). Disabled face sharply higher jobless rate. Wall Street Journal. Retrieved from http://online.wsj.com/news/articles/SB10001424052748704540904575451751896763276

National Center for Education Statistics (NCES). (2016). Fast facts: Income of young adults. Retrieved from https://nces.ed.gov/fastfacts/display.asp?id=77

National Bureau of Economic Research (NBER). (2010). US business cycle expansions and contractions. Retrieved from https://nber.org/cycles/cyclesmain.html

Needs Theory of Negotiation. (2002). In D. Yarn (Ed.), Dictionary of conflict resolution, Wiley. Hoboken, NJ: Wiley. Retrieved from http://0-search.credoreference.com.library.regent.edu/ content/entry/wileyconfres/need_theory_ofnegotiation/0

Newman, L., Wagner, M., Cameto, R. & Knokey, A. M. (2009). The post-high school outcomes of youth with disabilities up to 4 years after high school. A report from the National Longitudinal Transition Study-2 (NLTS2) (NCSER 2009–3017). Menlo Park, CA: SRI International. Retrieved from www.nlts2.org/reports/2009_04/nlts2_report_2009_04_complete.pdf

Nichols, L., & Islas, . A. (2016). Pushing and pulling emerging adults through college: College generational status and the influence of parents and other in the first year. Journal of Adolescent Research, 32(2), 59–95.

North, R. J., Lewis, D. G., Capecelatro, M. R., Sherrill, B. N., Ravyts, S. G., & Fontan, G. (2016). The things they carry: Characterizing the biggest problems in the lives of emerging adults. Journal of Social & Clinical Psychology, 35(6), 437–454.

Orlofsky, J. L., Marcia, J. E., & Lesser, I. M. (1973). Ego identity status and the intimacy versus isolation crisis of young adulthood. Journal of Personality & Social Psychology, 27(2), 211–219.

O'Shea, A., & Meyer, R. H. (2016). A Qualitative investigation of the motivation of college students with nonvisible disabilities to utilize disability services. Journal of Postsecondary Education & Disability, 29(1), 5–23.

Ouyang, B., Jin, S., & Tien, H. S. (2016). Vocational identity formation of college students in Macau. Career Development Quarterly, 64(3), 244–258. doi:10.1002/cdq.12058

Papp, R. (2010). Virtual worlds and social networking: Reaching the millenials. Journal of Technology Research. Retrieved from http://www.aabri.com/manuscripts/10427.pdf

Paul, K., Geithner, E., & Moser, K. (2009). Latent deprivation amount people who are employed, unemployed or out of the labor force. Journal of Psychology, 143(5), 477–491.

Payment, M. (2008). Millenials: The emerging workforce. Career Planning and Adult Development Journal, 24(3), 23–32.

Piumattis, G., & Rabaglietti, E. (2015). Differnt types of emerging adult university students: The role or achievement strategies and personality for adulthood self-perception and life and education satisfaction. International Journal of Psycholgy and Psychological Therapy, 15(2), 241–257.

Popa, I. L., & Kordes, U. (2014). Looking into self-exploration attitudes and ways of constructing experience. Interdisciplinary Description of Complex Systems, 12(4), 314–322. doi:10.7906/indecs.12.4.5

Praskova, A., Creed, P., & Hood, M. (2015). The development and initial validation of a career calling scale for emerging adults. Journal of Career Assessment, 23(1), 91–106.

Prensky, M. (2001). Digital natives, digital immigrants. MCB University Press, 9(5), Retrieved from https://www.marcprensky.com/writing/Prensky%20-%20Digital%20Natives,%20Digital%20Immigrants%20-%20Part1.pdf

Queenan, J. (2010, May 15). A lament for the class of 2010. The Wall Street Journal. Retrieved from http://www.wsj.com/articles/SB10001424052748704250104575238692439240552

Rasminsky, S., & Chan, V. (2015). Managing the suicidal college student: Advice for community providers. Psychiatric Times, 32(11), 24F-24H.

Savickas, M. (2002). Career construction: A developmental theory of vocational behavior. In D. Brown and Associates (Eds.), Career choice and development 4th ed.(pp. 149–205). San Francisco, CA: Jossey Bass.

Savickas, M. (2005). The theory and practice of career construction. In S.D. Brown and R.W. Lent (Eds.), Career development and counseling: Putting theory and research to work (pp. 42–70). Hoboken, New Jersey: John Wiley & Sons, Inc.

Savickas, M. (2012). Life design: a paradigm for career intervention in the 21st century. Journal of Counseling & Development, 90(1), 13–19.

Schiffrin, H. H., Liss, M., Miles-McLean, H., Geary, K. A., Erchull, M. J., & Tashner, T. (2014). Helping hovering? The effects of helicopter parenting on college students' well-being. Journal of Child and Family Studies, 23(3), 548–557. doi:10.1007/s10826-013-9716-3

Schlossberg, N. K., Waters, E. B., & Goodman, J. (1995). Counseling adults in transition: Linking practice with theory, 2nd ed. New York, NY: Springer.

Schwartz, S. J. (2002). Convergent validity in objective measures of identity status: Implications for identity status theory. Adolescence, 37(147), 609–25. Retrieved from http://eres.regent.edu:2048/login?url=https://search-proquest- com.ezproxy.regent.edu/docview/195946859?accountid=13479

Semplonius, T., Good, M., & Willoughby, T. (2015). Religious and non-religious activity engagement as assets in promoting social ties throughout university: The role of emotion regulation. Journal of Youth & Adolescence, 44(8), 1592–1606. doi:10.1007/s10964-014-0200-1

Setran, D., & Kiesling, C. (2013). Spiritual formation in emerging adulthood: A practical theology for college and young adult ministry. Grand Rapids, MI: Baker Academic.

Shallcross, L. (2016). Validating the quarter-life crisis. Counseling Today, 58(11), 36–42.

Siennick, S. E. (2013). Still the favorite? Parents' differential treatment of siblings entering young adulthood. Journal of Marriage and Family, 75(4), 981–994. 10.1111/jomf.12048

Sirniö, O., Martikainen, P., & Kauppinen, T. M. (2016). Entering the highest and the lowest incomes: Intergenerational determinants and early-adulthood transitions. Research in Social Stratification & Mobility, 44, 77–90. doi:10.1016/j.rssm.2016.02.004

Slater, C. L. (2003). Generativity versus stagnation: An elaboration of Erikson's adult stage of human development. Journal of Adult Development, 10(1), 53–65.

Sneed, J. R., Whitbourne, S. K., & Culang, M. E. (2006). Trust, identity, and ego integrity: Modeling Erikson's core stages over 34 Years. Journal of Adult Development, 13 (3–4), 148–157. doi:10.1007/s10804-007-9026-3

Sniatecki, J. j., Perry, H. h., & Snell, L. l. (2015). Faculty attitudes and knowledge regarding college students with disabilities. Journal of Postsecondary Education & Disability, 28(3), 259–275.

Spear, L. P. (2000). Neurobehavioral Changes in Adolescence. Current Directions in Psychological Science, 9(4). 111–114.

Super, D. (1975). Career education and career guidance for the life span and for life roles. Journal of Career Education, 2(2), 27–42.

Super, D. (1980). A life-span, life-space approach to career development. Journal of Vocational Behavior, 16(3) 282–298. doi: 10.1006/nimg.1999.0436

Tatum, J. L., Fuqua, D. R., Foubert, J. J., & Ray, C. M. (2013). The relationship between first year college men's religious affiliation and their moral development. College Student Affairs Journal, 31(2), 101–110.

Taylor, A., Rappleyea, D., Fang, X., & Cannon, D. (2013). Emerging adults' perception of acceptable behaviors prior to forming a committed, dating relationship. Journal of Adult Development, 20(4), 173–184.

The Center For Generational Kinetics. (2016). Generational breakdown: Info about all of the generations. Retrieved from http://genhq.com/faq-info-about-generations/

Tsunokai, G., Kposowa, & Adams, M. (2009). Racial preferences in interne dating: A comparison of four birth cohorts. The Western Journal of Black Studies, 33(1), 2009.

Talbot, A. L. (2015). Emerging adult financial capability (Order No. 3739715). Available from ProQuest Dissertations & ThesesGlobal. (1749781180). Retrieved from http://eres.regent.edu:2048/login?url=https://search-proquest- com.ezproxy.regent.edu/docview/1749781180?accountid=13479

Twenge, J., Sherman, R., & Wells, B. (2016). Sexual Inactivity During Young Adulthood is more common among U.S. millennials and iGen: Age, period, and cohort effects on having no sexual partners after age 18. Archives of Sexual Behavior, 1–8.U.S. Census Bureau. (n.d.). U.S. Census Bureau, American Community Survey, 2009–2013 and decennial census 1980, 1990, 2000. Retrieved from https://www.census.gov/content/dam/Census/newsroom/cspan/2015/20150130_cspan_youngadu lts.pdf

U.S. Department of Health and Human Services, Office of Adolescent Health. (2018). Adolescent health: Think, act, grow playbook, Washington, D.C.: U.S. Government Printing Office. Retrieved from https://www.hhs.gov/ash/oah/sites/default/files/tag-playbook-2018.pdf

van der Walt, F., & de Klerk, J. J. (2014). Workplace spirituality and job satisfaction. International Review of Psychiatry, 26(3), 379–389.

Vedder, R., Denhart, C., & Robe, J. (2013). Why are recent college graduates underemployed? University enrollments and labor-market realities. Center for College Affordability and Productivity.Retrieved from http://centerforcollegeaffordability.org/uploads/Underemployed%20Report%202.pdf

Verbruggen, M., Dries, N., & Van Laer, K. (2016). Challenging the uniformity myth in career counseling outcome studies: Examining the role of clients initial career counseling goals. Journal of Career Assessment, doi:10.1177/1069072716657797

Waits, N. M., & Pruitt, B. (2009). Hooking up: College students and no-rules relationships: A review of: "Hooking up: Sex, dating, and relationships on campus, by Kathleen Bogle.": New York: New York University Press, 2008, 223 pages, hardcover, $17.75. Journal of Sex Research, 46(4), 376–377. doi:10.1080/00224490902979411

Waldron, V. R., Kloeber, D., Goman, C., Piemonte, N., & Danaher, J. (2014). How parents communicate right and wrong: A study of memorable moral messages recalled by emerging adults. Journal of Family Communication, 14(4), 374–397. doi:10.1080/15267431.2014.946032

Weiland, S. (1993). Erik Erikson: Ages, stages, and stories. Generations, 17(2), 17.

Wiedmer, T. (2015). Generations do differ: Best practices in leading traditionalists, boomers, and generations X, Y, and Z. Delta Kappa Gamma Bulletin, 82(1), 51.

Winter, K. (2014). Understanding and supporting young children's transitions into state care: Schlossberg's transition framework and child-centred practice. British Journal of Social Work, 44(2), 401–417. doi: 10.1093/bjsw/bcs128

Workman, J. (2015). Parental influence on exploratory students' college choice, major and career decision making. College Student Journal, 49(1), 23–30. Retrieved from http://digitalcommons.brockport.edu/cgi/viewcontent.cgi?article=1087&context=edc_the

Yonker, J. E., Schnabelrauch, C. A., & DeHaan, L. G. (2012). The relationship between spirituality and religiosity on psychological outcomes in adolescents and emerging adults: A meta-analytic review. Journal of Adolescence, 35(2), 299–314. doi: 10.1016/j.adolescence.2011.08.010

Zhao, X., Selman, R. L., & Haste, H. (2015). Academic stress in Chinese schools and a proposed preventive intervention program. Cogent Education, 2(1).doi:10.1080/2331186X.2014.1000477

10

Job Loss and Transitions

Kiesha Ford, MA, LPC and Dixie Meyer, PhD, LPC

Remember that I have commanded you to be determined and confident! Do not be afraid or discouraged, for I, the Lord your God, am with you wherever you go.

Joshua 1.9, Good News Translation with Apocrypha

LEARNING OBJECTIVES

In this chapter, students will learn about

- The difference between types and categories of transitions
- Major theories used to analyze transitions
- Various ways people cope with transitions
- The stages of transition

LEARNING OUTCOMES

At the end of this chapter, students will be able to

- Recognize how to deconstruct the type and category of transition a person in a career change is experiencing
- Demonstrate the ability to apply Schlossberg's theory of transition to a client in a career transition
- Implement Super's theory of career development when working with a client in a career transition
- Identify what stage of transition a client in a career transition is facing

CHAPTER HIGHLIGHTS

- Categories of transitions
- Types of transitions
- Schlossberg's transition theory
- Super's career development theory
- Hopson and Adams's model of adult transitions

ADULT CAREER CRISES AND TRANSITIONS

John is a thirty-five-year-old factory worker from a suburban area near a large Midwestern city. He was hired at the factory after he graduated high school. He is married with two children and his wife is a homemaker. After working at the factory for seventeen years, John was called into the office and informed that the company would be giving layoffs to workers within the next few weeks due to reduction in company profits. John had expected to remain at his company until he retired. His employer informed him that he would be given severance pay and the opportunity for some tuition assistance if he chooses to return to school. John is angry his employer did not notify him sooner about the layoffs and is concerned he will not be able to provide for his family. He had previously considered returning to school for more training, but he never pursued the opportunity due to his work schedule. John has conflicting thoughts about his next steps and his future career decisions.

As a part of life, sometimes there are unexpected events that signal a life transition (e.g., loss of job, divorce). John expected to keep the same job until retirement. Job loss is usually cited as a negative life event, but there are times when job loss might signal an opportunity for positive change (Hartley, 1980; Little, 1976). John was frightened about how being without a job would negatively affect his family. People who perceive career transitions as an opportunity for new direction or new possibilities protect themselves from negative psychological effects (Eby & Bush, 1995). As John assumed he would go back to school, this transition could provide the opportunity to further his education to help him view this transition as the impetus needed to have his career move in a new positive direction.

TYPES OF TRANSITION

Scholars have defined transitions. Schlossberg (2011) defined transition as an event or a nonevent that results in a change of relationships, assumptions, routines, and roles. These identified changes majorly disrupt lives. John's relationship with his wife and family may change. Will his family see him as able to provide for the family? Will the family routine of John going off to work and his wife maintaining the home and caring for their children remain unchanged? Will John's wife need to pursue a job, with John needing to provide more familial and at-home support for his family?

For an experience to be classified as transitional, there should be personal awareness of discontinuity in one's life and a requirement for change in behavioral responses because the situations are new and novel (Adams, Hayes, & Hopson, 1976). In a transition, new behaviors are required to adjust, adding to the disruptions in lifestyle. How discontinuity in one's life is experienced may be perceived differently dependent on culture and how people personally internalize the event (Schlossberg, 2011). For example, Native Americans are more likely than people from other cultures to view change as continuous (Meyer & Cottone, 2013). Therefore, people from this culture may expect transition and thus more easily accept the transition.

Most transition frameworks convey that life events (or nonevents) are experienced as an enduring phenomenon with challenges (Evans, Forney, Guido, Patton, & Renn, 2010; Merriam & Caffarella, 1999). Transitions such as changing a job, being promoted within a company, returning after maternity leave, or taking early retirement seem to have very little in common. John's expectation to stay at his place of employment until retirement may suggest that until retirement and beyond, he may reflect on how his life did not turn out the way he expected. Each person must attach their own meaning to a transition. Often, meaning is understood by the type, context, and impact the transition has on the person. The context refers to the person's relationship with the transition and the setting in which the transition takes place. The impact can be determined by the amount of change required in one's daily life by the transition (Schlossberg, 2011). For John, his job loss was personal and required a large adjustment in daily functioning. John may be directed by Christian counselors and other professionals (ministers, pastors) to examine James 2:14–17 Bible verse regarding faith and deed. James 2:14–17 emphasizes the importance of putting faith to work. Faith should be worked out in everyday struggles and opportunities of life; faith itself prepares a person for salvation.

CATEGORIES OF CAREER TRANSITIONS

 Schlossberg (2009) described three career events that cause strain on a person's perception of how they define themselves in different life roles (son or daughter, husband or wife, coworker or friend): normative role transitions, nonnormative career events, and persistent occupational problems. Each type of career event is managed differently. How a person and their family cope with the transition is dependent on type. Certain types may produce more mental health challenges than others.

Normative Role Transitions

Normative transitions tend to be anticipated and voluntary. Examples of these transitions include entering or reentering a labor pool after maternity leave, starting your first full-time job, and moving from one organization to another. Louis (1980) acknowledged five normative transitions: entering or reentering the workforce, changing jobs within an organization, changing organizations, changing careers, and leaving the workforce. Normative transitions become crises when an event is not anticipated. An example could be a person ignoring pending retirement and then being shocked by the change of role due to retirement. For instance, Rick is a sixty-year-old supervisor who was planning to retire from his job in four years. His retirement would be considered a normative transition because he anticipated and planned for the transition. However, Rick was notified by his employer that his position was being eliminated within the next couple of months. Rick's normative transition (a planned retirement) has become a crisis situation because he must make the decision to either retire early or change to another job.

Nonnormative Career Events

Nonnormative career events are more likely to become crises than normative transitions because they are unexpected and involuntary (e.g., loss of a job or a demotion). For example, Alexandria, a counselor with a community college, was informed that the college was transitioning from counselors to advisors. Alexandria was told that if she wanted to keep her position, she would need to apply for an advisor role. The advisor position was for less pay and required more work hours per week. Alexandria was not expecting a change in her position and she would have not voluntarily applied for an advisor position at a college. She was trained as a counselor and she expected to retire from the college as a counselor. The college also has a policy that does not guarantee her the advisor position. She is now dealing with feelings of anxiety and anger. Her anxiety stems from the college policy and she is angry that her supervisor did not warn her about the pending changes.

Persistent Occupational Problems

All employees can expect challenges at work. Most work challenges ebb and flow. The level of difficulty experienced by the employee will change depending upon the intensity of the problem and how long the problem lasts. Persistent occupational problems create prolonged career problems. Persistent problems produce a cumulative effect that may lead to a transition crisis (Schlossberg, 2009). For example, Tracy, an administrative assistant, has been working with her company for several years. Her supervisor hired a new community coordinator for the department. The new community coordinator began assigning Tracy tasks not included in her job description. The additional assignments created what felt like a hostile environment for Tracy. Tracy did not report her grievances about the new employee to her supervisor because she did not want to be seen as a "problem" in her department. Tracy has been experiencing physical issues (e.g., headaches, shoulder pain) for the last several months. Her physician could not find a physical cause for her headaches and shoulder pain. Tracy was told to reduce her stress levels to possibly experience some symptom relief. Her physical issues have caused her to be tardy for or absent from work. The persistent issues at work have caused her to reevaluate her position within the company. Her supervisors have given her a warning about her tardiness and absences. Tracy is concerned she will need to find another job.

Overall, the type of career event (normative role transition, nonnormative career events, and persistent occupational problems) that facilitates a career transition can evoke a crisis situation for a person if the career transition impacts how the person defines themselves in life roles such as a wife or husband and son or daughter. In addition to life roles, the expectancy of the career transition may cause a person to reevaluate how they perceive their role within the workforce.

TYPES OF TRANSITIONS

Merriam (2005) identified four types of life transitions: anticipated, unanticipated, nonevents, and sleeper events. Each type of transition does not have to be related to a career transition. Yet, transitions at work or in one's career impact one's life with the possibility of a ripple effect in family life.

Anticipated Transitions

Anticipated transitions occur predictably or in the lifespan of most people (e.g., graduating high school, leaving home, marriage, having children, or starting a first job). However, in some countries such as Germany, Austria, and other German-speaking countries, anticipated transitions occur at a different rate or transitions leading to adulthood are fostered by the government or culture of the society. In Germany, for example, the transition into adulthood is shaped by early decisions regarding future educational goals. Children are evaluated by test scores and interested in determining their course of education after secondary school. Some students will be prepared for university while others may be directed toward vocational interests leading to apprenticeships. Nevertheless, regardless of the country, anticipated transitions will occur as adulthood is achieved and people accomplish goals within their lifespan (Cook & Furstenberg, 2002).

Anticipated transitions are expected events. For example, the process of obtaining your first job usually occurs in early adulthood. For many, it is a rite of passage from childhood to adulthood (Merriam, 2005). People can make their own money and can make decisions about how to spend their money. The emotions experienced from anticipated transitions can range from excitement to fear. The person can be excited for the prospect of gaining income and work experience but fear the responsibility of adulthood.

Unanticipated Transitions

Unanticipated transitions are not predictable or scheduled (e.g., a divorce, sudden death, or major surgery). These events blindside the person and are outside the person's control. The person has no choice in transition. The lack of ability to prepare for an unanticipated event often leads to emotional distress. Unanticipated transitions may lead to psychological concerns like depression, anxiety, or insomnia (Pearlin, Schieman, Fazio, & Meersman, 2005). In our earlier example, John was laid off from his factory job after being with the company for seventeen years. He did not expect to consider a job or career change. He had no idea he would need to redefine his role in the workforce. Emotionally, he was experiencing anger and fear about this new transition in his life. His family experienced similar emotional concerns.

Nonevent Transitions

Nonevent transitions are expected but do not occur (e.g., a promotion that never happens, not being able to afford to retire). Like the unanticipated events, the nonevents are also outside the person's control. People similarly experience emotional distress like depression or anxiety, but now the effect is a profound disappointment or loss of what they thought would be. In nonevents, the anticipated transition never happens. There are four types of nonevents: personal nonevents that are related to a person's aspirations, ripple nonevents that are experienced due to a nonevent of someone else, resultant nonevents that are caused by an event that did occur, and delayed nonevents that are anticipated events that might still happen (Schlossberg, 1984). Again, let's examine John and how he expected to stay with his company until retirement. The nonevent is a resultant event because John was laid off due to the company's lack of financial stability. Yet, it is also a personal nonevent because John had aspired to retire from his company.

Sleeper Events

Sleeper events are events that happen gradually and are outside the person's awareness. Sleeper events can be both positive and negative. To parents, it may seem like overnight that their children became adults, but in actuality the transition was constantly happening. Parents see their infants roll over and before the parents recognize the transition, their now toddler is running. When couples divorce, most couples rarely notice the transition from rarely fighting to fighting everyday. Sleeper events also happen at work. For example, when Selma began her job as an architect, she felt incompetent and was confused about how to approach design models with clients. Selma thought she would never become the lead architect on a major building project. The years passed and she is now the vice president of her company. Now, it is hard for her to remember a time before she felt confident in her ability to design any project.

MODELS OF TRANSITIONS AND CRISES

There are multiple models of career transitions. Schlossberg, Super, and Adams and Hopson have developed comprehensive theories to describe and examine a career transition. Schlossberg notes the systemic influences on career transitions and the coping mechanisms people use during a career transition. Super notes the importance of career across the lifespan and how career impacts self-concept. Adams and Hopson are concerned about the stages people pass through as they heal from a transition.

Schlossberg's Transition Theory

Schlossberg's transition theory (Schlossberg, 1984) is a psychosocial theory examining the impact of life events in the context of personal lives and societal expectations. Like Merriam (2005), Schlossberg acknowledges how the type of transition, whether it is anticipated, unanticipated, or a nonevent, affects the person. Schlossberg believes it is not the transition but rather the perception of the event that informs the psychological impact. Schlossberg further noted that to understand the meaning of a transition, one must understand the type, context, and impact of the transition. The context of the transition examines one's relationship with the transition and the setting where the transition occurs. The impact of the transition specifically assesses the personal effect and alterations in daily life.

There are two basic phases of transition in Schlossberg's model: ① processing the transition and decreasing the stress associated with the transition and ② deconstructing the details of the transition to recreate a new normal (Schlossberg, 2011). At the beginning of the transition, people are faced with major transitions in the workplace (loss of job) and may suffer from depression, reduced self-esteem, and anxiety. The mental health concerns associated with this phase are often related to the misunderstanding of how the transition process will occur. Essentially, the person needs to endure until the transition becomes manageable. Nonetheless, this cannot happen until this person's stress levels decrease. Once people develop effective coping skills, they can move on to establishing their new life. Transitions often mean that life will not go back to how it was before. But with a career counselor, social support, or help from loved ones, people can begin to decide how to best get past the transition and create happiness in life. In the basic phases of Schlossberg's model, John first needed to reduce the stress related to being laid off. John will have to navigate through his initial feelings of stress and anger to develop possible solutions, which may include seeking new employment or returning to school. Some of his concerns are related to lack of income, having to find new employment, and telling his wife about being laid off. But many of the same issues causing his stress may help alleviate it. Together with his wife and children, they can all be a source of support for one another during the phase of transition.

Coping with Transitions

Schlossberg (2011) identified features of the coping process common to all transition events. The components that contribute to coping include examining the situation, self, social support, and strategies related to dealing with stress (Chickering & Schlossberg, 1995). The situation describes the factors at the time of the transition. Concerns affect how troubled one is about, or how easily one will process, the transition. Examples of concerns include the impetus of the event; the timing, whether consistent with one's life or not; what the person's perceived control over the situation is; how one's roles might change as a result of the transition; how long the transition will last; and what previous and current stressors contribute to the transition. If a person is coping with job loss and a significant other is struggling with an illness, coping with a significant other's illness can make the process much more difficult. Self factors examine the person's inner strength when coping with a stressful situation. Personal external factors like income, resources, and age may contribute to increasing or reducing the stress produced from the transition. Personal, internal factors like the psychological health of the person also change how a person processes stress.

The social support a person has at the time of transition is critical for a sense of well-being. Romantic partners, family, friends, and community can each provide support for the person throughout the transition. Most people expect romantic partners, family, and friends to be there for them, but others outside this network may supply a unique type of support to validate the person facing the transition. For example, if a person's position within a company is redefined and they are demoted to a lower-paid position, the support obtained from supervisors, coworkers, or other professionals can lessen the stressful situation within the work environment. Strategies are used to cope with the stress of the transition. Here people identify what strategies are helpful to them. Strategies help alleviate personal stress levels, create meaning out of the transition, or alter the situation to make it more manageable.

Super's Theory of Career Development

It might be beneficial to analyze career transitions based on the stage of career development. People may more easily process the transition if is it consistent with the career stage; conversely, they may struggle more during the transition when it is not anticipated at that career stage. Two essential components of Super's (1980) theory of career development particularly salient to career transition include the stages of career development and self-concept. An extensive review of Super's theory of career development is outside of the scope of this chapter. For more information on Super's theory, please see Chapter 7.

Each career stage has different developmental tasks to present challenges. The five stages—exploration, growth, establishment, maintenance, and decline—are sequential, build on each other, and add unique contributions to career development (Super, 1980). The growth stage is where people begin to think about future careers; there is limited application to this stage and transitions. In the exploratory stage, people are entering the workforce. Acquiring a first job and multiple jobs during this stage are normative. In the establishment stage, people are solidifying their career decisions. People establishing their career are settling into and advancing their careers. The maintenance phase is one the longest stages. Here people will continue to advance their careers and may hit a plateau. The final stage, disengagement, encompasses a limited number of years prior to retirement. In this stage, people search for meaning outside of career.

At each stage of career development, a person's self-concept expands. Self-concept is interwoven into the stages and develops across the lifespan. Self-concept refers to how people view themselves and their situations (Super, 1980). Self-concept is how one images oneself in the roles, relationships, functions, and positions. Views of oneself are derived from needs, intelligence, aptitudes, values, and interests. How one views oneself changes how one will approach career choices. As the self-concept becomes more solidified, so do career choices. Career transitions cause people to drastically question their identity.

In the case study of John, while he was in the growth phase he began to think of himself as someone who would enjoy factory work. He understood that this career would enable him to have the type of life he desired. He was hired at the factory early in the exploratory phase of career development. When John was newly in the establishment phase, he considered furthering his education but was comfortable in his work. The news of his layoff came after his identify and self-concept were already firmly established as a factory worker. Now, this transition would strongly challenge that view of himself. John questioned who he would be if he was not the primary breadwinner for his family. He had already invested many years in his career and was not ready to begin the disengagement process with this company.

Hopson and Adams's Model of Adult Transitions

Hopson and Adams (1977) developed a model of the process people experience during a transition. The model of adult transitions states that adult transitions occur in a cycle of seven phases: immobilization, minimization, self-doubt, letting go, testing out, meaning, and internalization (Adams et al., 1976). The model is consistently applied regardless if the transition is positive or negative. The transitions may be a predicted change in routine (e.g., marriage) or an unexpected change that is forced on someone due to life circumstances (e.g., being laid off). These transitions may vary in intensity depending on the person and the situation.

Immobilization

Immobilization is feeling overwhelmed, shocked, and unable to act or make plans about the future. The person may feel frozen under the stress. Hopson and Adams (1977) described this first phase as a person feeling unable to comprehend and make decisions about the next phase of transitioning to a new life. The intensity and duration of this phase depends on the novelty of the situation and how the person views the situation. For one, there is interest to know whether the person has any expectations. In the example of John, in the beginning phase of this transition (redefining employment), he felt overwhelmed due to the unfamiliarity and negative expectation of the next transition with employment.

Minimization

Minimizing occurs when the person denies the change is going to occur or states that the change does not matter. The denial that the person experiences may be necessary in order to manage a troubling situation. Krantzler (1973) stated denial is a coping mechanism that provides time to temporarily retreat from reality while our biological and cognitive forces regroup and regain the strength to comprehend the new life or loss forced upon us. The same example of John being laid off could be characterized in this phase as John minimizing the situation by stating that he was going to leave the job anyway later in life. The denial component becomes a way to cope with possible stressors of locating new employment or redefining self without employment.

Self Doubt

Self-doubt occurs when people no longer trust their own abilities. They may fear that they cannot provide for their family or ever hold down another job. Self-doubt may turn into depression, anger, anxiety, or all three. The mental health concerns may be related to the current situation or fear about the future. For John, he felt angry about his situation. Part of that anger was related to his lack of trust in himself. Once the last day of employment comes for John, he will realize the reality of dealing with less or no income. This will most likely lead to an even stronger emotional response.

Letting Go

Letting go occurs once the person lets go of the anger, anguish, and frustrations about the transition. When people let go, they begin to accept the current and future situation. The person can become more optimistic about their future. They are able to successful consider the next phase in the transition. This may lead to examining the next opportunity (e.g., going to school, locating a better-paying job). When John is able to let go of his anger, he might realize he does want to return to school. He may be able to let go of his plans to return from the factory and consider other fields that are appealing to him.

Testing Out

Test(ing) out allows the person to test out new behaviors, new life styles, and new ways of coping with the transition. People in this phase may have a burst of energy to recreate their self-identity and may give advice to others who face the same challenges transitioning to a new situation. When John is laid off, as a newly unemployed person he may begin going on job interviews or may speak with a school advisor about how to register for college courses. John may also want to see a career counselor to guide him through this transition. After testing out new behaviors, as John now has a new situation, he may struggle to make meaning out of the transition.

Searching for Meaning

Meaning provides understanding of how things are different and why changes occurred. Many people have to find a purpose for a negative event or the trauma from the event may remain unbearable. The understanding of change in one's life begins the process of the person understanding their feelings about the change. Searching for meaning also helps to process the challenge to their status quo. This stage could be characterized as the person understanding their emotions, thoughts, and activities around the transition and what the changes mean for the next phase of life. When John is able to go a new direction in his life—possibly going to school or finding another position—he may realize his life is much better in the new situation compared to his previous situation. John may see the purpose of the lay-off was to force him to a new life that is much better for him, his family, and their future.

Internalization

Internalizing is the final stage of the transition. Internalizing allows a deeper understanding of the transition. The person has processed the transition and emerged on the other side with new coping mechanisms and cognitive growth. What is important is the person will incorporate new behaviors learned throughout the transitional process. After John processed the transition, he felt better about his life situation. He was now happy with his life. What he appreciated about life changed. His values changed. John quit placing all of his energy on work and began to spend more time with his family. John realized that his work did not provide stability in his life, but his family did.

Change Curve

To further process the change that is experienced when moving through the seven stages, Adams et al. (1976) developed a change curve encompassing the emotional turmoil experienced during transition (see Figure 10.1). On the curve, one can see how the cognitive process fluctuates across time. As time passes, the person becomes more confident and self-esteem may increase. The change curve culminates with integration of all of the thoughts, feelings, and behaviors encapsulating the transition.

FIGURE 10.1 Personal change impacts self-esteem and time. *Source*: John Adams, John Hayes, and Barrie Hopson, from Understanding and Managing Personal Change. Rowman & Littlefield Publishing Group, 1976.

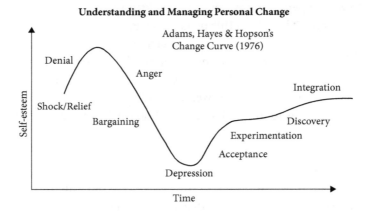

CONCLUSION

Transitions can be described as a discontinuation of a current path or behavior. Transitions may be either anticipated, unanticipated, nonevents, or sleeper events. People experiencing transitions may report life adjustments ranging from changes in roles, relationships, routines, and assumptions. A career transition for a person can cause anxiety, anger, and uncertainty about how to proceed with life goals. Hopson and Adams' model of transition, Super's theory of career development, and Schlossberg's theory of transition are frameworks that capture the process of change that can occur when a career crisis (transition) happens in adulthood. Schlossberg's theory of transition suggests that how people cope with the transition depends on the situation, self (internal and external resources), social support, and what strategies are employed to manage the transition. Super's theory of career development examines transitions based on stage of career development and self-concept. More challenges may be present for the person in transition depending on the stage of career development. Hopson and Adam's model of adult transition identifies seven phases a person travels through to accept the transition.

KEY TERMS

Categories of career transitions: there are three categories of career transitions: normative, nonnormative, and persistent occupational problems

Change curve: developed by Adams, Hayes, and Hopson to examine how time influences changes in self-esteem across the seven stages of transition and the emotional turmoil experiences across those stages

Model of adult transitions: developed Hopson and Adams, this model examines the process people experience during a transition across seven phases: immobilization, minimization, self-doubt, letting go, testing out, meaning, and internalization

Theory of career development: developed by Super to examine to the stages people face across their career development and how career influences life roles, self-concept, and developmental tasks

Theory of transition: developed by Schlossberg, this model examines the systemic influences on career transitions including how situation, self factors, social support, and strategies employed affect how well people cope with a transition

Transition: a discontinuation of a life path from an event or nonevent that results in a change of relationships, assumptions, routines, and roles

Types of life transitions: there are four types of life transitions: anticipated events, nonanticipated events, nonevents, and sleeper events.

REFLECTION AND DISCUSSION

1. How are the categories of transitions different from the types of career transitions?
2. Compare and contrast Schlossberg's and Hopson and Adam's models of transition.
3. How does one stage of career development affect how one copes with a transition?
4. According to Schlossberg, how well someone copes with a transition depends on what?
5. What are the seven phases identified in Hopson and Adam's model?

ADDITIONAL READINGS, RESOURCES, AND WEBSITES

Texts

Anderson, M., Goodman, J., & Schlossberg, N. (2012). Counseling adults in transition: Linking Schlossberg's theory with practice in a diverse world (4th ed.). New York, NY: Springer Publishing.

Chen. C. (2006). Career endeavor pursuing a cross-cultural life transition. New York, NY: Routledge.

Instruments

Instruments may be necessary to identify how one is coping with the transitions. Here is a list of well-known and respected instruments to be used in career counseling:

1. The **Career Transition Inventory** assesses how well people have made their career transitions. The instruments tests across five subscales: readiness, confidence, control, perceived support, and decision independence.

2. The **Career Decision Scale** estimates career indecision, career antecedents, and outcome measures to determine the effects of relevant interventions.

3. The **Career Decision Diagnostic Assessment (Life/Goal Awareness Subscales)** is a measurement of the psychological blocks to career decision-making.

4. The **Career Decision-Making Self-Efficacy Scale** measures a person's degree of belief that he or she can successfully complete tasks necessary to make career decisions.

5. The **Career Commitment Measure (Career Resilience and Career Identity Subscales)** detects differences in career commitment levels associated with varying levels of professionalism across occupational groups.

TRADITIONAL ACTIVITY

Case Study

Rosa is a 36-year-old, single Latina female. She has always taken pride in her work. She was laid off from her job as a human resource manager three months ago. She has been looking for work in human resources without success. Her severance pay has almost run out. She is drawing unemployment. She has sought unemployment counseling but reports that the case manager is not helpful and is forcing positions on her for which she is overqualified. She comes to counseling severely depressed and has difficulty meeting the unemployment agency's requirement of applying for the designated number of jobs.

1. What goals should you focus on in counseling Rosa?
2. How would you help guide Rosa in finding a position?

SPIRITUAL ACTIVITY

What is your calling?

Samuel heard God calling him in the night. But Samuel did not recognize God's voice. Samuel thought Eli was calling him. The third time Samuel heard the calling, Eli told Samuel it was God calling him. Have you heard God calling you? When do you recognize and not recognize God's voice?

1. How can you tell the difference between what you want to do in life for your gain and what you want to do in life for God's gain?
2. How can your career choice include God?

REFERENCES

Adams, J. D., Hayes, J., & Hopson, B. (1976). Transition: Understanding & managing personal change. London, UK: Martin Robertson.

Chickering, A. W., & Schlossberg, N. K. (1995). Getting the most out of college. Needham Heights, MA: Allyn and Bacon.

Cook, T. D., & Furstenberg Jr, F. F. (2002). Explaining aspects of the transition to adulthood in Italy, Sweden, Germany, and the United States: A cross-disciplinary, case synthesis approach. The Annals of the American Academy of Political and Social Science, 580(1), 257–287.

Eby, L. T., & Buch, K. (1995). Job loss as career growth: Responses to involuntary career transitions. The Career Development Quarterly, 44(1), 26–42.

Evans, N. J., Forney, D. S., Guido, F. M., Patton, L. D., & Renn, K. A. (2010). Student development in college: Theory, research, and practice (2nd ed.). San Francisco, CA: Jossey- Bass.

Hartley, J. F. (1980). The Impact of Unemployment upon the Self-esteem of Managers. Journal of Occupational Psychology, 53(2), 147–155.

Hopson B. (1981) Transition: Understanding and managing personal change. In Psychology and Medicine. Psychology for Professional Groups (pp. 187–213). London, UK: Palgrave.

Hopson & Adams. (1977). Toward an understanding of transition. In J. Adams and B. Hopson, eds., Transition: Understanding and managing personal change Montclair, NJ: Allenhald and Osmund.

Krantzler, M. (1973). Creative divorce: A new opportunity for personal growth. New York: M. Evans; [distributed by Lippincott, Philadelphia.

Little, C. B. (1976). Technical-professional unemployment: Middle-class adaptability to personal crisis. The Sociological Quarterly, 17(2), 262–274.

Louis, M. (1980). Career transitions: Varieties and commonalities. Academy of Management Review, 5, 329–340.

Merriam, S. B., & Caffarella, R. S. (1999). Learning in adulthood (2nd ed.). San Francisco, CA: Jossey-Bass.

Merriam, S. B. (2005). New adult life transitions foster learning and development. New Directions for Adult and Continuing Education, 108, 3–13.

Meyer, D., & Cottone. R. (2013). Solution-focused therapy as a culturally acknowledging approach with American Indians. Journal of Multicultural Counseling and Development, 41(1), 47–55. doi: 10.1002/j.2161-1912.2013.00026.x

Pearlin, L. I., Schieman, S., Fazio, E. M., & Meersman, S. C. (2005). Stress, health, and the life course: Some conceptual perspectives. Journal of Health and Social Behavior, 46(2), 205–219.

Schlossberg, N. K. (2011). The challenge of change: The transition model and its applications. Journal of Employment Counseling, 48(4), 159–162.

Schlossberg, N. K. (2009). Revitalizing retirement: Reshaping your identity, relationships, and purpose. Washington, DC: American Psychological Association.

Schlossberg, N.K. (1984). Counseling adults in transition: Linking practice with theory. New York, NY: Springer Publishing Company.

Super, D. (1980). A life-span, life-space approach to career development. Journal of Vocational Behavior, 16, 282–298.

Credit

Figure 10.1: Source: John Adams, John Hayes, and Barrie Hopson, from Understanding and Managing Personal Change. Rowman & Littlefield Publishing Group, 1976.

SECTION IV

Counseling Multicultural and Distinctive Populations

The Purpose of Multiculturalism and Social Justice in Holistic Career Development

S. Kent Butler, PhD, Nevin J. Heard, MA, and Michelle D. Mitchell, MS.Ed, LPC

Commit your work to the Lord, and your plans will be established.

Proverbs 16:3, New International Version

LEARNING OBJECTIVES

In this chapter, students will learn about

- How social justice and career development is connected
- The relationship between multicultural and career development
- A new model for viewing multiculturalism in regards to career counseling
- How to discern social justice issues' impact on career development
- How to integrate multicultural and social justice issues
- Applying interventions that are aligned with researched methods of mental health and social justice
- Creating advocacy plans and how to implement them accurately

LEARNING OUTCOMES

At the end of this chapter, students will be able to

- Identify key terms and definitions related to multicultural counseling
- Recognize and demonstrate the basic tenets of the multicultural social justice competencies
- Identify ways of integrating multicultural perspectives and career theory
- Recognize cultural elements involved in career decision-making

CHAPTER HIGHLIGHTS

- Social justice issues and career development
- Interweaving multicultural and social justice into career counseling
- Multiculturalism model
- Practical application of social cognitive career theory with multiculturalism

The tapestry of the United States is becoming increasingly more diverse, which has in some ways negatively impacted cultural isolation and insulation within present day society (Hirschman & Panther-Yates, 2008). As we interact with diverse clients from unique and differing cultural backgrounds than our own, it is imperative that we remain sensitive to their needs. To this end, it becomes even more vital when there are institutionalized barriers present when we assist our clients through important life-changing career decisions. For this reason, evidenced-based counseling practices that counselors implement with clients take on even greater importance as it relates to their past or present-day experiences.

SOCIAL JUSTICE ISSUES THAT COMPOUND CAREER DEVELOPMENT

The purposes of a person's heart are deep waters,
but one who has insight draws them out.

Proverbs 20:5, NIV

The National Economic and Social Rights Initiative proposes effects due to an absence of appropriate career planning for those who have been disregarded in diverse communities:

> While human rights movements have global visions, most are locally anchored and emerge out of concrete abuses and struggles of communities that are poor or otherwise marginalized. What these movements have in common is their belief in a universal vision of justice and understanding that their struggles are bound up in other human rights struggles around the world. (National Economic and Social Rights Initiative, 2011)

Fouad, Gerstein, and Toporek (2006) proffer that power, opportunity, and suppression have a detrimental impact on client lives and have called to action counselors who mightily embrace a social justice worldview to help change the narrative. Social justice activists must employ social advocacy and commitment to help eliminate inequitable social, political, and economic circumstances that impede the scholastic, vocation, and personal-social development of diverse populations. This aligns with the American Counseling Association's (ACA) ethical code: "When appropriate counselors advocate at the individual, group, institutional, and societal levels to examine potential barriers and obstacles that inhibit access and/or the growth and development of clients" (American Counseling Association, 2005, p. 5).

As culturally responsive helping professionals, we need to remain cognizant of the fact that mental health is adversely affected by oppressive behaviors (Jacobs, 1994).

Lent, Brown, and Hackett's 1987 social cognitive career theory (SCCT) (Savickas & Lent, 1994) is a derivative of Bandura's social cognitive theory. SCCT provides openings for dialogue on culture, sex roles, inherited wealth, social environments, and unanticipated life conditions that may amalgamate and supersede the effects of career decision-making (Stitt-Gohdes, 1997). To successfully navigate one's career options, individuals need to strongly embrace self-efficacy, envision positive outcomes, and believe in the goals they set. The ultimate reward stemming from the embracing of individual accomplishments, learning through direct and indirect opportunities, collectivistic influences shared in one's community or environment, and the physiological conditions one finds themselves responding to. The SCCT diverges from other career theories that suggest the self is a system and beliefs are intrinsically influenced from societal and financial frameworks (Stitt-Gohdes, 1997). Consequently, counseling from a social justice lens empowers counselors to nurture a more well-rounded perspective of clients within their social circles (Ratts, 2009). Discerning clients, who are often living within their own realities, benefit from counselors who make wise and often ethical decisions based on whether an issue requires counseling or advocacy work (Butler, 2012).

The isms—racism, sexism, heterosexism, and classism, to name a few—may environmentally impede growth and development and encumber opportunities for clients to reach their optimum potential. Counseling from a whole-person perspective incorporates both personal and professional viewpoints and affords clients opportunities to see themselves holistically as they move forward making knowledgeable and cogent career decisions (Zunker, 2006). The ultimate goal should be client satisfaction related to their right of autonomy, alluding to the feeling of having purpose. Maccoby and Terzi (1981) proffer that this self-fulfillment ethic obtained by trusting the counseling process may provide an improved sense of empowerment and autonomy.

INTERWEAVING MULTICULTURAL AND SOCIAL JUSTICE CONCERNS INTO CAREER COUNSELING

Put your outdoor work in order and get your fields ready; after that build your house.

Proverbs 24:27, NIV

In the psychotherapeutic professions, there was a paradigm shift which marked the need to incorporate multiculturalism into the counseling profession, especially as it relates to career counseling. Multiculturalism is the relating to and inclusion of different cultures while acknowledging the inherent complexity of cultures. Social justice is ultimately viewed as an inseparable part of multiculturalism and vice versa (Chang, Crethar, & Ratts, 2010). The role of multiculturalism is prioritized in the counseling field as evidenced within the ACA's ethical code.

The mission statement of the ACA's code of ethics prioritizes "using the profession and practice of counseling to promote respect for human dignity and diversity," a requirement which supersedes solitary discussion and beseeches action (ACA, 2014, p. 2). Additionally, the code calls for counselors to adopt the field's core professional values where diversity is honored and a multicultural approach is embraced. Doing so supports the worth, dignity, potential, and uniqueness of people within their social and cultural contexts. The conditions of the counseling profession insist upon the need of social justice as a value, calling on counseling professionals to be promoters of social justice (ACA, 2014).

Social justice is "the promotion of equity for all people and groups for the purpose of ending oppression and injustice affecting clients, students, counselors, families, communities, schools, workplaces, governments, and other social and institutional systems" (ACA Code of Ethics, 2014, p. 21). The importance of multiculturalism is revealed throughout the ACA Code of Ethics and is asserted with great significance within the code's mission statement and statement of professional values.

Historically, psychotherapists furthered multiculturalism and social justice in various ways. Social justice was discussed in the counseling literature as early as the late 1800s and became a focus in the 1990s (Kiselica & Robinson, 2001; Smith, Reynolds, & Rovnak, 2009). Traditionally, the focus of social justice was related to significant events in the history of the United States (e.g., war, revolution) and the impact these events have had on society. Influential leaders in the field such as Frank Parsons, Karen Horney, and Carl Rogers covered topics like immigration, public health, and sexism (Kiselica et al., 2001). Additionally, counseling journals have dedicated journal issues to relevant multiculturalism and social justice causes of the time, which was seen as early as 1971. Multiculturalism and social justice were viewed as social responsibilities for the new millennium (Lee & Sirch, 1994).

Multiculturalism and social justice have been viewed as a responsibility of mental health professionals because of the harmful effects that inequity brings about (Smith et al., 2009). Social injustice may have adverse psychological effects on individuals in that oppression can hinder the potential for human growth and development. Problems that hinder people's effective decision-making may be better understood as a reflection of their environment rather than an internal complication within the individual (Lee & Walz, 1998). Thus, the etiology of some mental health issues can be conceptualized as a manifestation of systems of social injustice from classism, racism, sexism, ableism, homophobia, xenophobia, and other forms of discrimination and oppression rather than of internal origin (Lee et al., 1998; Smith et al., 2009).

Therefore, counseling professionals may impact mental health through diminishing social injustice. By opposing social injustice, counseling professionals have the potential to foster human development. The concept of societal- and systemic-based work can create positive benefits derived from social justice-informed interventions. As is, the community engagement mental health approaches and safe spaces are the oppressive systems, which I doubt is their intent (Ratts et al., 2016). Such an approach may be viewed as a shift, as it is moving away from focusing primarily on the promotion of concerns traditionally seen solely as mental health issues at the individual level, with an addition of an embedded working ideology—all of which includes combating social injustices in the broader contexts of society.

However, because of the complexities of culture and its influence on a person's worldview, it is important to be culturally competent when counseling clients. Familiarity with one's own cultural competence, awareness, and skill set is important when analyzing multicultural and social justice-based cases. Tate, Fallon, Casquarelli, and Marks (2014) examined the career and work-life challenges confronted by traditionally marginalized populations and found these challenges occurred at individual and systemic levels, making it even more crucial for positive action.

MODEL FOR UNDERSTANDING MULTICULTURALISM

Though it has been theorized that a unified belief of cultural competence is impossible, it can be thought of as the capability to create conditions and engage in actions which maximize the optimal development of our clientele. Sue (2001) defines multicultural counseling competence as

> The counselor's acquisition of awareness, knowledge, and skills needed to function effectively in a pluralistic democratic society (ability to communicate, interact, negotiate, and intervene on behalf of clients from diverse backgrounds), and on an organizational/societal level, advocating effectively to develop new theories, practices, policies, and organizational structures that are more responsive to all groups. (p. 802)

The way counselors view and evaluate cultural competence has shifted over time. However, it has generally included the awareness, knowledge, and skills constructs. A counselor's awareness refers to the acknowledgement of attitudes, beliefs, assumptions, values, biases, and worldview (Sue, Arredondo, & McDavis, 1992). The counselor's knowledge embraces the counselor's understanding of society as it relates to identity, power, privilege, and marginalization. Generally, culturally competent counselors also possess skills that integrate culture and aid in the betterment of the client.

The 2015 Multicultural Social Justice Counseling Competencies (MSJCC) add an action component to the original constructs of awareness, knowledge, and skills. The conceptual framework intersects them with self-awareness, client worldview, counseling relationship, and counseling and advocacy interventions and takes privileged and marginalized identities of both the counselor and the client into account. Figure 11.1 depicts the multicultural counseling competencies from a privileged and marganilized counselor and client dynamic and how these two intercede in the multicultural competencies of Sue et al. (1992).

FIGURE 11.1 This is a competency cycle of counselor and client interaction with each of the counseling comptencies. Adapted from American Counseling Association, 2014 ACA Code of Ethics. Copyright 2014 by American Counseling Association. *Source*: https://ct.counseling.org/2016/01/multicultural-and-social-justice-counseling-competencies- practical-applications-in-counseling/.

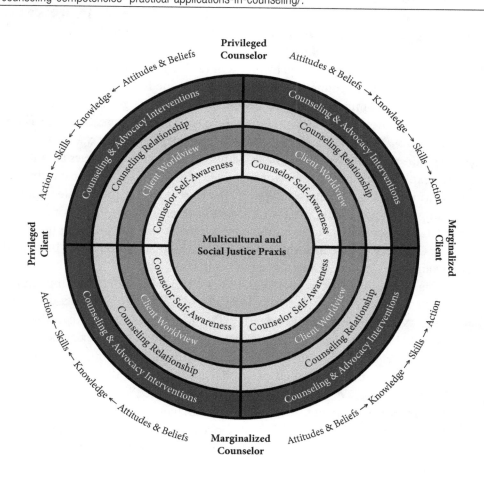

Through the MSJCC framework, Ratts, Singh, Nassar-McMillan, Butler, and McCullough, (2016) proffer that cultural and social justice competence needs to be viewed on a spectrum where self-awareness, client worldview, counseling relationship, and advocacy levels converge with attitudes, knowledge, skills, and action.

SELF-AWARENESS

The MSJCC suggests that counseling professionals engage in self-awareness development of their own attitudes and beliefs, knowledge, skills, and action levels to explore these competencies relative to their own worldviews. According to Ratts et al. (2016), this point is where the increased awareness of one's social location and all aspects of one's identity (gender, race, social class, age, ability, religion, sexual orientation, and geographic location) converge, conferring a certain set of social roles and rules, power, privilege, and marginalization, which govern the individual's identity and worldview is established (Ratts et al.). Such self-awareness allows one to become conscious of the beliefs, assumptions, attitudes, and biases they hold about their identities and the identities of others.

Although explicit bias is prohibited by the ACA (2005, 2014) ethical guidelines, it would be naïve to believe that no counselor has bias to which one is conscious. Explicit bias has been shown to be uncommon among counselors, although the extent is uncertain due to inconsistent and self-report research methods (Boysen, 2009). When addressing a counselors' own explicit bias, generally one of the most common responses is one of avoidance, of not working with a specific type of clientele. Multicultural training courses are intended to reduce such explicit bias and have been effective in doing so (Smith, Constantine, Dunn, Dinehart, & Montoya, 2006); however, typically there are no set, state-by-state requirements for continuing multicultural training for counselors after the completion of coursework. Thus, it is vital for counselors to continue exploration of self and edifying their cultural competence. One may engage in similar techniques to combat implicit bias, but additional strategies would need to be successfully implemented.

Implicit bias is distinct from explicit bias, thus strategies for addressing implicit bias are unique to the complexities of implicitness. Because implicit biases are generally outside of consciousness, they may differ from declared beliefs. Implicit biases may even be in opposition of explicit views, which can make it difficult to acknowledge the existence of implicit biases held (Smith et al., 2006). Implicit bias could manifest by treating people of differing faiths in a less friendly manner than people with whom you share the same faith. However, if implicit bias is confronted, individuals may unlearn their beliefs and replace them with more appropriate ones (Dasgupta, 2013). One of the biggest barriers to combating implicit bias could be the fact that bias attitudes exist. Once these biases become explicit, one may engage in the strategies mentioned in combating explicit bias such as partaking in trainings and programming, which counter negative beliefs and attitudes.

CLIENT WORLDVIEW

Counselors striving for multicultural and social justice competency toward their clients' worldview at the attitudes and beliefs, knowledge, skills, and action levels are aware, well-informed, experienced, and proactively oriented in understanding clients' worldviews regardless of the counselor's own privileged and marginalized status. When working with clients, taking a phenomenological approach is essential in providing effective, appropriate, and adequate support. Yet, coming to be knowledgeable about clients' worldviews is an endeavor in and of itself. Two ways in which counseling professionals can become more knowledgeable about their clients' worldview include broaching and community immersion.

Day-Vines et al. (2007), defines (broaching) as the "ability to consider the relationship of racial and cultural factors to the client's presenting problem" (p. 401). By initiating conversations about differences, one creates the opportunity to gain awareness, knowledge, and skills and to take action that best serves the client. Such communications may not occur if they are not actively initiated by counseling professionals. Another way for counseling professionals to become more knowledgeable of their clients' worldviews is to immerse themselves into the communities and contexts from which the clients come. Such immersions are similar to cultural immersion assignments, which may have presented themselves in multicultural coursework taken by the counselors-in-training during their degree programs. Engaging and sustaining such immersion activities may moderate bias, increase awareness, and lessen tension and misunderstandings between social groups (DeRicco & Sciarra, 2005; Hipolito-Delgado, Cook, Avrus, & Bonham, 2011). By immersing oneself in the community of their clients, a counselor's knowledge base about the client and their worldview may be gained and possibly seen in real time, first-hand. Before engaging in such involvement, counseling professionals should take appropriate steps to maintain ethical responsibility.

COUNSELING RELATIONSHIP

The MSJCC indicate the importance of acknowledging the identities and cultural realities of both the counseling professional and the client and their impact on the therapeutic relationship. Thus, counselors competent in multiculturalism and social justice within the counseling relationship at all levels are aware, knowledgeable, skilled, and action oriented in understanding how client and counselor identities along with privileged and marginalized statuses impact the therapeutic alliance.

Broaching and seeking supervision would also be effective to use when making efforts toward competence at this stage. Continually exploring issues of diversity includes the diversity in the room and counselor's willingness to consider and discuss how one's own identity and that of the client's affect therapy. One way counselors need to do this is by broaching the subject with their client even if it is not believed to be an issue. Additionally, counselors should seek understanding outside of the counseling relationship through supervision or consultation. Being open to knowing your client and their surroundings has the potential of strengthening your rapport and improving the counseling relationship. This ultimately benefits both parties, as putting the work in empathically reveals an outlook the professional counselor and client may build upon (Estrada, 2005).

COUNSELING AND ADVOCACY

At the counseling and advocacy action level, multiculturally competent counseling professionals intercede with and for clients on numerous levels (i.e., intrapersonal, interpersonal, institutional, community, nationally, and internationally) (Ratts et al., 2016). Ordinarily viewed through hypercritical lenses, advocacy measures get a bad rap and are often portrayed as loud, confrontational, and political. While advocacy may sometimes be representative as such, advocacy should be thought of on a spectrum. Examples of this may look like requesting that the mental health facility site honor your Muslim client's religious obligations or your Jewish client's dietary restrictions. The multicultural and social justice competency at the counseling and advocacy level involves action outside of the therapeutic relationship and may be outside the realm of what many consider to be traditional counseling. Oftentimes, social work is seen as a profession, one that engages in advocacy at institutional, community, public policy, and international levels. Counselors should embrace this opportunity and join in with social workers in the fight for a better society.

Culturally appropriate career development theories should embrace the aforementioned considerations and ensure they are integral elements for clients to explore when making significant career choices in a comprehensive manner. As noted, SCCT achieves this with great success. Instead of focusing primarily upon an individuals' behavior, performance, self-efficacy, interests, or experiences, SCCT integrates and builds a relationship among these variables to appropriately safeguard clients' needs.

SOCIAL COGNITIVE CAREER THEORY THROUGH A MULTICULTURAL LENS

The social cognitive career theory was originally presented by Lent, Brown, and Hackett as a learning theory within the field of career development (Duggar, 2015; Lent, Brown, & Hackett, 1994). SCCT emphasizes self-referent thinking in guiding human motivation and behavior (Lent et al., 1994). Moreover, the SCCT framework emphasizes a triadic relationship incorporating people, their behaviors, and their environment in an effort to understand academic and career interests, choice, and performance (Duggar, 2015; Lent & Brown, 1996). Each emphasis makes SCCT an ideal theoretical approach for counselors to utilize when working with diverse populations. The following section will provide an overview of SCCT and how it may be applied among diverse populations exploring career options.

Person Variables
SCCT person variables outline various aspects of an individuals' self-perspective. These variables are a great example of how counselors may integrate a multicultural viewpoint into the counseling relationship. Self- efficacy, outcome expectations, and goal representation help to guide a person's self-perspective.

Self-efficacy beliefs. SCCT defines self-efficacy as a self-judgement concerning capabilities that ultimately produces the action required to attain adequate performance (Bandura, 1986). This imperative variable is essential when working with diverse populations; to this end, self-efficacy involves judgements about one's personal abilities and does not focus heavily upon objective assessed skills (Lent et al., 1994).

Outcome expectations. Outcome expectations focus on judgements and one's beliefs about what they can accomplish and the consequences of those actions (Bandura, 1986). Therefore, the outcome expectations component operates independently from self-efficacy according to SCCT (Lent et al., 1994). To illustrate, self-efficacy beliefs focus on one's thoughts concerning their ability (e.g., "Am I able to complete this task?"). More practically, outcome expectations refer to the imagined results of particular behaviors (e.g., "If I complete this task, I believe this will happen.") (Lent, Brown, & Hackett, 2000). The dynamics between self-efficacy and outcome expectations are particularly relevant for counselors exploring career development with diverse clients because high self-efficacy does not always produce favorable outcomes. For instance, it should not be difficult to understand a person with high self-efficacy in mathematics avoiding a career as an accountant if they anticipate negative outcomes associated with the decision (e.g., lack of family or social support) (Lent et al.).

Goal representations. Goal representations determine whether one should engage in particular activities that will have an inherent impact or possibly impede future outcomes (Bandura, 1986; Lent et. al., 2002). SCCT states that goals play an important role in the self-regulation of behavior (Lent et al., 1994). Furthermore, goal representations operate primarily through symbolical desired outcomes (e.g., forethought), which allow for evaluative reactions to client's behavior based on internal standards of performance (Duggar, 2015). Consequently, SCCT suggests that reciprocal interactions among self-efficacy, outcome expectations, and goal representations are imperative forces in career development (Bandura, 1986).

Contextual Factors

Within SCCT literature, environmental variables are termed contextual factors that are explored within two subsets. The first subset examines a person's learning experiences based on their early life influences as compared to the second subset, which takes into account these same person's personal variables (self-efficacy, outcomes, and goals). Personal variables are labeled distal contextual factors, while career-related behaviors and current factors are considered proximal contextual factors (Duggar, 2015; Lent, Brown, & Hackett, 2000).

Distal contextual factors. By definition, distal contextual factors refer to variables that are more distant from career decision-making (Duggar, 2015). As a person considers their career choice, earlier factors (e.g., support, self-established goals) are applicable in the present. The literature also speaks to how contextual affordances affect learning experiences through which career-relevant self-efficacy and outcome expectations develop (Lent et al., 2000). Consequently, the cultural context pertaining to how people are raised directly influences their career-related exposure. Providing access to quality education and mentorship as well as understanding which socially accepted behaviors were affirmed or not affirmed during rearing years (Dugger, 2015) has a positive impact on diverse clients.

Proximal contextual factors. In addition, SCCT acknowledges the influence of a person's current environment as an element in career decision-making. Proximal contextual factors can either encourage or impede one's ability to transform career interests into goals and career goals into actions (Dugger, 2015). For instance, a student may develop an interest in being an educator; however, if their environment is not conducive or adequately resourced, the student may never establish worthwhile career goals or actions. In this scenario, the student's contextual factors involved barriers in the formation of previously desired career aspirations.

Triadic Reciprocity

The interaction between SCCT elements in career decision-making is termed triadic reciprocity (Dugger, 2015; Lent et al., 1994). This term was originally coined within Bandura's social cognitive theory and later adapted for SCCT use. The interactive relationship between a person, their environment, and their behavior is an imperative aspect in career decision-making. While the previously explored variables are important, they all work in tandem in the formulation of academic and career interests, goals, and actions. In this way, each SCCT element is impactful in one's overall conceptualization of career decision-making (Dugger, 2015; Lent et al., 1994).

CONCLUSION

As individuals begin to choose particular career or occupational paths beneficial for them, masterful clinicians help to contribute to successful conclusions. Sadly, given their worldviews, often based on relevant life experiences, clients from diverse populations may fail in making appropriate career decisions that directly reflect their hopes, gifts, and prayers. Therefore, it is essential that counselors utilize strength-based career theories, interventions, and counseling approaches that take the interplay of these dynamics into account when working with diverse clientele.

KEY TERMS

2015 Multicultural Social Justice Counseling Competencies (MSJCC): a set of guidelines that added an action component to the original constructs of awareness, knowledge, and skills

Broaching: the ability to consider the relationship of racial and cultural factors to a client's presenting problem

Distal contextual factor: related to factors that refer to constructs that are more distant from career decision-making

Goal representations: determinations as to whether one should engage in particular activities that will have an inherent impact or possibly impede future outcomes

Multicultural counseling competence: the counselor's awareness, knowledge and skills in the communities in which they work and interact to demonstrate knowledge in diverse arenas.

Outcome expectations: judgements and one's beliefs about what they can accomplish and the consequences of those actions

Person variables: the outline of various aspects of an individuals' self-perspective

Self-efficacy: self-judgement concerning capabilities that ultimately produces the action required to attain adequate performance

Social cognitive career theory (SCCT): emphasizes self-referent thinking in guiding human motivation and behavior

Triadic reciprocity: the interaction between the SCCT elements in the career decision

ADDITIONAL READINGS, RESOURCES, AND WEBSITES

Ratts, M. J., Toporek, R. L., & Lewis, J. A. (Eds.). (2010) ACA advocacy competencies: A social justice framework for counselors. Alexandria, VA: American Counseling Association.

Arthur, N., & McMahon, M. (2005), Multicultural career counseling: Theoretical applications of the systems theory framework. Career Development Quarterly, 53, 208–222. doi:10.1002/j.2161- 0045.2005.tb00991.x

Association for Multicultural Counseling and Development http://www.multicultural-counseling.org/index.php?option=com_content&view=article&id=62&Ite mid=82

Chung, R. C., & Bemak, F. P. (2012). Social justice counseling: The next steps beyond multiculturalism. Los Angeles, CA: SAGE.

Carter, R. (Ed.). (2005). Handbook of racial-cultural psychology and counseling, training and practice (Vol. 2, 7th ed.). Hoboken, NJ: John Wiley & Sons.

Lewis, J. A., Lewis, M. D., Daniels, J. A, & D'Andrea, M. J. (2011). Community counseling: A multicultural- social justice perspective. Belmont, CA: Brooks/Cole.

Case Study

Jessica is a 17-year-old, multiracial high school student. She was born in a small rural community, which lacked racial diversity. Jessica lives with her two parents and one younger sibling. Jessica currently works at the corner store to make extra money to assist her family. She is no stranger to hard work and has been working since she was 16-years-old. When faced with financial hardships, Jessica and her family lean on their faith in God. The family, as a whole, identifies as nondenominational Christian. They are active participants within their church home and generally do not miss opportunities to attend weekly services.

As a junior in high school, Jessica has begun considering her post-graduation career options. Despite her strong proficiency in math and science, Jessica's mother has been very vocal about her daughter becoming a hairstylist. Jessica's mother currently works at a hair salon and no one in their immediate family has ever attended a post-secondary institution. Jessica secretly aspires to attend a state university to pursue engineering. Due to family influence, she continues to vacillate between continuing with her family's tradition within the hair salon and seeking a higher degree. The hair salon is a family custom steeped in pride; however, Jessica must also consider the advantages of pursuing new educational opportunities. Going off to school will allow her to mature and grow, but it also comes with the issue of seeking a new career path that is away from her hometown and family.

Individually or within a group designated as career counselors, please discuss the following questions and decide what would be the best approach to take in helping Jessica to choose a career pathway.

TRADITIONAL ACTIVITY QUESTIONS

1. Considering the cultural dynamics that are prevalent within Jessica's narrative, what factors are important to understand when assisting her in choosing a meaningful career path?
2. How might these factors assist a career counselors' conceptualization of Jessica case?
3. How would you utilize social cognitive career theory to support Jessica?
4. How might a career counselor include Jessica's family in the therapeutic and career decision-making process?

SPIRITUAL ACTIVITY QUESTIONS

1. From a spiritual perspective, what role might Jessica's faith and beliefs play in her career decision-making process?

2. What scripture(s) might assist your work with Jessica, utilizing social cognitive career theory?

3. Applying the story of Jesus and the miraculous catch of fish (John 21:1–19), explore its relation to Jessica and the impending decision-making process and eventual career choice.

REFERENCES

American Counseling Association. (2005, 2014). ACA code of ethics. Alexandria, VA: Author. Retrieved from https://www.counseling.org/resources/aca-code-of-ethics.pdf

Bandura, A. (1986). Social foundations of thought and action: A social cognitive theory. Englewood Cliffs, NJ: Prentice-Hall.

Boysan, G. A. (2009). A review of experimental studies of explicit and implicit bias among counselors. Journal of Multicultural Counseling and Development, 37(4), 240–249. doi:10.1002/j.2161- 1912.2009.tb00106.x

Butler, S. K. (2012). Issues of social justice and career counseling. Career Planning & Adult Development Journal, 28(1), 140–151.

Chang, C. Y., Crethar, H. C., & Ratts, M. J. (2010). Social justice: A national imperative for counselor education and supervision. Counselor Education and Supervision, 50(2), 82–87. doi:10.1002/j.1556-6978.2010.tb00110.x

Day-Vines, N. L., Wood, S. M., Grothaus, T., Craigen, L., Holman, A., Dotson-Blake, K., & Douglass, M. J. (2007). Broaching the subjects of race, ethnicity, and culture during the counseling process. Journal of Counseling & Development, 85(4), 401–409. http://dx.doi.org/10.1002/j.1556- 6678.2007.tb00608.x

Dugger, S. E. (2015). Foundations of career counseling: A case-based approach. Upper Saddle River, NJ: Pearson Education.

Estrada, D. (2005). Multicultural conversations in supervision: The impact of the supervisor's Racial/Ethnic background. Guidance & Counselling, 21(1), 14.

Fouad, N. A., Gerstein, L. H., & Toporek, R. L. (2006). Social justice and counseling psychology in context. In R. L. Toporek, L. H. Gerstein, N. A. Fouad, G. Roysircar, & T. Israel (Eds.), Handbook for social justice in counseling psychology: Leadership, vision, and action (pp 1–16). Thousand Oaks, CA: Sage.

Hipolito-Delgado, C. P., Cook, J. M., Avrus, E. M., & Bonham, E. J. (2011). Developing counseling students' multicultural competence through the multicultural action project. Counselor Education and Supervision, 50(6), 402–421. doi:10.1002/j.1556–6978.2011.tb01924.x

Hirschman, E., & Panther-Yates, D. (2008). Peering inward for ethnic identity: Consumer interpretation of DNA test results. Identity: An International Journal of Theory and Research. 8, 47–66.

Jacobs, D. H. (1994). Environmental failure: Oppression is the only cause of psychopathology. Journal of Mind and Behavior, 15, 1–18.

Lee & Sirch. (1994). Counseling in an enlightened society: Values for a new millennium. Counseling and Values, 38(2), 90–97. doi:10.1002/j.2161-007X.1994.tb00826.x

Lee, C. C., Walz, G. R., & American Counseling Association. (1998). Social action: A mandate for counselors. Alexandria, VA: American Counseling Association.

Lent, R. W. & Brown, S. D. (1996). Social cognitive approach to career development: An overview. The Career Development Quarterly, 44, 310–321.

Lent, R. W., Brown, S. D., & Hackett, G. (1994). Toward a unifying social cognitive theory of career and academic interest, choice, and performance. Journal of Vocational Behavior, 45, 79–122.

Lent, R. W., Brown, S. D., Talleyrand, R., McPartland, E. B., Davis, T., Chopra, S. B., Alexander, M. S., Suthakaran, V., & Chai, C. (2002). Career choice barriers, supports, and coping strategies: College students' experiences. Journal of Vocational Behavior, 60, 61–72.

Kiselica, M. S., & Robinson, M. (2001). Bringing advocacy counseling to life: The history, issues, and human dramas of social justice work in counseling. Journal of Counseling & Development, 79(4), 387–397. doi:10.1002/j.1556-6676.2001.tb01985.x

Maccoby, M., & Terzi, K. (1981). What Happened to Work Ethic? In J. O'Toole, J. L. Scheiber, and L. C. Wood (Eds.), Working, Changes, and Choices, (pp. 162–171). New York, NY: Human Sciences Press.

National Economic and Social Rights Initiative. (2011). Human Rights: A Global Vision. Retrieved from http://www.nesri.org/human-rights/human-rights-a-global-vision

Ratts, M. J. (2009). Social justice counseling: Toward the development of a fifth force among counseling paradigms. Journal of Humanistic Counseling, Education and Development, 48(2), 160–172. Retrieved from http://ezproxy.lib.ucf.edu/login?URL=http://search.ebscohost.com/ login.aspx?direct=true&d-b=eric&AN=EJ866887&site=ehost-live; http://www.counseling.org/Publications/Journals.aspx

Ratts, M. J., Singh, A. A., Nassar-McMillan, S., Butler, S. K., & McCullough, J. R. (2016). Multicultural and social justice counseling competencies: Guidelines for the counseling profession. Journal of Multicultural Counseling & Development, 44(1), 28–48. doi:10.1002/jmcd.12035

Savickas, M. & Lent, R. (1994). Convergence in Career Development Theories. Palo Alto, CA: Consulting Psychologists Press, Inc.

Sciarra, D. T., & DeRicco, J. N. (2005). The immersion experience in multicultural counselor training: Confronting covert racism. Journal of Multicultural Counseling and Development, 33(1), 2–16. doi:10.1002/j.2161-1912.2005.tb00001.x

Smith, S. D., Reynolds, C. A., & Rovnak, A. (2009). A critical analysis of the social advocacy movement in counseling. Journal of Counseling & Development, 87(4), 483–491. doi:10.1002/j.1556- 6678.2009.tb00133.x

Smith, T. B., Constantine, M. G., Dunn, T. W., Dinehart, J. M., & Montoya, J. A. (2006). Multicultural education in the mental health professions: A meta-analytic review. Journal of Counseling Psychology, 53(1), 132–145.

Stitt-Gohdes, W. L. (1997). Career development: Issues of gender, race, and class. Information Series no. 371). Columbus, OH: ERIC Clearinghouse on Adult, Career, & Vocational Education, The Ohio State University.

Sue, D. W. (2001). Multidimensional facets of cultural competence. The Counseling Psychologist, 29(6), 790–821. http://dx.doi.org/10.1177/0011000001296002

Sue, D. W., Arredondo, P., & McDavis, R. J. (l992). Multicultural competencies/ standards: A pressing need. Journal of Counseling & Development, 70, 477–486.

Tate, K. A., Fallon, K. A., Casquarelli, E. J., & Marks, L. R. (2014). Opportunities for Action: Traditionally Marginalized Populations and the Economic Crisis. The Professional Counselor, 4(4), 285–302.

Zunker, V. G. (2006). Career counseling: A holistic approach (7th ed.). Belmont, CA US: Thomson Brooks/ Cole Publishing Co.

Credit

Figure 11.1: Source: https://ct.counseling.org/2016/01/multicultural-and-social-justice-counseling-competencies-practical-applications-in-counseling/

12

Career Counseling and Gender Issues

Kathie Erwin, EdD, LMHC and Matt Casada, MA, LMHC

But from the beginning of the creation, male and female he made them.

Mark 10:6, New King James Version

LEARNING OBJECTIVES

In this chapter, students will learn about

- The influence of gender on career decision-making
- The issues of gender stereotypes, dual-career couples, and the impact of career choices on the family

LEARNING OUTCOMES

At the end of this chapter, students will be able to

- Identify current issues of male and female career decision-making
- Recognize impact of social gender norms on career choice
- Become aware of the stressors of dual-career couples on their relationship and their parenting

CHAPTER HIGHLIGHTS

- Gender development and stereotypes
- Stereotypes and gender
- Counseling men, women, and couples
- Dual-career couples
- Practical application of social cognitive career theory and multiculturalism

INTRODUCTION

Career decision-making is an area in which changing social roles have a dramatic impact. The influences of political ideologies and socioeconomic pressures have blurred the lines of work roles that were traditionally considered suitable for men and women. The scripture verse from Mark 10:6—"But from the beginning of creation, male and female he made them"—has been used as exclusionary for persons seeking to break out of gender-defined work roles. However, this scripture does not place such restrictions.

As the opportunities are less restricted by gender norms, individuals have wider choices to pursue the career best suited to their talents and passion. The impact of broader career options is not only an individual matter but also impacts the individual in a relationship and as a parent.

GENDER DEVELOPMENT AND STEREOTYPES: IMPACT ON CAREER CHOICES

Abbott's 1884 novel, "Flatland," tells a story of a set of shapes living in a two-dimensional world. The narrator of the story, A Square, happily dwells in Flatland until he dreams one night of visiting a one-dimensional world, Lineland. While visiting the lines of Lineland, A Square tries to convince the one-dimensional inhabitants of his two-dimensional world, to change perspective. Constrained by their limited understanding and comprehension of anything beyond their one-dimensional world, the leaders of Lineland attempt to execute A Square (Abbott, 1963).

When held in a rigid and restrictive manner, stereotypes function in a manner similar to the inhabitants of Lineland by reducing complex, multidimensional people to simple, one-dimensional caricatures. As a result, their visible appearance, gender, and race function as "almost automatic bases of categorization" (Reskin, 2000, p. 320). These over-simplified categories create a set of expectations for how individuals of each gender are expected to act, think, and feel (i.e., prescriptive stereotypes) and prohibitions on how to act, think, or feel (i.e., proscriptive stereotypes) as well as potential consequences for those who break those expectations (Moss-Racusin, Phelan, & Rudman, 2010; Reskin, 2000).

For too long, stereotypes have translated to discrimination: a harmful action against a person or group of people on the basis of gender, race, or other characteristics. Addressing discrimination begins with recognizing and acknowledging the ways in which stereotypes lead to cognitive categories that reduce men and women to simplistic, one-dimensional characters (Reskin, 2000). As part of the discussion of gender issues in career counseling, this chapter will explore gender stereotypes, direct implications for men and women in the workplace, career choices as part of the calling of God, and the implications for seeking career counseling.

Male Stereotypes

Historically, men have been expected to demonstrate an orientation toward achievement, autonomy, and rationality (Heliman, 2012). To effectively live in this traditional stereotype, a man must learn to present traits such as competence, ambition, assertiveness, dominance, independence, self-reliance, a stoic demeanor, objectivity, and logical thinking. Additionally, men are expected to avoid feelings and expressions that portray weakness or vulnerability (Moss-Racusin et al., 2010). These stereotypes work together to create a male narrative that presents men as physically, mentally, and emotionally strong, displaying power and dominance across all fields of life. This narrative is one that disproportionately benefits men across many career settings because the traits associated with success narratives are the same associated with masculinity.

One of the ways that men benefit from the male stereotype is in the utilization of aggression as a means of gaining and retaining power. When part of the male socialization process includes the avoidance of weakness, men may funnel softer emotions into more aggressive feelings such as anger, using them to gain power and control (Blazina & Watkins, 1996). Conversely, women who display similar aggression are subject to backlash because these traits are not a part of the female stereotype (Moss-Racusin et al., 2010).

This dichotomy was captured by a study on male and female agreeableness in the workplace (Judge, Livingston, & Hurst, 2012). Men and women who demonstrated higher levels of agreeableness, a trait associated with the feminine communal traits, were viewed as more likeable. But this likeableness came at the expense of perceived competence, as those who showed more disagreeableness exchanged likeableness for competence, especially in competitive environments.

Scoring lower on agreeableness does not imply that one is rude, as only a minor difference exists between agreeable and disagreeable people. But for men, that minor difference is in alignment with the traditional stereotype that view men as oriented toward success. Because of this, the level of agreeableness displayed by a man will impact income and promotion. Those low in agreeableness are most strongly rewarded due to congruence with the male stereotype.

These same traits that reward men by placing them in roles of power and authority become the same structures that allow men to maintain power and control. These patterns of reward and reinforcement may lead to a boys' club for men within in the work place where those who have privileges work to protect them by controlling or excluding members from lower-ranking groups (Reskin, 2000).

Therefore, the man naturally aligning with the male stereotype benefits from the societal and vocational structures in place that function like an elevator, enabling men to ascend to culturally valued and esteemed positions. But this ascension does not come without cost. Although men may disproportionally benefit from gender stereotypes, it can be viewed as a "double-edged sword" that can negatively impact men and women alike (Johnston & Diekman, 2015). This is particularly true when gender stereotypes are held in a rigid manner.

Because men (and women) are far more complex than the one-dimensional caricatures, the reduction created by stereotypes can lead to intrapersonal conflict around one's gender identity. Gender-role conflict (GRC) (O'Neil, Helms, Gable, David, & Wrightsman, 1986) occurs within men who feel the negative implications of traditional gender roles. This conflict negatively impacts men and women alike by limiting or restricting their potential based on gender roles (O'Neil et al., 1986). Functioning primarily on a subconscious level, GRC influences thoughts, feelings, and behaviors.

Female Stereotypes

From suffragettes to Rosie the Riveter to the feminist movement, the role of women in the workforce was historically a matter of conformity and convenience. The political changes related to expanding rights for women is intricately linked to progression of women's career opportunities. The suffragettes ushered in the 20th century by literally putting their lives and marriages on the line to campaign for women's right to vote, which was finally earned in 1920 with passage of the 19th Amendment. These women broke from the socially expected roles of wife, mother, and hostess to gain a voice in the electorate. The next milestone event was during World War II when women were actively recruited to take over formerly male jobs. As the pressures of World War II drained the male workforce to the point of compromising manufacturing and support for the military, women stepped up to show their abilities in previously unexpected ways. Thus, Rosie the Riveter emerged as a symbol for women who worked in factories, shipyards and aircraft plants. Once thought too frail or incompetent to fly airplanes, the Women's Air Force Service Pilots, known as WASPS, was launched with women becoming test pilots for military aircraft and flying noncombat air support. But after the war ended, Rosie put down her tools and returned to the kitchen while the men resumed jobs in the civilian and military workforce. As the skills and expertise of women were no longer needed, these opportunities ended. Some occupations were still open to women, predominately teacher, nurse, maid, or other work that did not interfere with the homemaker role nor eclipse the status of their husbands.

The baby boomers' (refer to Chapter 9 for a more in-depth understanding the baby boomer generation) penchant for breaking down social barriers became the incubator for the civil rights and feminist movements of the 1960s and 1970s. Largely due to the efforts of these movements, Title VI of the Civil Rights Act was approved, prohibiting discrimination in the workforce based on race or gender. To enforce this provision, the Equal Employment Opportunity Commission (EEOC) was established to review complaints of job discrimination. As young women broke glass ceilings to get advanced education and compete in fields that were formerly male-only domains, the balance in the U.S. workforce changed. Working women were stereotyped as inadequate mothers and blamed for the problems of "latchkey children" who came home from school to spend on hours alone until mothers returned from work.

The female generational cohorts seemed to split over Gail Sheehy's (1974) description of "achievers who defer nurturing" versus "nurturers who defer achieving." Some in the Christian community went beyond decrying feminism and extended a spiritual indictment to all women who worked rather than fulfill traditional wife and mother roles. Feminist leaders Betty Friedan and Gloria Steinham clashed with Phyllis Schafly, the antifeminist, traditionalist voice. In the background, the nation spiraled toward inflation; incurred added expenses of military conflicts; and left more families struggling financially, prompting many to become dual-wage earners out of necessity. The increase of single mothers as head of household who joined the full-time workforce in order to survive led to a new crisis in the high cost and low availability of childcare.

Attitudes toward women who work went from early stereotypes of being less feminine and aggressive, angry, and anti-male to the ongoing 21st-century problem of sexual harassment and wage discrimination in the corporate and military workforce. At the core of work-related gender stereotypes are the long-standing social beliefs that associate men with agency (self-oriented, competitive) and women with communion (other-oriented, nurturing) (Fiske, Cuddy, Glick, & Xu, 2002; Johnston & Diekman, 2015). This is the social context in which boys are taught to be competitive while girls are admonished to be cooperative. As adults, these early influences become part of what drives or restricts the choice and progress of careers for women and men.

CAREER COUNSELING AND GENDER STEREOTYPES

From as early as elementary school, the myths of gender abilities can program men and women for success or failure in career choices. For example, the myth that girls are better suited for the study of liberal arts while boys excel in math and science can be a factor preventing each gender from choosing careers that are outside the socially transmitted gender norms. Bandura's (1977) model of perceived self-efficacy specifies four principle sources of efficacy information as performance accomplishments, vicarious learning, social persuasion, and psychological arousal. Regardless of cultural background, social persuasion is a powerful influence on gender stereotypes that leads to gender-role assumptions in career decision-making. Betz and Hackett (2006) suggest that the elements of self-efficacy in career decision-making are not just applicable to prior research on women's career choices but also significant in the career choices of men and minorities.

DUAL-CAREER COUPLES

Conflicts over time, money, and childcare responsibilities are common factors that can strain the relationship of dual-career couples with each other and with their children. Even among couples who are supportive of the dual-career lifestyle, work-family conflicts intercede with the expectations of gender roles and ideologies, which ultimately effect how spouses view family conflict (Minnotte, Minnotte, & Pedersen, 2013.). Casting aside the old ideals of the cookie baking, stay-at-home mother and the wage-earning father, dual-income households include 60% of married couples in the United States with children under the age of 18 compared with 31% where the father is the only wage earner (Pew Research Center, 2015).

For the dual-career couple, work-family conflicts are essentially role conflicts, which can be as basic as who stays home from work to care for a sick child to the complexity of whose promotion opportunity is viewed as justification for the family to move and leave the other spouse to deal with a job search after relocation. This decision often comes down to "gender ideology," or what each partner believes about the role of husband and wife, which impacts career decisions (Greenstein, 1996). Couples can respond with cooperation or contention based on early beliefs about gender roles as an amalgamation of the examples of family of origin, work experience, and self-perception of gender roles.

Regardless of work status (professional or labor), a meta-analysis of factors leading to work-family conflict showed that overload from work followed by role conflicts in the workplace were the greatest potential pressures that adversely impact working parents and, by extension, their interfamily relationships (Michel, Kotrba, Mitchelson, Clark, & Baltes, 2011).

Childcare can be the major issue that strains the relationship of dual-career couples. The ideal of shared parenting is not the common reality. Even among middle-class working couples, mothers spend 70% of nonwork time attending to routine needs of young children compared with the less than 50% of nonwork time given by fathers. The need for childcare during work hours is essential for parents to sustain jobs yet a major issue for working parents. The limited availability of affordable, quality daycare stresses both the time and finances of dual-career couples. The high costs of daycare, particularly for infants, toddlers, and multiple children, may be the impetus for a slight increase in families where one parent stays home. Mothers are more likely to leave their careers to stay home until children reach school age (Kreider & Elliott, 2010). While the decision of whether mother or father stay home to provide childcare may be made based on amount of income generated, it is also a matter of long-term consequences to the career re-entry

COMPONENTS FOR COUNSELING MEN

One deeply problematic reality among men is the stigma that exists around seeking help from others (O'Neil, 2008). To work effectively with men, career counselors must thoughtfully explore the implications of the male narrative as it relates to help-seeking attitudes. Foundational to this understanding are the ways in which socialization informs a man's attitude, therefore the likelihood of pursuing help services like counseling (Heppner & Heppner, 2005).

Engaging in counseling in any form encourages traits such as emotional awareness, self-disclosure, and admission of personal problems, traits that are dissonant with traditional male gender roles (Good & Wood; 1995). Men hold more negative attitudes toward counseling, which may account for their underrepresentation in career counseling compared with women (Tsan & Day, 2007).

These negative attitudes exist particularly among those whose GRC manifests in the form of restricted emotionality (Tsan, Day, Schwartz, & Kimbrel, 2011). This conflict means that men may not have information and direction that would be helpful to them, leaving them to figure out career issues in isolation. It also means that they may feel the need to present a stronger sense of security than actually exists. The understanding of these possible insecurities should inform the career counselor's approach to working with men (Rochlen, Blazina, & Raghunathan, 2002).

To address these realities, competent career counselors ought to name possible insecurities and gender incongruence by enquiring about the ways in which GRC may manifest uniquely for each client (Tsan et al., 2011). Career counselors may also address these issues by being prepared to employ a task-oriented approach rather than focusing on emotional connectivity (Good & Wood, 1995).

This approach appears relevant in working with men and women as a discrepancy exists between the preferred emphasis of career counseling (i.e., task-focused) and what the anticipated focus (i.e., person-focused). To address this, clinicians are encouraged to begin the career counseling process by giving clients space to discuss their desires for the process before discussing what they might expect from the process (Galassi, Crace, Martin, James, & Al, 1992). This type of opening allows the client to have choice and autonomy in relation to the direction of their time in career counseling and allows each client to experience a uniquely tailored process.

An additional benefit to this approach is that it encourages a collaborative approach. Maintaining an ongoing dialogue about the nature of the counseling process is an approach particularly beneficial while working with men. By monitoring the alliance and direction of treatment, clinicians are able to determine how clients are experiencing counseling and if they are receiving the style of treatment and care they desire (Heppner & Heppner, 2005).

COMPONENTS FOR COUNSELING WOMEN

Women tend to define themselves and, by extension, their career choices in terms of self-esteem, security, and significance (Clinton & Langberg, 2010). For women, high perception of self-worth is linked to willingness to make bold, potentially nontraditional career choices compared with lower self-worth that is more likely to submit to the demands of others. As nurturers, women are concerned with security, particularly for their children, which may limit career risk-taking options. While women can be sacrificial to the needs of family, they may also want a significant role in career and society. In career counseling with women, these three elements need to be explored so that the client comes to terms with her own views, not merely reflect the views of others.

When exploring careers in which women are underrepresented, counselors can work to focus on helping their female clients know how to cope with the stressors of being different and discrimination in the workplace. Making a choice to go against the social norm requires engaging supportive spouse and family resources to cope with anticipated gender-based microaggressions. Apart from emotional stress, gender microaggressions toward women in male-dominated careers become the forerunner of sexual harassment and sexual assault (Garner & Sterzing, 2016).

Women entering or progressing in the workforce also have to deal with the guilt of not being a full-time mother. Guilt may be internalized based on familial or religious norms as well as actively imposed guilt from family or friends. Perhaps the most devastating guilt about childcare comes from friends who flaunt their full-time motherhood as a badge of honor, which condemns women who work by choice or financial necessity. Single mothers who lack the option of staying at home also face an added stress of fulfilling a dual role in the family plus working. What may not be considered is that a woman's career choice can be her God-given calling to a specific field, which is a greater issue than choice or money. Regardless of the reasons a woman with children is in part-time or full-time work, career counseling with women needs to address issues of guilt, time constraints, role fulfillment, accepting limitations, avoiding neglecting herself, and how to assertively ask for help in parenting and career.

COMPONENTS FOR COUNSELING DUAL-CAREER COUPLES

Values and roles are the underlying issues in many conflicts experienced by dual-career couples regardless of their career status or income. The sociocultural values that each partner brings into the marriage is integral in defining the respective roles for the couple. Those values define what each partner expects the other to do in terms of work commitment, work-related travel, sacrifices when seeking promotion, and childcare responsibilities. When the dual-career family does not function well, the imbalance can threaten the couple's marriage. Whether real or perceived, the imbalance in values and roles is what is behind the daily frustrations that are expressed when couples enter into joint career counseling. One or both of the partners may be experiencing career burnout or couple burnout, which have similar symptoms of mental, physical, and relationship exhaustion (Pines & Nunes, 2003). The connection between career burnout and couple burnout is stronger than many couples want to admit yet it is a systemic issue, not an isolated one.

Cross-cultural value differences are significant when partners come from significantly different backgrounds. These issues remain as important today for the management of the household as those Hofstede (1993) defined for business management, including "individualism versus collectivism, power distance, uncertainty avoidance and masculinity versus Femininity." The counselor needs to invite each partner to describe what these differences mean from their perspective, how they play out in the relationships, and how they advance or restrict each partner's career progression. Pines and Nunes's (2003) study found that partners tend to confuse career burnout and couple burnout, which can lead to the build up of conscious or unconscious resentments against the partner. Helping the dual-career couple untangle their feelings about career from feelings about the relationship is important for family preservation and marital satisfaction while continuing to progress in a chosen career.

CONCLUSION

As is the case with many social constructs, gender roles, norms, and stereotypes are constantly evolving. This evolution requires that career counselors embody a deep sense of humility as it relates to cultural understanding and an open-minded curiosity in relating to clients.

These traits will allow a counselor to maintain a current understanding of culture, gender-role development and socialization, and the potential impact upon the vocational directions for men and women (Heppner & Heppner, 2005).

REFLECTION AND DISCUSSION

1. How has your gender socialization been congruent or incongruent with the traditional socializations discussed within the chapter?

2. Why is it important to consider gender roles and norms as they relate to career counseling?

3. What are the advantages and disadvantages each gender must address over the course of a vocational life?

4. What are some of the issues a person needs to consider when choosing a career that is traditionally performed by the opposite gender?

5. What are stressors on the couple's relationship when one person's career progresses faster or more successfully than the other person's career?

TRADITIONAL ACTIVITY

Interview an experienced professional in any field about the impact that gender has on their career. Discuss with them the pertinent information from this text to discover elements that have applied to their career trajectory.

SPIRITUAL ACTIVITY

Consider the ways in which religion and spirituality have informed gender rules, norms, and socialization. How does your spirituality address gender? Perhaps consult a religious leader in your community to continue this discussion.

REFERENCES

Abbott, E. A. (1963). Flatland: A romance of many dimensions. New York, NY: Barnes & Noble.

Bandura, A. (1977). Self-efficacy: Toward a unifying theory of behavior change. Psychology Review, 84, 191–215.

Betz, N.E. & Hackett, G. (2006). Career self-efficacy theory: back to the future. Journal of Career Assessment, 14 (1), 3–11.

Blazina, C., & Watkins, C. E. (1996). Masculine gender role conflict: Effects on college men's psychological well-being, chemical substance usage, and attitudes towards help-seeking. Journal of Counseling Psychology, 43(4), 461–465. doi:10.1037//0022-0167.43.4.461

Clinton, T.E. & Langburg, D. (2011). Counseling women. Grand Rapids, MI: Baker Books.

Fiske, S. T., Cuddy, A. J. C., Glick, P., & Xu, J. (2002). A model of (often mixed) stereotype content. Journal of Personality and Social Psychology, 82, 878–902. doi:10.1037/0022-3514.82.6.878.

Galassi, J. P., Crace, R. K., Martin, G. A., James, R. M., & Al, E. (1992). Client preferences and anticipations in career counseling: A preliminary investigation. Journal of Counseling Psychology, 39(1), 46–55. doi:10.1037//0022-0167.39.1.46

Garner, R.E. & Sterzing, P.R. (Nov 2016). Gender microaggressions as a gateway to sexual Harassment, Journal of Women & Social Work, 31 (4), 491–503 DOI: 10.1177/0886109916654732

Good, G. E., & Wood, P. K. (1995). Male Gender Role Conflict, Depression, and Help Seeking: Do College Men Face Double Jeopardy? Journal of Counseling & Development, 74(1), 70–75. doi:10.1002/j.1556-6676.1995.tb01825.x

Greenstein, T. N. (1996). Gender ideology and perceptions of the fairness of the division of household labor: Effects on marital quality. Social Forces, 74, 1029–1042.

Heilman, M. E. (2012). Gender stereotypes and workplace bias. Research in Organizational Behavior, 32, 113–135. doi:10.1016/j.riob.2012.11.003

Hofstede, G. (1993). Cultural constraints in management theories. Academy of Management Executive, 7, 81–87.

Heppner, M. J. & Heppner, P.P (2005). Addressing the Implications of Male Socialization for Career Counseling. In G. R. Brooks & G. E. Good (Eds.), The New Book of Psychotherapy and Counseling With Men:

A Comprehensive Guide to Settings, Problems, and Treatment Approaches (pp. 369–388). San Francisco, CA: Jossey-Bass.

Johnston, A.M & Diekman, A.B. (2015). Pursuing desires rather than duties? The motivational content of gender stereotypes. Sex Roles, 73, 16–28.

Judge, T. A., Livingston, B. A., & Hurst, C. (2012). Do nice guys—and gals—really finish last? The joint effects of sex and agreeableness on income. Journal of Personality and Social Psychology, 102(2), 390–407. doi:10.1037/a0026021

Kreider, R.M. & Elliott, D.B. (2010). Historical changes in stay-at-home mothers: 1969–2009. U.S. Census Bureau. http://www.census.gov/hhes/families/files/ASA2010_Kreider_Elliott.pdf

Michel, J. S., Kotrba, L. M., Mitchelson, J. K., Clark, M. A., & Baltes, B. B. (2011). Antecedents of work–family conflict: A meta-analytic review. Journal of Organizational Behavior, 32, 689–725. doi:10.1002/job.69

Minnotte, K.L., Minnotte, M.C. & Pedersen, D.E. (October 2013). Marital satisfaction among dual-earner couples: Gender ideologies and family to work conflict. Family Relations, 62, 686–698.

Moss-Racusin, C. A., Phelan, J. E., & Rudman, L. A. (2010). When men break the gender rules: Status incongruity and backlash against modest men. Psychology of Men & Masculinity, 11(2), 140–151. doi:10.1037/a0018093

O'Neil, J. M. (2008). Summarizing 25 Years of Research on Men's Gender Role Conflict Using the Gender Role Conflict Scale: New Research Paradigms and Clinical Implications. The Counseling Psychologist, 36(3), 358–445. doi:10.1177/0011000008317057

O'Neil, J., Helms, B., Gable, R., David, L., & Wrightsman, L. (1986). Gender-role conflict scale: College men's fear of femininity. Sex Roles, 14(5–6), 335. doi:10.1007/BF00287583

Pew Research Center. (June, 2015). The rise in dual income households. Retrieved from http://www.pewresearch.org/ft_dual-income-households-1960-2012-2/

Pines, A.M. & Nunes, R. (2003). The relationship between career and couple burnout: Implications for career and couple counseling. Journal of Employment Counseling, 40(2), 50–54.

Reskin, B. F. (2000). The proximate causes of employment discrimination. Contemporary Sociology, 29(2), 319–328. doi:10.2307/2654387

Rochlen, A. B., Blazina, C., & Raghunathan, R. (2002). Gender role conflict, attitudes toward career counseling, career decision-making, and perceptions of career counseling advertising brochures. Psychology of Men & Masculinity, 3(2), 127–137. doi:10.1037/1524-9220.3.2.127

Sheehy, G. (1974). Passages: predictable crisis of adult life. New York, NY: Ballantine Books.

Tsan, J. Y., & Day, S. X. (2007). Personality and gender as predictors of online counseling use. Journal of Technology in Human Services, 25, 39–55.

Tsan, J. Y., Day, S. X., Schwartz, J. P., & Kimbrel, N. A. (2011). Restrictive emotionality, BIS, BAS, and psychological help-seeking behavior. Psychology of Men & Masculinity, 12(3), 260–274. doi:10.1037/a0021636

13

Counseling LGBTQ Groups

Teri Hourihan, LPC, NCC

Do not judge and you will not be judged. Do not condemn and you will not be condemned. Forgive and you will be forgiven

Luke 6:37, NIV

Homosexuality was well known in the ancient world, well before Christ was born and Jesus never said a word about homosexuality. In all of his teachings about multiple things—he never said that gay people should be condemned. I personally think it is very fine for gay people to be married in civil ceremonies.

President Jimmy Carter (2012)

LEARNING OBJECTIVES

In this chapter, students will learn about

- Lesbian, gay, bisexual, transgender, and queer (LGBTQ) definitions and history
- How to work with LGBTQ clients through a multicultural lens
- The discrimination and oppression experienced by LGBTQ in the workforce
- Career counselor's responsibilities to standards and ethics when working with LGBTQ clients

- The Council of Accreditation of Counseling and Related Educational Programs (CACREP) standards, the American Counseling Association (ACA) code of ethics, spiritual competencies, multicultural competencies, the Association of Lesbian, Gay, Bisexual, and Transgender Issues in Counseling (ALGBTIC) competencies, and how these entities each support LGBTQ client care

LEARNING OUTCOMES

At the end of this chapter, students will be able to

- Successfully apply career theory to LGBTQ clients
- To apply the knowledge learned from the chapter to real-life client cases
- Identify areas of advocacy that are paramount for LGBTQ clients that counselors can promote in the community
- Set up their counseling room to support LGBTQ clients, counsel to support therapeutic rapport, and know how to assess for desired client pronouns
- Supervise from a clinical perspective to support LGBTQ clients, LGBTQ supervisees, or supervisees working with LGBTQ clients

CHAPTER HIGHLIGHTS

- LGBTQ acronym defined
- LGBTQ history—oppression and discrimination
- Standards and ethics supporting LGBTQ
- Career counseling with LGBTQ through a Christian perspective
- Work and healthcare discrimination
- LGBTQ marriage and workplace discrimination

INTRODUCTION

Counselors are not called upon to judge whether their clients' decisions are right or wrong. Instead, counselors are asked to take an unbiased stance as they help their clients' work toward wellness (ACA, 2014, A.11.b). When it comes to overall session evaluation, mental health counseling and career counseling are similar (Magee & Whiston, 2010). Each counselor engages their client in a therapeutic relationship to help meet the goals and objectives of counseling.

Lesbian, gay, bisexual, transgender, and queer (LGBTQ) people, groups, and communities are the population focus of this chapter. Because this book is about career counseling with a spiritual emphasis and integration, this chapter will detail how career counselors can work competently with LGBTQ people and groups. In order to provide a well-built perspective on this topic, it is necessary to detail several areas. Therefore, the first section will attend to the history of LGBTQ over the last century. Small sections of LGBTQ history will be summarized with the goal to provide insight concerning how stigmas, opportunities, ethics, and laws that have changed over the years.

Next, a thorough list of terms will be provided regarding LGBTQ-competent care. Following, some suggestions for how to set up a counseling room to support LGBTQ will be outlined as well as the importance of building rapport with such clients. Throughout this chapter the concept of discrimination in regards to LGBTQ people is detailed. Topics of discrimination include marriage and healthcare in the workplace. As it remains, the topic of discrimination is spread out throughout the chapter.

There are several highlights and examples of standards and ethics for career counselors regarding the treatment they provide for LGBTQ. These include the ACA Code of Ethics, Council for Accreditation of Counseling and Related Educational Programs (CACREP) Standards, Multicultural Competencies produced by the Association for Multicultural and Counseling Development (AMCD) (Arredondo et al., 1996), Spiritual Competencies (ASERVIC), and the Association of Lesbian, Gay, Bisexual, and Transgender Issues in Counseling (ALGBTIC).

LGBT TERMS AND DESCRIPTIONS

LGBT

To begin with, a few terms need to be defined: lesbian refers to a woman who is sexually, emotionally, and physically attracted to women; gay refers to a man who is sexually, emotionally, and physically attracted to men; bisexual refers to a man or woman who is sexually, emotionally, and physically attracted to both male and female; transgender refers to a person who does not feel their assigned sex at birth describes their assigned gender; and queer refers to a man or woman who does not identify as male or female but rather as gender neutral (ALGBTIC, 2012).

LGBT stands for lesbian, gay, bisexual, and transgender and it represents the group as a whole. The letter Q was added to the LGBT acronym around the year 1980 (Nelson, 2009). The letter Q represents the term queer, meaning strange, different, and fitting in with the LGBT lifestyle (Nelson). Each letter in the acronym LGBTQ is capitalized to represent each group as unique; yet, each letter is combined into the full term to represent the similar experiences each represents (Nelson). However, this acronym was not always used to describe this group (Freeman & Rupp, 2015).

Originally, the term homosexual was used to describe same sex relationships (Freeman & Rupp, 2015). The term homosexuality was coined in 1869 by Hungarian journalist David Ulrichs and used in English literature in 1880 (Ulrichs & Lombardie-Nash, 1994). Nonetheless, the term was certainly around prior to 1869, as it shows up within the text of the Bible (Leviticus 18:22, 20:13; 1 Timothy 1:10; 1 Corinthians 6:9). In 1970, the term gay replaced the term homosexuality (Drescher, 2015; Weeks, 1998). This occurred because of the negative connotation of how the term homosexuality was used in mainstream society as a pathological disease (Gay and Lesbian Alliance Against Defamation [GLAAD], n.d.; Stewart, 2009). Terms representing only women attracted to other women were developed to stand separate from that which meant men attracted to other men. Again, the term lesbian represents a woman sexually, emotionally, and physically attracted to women, not men. Before 1970, the terms gay and homosexual represented both men and women attracted to the same sex (Freeman and Rupp, 2015). Heading into the 1980s, new terms such as bisexual, transgender, and queer were formed to represent that which was different from gay and lesbian (Freeman & Rupp, 2015).

Sexuality and Gender Terms

There are numerous terms to describe sexuality and gender types (Eliason, 2014; GLAAD). Some are very outdated (e.g., dyke) and some are brand new (e.g., pansexual, gender fluid) (GLAAD). As times change, people change in how they speak about sexual and gender minorities. For the career counselor, this is important to understand because they are likely going to directly come into contact with this population at some point in their careers (Troutman & Packer-Williams, 2014).

Eliason (2014) was interested in understanding how published research would define sexuality and gender. He discovered that researchers in general have not agreed-upon definitions for these terms. This suggests the terms to describe the LGBTQ person and community are somewhat undistinguished. Therefore, the terms used to provide competent care to LGBTQ persons can be argued against. Nonetheless, they are terms which are deemed most appropriate to use (ALGBTIC, 2012). Due to the term homosexual no longer being appropriate, especially with the newer generations of LGBTQ people, the term queer is being used instead. However, some are rejecting terms altogether, believing, instead, that terms used to describe their sexual and gender identities are too labeling (Eliason, 2014). This goes for youth too. For instance, in surveys completed by youth, there were more acceptances of nongeneral LGBTQ terms as opposed to the terms lesbian, gay, and bisexual (Almeida, Johnson, Corliss, Molnar, & Azrael, 2009). To youth and millennial generations, supposedly, these terms are stigmatizing. There are cultural variations in regards to terms as well.

Culture and LGBTQ Terms

The University of Wisconsin-Madison (2016) compiled a list of terms used in U.S. culture that are considered current for 2016. All terms compiled on this list represent terms and acronyms representing LGBTQ persons in one form or another. There are several which show up more often in certain racial and ethnic cultures. A few of these terms include same gender loving, stud, and ag to represent Black females or males sexually attracted to their same sex. Stud and Ag refer only to lesbians, more often Black women, who appear masculine. Native Americans are more often referred to as two-spirited to label the queer or transgender person (University of Wisconsin-Madison, 2016).

There are also terms used to describe transgender people. Transgender people are those who feel their bodies do not reflect their sexual development (Eliason, 2014). Using terms such as transsexual, transvestite, gender queer, man-to-female, female-to-man, gender crosser, and transmasculine are appropriate to describe someone who identifies as transgender (Eliason, 2014). Additional terms for transgender people include crossdresser and gender nonconforming (University of Wisconsin-Madison, 2016). There are also terms to describe where on the gender continuum a person falls: "butch, femme, nelly queen, fairy, androgynous, effeminate, and lipstick lesbian" (Eliason, 2014, p. 169). The gender continuum is that which represents femininity on one side and masculinity on the other.

In and of itself, the acronym LGBTQ is used so often that it has become a term which describes a general community or person. Nonetheless, using the term LGBTQ to refer to the group as a whole can promote stigma or reduce stigma (Almeida et al., 2009). The promotion of stigma is clear. The literature supports the notion that minority status reflects stigma, especially for those who are part of the LGBTQ community (Almeida et al., 2009; Pollard, 2014). In effect, when the terms are clumped together, there is little room to notice the uniqueness of each group (Eliason, 2014). The acronym LGBTQ can reduce stigma, however, by its inclusion of all groups into one. Two terms considered safe to use to refer to the group or person is gender minority or sexual minority (Almeida et al., 2009).

New Millennial Terms

Two terms have been growing more popular in recent times: pansexual and gender fluid. These terms are typically represented in younger generations of adolescents (Gonel, 2013). The meaning behind these terms is that the sexual and gender identity of a person is neutral with no sexual or gender preference but instead attraction toward all (Boom, 2008; Gonel, 2013). In other words, this person has no preference for dating male, female, transgender, or queer persons. The change is often reflected in who they are dating at any particular time (Better, 2014; Gonel, 2013).

About 5% to 10% of youth represented in the United States are LGBT (Quintana, Rosenthal, & Krehely, 2010). For these youths who identify as transgender or gender fluid, they experience a high amount of discrimination and victimization online and in person ("Mental Health Diseases and Conditions," 2017). Largely for this reason, they are not likely to come out (disclose their sexual and gender identity status) (Guittar, 2013) before they reach adulthood (Guittar, 2013). According to the ALGBTIC (2012) competencies, LGBTQ clients are potentially vulnerable. Research also supports the ALGBTIC statement of vulnerability (Almeida et al., 2009; Silvestre, 2003; Troutman & Packer-William, 2014). In addition, counselors working with LGBTQ adults and adolescents who are struggling with the coming-out phase should not force them to disclose their sexual orientation or gender identity before they are ready because of the potential harm that can happen to the client (ALGBTIC, 2012; "Lesbian, gay, bisexual and transgender (LGBT) members spoke...," 2008).

Terms and labels are features of counseling that counselors should educate themselves on first before attempting counseling with any clients (ALGBTIC, 2012). All clients have specific terms, labels, and pronouns they prefer over others. The counselor preparing to career council may think that these areas are not important to assess for. However, if counselors do not assess for sexual orientation and gender-identity preference, they likely will not understand the barriers their clients are experiencing in preparing for career transitions (ALGBTIC, 2012). It is interesting to remember that Christ was very careful and cautious about how he interacted with the people around him. He stopped, waited, and took time to know the problem and thought before he reacted. Consider Matthew 8:5–13:

> When Jesus had entered Capernaum a centurion came to him and asked for help. "Lord," he said, "my servant lies at home paralyzed, suffering terribly." Jesus said to him, "Shall I come and heal him?" The centurion replied, "Lord, I do not deserve to have you come under my roof. But just say the word, and my servant will be healed. For I myself am a man under authority, with soldiers under me. I tell this one, 'Go,' and he goes; and that one, 'Come,' and he comes. I say to my servant, 'Do this,' and he does it." When Jesus heard this, he was amazed and said to those following him, "Truly I tell you, I have not found anyone in Israel with such great faith. I say to you that many will come from the east and the west, and will take their places at the feast with Abraham, Isaac and Jacob in the kingdom of heaven. But the subjects of the kingdom will be thrown outside, into the darkness, where there will be weeping and gnashing of teeth." Then Jesus said to the centurion, "Go! Let it be done just as you believed it would." And his servant was healed at that moment (NIV).

This part of scripture shows evidence that Christ was open to anyone—even apart from his disciples—approaching him and asking for help, that he responds with great detail, shows compassion, listens, and produces a behavioral response that helps aid the person in their struggle. Career counselors also need to be willing to listen, show empathy, and help clients on the vocational journey they are on.

Now that an exhaustive section on terms and correct verbiage to use with LGBTQ has been provided, the next section will detail some of the LGBTQ history and trends leading to this point in time. Essentially, it is important to know the context of current times.

LGBTQ HISTORY

There is a long history behind the LGBTQ community (Stewart, 2009, 2010). Weeks (1998) provides an in-depth summary of the last century regarding LGBTQ history. In terms of literary novelists and writers on homosexuality and sexuality, the earliest Weeks mentions in was in 1914. Literary writers such as Edward Carpenter, Havelock Ellis, and Iwan Bloch are mentioned. These writers, suggested Weeks, were some of the first to speak and write openly about the LGBTQ lifestyle. In the historical times of these writers, LGBTQ represented something unfamiliar; today, however, this population is common (Williams & Deyoe, 2015). Furthermore, same-sex relationships are documented in ancient history in texts such as the Bible. For instance, 1 Timothy 1:10 states "for the sexually immoral, for those practicing homosexuality, for slave traders and liars and perjures—and whatever else is contrary to the sound doctrine…" and Leviticus 18:2 states "do not have sexual relations with a man as one does with a woman; that is detestable" (NIV). Unfortunately, the Bible does not support a positive outlook on LGBTQ on face value. More recently, the Diagnostic Statistical Manual (DSM) which is used by professional counselors—among other healthcare professionals—to provide care to clients and patients also does not support the LGBTQ lifestyle (American Psychiatric Association [APA], 2013; Arthur, McGill, & Essary, 2014). The DSM labels homosexuality in the first and second editions of 1952 and 1968 as a psychological mental disorder and in 2013—the latest edition, DSM-V—the term **gender dysphoria** is used to describe a person not comfortable in their gender by birth (APA, 1952, 1968, 2013). Consider the DSM I (1952) definition of sexual deviancy:

> This diagnosis is reserved for deviant sexuality which is not symptomatic of more extensive syndromes, such as schizophrenic and obsessional reactions. The term includes most of the cases formerly classed as "psychopathic personality with pathologic sexuality." The diagnosis will specify the type of the pathologic behavior, such as homosexuality, transvestism, pedophilia, fetishism and sexual sadism (including rape, sexual assault, mutilation). (p. 38–39)

Therefore, for the Christian professional counselor, it can be especially difficult to differentiate a sinful lifestyle versus a mental health concern when both of their texts (Bible and DSM) depict the LGBTQ lifestyle as sinful or a psychological illness. Furthermore, the Christian career counselor may feel a lack of support from each of their communities (Christian and counseling) when they begin to work with LGBTQ people through an integration of each of the areas. During the early stages of the DSM I and II, LGBTQ people entering treatment were diagnosed as "homosexual" and provided treatment to correct their disorder (Drescher, 2015). The focus of treatment was on the person's sexuality and gender identity versus, for example, their depression, anxiety, or any other issue the person presented with in treatment. In 1973, via much support from medical professionals and the American Psychiatric Association, homosexuality was removed when the DSM II was updated to the DSM III (Drescher, 2015). This was a win for the LGBTQ community and for professionals. Nonetheless, during the era when homosexuality was viewed as a mental disorder, specific types of therapies were introduced to try to change a person's sexual orientation from gay to straight. One such theory was reparative therapy (McGeorge, Carlson, & Toomey, 2015).

Reparative therapy. Now considered an unethical therapeutic approach, reparative therapy, also named conversion therapy, was used by professional counselors and psychologists to change the sexual orientation of a person from gay to straight. The art of this therapy was to reverse what was then considered a deviant behavior, or mental disorder (McGeorge et al., 2015). LGBTQ clients entering into therapy could request reparative therapy or seek out a counselor specifically trained. Reparative therapy began in the 1970s, again, likely the result of the DSM I and II listing homosexuality as a mental disorder (Arthur et al., 2014).

In 2012, California passed a new bill prohibiting any professional treatment provider to use reparative therapy with minors under the age of 18. Fowler's (2012) article includes an interview with former reparative therapy client Peter Drake, who told his story of reparative therapy, which resulted in greater depression for Drake. Fowler's article was written just prior to the California bill passing. Bill 1172 prohibited only professional providers from using reparative therapy with minors. It did not, however, prohibit church organizations and pastoral personnel from using it (Arthur et al., 2014; Moss, 2014; McMurchie, 2014). It can also still be used with adults. Currently, reparative therapy is prohibited from being used with minors in California, Vermont, the District of Columbia, New Jersey, Oregon, and Illinois (Movement Advanced Project [MAP], 2016).

The American Counseling Association (ACA, 2014), the American Psychological Association (APA, 2000), and the American Psychiatric Association (2000) have rendered reparative therapy as unethical with all clients, nonetheless. These organizations, among many more, support the fair and ethical treatment of LGBTQ clients and patients. Most recently, the ACA made a tremendous statement regarding the unfair treatment of LGBTQ persons and groups by changing their annual 2017 conference venue from Nashville, Tennessee to San Francisco, California. This was in response to Tennessee Governor Bill Haslam signing into law Senate Bill 1556 and House Bill 1840 that stated counselors are able to deny services to clients based on the differences of their beliefs and values (ACA, 2016). This law goes against the 2014 ACA Code of Ethics rendering counselors ethically responsible to provide services to clients regardless of their differences of beliefs and values (A.11.b).

History: Gender Neutral in the 1800s

Continuing with the historical trends, in 1855 Times Magazine published an article titled "The Baby Show" ("The Baby Show," 1855). This was a time when parents all around the United States brought their infants and toddlers to New York City to have them judged based on areas such as size, temperament, and appearance. The author of the article details the specifics of what each of the babies was wearing, in which it becomes clear that no type or color of clothing was specific to either gender. For instance, some of the male babies were wearing pink and dresses and some of the female babies were wearing blue and slacks. Therefore, what becomes apparent from articles such as this is that gender based on colors and appearance has changed over the years. Today, it is widely accepted that in the United States, society perceives blue is for boys and pink is for girls. For LGBTQ, especially transgender and queer persons, these color-by-gender specifics may be a source of discrimination.

Early Historical Gateways for LGBTQ

The rights of LGBTQ have developed through various amendments and laws that were largely created for reasons and people outside of LGBTQ causes. Nonetheless, as a result of these laws and amendments in place, LGBTQ have also been supported in these causes. Two such examples include the Title IX Education Amendment of 1972 and the Equal Access Act of 1984 (Kimmel, 2016; Stewart, 2009). Each of these were created to provide a safe school environment for all kids. LGBTQ youth were not directly part of these causes; however, they benefited from them (Stewart, 2009). The Title IX Education Amendment states that no public school that receives federal funding can discriminate based on sex—for instance, no child can be told they cannot participate in a sport or school activity based solely on their sexual identity (Stewart, 2009; U.S. Department of Justice, 2015). Over a decade later, Christian groups were pushing for the right to form Bible study and church groups on school grounds during breaks or after school. Not even created with all students in mind—especially LGBTQ students—the Act passed and groups could begin to form on school grounds based on certain criteria. LGBTQ groups started to request to form their own clubs, specifically gay-straight-alliance clubs, on school grounds but, unfortunately, they received much backlash from school administrators. Eventually, the courts upheld the right of LGBTQ groups to form on school grounds under the act. Consequently, many schools chose to shut down the group opportunity for all (Stewart, 2009). As it was, the act gave permission to schools to either open up the opportunity for all or close it to all.

Currently, the LGBTQ community is making its way toward greater rights and opportunities. Next, a consideration of how career counselors can utilize a counselor checklist during their work with LGBTQ clients is explored.

CAREER COUNSELOR CHECKLIST

Shifting focus, career counselors should consider developing a personal checklist for providing treatment to clients from diverse backgrounds. There is a lot of evidence that counselors in clinical fields are not feeling adequately prepared to counsel LGBTQ clients with competence (Farmer, Welfare, & Burge, 2013). This is concerning since counselors are required to provide services that are aligned with ethical standards (ACA, 2014). Nonetheless, the field is rather new regarding evidenced-based treatment for LGBTQ. Therefore, it is not surprising that in recent surveys counselors and counselors-in-training are confirming their lack of training to work with this diverse population. The counselor checklist is simply a way for counselors to develop a plan for their counseling approach when working with LGBTQ clients (Holcomb-McCoy, 2004). Essentially, if there are areas where counselors believe their skills are underdeveloped, this can indicate to them that they need training or to engage in research or consultation as they continue working with these diverse populations.

The checklist proposed by Holcomb-McCoy considers counselor competencies as a priority. Her article reflects on the school counselor; nonetheless, multicultural and diverse competencies are also meaningful to the career counselor (Ebin & Belyeu, 2016). One of the first ways counselors can show competency to work with LGBTQ clients is knowing the correct terms to use when referring to LGBTQ. Counselors can also be educated about the names of different sexual and gender identities in circulation as well as how to respect the pronouns each client wants to be called by. The counselor checklist could also include how to set up the counseling room, provide unconditional positive regard to clients, and check in with clients regarding their spiritual and religious involvement. Checking off each box for counselor competency and goals is one way career counselors can make sure their focus stays in the context of LGBTQ.

THREE AREAS OF CONSIDERATION FOR COUNSELING LGBTQ CLIENTS

Setting Up the Counseling Room

The first consideration is a how a counseling room should be arranged. This room should be set up as inclusive for all and for all to feel welcome. The Gay, Lesbian, and Straight Education Network (GLSEN) (2016) is a resource for professionals working with LGBTQ youth, more often professionals such as teachers and administrators working in K–12 school systems. The GLSEN mentions the importance of context regarding inclusiveness of all youth. The GLSEN can also provide meaning to the counseling context as counselors engaging in career counseling consider the setting clients will enter.

Moreover, counselors should set up the counseling room with supportive material for LGBTQ inclusiveness. Supportive material might include quotes, community pamphlets for LGBTQ-related events, and wearing small trinkets—a bracelet or a sticker—stating LGBTQ support (GLSEN, 2016). Simply wearing a bracelet with a rainbow on it or posting a rainbow in your office could be enough to signify your support and ward off unwanted colleague or community discrimination. In addition, the counseling context can promote client safety by using terms such as **partner** when referring to a romantic relationship and the nongender pronouns "they" versus "him" or "her" (GLSEN, 2016). Using language that respects the client's wishes is key to providing competent care to LGBTQ clients (Harper et al., 2004). Counselors should also have an idea about local employers' stance on LGBTQ inclusiveness. In addition, knowing where support in the community is regarding career development and social events can be useful for counselors to know offhand rather than having to take time from counseling to come up with these resources.

Unconditional Positive Regard for the Minority Client

The second consideration is the counselor recognizing the importance of unconditional positive regard toward their minority clients. There are natural stressors that occur as a result of being part of a minority group (Blume & Lavato, 2010; Harper et al., 2004). Minority status is a source of discrimination and oppression compared to holding majority status. LGBTQ persons are considered a minority population in the United States and in most parts of the world. Each of the entities encased within LGBTQ—lesbian, gay, bisexual, and transgender—experiences oppression and discrimination at their own level and at the system's level (Kelleher, 2009).

LGBTQ persons and communities experience oppression and discrimination because of the identity they stand for. They represent something unique to the majority population. Their sexual preference, choice of attire, and often "loud" appearance demonstrates against the norm standards compared to the typical American culture that is composed and even-keeled (Individualistic Cultures, 2016). LGBTQ persons and groups are many times harassed both physically and verbally as well as emotionally abused by the everyday, common person. In fact, many times they are harassed by complete strangers. Their families also become a source of contempt, hate, and rejection (Stewart, 2009). Especially for the LGBTQ person who comes out to their family, it is they who are at great risk for ostracism by their family members, sometimes their whole families. This is the reality for many LGBTQ people. That is why having the LGBTQ community as well organizations to support their social and emotional needs becomes critical (Paceley, Oswald, & Hardesty, 2014).

Also a concern, many LGBTQ persons are subject to rejection and discrimination in churches and in their faith communities (Stewart, 2009). There are times when LGBTQ persons will not be allowed to attend church, join in holy communion, or become a leader within church bodies, and they may be subjected to being told their sexual orientation is sin and an abomination to God. No wonder people from this community report struggling in their faith and with the Christian community in general (Paprocki, 2014).

Church and LGBTQ. LGBTQ in the context of church is somewhat of a sensitive issue in mainstream society. Watson (2015), for example, found through interviews of church pastors that there is an internal struggle within pastors who are providing care to LGBTQ members. Additionally, most churches in the United States are not openly accepting, or LGBTQ-affirming, of LGBTQ members (gaychurch.org, 2017). Therefore, counselors must recognize that when an LGBTQ person comes to receive counseling, they are bringing with them the pain from years of societal injustice. These are some of the issues counselors must be aware of as they journey to provide career counseling to these populations. Counselors also need to realize that they too bring into counseling their own biases and discriminatory beliefs (Harper et al., 2004). Therefore, it is notably critical for the counselor-in-training who identifies as religious to have training on providing counseling to the LGBTQ client.

Therapeutic Relationship with the LGBTQ Client

Finally, with this third consideration, it is just as meaningful to acknowledge the relationship between counselor and LGBTQ client as it is to acknowledge the value in skill development to work with this client. The relationship between client and counselor is perhaps the most important area of counseling LGBTQ clients (Fulton, 2016; Lamprecht, 2015; Sackett & Lawson, 2016). To continue, the relationship factor between a counselor and an LGBTQ client is built on trust and, at times, counselor self-disclosure (Evans & Barker, 2010). Evans and Barker were interested to know if LGBTQ clients considered it important for counselors to self-disclose their sexual orientation. While few clients in their qualitative study stated self-disclosure by the counselor was important to the counseling process, most of the comments by clients reflected how important it was to the client to feel they could trust their counselor. When LGBTQ clients felt their counselor was judgmental toward their sexual orientation, the counseling relationship suffered and trust for the counselor diminished. It is important to know that most of the LGBTQ clients in Evans and Barker's study did not state that the sexual orientation of the counselor was essential—they were open to working with heterosexual or LGBTQ counselors—but, instead, it was the counselor's comfort, knowledge, and openness to the client's sexual orientation that was paramount to the client's progress in counseling.

COUNSELOR AND THE LGBTQ CLIENT

Counselors should be intentional to receive specific training on working with LGBTQ clients (Troutman & Packer-Williams, 2014). This may mean they engage in training outside of their educational programs or register for continuing education courses that focus on providing treatment to LGBTQ clients. Again, it is also important that counselors reflect on their potential biases, especially for the counselor who is heterosexual. Troutman and Packer-Williams mention the necessary steps heterosexual counselors need to take to address their heterosexual privilege. Heterosexual privilege is an automatic privilege of heterosexual people. This privilege includes the ability to marry the person you love without judgement, the open rights to fostering and adopting children, the public showing of affection to a spouse, the freedom to express your sexuality openly to your coworkers, and the right to apply for higher tax accommodations each year. For the counselor, this privilege might include the power in the counseling relationship when working with sexual-minority clients (Troutman & Packer-William).

CAREER DEVELOPMENT FOR THE LGBTQ CLIENT

LGBTQ people experience barriers in their career development (Schmidt, Miles, & Welsh, 2011). Perhaps one of their first experiences with career developmental barriers is on college campuses. Oppression and discrimination on college campuses is happening. These potential barriers can come in many forms, such as through verbal statements. Consider the research by Powell (2013), for instance, who discovered that although both heterosexual and LGBTQ college students hear discriminatory terms on college campuses, each heard different terms. Further, the propensity for certain terms to be used in one context (LGBTQ) versus another context (heterosexual) is considered. In essence, LGBTQ people were more likely hear statements such as "you are so gay," whereas heterosexual students heard terms such as **faggot** and **dyke**. Seemingly this suggests that all students hear oppressive LGBT terms yet the terms are different depending on the social environment. Powell's research suggests not that discriminatory statements happen but they happen in a way that is different depending on the sample of people. When the context changes, the comments change too.

Feeling the sense of acceptance as an LGBTQ college student is a necessary developmental milestone. Verbal statements reflect just one way through which acceptance versus rejection is often experienced. Support and acceptance can also be shown through action. For students, support allotted to them through administrators and professors is far-reaching. At Iowa State University, for instance, 18 professors and administrators signed a proposal allowing for a new project on campus to take effect (Evans, 2002). This project, called the Safe Zone Project, was developed for the sole purpose of giving LGBTQ students a feeling of safety in their school. This project developed community support, which is something valuable for career counselors to emphasize with LGBTQ clients (Schmidt et al., 2011).

However, many LGBTQ students do not feel they have the support of allies like some of their heterosexual peers do (Joyce, 2014). Joyce's article pinpoints areas of concern related to students feeling less overall support from professors and administrators and a need to hide their sexual orientation. For these students, so-called underground support groups have risen up so the necessary community support is provided to these students (Joyce, 2014). Especially for Christian LGBTQ students, these underground support groups could mean their only lifeline to be open to peers about their sexual and gender identities. For these students, coming out to family and friends and in their universities may not be the safest choice (Joyce, 2014).

RELIGION, SPIRITUALITY, AND THE LGBTQ CLIENT

Religion and spirituality can and does exist in the lives of LGBTQ persons. Despite the tremendous difficulty of the coming out experience for most LGBTQ persons, the religion of the LGBTQ person's parents has only some influence (Pastrana, 2015). Perhaps the most interesting piece of Pastrana's findings was that religion was not the influence which drove or negated the coming out experience for LGBTQ persons; in fact, many LGBTQ people believe religion and spirituality to be important (Mili, 2005). Mili, furthermore, provides an interesting way to look at scripture as a way to support LGBTQ people. For example, Jeremiah 31:33 states, "I will put my law within them and on their heart I will write it…" (English Standard Version (ESV). Mili states there are two interpretations: (1) God accepts LGBTQ persons because they were born with such desires and (2) God wills the LGBTQ person into becoming a straight person. Helping professionals can utilize Mili's interpretations as a way to help LGBTQ persons to find the faith circle they might wish to join.

Christian career counselor dilemmas. Christian career counselors working with LGBTQ clients have a challenging role to fill. For starters, they are bridging the gap for these clients in many dynamic ways. Barriers exist that counselors have to learn to navigate for and with their clients. Just consider Christian counseling by itself; this is its own niche in counseling (Gaehring, 2011). Adding in LGBTQ becomes even more demanding for the counselor. Therefore, it is precisely this career counselor who needs training in LGBTQ issues. Christian career counselors, likewise, have a responsibility to engage in counseling from a religious and spiritual perspective as found in the competencies developed by the Association for Spiritual, Ethical, and Religious, Values in Counseling (ASERVIC, 2009; Cashwell & Watts, 2010).

However, Christian counselors are presented with a dilemma: they are ethically obligated to provide counseling to an LGBTQ person even when their religious beliefs and values may differ (ACA, 2014, A.11.b). This ACA ethic is true in 49 out of the 50 states in the United States. As already mentioned, Tennessee law now states that counselors can refer based on the differences of values and beliefs (ACA, 2016). Along with this, the ASERVIC stated within their 2010 competencies that they fully support the ACA code of ethics and multicultural competencies, and the ALGBTIC competencies (Cashwell & Watts, 2010). Arguably, the

Christian counselor does have an obligation to provide competent counseling to the LGBTQ client in every state of the United States, not including Tennessee.

It is reasonable to assume that career counseling for many Christian counselors is a trying time. Francis and Dugger (2014) recognized that counselors wanting to stay true to their career standards while also holding true to their faith are in a difficult situation. Their article summarized some of the dilemmas Christian counselors face to uphold both their Christian beliefs and the ACA code of ethics at the same time. A highlight is that counselors have the unique perspective of seeing from two lenses: the lens of Christianity and the lens of counseling. From this perspective, it is the Christian counselor who actually is in the best position to create change. Certainly, once the Christian counselor moves into a position of neutrality—being open to accepting all clients—their position can become more influential in the counseling room with clients.

Regardless of religious or nonreligious background, career counselors have a role to play in the career development of their clients. Stoltz and Young (2013) present a model of career development utilizing motivational interviewing (MI). They suggest a stage approach with MI as a leading component. These stages with the client are establishing rapport, assessment, "rolling with resistance," focus on self-efficacy, empathy, and termination (Stoltz & Young, 2013). This approach is a useful model for any counselor working in the field of career counseling. Particularly for the Christian counselor (not the career counselor), MI is an approach to counseling that is supported in the literature for their use (Martin & Sihn, 2009) and use with LGBTQ clients (Chen et al., 2016; Harding, Dockrell, Dockrell, & Corrigan, 2001). However, although MI in career counseling is shown to be useful with general samples with unknown sexual or gender orientations, at this time no studies could be located that focused on career counselors using MI with LGBTQ clients. Therefore, this is a suggested research area for future studies. It would be very interesting to see a study completed on the use of MI by a Christian career counselor engaging in counseling with LGBTQ clients.

GENERAL CAREER COUNSELING ISSUES AND SUPERVISION

Lack of Counselor Training to Work with LGBTQ

Counselors need to be trained on specific ways to offer career counseling to their LGBTQ clients. (Troutman & Packer-Williams, 2016). Once reparative therapy was considered unethical, counselors were left floundering to find techniques to use with persons who came into counseling wanting help with their sexual orientation. Luckily, the response has been positive from counselor educators who have provided responses for what to do in the midst of the new ethical standards in the field of counseling. These responses included ways to provide counseling through empathic regard, client-centered care, concern for treatment planning to be focused on client concerns and not counselor concerns, and ways to guide the counseling direction through techniques used with other client populations (Troutman & Packer-Williams, 2016).

Essentially, a counselor-in-training struggles with the questioning of what to do with an LGBTQ client. Nonetheless, although LGBTQ clients are certainly their own population, an

LGBTQ client can go through the same life struggles as a heterosexual person goes through (e.g., marriage, bereavement, loss, grief). As it remains, just because a person is LGBTQ does not mean their experience of life is completely unlike a heterosexual person's life. Moreover, the difference often lies in how they each experience the event—their perception.

Troutman and Packer-Williams (2014) describe the importance of counselors-in-training receiving specific training to work with the LGBTQ client within their schooling curriculum or private workshops. However, the Council for Accreditation of Counseling and Related Educational Programs (CACPREP) recommendations, as summarized by Troutman and Packer-Williams, are for the focus of these training agendas to not necessarily reflect a different counseling paradigm to use with LGBTQ clients but instead to train counselors on the LGBTQ-person experience within a cultural and systematic context. There needs to be more focus on the LGBTQ identity development and mental health concerns related to this population while reducing the focus on sexual orientation (Alessi, 2013). Just like knowing the suicide risk factors for youth versus adults in the general population, counselors are to know the risk and protective factors for the LGBTQ population.

Meyers (2016) supports the view regarding counselors focusing on LGBTQ client concerns as opposed to their sexual identity (unless the client wants to focus on their sexual identity). Meyers reports that LGBTQ clients respond well to affirmative therapies. This report indicated that affirmative therapies were useful to LGBTQ clients because they acknowledge the discrimination and stigma experienced by LGBTQ persons and they tend to focus on the concerns of the client rather than on their sexual orientation. In effect, how to work competently with LGBTQ clients should be a focus of counselor training (Alessi, 2013). Consequently, at this time, there are instances when counselors-in-training and professional counselors think they have zero experience to work with the LGBTQ client, so they either refuse to work with this population altogether (Meyers, 2016) or flounder within the counseling room when working with them.

Counselor Education

Counselor education lacks clear attention to LGBTQ literature and training (Farmer et al., 2013). Up until 15 years ago, there was little emphasis for providing specific training for LGBTQ focus. As a result, there was not a lot of opportunity for counselors to receive this training. The field of counseling as well as other fields—psychology and social work—began to take notice that there was a need for training in these areas of diversity. As educational institutions widen their programs to include more multicultural and diversity courses, LGBTQ focus will likely expand too. Until this occurs, counselors entering the counseling field may continue to feel discomfort working with LGBTQ people. Thus, early supervision is important.

Supervision of the Counselor-in-Training

Supervision is a path to career development and wellness (Meany-Walen, Davis-Gage, & Lindo, 2016). Meany-Walen et al.'s study sought to find out if a supervisory approach that focused on supporting counselors-in-training through a wellness model was effective at increasing total wellness. Total wellness was measured by the Five Factor Wellness Inventory created by Myers and Sweeney (2008). This scale measures coping, creativity, sociability, physical, and essential of self. This was a supervisor relationship over the course of counselors-in-training practicum semesters that included weekly supervision using curriculum focused on wellness. Their research suggests that counselors-in-training need the supportive foundation to explore their own wellness first, following with the wellness of their clients. Essentially, career counselors too need to have their own sense of wellness before providing wellness to others.

Counselors-in-training should have supervisory training experiences that help them to understand their own true or potential biases, engage in self-exploration, learn about the discrimination and oppression of LGBTQ groups, and hold an expectation that their supervisor has a large cultural worldview regarding LGBTQ communities (Owen-Pugh & Baines, 2014). Supervisees should also be given the chance to learn about possible countertransference that can occur in counseling. And, if the counselor-in-training is heterosexual, they need to understand the risk of their own potential heterosexist oppression that can become a barrier to their effectiveness in counseling (Owen-Pugh & Baines, 2014). Unfortunately, many training counselors come out of their training still stating they lack comfort to work with LGBTQ. In addition, they often state their frustration concerning supervisors who were not comfortable or knowledgeable about LGBTQ issues. Of course, the only thing fear and avoidance from the supervisor breeds is fear and avoidance from the counselor (Owen-Pugh & Baines, 2014).

Graham, Carney, and Kluck (2012) state in their article that the competency level of counselors-in-training—a competency measured by the Sexual Orientation Counselor Competency Scale developed by Bidell (2005) to work with LGB clients was influenced by their level of skill, knowledge, and awareness of LGB culture and identity. Therefore, the first step is to provide counselors-in-training with a supervisor who is knowledgeable about LGBTQ issues. The second step is to increase counselor-in-training competency by providing opportunities for them to learn about LGBTQ through direct community experience. Graham et al. (2012) stated counselors-in-training can increase their skill, knowledge, and awareness of LGB culture by involving themselves in workshops, having LGB friends, and seeking ways to involve themselves in the community to promote LGB awareness. This can also hold true for counselors working within the confounds of career counseling with LGBTQ clients. Counselors, for instance, can encourage their LGBTQ client to explore career options in LGBTQ communities, develop relationships with other LGBTQ professionals, seek training to increase their self-esteem for job placement, and begin identifying ways to interview that reflect their own personal self.

Counselor Training to Work with LGBTQ Clients
Counselors who receive training to work with LGBTQ people and communities report more comfort when working with this group (Goodrich & Luke, 2010; Love, Smith, Lyall, Mullins, & Cohn, 2015). Love et al. (2015) found that as counselor empathy scores increased, competency to work with LGB clients also increased. When counselors lack empathy, furthermore, they

can simply engage in personal reading about LGB lifestyles to enhance their empathy and competency (Love et al., 2015). Then with training counselors report feeling more competence and empathy (Love et al., 2015); hold fewer biases resulting in discriminatory actions; and have competency (skill, knowledge, and attitudes, as measured by the ACA competencies) to work with LGBTQ population (Hall, McDougald, & Kresica, 2013).

Novice Counselor Qualms

Over 90% of school counselors have worked with an LGBTQ student at some point in their careers. However, 34% of this sample reported feeling somewhat to very unprepared to work with the LGBTQ student population (Hall et al., 2013). Incredibly, school counselors already working in the field who reported no training to work with LGBTQ populations were also expected to work at a competent level with such groups. As evidence of this, the ALGBTIC states within their competency statement that counselors must have training, knowledge, and skill to meet full competency to work with LGBTQ clients (Harper et al., 2009). Therefore, counselors need training, and those without training are left trying to navigate the system on their own. Counselors competent enough to work with LGBTQ clients are aware of the counselor competencies located in the ALGBTIC competency statement, are aware of the discrimination and oppression experienced by this group, and are comfortable providing counseling to LGBTQ persons (Harper et al., 2009; Owen-Pugh & Baines, 2014).

CAREER COUNSELING WITH LGBTQ CLIENTS

Relational Cultural Theory (RCT)

RCT is an approach with LGBTQ clients that has an evidenced-based foundation (Duffey, Haberstroh, & Trepal, 2009; Duffey, Haberstroh, Ciepcielinski, & Gonzales, 2016; Schultheiss, 2003; Duffey & Trepal, 2016; Singh & Moss, 2016). Further, it is an approach that reflects the opportunity for counselors to gain skills and to set in place a foundation for career counseling to take place (Schultheiss, 2003).

The primary focus of RCT is on the relationship between the counselor and the LGBTQ client. It directs attention to how relationships are formed together and how they continue for a period of time (Duffey et al., 2009, 2016). It is the framework by which the ACA division Association for Creativity in Counseling was established. The theory holds that counselors are responsible for fostering the therapeutic relationship with their clients in ways that promote the development of their clients in positive ways (Duffey et al., 2009, 2016). RCT has shown to be effective not only with people from the general public but also specifically with LGBTQ clients. Singh and Moss (2016) conducted a study with LGBTQ participants who made up their study sample and discovered that RCT helped the counselor and client to relate, helped counselors to show accurate and genuine empathy, and fostered trust between the client and the counselor.

How to facilitate RTC. Counselors begin by assessing for how their client tends to build relationships in their life and work settings (Schulthesis, 2003). To facilitate such an assessment, the career counselor should begin by engaging their client in a conversation about how their client perceives their own current work-related relationships. The career counselor is especially interested in understanding their client's strengths and vulnerabilities when it comes to building relationships (Schulthesis, 2003). Once the formal assessment is complete, the counselor moves toward the intervention stage. This assessment process is in the form of questions asked by the counselor to the client.

RCT interventions in career counseling are purposeful. They revolve around helping the client build relational support, utilize their skills to form helping relationships, and to use these formed relationships to overcome career predicaments (Schulthesis, 2003). The intervention phases also consist of counselors encouraging clients to ponder the relationships they have currently and how they could use these relationships to their advantage.

General Career Counseling with LGBTQ Clients

Chung (2003) stated there is a need for researchers to study and publish articles concerning career development and theory with LGBTQ. Since 2003, it seems there has only been minor development in these areas. Pope et al. (2004) recognized the amount of available research on career counseling with LGBTQ had grown since 1900; nonetheless, at the time this chapter was written, the field seems to be struggling overall with focusing on career counseling with LGBTQ. Dagley and Salter (2003) concur with Chung regarding the need for more career counseling research with LGBTQ. It is vital to recognize that career counseling with heterosexual people versus LGBTQ people is different. The same career counseling agenda does not fit each of these groups equally (Gedro, 2008). Consequently, it is not appropriate to explore career counseling in general when referring to the LGBTQ population and what is valid for this group.

Counselors working with LGB people and groups need to be knowledgeable and skilled and have an attitude willing to explore their own biases and countertransference risks during the treatment process (Israel & Selvidge, 2003). Irael and Selvidge summarize the counselor competencies developed by Arredondo et al. (1996). Because of the need for counselors to be knowledgeable and skilled and have the aligned attitude to work with multicultural groups, it can be assumed that this also goes for the counselor working with LGBTQ groups. These groups are considered under the umbrella of multicultural and diverse groups, as mentioned above.

Career counseling with LG groups needs to focus first on counselors understanding the areas of concern of the client (Pope et al., 2004). Pope et al. only mention career counseling with lesbian and gay clients. Chung (2003) stated bisexual and transgender individuals are almost completely ignored. Counselors need to fully assess their client's life circumstances and reasons for coming into counseling from the client's perspective before assuming the direction to take with them. Counselors also need to assess whether their LGBTQ client has come out to family and friends. Additioning, counselors can assess how open their LGBTQ clients are in professional settings, such as in work settings. Counselors wanting to increase their multicultural knowledge and skill should make it a priority to congregate in areas that support LGBTQ lifestyles.

Fortunately, today employers cannot directly ask whether their interviewee is married or has children but they can be discreet about these areas. Pope et al. (2004) suggests counselors cover all areas of potential concern in interviewing for a position that an LGBTQ person might experience. Israel and Selvidge (2003) highlight the same areas in their article. It seems that, overall, the recommendation is for career counselors to understand what LGBTQ lifestyle and culture is in order to better support their clients' needs.

TRANSITIONING INTO THE WORKFORCE

College support from family, friends, and professors helps transition college students from academia to career roles (Schmidt et al., 2011). Even just the perception of low social acceptance by LGBTQ college students can be detrimental to their career development (Schmidt et al., 2011). Schmidt et al. surveyed 189 LGBTQ college students to find out how their career development was negatively impacted by their perception of discrimination versus positively impacted by their perception of social support. At the outcome of their study, it was discovered that the greater the perception of discrimination, the harder it was to make career related decisions. Determined also was that perceived social support was not able to moderate high perceived discrimination to impact career decision-making positively. Schmidt et al.'s research suggests that career counselors should assess for perception of social support and discrimination and use interventions to address these issues. This perception of discrimination, unfortunately, may have been there since adolescence (Almeida et al., 2009); therefore, counselors should assess for length of time of discrimination in each of their clients.

Schmidt et al. (2010) suggest that Super's and Savickas' models of career counseling work well with LGBTQ populations because they were developed to work also with marginalized clients. Each of these models of career counseling have been highlighted throughout this book. Schmidt et al., furthermore, aim to propose that Super's and Savickas' models allow clients to feel safe and heard within their own worldviews and perspectives, leading to an opportunity for these models to work well with LGBTQ clients. In addition, these two models provide an explanation for why LGBTQ clients tend to feel overwhelmed by discrimination in the workforce to a degree that they choose not to attempt to promote within their career roles (Schmidt et al., 2010). A great source for a more in-depth review is the article by the APA (2012) on guidelines for psychological practice with LGB clients. Highlighted in this article are ways to assess LGB clients before and during counseling treatment, complete a thorough psychosocial with clients, provide client-centered care, pay attention to disabilities and medical concerns (seeing potential barriers for career attainment), and assess clients' socioeconomic standards of living (APA, 2012).

Discrimination of Sexual Minorities at Work

On college campuses, trans and queer students are prone to have a negative perception of the school context (in class assignments, help from professors, and curriculum inclusion) when they are more open with their sexuality. Additionally, they were less likely to utilize on-campus resources (Garvey & Rankin, 2015). Whether true or false, these students are also more likely to have lower career expectations following graduation. Ng, Schweitzer, and Lyons (2012) found there to be a correlation between perception of discrimination in college and career expectations. In Ng et al.'s study, the perception was measured by their "anticipated stigma," as defined by Quinn and Chaudoir (2009). These studies suggest that discrimination is experienced both through perception and anticipation, or expectation, of it.

Interesting to discover, in Ng et al.'s study, gay men surveyed had a lower expectation of pay and lesbian women had a higher expectation of pay, each over their heterosexual counterparts. The results at the end of the study found that gay men earn 11% to 27% less than heterosexual men and lesbian women earn 17% to 23% more than heterosexual women. The reason for the change in pay rates across these findings may reflect the pay differential between men and women (Hegewisch & DuMonthier, 2016) over the course of most, if not all, centuries of time (Women's Policy Research, 2016). Hegewisch and DuMonthier suggest the wage gap between men and women may become more equal around year 2059. The lack of parity regarding earnings and gender is not a new finding. Also not new, men are characterized as "masculine" more often than women are. Therefore, the connection could be that lesbian women earn higher wages over and above heterosexual women because lesbian women are more likely to take on the traits of men, such as masculinity, then heterosexual women (Finlay & Scheltema, 1999; Nguyen, 2008). These traits can also reflect heterosexual women who look manlier. The same goes for these women—they threaten the power of the heterosexual male (Nguyen, 2008).

Finlay and Scheltema (1999) caution people not to overthink the term masculine for lesbian women, as in their study, masculinity equaled independence and aggressiveness. Therefore, they suggest naming the traits as independence and aggressiveness rather than masculine. However, the question arises: Would these traits be observed in heterosexual men as independence and aggressiveness too, or as masculine? Despite traits and gender orientation, however, heterosexual men by far experience less work discrimination—perceptual and real—then LGBTQ (Chung, Williams, & Dispenza, 2009). It should be noted, Chung et al. (2009) found that all study participants reflected their own experience of perception.

Promotion and Career Development for LGBTQ

Employment is a context where professional growth is experienced, new college graduates get the opportunity to put their skills into practice, and promotion within organizations exists. It can also be a place where discrimination, oppression, and lack of opportunity can occur for some people. LGBTQ people are subject to these negative experiences (Parnell, Lease, & Green, 2012, 2010; Rumens, 2011). If they are openly gay or lesbian, their chances of discrimination increases (Rosario, Schrimshaw, & Hunter, 2006). Many bisexual people can go unnoticed as part of the LGBTQ community and report overall less discrimination because of their sexual identity (Parker, 2015). Parker stated that bisexual people are much more likely to marry the opposite sex, suggesting that they are much more likely to fit into the societal norm of heterosexual.

Career development is important to the college student as they journey through their degree programs. Generally, one of the goals of attending college is to have career opportunities and use their obtained skillset in a position of choice. Tate et al. (2015) agree, mentioning that college students are attracted to the success college can bring. However, Tate et al. also state that college attainment is linked to the student's beliefs about their own employability once graduated. LGBTQ college students oftentimes lack the confidence in their ability to enter the world of work as both a professional and as an LGBTQ person (Schmidt et al., 2011).

To end this section, the National Center for Transgender Equality (NCTE) is a source on transgender issues and advocacy efforts. The NCTE website provides data on surveys regarding a transgender person's experiences in employment. These surveys report that 23% of transgender people are denied promotion within their jobs because of their gender identity; 50% report discrimination at work; and 45% reported being called by the wrong pronouns at their jobs, either purposely or accidently (NCTE). Therefore, promotion in the workplace is difficult for LGBTQ. It seems the least matched up a person's gender and sexual orientation is to society's expectations, the less likely they are to be promoted. However, some choose to be open at work despite the possibility of discrimination and demotion.

Openly Gay at Work

The decision to be openly gay at work is a tough decision for LGBTQ professionals (Ward, 2015). Teachers especially have a difficult time deciding whether to share their sexual or gender identity with colleagues, students, and the parents of students due to the engrained stigma that LGBTQ people are perverted and child molesters. When we focus on the Christian versus secular work setting, the idea of having an LGBTQ person working within the organization is not common. Dabrowski (2014) mentions that those persons who work in religious organizations and identify as LGBTQ face the real possibility of losing their job as a result of their sexual and gender orientation.

LGBTQ persons feeling safe in their communities and in their work settings has a direct effect on their well-being. Rosario et al. (2006) discovered in their study that the more positive outlook and openness gay men had concerning their sexual orientation, their risk for engaging in unsafe sex decreased and they reported fewer symptoms of anxiety. Rosario et al. suggested that the less anxious the gay men in their study felt, the less their desire to engage in substance abuse was present. However, Rosario et al.'s study found an unexpected result of the coming out experience for gay men: engagement in unprotected anal sex increased. As it turns out, it was the positive attitude they had about being gay which lowered their risk for unprotected sex rather than the coming out process itself. These results were also found in an earlier study led also by Rosario on LGB youth (Rosario, Hunter, Maguen, Gwadz, & Smith, 2001). Again, the more positive outlook an LGB youth had about their sexual orientation after the coming out experience, the lower their stress and their engagement in unprotected sex was. These two studies show that the coming out experience coupled with a positive outlook positively impacts an LGB person's mental health. This has implications for work settings.

When LGB employees are faced with a double minority status—for example, ethnic minority and LGB sexual orientation—accompanied by a fear of discrimination, they are less likely to reveal their sexual identity in their work setting (Perez, 2015). In addition, the double stigma of ethnicity and sexual orientation increases their risk of depression and anxiety. As a result, their coping skills may include trying to pass as heterosexual or taking on the characteristics of their White colleagues (Perez, 2015). Please note here that the relationship between disclosing sexual orientation to others—for instance, in community and work settings—does not equal mental health wellness. Rather, it is the positive reactions from others after coming out and their own self-disclosure experience as positive that directly effects their mental health wellness (McLane Lyons, 2013; Perez, 2015; Rosario et al., 2001, 2006). Suggestive of the research, LGB employees need to be very cautious concerning their wish to self-disclose to their employers and colleagues, understanding that the threat of job loss and discrimination is real. This is especially the case when the LGB person does not feel comfortable with their sexual identity. Unfortunately, at this time in the United States there is not full safety in the work context for LGBTQ to come out to colleagues. The world is certainly moving in that direction but it is not there yet.

Healthcare and LGBTQ. Concerning the topic of healthcare and LGBTQ, Compton and Whitehead (2015) point out the importance of providers having knowledge of LGBTQ disparities, health issues, and community hardships. As their article poses, doctors and nurses need to be able to discern the health disparities of all the populations they serve, including that of LGBTQ (Compton & Whitehead, 2015). Some of these health disparities include HIV/AIDS, depression, substance abuse, obesity, higher nicotine use, and workplace discrimination (Ard & Makadon; Lambda Legal, 2010). Likewise, Brathwaite, Jebb, Payne, and Crumbie (2014) state healthcare discrimination is current for LGBTQ people employed in healthcare and who try to access healthcare. Moreover, their research points out the critical need for employers to recognize the potential for stress in the workforce of LGBTQ staff or clients (Burns & Krehely, 2011).

Accessing healthcare within a place of employment is also a source of discrimination for LGBTQ people (Ard & Makadon; Lambda Legal, 2010). The National Women's Law Center (2003) published an article concerning the Affordable Care Act and LGBTQ persons. The Affordable Care Act extended to meet the healthcare needs and disparities of marginalized people, including LGBTQ people who otherwise were not receiving the benefits of healthcare as readily as their heterosexual counterparts. The worry with President Trump taking office is that this type of care act will be taken away and no other system will be put in its place to protect LGBTQ people from having to be without healthcare (Human Rights Campaign, 2016). Without the Affordable Care Act, managed-care companies are at times reluctant to provide care to LGBTQ people with what they call a preexisting diagnosis of HIV/AIDS. In addition, LGBTQ people with HIV/AIDS are more likely than heterosexual people living with HIV/AIDS to experience medical providers' reluctance to touch them and who indirectly state to them that they are to blame for contracting the disease (Lambda Legal, 2010). Lambda Legal shares stories of LGBTQ people being denied access to medical services for reasons of their sexual orientation and gender identity. Therefore, regardless of whether they have healthcare insurance, they are being denied services based on their sexual and gender identities (Krehely, 2009; Lambda Legal, 2010).

Marriage in the workforce. There are several discrimination factors related to LGBTQ people being married and open about their sexual orientation and gender identity. The first risk is that in 2017 there are only 19 states fully protecting LGBTQ people in the workforce (California, Oregon, Washington, Nevada, Utah, Colorado, New Mexico, Massachusetts, Minnesota, Iowa, Illinois, Maine, Vermont, Maryland, New Jersey, Rhode Island, Connecticut, Delaware, and Hawaii) (Freedom for All Americans, 2016). In addition, three states—Wisconsin, New York, and New Hampshire—protect people based on their sexual orientation but not gender identity and two other states (Utah and Indiana) have only some protection for LGBTQ people (Freedom for All Americans, 2016). At any time, within the states and cities that do not protect a person who is gay, for example, an LGBTQ person could be fired because of their orientation (APA, 2012; Badgett, Lau, Sears, & Ho, 2007; Fredriksen-Goldsen et al., 2014; Freedom for All Americans, 2016; Hebl, Tonidandel, & Ruggs, 2012; Ng et al., 2012; Thompson, 2015). Moreover, about 52% of the LGBTQ population lives within the 32 states not protected (MAP, 2016).

The Movement Advancement Project (MAP) was developed specifically for advocacy purposes for LGBTQ rights. The project seeks to protect LGBTQ people in all 50 states in the United States. ONE Community (ONE Community, 2017) is another organization lobbying for LGBTQ rights in the workforce and public venues such as restaurants. ONE Community, located in Arizona, provides an open forum for owners to market their business as open to all. Once businesses register, ONE Community provides them with a sign to post in their store window which reads "Open for Business to Everyone!" The reason this is so important is because Arizona is one of the 30 states where LGBTQ people are not fully protected against discrimination in the workforce (ONE Community, 2017; Stewart, 2009, 2010). In fact, in 2017 only five out of the 96 cities in Arizona fully protect LGBTQ people from this type of discrimination. Catherine Alonzo in a Phoenix New Times article stated to interviewer Elizabeth Stuart that the only cities protected in Arizona are Phoenix, Tucson, Sedona, Flagstaff, and Tempe (Stuart, 2016).

Subsequently, as career counselors work with LGBTQ clients who are desiring to come out in their workplace, the counselor could provide education to their client about the risk factors based on their state laws. When career counselors are working with clients from a Christian perspective, it is even more important to help clients navigate this journey because LGBTQ Christians experience an increase of discrimination because of their LGBTQ status and religious identity (Watson, 2015). Clients may have encountered shaming experiences within churches prior to entering counseling (Lancet, 2015; Lapinski & McKirnan, 2013) that is impacting their self-esteem and ability to engage in seeking employment due to increased depression (Lapinski & McKirnan, 2013).

REMEMBERING THE VALUES AND ETHICS OF COUNSELING

Coming to the end of this chapter, there is a need to pinpoint the support for LGBTQ people in current counseling competencies and ethical codes. This is needed because at this time, as shown already, the laws in most states do not fully protect LGBTQ people from being fired, discriminated against, and treated unfairly. However, counselors are required to work under the precepts of the ACA code of ethics. The ACA code of ethics, the CACREP standards, multicultural competencies, LGBTQ competencies, and religious and spiritual competencies will be summarized next as they relate to the obligation of counselors to know what to consider when working with LGBTQ populations. It is truly an obligation of counselors working in the field to be competent in each of these areas.

ACA Code of Ethics[1]

The ACA code of ethics serves to protect clients from the unethical practice of counseling. Counselors licensed in the United States and who are practicing counseling are expected to work under these ethical codes. Most state counseling boards use these ethical standards when settling complaints and attending to ethical issues (Kaplan et al., 2009). There are nine sections within the ACA code of ethics: (a) The Counseling Relationship; (b) Confidentiality and Privacy; (c) Professional Responsibility; (d) Relationships with Other Professionals; (e) Evaluation, Training, and Teaching; (g) Research and Publication; (h) Distance Counseling, Technology, and Social Media; and, (i) Resolving Ethical Issues (ACA, 2014). Each section imparts the expectation of counseling students and professional counselors who are working in the field of counseling.

Aligning the ACA Code of Ethics with the LGBTQ population. There are several ethical codes from the ACA Code of Ethics (2014) that directly align with the ethical practice of counseling with LGBTQ people. A summary of these codes is included next. Although LGBTQ is not explicitly stated in the ACA code of ethics, the term client is meant to encompass all clients, not just heterosexual clients. Therefore, it can be assumed that the ethical codes are written also for counselors working with LGBTQ clients. These will be succinctly summarized. For further review of any section listed, please reference the resources provided below.

Counselors, first and foremost, are to seek opportunities to provide counseling in ways that promote the positive developmental growth of their clients. To do so, counselors working with LGBTQ clients can encourage these clients to sign a release for the inclusion of the client's family and friends (A.1.d), provide ongoing informed consent (A.2.a), and communicate their counseling objectives and goals in ways that are aligned with their LGBTQ client's cultural context (A.2.c). Counselors also are aware of their own personal values and biases that impede counseling (A.4.b.) and strictly guard against imposing their values on their clients (A.b.11). Seeking ways to advocate for LGBTQ clients to reduce the barriers in the community is important (A.7.a.). Moreover, counselors can provide additional resources

---

1   Adapted from American Counseling Association, 2014 ACA Code of Ethics. Copyright © 2014 by American Counseling Association.

and referrals when they decide their competence and skill to work with LGBTQ clients is not adequate. However, this does not include a counselor's discomfort to work with LGBTQ persons (A.11.b.); rather, this means counselors look at the issue for treatment as the need for the referral (A.11.a.). Counselors also seek ways to increase their knowledge of multicultural competencies (C.2.a.).

The profession of counseling expects counselors to seek ways to increase their expertise to help LGBTQ clients (C.2.d.); to consult experts in the field (C.2.e.) when questioning their competency to work with a client; and to not show disfavor against any client or potential client, including against a person's sex or gender (C.5.). When it comes to counseling techniques, counselors are to use techniques and theories that align with LGBTQ evidenced-based practice (C.7.a.); use the least restrictive means to treatment (C.7.b.); and not use techniques that have the potential to harm an LGBTQ client (C.7.c.), such as reparative therapy.

When it comes to career counseling, the ACA is not silent. First, career counselors should utilize only those career assessment tools that have been shown to be effective with LGBTQ clients (E.1.a.); not misuse assessment tools (E.1.b.); diagnose properly (E.5.a.); consider the cultural context of clients when diagnosing (E.5.b); recognize potential risks for discriminatory factors (E.5.c.); refrain from making a diagnosis when it could harm clients or others (E.5.d.); and, finally, supervise counselors-in-training with the same precautionary procedures (F.1.).

CACREP Standards

Council for Accreditation of Counseling and Related Educational Programs (CACREP) is a highly respected accrediting organization in the United States (Troutman & Packer-Williams, 2014). It is the hope that over time CACPREP will allow for the reciprocity of counseling licenses across state lines. Graduate programs accredited by CACREP must operate under CACREP standards. CACREP includes six sections: (a) The Learning Environment, (b) Professional Counseling Identity, (c) Professional Practice, (d) Evaluation in the Program, (e) Entry-Level Specialty Areas, and (f) Doctoral Standards Counselor Education and Supervision (CACREP, 2016).

The six sections just mentioned encompass all CACREP-accredited programs. These programs educate counselors from all different sexual and gender orientations as well as train counselors to work with all types of client populations. The LGBTQ client and counselor can be assumed to fall under these guidelines as well. Therefore, counselors are prepared by their educational institution to work with LGBTQ clients (1.A.). Educational institutions teach from multicultural and diversity lenses (2.a-h.); educate counseling students on the developmental patterns of LGBTQ youth (3.a-i.), and career counseling theory relating to the LGBTQ client is taught (4.a-j.). Additionally, theories of counseling are fixed to include LGBTQ models of counseling as related to evidenced-based practice. This includes counseling programs developing their curriculum to incorporate educating counseling students on ways to conceptualize LGBTQ clients, and models for suicide prevention, trauma-informed care, and group counseling for LGBTQ clients (5.a-n.; 6.a- h.) (CACREP, 2016).

Multicultural Competencies

Sue, Arredondo, and McDavis (1992) proposed the first multicultural counseling competencies. These were created to provide direction to the counselor working with clients from diverse backgrounds. In 1996, Arredondo et al. updated the 1992 competencies, restructuring them to identify areas missed in the first edition. There are five major groups of people addressed in these competencies: African/Black, Asian, Caucasian/European, Hispanic/Latino, and Native American or indigenous people (Arredondo et al., 1996). Despite Arredondo et al.'s focus on racial and ethnic groups, the primary goal was also met—introducing the need for counselors to consider the differences projected within each group of people.

Most recently, in 2016 a new set of multicultural counseling competencies was introduced. Ratts, Singh, Nassar-McMillan, Butler, and McCullough (2015) developed the Multicultural and Social Justice Counseling Competencies; this is the newest edition of the original competencies introduced in 1992 by Sue et al. Moreover, the newest edition encompasses all groups of people, suggesting LGBTQ people are included. This is evidenced by the vast amount of research that uses the term multicultural as an umbrella term to direct attention to LGBTQ groups (Cochran & Robohm, 2015; Flores, 2012; Missouri State University, 2016; Vecellio, 2012). Therefore, the 2016 competencies will be suggested here as also applying to counselors working with LGBTQ groups. As such, the term LGBTQ will be stated here but is not directly stated within the competencies themselves.

Counselors working with LGBTQ groups need to be self-aware of their own biases, either potential or real (Ratts et al., 2015). Counselors should acknowledge their own values, beliefs, and privilege prior to engaging in the therapeutic relationship with an LGBTQ client. This includes continuing to educate themselves along the way as they work with clients whose values, beliefs, and cultural frameworks vary from their own. In order for counselors to work from a culturally inclusive view, they need to be open to learning about their clients' worldviews, participate in trainings that build their cultural awareness, and understand how the relationship between themselves and their LGBTQ clients might take time to build because of the counselor's privilege, and multicultural informed counselors need to initiate advocacy missions to empower LGBTQ clients in their communities and employment contexts (Ratts et al., 2015).

Spiritual Competencies

Equally important to recognize are the spiritual competencies developed in 2009 by the Association for Spiritual, Ethical, and Religious Values in Counseling (ASERVIC) and endorsed by the ACA. The preamble included in the competencies states ASERVIC's commitment to diversity as subjected to the AMCD competencies and ALGBTIC competencies (ASERVIC, 2009). Suggestive within the statement of the preamble is the inclusion of LGBTQ groups. For this reason, as in the prior sections, the term LGBTQ will be implied within these competencies.

Counselors working with LGBTQ groups are to have competency in areas of culture and worldview which describes a client's beliefs, values, and religious orientations (ASERVIC, 2009). Counselors, furthermore, will understand major religions and spiritual orientations of LGBTQ clients and understand barriers that impede spiritual and religious growth among

LGBTQ groups. When working with LGBTQ clients, counselors engage in self-reflection concerning the potential for their own beliefs and worldviews about religion to intercede the counseling relationship. Counselors are able to apply spiritual and religious developmental models to LGBTQ client development, and counselors are able to discern how the LGBTQ person develops in relationship to religious and spiritual development. Self-aware and spiritually competent counselors are also able to guide LGBTQ clients toward growth in spiritual dimensions even when these dimensions differ from those of the counselors. Regardless of beliefs, spiritually competent counselors are able to assess spiritual perspectives of clients at the initial assessment period. And, finally, spiritually competent counselors take into consideration the spiritual and religious beliefs of their LGBTQ clients before applying a diagnosis (ASERVIC, 2009).

ALGBTIC Competencies

Lastly, it is paramount to provide a critique of the ALGBTIC competencies that address counselor competency to work with LGBTQ clients and groups. The ALGBTIC (2012) taskforce headed by Harper et al. supports the importance of counselors receiving training to work with LGBTQ individuals. Counselors must be aware of their own conduct in the counseling realm. Without knowing some of the issues embedded in historical trends of discrimination, developmental segments, and minority statuses of LGBTQ persons and groups, counselors will have a difficult time discerning the issues their LGBTQ clients are going through (ALGBTIC, 2012).

A counselor competent to work with LGBTQ persons, groups, and communities will be able to use the correct terminology and language with each of their clients. This means that when a client wishes for their counselor to use certain pronouns, the counselor obliges to such a request. Counselors are also to recognize that their LGBTQ clients have likely experienced years of discrimination, oppression, and injustice through the actions and words of people. Therefore, counselors take time to discern the impact their words have on a client's ability to build trust and rapport with that counselor. A counselor who does not consider the prejudices and societal pressures to conform that may have impeded the developmental growth of their LGBTQ clients is neglectful. Consequently, when counselors acknowledge these areas of injustice, it can help build rapport. As we consider LGBTQ groups in career counseling, it is an important task for counselors engaging in career counseling with LGBTQ clients to understand the social injustice within employment for LGBTQ. In addition, providing counseling in the same fashion to an LGBTQ client as one does for the heterosexual client is not going to be efficient (ASERVIC, 2009). Therefore, although there are certainly similar life experiences that are not sexual-orientation or gender-identity specific, each person's experience of societal pressures and norms vary. Hence, career counselors are to view their LGBTQ clients as human beings within context.

CONCLUSION

This chapter reflected the experience of LGBTQ people, groups, and communities in the context of history, society, and personal settings from a career counseling perspective. The overall goal of this chapter was to provide a comprehensive critique of LGBTQ people and ways counselors can competently provide care within a career counseling scope. Several areas were reviewed: discrimination and marriage in the workforce and in college life, considerations for rapport and setting up the counseling room, the church in relationship to LGBTQ groups, issues in supervision, new counselor dilemmas, and counselor training to work with LGBTQ people. Each section was integrated into the full picture of career counselor competencies to work with LGBTQ people and groups. Furthermore, the ethical standards and competencies in use today were also summarized in relationship to career counseling with LGBTQ clients.

REFLECTION AND DISCUSSION

1. What do you think is the most important thing to remember as a counselor or future counselor working with LGBTQ clients?
2. Reflect on the historical context of the LGBTQ person and community in a way that builds support and direction for your method of counseling with LGBTQ clients?
3. How closely aligned do you believe career counseling with LGBTQ client is with career counseling with the heterosexual client? After reading this chapter, is there reason for changing your method based on the client?
4. Reflect on the effect of discriminatory practices in the work place that subject LGBTQ people to unfair practices and termination based on their sexual and gender identities. Were you aware of these discriminatory work practices prior to reading this chapter?
5. How familiar are you with the ethical standards and competencies in the field of counseling regarding LGBTQ people, groups, and communities?

ADDITIONAL READINGS, RESOURCES, AND WEBSITES

CenterLink: The Center of LGBT Centers. (2017). Retrieved from http://www.lgbtcenters.org/

Gay and Lesbian Alliance Against Defamation (GLAAD). (2017). Retrieved from http://www.glaad.org/about

Gay, Lesbian, Straight, Education Network (GLSEN). (2017). Retrieved from https://www.glsen.org/ Human Rights Campaign. (2017). Retrieved from http://www.hrc.org

Human Rights.gov. (2017). Retrieved from https://www.humanrights.gov/dyn/issues/lgbt.html

TRADITIONAL ACTIVITY

The Case of Steve

Steve is a 26-year-old transgender male. He is currently in a PhD program for cultural studies and hopes to develop the field in areas of transgender awareness in his community. The community is a well-developed college town with a high population of LGBTQ people. He feels good about being transgender, has a girlfriend, and speaks openly about his sexual and gender orientation. He works in an organization that focuses on advocacy for reducing discrimination against LGBTQ people. Life for Steve at age 26 is something he looks forward to each day; however, this was not always the case. At 12 years old, Steve was depressed and suicidal because he felt different. He knew he was born with the sex parts of a female, but he felt male. It was not until age 22 when Steve told his family and community about his feelings for identifying as trangender. Within two years, Steve had sex reassignment surgery and was fully transformed into a male. Steve enters therapy with his girlfriend as his support. Steve is going through a career change and wants help from you as the career counselor regarding the change. You are a Christian and have never worked with a transgender person, let alone one who is in a heterosexual relationship. What are the first steps that you can take to ensure you provide competent career counseling to Steve while acknowledging the support and relationship of his girlfriend?

Envision

- The student may initially want to refer the client out of therapy
- The student may feel uncomfortable providing counseling to Steve because he is a transgender male with a girlfriend

Case Intervention

- Counselor needs to first seek consultation to work with Steve
- Counselor needs to read up on the ethical standards related to counseling in their state
- Begin with assessment and follow the course of therapy taking into consideration the literature on LGBTQ history and life.

Respond

After reading the story about Steve, what are your initial thoughts? What did you feel and think as you read his story? Did you feel compassion, hurt, or disgust?

What are your thoughts as a counselor-in-training regarding the transition from one gender to the next?

SPIRITUAL ACTIVITY

Read the story about Steve again; however, this time have one of your peers read it to you as you close your eyes. What do you feel and think? Does the experience of having it read to you bring up a different perspective? You might also want to try reading the story out loud or separate the developmental periods of Steve's life to develop meaning from each stage. Now, compare the above ethical codes, standards, and competencies. What does the counseling literature state is your responsibility as a future counselor regarding the treatment you provide to Steve?

Let us, again, look at Steve's case. This being a book dedicated to emerging adults receiving career counseling with a spiritual integration, there is a need for readers to consider their views on providing counseling to LGBTQ people when their religious beliefs differ. What if you found out Steve was a practicing Christian, and you, his counselor, are a practicing Christian as well? Would this change your approach? How likely would you be to think about the Bible verses that reflect a negative viewpoint of the LGBTQ lifestyle as you provided counseling to Steve? Understanding how your religious beliefs might promote bias is an important step a counselor must take to become a competent counselor.

Questions for reflection.

1. At this time in your counseling career, do you find yourself hoping you do not have to work with the LGBTQ population?

2. How do you reflect on your own insecurities about counseling certain populations as a result of your religious beliefs? How will you work through your biases and misunderstandings?

Movement Advancement Project (MAP). (2017). Retrieved from http://www.lgbtmap.org/

ONE Community. (2017). Retrieved from https://www.onecommunity.co/

Out & Equal: Workplace Advocates. Retrieved from http://outandequal.org/lgbt-careerlink/

REFERENCES

Alessi, E. J. (2013). Acknowledging the impact of social forces on sexual minority clients: Introduction to the special issue on clinical practice with LGBTQ populations. Clinical Social Work Journal, 41(3), 223- 227. doi:10.1007/s10615-013-0458-x

Almeida, J., Johnson, R. M., Corliss, H. L., Molnar, B. E., & Azrael, D. (2009). Emotional distress among LGBT youth: The influence of perceived discrimination based on sexual orientation. Journal of Youth and Adolescence, 38(7), 1001–1014. doi:10.1007/s10964-009-9397-9

American Counseling Association (ACA). (2014). ACA code of ethics. Retrieved from https://www.counseling.org/resources/aca-code-of-ethics.pdf

American Counseling Association (ACA). (2016). ACA takes a firm stand against Tenn. bill that would allow discrimination within counseling profession. Retrieved from https://www.counseling.org/news/updates/2016/02/09/aca-takes-firm-stance-against-tenn.-bill- that-would-allow-discrimination-within-counseling-profession

American Counseling Association (ACA). (2016). News Archive for 2016: Tennessee advances bill that tells counselors to discriminate. Retrieved from https://www.counseling.org/news/news-release-archives/by- year/2016/2016/03/24/tennessee-advances-bill-that-tells-counselors-to-discriminate

American Psychiatric Association. (1952). Diagnostic and statistical manual of mental disorders (1st ed.). Washington, DC: Author. Retrieved from http://www.turkpsikiyatri.org/arsiv/dsm-1952.pdf

American Psychiatric Association. (1968). Diagnostic and statistical manual of mental disorders (2nd ed.). Washington, DC: Author. Retrieved from http://www.behaviorismandmentalhealth.com/wp- content/uploads/2015/08/DSM-II.pdf

American Psychiatric Association. (2000). Sexual orientation, therapies focused on attempts to change (reparative or conversion therapies). Washington, DC: Author

American Psychological Association (APA). (2000). Guidelines for psychotherapy with lesbian, gay, and bisexual clients. Retrieved from http://www.apa.org/pi/lgbt/resources/guidelines.aspx

American Psychological Association (APA). (2012). Guidelines for psychological practice with lesbian, gay, and bisexual clients, 67(1), 10–42 DOI: 10.1037/a0024659. Retrieved from http://www.apa.org/pubs/journals/features/amp-a0024659.pdf

American Psychiatric Association (APA). (2013). Diagnostic and statistical manual of mental disorders (5th ed.). Washington, DC: Author

Ard, K., & Makadon, H. (n.d.). Improving the health care of lesbian, gay, bisexual and transgender (lgbt) people. The Fenway Institute. Retrieved from https://www.lgbthealtheducation.org/wp- content/uploads/Improving-the-Health-of-LGBT-People.pdf

Arredondo, P., Toporek, R., Brown, S. P., Sanchez, J., Locke, D. C., Sanchez, J., & Stadler, H. (1996). Operationalization of the multicultural counseling competencies. Journal Of Multicultural Counseling & Development, 24(1), 42–78.

Arthur, E., McGill, D., & Essary, E. H. (2014). Playing it straight: Framing strategies among reparative therapists. Sociological Inquiry, 84(1), 16–41. doi:10.1111/soin.12026

Association for Lesbian, Gay, Bisexual, and Transgender Issues in Counseling (ALGBTIC). (2012). ALGBTIC competencies for counseling lesbian, gay, bisexual, transgender, queer, questioning, intersex, and ally individuals. Retrieved from http://www.algbtic.org/images/stories/ALGBTIC_Comps_for_Counseling_LGBQQIA_Individuals_Fin al.pdf

Association for Spiritual, Ethical, and Religious Values in Counseling (ASERVIC). (2009). Spiritual competencies. Retrieved from http://www.aservic.org/resources/spiritual-competencies/

Badgett, M. V. L., Lau, H., Sears, B., & Ho, D. (2007). Bias in the workplace: Consistent evidence of sexual orientation and gender identity discrimination. UCLA Law. Retrieved from http://www.law.ucla.edu/williamsinstitute/publications

Better, A. (2014). Redefining queer: Women's relationships and identity in an age of sexual fluidity. Sexuality & Culture, 18(1), 16–38. doi:http://0-dx.doi.org.library.regent.edu/10.1007/s12119-013-9171-8

Blume, A. W., & Lovato, L. V. (2010). Empowering the disempowered: harm reduction with racial/ethnic minority clients. Journal of Clinical Psychology, 66(2), 189–200. doi:10.1002/jclp.20668

Boom, J. (2008). T03-P-02 the philosophy of pansexuality. Sexologies, 17, S73-S73. doi:10.1016/ S1158- 1360(08)72717-8

Brathwaite, B., Jebb, P., Payne, D., & Crumbie, A. (2014). Essential lessons in respect: Should all healthcare staff have LGBT awareness training? Nursing Standard, 28(23), 28.

Burns, C., & Krehely, J. (2011). Gay and transgender people face high rates of workplace discrimination and harassment. Center of American Progress. Retrieved from https://www.americanprogress.org/issues/ lgbt/news/2011/06/02/9872/gay-and-transgender-people-face-high-rates-of-workplace-discrimination-and-harassment/

Carter, J. (2012). NIV lessons from life Bible: Personal reflections with Jimmy Carter. Grand Rapids, MI: Zondervan.

Cashwell, C. S., & Watts, R. E. (2010). The new ASERVIC competencies for addressing spiritual and religious issues in counseling. Counseling and Values, 55(1), 2–5. doi:10.1002/j.2161-007X.2010.tb00018.x

Chen, J., Li, X., Xiong, Y., Fennie, K. P., Wang, H., & Williams, A. B. (2016). Reducing the risk of HIV transmission among men who have sex with men: A feasibility study of the motivational interviewing counseling method. Nursing & Health Sciences, 18(3), 400–407. doi:10.1111/nhs.12287

Chung, Y. B. (2003). Career counseling with lesbian, gay, bisexual, and transgendered persons: The next decade. The Career Development Quarterly, 52(1), 78–86.

Chung, Y. B., Williams, W., & Dispenza, F. (2009). Validating work discrimination and coping strategy models for sexual minorities. The Career Development Quarterly, 58(2), 162–170. doi:10.1002/j.2161-0045.2009.tb00053.x

Cochran, B. N., & Robohm, J. S. (2015). Integrating LGBT competencies into the multicultural curriculum of graduate psychology training programs: Expounding and expanding upon Hope and Chappell's choice points: Commentary on "Extending training in multicultural competencies to include individuals identifying as lesbian, gay, and bisexual: Key choice points for clinical psychology training programs". Clinical Psychology: Science and Practice, 22(2), 119–126. doi:10.1111/cpsp.12095

Compton, D. A., & Whitehead, M. B. (2015). Educating healthcare providers regarding LGBT patients and health issues: The special case of physician assistants. American Journal Of Sexuality Education, 10(1), 101–118. doi:10.1080/15546128.2015.1009597

Council for Accreditation of Counseling and Related Educational Programs (CACREP). (2016). CACREP Standards. Retrieved from http://www.cacrep.org/for-programs/2016-cacrep-standards/

Dabrowski, J. (2014). The exception that doesn't prove the rule: Why congress should narrow Enda's religious exemption to protect the rights of LGBT employees. American University Law Review, 63(6), 1957–1984. Retrieved from http://0-search.proquest.com.library.regent.edu/docview/1629660683?accountid=13479

Dagley, J. C., & Salter, S. K. (2004). Practice and research in career counseling and development-2003. The Career Development Quarterly, 53(2), 98–157. doi:10.1002/j.2161-0045.2004.tb00986.x

Drescher, J. (2015). Out of DSM: Depathologizing homosexuality. Behavioral Sciences (2076–328X), 5(4), 565–575. doi:10.3390/bs5040565

Duffey, T., Haberstroh, S., & Trepal, H. (2009). A grounded theory of relational competencies and creativity in counseling: Beginning the dialogue. Journal of Creativity in Mental Health, 4(2), 89–112. doi:10.1080/15401380902951911

Duffey, T., Haberstroh, S., Ciepcielinski, E., & Gonzales, C. (2016). Relational-Cultural Theory and supervision: Evaluating developmental relational counseling. Journal of Counseling & Development, 94(4), 405–414.

Duffey, T., & Trepal, H. (2016). Introduction to the special section on relational-cultural theory. Journal of Counseling & Development, 94(4), 379–382. doi:10.1002/jcad.12095

Ebin, J., & Belyeu, N. (2016). Key competencies for working with LGBTQ clients. Counselor: The Magazine for Addiction Professionals, 17(3), 60–64.

Eliason, M. J. (2014). An exploration of terminology related to sexuality and gender: Arguments for standardizing the language. Social Work in Public Health, 29(2), 162–175. doi:10.1080/19371918.2013.775887

Evans, N. J. (2002). The impact of an LGBT safe zone project on campus climate. Journal of College Student Development, 43(4), 522–539.

Evans, M., & Barker, M. (2010). How do you see me? Coming out in counselling. British Journal of Guidance & Counselling, 38(4), 375–391.

Farmer, L. B., Welfare, L. E., & Burge, P. L. (2013). Counselor competence with lesbian, gay, and bisexual clients: Differences among practice settings. Journal of Multicultural Counseling & Development, 41(4), 194–209.

Finlay, B., & Scheltema, K. E. (1999). Masculinity scores as an artifact of feminist attitude: Evidence from a study of lesbians and college women. Journal of Homosexuality, 37(4), 139–147. doi:10.1300/J082v37n04_09

Flores, G. (2012). Toward a more inclusive multicultural education: Methods for including LGBT themes in K-12 classrooms. American Journal of Sexuality Education, 7(3), 187–197. doi:10.1080/15546128.2012.707072

Fowler, G. (2012). California bill bans gay-conversion therapy. Wall Street Journal. Retrieved from http://www.wsj.com/articles/SB10000872396390444914904577622153696305504

Francis, P. C., & Dugger, S. M. (2014). Professionalism, ethics, and value-based conflicts in counseling: An introduction to the special section. Journal of Counseling & Development, 92(2), 131–134. doi:10.1002/j.1556-6676.2014.00138.x

Fredriksen-Goldsen, K. I., Simoni, J. M., Kim, H.-J., Lehavot, K., Walters, K. L., Yang, J., & Hoy-Ellis, C. P. (2014). The health equity promotion model: Reconceptualization of lesbian, gay, bisexual, and transgender (LGBT) health disparities. The American Journal of Orthopsychiatry, 84(6), 653–663. http://doi.org/10.1037/ort0000030

Freedom for All Americans. (2016). LGBT Americans aren't fully protected from discrimination in 32 states. Retrieved from http://www.freedomforallamericans

Freeman, S. K., & Rupp, L. J. (2015). Understanding and teaching U.S. lesbian, gay, bisexual, and transgender history. Madison, WI: University of Wisconsin Press.

Fulton, C. L. (2016). Mindfulness, self-compassion, and counselor characteristics and session variables. Journal of Mental Health Counseling, 38(4), 360. doi:10.17744/mehc.38.4.06

Gaehring, K. M. (2011). Christian counselor training: Perceptions and experiences of licensed Christian counselors (Order No. 3485967). ProQuest Dissertations & Theses Global. (909023241). Retrieved from http://0-search.proquest.com.library.regent.edu/docview/909023241?accountid=13479

Garvey, J. C., & Rankin, S. R. (2015). The influence of campus experiences on the level of outness among trans-spectrum and queer-spectrum students. Journal of Homosexuality, 62(3), 374–393. 10.1080/00918369.2014.977113

Gaychurch.org. (2017). Retrieved from https://www.gaychurch.org/find_a_church/

Gay and Lesbian Alliance Against Defamation (GLAAD). (n.d.). GLAAD media reference guide-terms to avoid. Retrieved from http://www.glaad.org/reference/offensive

Gay, Lesbian, and Straight Education Network (GLSEN). (2016). Safe space kit: A guide to supporting lesbian, gay, bisexual, and transgender students in your school. Retrieved from Retrieved from http://www.glsen.org/

Goodrich, K., & Luke, M. (2010). The experiences of school counselors-in-training in group work with LGBTQ adolescents. Journal for Specialists In Group Work, 35(2), 143–159. doi:10.1080/01933921003705966

Graham, S. R., Carney, J. S., & Kluck, A. S. (2012). Perceived competency in working with LGB clients: Where are we now?. Counselor Education & Supervision, 51(1), 2–16.

Gedro, J. (2008). LGBT career development. Advances in Developing Human Resources. Empire State College. doi: 10.1177/1523422308328396

Gonel, A. (2013). Pansexual identification in online communities: Employing a collaborative queer method to study pansexuality. Graduate Journal of Social Science, 10(1), 36–59.

Guittar, N. A. (2013). The meaning of coming out: From self-affirmation to full disclosure. Qualitative Sociology Review, 9(3) Retrieved from http://0-search.proquest.com.library.regent.edu/docview/1458957034?accountid=13479

Hall, W. J., McDougald, A. M., & Kresica, A. M. (2013). School counselors' education and training, competency, and supportive behaviors concerning gay, lesbian, and bisexual students. Professional School Counseling, 17(1), 130–158.

Harding, R., Dockrell, M. J. D., Dockrell, J., & Corrigan, N. (2001). Motivational interviewing for HIV risk reduction among gay men in commercial and public sex settings. AIDS care, 13(4), 493–501.

Hebl, M. R., Tonidandel, S., & Ruggs, E. N. (2012). The impact of like-mentors for Gay/Lesbian employees. Human Performance, 25(1), 52–71. doi:10.1080/08959285.2011.631645

Hegewisch, R., & DuMonthier, A. (2016). The gender wage gap: 2015; annual earnings differences by gender, race, and ethnicity. Institute for Women's Policy Research. Retrieved from http://www.iwpr.org/initiatives/pay-equity-and-discrimination

Holcomb-McCoy, C. (2004). Assessing the multicultural competence of school counselors: A checklist. Professional School Counseling, 7(3), 178.

Huffington Post. (2012). President Jimmy Carter authors new Bible book, answers hard biblical questions. Retrieved from http://www.huffingtonpost.com/2012/03/19/president-jimmy-carter-bible-book_n_1349570.html

Individualistic Cultures 2nd ed. (2016). Oxford, UK: Oxford University Press.

Israel, T., & Selvidge, M. M. D. (2003). Contributions of multicultural counseling to counselor competence with lesbian, gay, and bisexual clients. Journal of Multicultural Counseling and Development, 31(2), 84–98. doi:10.1002/j.2161-1912.2003.tb00535.x

Joyce, K. (2014). LGBT Christian college students fight for a voice. The Daily Beast. Retrieved from http://www.thedailybeast.com/articles/2014/02/14/lgbt-christian-college-students-fight-for-a- voice.html

Kaplan, D. M., Kocet, M. M., Cottone, R. R., Glosoff, H. L., Miranti, J. G., Moll, E. C., . . . Tarvydas, V. M. (2009). New mandates and imperatives in the revised ACA code of ethics. Journal of Counseling and Development: JCD, 87(2), 241–256. Retrieved from http://0- search.proquest.com.library.regent.edu/docview/219030918?accountid=13479

Kelleher, C. (2009). Minority stress and health: implications for lesbian, gay, bisexual, transgender, and questioning (LGBTQ) young people. Counselling Psychology Quarterly, 22(4), 373–379. doi:10.1080/09515070903334995

Kimmel, A. P. (2016). Title IX: An imperfect but vital tool to stop bullying of LGBT students. Yale Law Journal, 125(7).

Krehley, J. (2009). How to close the LGBT health disparities gap. The Center for American Progress. Retrieved from https://www.americanprogress.org/issues/lgbt/reports/2009/12/21/7048/how-to- close-the-lgbt-health-disparities-gap/

Lambda Legal. (February, 2010). When health care isn't caring: Lambda Legal's survey on discrimination against LGBT people and people living with HIV. Retrieved from http://www.lambdalegal.org/publications/when-health-care-isnt-caring

Lamprecht, L. M. (2015). A phenomenological inquiry of clients' experiences of receiving a humanistically oriented therapeutic letter from their counselor between counseling sessions. Journal of Humanistic Counseling, 54(3), 187–202.

Lancet, T. (2015). Ending LGBT conversion therapies. The Lancet, 385(9977), 1478. doi:http://0- dx.doi. org.library.regent.edu/10.1016/S0140-6736(15)60737-1

Lapinski, J., & McKirnan, D. (2013). Forgive me father for I have sinned: The role of a Christian upbringing on lesbian, gay, and bisexual identity development. Journal of Homosexuality, 60(6), 853–872. doi:10.1 080/00918369.2013.774844

Lesbian, gay, bisexual and transgender (LGBT) members spoke of how they had been attacked, bullied and even put into care after coming out as gay during their youth. (RCN CONGRESS IN BRIEF)(brief article). (2008). Nursing Standard, 22(35), 8.

Love, M. M., Smith, A. E., Lyall, S. E., Mullins, J. L., & Cohn, T. J. (2015). Exploring the relationship between gay affirmative practice and empathy among mental health professionals. Journal of Multicultural Counseling & Development, 43(2), 83–96.

Magee, I. M., & Whiston, S. C. (2010). Casting no shadow: Assessing vocational overshadowing. Journal of Career Assessment, 18(3), 239–249. doi:10.1177/1069072710364790

Martin, J. E., & Sihn, E. P. (2009). Motivational Interviewing: Applications to Christian therapy and church ministry. Journal of Psychology and Christianity, 28(1), 71.

McGeorge, C. R., Carlson, T. S., & Toomey, R. B. (2015). An exploration of family therapists' beliefs about the ethics of conversion therapy: The influence of negative beliefs and clinical competence with lesbian, gay, and bisexual clients. Journal of Marital & Family Therapy, 41(1), 42–56. doi:10.1111/jmft.12040

McLane Lyons, S. M. (2013). Disclosure, sexuality-specific social support, and LGB psychological health (Order No. 1549766). ProQuest Dissertations & Theses Global.Retrieved from http://0- search.proquest. com.library.regent.edu/docview/1491381031?accountid=13479

McMurchie, M. (2014). "The dustbin of quackery"? Senate bill 1172 and the legal implications of banning reparative therapy for homosexual minors. Southern California Law Review, 87(6), 15–19.

Meany-Walen, K. K., Davis-Gage, D., & Lindo, N. A. (2016). The impact of Wellness-Focused supervision on mental health counseling practicum students. Journal of Counseling & Development, 94(4), 464–472. doi:10.1002/jcad.12105

Mental health diseases and conditions—depression; transgender and gender-fluid teens left with few safe harbors. (2017). Mental Health Law Weekly, 151. Retrieved from http://0- search.proquest.com.library. regent.edu/docview/1875470122?accountid=13479

Mili, D. (2005). The house of god—heaven and hell: A Canadian perspective on the empowerment of lesbian, gay, bisexual, and transgendered (LGBT) people through religion and subjugated knowledge. Reflections: Narratives of Professional Helping, 11(3), 73–83.

Missouri State University—coordinator, multicultural programs/LGBT student services. (2016). Journal of Blacks in Higher Education (Online). Retrieved from http://0-search.proquest.com.library. regent.edu/docview/1802516118?accountid=13479

Moss, I. (2014). Ending reparative therapy in minors: An appropriate legislative response. Family Court Review, 52(2), 316–329. doi:10.1111/fcre.12093

Movement Advancement Project (MAP). (2016). Conversion therapy laws. Retrieved from http://www. lgbtmap.org/equality-maps/conversion_therapy

Movement Advancement Project (MAP). (2017). Retrieved from http://www.lgbtmap.org/

Myers, J. E., & Sweeney, T. J. (2008). Wellness counseling: The evidence base for practice. Journal of Counseling & Development, 86(4), 482–493. doi:10.1002/j.1556-6678.2008.tb00536.x

National Center for Transgender Equality (NCTE). Retrieved from http://www.transequality.org/issues/ employment

National Women's Law Center: Extending the Possibilities. (2003). Fact sheet: LGBT Americans and the affordable care act. Retrieved from http://www.namihelps.org/LGBT-Americans-and-the-ACA-Fact-Sheet.pdf

Nelson, E. S. (2009). Queer. In Encyclopedia of Contemporary LGBTQ Literature of the United States. Santa Barbara, CA: Greenwood Press.

Ng, E. S. W., Schweitzer, L., & Lyons, S. T. (2012). Anticipated discrimination and a career choice in non-profit: A study of early career lesbian, gay, bisexual, transgendered (LGBT) job seekers. Review of Public Personnel Administration, 32(4), 332–352. doi:10.1177/0734371X12453055

Nguyen, A. (2008). Patriarchy, power, and female masculinity. Journal of Homosexuality, 55(4), 665–683. doi:10.1080/00918360802498625

ONE Community. (2017). Retrieved from https://www.onecommunity.co/

Owen-Pugh, V., & Baines, L. (2014). Exploring the clinical experiences of novice counsellors working with LGBT clients: Implications for training. Counselling and Psychotherapy Research, 14(1), 19–28. doi:10.1080/14733145.2013.782055

Paceley, M. S., Oswald, R. F., & Hardesty, J. L. (2014). Factors associated with involvement in nonmetropolitan LGBTQ organizations: Proximity? Generativity? Minority stress? Social location?. Journal of Homosexuality, 61(10), 1481–1500. doi:10.1080/00918369.2014.928582

Paprocki, C. M. (2014). When personal and professional values conflict: Trainee perspectives on tensions between religious beliefs and affirming treatment of LGBT clients. Ethics & Behavior, 24(4), 279–292.

Parker, K. (2015). Among LGBT Americans, bisexuals stand out when it comes to identity acceptance. Pew Research Center. Retrieved from http://www.pewresearch.org/fact-tank/2015/02/20/among-lgbt-americans-bisexuals-stand-out-when-it-comes-to-identity-acceptance/

Parnell, M. K., Lease, S. H., & Green, M. L. (2012;2010;). Perceived career barriers for gay, lesbian, and bisexual individuals. Journal of Career Development, 39(3), 248–268. doi:10.1177/0894845310386730

Pastrana, A. (2015). Being out to others: The relative importance of family support, identity and religion for LGBT latina/os. Latino Studies, 13(1), 88–112. doi:10.1057/lst.2014.69

Perez, K. M. (2015). The effects of gender conformity/nonconformity and ethnic identity on workplace sexual identity management among LGB African Americans (Order No. 3729779). ProQuest Dissertations & Theses Global. Retrieved from http://0-search.proquest.com.library.regent.edu/docview/1734473937?accountid=13479

Pollard, S. M. (2014). Coping mechanisms as a moderator between stigmatizing experiences related to sexual minority status and psychological distress in the LGBTQ population (Order No. 1557573). ProQuest Dissertations & Theses Global. Retrieved from http://0-search.proquest.com.library.regent.edu/docview/1548008822?accountid=13479

Pope, M., Barret, B., Szymanski, D. M., Chung, Y. B., Singaravelu, H., McLean, R., & Sanabria, S. (2004). Culturally appropriate career counseling with gay and lesbian clients. The Career Development Quarterly, 53(2), 158–177. doi:10.1002/j.2161-0045.2004.tb00987.x

Powell, M. K. (2013). Perception of environment by lgbt students on a college campus (Order No. 1549694). ProQuest Dissertations & Theses Global. Retrieved from http://0-search.proquest.com.library.regent.edu/docview/1491152389?accountid=13479

Ratts, M. J., Singh, A. A., Nassar-McMillan, S., Butler, S. K., & McCullough, J. R. (2015). Multicultural and Social Justice Counseling Competencies. Multiculturalcounseling.org Retrieved from http://www.multiculturalcounseling.org/index.php?option=com_content&view=article&id=205:amcd-endorses-multicultural-and-social-justice-counseling-competencies&catid=1:latest&Itemid=123

Rosario, M., Hunter, J., Maguen, S., Gwadz, M., & Smith, R. (2001). The coming-out process and its adaptational and health-related associations among gay, lesbian, and bisexual youths: Stipulation and exploration of a model. American Journal of Community Psychology, 29(1), 133–60. Retrieved from http://0-search.proquest.com.library.regent.edu/docview/205337893?accountid=13479

Rosario, M., Schrimshaw, E. W., & Hunter, J. (2006). A model of sexual risk behaviors among young gay and bisexual men: Longitudinal associations of mental health, substance abuse, sexual abuse, and the coming-out process. AIDS Education and Prevention, 18(5), 444–460. doi:10.1521/aeap.2006.18.5.444

Rumens, N. (2011). Minority support: Friendship and the development of gay and lesbian managerial careers and identities. Equality, Diversity and Inclusion: An International Journal, 30(6), 444–462. doi:10.1108/02610151111157684

Quinn, D. M., & Chaudoir, S. R. (2009). Living with a concealable stigmatized identity: The impact of anticipated stigma, centrality, salience, and cultural stigma on psychological distress and health. Journal of Personality and Social Psychology, 97(4), 634–651.

Quintana, N., Rosenthal, J., & Krehely, J. (2010). On the streets: The federal response to gay and transgender homeless youth. The Center for American Progress. Retrieved from https://www.americanprogress.org/issues/lgbt/reports/2010/06/21/7983/on-the-streets/

Sackett, C. R., & Lawson, G. (2016). A phenomenological inquiry of clients' meaningful experiences in counseling with counselors-in-training. Journal of Counseling & Development, 94(1), 62–71. doi:10.1002/jcad.12062

Schmidt, C. K., Miles, J. R., & Welsh, A. C. (2011). Perceived discrimination and social support: The influences on career development and college adjustment of LGBT college students. Journal of Career Development, 38(4), 293–309. doi:10.1177/0894845310372615

Schultheiss, D. E. P. (2003). A relational approach to career counseling: Theoretical integration and practical application. Journal of Counseling & Development, 81(3), 301–310. doi:10.1002/j.1556- 6678.2003.tb00257.x

Silvestre, A. J. (2003). Ending health disparities among vulnerable LGBT people. A commentary. Clinical Research and Regulatory Affairs, 20(2), ix-xii. doi:10.1081/CRP-120021077

Singh, A. A., & Moss, L. (2016). Using relational-cultural theory in LGBTQQ counseling: addressing heterosexism and enhancing relational competencies. Journal Of Counseling & Development, 94(4), 398–404. doi:10.1002/jcad.12098

Stewart, C. (2009; 2010). The greenwood encyclopedia of LGBT issues worldwide. Santa Barbara, CA: Greenwood.

Stoltz, K. B., & Young, T. L. (2013). Applications of motivational interviewing in career counseling: Facilitating career transition. Journal of Career Development, 40(4), 329–346.

Stewart, C. (2009). The Greenwood Encyclopedia of LGBT Issues Worldwide [3 volumes]. Retrieved from http://publisher.abc-clio.com.ezproxy.regent.edu:2048/9780313342325

Stuart, E. (2016). Best and worst Arizona cities for LGBT rights. Phoenix New Times. Retrieved from http://www.phoenixnewtimes.com/news/best-and-worst-arizona-cities-for-lgbt-rights-7955082

Sue, D. W., Arredondo, P., & McDavis, R. J. (1992). Multicultural counseling competencies and standards: A call to the profession. The UNM College of Education. Retrieved from http://coe.unm.edu/uploads/docs/coe-main/faculty- staff/MultiCultural%20Counseling%20Competencies%20and%20Standards.pdf

Tate, K. A., Fouad, N. A., Marks, L. R., Young, G., Guzman, E., & Williams, E. G. (2015). Underrepresented first-generation, low-income college students' pursuit of a graduate education: Investigating the influence of self-efficacy, coping efficacy, and family influence. Journal of Career Assessment, 23(3), 427–441. doi:10.1177/1069072714547498

The Baby Show. (1855). New York Times. Retrieved from https://timesmachine.nytimes.com/timesmachine/1855/06/06/issue.html

Thompson, E. S. (2015). compromising equality: An analysis of the religious exemption in the employment non-discrimination act and its impact on LGBT workers. Boston College Journal of Law & Social Justice, 35(2), 285.

Troutman, O., & Packer-Williams, C. (2014). Moving beyond CACREP standards: Training counselors to work competently with LGBT clients. Journal of Counselor Preparation & Supervision, 6(1), 1–19. doi:10.7729/51.1088

Troutman, O., & Packer-Williams, C. (2014). Moving beyond CACREP standards: Training counselors to work competently with LGBT clients. Journal of Counselor Preparation and Supervision, 6(1) doi:http://dx.doi.org.ezproxy.regent.edu:2048/10.7729/51.1088

Ulrichs, K. & Lombardi-Nash, M. (1994). The riddle of "man-manly" love.Buffalo, NY: Prometheus Books.

University of Wisconsin-Madison. (2016). Trans, genderqueer, and queer terms glossary. Retrieved from https://lgbt.wisc.edu/documents/Trans_and_queer_glossary.pdf

Vecellio, S. (2012). Enacting FAIR education: Approaches to integrating LGBT content in the K-12 curriculum. Multicultural Perspectives, 14(3), 169–174. doi:10.1080/15210960.2012.697015

Ward, D. M. (2015). A grounded theory study to describe approaches gay K-8 teachers take to living openly at work (Order No. 3710750). ProQuest Dissertations & Theses Global. Retrieved from http://0- search.proquest.com.library.regent.edu/docview/1706284339?accountid=13479

Watson, R. G. (2015). Nazarene clergy responses to homosexuality and interactions with LGBT people (Order No. 3700870). Dissertations & Theses @ Regent University; ProQuest Dissertations & Theses Global.\Retrieved from http://0- search.proquest.com.library.regent.edu/docview/1680593312?accountid=13479

Weeks, J. (1998). CHAPTER 8: Discourse, desire and sexual deviance: Some problems in a history of homosexuality. In, Culture, Society & Sexuality (pp. 119–142). Abingdon, Oxon Ox, England: Taylor & Francis Ltd / Books.

Williams, V. K., & Deyoe, N. (2015). LGBTQ titles in academic library youth collections. Library Resources & Technical Services, 59(2), 62–71.

Women's Policy Research. (2016). Women's median earnings as a percent of men's median earnings, 1960–2015 (full-time, year-round workers) with projection for pay equity in 2059. Retrieved from http://www.iwpr.org/initiatives/pay-equity-and-discrimination

14

Career Counseling and Individuals with Disabilities

Helen Runyan, PhD and Jasmine L. Knight, PhD

Do not curse the deaf or put a stumbling block in front of the blind, but fear your God. I am the LORD.

Leviticus 19:14, New International Version

LEARNING OBJECTIVES

In this chapter, students will learn about

- The impact of spirituality on career counseling people with disabilities (PWD)
- Appropriate terminology to use in career counseling regarding disabilities
- Special career counseling needs of the widely diverse PWD population
- Unique best practices to help with career counseling individuals with exceptional needs
- The role and responsibilities of professional career counselors regarding PWD

LEARNING OUTCOMES

At the end of this chapter, students will be able to

- Explain and utilize empowering terminology concerning PWD
- Discern special career counseling needs of a client in a culturally appropriate manner
- Identify and describe at least one best practice to utilize when career counseling people with specific needs
- Identify the roles and responsibilities of a career counselor regarding PWD

- Share which of these responsibilities career counselors feel tap into their personal strengths
- Share which career counseling responsibilities provide them with an opportunity for personal growth

CHAPTER HIGHLIGHTS

- Americans with Disabilities Act (ADA)
- Appropriate terminology for disabilities
- Disability
- Individuals with Disabilities Education Act (IDEA)
- People with Disabilities (PWD)

INTRODUCTION TO CONCEPT

What is a disability? What exactly is included when we are speaking about disabilities? How do disabilities impact career counseling? First, let's think about our individual answers. Get a blank sheet of paper and write down your answers to the following:

- List the words that come to mind when you hear the word **disability**
- List all the disabilities you can think of
- List how these disabilities might affect career counseling processes
- List the names of everyone you know with a disability
- List how their disabilities might impact them if they pursued career counseling

Keep this paper available as you read through this chapter. We will refer to it periodically.

Back to the original question: What is a disability? In Biblical times, any imperfection disqualified someone from entering the temple. Leviticus 21:17–23 (NIV) lists many of the specific "imperfections": blind, lame, a marred face, any limb too long, a broken foot or hand, a hunchback, a dwarf, a defect in his eye, eczema, scab, or eunuch. Fortunately, that did not disqualify people with "defects" from doing many other types of jobs available in biblical times.

More recently, the U.S. Census Bureau considers hearing, vision, ambulatory, cognitive, self-care, and independent living challenges to define functional disabilities in its annual census (Strauser, 2013). Per the Americans with Disabilities Act (ADA; 1990), a disability is having a "physical or mental impairment" that noticeably restricts at least one "major life activity." The tripartite definition utilized in this law was modeled after the Rehabilitation Act of 1973 with the expectation that the courts would continue to interpret the term "disability" in the same broad fashion they formerly used. Unfortunately, the courts viewed the language in a very narrow scope. Because many people with great limitations were no longer being protected, Congress enacted the ADA Amendments Act of 2008. This amendment was further enhanced by the Amendment of ADA Title II and Title III Regulations, which went into effect on October 11, 2016.

Why do you need to know these facts? It's important to not only know what the current legal definition of disability is, but to know when it took effect. If you have a client who might benefit from ADA protection but claims they already tried and failed to meet the definition, your knowledge of the history of the ADA will help them.

Despite that extensive, albeit brief history, the definition of disability is broadly defined as having an impairment (either mental or physical) that significantly limits a major life activity, which for our purposes is career development. Let's refer to your initial list.

- Do your words related to the word **disability** fall within this broad definition?
- Do your listed disabilities meet this description?
- Which of the listed terms might significantly limit a person's career trajectory?
- Puzzle through the discrepancies (if any) between the ADA definition and your lists.

As you read through the rest of this chapter, continue to measure your perceptions. The knowledge you gain should inform your opinions of people with disabilities as well as give you more options to counsel them regarding careers.

What do you think when you see someone with a visible disability? When we are young, we tend to ask questions and stare with curiosity. At some point as we mature, we are expected to shed this hyperawareness and replace it with a laissez-faire attitude. To meet cultural expectations, we pretend that everything is "typical." This might work if we are simply passing someone on the street; however, as counselors, we are ethically bound to individuate and utilize best practices for each clients' needs (see American Counseling Association [ACA], 2014, C.5., E.8., H.5.d.; National Career Development Association [NCDA], 2015). Besides, it does not seem practical to practice career counseling with a client while ignoring her or his abilities or challenges. When we add our calling as a Christian to love people as God loves people to this mix—"The Lord is gracious and compassionate, slow to anger and rich in love" (Psalm 145:8, NIV)—we must remember to be compassionate regardless of others' challenges, maybe even more so because of their challenges. Add to this mixture the prevalence of invisible disabilities (e.g., some mental health challenges) and you might begin to see the relevance and the importance of spirituality for PWD.

THE INTERSECTION OF SPIRITUALITY, DISABILITY, AND CAREER

In general, PWD regard spirituality as an important concept throughout all aspects of their lives (Camden-Smith, 2014). Research also suggests that professionals should broach the topic of spirituality with PWD to provide holistic care, which obviously includes career counseling (Bogdashina, 2013; Camden-Smith, 2014). Despite this need, research remains sparse regarding spirituality, disability, and career counseling (Bogdashina, 2013; Camden-Smith,

2014). Because PWD have often dealt with numerous losses, including many in the career arena, introducing spirituality seems entirely appropriate (Boswell, Hamer, Knight, Glacoff & McChesney, 2007). In fact, failing to introduce it might seem unethical. PWD seem to accept their losses, within and without career development, easier when they feel their disabilities and their lives have purpose (Boswell et al., 2007). The same hope gained by increased spirituality is also enhanced by employment, making the intersection of spirituality, disability, and career particularly useful in counseling (Sears, Jones, & Strauser, 2013). Since gainful employment can be central to identity and enhances a person's self-esteem, sense of well-being, and quality of life (Sears et al., 2013), using spirituality to enhance career counseling seems particularly effective. Utilizing appropriate language throughout this counseling process is also helpful, as you will see in the next section.

TERMINOLOGY

> *The difference between the right word and the almost-right word is the difference between lightning and a lightning bug.*
>
> Mark Twain

Being convinced of the necessity of disability knowledge, career counselors might still be taken aback by the sheer mass of "politically correct" language they need to learn. This section will quell those fears and add to cultural competence through appropriate language.

The broad definition of disability has a plethora of related terms. The following are terms most commonly used in career counseling, in this chapter, or both:

Americans with Disabilities Act of 1990 (ADA): Public Law 101–336, intended to increase employment opportunities for PWD

ASD: autism spectrum disorders

BLS: Bureau of Labor Statistics

CIP: cognitive information processing, a career counseling approach (Dipeolu, 2015)

Disability: having a "physical or mental impairment" that noticeably restricts at least one "major life activity" (ADA, 1990)

DWP: Developmental Work Personality; newer theory suggesting childhood learning and behavior affects future work personality (Ritter, Strauser, O'Sullivan, Reid, Khosravisnasr, & Cronin, 2013)

IDEA: Individuals with Disabilities Education Act (IDEA; 2006)

IEP: individualized education program

LD: learning disabilities

NBD: neurological-based disabilities, including ADHD, LD, ASD, and dyslexia (Dipeolu, 2015)

PWD: people with disabilities (Kulkarni & Gopakumar, 2014)

TWA: Minnesota theory of work adjustment; a theory matching person and environment in careers (Swanson & Schneider, 2013)

In general, when referring to people with disabilities (PWD), the same rules apply as those common in counseling. Namely, use person-first language (American Psychological Association, 2010; Dunn & Andrews, 2015). Do not refer to the mentally ill client; rather, refer to the client with a mental illness. To be language conscious, it would be better to not use the term **disabled** at all. I prefer the term **differently abled**, which refers to the fact that everyone has different abilities. To simplify the terminology for this chapter, though, we will utilize the term **disability** to correlate with the American laws and common research terms. This terminology matters because language has a powerful effect on empowerment and self-determination. By promoting person-first language, you are advocating for PWD. By promoting self-determination, you are advocating for successful outcomes for PWD (Shogren & Shaw, 2016), who are a growing population.

PREVALENCE

Return to the lists you created at the beginning of the chapter. How many people were you able to name who had a disability? How would this number compare to the number of people you could name, if you made a list of all people you knew?

Why does this matter? Over one tenth of the world's population have a disability (Kulkarni & Gopakumar, 2014; Sterner, 2016; World Bank, 2011). The World Health Organization (WHO, 2015) estimates this number to be even higher, finding that approximately 15% of the world's population have disabilities. The Bureau of Labor Statistics (BLS; 2015) reported that only 17.5% of PWD were employed in 2015, compared to 65% of people with no disability. Younger PWD sometimes neglect attempting to find work due to lowered expectations and attitudes (Lindsay, McDougall, Menna-Dack, Sanford & Adams, 2015). As people age, they are more likely to have a disability (BLS, 2015). In general, PWD younger than 40 tend to have cognitive disabilities and those over 40 tend to have trouble with ambulation (Strauser, 2013). PWD tend to be equally men and women (Strauser, 2013). As for race and ethnicity, being African American correlates with the highest percentage of disabilities, while Asian

Americans have the lowest number of disabilities (Strauser, 2013). As noted above, PWD are diverse. Per the 2011 U.S. Census, ambulation difficulties accounted for the highest number of disabilities (5.3%) within the number of working age adults (Strauser, 2013). Comparing PWD according to education attained, those who gained less than a ninth-grade education comprise the highest percentage, while people with bachelor's degrees are least likely to have disabilities. When compared by type of disability, those with a hearing disability are most likely to be unemployed (Strauser, 2013). Research has suggested that having a disability is the strongest predictor of unemployment (Smith, 2014). Unfortunately, a recent content analysis of ten ACA journals over a 10-year period exposed a severe lack of literature on the topic (i.e., 1% of total articles; Woo, Goo, & Lee, 2016). Despite this dearth of information, chances are that you will have clients with disabilities regardless of your intended counseling setting.

SPECIAL NEEDS

Because of the wide variety of possible disabilities, the diverse population of PWD necessitates counselor flexibility. Possibly complicating the work of career counseling the already-challenging clientele, disability status is heterogeneous (Houtenville, Sevak, O'Neill, & Cardoso, 2013). Most of the research (41%) concerning career counseling for PWD has focused on physical disabilities (Woo et al., 2016). In addition to physical disabilities, the most commonly researched disabilities include neurological-based disabilities (Diakogiorgi & Tsiligirian, 2016; Dipeolu, 2015; Stipanovic, 2015), mental health disorders (Hayden & Buzzetta, 2014; Matthews, Harris, Jaworski, Alam, & Bozdag, 2014; Sterner, 2016; Strauser, 2013), and intellectual disabilities (Gibbons, Hyfantis, Cihak, Wright, & Mynatt, 2015). Career counselors need to be aware of all disabilities, including invisible disabilities such as chronic pain and invisible wounds of war (e.g., PTSD and TBI; Hayden & Buzzetta, 2014). In the following subsections, we will take a closer look at these diverse disabilities, one at a time.

NEUROLOGICAL-BASED DISABILITIES

Neurological-based disabilities include ADHD, ASD, dyslexia, and LD (Dipeolu, 2015). While these disabilities fall underneath the bigger umbrella of NBD for this chapter, research supports the use of a variety of career counseling methods depending on the specific disability (Dipeolu, 2015). One point of agreement is the need for strengths-based career counseling, which highlights the abilities of PWD (Dipeolu, 2015). Another common idea is the helpfulness of early intervention, especially while children are still in school (Dipeolu, 2015).

People with ADHD often have challenges concerning career decision-making, a critical factor in successful careers (Brooks, 2016). ADHD is listed in this special needs section because of its accompanying career indecision, as decision-making is one of the most important steps in career planning (Brooks, 2016). Some of the typical challenges people with ADHD have in career decision-making include less self-efficacy, executive functioning deficits, decreased attention, depression, and anxiety (Brooks, 2016). Some of the common aids to career counseling people with ADHD are keeping a positive focus and helping them to arrive at careers on their own, which will empower them (Brooks, 2016). Brooks (2016) claims that people with ADHD respond more favorably to specific techniques such as cognitive behavior therapy (CBT), normalizing the lack of a career plan, reframing, focus on the transitory nature of decision-making, and "paradoxical intent" (Brooks, 2016, p. 56). He also reports successfully creating and developing a technique called "Possible Lives Mapping" (for more detail on this exercise, see Brooks, 2016).

Consideration for work satisfactoriness needs to accompany competent career counseling. Career counselors should help clients enhance their strengths while downplaying their disabilities. Occupations requiring low written-language skills might be more suitable for people with dyslexia (Diakogiorgi & Tsiligirian, 2016). For children with dyslexia, career choices can be more limited by parents' and teachers' stereotypical thoughts about the learning disability than by the disability itself (Diakogiorgi & Tsiligirian, 2016).

Another group often limited by the short-sighted expectation of others includes adolescents with LD. They are often ill-prepared to transition out of high school (Stipanovic, 2015). Increasing metacognitive abilities of adolescents with LD positively impacts their career development (Stipanovic, 2015).

When considering the neurological-based disabilities, the disability might guide the career counseling somewhat; however, they all have some things in common. Strengths-based career counseling is helpful for highlighting the abilities PWD have (Dipeolu, 2015). Early intervention is also helpful, especially while children are still in school (Dipeolu, 2015).

MENTAL HEALTH NEEDS

Although career development is not always viewed as a priority in treatment planning with clients with mental health challenges, there is a strong correlation between employability and self-esteem (Cábelková, 2015; Hayden & Buzzetta, 2014; Luke & Redekop, 2016; Sterner, 2016; Lustig, Zanskas, & Strauser, 2012). People who have mental health issues are less likely to be employed (Hayden & Buzzetta, 2014; Matthews et al., 2014; Sterner, 2016). When clients with severe mental health challenges are counseled with a vocational focus, the resulting sense of purpose can increase their mental health (Hayden & Buzzetta, 2014; Lustig et al., 2012; Sterner, 2016). The reverse is also true. When clients with mental health needs did not receive adequate career counseling, their mental health and employability tended to decrease (Cábelková, 2015; Hayden & Buzzetta, 2014; Lustig et al., 2012; Sterner, 2016).

K–12 STUDENTS

The reauthorization of the Individuals with Disabilities Education Act (IDEA, 2006) specified by law the importance of secondary school programs to assist children with IEPs with their transitions to college or to career after graduation (Gothberg, Peterson, Peak, & Sedaghat, 2015). Unfortunately, there remains a lack of funding and awareness concerning youth with disabilities (Lindsay et al., 2015). One of the most recent, promising tools to assist in developing IEP goals that better prepare students for college or career after graduation is the Triangulated Gap Analysis Tool (TGAP; Gothberg et al., 2015). The TGAP (Gothberg et al., 2015) is a 5-step process that is described more in the Interventions section below.

If special education is not involved, career counselors can still help youth with disabilities by improving their life skills such as self-care and using public transportation, self-confidence, self-advocacy, and communication (Lindsay et al., 2015). Counselors could serve youth with disabilities by using assessments to increase career decision-making (Osborn, Finklea & Belle, 2014) and suggesting extracurricular activities and volunteer positions, which could also aid in the improvement of these life skills (Lindsay et al., 2015).

VETERANS

Veterans are included in the special needs groups because their employment is interwoven into their lives more intricately than many others, and while many return home from war unscathed, a substantial number of postwar veterans suffer with disabilities (Hayden & Buzzetta, 2014; Smith, 2014; Zalaquett & Chatters, 2016). Veterans who separate from the military with physical and mental health needs find transitioning to the regular workforce a daunting task (Hayden & Buzzetta, 2014; Smith, 2014; Zalaquett & Chatters, 2016). They also face possible stigma being a veteran (Hayden & Buzzetta, 2014; Zalaquett & Chatters, 2016).

BEST PRACTICES

Barriers

In addition to the special needs listed above, many commonalities exist as barriers to effective employment for PWD. These include prejudice, discrimination, stigma, lack of social support, absence of role models, less education, decreased independence, negative thinking, and environmental barriers (Ebener, Fioramonti, & Smedema, 2016; Hampton, Li, & Denninger, 2015; Hayden & Buzzetta, 2014; Lindsay et al., 2015; Lustig et al., 2012). These barriers can be seen on all levels, from individual to policy level (Sears et al., 2013).

Individual level. The barriers at the individual level include a possible lack of awareness (Sears et al., 2013). PWD often lack understanding about the appropriate timing of disability disclosure (Sears et al., 2013). They have often missed opportunities to develop self-advocacy abilities and self-awareness considering their unique disabilities (Sears et al., 2013). They often need better understanding of available accommodations, have fewer social interactions, and participate less in school, leaving them with less of a foundation as far as careers go (Sears et al., 2013). In fact, the earlier the onset of the disability, the less likely it is that PWD have developed a strong work-identity (Sears et al., 2013).

Societal level. Despite the prevalence of disabilities, many PWD face stigmatization (Sears et al., 2013). Because of fear of being viewed as less capable by their employers, many PWD fail to disclose their disabilities to their employers (Sears et al., 2013). The result of this fear and lack of disclosure can be devastating, leading to the loss of employment. On the other hand, PWD who disclose their disabilities can receive simple accommodations and increased work satisfaction. Although stigmas exist, many companies are recruiting PWD to diversify their workforce (Sears et al., 2013).

Policy level. At the policy-making level, the system that was developed to help PWD has had the opposite effect as far as employment is concerned (Sears et al., 2013). PWD often fear losing their disability benefits by finding employment, so they are resistant to seeking employment (Sears et al., 2013). Despite laws like the ADA (1990), PWD remain averse to disclosing their disabilities to their employers (Sears et al., 2013).

Strategies

PWD who are successfully employed tend to utilize career management strategies proactively (Kulkarni & Gopakumar, 2014). Some of the more common strategies include sustaining optimism, informing others about abilities, advocating for disability awareness, and building and participating in disability support systems (Kulkarni & Gopakumar, 2014).

PWD have better opportunities once they have adapted to the modifications necessary after the onset of the disability (Ebener et al., 2016). The barriers listed above influence this adaptation (Ebener et al., 2016). Career counselors can positively affect the client's adaptation by advocating for him or her, teaching them to self-advocate, and helping locate mentors or role models (Ebener et al., 2016). Some specific theories that might be useful with PWD include DWP (Ritter et al., 2013), TWA (Swanson & Schneider, 2013), SCCT (Hayden & Buzzetta, 2014) and CIP (Hayden & Buzzetta, 2014).

INCOME Framework

Sears et al. (2013) created the INCOME framework because they believed the diversity of PWD caused the other career theories challenges. There are three specific drawbacks to mainstream career theories:

1. PWD often lack early career exploration.
2. PWD tend not to develop decision-making skills as well as others.
3. PWD often have a negative self-image due to stigma.

Additionally, INCOME forgoes the stages of prior theories to facilitate the use of statuses, which are more flexible and nonsequential.

INCOME includes the following six statuses:

1. Imagining—developing work awareness
2. Informing—gaining self-awareness, more work information, opportunities, and context
3. Choosing—using information to choose occupation
4. Obtaining—seeking and gaining desired work

5. Maintaining—sustaining work

6. Exiting—considering leaving work

Motivational Interviewing

Motivational interviewing (MI; Miller & Rollnick, 1991) is a positive, client-centered approach that can increase motivation (Sears et al., 2013). While concentrating on a client's knowledge, beliefs, goals, and strategies, career counselors can promote client self-empowerment to increase motivation (Sears et al., 2013).

MI is built on four original principles (Sears et al., 2013):

1. Express understanding by listening nonjudgmentally.

2. Roll with resistance by accepting beforehand that clients will have opposing motivations.

3. Explore discrepancies between client's behavior and core values.

4. Reinforce self-efficacy by creating a hopeful, positive atmosphere and celebrating small successes.

Developmental Work Personality

Developmental work personality (DWP) is a newer career counseling theory suggesting childhood learning and behavior affects future work personality (Ritter et al., 2013). DWP suggests that the environment at home and school and the mentors during grade school have an impact on adult careers (Ritter et al., 2013). Because this career theory applies to middle school through adulthood, it is much more extensive than other developmental models in the field (Ritter et al., 2013). DWP has worked well with children whose disability began between the ages of six and 13 (Ritter et al., 2013). The theory is that this developmental age is critical to career development (Ritter et al., 2013). When this critical development is waylaid due to the onset of a disability, it often results in a negative work identity (Ritter et al., 2013). Following this theory, it makes sense that working on reframing earlier experiences into a positive identity can make a big impact on work personality (Ritter et al., 2013).

Minnesota Theory of Work Adjustment

The Minnesota theory of work adjustment (TWA) has been shown effective for people with intellectual disabilities (Swanson & Schneider, 2013). In this theory based on person and environment match or fit, there are reciprocal effects between PWD and their vocational environments (Swanson & Schneider, 2013). TWA works well with PWD because it is assumed that people naturally gain and maintain interest in things they can do. Thus, PWD naturally lose interest in activities they can no longer do due to their disabilities. TWA also focuses on two main ideas: a person's job satisfaction and a workplace's satisfaction with the person (Swanson & Schneider, 2013).

Social Cognitive Career Theory

Social cognitive career theory (SCCT) focuses on career self-efficacy and is helpful when counseling clients who have foreclosed on certain occupational choices (Hayden & Buzzetta, 2014). When PWD eliminate possible job options due to faulty beliefs concerning their abilities, career counselors can augment the clients' ideas concerning possible occupations (Hayden & Buzzetta, 2014). Once clients believe they can do more and perform in more places, they are more capable of finding meaningful employment (Hayden & Buzzetta, 2014).

Models for Assessment Integration

CIP. Cognitive Information Processing (CIP) is a bit more structured than SCCT. The focus in CIP is career decision-making and problem solving (Hayden & Buzzetta, 2014). One of the reasons that CIP is such a good choice when counseling PWD is its individualized attention (Hayden & Buzzetta, 2014). CIP has been used effectively in career counseling people with ADHD (Dipeolu, 2015).

CIP has seven steps (Osborn et al., 2014):

1. Conduct initial interview.
2. Make a comprehensive, preliminary assessment.
3. Collaboratively define challenges and causes.
4. Formulate goals to overcome those challenges.
5. Develop an Individual Learning Plan (ILP).
6. Execute the ILP.
7. Review the ILP.

Stages of change model. The stages of change model (SOC; Prochaska & DiClemente, 1983) has implications for many aspects of counseling. Like CIP, the SOC is structured. Career counselors can use the SOC to understand diverse PWD (Sears et al., 2013). Because the SOC has been well-researched with diverse people, its use with PWD fits well (Sears et al., 2013).

The SOC has five stages (Prochaska & DiClemente, 1983):

1. Precontemplation—client is not considering change
2. Contemplation—client is thinking about changing
3. Preparation—client becomes more committed to change
4. Action—client begins making calculated changes
5. Maintenance—client attempts to sustain satisfactory changes

While SOC can be used for any major change, it is often used in substance abuse counseling to access if clients are ready to stop abusing substances. In career counseling, it is helpful to guide the counselor in becoming aware of how ready the client is to change (Sears et al., 2013).

Zunker model. The Zunker model has four important steps (Osborn et al., 2014)

1. Analyze client's needs.
2. Collaborate about testing purposes.
3. Determine which assessment(s) will be most helpful.
4. Use the results of the assessment(s) to help client make career decisions.

Assessments

One caveat for career counselors when it comes to assessments: assessments are not often normed on PWD. Please use caution when utilizing these assessments (see NCDA, 2015, section E8). Another caution is to utilize assessments as a part of a larger career counseling process rather than a cut-and-dry answer (Osborn et al., 2014). There are many assessments available in career counseling: the Career Thoughts Inventory, Positive and Negative Affective Scale, SDS, Veterans and Military Occupations Finder, value card sorts, and transferable skills scales and activities (Hayden & Buzzetta, 2014). Career assessments can help clarify clients' interests and self-knowledge, identify barriers, increase career decisiveness, and decrease negative thoughts about the career process (Osborn et al., 2014).

CAREER THOUGHTS INVENTORY

The Career Thoughts Inventory (CTI) is an assessment of negative/dysfunctional thinking and is often used in CIP (Hayden & Buzzetta, 2014; Lustig et al., 2012). Besides offering a measure of dysfunctional thinking, the CTI measures three subscales: decision-making confusion, external conflict, and commitment anxiety (Hayden & Buzzetta, 2014; Kim, Lee, Ha, Lee, & Lee, 2015; Lustig et al., 2012). The CTI assessment is often used with the CTI workbook as an intervention (Hayden & Buzzetta, 2014; Lustig et al., 2012).

POSITIVE AND NEGATIVE AFFECT SCALE

Although not only a career assessment, the Positive and Negative Affect Scale (PANAS; Watson, Clark, & Teilegen, 1988) is a helpful assessment to determine if the client is likely to be having negative career thoughts (Sears, Strauser, & Wong, 2014). Sears et al. (2014) reported that negative career thoughts correlated with decreased positive affect and increased negative affect. Their research also adds to the research supporting the use of cognitive and affective assessments for career counseling (Sears et al., 2014).

SELF-DIRECTED SEARCH

The Self-Directed Search (SDS; Holland, 1994) is an assessment useful once clients have been able to open up their thinking to more prospective jobs (Hayden & Buzzetta, 2014).

By aligning clients' interests with occupations, the SDS might help them gain interest in careers they had not yet considered (Hayden & Buzzetta, 2014).

Interventions

CTI WORKBOOK

The CTI workbook is an intervention often used in CIP to reframe negative/dysfunctional thinking concerning careers (Hayden & Buzzetta, 2014). The CTI workbook is often used in conjunction with the CTI (Hayden & Buzzetta, 2014).

CASVE CYCLE

The CASVE cycle is useful in structuring helpful career counseling and used in CIP (Hayden & Buzzetta, 2014). It consists of 5 steps, before cycling back to the first (Hayden & Buzzetta, 2014):

C—Communication; recognize client's issue

A—Analysis; analyze the issue

S—Synthesis; synthesize a list of possible, acceptable career choices

V—Valuing; pare synthesized list down to the one most consistent with client's values

E—Execution; attempt to gain chosen employment

C—Communication; review results of decision made

TRIANGULATED GAP ANALYSIS TOOL

The Triangulated Gap Analysis Tool (TGAP) is a useful tool when developing IEPs for children identified as having disabilities (Gothberg, 2015). The TGAP specifies five distinct steps to triangulate data and analyze gaps to aid in postsecondary transitions (Gothberg et al., 2015). The five steps (Gothberg et al., 2015) are delineated next:

1. Record at least one of the student's postsecondary goals.
2. Align this goal with state standards and postsecondary expectations (e.g., industry standards or higher education expectations).
3. Analyze the gap between the ideals to be achieved in Step 2 and the student's present circumstances.

4. Outline the steps necessary to close this gap.

5. Develop an annual goal based on the knowledge gained with the first four steps.

Regardless of the strategies, assessments, or models used, professional career counselors must practice the below roles and responsibilities in order to competently counsel PWD.

ROLES AND RESPONSIBILITIES OF PROFESSIONAL CAREER COUNSELORS

- Understand and utilize appropriate, empowering terminology.
  - Use people-first language.
- Understand unique culture of PWD.
  - Remember the diversity, even among PWD.
- Know that career counseling need not be a mutually exclusive field.
  - Utilize your counseling skills to improve mental health.
  - Collaborate with other professionals to holistically help clients.
- Learn about strategies and resources that can benefit those with special needs.
  - Know who and what are most able to aid in career development of PWD.
- Know when to refer.
  - An important new study in the field suggested that (at least with a small sample of youth with disabilities) some clients might need "customized employment," consisting of developing relationships with employers and finding ways that PWD can benefit employers (Simonsen, Fabian, & Luecking, 2015, p. 15).
- Advocate for greater awareness and funding for PWD (Lindsay et al., 2015).

CONCLUSION

In this chapter, we discussed appropriate, empowering terminology regarding PWD. In addition to using people-first language, we also discussed the special needs of the widely diverse population of PWD. Because of this diversity, we discussed the unique best practices to help individuals with exceptional needs. Finally, we went over the role and responsibilities of professional career counselors regarding PWD.

KEY TERMS

Americans with Disabilities Act of 1990: Public Law 101–336, intended to increase employment opportunities for PWD

Career Thoughts Inventory: an assessment of negative/dysfunctional thinking; often used in CIP

CASVE cycle: useful in structuring helpful career counseling; used in CIP

Cognitive information processing: a structured form of career counseling focused on career decision-making and problem solving

Disability: having an impairment (either mental or physical) that significantly limits a major life activity

LD: learning disabilities such as ADHD or dyslexia

PWD: people with disabilities

Social cognitive career theory: a career theory that focuses on career self-efficacy

Special needs: the wide variety of possible disabilities

REFLECTION AND DISCUSSION

1. Give a brief history of the ADA.
2. Explain the meaning of empowering terminology.
3. Identify and describe at least one best practice to utilize with PWD.
4. Identify one of the roles and responsibilities of a career counselor when helping PWD.
5. Discuss an appropriate reason to refer PWD to another helper.

ADDITIONAL READINGS, RESOURCES, AND WEBSITES

American Association on Intellectual and Developmental Disabilities; https://aaidd.org/

Brown, S. D., & Lent, R. W. (2013). **Career development and counseling: Putting theory and research to work** (2nd ed.). Hoboken, NJ: Wiley.

Drummond, H. (2012). Guide to decision making: Getting it more right than wrong. London: Profile Books.

Information and technical assistance on the American with Disabilities Act; https://www.ada.gov

National Council on Disability; http://www.ncd.gov/

Occupational Outlook Handbook; http://www.bls.gov/ooh/, assistance with career information

O*NET; sponsored by the U.S. Department of Labor, Employment and Training Administration, and developed by the National Center for O*NET Development; https://www.onetonline.org/

U. S. Department of Labor Office of Disability Employment Policy; https://www.dol.gov/odep

TRADITIONAL ACTIVITY

Envision

People with disabilities can be assisted by career counselors. Their disabilities do not automatically make them unemployable.

Instead of focusing on disabilities, focus on abilities. Reframe disabilities by focusing on strengths.

Case Study/Intervention

Francine is a 29-year-old female veteran who is seeking help getting a better job. Francine separated from the Marines with an honorable discharge after serving three years of a 4-year enlistment. She was discharged due to PTSD and a traumatic brain injury (TBI) she received while serving in Afghanistan. Prior to her discharge, Francine received help at the local VA hospital. She had worked hard during counseling because she believed she was going to be allowed back to work as a Marine. She felt like her PTSD symptoms were under control; however, she was surprised to receive intensive transitional support to aid in her transition back to civilian life. She continued working on these new challenges with her VA counselor while receiving vocational rehabilitation services. She reported having taken several assessments, which made her think she would be able to gain employment as a teacher (the job she had prior to joining the Marines). Francine said she knew right away that she wouldn't be able to continue as a teacher. She reported feeling exhausted before lunch and feeling like she had very little patience for her sixth-graders.

Francine has come to Joe stating she no longer trusts the VA. She feels like she was set up for failure. After building rapport with Francine and listening to her story, Joe realizes that the problems she was having at work were not innate failure. Rather, she was exhibiting symptoms typical of someone with TBI. After Joe poses this as a possibility to Francine, he asks her to do research on TBI symptoms. She returns to the next session with brand-new optimism. She reports how great it feels to know she's "not crazy." After an SDS and value card sort, Joe discusses the probability that she is gifted in teaching. Francine agrees heartily, but she explains she just isn't capable of doing it. Joe researches what accommodations might be available to assist Francine. By speaking with human resources at the local public school district, Joe is able to ascertain their existing knowledge concerning TBI accommodations. Francine applies for a unique position that suits her special needs and gets the job. She reports being very grateful that Joe helped her "be normal again."

Envision yourself as Francine's counselor:

1. If Francine was embarrassed about her TBI and failed to disclose it, would you deal with her differently than Joe did? Would you be able to figure out her disability?

2. Do you think that Joe did too much for Francine? Too little? Why?

SPIRITUAL ACTIVITY

Envision

Spirituality can give meaning to challenges: "Before I was afflicted I went astray, but now I keep your word… It is good for me that I was afflicted, that I might learn your statutes" (Psalm 119:67, 71, NIV).

Spirituality can also leave people feeling they are being punished and not deserving of good work: "And the Lord spoke to Moses, saying, 'Speak to Aaron, saying, none of your offspring throughout their generations who has a blemish may approach to offer the bread of his God'" (Leviticus 21:16, ESV).

How can God use persons with disabilities?

PWD sometimes have difficulty believing in God's grace. They may get stuck wondering how a loving God would allow their challenges and issues. Negative thinking is shown to impact employment negatively. It might help to remind a client who is questioning God's love that He used Paul to deliver the Good News to the Gentiles in spite of his disability:

> Therefore, in order to keep me from becoming conceited, I was given a thorn in my flesh, a messenger of Satan, to torment me. Three times I pleaded with the Lord to take it away from me. But he said to me, "My grace is sufficient for you, for my power is made perfect in weakness." Therefore I will boast all the more gladly about my weaknesses, so that Christ's power may rest on me. That is why, for Christ's sake, I delight in weaknesses, in insults, in hardships, in persecutions, in difficulties. For when I am weak, then I am strong. (2 Corinthians 12:7b–10, NIV)

1. Is it ethical to talk about the Bible with a client? If so, under what circumstances?

2. How would you help Francine (from the case study above) differently if you were a Christian career counselor?

REFERENCES

American Counseling Association. (2014). ACA Code of Ethics. Alexandria, VA: Author.

American Psychological Association. (2010). Publication manual of the American Psychological Association (6th ed.). Washington, DC: Author.

Americans with Disabilities Act (1990), Pub. L. 101–336, 42 U.S.C. §§ 12101 et seq. The U.S Equal Employment Opportunity Commission.

Bogdashina, O. (2013). Autism and spirituality: Psyche, self and spirit in people on the autism spectrum. London, UK: Jessica Kingsley.

Boswell, B., Hamer, M., Knight, S., Glacoff, M., & McChesney, J. (2007). Dance of disability and spirituality. Journal of Rehabilitation, 73(4), 33–40.

Brooks, K. S. (2016). Breaking through career indecision in clients with ADHD. Career Planning & Adult Development Journal, 32(1), 54–62.

Bureau of Labor Statistics. (2015). Persons with a disability: Labor force characteristics summary. Retrieved from: www.bls.gov/news.release/disabl.nr0.htm

Cábelková, I. (2015). The effect of social transfers on the level of unemployment of disabled in EU. Economics & Sociology, 8(1), 298–307. http://dx.doi.org/10.14254/2071-789X.2015/8-1/23

Camden-Smith, C. (2014). Private lives, public policy–a commentary on "spirituality and learning disability: A review of UK government guidance". Tizard Learning Disability Review, 19(4), 178–180. Retrieved from http://0-search.proquest.com.library.regent.edu/docview/1662747272?accountid=13479

Diakogiorgi, K., & Tsiligirian, E. (2016). Parents' and school career counsellors' evaluations of the occupational competence of children with dyslexia. European Journal of Counselling Psychology, 4(1), 32–61. doi:10.5964/ejcop.v4i1.97

Dipeolu, A. (2015). Career development, work-based transitions, and individuals with neurological-based disabilities. Career Planning & Adult Development Journal, 31(4), 6–11.

Dunn, D. S., & Andrews, E. E. (2015). Person-first and identity-first language: Developing psychologists' cultural competence using disability language. American Psychologist, 70(3), 255–264.

Ebener, D. J., Fioramonti, D. L., & Smedema, S. M. (2016). Career development in men with disabilities: A psychosocial perspective. Career Planning and Adult Development Journal, 32(1), 120–129. Retrieved from http://0-search.proquest.com.library.regent.edu/docview/1770933068?accountid=13479

Gibbons, M. M., Hyfantis, J., Cihak, D. F., Wright, R., & Mynatt, B. (2015). A Social-Cognitive Exploration of the Career and College Understanding of Young Adults with Intellectual Disabilities. Professional School Counseling, 19(1), 80–91. doi:10.5330/1096-2409-19.1.80

Gothberg, J. E., Peterson, L. Y., Peak, M., & Sedaghat, J. M. (2015). Successful transition of students with disabilities to 21st-century college and careers: Using triangulation and gap analysis to address nonacademic skills. Teaching Exceptional Children, 47(6), 344–351. doi:10.1177/0040059915587890

Hampton, N. Z., Li, Q., & Denninger, Y. Z. (2015). The influence of family of origin on the career development of outstanding women with disabilities in China. Journal of Rehabilitation, 81(4), 38–48. Retrieved from http://0- search.proquest.com.library.regent.edu/docview/1756229362?accountid=13479

Hayden, S., & Buzzetta, M. (2014). Hope for the future: Career counseling for military personnel and veterans with disabilities. Career Planning and Adult Development Journal, 30(3), 52–64. Retrieved from http://0-search.proquest.com.library.regent.edu/docview/1609375107?accountid=13479

Holland, J. L. (1994). Self-Directed Search. Odessa, FL: Psychological Assessment Resources.

Houtenville, A. J., Sevak, P., O'Neill, J., & Cardoso, E. D. (2013). Disability prevalence and economic outcomes. In D. R. Strauser (Ed.), Career development, employment, and disability in rehabilitation: From theory to practice.

Kim, B., Lee, B. H., Ha, G., Lee, H. K., & Lee, S. M. (2015). Examining longitudinal relationships between dysfunctional career thoughts and career decision-making self-efficacy in school-to-work transition. Journal of Career Development, 42(6). doi:10.1177/0894845315578903

Kulkarni, M. & Gopakumar, K. V. (2014). Career management strategies of people with disabilities. Human Resource Management, 53(3), 445–466. doi:10.1002/hrm.21570

Lindsay, S., McDougall, C., Menna-Dack, D., Sanford, R., & Adams, T. (2015). An ecological approach to understanding barriers to employment for youth with disabilities compared to their typically developing peers: Views of youth, employers, and job counselors. Disability & Rehabilitation, 37(8), 701–711.

Luke, C., & Redekop, F. (2016). Supervision of co-occurring career and mental health concerns: Application of an integrated approach. Career Planning and Adult Development Journal, 32(1), 130–140. Retrieved from http://0-search.proquest.com.library.regent.edu/docview/ 1770932562?accountid=13479

Lustig, D. C., Zanskas, S., & Strauser, D. (2012). The relationship between psychological distress and career thoughts. Journal of Rehabilitation, 78(4), 3–10. Retrieved from http://0- search.proquest.com.library.regent.edu/docview/1115595196?accountid=13479

Matthews, L. R., Harris, L. M., Jaworski, A., Alam, A., & Bozdag, G. (2014). Function, health and psychosocial needs in job-seekers with anxiety, mood, and psychotic disorders who access disability employment services. Work, 49(2), 271–279. doi:10.3233/WOR-131660

Miller, W. R., & Rollnick, S. (2002). Motivational interviewing: Preparing people for change (2nd ed.). New York, NY: Guilford Press.

National Career Development Association (NCDA). (2015). Code of ethics. Broken Arrow, OK: Author.

Osborn, D. S., Finklea, J. T., & Belle, J. G. (2014). Integrating assessments into the career decision-making conversation. Career Planning & Adult Development Journal, 30(4), 144–155.

Prochaska, J. O., & DiClemente, C. C. (1983). Stages and process of self-change in smoking: Toward an integrative model of change. Journal of Consulting and Clinical Psychology, 51, 390–395.

Ritter, E., Strauser, D. R., O'Sullivan, D., Reid, J., Khosravisnasr, S., & Cronin, T. (2013). Theories of career development and work adjustment. In D. R. Strauser (Ed.), Career development, employment, and disability in rehabilitation: From theory to practice (pp. 97).

Sears, S. H., Jones, A., & Strauser, D. R. (2013). Career counseling with people with disabilities. In D. R. Strauser (Ed.), Career development, employment, and disability in rehabilitation: From theory to practice (pp. 277–295).

Sears, S. H., Strauser, D. R., & Wong, A. K. (2014). Examining career readiness and positive affect in a group of college students with disabilities: A pilot study. Journal of Postsecondary Education & Disability, 27(3), 307–319.

Shogren, K. A., & Shaw, L. A. (2016). The role of autonomy, self-realization, and psychological empowerment in predicting outcomes for youth with disabilities. Remedial and Special Education, 37(1), 55–62. doi:10.1177/0741932515585003

Simonsen, M., Fabian, E., & Luecking, R. G. (2015). Employer preferences in hiring youth with disabilities. Journal of Rehabilitation, 81(1), 9–18. Retrieved from http://0-search.proquest.com. library.regent.edu/docview/1672757489?accountid=13479

Smith, D. L. (2014). The relationship between employment and veteran status, disability and gender from 2004–2011 Behavioral Risk Factor Surveillance System (BRFSS). Work, 49(2), 325–334. doi:10.3233/WOR-131648

Sterner, W. R. (2016). Integrating career planning in community and agency settings: Issues, factors, and considerations. Career Planning and Adult Development Journal, 32(1), 73–85. Retrieved from http://0-search.proquest.com.library.regent.edu/docview/1770933198?accountid=13479

Stipanovic, N. (2015). Metacognitive strategies in the career development of individuals with learning disabilities. Career Planning & Adult Development Journal, 31(4), 120–130.

Strauser, D. R. (2013). Career development, employment, and disability in rehabilitation: From theory to practice. New York, NY: Springer Publishing Company.

Swanson, J. L., & Schneider, M. (2013). Minnesota theory of work adjustment. In S. D. Brown & R. W. Lent (Eds.), Career development and counseling: Putting theory and research to work (pp. 29–53).

Watson, D., Clark, L. A., & Teilegen, A. (1988). Development and validation of brief measures of positive and negative affect: The PANAS scales. Journal of Personality & Social Psychology, 54(6), 1063–1070.

Woo, H., Goo, M., & Lee, M. (2016). A content analysis of research on disability: American counseling association journals between 2003 and 2013. Journal of Multicultural Counseling and Development, 44(4), 228–244. doi:10.1002/jmcd.12051

World Bank. (2011). Main report. Washington, DC: World Bank. http://documents.worldbank.org/curated/en/665131468331271288/Main-report

World Health Organization. (2015). WHO global disability action plan 2014–2021: Better health for all people with disability. Retrieved from http://www.who.int/disabilities/policies/actionplan/Disability_action_plan_faq.pdf

Zalaquett, C. P., & Chatters, S. J. (2016). Veterans' mental health and career development: Key issues for practice. Career Planning and Adult Development Journal, 32(1), 86–99. Retrieved from http://0- search.proquest.com.library.regent.edu/docview/1770933113?accountid=13479

Career Counseling with Special Populations

15

Career Counseling and the Military

Kaitlyn C. Stafford, LCSW and Yashika D. Neaves, M.Ed

Greater love hath no man than this, that a man lay down his life for his friends.

John 15:13, King James Version

LEARNING OBJECTIVES

In this chapter, students will learn about

- The different armed services' branches, rank structure, and military-specific language
- The background, in brief, regarding the wars American veterans have served in
- The scope of mental health issues and corresponding resources unique to service members and their families
- The distinctive career challenges services members and their families encounter and methods of assisting this population with navigating career concerns

LEARNING OUTCOMES

At the end of this chapter, students will be able to

- Execute culture-specific language dialogue with and advocate for service members and their families
- Recognize the mental health concerns prevalent with this population
- Categorize the unique challenges that service members and their families face regarding career choice and trajectory
- Identify resources for military service members and their families

- Definitions: service member, veteran, active duty, reservist, officer, enlisted, warrant officer, OEF, OIF, PTSD
- Military culture-specific language and terminology
- An overview of veterans from World War I to present
- The stigma of and struggle with PTSD
- Transitioning out of the military
- Licensure reciprocity for spouses

OVERVIEW OF THE MILITARY CULTURE

Imagine that you work at a local counseling agency and are greeted by your new client, Corporal Smith. He reports that the reason for his visit is due to communication issues with his wife and problems at work. After some discussion with Corporal Smith, you discover that he is just settling into his new home after his most recent Permanent Change of Station, or PCS, and that his wife and children currently reside with family members out-of-state due to Corporal Smith's upcoming deployment to Afghanistan. To build rapport with Corporal Smith and assess his current situation in more detail, you ask him, "How long have you been a soldier?" Corporal Smith immediately corrects you, "I'm not a soldier, I'm a Marine." This situation highlights the importance of understanding military-specific language and acronyms, branches and rank structure, common mental health issues and effective treatments, and career-specific knowledge when working with military service members and their families. In addition, Carolla and Corbin-Burdick (2015) stressed the importance of providing culturally integrated counseling with service members, whose military identities account for their worldview as much as other cultural factors like socioeconomic status, ethnicity, and gender. Thus, these themes will be explored throughout this chapter with the goal of increasing the reader's understanding of the unique, but rewarding, aspects of working with this population to discover their career calling by providing a framework for effective intervention.

The theme scripture, John 15:13 (KJV), resonates. "Greater love hath no man than this, that a man lay down his life for his friends" embodies the calling of our military persons who pledge their lives in sacrifice for the freedoms of others. A career calling like this comes with the extraordinary price of selflessness, one that is incomprehensible to most. Consider this spiritual aspect of sacrifice in every element of information as you get acquainted with the military culture throughout this chapter; it is an important aspect to reflect on in career counseling service members, veterans, and military families on their purpose and call to serve.

BRANCHES, RANK STRUCTURE, AND CULTURE-SPECIFIC LANGUAGE

The U.S. Department of Defense (DoD) formally recognizes the following uniformed services: Army, Marine Corps, Navy, Air Force, National Guard, and Coast Guard. Each branch of service has a unique identity, including the names each branches' members are referred to, rank or rate structure, career paths, and traditions. For example, while many people refer to those in the military as soldiers, like in the example with Corporal Smith at the start of the chapter, the term soldier is actually a reference to a member of the Army, Marine to a member of the Marine Corps, sailor to someone in the Navy, airman to someone in the Airforce, and Coast Guardsman to a member of the Coast Guard. Likewise, the term veteran is typically used for any former armed services members or current service members who have served in combat. In this chapter, you will see the term service member used, which is a reference to a member of the armed services who is currently serving either in the active duty or reserve component. Furthermore, each service member is typically referred to by the rank, rate, or rating specific to his or her branch of service and last name. Service members can maintain their respective roles full time, active duty, or as part-time reservists. Active-duty service members typically live on or near their assigned duty stations and serve in their specified job as their full-time occupation. Active-duty service members and their families receive all the benefits of being a full-time employee, whereas reservists do not. Reservists are required to report to their duty stations on a part-time basis, usually one weekend a month with some additional extended periods of training during the year (i.e., two weeks of annual training). Reservists receive occupational benefits like active-duty service members only when they are working in their reserve roles. Many reservists work full-time jobs or have careers outside of the military and usually live away from their assigned duty stations, which can create a unique set of challenges.

Additionally, service members are either identified as enlisted, warrant officers, or officers in their respective branches (see Tables 15.1 and 15.2 for a detailed list). Service members' ranks determine their level of pay as well as their level of responsibility. Traditionally, enlisted members and warrant officers are not required to have bachelor's degrees, whereas commissioned officers are required to have bachelor's degrees and often master's degrees as they move up in rank. Along with understanding the structure of the military and service branches, service members and their families often use acronyms or culture-specific language. While some of these acronyms change depending on the branch of service, there are many that are utilized across branches. Understanding these terms can be helpful when trying to assess a service member's or a family member's current or past culture-specific experiences. See Table 15.3 for a list of terms and acronyms commonly used.

TABLE 15.1. Department of Defense. Retrieved from http://www.defense.gov/About-DoD/Insignias/Enlisted. Copyright in the public domain.

Enlisted Rank with Corresponding Insignias

	Army	Navy / Coast Guard	Marine Corps	Air Force	
E1	Private	Seaman Recruit (SR)	Private	Airman Basic	
E2	Private E-2 (PV2)	Seaman Apprentice (SA)	Private First Class (PFC)	Airman (Amn)	
E3	Private First Class (PFC)	Seaman (SN)	Lance Corporal (LCpl)	Airman First Class (A1C)	
E4	Corporal (CPL) / Specialist (SPC)	Petty Officer Third Class(PO3) **	Corporal (Cpl)	Senior Airman (SrA)	
E5	Sergeant (SGT)	Petty Officer Second Class (PO2) **	Sergeant (Sgt)	Staff Sergeant (SSgt)	
E6	Staff Sergeant (SSG)	Petty Officer First Class (PO1) **	Staff Sergeant (SSgt)	Technical Sergeant (TSgt)	
E7	Sergeant First Class (SFC)	Chief Petty Officer (CPO) **	Gunnery Sergeant (GySgt)	Master Sergeant (MSgt)	First Sergeant

E8	Master Sergeant (MSG)	First Sergeant (1SG)	Senior Chief Petty Officer (SCPO) **	Master Sergeant (MSgt)	First Sergeant	Senior Master Sergeant (SMSgt)	First Sergeant
E9	Sergeant Major (SGM)	Command Sergeant Major (CSM)	Master Chief Petty Officer (MCPO) ** ***	Fleet/Command Master Chief Petty Officer ** ***	Master Gunnery Sergeant (MGySgt)	Sergeant Major (SgtMaj)	Chief Master Sergeant (CMSgt)	First Sergeant	Command Chief Master Sergeant
E9	Sergeant Major of the Army (SMA)		Master Chief Petty Officer of the Navy (MCPON) and Coast Guard (MCPOCG)		Sergeant Major of the Marine Corps (SgtMajMC)		Chief Master Sergeant of the Air Force (CMSAF)	

TABLE 15.2. Department of Defense. Retrieved from http://www.defense.gov/About-DoD/Insignias/Officers. Copyright in the public domain.

Officer Rank with Corresponding Insignias

	Army	Navy	Marine Corps	Air Force
		Coast Guard		
W1	Warrant Officer 1 WO1	USN Warrant Officer 1 — WO1	Warrant Officer 1 WO	NO WARRANT

W2	Chief Warrant Officer 2 CW2	USN Chief Warrant Officer 2 — CWO2 USCG	Chief Warrant Officer 2 CWO2	NO WARRANT
W3	Chief Warrant Officer 3 CW3	USN Chief Warrant Officer 3 — CWO3 USCG	Chief Warrant Officer 3 CWO3	NO WARRANT
W4	Chief Warrant Officer 4 CW4	USN Chief Warrant Officer 4 — CWO4 USCG	Chief Warrant Officer 4 CWO4	NO WARRANT
W5	Chief Warrant Officer 5 CW5	USN Chief Warrant Officer 5 — CWO5	Chief Warrant Officer 5 CWO5	NO WARRANT

	Army	Navy	Marines	Air Force
		Coast Guard		
O1	Second Lieutenant 2LT 	Ensign ENS 	Second Lieutenant 2nd Lt 	Second Lieutenant 2d Lt
O2	First Lieutenant 1LT 	Lieutenant Junior Grade LTJG 	First Lieutenant 1st Lt 	First Lieutenant 1st Lt
O3	Captain CPT 	Lieutenant LT 	Captain Capt 	Captain Capt
O4	Major MAJ 	Lieutenant Commander LCDR 	Major Maj 	Major Maj

	Army	Navy Coast Guard	Marines	Air Force
O5	Lieutenant Colonel LTC	Commander CDR	Lieutenant Colonel LtCol	Lieutenant Colonel Lt Col
O6	Colonel COL	Captain CAPT	Colonel Col	Colonel Col
O7	Brigadier General BG	Rear Admiral Lower Half RDML	Brigadier General BGen	Brigadier General Brig Gen
O8	Major General MG	Rear Admiral Upper Half RADM	Major General MajGen	Major General Maj Gen

	Army	Navy / Coast Guard	Marines	Air Force
O9	Lieutenant General LTG	Vice Admiral VADM	Lieutenant General LtGen	Lieutenant General Lt Gen
O10	General GEN Army Chief of Staff	Admiral ADM Chief of Naval Operations and Commandant of the Coast Guard	General Gen Commandant of the Marine Corps	General Gen Air Force Chief of Staff
	General of the Army (Reserved for wartime only)	Fleet Admiral (Reserved for wartime only)		General of the Air Force (Reserved for wartime only)

TABLE 15.3. This is not an exhaustive list of terms, phrases, or acronyms. Many of these are either common knowledge or phrases used among military service members and providers or are obtained from the U.S. Department of Defense (2016).
Source: http://www.dtic.mil/doctrine/new_pubs/jp1_02.pdf.

Common Military Terms, Acronyms, Language

Term/Acronym	Explanation
AD (active duty)	Full-time duty in the military or full-time service in the Reserve component
Article 15	An in-house, non-legal hearing to determine a service member's punishment (or NJP non-judicial punishment) when he/she has engaged in misconduct

Term/Acronym	Explanation
AWOL (absent without leave)	When a service member has not had prior approval from his/her command or unit to be off duty or away from work; also referred to as unauthorized absence (UA)
Base	An area from which operations are planned or sustained or in which military installations are located; also referred to as camp, post, etc. depending on the branch; e.g., a family may state that they live on base or on post, which means that they live in housing that is located within the restricted area of land within which the service member is also required to work; examples of military bases include Ft. Benning, Camp Pendleton, and Lackland Air Force Base
CASEVAC (casualty evacuation)	The effort of moving casualties (persons who are deceased, unaccounted for, sick, or wounded) to and from medical treatment centers
Chain of command	The lineage of rank structure through which authority of decision-making succeeds
Chaplain	Military personnel whose job is to provide religious or spiritual counseling within a command or unit
Civilian	A nonmilitary person, although not referring to military personnel spouses or children
Combat and operational stress	Physical, mental, psychological, emotional, or behavioral reactions typically expected after one has been exposed to wartime activities
Command	Referring to either an official order or the structure or unit of authority issuing official orders over subordinates; e.g., a service member may state that he or she is having issues within his/her "command," referring to the climate or his/her work environment or unit
CONUS	Continental United States, U.S. Territory and surrounding waters
Convoy	A systematized group of military vehicles that typically takes the same route in an effort to establish a controlled movement in an area; also referred to a group of merchant ships escorted by military ships/aircraft; "We were on our usual convoy when an IED blew up in front of us."
Court-martial	A legal proceeding for more serious crimes or wrongdoings
Dependent	A service member's spouse, children who are under 21 years old, and children/immediate family members (siblings, children, parents) who are unable to care for themselves mentally or physically
Deployment	The movement of service members to and from an operational area, aka down range or in theater.
Direct fire	Referring to weapons of some sort being aimed at a specific mark, either other weapons/fire or persons; "We were under direct fire for over an hour."
Drop zone	Referring to the area where airborne personal or supplies will land on the ground
EOD (explosive ordnance disposal)	Referring to the detection and removal of explosives or other harmful nuclear, biological, and chemical means to ensure safety; "The EOD tech found and disposed of three IEDs the day before on that same route."
FOB (forward operating base)	A tactical support area with less than usual accommodations

Term/Acronym	Explanation
IED (improvised explosive device)	A weapon/bomb utilized to harm, kill, or cause interruption of mission operations
In theater	Referring to being deployed or on a mission outside of the United States; "When we were in theater, our team used to play cards when we came back from a mission."
JA or JAG (Judge Advocate General)	A reference to military attorneys or lawyers
Leave	When a service member has been approved to be off work or duty; similar to paid time off (PTO)
MASCAL (mass casualty)	Referring to a large incident including sudden loss of life or injury that requires operation support
MEB (Medical Evaluation Board)	A review board that determines whether a service member's physical or mental health will permanently interfere with his/her duty
MOS (military occupational specialty)	A service member's job in their respective branch; "Eli's MOS was an EOD technician in the Navy and John's MOS was a Reconnaissance "Recon" Marine."
MWR (morale, welfare, recreation)	An area or set of programs focused on recreational activities in order to promote wellness
OCONUS (outside the continental United States)	Any area outside of the United States and its surrounding waters
OCS (Officer Candidate School)	Refers to the initial training and education program that prepares officers in the military
PCS (permanent change of station)	When service members are ordered to relocate to a new duty station
POTUS	President of the United States
POW (prisoner of war)	A person who while deployed is detained by enemy forces
Reserve Component	Members of a branch of the armed services who maintain part-time training and can be called to active duty at any time
Security Forces	Service members whose job is to provide protection and enforce the laws; i.e., military police
SOI (School of Infantry)	The training and education program intended for enlisted members who have graduated basic training
TDY (temporary duty)	When a service member has official orders to train or re-locate, temporarily, away from his/her permanent duty station; also referred to as TAD (temporary assignment of duty).
VBEID (vehicle-borne improvised explosive device)	An IED (see definition) specifically placed in correlation with a vehicle.
Wire (inside or outside)	Inside the wire refers to the secured area or base on a deployment; outside the wire refers to a nonsecured area on deployment.

Service members and their families do not necessarily expect off-base or civilian providers to engage in military-specific language; however, understanding culture-specific terminology does make building rapport and evaluating the context of your client's issues easier and more efficient. In fact, if a service member is coming to you for help as an off-base provider without a referral from an on-base provider, he or she is likely seeking confidential support that is not connected to the work environment. Thus, inquiring about military-specific language in a curious way may be a manner in which to strengthen the career counseling experience and show a true interest in understanding where he or she is coming from and the context of the current problem(s) he or she is presenting with. If you are a military provider or are affiliated with the DoD or Veteran's Affairs (VA), your client will likely expect you to be familiar with commonly used military language; having a lack of knowledge in this area could hinder the therapeutic process. Nonetheless, if you expect to work with this population, familiarize yourself with culture-specific language and terms, and do not assume that something you have watched in a movie or seen in the media is an accurate portrayal of a service member's experience, as his or her experience is specific to his or her branch, rank or rate, job, and other personal cultural factors such as gender, race, ethnicity, and sexual preference.

BRIEF HISTORY AND OVERVIEW OF SOCIETAL PERCEPTION OF THIS POPULATION

While there have been great advances in research and intervention with military service members since Operation Iraqi Freedom (OIF) and Operation Enduring Freedom (OEF), it has historically taken a considerable amount of time for providers and scholars to distinguish the unique mental health, career, financial, and interpersonal concerns specific to service members and their families. At present, there continues to be much more to learn in order to efficiently and effectively help this population of men and women. While this section does not provide an extensive historical context for the societal, provider, and service members' responses to each war, it is intended to afford a framework or context for help-seeking behaviors among this population as well as the evolution of provider responses, interventions, and resources for service members and their families.

World War I and World War II. In the context of World War I, American society focused on the healing aspects of shell-shock, a term coined in 1915 to describe a condition that was thought to be a short term, curable wound rather than the problem itself for war veterans (Stagner, 2014). The treatment of shell-shock ranged from a focus on diaphragmatic breathing, faith-based interventions, and the necessity of having a female caregiver (Stagner, 2014). From 1920 to 1930, societal attitudes about veterans' responses to war shifted drastically from supportive to viewing these former service members as criminals, mentally ill, and dangerous. Simultaneously, veteran suicide rates increased to two per day (Stagner, 2014). The overarching view regarding shell-shock was that it was incurable for service members who had some kind of predisposition to mental illness; thus, policy makers shifted their focus from treatment to screening so that service members with alleged predisposing factors did not enter into the military. However, this response was met with opposition from the newly formed American Legion, which advocated for veteran's rights (Stagner, 2014). For World War II veterans, Langer (2011) highlighted the increasing number of veterans being misdiagnosed with disorders like schizophrenia due to the lack of research and understanding about the impact of war on those who served. Shell-shock eventually became known as combat fatigue, specifically during the World War II and Korean War eras, until the third edition of the Diagnostic and Statistical Manual of Mental Disorders identified this disorder as posttraumatic stress disorder, or PTSD as we know it today (Langer, 2011). Although there is much less research regarding the impact of war on First and Second World War veterans, the foundations of advocacy and knowledge about the effects of war on quality of life and mental health for veterans began during these war eras. As research interest has increased over the years, we are afforded improved information about the unique dynamics of each veteran population for each period of war or conflict.

Korea. At present, Korean War veterans are the largest group of the oldest of survivors of previous of wars; thus, normal aging issues coupled with increasing attention regarding OIF and OEF service members returning with PTSD and other mental health issues may be contributing to an increase in this particular veteran population seeking help (Brooks & Fulton, 2009). Brooks and Fulton (2009) found that Korean War veterans reported greater mental health and quality of life concerns than veterans of other wars and that they were also more likely to seek treatment from the VA than other war veterans. This may be because many Korean War veterans have felt that less attention was given to them regarding their participation in the war over the years; accordingly, they may feel more deserving than other veteran populations to receive assistance that they perceive has long been ignored. Consider this perspective from James Dalton Carpenter (personal communication, October 16, 2016), a veteran who served for 11 months during the height of the Korean War: "I was proud, we liberated a country, but we weren't appreciated by our society or our country, the same country that sent us there ... we were forgotten." Carpenter mentioned that the Korean War was different from other wars in that initially there was only one enemy—North Korea—to fight, but that this eventually changed to include China. He also explained that unlike the wars that followed, there were no helicopters to deliver food and other items, so mail and supplies moved in at a much slower pace (James Dalton Carpenter, personal communication, October 16, 2016). Additionally, as Korean War veterans are getting older and experiencing greater difficulty coping and managing the challenges that come with normal aging, perhaps there is a sense of resilience and the ability to seek help for these difficulties that differs from other veteran populations. Although forgotten, as mentioned by Carpenter (personal communication, October 16, 2016), it is likely that Korean War veterans feel much more pride associated with their time of service compared to other populations, such as Vietnam veterans.

Vietnam. The Vietnam era sparked societal attention and activism, with large numbers of nonsupporters for the United States' involvement in the war. Many Vietnam veterans were met with hostility, shaming, and a lack of support upon their return, the result of which has contributed to unique mental health issues prevalent in this particular veteran population. Additionally, as noted by Flores (2014), the Vietnam War was different from other wars such as World War II in that the enemy was ill defined and veteran experiences encompassed more than mere combat, including exposure and participation in unwarranted crimes. Flores (2014) also noted that the political attitudes of Vietnam veterans influenced by cultural debates and veterans' experiences in combat has shaped the way that these veterans remember and perceive their personal narratives as well as the degree of support they received after the Vietnam War. When working with this population, then, it is important to gain a greater understanding of each veteran's own perception of specific political and societal attitudes regarding the war. Likewise, Link and Palinkas (2013) noted several studies that have found that combat exposure had adverse effects for not only the Vietnam veterans exposed to it but the children and spouses of those veterans as well. Similarly, Magruder and Yeager (2009) conducted a meta-analysis and found that Vietnam veterans seemed to show greater prevalence of PTSD when compared to Gulf War, OIF, and OEF veterans.

OIF and OEF. As research has continued beyond Vietnam era veterans, there seem to be additional studies that are finding an array of difficulties associated with deployment for OIF and OEF veterans as well (Link & Palinkas, 2013). Regardless of war period, according to Magruder and Yeager (2009), veterans with exposure to combat present with higher rates of PTSD than those without. Fortunately, changes in legislation over time and increased attention to service members' needs has permitted better benefits as well as access to care (although the need for continued improvements in the system remains vast). For OEF and OIF service members, these shifts have led to an increasing amount of consideration regarding traumatic brain injury and PTSD (Amara, 2013). In fact, unique to OIF and OEF veterans has been the increased occurrence of service members returning home with physical and psychological injuries (Link & Palinkas, 2013). This has created a distinctive set of challenges and barriers for OIF and OEF service members and their families, which will be explored throughout the remainder of this chapter.

Overall, societal perceptions and the nature of warfare due to geographical locations, time and war periods, and advances in technology have indeed impacted service member's opinions of their participation in the military, war, and combat. Figure 15.1 provides information regarding the current population of veterans across war periods as well as projections for 10 and 20 years in the future, respectively. As mentioned previously, each service member's or veteran's (and their families') experiences differ based on the period of time in which he or she served as well as his or her participation in combat; thus, the needs of each veteran population will continue to shift with time and changes in the economy, and as these veterans age. Understanding these dynamics provides a foundational understanding throughout the career counseling process to establish quality within the working alliance and minimize premature counseling termination found to be common among in OIF and OEF PTSD veterans (Szafranski, Gros, Menefee, Wanner, & Norton, 2014).

FIGURE 15.1 Represents projected number of veterans from the Gulf War to the period of 911. Data was obtained from the National Center for Veterans Analysis and Statistic 2014 Veteran Population Data which is public information and can be retrieved at http://www.va.gov/vetdata/veteran_population.asp.

Overview of Projected Veteran Populations by Gulf War Post-9/11 from 2016–2036

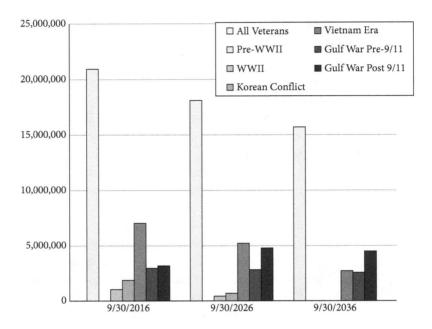

CAREER AND MENTAL HEALTH DYNAMICS

To appropriately help service members, veterans, and their families with their careers, it is important to understand that there are unique mental health concerns that exist for members within this population because of their cultural experiences. Whether you are counseling a spouse who is trying to find a meaningful career path or a service member who is struggling to decide whether to get out of the military or stay in, understanding the mental health dynamics that are present for these clients while exploring career goals is necessary to help members of this population competently. For example, if you are working with a veteran who has been diagnosed with a TBI, it is important to understand how this disorder impacts your client cognitively, emotionally, and behaviorally as this will likely impact his or her success in whatever career path you are exploring in your sessions. Additionally, if you are working with active- duty service members, the presence of mental health concerns can directly impact their careers, especially if the service member does not respond positively to treatment or if the mental health concerns persist, therefore interfering with the performance of military duties. Understanding the mental health dynamics of this population will give you a better understanding of the challenges that may impact your military clients' career and career decisions as well as provide you with information to appropriately assess and refer your client if mental health concerns are impacting your ability to focus on career-related goals.

UNDERSTANDING MENTAL HEALTH DYNAMICS WITH THIS POPULATION

While there are a range of mental health concerns among this population, as mentioned previously, issues like PTSD and TBI are especially associated with veterans and seen as topics of interest throughout the existing research. However, it is important to consider that the treatment of veterans, just like the majority of mental health treatment today, is influenced by an overwhelming emphasis on the medical model, which can lead to a tendency to overly pathologize these consumers and offer quick treatment solutions when longer and more holistic approaches may be warranted (Carolla & Corbin-Burdick, 2015). For that reason, while this chapter presents some of the existing research and resources, we encourage you to enter the therapeutic realm with your service member, veteran clients, and their families with a phenomenological and holistic perspective. Nonetheless, military service members are often subjected to distinctive traumatic experiences as a result of combat exposure; this, coupled with recurrent transitions due to training, change of duty stations, and deployment, adds additional stressors and adjustment concerns for these service members and their families. Thus, understanding these exclusive issues is warranted for ethical and competent practice with this population. The following section will explore the impact of trauma and transition on service members and their families; the stigma associated with counseling; and resources for providers, service members, and their families.

Themes of Trauma and Transition

Only half of one percent of Americans served in the military within the past decade, and of that, 56% experienced a traumatic event and say that they have flashbacks or repeated distressing memories (Morin, 2011). Over two million U.S. service members have deployed to Iraq or Afghanistan since September 11, 2001, and of that, 27% deployed more than once (Sayer et al., 2010). The mental health considerations of the military population of OEF and OIF veterans in transition include post-traumatic stress disorder (PTSD), traumatic brain injuries (TBI), other service-connected disabilities (both physical and psychological), and military sexual trauma (MST), which is reported as a war-related stressor (Schreiber & McEnany, 2015). Forty-six percent of these military members over the past 10 years suffered from posttraumatic stress, with 71% dealing with combat zone experiences that will decrease their chances of an easier transition to their civilian life (Morin, 2011). Serving on active duty with PTSD complicates the military experience due in part by traditional masculine gender role norms (TMGRNs) experienced by both military men and women; this promotes and reinforces the value of "competition and power, hiding perceived weakness as well as maintaining self-reliance and emotional control" (Lorber & Garcia, 2010, p. 297). These perceptions often mean that active duty military will conceal their perceived weakness, tamper in substance abuse as a coping mechanism, and avoid or drop out of psychotherapy. Ninety-five percent of males who served in OEF and OIF dropped out of psychotherapy, more than twice the rate of male Vietnam veterans. These compelling numbers of improperly or untreated military members have led to marital and occupational difficulties on active duty and when it is time for these service members to transition from military (Sayer et al., 2010).

In addition to the heightened prevalence regarding trauma-based problems for service members, frequent moves and periods of transition from deployment to home or home to a new duty station can complicate coping abilities and interpersonal relationships. Likewise, for reservists, transitioning from deployment or training to civilian life with even less support from the military community has its separate set of challenges. As avoidance constitutes one of four symptom clusters of PTSD per the American Psychiatric Association (2013a), frequent moves and adjustment periods can complicate service members accessing treatment; such transitions compound additional stressors and may worsen symptom severity. In addition, the American Psychiatric Association (2013b) pointed out that some military veterans and psychological professionals disagreed on the terminology for the disorder when revising the fifth Diagnostic and Statistical Manual of Mental Disorders (DSM-5). Some military veterans believed the term **disorder** influenced the stigma of receiving help whereas some psychological professionals were of the opinion that the military community needs to evolve in a way that lessens the stigma (American Psychiatric Association, 2013b). Nonetheless, it's apparent that in addition to all the previously mentioned barriers regarding veterans utilizing and accessing mental health treatment, the stigma associated with war-related disorders and mental health issues remains an area of concern for both the military community and providers.

The Stigma Associated with Counseling

For the military service member, the stigma, or the anxiety of an anticipated stigmatized label associated with seeking mental health counseling, is linked to levels of resistance, personal beliefs about mental illness, and self-reliance TMGRN attitudes that have manifested through institutionalization, combat training, and the desire to emulate strength depicted in being a member of the U.S. Armed Forces. These misguided cognitions transfer into perceptions and follow-on behaviors that reject clinical treatment when warranted. A large portion of Armed Forces members who served during combat-related tours view the need for counseling or mental health care as a sign of weakness that goes against their presumed view of military traditions. These misconceptions and predispositions cause opposition to normalizing stress levels when they arise, which coupled with individual and family distress can lead to suicidal thoughts, increased substance abuse, major depression and a greater opposition toward follow-up counseling (Lorber & Garcia, 2010; Vogt, Fox, & Di Leone, 2014). Overall, behavioral health counseling is viewed negatively by a large majority of military service members as a forum for just complaining and that comes with a trepidation of being labeled and discredited by their unit. This results in suppression of emotions, psychological challenges, and maladaptive behaviors that distort purpose and calling.

Social desirability in the military workplace among fellow comrades is one of the biggest barriers that redirects the necessity to seek mental wellness for service members; OEF and OIF veterans fear being viewed as incompetent in the workplace and avoided, or rejected by others because of a mental diagnosis (Vogt, Fox, & Di Leone, 2014). The military service member then justifies their invalid belief that mental illness can be resolved without professional mental health care. This island mentality of isolation also guarantees that there will be no breach of confidentiality; with TMGRN attitudes, sharing vulnerabilities would be detrimental to the psyche, especially if therapeutic trust is broken, putting their active duty or reserve career in jeopardy. This is particularly the case for male service members who feel pressure to prove themselves for promotion and mission readiness and to have the mental stamina suited to depict the image of an iconic military leader (Morin, 2011; Schreiber & McEnany, 2015). Anonymity is viewed as the coveted path to escape stigmas and remain intact within the workplace. This type of internalized behavior, however, is the cause of nearly 1.5 million service members diagnosed with a mental disorder failing to seek help, and those who did, did so over a year after their diagnosis and did not continue with follow-up care (Hodge, Auchterlonie, & Milliken, 2006; Milliken, Auchterlonie, & Hodge, 2007).

Psychological or stress-related difficulties that are not properly prevented or treated as a consequence of negative internal beliefs about mental health care, societal perceptions regarding mental illnesses, and institutionalized military culture association have to be exposed in order to reduce the mental health care stigma. Stigma reduction for military men and women is a necessity to prevent social, emotional, and personal impediments that impact active-duty service performance and post-military reintegration within the civilian sector. This section is calling for military sensitivity, awareness, and competence as imperative for counselors to identify and utilize effective practices that will operate to diminish stigmas that hinder work-life balances of transition, reintegration, and mental wellness that impede career purpose and development. Mental health care workers who label the illness—for example, the person has post-traumatic stress disorder, rather than the person is a PTSD soldier—help reduce internal, societal, and institutionalized stigmas about seeking counseling (Schreiber & McEnany, 2015). Properly communicating clinical terms to normalize mental illnesses, similar to other medical terms (e.g., catching a cold, having the flu, or experiencing a migraine), can be the linkage to promoting posttraumatic growth (PTG), the positive psychological change that produces growth in confidence, purpose, and calling subsequent to trauma exposure (Tedeschi & Calhoun, 2004).

Military Spouses and Families

While service members themselves experience the impact of trauma and transition, their spouses and children are undoubtedly affected by the reactions of their service members and the dynamics of military culture. As pointed out by Carolla and Corbin-Burdick (2015), studies have highlighted the influence that a change in a system can create, and this concept is illustrated by research showing that military children experienced increased levels of anxiety as a result of parental or spouse separations due to deployments and that spouses experienced similar rates of depression as their service members. Likewise, Eaton et al. (2008) found that Army spouses experienced equivalent rates of mental health issues as combat soldiers; yet, spouses were more likely to seek mental health treatment than Army service members. Notably, many spouses in Eaton et al.'s (2008) study received their mental health care from primary care facilities, which may not necessarily be fully equipped to respond fully to the spouses' mental health needs.

Also, marked alterations in combat veterans' behaviors such as irritability, angry outbursts, verbal and physical aggression, or reckless self-destructive behavior symptoms lead to emotional impairments that interfere with family relationships and cause disconnection (APA, 2013a; 2013b). Marital dissatisfaction due to altered behavior or the onset of aggression causes impairments in open communication. Military veterans with PTSD are twice as likely to divorce than veterans without PTSD and three times more likely to divorce more than twice (Price & Stevens, 2014). Combat veteran spouses also report a greater sense of anxiety around intimacy (Cosgrove et al., 2002). Sexual dysfunctions tend to be higher for combat veterans with PTSD, which in turn causes diminished sexual interest, contributing to the decrease in couple satisfaction and adjustment (Price & Stevens, 2014). Moreover, male spouses of military wives (who are a minority) also experienced challenges and mental health issues like depression, anxiety, and PTSD, especially for those husbands who had prior service in the military, and at times felt less support due to the lack of resources in the military community for male spouses (Southwell & MacDermid Wadsworth, 2016). Thus, it is imperative that career counselors collaborate with psychotherapists and behavioral health clinicians to address both short- and long-term career goals with these family considerations in mind when assisting their married military clients with PTSD (Lorber & Garcia, 2010).

In regards to military service members' children, Campbell, Brown, and Okra (2011) noted that children experienced a greater risk of witnessing intimate partner violence than civilian children, and that child maltreatment increased during deployment episodes. Risk factors for military service member child maltreatment include caregiver depression, PTSD, and substance abuse according to Campbell et al. (2011). For younger children, from birth to age five, Osofsky, Molinda, and Chartrand (2013) stressed the impact that caregiver absence and increased stress due to deployment has on a child's attachment to his or her parents, which can lead to symptoms of anxiety and behavior issues. As young children are vulnerable to the absence of the deployed parent, the mental health of the at-home caregiver is increasingly important for these children; thus, support for this caregiver is crucial not only for his or her well-being but for his or her young children (Osofsky et al., 2013). Additionally, many military children must get accustomed to frequent interstate and international moves, which can impact their mental health, worldview, and cultural identity in a way that is unique from civilian children. Research supports the concept that many military children identify as third culture kids (TCK), which can present challenges but also a sense of independence, adaptability, and resilience. For more information regarding this concept, please refer to the TCK chapter in this textbook. These are important considerations when working with adolescents or college students who are military children.

On a different note, in their study of military spouses, Wang, Nyutu, Tran, and Spears (2015) found that positive affect, especially when shared in relationships; support from friends, especially within the community rather than family; and military community support contributed to a spouses' feelings of mastery and control in their environments as well as a sense of psychological well-being. As well, Southwell and MacDermid Wadsworth (2016) conducted qualitative analyses of husbands of female service members and identified some positive aspects associated with this minority spouse population including pride in their wives, closer relationships due to overcoming the unique challenges that military life places on the couple, and strengthened father-child relationships due to fathers taking on the primary parenting role when spouses were away.

WOMEN AND LGBT IN THE MILITARY

While these subsections will in no way cover the vast amount of information on the following subject, we do hope to give you an overview that will pique your interest in reading more on these topics as well as provide enough understanding about the challenges within the military culture specific to women and LGBT populations so that you, as a provider, will have an appropriate framework from which to practice with these minority groups.

Women

Women have worked in the military for quite some time in various roles, and the history of women's interest in serving in the Armed Forces is quite rich. Women in the U.S. military have come a long way from their official participation in World War II via the Women's Army Corps (WAC), Navy's Women Accepted for Volunteer Emergency Service (WAVES), U.S. Marine Corps Women's Reserve (MCWR), Women Airforce Service Pilots (WASP), and the U.S. Coast Guard Women's Reserves (aka SPARS). In fact, in 2013 the rescinding of the 1994 Direct Ground Combat Definition and Assignment Rule (DGCDAR) opened positions that were previously closed to women in the military (U.S. Department of Defense, n.d.c). Because these changes were implemented in 2016, this topic remains quite new and controversial; thus, researchers have undoubtedly responded with inquiries. There are thousands of scholarly articles one can read on this subject and a number of other resources and periodicals discussing the issue. The DoD alone noted over 33 extensive studies dedicated to reviewing the impact, implications, and integration of women in the Armed services in a fact sheet available to the public (U.S. Department of Defense, n.d.c).

Prior to the repeal of 1994 DGCDAR, McNulty (2012) noted the historical misconceptions of the roles women have played during war in regards to combat as well as the ever-changing public and service member opinions on the matter. McNulty (2012) described how Lioness teams, later known as Female Engagement Teams (FET), are examples of how women can and did play integral roles in the wars in Iraq and Afghanistan by engaging with the local women while being exposed to combat. Yet, policy has changed regarding women serving in combat roles, and with it comes myriad opinions and challenges that women who currently serve or are wanting to serve, especially in combat roles, continue to face. For example, Nindl et al. (2016), discussed the physical and physiological differences between men and women and that there are several studies on, and suggestions with regard to, physical training that can be implemented to assist women in the military (who are physically inferior to men in most cases) to perform jobs requiring intense physical fitness that basic trainings, like the Army's, might not be able to train them to do. Another area of concern is the impact that women integration has on unit cohesion and competence. It appears that some of the recent and more historical research is mixed on this issue (Schaefer et al., 2015; U.S. Army Institute for the Behavioral and Social Sciences, 1977; U.S. Army Institute for the Behavioral and Social Sciences, 1978). Nonetheless, leadership plays a large role in the success of integrating women into combat roles and units (Klenke, 2016; Schaefer et al., 2015).

According to the DoD (2016), women currently make up about 16% of the military, so while numbers have grown over the years and policy has progressed, women remain a minority in the military culture, which is dominated by the male gender. King (2015), in his critique of an article on women in the military, mentioned the unique challenges that women have faced in the Marine Corps as a result of the derogatory language sometimes used by men to define these women's roles. Klenke (2016) pointed out that despite new positions being opened to women, women remain hesitant to fully approach these new opportunities for fear that they will not be fully accepted by their male counterparts or that there will be some assumption of being accepted because of their gender rather than qualification. Other unique issues for women in the military include juggling their careers with child-rearing, especially during deployments; military sexual trauma (MST), mentioned previously in this chapter; and trying to navigate the gender bias that exists despite recent and overdue changes made toward equivalence. As mental health and career counseling professionals serving this population, the overwhelming research shows that the challenges unique to women in the military are vast.

LGBT Service Members

The lesbian, gay, bisexual, and transgender (LGBT) community within the United States make up approximately 3.8% of the population, implying that there is an estimated nine million LBGT Americans (Gates, 2011); of that, there are approximately 70,000 LGBT Armed Forces active-duty service members, veterans, and reservists who have disclosed their sexual orientation or sexual identity (Gates, 2010). Historically, homosexual and transgender individuals were rejected by the military, which at the time considered gender identity or sexual orientation a private matter of preference; LGBT active-duty service members were silenced by laws that determined homosexuality incompatible with their military service (Secretary of Defense, 1993). Don't Ask Don't Tell (DADT), which prohibited U.S. military forces from openly sharing their sexual orientation, was ended after a political move in 2011 in one of the first major actions that lead to an open LGBT population within the military (Ramirez et al., 2013). The repeal of Section 3 of the Defense of Marriage Act (DOMA) in 2013 was the next major advance, which opened up sanctions to federal entitlements for same-sex couples to include health insurance, social security benefits, joint tax filing with exemptions, and immigration protections for binational couples. The repeal of Section 3 of DOMA did not impact state laws automatically, thus 13 states continued not recognizing same-sex marriage following the repeal (Karimi & Pearson, 2015). This required additional considerations for same-sex military couples who prepared for military reassignments to those states and overseas countries that did not acknowledge same-sex marriage. In spite of these known challenges, upon the Supreme Court ruling in favor of same-sex marriage nationwide (Obergefell et al. v. Hodges, 2015), the Armed Forces initiated special task forces within each branch of service to carry out policies associated with the changes in the federal law.

One of the most controversial topics within the LGBT population is transgender individuals, who are viewed differently from lesbians, gays, and bisexuals in that their discrimination is not a matter of sexual orientation but rather gender identity, in which they fail to conform to gender stereotypes (Carroll, Gilroy, & Ryan, 2002). In recent years, lesbian, gay, and bisexual organizations' inclusiveness has expanded to embrace the transgender population (Chung, 2003). The conflict of sexual orientation versus gender identity present societal bias, which resonates immensely within the military due to the overarching theme of TMGRNs (Lorber & Garcia, 2010). As TMGRNs are slowly phasing out due to mental health efforts in the aftermath of OIF and OEF, the military cultural transition and awareness of the transgender population as part of the Armed Forces is becoming evident. In 2015, the social disparities within the workforce led the Equal Employment Opportunity Commission (EEOC) to extend Title VII's protection, which prohibits sex discrimination, to cover sexual orientation for federal sector employees (Minoz & Kalteux, 2016). An EEOC Equal Protection Clause ruling based on several court cases held that "discrimination against a transgender individual because of [her] gender non-conformity is sex discrimination … whether its described as being on the basis of sex or gender" (Glenn v. Brumby, 2011). The EEOC and Equal Protection Clause rulings commanded the Armed Forces to reevaluate their policies that failed to recognize transgender service members even in the aftermath of DADT. Additionally, a memorandum signed by the Secretary of the Army and distributed in July 2016 entailed a number of initiatives set in place by the military to expand their inclusion of transgender personnel in the military.

Despite the progressive movements that now give legal equality to military LGBT individuals, the LGBT service members and veterans who concealed their sexual orientation and identity during DADT lacked full disclosure during counseling and mental health support. In the aftermath of DADT, this secrecy has exposed significant considerations for this population, to include elevated rates of depression, isolation, and social exclusion within the military community (Ramirez et al., 2013). Research has shown higher prevalence rates of substance abuse, anxiety, sexual harassment, victimization, physical health problems, and suicide associated with LGBT veterans and active-duty members (Carroll & Gilroy, 2002; Chung, 2003; Lorber & Garcia, 2010; Moradi, 2009; Ramirez et al., 2013). The road to a military culture that fully embraces what was once prohibited may be a path with more hurdles than others. Although new legislation is in place to implement inclusion for these military members, mental health counselors working with military LGBT clients must have the competency to recognize the compounding cultural considerations associated with past rejection embedded in military forces that have produced heightened mental and psychological impediments. The internal discrimination that intersects gender identity and sexual orientation, like racism, religious affiliations, and rank hierarchy within the military, are added challenges that mental health workers must be prepared to address. The residual effects of this discrimination throughout transition and civilian reintegration toward veteran status, and its influences on career pursuits and psychological considerations, still haunts the LGBT military service member today; thus, the Veterans Health Administration (VHA) through collaborative aid of interdisciplinary providers is working to transform LGBT healthcare, clinical services, and consultation resources. Although this transformation is still in the early stages, it is one step closer to healing the mental wounds of LGBT military veterans (Kauth & Shipherd, 2016).

IMPLICATIONS FOR CAREER COUNSELING WITH THE MILITARY

The career culture of the military is multidynamic; the term that the DoD has coined is **Military Life Cycle** (MLC) to address the multidimensional career considerations associated throughout the life of a service member from new recruit to separation after the end of contractual military service. This concept comes with a model approach that has implications for career counseling military personnel for private-sector practitioners, DoD-contracted counselors, federal government behavioral health workers, and military career counselors. Components of the MLC model were discussed in legislation following OIF and OEF and implemented in all branches of service in 2015 to address Career Readiness Standards (CRS) of active duty service members and reservists (see Figure 15.2). This MLC model assists with fulfilling career callings, both short- and long-term, with regards to optimal career outcomes amid career challenges.

New recruits to military service are introduced to the MLC model when they take the Armed Services Vocational Aptitude Battery (ASVAB), which determines their basic qualifications to enter the military and the best occupational choices based on their test scores

FIGURE 15.2 This MLC model addresses career tenets throughout the tenure of the military member's service as they progress in their active or reserve duty. Department of Defense Transition Assistance Program. Copyright in the public domain. Retrieved from https://www.dodtap.mil/mlc.html.

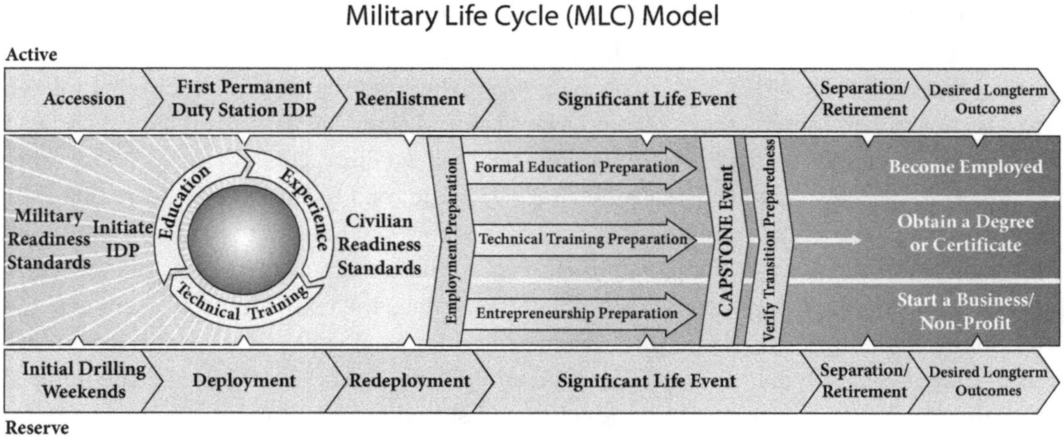

Military Life Cycle (MLC) Model

(Roberts et al., 2000). If new recruits receive a qualifying score on their ASVAB, they are given the opportunity to then select a specific career path for a vocation of choice prior to signing their contract; however, this process can get convoluted at Military Entrance Processing Stations (MEPS) and recruiting offices, where career counseling is minimal for new recruits. This is due in part to DoD mission requirements to fill certain occupations that have shortages versus occupations that are over strength, which by default places new recruits in positions where their career path could be determined by chance, not choice. If a new recruit desires to serve their country, they may only be presented with military mission career options given to them at MEPS, even if this means electing a profession that is not associated with their interest, personality, skills, or civilian market trends. This includes vocations limited to the military settings (e.g., infantryman, amphibious combat vehicle Marine, tank driver) that do not easily translate into civilian occupations. Military recruiters who are tasked with meeting mission-related quotas will assure new enlisted recruits that after they sign their contract and get to their first duty station, they can change their occupation or apply to become a military officer. Although this is true to a degree, the process of changing careers paths once in the military still comes with military mission constraints, prerequisites, and additional service obligations that may limit changing jobs or positions easily.

The DoD's announcement of military downsizing by 40,000 troops significantly impacted the career and transition milestones of the Armed Forces (Klimas, 2015); the drawdown due to budget constraints has reduced U.S. military forces in 2016, with projected cuts for Army soldiers well into 2018. This transformation has lowered the overall personnel quota for military mission requirements and placed higher qualifications on the type of new recruits entering the military. This has considerable effects on thousands of active-duty service members who consider the military their career choice for employment and retirement. The MLC is a holistic military career model that legislative leaders realized was necessary in order to address the consequences of this phenomenon on its service members' career concerns in hopes to mitigate a lack of preparedness toward transition. Military career counselors, active-duty and reserve service members who function as career advisors to their fellow service members (see Table 15.4), are embedded in almost

TABLE 15.4. Career advising reference graph for occupations by branch.

Career Advising Occupational Titles by Branch

Branch of Service	MOS/Rating Code/Designator Code	Career Advising Occupational Titles
Army	79S	Career Counselor
Army Reserves	79V	Army Reserve Career Counselor
Marines	4821	Career Planner
Navy	NCC	Navy Career Counselor

every branch of service. Military career counselors address the needs of military service members to assist with career advancement, promotion, retention, assignment choices, and options after their service; however, their training is mission-oriented, based on the needs of their branch of service. The federal government, through the Transition Assistance Program (TAP) offices, also has civilian career counselors who are trained to address the CRS (see Figure 15.3) and benchmark certain objectives as part of the career counseling process; however, the CRS requirements, if not coupled with vocational rehabilitation and psychotherapy, can overlook a service members' mental, emotional, and psychological needs in the process. Military college career counselors have been affected by the budget cuts as well, since education falls into a voluntary category for service members. One clear example of this is the Virtual Education Centers (VEC), established in the Navy and which also support the Marine Corps, that are replacing face-to-face academic and career counseling at 16 of the 20 Navy College offices (military.com). The Army has started their realignment of education and career centers, but additional educational and career centers are projected to have cuts until 2019.

Career counseling with the military requires strategies to address the multi-tiered considerations, challenges, and of service members to build a cohesive holistic mental health and wellness approach. This includes identifying prior military skills, experience gained from the service, education levels, interests, and personality tendencies in conjunction to combat-related factors of PTSD, TBI, major depression, military sexual trauma (MST), suicidal ideations, or physical disabilities that add to the complexity of career counseling this population. Service members in default occupations need additional guidance to bridge the challenge of leaving the military after years of serving in an occupation chosen based on the needs of their branch. Career counselors must account for this during the initial assessment phase as well as consider other career development services that the military client has undergone. This could account for any perceived apprehensions or areas that need to be readdressed due to reorganization of military career services available face-to-face and career counselor objectives based on legislative benchmark laws. Career counseling with the military has to embrace the story of the service member, identify any underlying psychological stressors, and validate experiences of those who seek help (NCDA, 2014). Capturing a deeper sense of how to facilitate counseling sessions based on the initial counseling session will deepen the established rapport, strengthen military cultural competency for the counselor, and develop PTG throughout the MLC into the life-career path for the veteran. The career construction theory (CCT) takes a narrative approach toward career development utilizing a thematic analysis model, which is one way to bind the layers of military culture into a story for the service member to help them identify their career calling (Betz, 1994; Chan et al., 2015; Corso & Rehfuss, 2011; Super, 1980). Additional resources and intervention will be explored toward the end of the chapter.

FIGURE 15.3 Civilian counselors trained to help service members with CRS. Department of Defense Transition Assistance Program. Copyright in the public domain. https://www.dodtap.mil/rest/docs?filename=CRS_and_Capstone.pdf.

Transition Assistance Program (TAP) Overview

Career Readiness Standards

Career Readiness Standards (CRS) are a set of career preparation activities Service members must complete to depart from Active Duty and be considered "career ready." The standards provide Service members with a clear, comprehensive set of activities to ensure they have the training and skills needed to transition successfully into civilian life. Completion of CRS activities is mandatory for all Service members retiring, separating, or being released after 180 days or more of Active Duty. Commanders or their designees verify CRS completion during a mandatory event called "Capstone."

KEY ROLES AND RESPONSIBILITIES

Service Members

Consider your post-military goals and aspirations and the income needed to support your lifestyle

Be proactive: Plan ahead and learn about the services available on your installation to assist you in meeting CRS

Complete all CRS requirements prior to Capstone and transition

Commanders

Educate your Service members about CRS and the importance of responsible transition planning

Ensure your Service members are provided time and access to resources needed to meet CRS

Work with your local TAP office to balance your mission needs with Service member transition requirements

Verify CRS during Capstone – no later than 90 days prior to Service member's separation by using the ITP Checklist *(DD Form 2958)*

Initiate a "warm handover" between a Service member and relevant partnering agency *(as necessary)*

TAP Managers

Ensure your office supports transitioning Service members and resources are available to meet expected throughput at your installation

Communicate with Commanders and Service members about CRS; educate them about what resources or training you can provide to assist Service members in meeting the standards

Encourage Service members to complete CRS activities early

TO MEET CRS, SERVICE MEMBERS MUST:

>> Prepare a DoD standardized 12-month post-separation budget

>> Complete a standardized DoD Individual Transition Plan (ITP)

>> Register on eBenefits *(https://www.ebenefits.va.gov)*

>> Complete Continuum of Military Service counseling *(active component only)*

>> Evaluate transferability of military skills to the civilian workforce *(complete Military Occupational Code Crosswalk and DoD standardized gap analysis)*

>> Document requirements and eligibility for licensure, certification, and apprenticeship

>> Complete an assessment tool to identify personal interests and leanings regarding career selection

>> Complete a job application package or present a job offer letter

>> Receive a Department of Labor (DOL) Gold Card and demonstrate understanding of post 9/11 Veteran priority at DOL American Job Centers

>> Complete pre-separation counseling *(using the DD Form 2648/2648-1)*

>> Attend VA Benefits I and II Briefings

>> Attend the DOL Employment Workshop (unless exempt)

CAPSTONE
CRS VERIFICATION PROCESS

>> No later than 90 days before transition, Service members participate in Capstone to verify they meet CRS and ensure they have a viable ITP

>> If a Service member does not meet CRS or present a viable ITP, they will be provided with assistance through a "warm handover" to a relevant partnering agency

For more information about TAP contact your local installation Transition Assistance Office or visit
www.DoDTAP.mil

PREPARE TO
SUCCEED

Transitioning Out of the Military

In 2008 following the return home of OEF and OIF service members, the federal budget paid out $467 million in unemployment compensation to active-duty military members who were discharged honorably as part of Public Law 102–164 that made provisions to ex-service members on the same basis of unemployment insurance paid out to civilians (DiSimone, 1992). According to the U.S. Bureau of Labor Statistics (2016), the amount of federal government compensation paid out to military service members increased in 2009 to $710 million, in 2010 to $923 million, and in 2011 to $944 million. In October 2011, the unemployment rate of veterans was at 7.7% with 12.1% of that number being veterans returning from Iraq and Afghanistan; this accounted for several thousands of unemployed veterans (Burearu of Labor and Statistics, 2018). Subsequently, after reaching nearly one billion dollars of unemployment compensation, in November 2011 the Veterans' Opportunity to Work (VOW) Act was passed, and a year later it was implemented across all military branches. This law applied education and training expansions, TAP-mandated benchmarks, federal employment preferences and provisions, and veteran tax credits as well as Department of Labor (DOL) skills training for translating military skills to civilian sector occupations. One section of the VOW Act makes it mandatory for service members to complete an Individual Transition Plan (ITP), which addresses set benchmarks in their transition that must be started no later than 12 months from their anticipated military separation date (Burearu of Labor and Statistics, 2018).

The VOW Act was put in place to ease the federal budget of government while simultaneously assuring our service members the best opportunity and training to transition into the next phase of their life. As a quality control measure, in 2013 the Office of Secretary of Defense (OSD) put in place the CRS to ensure that all military branches, transition centers, soldiers, units, and commanders are doing their part to care for the mental wellness of military personnel during their exit from the military as a top priority. This has placed a major shift on TMGRNs attitudes as the military is being acclimated to a new norm when it comes to transitional assistance, career counseling, and care for military personnel reintegrating into civilian life. The mental health considerations of taking off the uniform is not one to take lightly; there are many factors in each client case that require career counseling sensitivity, awareness, and competency of military culture. With the help of legislative support, military personnel TMGRN, customs, and traditions are shifting attitudes toward the wellness of the service member beyond their years of active and reserve service. The ITP benchmarks require that military members look at the issues that complicate transition in a psychoeducational setting and address their personal, financial, and family needs to include the psychology of taking off the uniform (NCDA, 2014).

Difficulty with Career Paths for Spouses

As a result of unique caregiving roles due to service members' absences and frequent moves, spouses often have to put their own careers aside or on hold, or struggle to balance their education and careers aspirations amid frequent transitions and stressors specific to the military lifestyle. Marshall (2014) proposed the following challenges and opportunities for military spouses: temporary duty stations; constant job changes and how this impacts the spouses resume; learning from outliers (i.e., jobs that do not seem to line up); laying a future path and being entrepreneurial; reliable and workable references, and professional development. For instance, spouses choosing to go to college or seeking professions with additional education requirements have to take into account that he or she may experience relocation during this period, in which case the spouse will have to facilitate transferring education credits or continuing his or her education at a location apart from the service member.

Additionally, for spouses who have obtained the necessary education or career training, getting promoted can be difficult when he or she is only located in an area for several years (or less). Spouses can also experience frustration and grief as a result of having to leave a job they love only to endure the stressors that come with applying for and obtaining a new job in the new area of relocation. As a result, providers working with military spouses play an important role in being present with their personal struggles while also assisting them in acquiring and maintaining careers that are not only meaningful but flexible as well. In addition to some of the matters mentioned previously, another area of concern for military spouses is obtaining and maintaining appropriate licensure or credentials for their careers. The following section will discuss this issue in detail.

Credentialing Portability Due to Frequent Moves

As current and future providers of mental health and career services, we are sure you can appreciate the importance of licensure and the impact that your own licensure or credentialing status has on the amount you are paid and the responsibilities you carry as well as your ability for growth and promotion in your profession. So, consider the following scenario: Jackie is the wife of a Corpsman (enlisted medical specialist) in the Navy. The couple and their children have orders to move to California within the next six months. Jackie recently passed the bar exam to practice law in the state of North Carolina and began working at a small law firm prior to finding out about her family's new orders to PCS. Jackie is experiencing hopelessness that she will never find a steady path in her career. While she has much to be proud of—graduating law school while raising her two young children away from family support, passing her bar exam, and getting a job in her field—in many ways she feels like she has to start over and in some regards, unfortunately, Jackie is correct. Each time Jackie has to move with her husband, she will likely have to take a new bar exam; there is a possibility that, as a result, she will fall behind her peers in that she may not be able to gain experience as quickly or as regularly as others who do not have to move so frequently.

The U.S. Department of the Treasury and U.S. Department of Defense (2012) issued a report stating that nearly 35% of military spouses hold an occupation that requires some type of licensure or certification and that military spouses are 10 times more likely to move between states than civilian spouses. As the focus of this book is on the importance of career calling, we can only reiterate the impact that such barriers on careers have on military spouses' and their families' psychological and financial well-being. For professions requiring licensure and certification, such as education, law, nursing, mental health, medicine, real estate, and cosmetology, every state has a unique set of requirements. The DoD recommends the following best practices for states in order to assist with improved licensure portability for military spouses in such career pursuits: licensure by endorsement, temporary or provisional licensing, or an expedited application process (U.S. Department of the Treasury & U.S. Department of Defense, 2012). As a result of this initiative, 35 states now recognize a new endorsement policy, 43 states provide temporary licenses, and 34 states are expediting procedures for regulatory department or board approval (USA4MilitaryFamilies, 2016).

Accordingly, while there have been improvements in states' licensure and certification policies, there still remain barriers for spouses that differ based on the individual's specific career, experience, and location. As an example, let us review a mental health professional's licensure portability by considering the difference in two states' laws and rules: Hawaii and Florida's requirements for postgraduate supervision. Hawaii's statutes state

> completion of not less than **three thousand hours of post-graduate experience in the practice of mental health counseling** with one hundred hours of face-to-face clinical supervision that shall be completed in no less than two years and in no more than four years, under the clinical supervision of a person who is a licensed mental health counselor, psychologist, clinical social worker, advanced practice registered nurse with a specialty in mental health, marriage and family therapist, or physician with a specialty in psychiatry (Mental Health Counselors, 2007, p.5).[1]

Florida's website states that, based off of their statutes, the requirements for licensure of a mental health counselor consists of

> two (2) years of post-master's supervised experience under the supervision of licensed mental health counselor or the equivalent who is qualified as determined by the Board. The supervision experience must have consisted of **at least 1,500 hours providing psychotherapy face-to-face with clients for the profession for which licensure is sought**, and shall be accrued in no less than 100 weeks. At least 100 hours of supervision per 1,500 hours of psychotherapy face-to-face with clients provided by the intern; At least one (1) hour of supervision every two (2) weeks; at least one (1) hour of supervision per fifteen (15) hours of psychotherapy, with a minimum of one (1) hour of supervision every two (2) weeks. If the applicant obtained group supervision, each hour of group supervision must alternate with an hour of individual supervision. Individual supervision is defined as one supervisor supervising no more than two (2) interns and group supervision is defined as one supervisor supervising more than two (2) but a maximum of six (6) interns in the group (Florida Board of Clinical Social Work, Marriage & Family Therapy, and Mental Health Counseling, n.d.).[2]

---

1   Source: http://cca.hawaii.gov/pvl/files/2013/08/hrs_pvl_453d.pdf

2   Source: http://floridasmentalhealthprofessions.gov/licensing/licensed-mental-health-counselor/

So, while one state (Hawaii) clarifies a total number of hours in mental health counseling, another state (Florida) specifies the total hours of psychotherapy. As well, each state's definitions of the activities that qualify as mental health counseling differ. Thus, although Hawaii assists spouses coming into the state via military orders with current licensure requirements equivalent or exceeding those of the state of Hawaii via temporary and expedited licensure, how does the licensure equivalency get translated when the language from state to state differs? Consider that a military spouse was licensed in the state of Florida as a mental health counselor for over four years. When he moves to Hawaii, he technically has only 1,500 hours of psychotherapy documented with the Florida board under supervision because this activity was the only activity required for submission by that board (and excludes other hours that he was engaging in that may very well be considered mental health counselor activities for another board). According to the laws and rules, this spouse, if moving to Hawaii from Florida, will have to work under supervision despite his six years of total postgraduate experience in counseling to obtain a license in his new state. These are the small details that plague spouses as they prepare to move to new states, details that can influence the course of spouses' careers and their families' quality of life.

In conclusion, military spouses face significant challenges when it comes to establishing their careers. Licensure and certification reciprocity concerns are one of many obstacles that spouses face that may contribute to psychological distress as they seek to support their service member, raise their children, and attempt to establish their own career autonomy. An important role that professionals can take is advocating for military spouses to legislators and state licensing and certification boards. Professionals can also join professional organizations, like the National Military Family Association, and sign up to advocate for military families (http://www.militaryfamily.org/).

RESOURCES AND INTERVENTIONS FOR THIS POPULATION

The following section is an overview of resources for service members, veterans, and their families as it pertains to mental health and wellness as well as career specific needs.

Service Members and Veterans

Carolla and Corbin-Burdick (2015) advocated for using a holistic approach when working with the military population and suggested the following recommendations for providers: evaluate and make conceptualization decisions based all experiences of the client, not just those from the military; include support systems; opt to utilize a less pathologizing approach like the posttraumatic growth (PTG) model; strive to develop rapport and a warm therapeutic relationship with your client; assist the client in positively reframing his or her roles within the civilian community; incorporate cultural identity models in order to better understand your client's problems; utilize evidenced-based approaches; and refer to VA and DoD practice guidelines. Likewise, the VA and DoD do provide an extensive list of clinical practice guidelines for the treatment of service members and veterans specific to his or her problem or disorder. These suggestions may help you connect your client, if needed, to the appropriate mental health treatment providers so that you can then continue to assist your client with his or her career goals. For example, for mild to moderate depression, the following intervention protocols are indicated for use as first-line treatment options: "Evidence-based psychotherapies: Acceptance and commitment therapy (ACT), Behavioral therapy/behavioral activation (BT/BA), Cognitive behavioral therapy (CBT), Interpersonal therapy, Mindfulness-based cognitive therapy (MBCT), or Problem-solving therapy (PST)" (Department of Veteran Affairs & Department of Defense, 2016). For PTSD, the following evidence-based therapies are listed as efficacious: Prolonged Exposure (PE), Cognitive Processing Therapy (CPT), Stress Inoculation Therapy, or Eye Movement Desensitization and Reprocessing Therapy (EMDR); Evidence-based pharmacotherapies: SSRIs, or SNRIs (Department of Veteran Affairs & Department of Defense, 2010).

Moreover, the VA and DoD stress the role of the patient in the decision of treatment modality, clinician competency in the modality, and symptom severity (Department of Veteran Affairs & Department of Defense, 2010). Also, be sure to consider other holistic approaches such as acupuncture, yoga, or equine therapy for service members or veterans who historically may not have responded to traditional psychotherapy or psychopharmacological interventions. Another resource to consider is Mental Health First Aid, which is a nationally recognized training and legislation to normalize mental health diagnosis such as PTSD, major depression, substance abuse, military sexual trauma (MST), and suicidal ideations—just as any other medical condition is commonly normalized—to alter the stigma of mental illness and bring about awareness for proper care for incidents that require first aid (https://www.mentalhealthfirstaid.org/cs/).

As military service members make their transition from service member to civilian, discovering resources and prevention and interventions treatment measures associated with positive psychological change is essential for effective reintegration through career counseling and psychotherapy. Utilizing an individual transition plan (ITP) and evidence-based treatment, coupled with benchmarks in psychoeducational group sessions, can contribute to closing the gaps of known dropout rates in counseling with military service members. For the army, the Army Master Resiliency Training is a train-the-trainer program that teaches positive psychology to handle stress-related circumstances with constructive coping skills (Reivich, Seligman, & McBride, 2011.) Additionally, credentialing websites to assist with certifications associated with military careers are useful:

- Army: www.cool.army.mil
- Navy: www.cool.navy.mil
- Marines: www.cool.navy.mil/usmc/
- Airforce: https://afvec.langley.af.mil/afvec/Public/COOL/

Spouses

Social and community support emerged as a common theme associated with psychological well-being for military spouses (Orthner & Rose, 2009; Wang et al., 2015). Hence, the importance of encouraging increased interpersonal relationships and empowering spouses to make social connections are interventions that providers can implement. Military OneSource is a good resource for spouses (and service members) as it provides short-term, confidential counseling either face-to-face, online, or via phone or video. There are also resources for spouses regarding career counseling via Military OneSource and organizations like the National Military Family Association that provide scholarships for education and licensure, funding, and other support such as retreats and deployment education for military spouses and children (see http://www.militaryfamily.org/).

Military Children

For military children, especially those exposed to trauma or who have witnessed IPV, Campbell, Brown, and Okra (2011) encouraged the use of trauma-focused cognitive behavioral therapy (TF-CBT), which is an evidence-based method that includes intervention with the children and the caregivers. In order to assist younger children (birth to 5 years) who may receive less community support than military children who are of school age, Osofsky and Chartrand (2013) offered some suggestions for the spouses who are providing caregiving in the absence of their service member, some of which are maintaining routines; finding ways to communicate and connect with the absent parent; and providing empathy, care, and active listening. Additionally, Osofsky and Chartrand (2013) proposed that there is a range of support resources and interventions to assist children and spouses, such as the FAP (Family Advocacy Program); Zero to Three: National Center for Infants, Toddlers, and Families (ZTT); Talk Listen Connect (TLC), which includes interactive videos and parental scripts for children explaining issues like deployment, changes, and grieving; and child-parent psychotherapy (CPP).

CONCLUSION

Service members, veterans, and their families are a rewarding population to work with. As our theme scripture from John 15:13 (KJV) states, "Greater love hath no man than this, that a man lay down his life for his friends." The sacrifices that our military men and women are willing to make in order to ensure our freedom is certainly heroic. Over time, our country has increased research efforts and access to services for this population, yet many current and former service members remain underserved or struggle to meet the demands of their careers at the expense of their mental health, their families, and their futures. It is our job as mental health professionals to gain a greater understanding of the needs of this population and to do all that we can to give back to those who are so willing to give up everything for us.

KEY TERMS

Active duty: signifies that a member of the armed services occupies his or her job in the military on a full- time basis

Enlisted: refers to a member of the military who has agreed for some period of time to serve his or her country in an official capacity; the enlistment period signifies the amount of time to which he or she has agreed to officially serve

Reservist: a member of the armed services who serves in the military on a part-time or as-needed basis but who can be called upon to serve on active duty orders at any time; because reservists typically train every month but are only paid while training or on active duty order, they typically hold a civilian job

OEF: Operation Enduring Freedom; a reference to the war in Afghanistan

Officer: a member of the Armed Forces who has a bachelor's degree or higher; typically refers to a commissioned officer, although enlisted members of the military, as they move up in rank, are deemed noncommissioned officers; officers typically have increased authority and responsibility

OIF: Operation Iraqi Freedom; a reference to the war in Iraq

PTSD: post-traumatic stress disorder; defined by symptoms of avoidance, hypervigilance, hyperarousal, negative cognitions and mood, and reexperiencing of traumatic events

Service member: refers to an individual who is currently serving as an active-duty or reserve affiliate in the Armed Forces

Veteran: a current or former member of the Armed Forces; can also define a current or former member of the armed service who has deployed to a combat zone

Warrant officer: a member of the Armed Forces in all branches but the Air Force who holds increased authority or responsibility, typically more than enlisted members but less than traditional commissioned officers; many warrant officers are not required to have a bachelor's or higher degree

REFLECTION AND DISCUSSION

1. Consider three benefits of understanding military-specific language and cultural dynamics.
2. What are some of the unique mental health challenges that service members, veterans, military spouses, and their children experience?
3. What are potential resources that you can use as a provider to assist service members and their families?
4. Consider your perception of the military culture prior to reading this chapter. How has your understanding of the military culture changed? Examine any biases or beliefs that you may have when working with this population.
5. How will your knowledge of military culture impact your future work with this population?

ADDITIONAL READINGS, RESOURCES, AND WEBSITES

Center for Deployment Psychology: http://deploymentpsych.org/

Give an Hour: https://www.giveanhour.org

Grossman, D., & Christensen, L. W. (2008). On combat: The psychology and physiology of deadly conflict in war and in peace (3rd ed.). Warrior Science Publications.

Grossman, D. (2009). On killing: The psychological cost of learning to kill in war and society (Revised ed.). New York, NY: Hachette Book Group.

Mental Health/Veteran Affairs: http://www.mentalhealth.va.gov

Military and Government Counseling Association (MGCA): http://acegonline.org/

Military Children: http://www.militarychild.org/

Military Families: http://www.militaryfamily.org

Military OneSource: http://www.militaryonesource.mil/

Real Warriors: http://www.realwarriors.net

Substance Abuse and Mental Health Services Administration (SAMSHA): http://www.samhsa.gov/veterans-military-families

USA4MilitaryFamilies: http://www.usa4militaryfamilies.dod.mil

U.S. Department of Defense: http://www.defense.gov

Van Der Kolk, B. (2014). The body keeps the score: Brain, mind, and body in the healing of trauma. New York, NY: Viking.

TRADITIONAL ACTIVITY

Envision

Consider the factors of this transitioning military service member:

Sergeant (SGT) Allen, a military combat medic, has been in the Army for 14 years. She is being involuntarily separated having met the retention control point (RCP) for SGT, which mandates that she can no longer serve if she has not been promoted to Staff Sergeant (SSG) by the time she reaches 14 years of Army service. SGT Allen will be released from the military and does not feel prepared for this unexpected transition; she wanted to complete 20 years serving in the Army, which would have made her eligible for retirement. SGT Allen deployed to combat twice since being on active duty, to Iraq and then to Kuwait; she states that excessive eating habits helped her cope with the high-stress environments during deployments. This caused her to become overweight and flagged with unfavorable actions, making her ineligible for promotion. With only six months from separation, SGT Allen comes to you, as her career counselor, and expresses feeling lost and unsure of her next steps. She tells you that her highest level of education is a high school diploma and that she has not completed any higher education courses since entering the military. She explains that her goal was to retire from the military and then go to school; this would have placed her in a financial position with retirement pay, allowing her to be a full-time student without working. SGT Allen shares that she is a single mom, and without bringing in some type of income once separated, she will not be able to support herself and her son. Although school is an option, she does not have the financial mobility to go to school full-time without working. After deploying and being constantly exposed to the deaths of comrades, she states she no longer has a desire to work in the medical field, although most of her military experience is within healthcare. She attributes her disordered eating as damaging her military career but says she is resilient and does not feel like she suffers from PTSD like some of her other colleagues. SGT Allen does not know what her career calling is because she joined the military right after high school and was given an occupation based on her ASVAB scores. She took the medic vocation so that she could serve her country; now, after 14 years of service, she is ready to go into a new career path of her choice but does not know what that means.

1. What are some resources and interventions that may help SGT Allen explore her career interest and goals? Take into account some of her transferable skills while also addressing her financial and educational concerns.

2. How could you help SGT Allen with identifying her purpose and career calling as a single mother and soon-to-be combat veteran?

3. What types of career counseling strategies do you believe will be most effective in helping SGT Allen identify who she is and how that correlates with where she will find career fulfillment?

SPIRITUAL ACTIVITY

As you read the following scenario, consider how the themes of trauma and transition presented in this chapter may be impacting David's struggle to find meaning and purpose in his life and work. As you read, keep in mind the scripture theme of this chapter: "Greater love hath no man than this, that a man lay down his life for his friends" (John 15:13, KJV).

David joined the Marine Corps at age 18; he felt a strong sense of duty to serve his country because his father served in the Army, his grandfather in the Marine Corps, and his uncle in the Navy. After the attacks of September 11, 2001, David was deployed to Iraq several times. Being in the infantry, he was frequently exposed to combat. Many years later, David is coming to you because he "feels exhausted," is having issues "connecting with" his wife and his children, and he has struggled with feeling like it was "all for nothing." He states that he often has panic attacks, can't sleep, and feels like he is weak because he "cannot handle the stress." He is wondering if he should get out of the military early even though he has several more years until he can retire. He thought that serving in the military was his calling, "to do something greater than" himself, but he just isn't sure anymore. He hopes you can help him navigate this decision.

1. What factors might be influencing David's current confusion regarding his career calling?

2. How might you assist David in reconnecting to the spiritual part of himself that chose this career to "do something greater than himself"?

MILITARY TRANSITION AWARENESS QUIZ

Read each statement and indicate whether you think it is true or false.	TRUE	FALSE
1. Of the one half of one percent of Americans who served in the military within the past decade, 56% experienced a traumatic event.		
2. Getting a job is the only thing that a military service member has to be concerned with as they reintegrate into civilian life.		
3. The unemployment rate of veterans is 7.7%, with 12.1% being veterans returning from Iraq and Afghanistan.		

4. There are many places you can go for help in your transition to civilian life.

5. The Department of Veterans Affairs pays for medical treatment for all veterans.

6. Civilian lifestyle is similar to peacetime military lifestyle, so little adjustment should be necessary.

7. Change in lifestyle always causes stress in human beings; therefore, counseling or therapy for soldiers in transition is not necessary.

8. The higher the military rank, the more respect a soldier will receive from civilians when they leave the service.

9. Soldiers setting goals too soon before leaving the military might limit their future possibilities.

10. Due to their trauma, military members diagnosed with PTSD cannot develop psychological growth.

REFERENCES

Amara, J., PhD, Iverson, K. M., PhD, Krengel, M., PhD, Pogoda, T. K., PhD, & Hendricks, A., PhD. (2014). Anticipating the traumatic brain injury–Related health care needs of women veterans after the department of defense change in combat assignment policy. Women's Health Issues, 24(2), e171- e176. doi:10.1016/j.whi.2013.12.004

American Psychiatric Association. (2013a) Diagnostic and statistical manual of mental disorders, (5th ed.). Washington, DC: Author.

American Psychiatric Association. (2013b). Posttraumatic stress disorder fact sheet. Retrieved from http://www.dsm5.org/Documents/PTSD%20Fact%20Sheet.pdf

America's Navy. (2009, June 28). Enlisted rating insignia. Retrieved from http://www.navy.mil/navydata/nav_legacy.asp?id=259

America's Navy. (2009, August 12). Rank insignia of navy commissioned and warrant officers. Retrieved from http://www.navy.mil/navydata/nav_legacy.asp?id=266

Bureau of Labor and Statistics. (2018). Employment situation of veterans summary. Retrieved from https://www.bls.gov/news.release/vet.nr0.htm

Brooks, M.S., & Fulton, L. (2009). Evidence of poorer life-course mental health outcomes among veterans of the Korean War cohort. Aging & Mental Health, 14(2), 177–183. doi: 10.1080/1360786090304656

Betz, N. E. (1994). Self-concept theory in career development and counseling. The Career Development Quarterly, 43(1), 32. Retrieved from http://0-search.proquest.com.library.regent.edu/docview/219440989?accountid=13479

Campbell, C.L., Brown, E.J., & Okwara, L. (2011). Addressing sequelae of trauma and interpersonal violence in military children: a review of the literature and case illustration. Cognitive and Behavioral Practice, 18, 131–143.

Carrola, P., & Corbin-Burdick, M.F. (2015). Counseling military veterans: advocating for culturally competent holistic interventions. Journal of Mental Health Counseling, 37(1), 1–14.

Carroll, L., Gilroy, P. J., & Ryan, J. (2002). Counseling transgendered, transsexual, and gender-variant clients. Journal of Counseling & Development, 80, 131–139.

Chan, K. Y., Uy, M A., Ho, M. R., Sam, Y. L., Chernyshenko, O. S., & Yu, K. T. (2015). Comparing two career adaptability measures for career construction theory: Relations with boundary less mindset and protean career attitudes. Journal of Vocational Behavior, 87, 22–31.

Chung, Y. B. (2003). Career counseling with lesbian, gay, bisexual, and transgendered persons: The next decade. The Career Development Quarterly, 52(1), 78–86.

Corso, J. D., & Rehfuss, M. C. (2011). The role of narrative in career construction theory. Journal of Vocational Behavior, 79, 334–339. doi: 10.1016/jvb.2011.04.003

Cosgrove, D. J., Gordon, Z., Bernie, J. E., Hami, S., Montoya, D., Stein, M. B., et al. (2002). Sexual dysfunction in combat Veterans with post-traumatic stress disorder. Urology, 60, 881–884.

Department of Commerce and Consumer Affairs. (2007). Mental Health Counselors, Hawaii Revised Statutes §453D-7. Retrieved from http://cca.hawaii.gov/pvl/files/2013/08/hrs_pvl_453d.pdf

Department of Defense. (n.d.). Department of Defense Transition Assistance Program. Retrieved from www.dodtap.mil

Department of Veteran Affairs. (2014). National Center for Veterans Analysis and Statistics: Veteran Population. Retrieved from http://www.va.gov/vetdata/veteran_population.asp

Department of Veteran Affairs, & Department of Defense. (2016). VA/DoD clinical practice guideline for the management of major depressive disorder. (Version 3.0). Retrieved from http://www.healthquality.va.gov/guidelines/MH/mdd/MDDCPGClinicianSummaryFINAL1.pdf

Department of Veteran Affairs, & Department of Defense. (2010). VA/DoD clinical practice guideline for the management of post-traumatic stress. (Version 2.0). Retrieved from http://www.healthquality.va.gov/guidelines/MH/ptsd/CPGSummaryFINALMgmtofPTSDfinal021413. pdf

DiSimone, R. L. (1992). Unemployment insurance: Recent legislation. Social Security Bulletin, 55(1), 47–50.

Eaton, K.M., Hoge, C.W., Messer, S.C., Whit, A. A., Cabrera, O.A., McGurk, D., Cox, A., & Castro, C.A. (2008). Prevalence of mental health problems, treatment need, and barriers to care among primary-care seeking spouses of military service members involved in Iraq and Afghanistan deployments. Military Medicine, 173(11), 1051–1056.

Flores, D. (2014). Memories of war: Sources of Vietnam Veteran pro- and antiwar political attitudes. Sociological Forum, 29(1), 98–119. doi 10.1111/socf.12071

Florida Board of Clinical Social Work, Marriage & Family Therapy, and Mental Health Counseling. (n.d.). Licensed mental health counselor. Retrieved from http://floridasmentalhealthprofessions.gov/licensing/licensed-mental-health-counselor/

Gates, G. J. (2011). How many people are lesbian, gay, bisexual, and transgender? The Williams Institute, ULCA School of Law. Retrieved from: http://williamsinstitute.law.ucla.edu/research/census-lgbt- demographics-studies/how-many-people-are-lesbian-gay-bisexual-and-transgender/

Gates, G. J. (2010). Lesbian, gay, and bisexual men and women in the US military: Updated estimates. The Williams Institute, ULCA School of Law. Retrieved from: http://williamsinstitute.law.ucla.edu/wp- content/uploads/Gates-GLBmilitaryUpdate-May-20101.pdf

Hodge, C. W., Auchterlonie, J. L., & Milliken, C. S. (2006). Mental health problems, use of mental health services, and attrition from military service after returning from deployment to Iraq or Afghanistan. Journal of the American Medical Association, 295, 1023–1032.

Kauth, M. R., & Shipherd, J. C. (2016). Transforming a system: Improving patient-centered care for sexual and gender minority veterans. LGBT Health, 3(3), 177–179.

Karimi, F. & Pearson, M. (2015, Feb 13). The 13 states that still ban same-sex marriage. CNN. Retrieved from http://www.cnn.com/2015/02/13/us/states-same-sex-marriage-ban/

Klenke, K. (2016). Women in combat: Contexts, terror management, and mortality salience: Implications for women's leadership. International Leadership Journal, 8(2), 38–67.

King, A.C. (2015). Women warriors: Female accession to ground combat. Armed Forces & Society, 41(2), 379–387. doi: 10.1177/0095327X14532913

Klimas, J. (2015). Lawmakers say they were blindsided by Army cuts. The Washington Times. Retrieved from: http://www.washingtontimes.com/news/2015/jul/8/obama-admin-cut-40k-army-soldiers/

Langer, R. (2011). Combat trauma, memory, and the World War II veteran. War, Literature & the Arts: An International Journal of the Humanities, 23(1), 50–58.

Lambda Legal. (2011). Glenn v. Brumby, 663 F. 3d at 1317. Retrieved from https://www.lambdalegal.org/in-court/cases/glenn-v-brumby-et-alLink, P. E., & Palinkas, L. A. (2013). Long-term trajectories and service needs for military families. Clinical Child & Family Psychology Review, 16, 376–393, doi:10.1007/s10567-013-0145-z

Lorber, W., & Garcia, H. A. (2010). Not supposed to feel this: Traditional masculinity in psychotherapy with male veterans returning from Afghanistan and Iraq. Psychotherapy: Theory, Research & Practice, 47(3), 296–305.

Magruder, K.M., & Yeager, D.E. (2009). The prevalence of PTSD across war eras and the effect of deployment on PTSD: a systematic review and meta-analysis. Psychiatric Annals, 39(8), 778–788. doi: 10.3928/00485713-20090728-04

Marshall, S. (2014). Helping military spouses address employment challenges through career communications. Career Planning and Adult Development Journal, 9, 85–90.

McNulty, S. S. (2012). Myth busted: women are servicing in ground combat positions. Air Force Law Review, 68, 119–166.

Milliken, C. S., Auchterlonie, J. L., & Hodge, C. W. (2007). Longitudinal assessment of mental health problems among active duty and reserve component soldiers returning from Iraq war. Journal of the American Medical Association, 298, 2141–2148.

Minoz, S. T., & Kalteux, D. M. (2016). LGBT, the EEOC, and the meaning of "sex". The Florida Bar Journal, (March Report), 43–48.

Moradi, B. (2009). Sexual orientation disclosure, concealment, harassment, and military cohesion: Perceptions of the LGBT military veterans. Military Psychology, 21, 513–533. doi: 10.1080/08995600903206453

Morin, R. (2011). The difficult transition from military to civilian life. Pew Research Center: Social & Demographic Trends. Retrieved from: http://www.pewsocialtrends.org/2011/12/08/the-difficult-transition-from-military-to-civilian-life/

National Career Development Association (NCDA). (2014). Career Planning and Adult Development Journal, 30 (3). San Jose, CA: Career Planning & Adult Devt. Network.

Nindl, B.C., Jones, B.H., Van Arsdale, S.J., Kelly, K., Kraemer, W.J. (2016). Women in combat: summary of findings and a way ahead. Military Medicine, 181, 109–118. doi:10.7205/MILMED-D-15-00409

Orthner, D.K. & Rose, R. (2009). Work separation demands and spouse psychological well-being. Family Relations, 58, 392–403.

Osofsky, J.D., & Chartrand, M.M. (2013) Military children from birth to five years. The Future of Children, 23(2), 61–77.

Price, J. L. & Stevens, S.P. (2014). Partners of Veterans with PTSD: Research Findings. US Department of Veterans Affairs. Retrieved from: http://www.ptsd.va.gov/professional/ treatment/family/partners_of_vets_research_findings.asp

Ramirez, M. H., Rogers, S. J., Johnson, H. L., Banks, J. Seay, W. P., Tinsley, B. L., & Grant, A. W. (2013). If we ask, what they might tell: Clinical assessment lessons from LGBT military personnel post-DADT. Journal of Homosexuality, 60, 401–418. doi: 10.1080/00918369.2013.744931

Reivich, K J., Seligman, M. E. & McBride, S. (2011). Master resilience training in the U.S. Army. American Psychologist, 66(1), 25–34. doi: 10.1037/a0021897

Roberts, R. D., Goff, G. N., Anjoul, F., Kyllonen, P. C., Pallier, G., & Stankov, L.(2000). The Armed Services Vocational Aptitude Battery (ASVAB): A little more than acculturated learning. Learning and Individual Differences, 12(1), 81–103. doi: 10.1016/S1041-6080(00)00035-2

Sayer, N. A., Noorbaloochi, S., Frazier, P., Carlson, K., Gravely, A., & Murdoch, M. (2010). Reintegration problems and treatment interests among Iraq and Afghanistan combat veterans receiving VA medical care. Psychiatric Services, 61(6), 589–597.

Schaefer, A. G., Wenger, J.W., Kavanagh, J., Wong, J.P., Oak, G.S., Trail, T. E., & Nichols, T. (2015). RAND implications of integrating women into the Marine Corps infantry report. Santa Monica, CA: RAND Corporation.

Schreiber, M., & McEnany, G. P. (2015). Stigma, American military personnel and mental health care: Challenges from Iraq and Afghanistan. Journal of Mental Health, 24(1), 45–59.

Secretary of Defense. (1993). Memorandum on policy on homosexual conduct in the armed forces. Retrieved from: http://www.qrd.org/qrd/usa/military/1993/Aspin.Directive.On.Ban

Southwell, K.H., & MacDermid Wadsworth, S.M. (2016). The many faces of military families: unique feature of the lives of female service members. Military Medicine, 181(1), 70- 79. doi: 10.7205/MILMED-D- 15-00193

Stagner, A.C. (2014). Healing the soldier, restoring the nation: Representations of shell shock in the USA during and after the First World War. Journal of Contemporary History, 49(2), 255–274. doi: 10.1177/0022009413515532

Szafranski, D. D., Gros, D. F., Menefee, D. S., Wanner, J. L., & Norton, P. J. (2014). Predictors of length of stay among OEF/OIF/OND veteran inpatient PTSD treatment noncompleters. Psychiatry, 77(3), 263–74. doi: http://0dx.doi.org.library.regent.edu/101521psyc2014773263

Super, D. E. (1980). A life-span, life-space approach to career development. Journal of Vocational Behavior 16:282–298

Tedeschi, R. G & Calhoun, L. (2004). Posttraumatic growth: Conceptual foundations and empirical evidence. Psychological Inquiry, 15(1), 1–18.

The George Washington Law Review. (2015). Obergefell et al. v. Hodges, 576 U.S. Retrieved from https://www.gwlr.org/obergefell-v-hodges/

U.S. Army Research Institute for the Behavioral and Social Sciences. (1977). Women content in units force development test (MAXWAC). Retrieved from http://www.dtic.mil/docs/citations/ADA050022

U.S. Army Institute for the Behavioral and Social Sciences. (1978). Women content in the Army reforger 77 (REF-WAC 77). Retrieved from http://www.dtic.mil/docs/citations/ADA055960

U.S. Department of Defense. (n.d.), Fact sheet: women in service review (WISR) implementation. Retrieved from: https://www.defense.gov/Portals/1/Documents/pubs/Fact_Sheet_WISR_FINAL.pdf

U.S. Department of the Treasury, & U.S. Department of Defense. (2012). Supporting our military families: best practices for streamlining occupational licensing across state lines. Retrieved from http://archive.defense.gov/home/pdf/Occupational_Licensing_and_Military_Spouses_Report_vFIN AL.PDF

Wang, M., Nyutu, P.N., Tran, K.K., & Spears, A. (2015). Finding resilience: the mediation effect of sense of community on the psychological well-being of military spouses. Journal of Mental Health Counseling, 37(2), 164–174.

MILITARY TRANSITION AWARENESS QUIZ ANSWERS

Read each statement and indicate whether you think it is true or false.	TRUE	FALSE
1. Of the one half of one percent of Americans who served in the military within the past decade, 56% experienced a traumatic event.	X	
2. Getting a job is the only thing that a military service member has to be concerned with as they reintegrate into civilian life.		X
3. The unemployment rate of veterans was at 7.7%, with 12.1% being veterans returning from Iraq and Afghanistan.	X	
4. There are many places you can go to get help in your transition to civilian life.	X	
5. The Department of Veterans Affairs pays for medical treatment of all veterans.		X
6. Civilian lifestyle is pretty much like peacetime military lifestyle, so little adjustment should be necessary.		X
7. Change in lifestyle always causes stress in human beings; therefore, counseling or therapy for soldiers in transition is not necessary.		X
8. The higher the military rank, the more respect a soldier will receive from civilians when they leave the service.		X
9. Soldiers setting goals too soon before leaving the military might limit their future possibilities.		X
10. Due to their trauma, military members diagnosed with PTSD cannot develop psychological growth.		X

1. Several studies over the years have identified that more than half of the veterans who served over the past decade have suffered or experienced a traumatic event; with growing and new studies that include service members coming forward, that number has shown to be higher in some cases.

2. Employment is only one factor with reintegration; service members also have to learn the psychology of taking off the uniform. Service member experience anxiety and heightened stress related to this adjustment coupled with their final military move (housing), family and medical concerns, and financial considerations as well as any combat-related considerations.

3. Unemployment was higher for those veterans who deployed during OEF and OIF and separated from the military with honorable discharges than those who did not experience combat.

4. There are numerous state, federal, and private organizations that can assist with military transition considerations; due to the VOW Act, each branch of service ensures

that there is a smooth hand-over to state veteran representatives to assist with the transition period.

5. The Department of Veterans Affairs may assist with medical treatment, but only veterans who have been released under conditions other than dishonorable are eligible to be considered.

6. Common acceptable terminology within the civilian workforce and professional dress attire is foreign to most military members who have been indoctrinated within their branch of service. The customs and traditions to include ceremonies, rank, and duties even during peacetime still impacted the adjustment for service members that are separating.

7. Change associated with TMGRN, TBI, PTSD, and MST should be taken into considerations for each military service member. Counseling or therapy is necessary during the transition period to address the possibility of overlooking conditions that may negatively affect reintegration.

8. The military community is small in comparison to the U.S. population, which knows very little about military rank structure; military language is thus unfamiliar to most civilians who do not consider their interactions to be impacted by the previous rank of a service member.

9. Setting goals early is recommended; legislation allows retirees up to two years to prepare for their transition and up to 18 months, but no later than 12 months, for separates (individuals not retiring from active duty). This provides sufficient time to address all the factors that may impede the transition period if too abrupt.

10. Although there is substantial emphasis on the harmful outcomes of post-event distress and posttraumatic reactions that overemphasizes PTSD in literature as it relates to the military population, this can lead to a bias in conceptualizing any type of posttraumatic exposure without regard to ego-resiliency (ER) or posttraumatic growth (PTG). "Most people who are exposed to trauma don't develop PTSD, and those who do usually have past symptomataology" (Paris, 2013, p. 125). In view of contextual dynamics of traumatic exposure, there are positive internal and external mechanisms that military service members experience (Harvey, 1996; Harvey &Tummala- Narra, 2007).

QUIZ REFERENCES

Harvey, M. R. (1996). An ecological view of trauma and trauma recovery. Journal of Traumatic Stress, 9, 3–23.

Harvey, M. R., & Tummala-Narra, P. (2007). Sources and expressions of resilience in trauma survivors: Ecological theory, multicultural perspectives. Journal of Aggression, Maltreatment & Trauma, 14(1/2), 1–7.

Paris, J. (2013). The Intelligent Clinician's Guide to the DSM-5. New York, NY: Oxford University Press.

16

Career Counseling and Third Culture Kids

Brenda Keck, LMFT and Joel Cagwin, LCPC

You are no longer foreigners and strangers, but
fellow citizens with God's people and also members
of his household.

Ephesians 2:19, New International Version

LEARNING OBJECTIVES

In this chapter, students will learn about

- Common third culture kid (TCK) characteristics
- Identity development related to growing up as a TCK
- Applications for career counseling with TCKs

LEARNING OUTCOMES

At the end of this chapter, students will be able to

- Define and describe different types of TCKs
- Articulate why TCKs are a relevant population for career counselors to study
- Describe different aspects of TCK identity development
- Explain influences on TCK career development
- List strengths and challenges TCKs face
- Identify recommendations for career counseling with TCKs

CHAPTER HIGHLIGHTS

- Defining TCK
- Cultural, personal, and identity development
- Distinguishing characteristics of adult TCKs
- Implications for counseling TCK career development

INTRODUCTION

In recent decades, the globalization of our world has been defined by an increase in multinational companies and international organizations operating across borders. The subsequent global mobility of families has become increasingly commonplace. This phenomenon has given rise to a growing group of adults presenting for career counseling with unique needs and attributes. Third culture kids (TCKs), the children of these families, spend a significant part of their formative years in one or more countries other than their passport country because of their parent's work choices (Pollock & Van Reken, 2009). As far back as the year 2000, it was estimated that 37,000 U.S. citizens return to the United States every year just to attend college (Gaw, 2000).

According to Melles and Frey (2014), the large numbers of TCKs will continue to rise as a result of expanding globalization of trade and business. This expansion is not a trend, fad, or isolated phenomenon. It is an inescapable force that has been referred to as a tsunami (Black, Morrison & Gregerson, 1999). With an estimated 45,000 U.S. citizens emigrating out of the U.S. every year (Costanza , Klekowski, & Koppenfels, 2013), a new generation of TCKs is now returning to the United States seeking education and employment.

TCKs are also referred to in the literature as adult third culture kids (ATCKs), transculturals, and global nomads (Pollock & Van Reken, 2009; McDonald, 2010; Schaetti, 2000). This population can be categorized into subgroups that include children of corporate employees, international business professionals, missionaries (MKs), government personnel, and military personnel ("military brats"), each with their own nuance of the TCK experience. The distinctive element of the TCK experience lies in the idea of a third culture. This term, coined by Ruth Useem (Useem & Downie, 1976), describes the unique cultural space that defines the world of a TCK. The first culture, or home culture, is the country from which the person holds a passport. The second culture is the culture which the person is living without citizenship. The third culture is a culture created within the individual that is an amalgam of all the cultures as well as unique aspects of expatriate living (Pollock & Van Reken, 2009). TCKs may not share specific national cultures with each other, but they share a third culture experience in which many find their primary sense of belonging (Pollock & Van Reken, 2009).

As a result of their unique cultural experience, TCKs have been referred to as an invisible minority or hidden immigrants of a culture that extends beyond the limits of either their native or host cultures (Pollock & Van Reken, 2009; Washington & Gadikar, 2016; Schaetti, 2000).

They have been identified as a distinct cultural group with particular characteristics that set them aside from their peers (Selmer & Lam, 2004). As such, according to the **American Counseling Association (ACA) Code of Ethics** (ACA, 2014), counselors have a professional responsibility to learn about the unique cultural experiences of TCKs. They must develop multicultural competencies in this domain in order to serve this growing population effectively and competently. Understanding the unique experiences and developmental path of TCKs is critical to helping them make constructive decisions about their career choices.

TCKs have sometimes been referred to as an invisible minority or a distinct cultural group with characteristics that set them aside from their non-TCK peers (Pollock & Van Reken, 2009; Washington & Gadikar, 2016; Schaetti, 2000; Selmer & Lam, 2004). As such, according to the **ACA Code of Ethics** (ACA, 2014), counselors have a professional responsibility to learn about the unique cultural experiences of TCKs. They must develop multicultural competencies in this domain in order to serve this growing population effectively and competently. Understanding the unique experiences and developmental path of TCKs is critical to helping them make constructive decisions about their career choices.

As the developmental path of TCKs is discussed in this chapter, it will become clear why many of them struggle to find a sense of home and belonging. A Biblical concept that can often be a meaningful source of comfort to a TCK is found in Ephesians 2:19: "you are no longer foreigners and strangers, but fellow citizens with God's people and also members of His household." Identifying their citizenship and sense of belonging with God's family located in heaven transcends the complex tangle of cultures, nationalities, and transitions of which they are trying to make sense.

In addition to the ethical responsibility to provide competent care for TCKs, Christian therapists may also find spiritual purpose and meaning in serving this population. Many TCKs come from families who have chosen the complex and challenging life of cross-cultural living in response to a spiritual commitment and calling. As you will see throughout this chapter, the commitment they have made has profound implications for their children, both positive and challenging. In fact, one of the primary reasons that missionaries return from the field prematurely is because of problems encountered by their children (Brierley, 1997). Providing competent and compassionate care for TCKs is a critical support for these families and subsequently for God's work around the world. Assisting a TCK to launch into a stable, successful career may be the very thing that enables a family to stay on the field, where literally hundreds of lives will continue to be touched by their ministry. Your work as a career counselor is an important ministry in the body of Christ with global implications!

DEFINING A TCK

Defining a TCK can be challenging because there is currently a lack of consensus on specific parameters within the definition regarding age when living in a host country, length of time in foreign context, or number of moves (Pollock & Van Reken, 2009). However, Pollock and Van Reken (2009) offer a commonly accepted definition in their seminal book on TCKs:

A Third Culture Kid (TCK) is a person who has spent a significant part of his or her developmental years outside the parents' culture. The TCK frequently builds relationships to all of the cultures, while not having full ownership in any. Although elements from each culture may be assimilated into the TCK's life experience, the sense of belonging is in relationship to others of similar backgrounds [other TCKs] (Pollock & Van Reken, 2009, p. 13).

The specific element of the TCK experience that sets them apart from their parents is the fact that their cross-cultural experiences are occurring during their developmental years. While their parents are generally experiencing the new culture from a developed identity embedded in the paradigm of an established worldview, the cross-cultural experience is the very thing that is forming the TCK's worldview and identity. During their developmental years when they are absorbing the cultural grammar that makes up their internal structure of the world and who they are in it, they are receiving complex, diverse, and changing information from multiple worldviews and cultures. It is the assimilation of all of the cultural experiences that they are exposed to that creates the unique cultural identity of TCKs.

There is no agreement regarding what length of time living outside of one's passport country results in the formation of TCK characteristics. Pollock and Van Reken (2009) pose that time itself doesn't determine the impact of the third culture experience on the development of a particular child. A combination of other variables such as the child's age, personality, and participation in the local culture can also influence how a child is impacted. While it is not known how long a child must live in a host country to develop TCK characteristics, Pollock and Van Reken state that "it is certainly more than a two-week or even a two-month vacation to see the sights" (Pollock & Van Reken, 2009, p. 21). Some people are identifiable as TCKs after spending as little as one year outside their parents' culture (Pollock & Van Reken, 2009).

Despite the fact that TCKs' individual experiences may be very diverse (e.g., a Korean TCK living in Africa or an American TCK living in Thailand), TCK demonstrates a surprising degree of cultural similarities. In addition to the common experience of synthesizing and internalizing their specific amalgam of cultural influences, there are several shared experiences that connect TCKs to each other: (1) an awareness of being distinctly different from those around them, (2) the expectation of eventually returning to their passport country (and therefore always temporary in their host country), (3) a privileged lifestyle, and (4) a system identity that is tied to the organization that has sent them (Washington & Gadikar, 2016).

The term adult third culture kid (ATCK) is used to refer to an adult person of any age who experienced a TCK childhood (Pollock & Van Reken, 2009). The term alludes to the permanent and sustained impact of the TCK experience across the lifespan. Precisely because it occurs during their developmental years, the imprint of the TCK experience has lasting effects on identity development and cultural worldview. When working in career counseling, the client is most likely an ATCK. However, for simplicity of terminology, this chapter will typically refer to individuals as TCKs.

CULTURAL, SOCIAL, AND PERSONAL IDENTITY DEVELOPMENT

Because identity development is a particularly difficult journey for TCKs (Davis, Edwards, & Watson, 2015; Fail, Thompson, & Walker, 2004; Schaetti, 2006; Walters & Anton-Cuff, 2009; Washington & Gadikar, 2013) and has such an important impact on career development, this chapter will thoroughly explore the developmental path of TCKs. In her research on TCK identity development, Schaetti (2000) goes so far as to say that the TCK experience is pervasively characterized by a search for a congruent identity. It is critical for career counselors to understand the complexity of a TCK's path of identity development because of the primacy of identity in career planning.

Contributing forces. Two overarching experiences of TCK life that influence their development are a high degree of mobility and the fact that they live within multiple cultures (Grimshaw & Sears, 2008; Pollock & Van Reken, 2009). At first glance, it may appear that the issues surrounding TCKs are similar to acculturation challenges faced by immigrants or refuges. However, when evaluated more closely, it is apparent that there are some fundamental differences. Immigrants and refugees move from one culture to another with intent to stay in the new culture. They are faced with the challenge of acculturation into the new, stable context. But TCKs are highly mobile, moving repeatedly between cultures. Therefore, acclimatization, rather than acculturation, becomes a part of the TCK identity (McDonald, 2010). The chronic experience of major transition is intensified by the magnitude of changing not only locations but cultures as well.

Cultural identity. The traditional path in which a person learns culture includes learning (through absorption) cultural rules as a child, testing those rules as an adolescent, internalizing a personal application of their own self as a young adult, and then operating within these norms as an adult (Pollock & Van Reken, 2009). These stages are sequential, building on the previous stage. When enough of the underlying cultural values, norms, and attitudes are absorbed so that an individual can operate intuitively within a culture and understand it, they are said to have achieved cultural balance. Having cultural balance is critical to feeling a sense of belonging and security in a culture (Pollock & Van Reken, 2009).

For a non-TCK, a consistent worldview is represented at each stage of cultural learning and by the various sources of cultural learning around them such as parents, teachers, peers, and media (Pollock & Van Reken, 2009). The TCK faces two challenges in this traditional path of cultural learning. First, the path is frequently interrupted by a cross-cultural move to an environment with completely different rules. This requires that they regress to the previous stages and start again. Second, their multicultural environment will likely have people representing contrasting and contradicting worldviews. Instead of unified cultural messages regarding worldview, values, and norms, they are bombarded with multiple worldviews and contradictory information about values and norms (Pollock & Van Reken, 2000).

Cultural identity strategies. TCKs utilize different strategies to cope with their complex cultural environments. They strive to define a cultural identity that transcends the cultures of either their passport or host country. Moore and Barker (2011) identified that most TCKs develop either a shifting identity or a blend of cultures identity. A shifting identity, sometimes called code-switching (Schaetti, 2000), describes an ability to adapt to different cultural settings through internally alternating between two or more cultural identities. This ability to shift communication, language, and behaviors in different cultural settings is intuitive and fluid (Moore & Barker, 2011). While it enables a person to move between cultural contexts and act appropriately in each, it is not the same as building intimate relationships. It is about behaving in ways sufficiently accepted by others in a culture so that everyone feels comfortable (Schaetti, 2000).

A blend of cultures identity incorporates elements of two or more cultures into a single, blended identity that remains consistent regardless of what country TCKs are in. They are unable to separate the disparate cultures and, therefore, behave in a consistent manner regardless of what country they are in (Moore & Barker, 2011).

"Chameleon" adaptation. The extensive experience TCKs have in multiple cultural settings often develops some level of cultural adaptability. They often use the self-identified label of chameleon to refer to their ability to quickly observe new environments and adapt their language, style of relating, appearance, and cultural practices to blend in and prevent rejection (Pollock & Van Reken, 2009). However, being a cultural chameleon has its challenges as well. It may enable them to appear to fit in and be 'one of the crowd', when, in fact, they are expending all of their energy observing and adapting instead of actually participating in life. The constant changing back and forth between various behavioral patterns can make it difficult for the TCK to develop their own solid value system that stays stable across settings (Pollock & Van Reken, 2009).

Repatriation. As we have stated, TCKs experience high mobility throughout their lives. However, most TCKs repatriate back to their passport country for at least a period of time, often for college. In fact, repatriation has been identified as a specific developmental task unique to TCKs (Schaetti, 2000). Schaetti describes this transition as a "typically psychoculturally shattering experience" (Schaetti, 2000, p. 127). There are two processes at work during repatriation. First, the TCK is coping with immediate requirements of the new environment and reverse culture shock. Second, they are coping with the internal dissonance precipitated by the encounter with their passport culture and the foreign culture (Schaetti, 2000). Unlike other cultural transitions they have made, repatriation is not viewed as a temporary visit. For the first time, they may be faced with the questions of acculturation as opposed to acclimation. An identity crisis is precipitated, as they have to consider to what degree they can assimilate into the passport culture without losing critical and defining aspects of themselves. Social identity issues during repatriation will be discussed in the section on social identity.

Nationality. A concept closely related to repatriation is nationality, another unique developmental task identified by Schaetti (2000). The transaction of nationality refers to the TCKs paradoxical experience of being defined in foreign cultures by their passport nationality while at the same time realizing that their nationality is relatively uninformative as a cultural descriptor of their experience (Schaetti, 2000). They often experience a "rubber band nationality" where their internal sense of national identity expands and contracts as they move among different cultural settings. They may at times feel a strong affiliation to their passport country and at other times feel critical, alienated, and foreign. Both repatriation and nationality can be a source of distress for TCKs until they construct a positive framework for navigating their emotional experience and resolving the dissonance (Schaetti, 2000). We will discuss strategies for promoting positive transactions of repatriation and nationality in the section on counseling competencies.

Implications for career counseling. The cultural identity development path for TCKs has several important implications for the career counseling process. First, a career counselor should always keep in mind that no matter how "typical" their TCK client appears, they are internally very different than their monocultural peers. Their cultural adaptability and capacity to blend in can belie the extent to which they differ from those around them. In addition, if the TCK presents for career counseling during their college years, the counselor should be aware that the years immediately following repatriation are some of the most tumultuous years of a TCK's life. The developmental tasks of repatriation and nationality become particularly distressing and salient during this transition (Schaetti, 2000).

Social identity. In addition to the overarching question of cultural identity, a more personal element of identity development for a TCK involves how they experience themselves in relationship to others around them (Schaetti, 2000; Pollock & Van Reken, 2009). Erikson's psychosocial model of development (see Table 16.1) is a useful model for conceptualizing TCKs because it extends the developmental stages throughout the lifespan and gives prominence to social factors influencing development (Erikson, 1959, 1964).

Erikson's Psychosocial Stages of Development

TABLE 16.1 Erikson's 8 stage developmental model.

Stages	Ego Strength & Age
1. Trust vs. Mistrust	Hope; 0–1 years
2. Autonomy vs. Shame & Doubt	Will; 1–3 years
3. Initiative vs. Guilt	Purpose; preschool
4. Industry vs. Inferiority	Competence; grade school
5. Identity vs. Role Confusion	Fidelity; adolescence
6. Intimacy vs. Isolation	Love; young adulthood
7. Generatively vs. Stagnation	Care; middle adulthood
8. Integrity vs. Despair	Wisdom; older adulthood

While there are eight stages of development in his model, of particular interest in understanding TCKs is his fifth stage, Identity versus Role Confusion. During this stage of development, adolescents are asking the question, Who am I? Friends, social groups, and cultural trends all play a role in shaping and forming identity. The social environment provides the context and parameters in which a personal identity is defined. In essence the question becomes, Who am I in relationship to you? Through a synthesis of childhood identifications, the adolescent achieves a reciprocal relationship with their society while maintaining a feeling of continuity within himself (Marcia, 1966). A successful outcome of this developmental phase results in a commitment to an occupational choice and becoming a fully participating citizen (Marcia, 1966).

In addition to the identity and confusion poles, Marcia (1966) expanded Erikson's fifth stage of development to include middle positions of moratorium, in which an individual is dealing with an identity crisis, but not having or making a vague commitment, and foreclosure, in which an individual has made a commitment without considering options or foregoing the crisis of the developmental stage. The foreclosed individual's commitments would likely be difficult to distinguish from his childhood beliefs. In Table 16.2 Marcia's Identity Development model is portrayed to show a common model used to indicate career adjustment and growth.

TABLE 16.2 Marcia's concepts have been useful for the study of career development concepts such as career commitment and career maturity (Blustein, Devenis, & Kidney, 1989; Linnemeyer & Brown, 2015; Vondracek, Schulenberg, Skorikov, Gillespie, & Wahlheim, 1995).

Marcia's Identity Development Positions

	Identity Crisis	No Crisis
Commitment	Identity Achievement	Foreclosure
No Commitment	Moratorium	Role Confusion (identity diffusion)

Variable reference group. TCKs face several challenges during this stage of social development. Because of the high mobility that characterizes their lives, the social groups that they are exposed to are constantly changing. The PolVan Cultural Identity Model (see Table 16.3) delineates four possible modes of relationship a TCK can have to their surrounding environment at any time: Foreigner, Hidden Immigrant, Adopted, or Mirror.

TABLE 16.3. PolVan Cultural Identity Box. Pollock & Van Reken, 2009, p. 55. Copyright 1996 David C. Pollock and RuthVan Reken.

The PolVan Cultural Identity Model
Cultural Identity in Relationship to Surrounding Culture

Foreigner	**Hidden Immigrant**
Look different	Look alike
Think different	Think different
Adopted	**Mirror**
Look different	Look alike
Think alike	Think alike

These designations describe the internal experience of the TCK in relationship to those around them. One day they may experience themselves as a Foreigner surrounded by others who both look different from them and think differently. On another day they may feel like a Hidden Immigrant who looks like the people around them but thinks very differently from them. In some environments the TCK may be immersed in a culture that mirrors them physically and shares their worldview, while at other times they may be in an environment where they look different, but internally they strongly identify with the surrounding culture (this is an example of the Adopted identity in Table 16.3). With every move, not only do they have to learn the new cultural rules but they also have to figure out who they are in relationship to the surrounding culture. With such a fluid context, they are missing the stable social conditions from which a solid sense of self emerges. In one setting, they may have language proficiency and operate as "the life of the party," able to be gregarious, witty, and humorous. In another setting, they may lack the communication and cultural proficiency needed to joke around, express their feelings, or assert leadership. Which one is the "real them"? It is easy to see how TCKs may be still be working through this stage of development well into their college years (Grimshaw & Sears, 2008).

Social implications of repatriation. To complicate things further, it is during this critical phase of social development that many TCKs are faced with repatriation, the most complex transition of their lives. The research delineates that at the time of entry into their passport country, TCKs strive to draw on their knowledge base of past experiences of successful navigation into new cultures and integrate it with observations of the new environment (Finn Jordan, 2002). Because the third culture is not recognized by most people, when the TCK honestly tries to answer the standard question, "Where are you from?", they find that their U.S. peers often terminate the conversation or become bored or disbelieving (Finn Jordan, 2002). As a result, TCKs often cope by suppressing or distancing from their third culture identity. Schaetti states that identity management is a typical strategy for TCKs who must "set aside their third culture identity in order to secure a more relevant social identity" (Schaetti, 2000, p. 111). She goes on to suggest that while this may initially seem inauthentic, it can be an effective adaptive strategy for coping socially as they develop a constructive identity that can integrate the new experience (Schaetti, 2000). As the TCKs navigate this complex transition, they are required to operate as more of an observer in a culture that generally calls for a highly participating self (Finn Jordan, 2002).

Difference and marginality. Whether in their passport country, as a foreigner in their host country, or in the multinational expatriate community, the TCK is often negotiating some form of difference in physical appearance, clothing, language (including accent or speech inflection), behaviors, and thought processes (Schaetti, 2000; Pollock & Van Reken, 2009). This pervasive experience of difference can form an integral part of their developing identity as they become accustomed to making friends across racial and ethnic lines and with peers holding differing worldviews (Washington & Gadikar, 2016; Pollock & Van Reken, 2009). In the expatriate community, the primary source of commonality among the members is specifically the experience of difference (Schaetti, 2000). They often experience simultaneously being a part of and apart from the cultural social mainstream in either their passport country or a host country (Schaetti, 2000). In effect, they become marginalized in both worlds. The paradox of difference is that while it can feel isolating and lonely, the lack of restraint from conforming to any one culture's expectations can also be an avenue to freedom and opportunity (Schaetti, 2000). A constructive resolution to difference, or the experience of marginality, can include embracing the freedom to make use of it for personal and professional fulfillment and a feeling of home in many places instead of feeling trapped in a lonely existence of feeling at home nowhere (Schaetti, 2000; Pollock & Van Reken, 2009). Many TCKs maintain a life-long awareness of difference from their passport country peers, with up to 74% reporting that they see themselves as outsiders to their "home" culture or very "different" because of the experience (Finn Jordan, 2002). For many TCKs, repatriation is a significant encounter with their "different" status and the first time they have to negotiate it without the third culture expatriate community around them to share the experience.

Organizational identity. A powerful component of a TCK's identity is the subculture of their parents' organization (i.e., military, missionary, diplomatic, business) (Useem, 1973; Pollock & Van Reken, 2009). In many cases the whole system of the sponsoring organization serves as both surrogate family and community. The clear demarcation of membership in the group can provide a significant experience of belonging in a world where the TCK seems to belong nowhere. At the same time, the subculture is often characterized by a hierarchical organization, which extends influence and authority over a family's life that far exceeds what they would ever experience by an employer in their passport country (Pollock & Van Reken, 2009; Useem, 1973). Education options, housing, city of residence, norms of behavior in the host country, and frequency of visiting passport country are just a few of the areas of life that are often dictated by the sponsoring organization. The influence of the organization can be similar to the influence of an extended family system in a non-TCK setting.

Implications for career counseling. The social identity development in TCKs has important implications for the career counseling process. Many TCKs will present for career counseling during college. The career counselor should be aware the TCK will likely be still working through Erikson's fifth stage of development, identity versus confusion. As Pollock and Van Reken (2009) explain that TCKs commonly have delayed adolescence, some of the identity development features would be good to evaluate beyond the college years as well. A career counselor may evaluate to what extent a TCK client has navigated through the identity versus confusion stage. They may also choose to refer to the moratorium or foreclosure position within Marica's (1966) developmental model.

Even if the client had previously made progress in the identity developmental stage, the reentry into the passport country will frequently complicate an identity crisis requiring a reworking of this developmental stage. The need to reconsider the sense of identity that they had previously achieved can be potentially distressing. In addition, the TCK may feel it necessary to repress their third culture identity in order to construct a more socially relevant identity in the new setting. Even though there are some long-term complications associated with this strategy, it can be an effective strategy during initial settling in to the passport culture. Finally, the career counselor should be aware that many TCKs experience profound loss when they repatriate to their passport country because as adults, they lose their membership in the sponsoring organization. They experience grief as well as a loss of identity in one of the only places of tangible belonging they have known.

Personal identity. Our Western, individualistic culture also asks the question of personal identity development. How is the personal identity of TCKs impacted by their multicultural upbringing?

TCK model of identity development. While there is currently no developmental model specifically for TCKs, Schaetti (2006) has suggested a broad five-stage model that she applies to the unique experience of TCKs:

1. **Stage 1: Pre-encounter.** During this stage, the TCK accumulates experiences without awareness of having or forming an identity.

2. **Stage 2: Encounter.** In this stage, the TCK has an experience or a series of experiences that cause them to recognize that they are different than others in their lives.

3. **Stage 3: Exploration.** In this stage, the TCK actively engages in an inquiry and exploration of their identity. It is during this time that a TCK may adopt the label "TCK" (or one of the alternatives). It is also when questions of national identity become poignant.

4. **Stage 4: Integration.** During Integration, the TCK assimilates a coherent internal identity that takes into account all the disparate components of their world. They formulate a satisfactory answer to the question, Who am I?

5. **Stage 5: Recycling.** This stage recognizes that identity formation does not occur at one point in time but continues throughout the lifespan. The TCK will need to return to the work of establishing and refining their identity at various times throughout their life.

An understanding of this model is helpful for career counselors in several ways. First, it provides a general framework for understanding where the client is in their identity formation. Second, it defines the experience of the encounter stage, a stage of development that often becomes salient with the experience of repatriation to the passport country for college and a time when career counselors are likely to interact with them. The experience of the encounter stage and the subsequent exploration stage can be very distressing until some level of integration is achieved. Finally, it underlines that life transitions and events can trigger additional encounter experiences and the need to cycle back through exploration and integration throughout the lifespan. As identity questions reemerge at different points of development, there is a new opportunity for greater depths of resolution and understanding with each cycle (Finn Jordan, 2002). Throughout the lifespan, new circumstances can spur internal conflict over a core sense of the self, a process largely determined by social interactions (Finn Jordan, 2002). Most TCKs will not have an awareness of these stages; they are just intuitively moving to resolve the dissonance they feel.

Distinct maturity patterns. In a more detailed aspect of personal identity, the complex life experiences of TCKs result in what is sometimes referred to as uneven maturity. This refers to a common developmental pattern in TCKs of maturing more quickly than non-TCK peers in some areas of development and more slowly in others (Pollock & Van Reken, 2009).

In some ways, TCKs will seem far older than their years (Pollock & Van Reken, 2009). They have a global awareness that rivals or surpasses many monocultural adults. Many have advanced communication skills, proficiency in multiple languages, and a comfort in communicating with adults that is uncommon for their age. In addition, they often develop early autonomy and independence through world travel, separation from family, or boarding school (Pollock & Van Reken, 2009).

On the other hand, TCKs can appear to lack sophistication or social skills when compared to peers in their passport country. The constraints of living as a guest in another country can limit the normal adolescent expressions of testing or pushing against the rules, values, and beliefs of the system, a normal part of adolescent development. While a parent may suffer personal embarrassment as a result of their child's behavior in their passport country, that same behavior could jeopardize a job or residence visa in a foreign country or even escalate into an "international incident" (Useem, 1973). The realities of expatriate life often lack real choices and autonomy for adolescents. One implication of these dynamics is that TCKs often go through delayed adolescence. After they return to their passport country during early adulthood, they experience an abrupt freedom that opens up a space for them to progress through adolescent rebellion and developmental stages that their peers transacted during high school (Pollock & Van Reken, 2009).

Discovering the term TCK. Throughout their lives, TCKs become painfully aware that they don't fit in any of the standard categories of group membership. They do not fit in either the host country culture where they are living or the passport culture to which they return. While there is increasing awareness of the TCK term and concepts, some of them do not get introduced to these while growing up. The simple and common question, Where are you from? can be answered in a word by most people, but it is one of the most complex questions to which TCKs worry about having to respond (Wang, 2015). A powerful moment in the life of a TCK is when they discover a "name" for their experience (Wang, 2015). In Wang's (2015) research on identity development in TCKs, she reports that many TCKs identify learning about the term TCK as a crucial point in their lives and some went so far as to say that it was "life changing." Having a term that identifies them provides a sense of identity accompanied by relief.

Faith as a resource. A significant percentage of TCKs are raised in families with strong religious commitment, and spirituality is a significant resource for them in their complex journey of identity development. Two areas of common distress for TCKs that can be effectively addressed through spiritual truths are national identity and finding a sense of belonging. The New Testament paints a powerful picture of our belonging and membership in God's family. Jesus' words in John 14:20–24 (ESV) describe our place within the community of the Trinity:

> I am in My Father, you are in Me, and I am in You.... If anyone loves Me, he will keep My word. My Father will love him, and We will come to him and make our home with him.

Grasping the reality of a permanent, eternal place of belonging in a community that will never be lost is a deeply meaningful truth to a TCK. This spiritual identity of belonging is also extended to the Body of Christ, which transcends any specific culture. While there will likely continue to be many "goodbyes" for the TCK, there is comfort in knowing that separations are only for a time and that they will have an eternity to be with the people they love. Their true identity is as a "fellow citizen with the saints, and members of God's household" (Ephesians 2:19, KJV).

Resolving the internal dissonance surrounding national identity is not simple. Everyone has a need to understand where they belong in this world and to feel a part of the greater humanity. However, many TCKs find some resolution to the question of national identity by holding on the idea that our true citizenship is in heaven (Philippians 3:30).

Implications for career counselors. The personal identity development of TCKs has important implications for career counselors. First, the encounter and exploration stages of TCK identity development, marked by high distress and preoccupation, are often triggered by repatriation or other significant life transitions during which the TCK might also engage in career counseling (Schaetti, 2000). Having an understanding of this process will inform the career counselor of important identity development processes that are impacting the TCKs capacity for career decision-making. Second, career counselors should keep in mind that TCK maturity patterns are unique and will not likely parallel the patterns expected of their non-TCK peers. Normal development for a TCK may look like immaturity and delayed adolescence when evaluated through a typical developmental lens (Pollock & Van Reken, 2009). However, when the context of their identity development is considered, their development path can be seen as adaptive and not pathological. Counselors should guard against ethnocentricity in assessing TCKs. Finally, sometimes a career counselor is the one who has the opportunity to provide a TCK with the vocabulary and paradigm to discover that they are part of a wider community of individuals who share their cultural heritage and experience. Providing the TCK with vocabulary and information about their life experience can contribute in a powerful way to their identity development and journey to find meaningful work in the world. The high value for difference, however, may also manifest as a resistance to be "pigeonholed" by another person's definition of them.

DISTINGUISHING CHARACTERISTICS OF ADULT TCKS

As with any cultural group, the values, attitudes, and behaviors that emerge from their common experiences result in a set of distinguishing characteristics.

Relationship patterns. TCKs typically have a wealth of relationships across the globe. However, like much of their lives, their relationship networks are plagued with continual change and loss inevitable in a transient community (Pollock & Van Reken, 2009). They learn patterns of relationship building that accommodate for the speed with which people come and go in their community as well as the unavoidable grief that accompanies the repeated loss of close friendships. Because of how quickly people come and go in the expatriate world, TCKs tend to approach relationships with an urgency and pace that would be considered intense by non-TCK standards. While non-TCK peers may spend months slowly getting to know each other, a TCK generally has little use for common early stages of relationship and may move quickly to deeper sharing. They are prone to interpret the prolonged early stage of relationship building common among non-TCKs as superficial and "shallow" (Pollock & Van Reken, 2009). On the other hand, some TCKs protect themselves from ongoing grief by not involving themselves emotionally in relationships. In addition, TCKs are known for developing a quick release in relationships. When they see any signs that a relationship may be coming to a close or an ending of some kind, they will quickly begin to lean away from the relationship and may even terminate the relationship prematurely (Pollock & Van Reken, 2009).

Plurality (3D) worldview. One of the results of the TCK's multicultural life is a multidimensional worldview sometimes referred to as plurality (Pollock & Van Reken, 2009). TCKs have often been exposed to a wide variety of environments including extreme poverty, slums, political instability, war, natural disasters, inadequate medical resources, and other conditions not normally encountered in the United States (Bikos et al., 2014). When they hear news stories world events, they hear them through a rich paradigm of life experiences. The chosen career path of a TCK will likely be impacted by their global awareness and exposure to lack of resources in much of the world (Bikos et al., 2014).

A multicultural worldview includes an understanding that truth can be contextual. Many TCKs have had to develop an appreciation for the paradox of different truths on the one hand while striving to find a solid ground for a commitment to personal truth (Schaetti, 2000). In one setting, "saving face" by not speaking the obvious is an honorable action; in another setting, the same action would be considered an insulting lie. TCKs have grown up processing the complexity of conflicting worldviews and it is second nature to them to see the world as multifaceted with few absolute truths (Pollock & Van Reken, 2009).

Disenfranchised grief. The pervasive quality of high mobility in the expatriate community results in a TCKs experiencing loss of people, places, pets, and possessions throughout their lives (Gilbert, 2008). In addition, Pollock and Van Reken (2009) have identified that there are many hidden losses such as familiar surroundings, familiar foods and smells, familiar routines and lifestyles, or presence at significant family events (Pollock & Van Reken, 2009). Gilbert (2008) expands the discussion by including what he terms "existential losses." Existential losses involve the loss of security that comes in knowing that what one has thought of as real is, in fact, a reflection of reality. The world as they have known it is reliable and predicable and will continue being so.

The losses they experience are often ambiguous, and the accompanying grief is frequently disenfranchised (Gilbert, 2008). Unprocessed grief can show up in adult TCKs' lives in various ways. Transitions of any kind often are emotionally intense for TCKs. They have been known to stop saying goodbye at partings and will simply disappear, compounding the unresolved grief. It is not uncommon for disenfranchised grief to result in high levels of anxiety or depression in adult TCKs.

Belonging and restlessness. One of the most challenging experiences of the TCK life is a feeling of belonging nowhere and everywhere at the same time. Some TCKs have a multiple sense of belonging and some have no sense of belonging (Fail et al., 2004). Because they frequently do not identify wholly with one particular culture, TCKs occupy liminal or "in-between" space (Bushong, 2013; Pollock & Van Reken, 2009). In addition, because of their mobility, geographic locations that hold treasured memories of their childhood are often spread across multiple countries and inaccessible to them later in life. Concepts of home and belonging are emotionally challenging for the TCK, who must find alternative ways to achieve a sense of belonging.

A further challenge to finding a place to belong is that TCKs become so accustomed to change and temporary residence in their lives that they have a difficult time settling down for any period of time. They feel chronically restless and rootless (McDonald, 2010; Pollock & Van Reken, 2009). Many of them develop a migratory instinct that compels them to inject change into their lives on a regular basis. While being open to change can be beneficial, restlessly moving from one place to another without legitimate reasons can have dire consequences on academic, career, and family life (Pollock & Van Reken, 2009).

Marginalization: encapsulating or constructive. The experience of difference combined with the challenge of finding a sense of belonging in a particular community is often experienced as marginalizing. The TCK feels as though they are encapsulated by the ways their life has separated them from others (Fail et al., 2004). However, some TCKs have built a constructive marginality by using their multicultural identities to their advantage and finding multiple places of belonging. They find joy and freedom in being able to connect in multiple places in spite of the tension of ongoing ambivalence (Fail et al., 2004).

IMPLICATIONS FOR COUNSELING

With the foundational understanding of the developmental path and experience of TCKs in mind, counselors should be mindful of several themes that need to be attended to when counseling TCKs.

Chronic transition. It is evident from the previous discussion that TCKs experience major transitions more frequently than other people. According to Pollock and Van Reken (2009), TCKs go through five stages with each transition. Because these stages are repeated frequently and become an integral part of their lives, the stages become almost automatic. It is very helpful for counselors to have a framework for understanding where a client may be in this process.

Stage 1: Involvement Stage. In the involvement stage, the TCK is a comfortable member of their current community. They have an identity in the community and tend to be focused on the present. They are known and easily involve themselves in traditions and customs of the community (Washington & Gadikar, 2013).

Stage 2: Leaving Stage. In this stage. the TCK realizes they will be leaving and begins to mentally and physically prepare. They begin to relinquish responsibilities they've had in the community and begin detaching from emotional ties. To make the leaving as painless as possible, TCKs may deny feelings of sadness or grief as a way of coping. However, this strategy is only a temporary solution and they carry the unprocessed grief over into the next phase of transition, compounding it with each move (Pollock & Van Reken, 2001). TCKs who have used the denial and detachment strategy to cope with chronic loss and grief will inevitably carry the unresolved grief with them. They may disengage emotionally from future relationships because they learn to associate relationships with loss (Melles & Frey, 2014). They may also have disproportionately strong emotional responses to future transitions.

Stage 3: Transition Stage. This transition stage commences when the TCK has left the first location and does not end until after they have made the internal decision to become a part of the new community. It is a time of significant chaos and ongoing adjustments as they cope with the loss of their last support system, the lack of identity in a new system, and the challenges of forging an identity in a new context. Counselors should be aware that one coping strategy sometimes employed by TCKs is to make intentional efforts to disengage with others and to be very selective in what they reveal about themselves (Washington & Gadikar, 2013). Their true level of distress can be camouflaged by their disengaged presentation. In fact, it is common to experience a severe loss of self-esteem with cultural transitions (Pollock & Van Reken, 2001).

Stage 4: Entering Stage. The entering stage is characterized by the TCK starting to adjust to their new environment. This stage is much less chaotic as the TCK moves back and forth between hopeful excitement about their new environment and continued feelings of loss (Washington & Gadikar, 2013). The TCK makes a conscious decision to engage in the new community.

Stage 5: Reinvolvement Stage. This is final stage of transition to the new location. They are at home in their new community and back to focusing more on the here and now instead of anticipating the future or reminiscing about the past (Pollock & Van Reken, 2009). However, no matter how long the TCK is in the new environment, they will still have feelings of being marginalized (Fail et al., 2004). But, feeling different does not have to mean uncomfortable or distressed (Fail et al., 2004).

Transition is such a central experience of the TCK's life that it is important for the counselor to understand how their life is currently being impacted by transition. In addition, the counselor should remain cognizant of the impact of past transitions that include unresolved grief. It is common for intense grief to be triggered for TCKs during any kind of transition.

Repatriation. We have already discussed the specific challenges involved with repatriation. Schaetti's (2000) research identified a number of ways TCKs typically cope with the stress of repatriation. Table 16.4 summarizes positive and negative ways that TCKs react to repatriation (Schaetti, 2000). A counselor can support the TCK by encouraging positive coping behaviors.

TABLE 16.4. Summary of positive and negative coping skills for repatriation. This graph was created by Brenda Keck based on information in Global Nomad Identity: Hypothesizing a developmental model (doctoral dissertation) by Barbara F. Schaetti, 2000.

Positive and Negative Coping with Repatriation

Positive Coping	Negative Coping
• Link to international groups and friends • Actively and intentionally engage in repatriation • Be open to new experiences • Seek to learn about popular music, pop culture, and current events • Take a reflective, anthropological stance that distances from identity • Intentionally bridge relationships with American peers	• Shut down—withdraw emotionally and relationally • Pass—actively encourage others to assume they are American to bypass the complexity of relating across cultures • Postpone—do not accept repatriation; continue to think of self as being part of life in another place • Insult—adopt a derogatory attitude and discussion of passport country

Nationality. There are also ways to assist TCKs in negotiating a satisfactory internal sense of national identification. Schaetti (2000) identified three typical ways that TCKs have found to conceptualize their national identity. The actual choice made is less important than going through the process of personal exploration to settle on a national identity (Schaetti, 2000). Table 16.5 summarizes the three options outlined in her research. It can be very helpful for a TCK to have these options articulated.

TABLE 16.5. Three forms of national identity experienced internally. This table was created by Brenda Keck based on information in Global Nomad Identity: Hypothesizing a developmental model (doctoral dissertation) by Barbara Schaetti, 2000.

Internal Sense of National Identity

National Identity	Description
Insular National Identity	The idea that nationality, language, and country of residence must be all the same. These TCKs adopt a single nationality with which to identity. This relieves them from having to integrate the complex and sometimes contra-dictory ideas of multiple cultures. It provides a place to "put down roots."
International National Identity	Identifying with being a citizen of the passport country based on agreement with the ideas and principles of the nation (such a freedom, democracy) but feel even stronger personal attachment to the process of traveling, meeting new and different people, and generally learning about alternative ways of doing things. National citizenship is the home base from which to explore the world.
Transnational national Identity	The idea of a national identity has lost much of its meaning beyond being a descriptive term or matter of functional necessity in the modern world. These TCKs have moved away from feeling allegiance or nostalgia for any one nation to the exclusion of others. These individuals retain their third culture as their primary identification.

Unresolved grief. The pervasive experience of loss and grief through chronic transition has been discussed in other sections. The important thing for counselors to remember when working with TCKs is that grief is often a defining component of their experience that they will be processing and negotiating much of their life. They may also be strongly defended against experiencing the grief. They will need support, encouragement, and strategies to work through the grief.

Incomplete developmental tasks. Wrobble and Pleuddemann's (1990) study on psycho-social adjustment in missionary kids indicated that they are not resolving the developmental crises described by Erikson as successfully as their non-TCK peers. The completion of Erikson's Stage 5 (identity versus confusion) may be delayed even longer as TCKs temporarily put their overseas experience behind them during the adjustment and completion of college. After the initial adjustments to their passport culture are made, the adult TCK can return to the unresolved tensions between the overseas experience and life in the passport culture (Wrobble & Pleuddemann, 1990). Some adult TCKs have never been given the vocabulary or categories to make sense of their experience, especially if they are from an earlier era of history when information was not as available as it is today. Even aging adult TCKs can continue to struggle significantly with issues of identity development if not given the tools and support to process their experience, as has been noted anecdotally by Useem and Cottrell (1999).

Normalizing and naming their experience. While some TCKs return to the United States armed with a lot of tools and information about themselves and how to cope with the transition they are facing, many are not given any information and may not have even heard of the term third culture kid (or other similar terms). One of the most powerful roles that a counselor can play in the life of a TCK is to normalize their experience and give them a vocabulary to name themselves (Wang, 2015). They can clearly see that they are different than their non-TCK peers but may not understand why. Helping them understand why their own developmental path has been so challenging and collaborating with them chart a course to explore how their history can inform their future is a powerful investment.

Termination. Given the previous discussion regarding unresolved grief and transition, the termination stage of therapy will require some special attention by the counselor. For the TCK, this will inevitably constitute another significant loss. Learning to "end well" may be a new skill for the TCK and this offers an opportunity to practice and model how to end a season in a way that provides good closure. The counselor should realize that the TCK is likely to be resistant to saying goodbye and will be prone to end therapy prematurely by no longer showing up for appointments. Ironically, the more meaningful the relationship has been, the more likely the TCK will be to disappear without saying goodbye. The termination process itself can become a treatment intervention. Bushong (2013) suggests several ways to leverage this phase of treatment for the TCK client. Among other things, she suggests taking this opportunity to explore how the TCK family handled goodbyes throughout their life. How were goodbyes handled in each place that they lived? Are there unfinished endings that need to be attended to? In addition to all the ethical considerations that always inform termination, closure with a TCK may call for additional ceremony and intentionality.

TCK CAREER DEVELOPMENT

In this final section we want to turn our attention specifically to the career counseling implications for TCKs.

General recommendations. In their study on career development in TCKs, Bikos et al. (2014) have made four recommendations for career counseling with this population:

1. Attend to sociocultural adaptation. The difficulties faced by repatriating TCKs are well documented (Brierley, 1997; Davis et al., 2010; Davis, Suarez, Crawford & Rehfuss, 2013; Finn Jordan, 2002; Pollock & Van Reken, 2001; Wrobbel & Pleuddemann, 1990). Therefore, it is recommended that career counselors inquire about educational and career development as well as overall repatriation. Successfully navigating the psychosocial tasks of this developmental stage is critical to career decision-making (Bikos et al., 2014). Explore whether the client has attended a reentry program, as they have been shown to help repatriating TCKs (Davis et al., 2010; Davis et al., 2013).

2. Offer empirically supported (standard) career services. Despite the atypical life experiences that TCKs bring to career counseling, they have effectively used traditional career planning (Bikos et al., 2014).

3. Use contextual and developmental approaches. The globalization and social complexity of the third culture experience are characteristic of postmodern pathways. Savickas' career adaptability model is a developmental approach that may have strong application with TCKs (Bikos et al., 2014). In addition, Biko et al. (2014) suggest the use of the framework proposed by Flum and Blustein, which considers identity formation as well as the cultural and relational context (Bikos et al., 2014).

4. Inquire about faith and calling. As stated earlier, many TCKs come with a rich tradition of spirituality and faith. In their research with missionary kids, Bikos et al. (2014) found that even though they did not inquire directly about spirituality or faith, the participants volunteered elements of faith across the domains of discussion. Faith and calling have deep meaning and implication for career path decisions. It is recommended that career counselors include topics of faith and calling when exploring career options.

Environmental, personal, and behavioral influences on career and educational planning. There is a range of components that influence the tasks involved with career and educational planning and decision-making in a TCK's life. Bandura's social cognitive career theory provides a useful framework for exploring these components from the perspectives of (a) external environmental factors, (b) personal attributes, and (c) overt behaviors (Bikos et al., (2014).

External environments. The external environments that impact a TCK's educational and career path are unique and varied. Growing up internationally exposes the TCK to a variety of environments that impact their values and view of work. They have often witnessed extreme poverty or slums, political instability, war, overt racism, natural disasters, and multiple languages. Because of their privileged status as an expatriate, they are often insulated from suffering personally in these situations (Bikos et al., 2014). In fact, many times the primary role models in their lives are people who are there specifically to serve the needs of people in these situations (Cottrell, 2002). These experiences often result in a deep awareness of the needs in the world and a desire or sense of responsibility to improve the state of the world.

Another environmental condition that impacts TCKs is their financial status. The TCK's parents may have been highly paid by their organization or may have lived on support that they raised. Even if they have lived on a level of raised support that would be considered quite low by U.S. standards, they may still be among the wealthiest people in the host country. Whatever their personal situation, it is likely to be quite different than would be experienced by their peers in the United States and will influence their expectations and view of money in career choice (Bikos et al., 2014).

Counselors should be aware that TCKs might have had limited access to a variety of role models growing up. The career options in the expatriate communities that they were exposed to would generally be professional careers but may not have included the spectrum of career options that most of their peers in the United States would be exposed to. Consequently, when making educational and career path decisions, they do not have an understanding of the range of options available to them (Bikos et al., 2014). They may benefit from trait and factor type assessments to broaden their ideas of options that may be a good fit for them.

Many TCKs will have a variety of educational experiences, possibly including home schools, boarding schools, local national schools, international schools, Christian schools, and schools in the United States. While their education may be varied and nontraditional, they generally have strong educational backgrounds (Bonebright, 2010). Cottrell (2002) describes TCKs as being raised by highly educated parents in educationally elite communities. Her research identified that over 80% of their parents have at least a bachelor's degree and almost 50% have advanced degrees (Cottrell, 2002). As would be expected, a large percentage of TCKs also pursue higher education, with more than 95% completing some college and 29% completing advanced degrees.

While TCKs generally have a high value for and a strong background in education, many schools overseas have limited career development resources (Bikos et al., 2014).

In many cases, the parents of TCKs attending college are still living abroad. The TCK will visit them on holidays or during breaks, but the parents rarely come to the school. It is not unusual for there to be long periods of time, even years, between visits (Bikos et al., 2014). However, in spite of the geographic challenges, the TCK may still feel significantly supported by their parents. The family system may have developed effective tools to compensate for geographic separations. The TCK may also rely more heavily on extended family in the United States, church members, church leaders, and family friends (Bikos et al., 2014).

Nobles (forthcoming) noted that military brats may have a difficult time adjusting due to the changes in environment upon repatriation, possibly having difficulty engaging in the home culture, which may feel dull in comparison to the thrilling experiences they had when living internationally. Considering this in career counseling with TCKs may assist in dealing with expectation management and engagement in the work environment.

Personal Attributes. The TCK brings some cultural values and attitudes to the career counseling decision- making process. Many TCKs are highly motivated to use their careers to help others and make a difference in the world. Because of their exposure to the needs and lack of resources in other parts of the world, they may have a sense of responsibility to use their career to help (Biko et al., 2014). TCKs are likely to see themselves as having global values, interests, and skills and are likely to choose careers that have an international component (Bikos et al., 2014).

Several have suggested that not only do TCKs show interest in international careers but they also make preferable international business people, particularly when there is a shortage of qualified international business people seeking jobs (Bonebright, 2010; Lam & Semler, 2004; Semler & Lam, 2004). Qualities in TCKs appealing for international careers include cross-cultural adaptability skills (Doran, Larsen, & Wolff, 2015), interpersonal skills, cultural flexibility, tolerance for ambiguity, decreased ethnocentrism (Tarique & Weisbord, 2013), social sensitivity in intercultural contexts (Lyttle, Barker, & Cornwell, 2011), and interethnic sensitivity skills (Nobles, 2015).

Because of the challenges that TCKs may be facing in their social adjustment at college, they may express a preference for organizations that allow independence and are tolerant of personal differences. They may gravitate toward less collectivist organizational cultures where fitting in is less significant (Bonebright, 2010).

Many TCKs come from backgrounds with a strong faith component. They are likely to include spiritual components in their career development explorations. They also attribute God's involvement to their experiences and decision-making (Bikos et al., 2014).

It is evident from this chapter that the TCKs background would be expected to be a primary consideration in career planning. However, a counselor will also need to be cognizant that during college, TCKs sometimes will cope with their adjustment by distancing from their TCK history and identity in order to fit in socially. They may resist discussions that highlight their background (Bikos et al., 2014). In this instance, the counselor must recognize that the needs of the psychosocial developmental work are taking precedence over the career planning decision-making. Career planning may need to slow down while the TCK continues to work out their adjustment to the new environment.

Behaviors. There are specific ways that TCKs can act to advance their career and educational planning and goals. They will benefit from traditional career planning activities such as interviewing others about educational and career opportunities, trying out career-related activities, and gaining work-related experience (Bikos et al., 2014).

It can be helpful for repatriated TCKs to stay connected to international communities. Some possible ways to stay involved internally would be through foreign language study, hosting international visitors, or volunteering for internationally related organizations.

When choosing educational majors, TCKs are likely to be drawn to selections that reflect their international heritage and that leave the door open to returning to work abroad. Cottrell's (2002) research revealed that some students choose majors that have general application to international settings, such as international relations, anthropology, foreign languages, or area studies. Others choose an international major that connects them specifically to their childhood home, often with a goal of returning. For others, they chose majors that reflected interests that were developed in the international setting. Finally, many TCKs choose majors less for the actual topic and more because it might lead to work abroad. The major is simply seen as a vehicle to international employment (Cottrell, 2002).

When making a decision about a career choice, TCKs tend to choose a career in which they can exercise expertise, leadership, and independence (Bonebright, 2010). Having an international component to their job remains important to them well into adulthood (Bonebright, 2010). They will be looking for jobs that allow them to travel and maintain international connections.

While TCKs are in college, counselors can support them by connecting them to other TCK peers or international students as well as organizations on campus with an international component. They are often ideal candidates to work in the international student office of the school.

STRENGTHS

In this chapter, we have delineated many challenges TCKs might experience in order to equip career counselors to support them effectively as they make educational and career decisions. Counselors may equip TCKs by minimizing negative aspects of the TCK influence while maximizing the positive. Recalling concepts like encapsulating versus constructive marginalization may help a career counselor leverage the TCK identity and connectivity with others. The many strengths of TCKs (see Figure 16.1) should also be highlighted and leveraged as they explore their options in the work place.

FIGURE 16.1 [Common strengths of TCKS.]

Common Strengths of TCKs

- Often multilingual
- Expanded, international worldview
- Cross-cultural skills
- Cultural flexibility and adaptability
- Independent
- Ability to cope with crises
- Religious commitment and spirituality
- Forms depth in relationships quickly
- Educated; values education
- High achieving
- Service oriented
- Lower ethnocentrism
- Qualified for international work

The opening chapter of this book discussed the role of work in fellowshipping with God. A TCK's experience through their life story may be considered an opportunity to connect with how God may interact with his or her experiences to form an occupation that continues a walk with God, as he has been present throughout the TCK's journey throughout the world. The consideration of how a TCK identity is formed may assist a TCK client with relating to God as well as determining a career path. It is our hope that career counselors will find enjoyment in serving this unique and privileged population.

CONCLUSION

The population of TCKs can be expected to continue to rise with expanding globalization. Multicultural influences and high mobility during their developmental years are powerful forces shaping their identity culturally, socially, and personally. TCKs possess distinctive characteristics that require specific competencies for counselors striving to serve them effectively. This chapter has provided foundational information for multicultural competency in working with this population as well as specific recommendations for counseling TCKs and guiding them in their educational and career paths.

KEY TERMS

Acclimatization: the process of adjusting to a culture by adjusting behavior to fit the current culture in which one is present

Acculturation: the process of adjusting to a culture by taking on aspects of the new culture

Adult third culture kid (ATCK): a grown person who has had the third culture kid experience in childhood

Cultural balance: an ability to navigate a culture intuitively

Foreign service kid: may also be called a diplomat kid; a TCK with parent(s) involved in government work internationally

Global nomad: a third culture kid (TCK); a person who has grown up in a culture other than his parents' passport culture, commonly due to the parents' occupation

Military brat: a military child; a TCK with parent(s) serving in the military; this term may sound offensive, but it is commonly the preferred term within the population

Missionary kid (MK): a TCK with parent(s) involved in international, faith-based ministry in a culture other than his or her parents

Reentry: sometimes used to be synonymous with repatriation, reentry is the process of entering the passport country; for TCKs, the term entry is often considered more accurate, as they have not previously lived there

Repatriation: the return of a person residing in a foreign country to their passport country

Third culture kid (TCK): a person who has spent a significant portion of developmental years growing up in a culture other than his or her parents' culture; a significant portion of the identity of a TCK is in relation to others who have also grown up outside of their parents' culture

REFLECTION AND DISCUSSION

1. What relationship do you see between transitions during developmental years and the development of identity?

2. How would you explain the term **third culture kid** to one who had not learned of the term before? How would you explain the term to a non-TCK who may be skeptical of the impact being a TCK has on development?

3. How can a career counselor assess a TCK's acculturation and relational needs in occupation, based on the PolVan cultural identity model?

4. How might the unique role of a TCK's parents' work organization (military, missions, foreign diplomatic service, business) impact their sense of identity and career choice?

5. What significance does belonging have for career choice?

6. How would you envision maximizing a TCK's experiences and minimizing their challenges in their career development?

ADDITIONAL RESOURCES

An exhaustive list of resources is not possible in this chapter, but a few readings, websites, and organizations that may be helpful for TCKs, their families, and those who treat them. For further resources, appendices of books for TCKs often have lists, such as in the book by Pollock and Van Reken (2009).

Readings:

Bushong, L. J. (2013). Belonging everywhere and nowhere: Insights into counseling the globally mobile. Indianapolis, IN: Mango Tree Intercultural Services.

Molinsky, A. (2013). Global dexterity: How to adapt your behavior across cultures without losing yourself in the process. Boston, MA: Harvard Business School.

Pascoe, R. (2006). Raising global nomads: Parenting abroad in an on-demand world. North Vancouver, BC: Expatriate Press. Includes a list of books on a number of different topics related to experiences of TCKs and their families.

Pollock, D. C., & Van Reken, R. E. (2009). Third culture kids: Growing up among worlds (Revised ed.). Boston, MA: Nicholas Brealey. Includes a list of publications and publishing houses dedicated to TCK issues.

Organizations:

There are many organizations that serve various TCKs; we highlight a few of the organizations that may be particularly useful for career counselors and their clients. Recognizing that TCKs are influenced by the organization that facilitated or sent their families abroad, organizations attending to the unique dynamics of missionary kid, military brat, foreign service dependent, or international business child may be particularly helpful. The sending organization may have their own resources dedicated to the care of the families sent abroad. In addition to activity of stand-alone websites, various organizations may have virtual community activity on social media sites such as Facebook. A few organizations with information applicable to career counselors follows.

Websites change frequently and resources associated with a website may change as well. Many websites are dedicated to specific populations, including smaller populations within the broader TCK community. For larger lists of websites, consult the list in the appendix of the Pollock & Van Reken (2009) or the Transitions Abroad website: http://www.transitions-abroad.com/listings/living/resources/expatriatewebsites.shtml#global

Barnabas: Geared toward MKs, Barnabas has transition seminars, retreats, and counseling and member care training for those who serve missions families. Visit Barnabas.org.

Families in Global Transition: A welcoming forum for international individuals, families, and those treating them. Has an annual multidisciplinary conference. Visit figt.org.

Foreign Services Youth Foundation: An organization serving children of diplomats or U.S. State Department employees living abroad. Their website has a number of resources, including information and connections to reentry programs. Visit fsyf.org.

Interaction International: An organization advocating for and serving TCKs. The organization has reentry seminars for TCKs, caregiver training, and educational planning for parents. Visit interactionintl.org.

Mu Kappa: A fraternal organization of MKs in college across North America. Visit Mukappa.org.

Operation We Are Here: With several websites dedicated to military brats, this website, dedicated to serving military families with a lengthy list of resources and links, offers military brat support. It includes links to other military brat support websites. Visit operationwearehere.com/MilitaryBrats.html.

Society for Intercultural Education Training and Research: An organization for professionals interested in learning how to address intercultural relations issues. Resources include conferences, webinars, and information such as an ethics code. Visit seitarusa.org.

TCKid: An online community for TCKs and other cross-cultural kids (CCKs) with many resources. Administration has changed, but resources continue to be present for the community. Visit tckidnow.com.

TCK International: A Christian website providing resources for TCKs and their parents to equip them for overseas service. Visit Tckinternational.com.

TCK World: A website dedicated to the legacy of Ruth Hill Useem, pioneer on TCK studies, and to the care of TCKs. Teleconference seminars, studies, professional links, and social connections are available. Visit tckworld.com.

TRADITIONAL ACTIVITY

Case Study

Jane is a 28-year-old who spent her childhood in Africa, the Middle East, and Europe due to having a diplomat as a father. She attended international schools, including an international boarding school for a few years in high school. She considers her education excellent. She received a prestigious international baccalaureate high school diploma and attended a reputable university in the United States where she performed well and achieved a 3.4 GPA in international relations.

Seeking career counseling, Jane is frustrated with her current employer in international business because the business seems to cash in on people's suffering. She also notes that she has changed jobs twice in the six years after graduating university because she was not satisfied with her previous work. She also notes that she her best friends are scattered around the world, and she does not have anyone in her area with whom she connects. She is considering returning to school for a master's degree; this is something she has considered doing since the middle of her BA.

Question 1: How might Jane's experience as a TCK impact her identity formation and relationship style? How would you conceptualize how these dynamics inform her career direction? Refer to concepts discussed in this chapter to discuss dynamics such as identity and belonging.

Question 2: How might career counseling approaches differ in responding to Jane's presenting career concerns? How might general counseling theoretical approaches contribute to career conceptualization with Jane?

SPIRITUAL ACTIVITY

David is the son of a Canadian mother and American father who met as missionaries. He grew up primarily in Latin America, specifically two main locations in South America, with two one-year home assignments (previously called furloughs) in North America. Now attending his senior year at university in the United States, David enjoys programming video games and computers, although he has a theology and linguistics double-major.

David had pictured himself serving as a Bible translator, like his parents were doing in Latin America, but finds himself less enthused about his major courses than he anticipated. Couple that with his enjoyment of programming and David is dealing with a crisis of direction that he says he has never faced before. Previously, he always had a clear sense of what he was supposed to be doing, but now the direction he has put so much energy into has no appeal. Studies about Biblical interpretation have caused him to question details of his faith, and he expresses some confusion about where he will end up. David says he continues to believe in God but that his belief "won't look like my parents.'"

Not having a person after whom he can model his career aspirations has been especially troublesome for David. Looking not only to his parents but also to others in the mission field as examples to pattern his life after, David feels without a rudder. He wants to pursue a career that incorporates the skills that have given him so much personal enjoyment, but he shares that he does not know anyone in the Christian world whose work in programming he can seek to emulate in both faith and professional work. David desires to know how to integrate his career interests with his faith.

Question 1: How might David be counseled regarding finding in his work an opportunity to walk with God, as Adam and Eve did in the garden prior to the fall? How does this relate to his enjoyment of the programming work that he may view as secular work as opposed to the mission work he had envisioned doing until recently?

Question 2: How might David's personal identity development impact his spirituality, and how does this relate to career counseling with David? How might national identity and belonging impact David's spiritual growth and career concerns?

REFERENCES

American Counseling Association (2014). ACA Code of Ethics. Alexandria, VA: Author

Bikos, L. H., Haney, D., Edwards, R. W., North, M. A., Quint, M., McLellan, J., & Ecker, D. L. (2014). Missionary kid career development: A consensual qualitative research investigation through a social cognitive lens. The Career Development Quarterly, 62, 156–174. doi: 10.1002/j.2161- 0045.2014.00077.x

Black, J.S., Morrison, A.J., & Gregersen, H.B. (1999). Global explorers: The next generation of leaders. New York, NY: Routledge.

Blustein, D. L., Devenis, L. E., & Kidney, B. A. (1989). Relationship between the identity formation process and career development. Journal of Counseling Psychology, 36(2), 196–202. Retrieved from http://0-psycnet.apa.org.library.regent.edu/journals/cou/36/2/196.pdf&productCode=pa

Bonebright, D. A. (2010). Adult third culture kids: HRD challenges and opportunities. Human Resource Development International, 13(3), 351–359. doi: 10.1080/13678861003746822

Brierley, P. W. (1997). Missionary attrition: The ReMAP research report. In W. D. Taylor (Ed.), Too valuable to lose: Exploring the causes and cures of missionary attrition (pp. 85–104). Pasadena, CA: William Carey Library.

Bushong, L. J. (2013). Belonging everywhere and nowhere: Insights into counseling the globally mobile. Indianapolis, IN: Mango Tree Intercultural Services.

Costanza , Klekowski, & Koppenfels. (2013). Counting the unaccountable: Overseas Americans. Retrieved from https://www.migrationpolicy.org/article/counting-uncountable-overseas-americans

Cottrell, A. B. (2002). Educational and occupational choices of American adult third culture kids. In M. G. Ender (Ed.), Military brats and other global nomads: Growing up in organization families (pp. 229–253). Westport, CT: Praeger.

Davis, P., Headley, K., Bazemore, T., Cervo, J., Sickinger, P., Windham, M., & Rehfuss, M. (2010). Evaluating Impact of Transition Seminars on Missionary Kids' Depression, Anxiety, Stress, and Well-being. Journal of Psychology and Theology, 38(3), 186–194. Retrieved from: http://0- search.ebscohost.com.library.regent. edu/login.aspx?direct=true&db=rfh&AN=ATLA0001805850&sit e=eds-live

Davis, P. S., Edwards, K. J., & Watson, T. S. (2015). Using process-experiential/emotion-focused therapy techniques for identity integration and resolution of grief among third culture kids. Journal of Humanistic Counseling, 54(3), 170–186. doi: 10.1002/johc.12010

Davis, P. S., Suarez, E. C., Crawford, N. A., & Rehfuss, M. C. (2013). Reentry program impact on missionary kid depression, anxiety, and stress: A three year study. Journal of Psychology & Theology, 41(2), 128–140. Retrieved from http://0-search.ebscohost.com.library.regent.edu/ login. aspx?direct=true&db=pbh&AN=88847591&site=ehost-live

Doran, R., Larsen, S., & Wolff, K. (2015). Different but similar: Social comparison of travel motives among tourists: Different but similar. International Journal of Tourism Research, 17(6), 555–563. doi:10.1002/jtr.2023

Erikson, E. H. (1959). Identity and the life cycle. New York, NY: Norton.

Erikson, E. H. (1964). Insight and responsibility. New York, NY: Norton.

Fail, H., Thompson, J., & Walker, G. (2004). Belonging, identity and third culture kids: Life histories of former international school students. Journal of Research in International Education, 3(3), 319–338. doi: 10.1177/1475240904047358

Finn Jordan, K.A. (2002). Identity formation and the adult third culture kid. In M.G. Ender (Ed.), Military brats and other global nomads: Growing up in organization families (pp 211–228). Westport, CT: Praeger.

Gaw, K. F. (2000). Reverse culture shock in students returning from overseas. International Journal of Intercultural Relations, 24, 83–104.

Gilbert, K. R. (2008). Loss and grief between and among cultures: The experience of third culture kids. Illness, Crisis & Loss, 16 (2), 93–109. doi: 10.2190/IL.16.2.a

Grimshaw, T., & Sears, C. (2008). 'Where am I from?' 'Where do I belong?' The negotiation and maintenance of identity by international school students. Journal of Research in International Education, 7 (3), 259–278. http://dx.doi.org/DOI: 10.1177/1475240908096483

Lam, H. & Semler, J. (2004). Are former "third culture kids" Ideal business expatriates? Career Development International, 9(2), 109–122. doi: 10.1108/13620430410526166

Linnemeyer, R. M., & Brown, C. (2010). Career maturity and foreclosure in student athletes, fine arts students, and general college students. Journal of Career Development, 37(3), 616–634. doi: 10.1177/0894845309357049

Lyttle, A. D., Barker, G. G., & Cornwell, T. L. (2011). Adept through adaptation: Third culture individuals' interpersonal sensitivity. International Journal of Intercultural Relations, 35(5), 686–694. doi:10.1016/j. ijintrel.2011.02.015

Marcia, J. E. (1966). Development and validation of ego identity status. Journal of Personality and Social Psychology, 3(5), 551–558. Retrieved from http://0-psycnet.apa.org.library.regent.edu/ journals/psp/3/5/551. pdf&productCode=pa

McDonald, K. E. (2010,). Transculturals: Identifying the invisible minority. Journal of Multicultural Counseling & Development, 38 (1), 39–20. Retrieved from http://0-eds.a.ebscohost.com. library.regent.edu/eds/pdfviewer/ pdfviewer?sid=a7b6f2c4-685b-46e6-b186- 26f9f8649f44%40sessionmgr4006&vid=3&hid=4111

Melles, E. A., & Frey, L. L. (2014). "Here, everybody moves": Using relational cultural therapy with adult third-culture kids. International Journal for the Advancement of Counselling, 36, 348–358. doi: 10.1007/ s10447-014-9211-6

Moore, A. M., & Barker, G. G. (2011). Confused or multicultural: Third culture individuals' cultural identity. International Journal of Intercultural Relations, 36(4), 553–562. doi: 10.1016/j.ijintrel.2011.11.002

Nobles, H. (2015). Models of the post-racial world? Rhetorics of race among U.S. military brats. Proceedings of the Third Conference on Veterans in Society. Texas Christian University. Retrieved from: https://vtechworks.lib.vt.edu/bitstream/handle/10919/72935/Nobles_Models_of_the_PostRacial_ World.pdf?sequence=1&isAllowed=y

Nobles, H. (forthcoming). Stories we didn't know to tell: A collective memoir from a lost tribe. Contact author for more details at heidi-nobles.squarespace.com.

Pollock, D. C., & Van Reken, R. E. (2009). Third culture kids: Growing up among worlds (Rev. ed.). Boston, MA: Nicholas Brealey Publishing.

Schaetti, B. F. (2000). Global nomad identity: Hypothesizing a developmental model (Doctoral dissertation). The Graduate College of The Union Institute.

Schaetti, B. F. (2006). A most excellent journey. In R. Pascoe (Ed.), Raising global nomads: Parenting abroad in an on-demand world (pp. 207–220). North Vancouver, BC: Expatriate.

Selmer, J., & Lam, H. (2004). "Third-culture kids" future business expatriates? Personnel Review, 33 (4), 430–445. doi: 10.1108/00483480410539506

Tarique, I. & Weisbord, E. (2013). Antecedents of dynamic cross-cultural competence in adult third culture kids (ATCKs). Journal of Global Mobility, 1(2), 139–160. doi: 10.1108/JGM-12-2012-0021

Useem, R.H., (1973). Third culture factors in educational change. In Cultural challenges in education: The influence of cultural factors in school learning (pp. 121–138). Lanham, MD: Lexington Books.

Useem, R. H. & Cottrell, A. B. (1999). TCKs four times more likely to earn bachelor's degrees (Originally posted 1993). TCK World. Retrieved from http://www.tckworld.com/useem/art2.html

Useem, R. H., & Downie, R. D. (1976, September-October). Third culture kids. The Journal of the National Education Association: Today's Education, 65 (3), 103–105.

Vondracek, F. W., Schulenberg, J., Skorikov, V., Gillespie, L. K., & Wahlheim, C. (1995). The relationship of identity status to career indecision during adolescence. Journal of Adolescence, 18(1), 17–29.

Walters, K. A. & Auton-Cuff, F. P. (2009). A story to tell: The identity development of women growing up as third culture kids. Mental Health, Religion & Culture, 12(7), 755–772. doi: 10.1080/13674670903029153

Wang, S. I. (2015). Third culture kids: The co-construction of third culture identity (Master's thesis, San Diego State University). Regent University Library Catalog. Retrieved from http://0- search.proquest.com.library.regent.edu/ pqdtglobal/docview/1712659820/5BF51E8145404C74PQ/1?accountid=13479

Washington, C. R., & Gadikar, A. J. (2016). Implications for professional counselors when working with adult third culture kids. American Counseling Association. Retrieved from https://www.counseling.org/knowledge-center/vistas/by-year2/vistas-2016/docs/default- source/vistas/article_19f9bf24f16116603abcacff0000bee5e7

Washington, C. R. & Gadiker A. J. (2013, October). Implications for professional counselors when working with adult third culture kids. Paper presented at the 2013 Association for Counselor Education and Supervision, Denver, CO, 1–12. Retrieved from http://www.counseling.org/ docs/default-source/vistas/article_19f9bf-24f16116603abcacff0000bee5e7.pdf?sfvrsn=6

Wrobbel, K. A. & Pleuddemann, J. E. (1990). Psychosocial development in adult missionary kids. Journal of Psychology and Theology, 18(4). 363–374. Retrieved from http://0- eds.b.ebscohost.com.library.regent.edu/ehost/pdfviewer/pdfviewer?vid=2&sid=39d4e3e2-ffc1- 4fd1-a281-a3e6e1bf1395%40sessionmgr102&hid=122

Credits

Career Counseling and Religious Vocations

Nicole G. Johnson, PhD, LPC

I therefore, the prisoner of the Lord, beseech you that ye walk worthy of the vocation wherewith ye are called.

Ephesians 4:1–3, King James Version

LEARNING OBJECTIVES

In this chapter, students will learn about

- Exploring the meaning of vocation as it relates to careers in ministry
- Fostering career development with people in religious vocations
- Special considerations for career development for people in religious vocations
- How careers in religious vocations impact life and family across the life span

LEARNING OUTCOMES

At the end of this chapter, students will be able to

- Foster a therapeutic relationship with people seeking a religious vocation
- Describe the unique work environment related to religious vocation
- Support career development across the lifespan of the client
- Help clients develop a career plan that addresses career challenges

CHAPTER HIGHLIGHTS

- Persons in religious vocations
- Call versus vocation versus job

- Special considerations in career counseling
- Assessment of spiritual and natural gifts
- List of religious vocations
- Current educational requirements for ministry
- Career dynamics
- Spirituality and the counseling process
- Religious vocation and the life span
- Religious vocations and the family
- Crossing Careers

CAREER COUNSELING FOR PERSON IN RELIGIOUS VOCATIONS

Career counseling for persons working in religious vocations requires the skilled career counselor to possess unique knowledge and awareness. Religious vocations can include careers as specific as the pastor of single local assembly in a city or as vast as a missionary overseeing multiple projects in a foreign country. Maintaining a client-centered perspective of vocation is important to foster the therapeutic relationship. When developing this relationship, the career counselor should be equipped to lead a guided conversation with their clients concerning vocation and the difference between a call and a job. A call can be considered a divinely inspired move toward a particular career path that is given by God, accepted, and followed. A job is considered a career path chosen without intentional divine inspiration. Understanding the factors that lead one to a religious vocation may clarify the process of defining the appropriate path to develop one's career. The counseling process should include the client's self-exploration of their spiritual beliefs around the religious vocation (Savickas, 1997). Assessments of natural and spiritual gifts and exploration of educational requirements and career dynamics will assist in the determination of which career path is appropriately matched to the clients' personality (Frame and Shehan, 2005) The strategies needed to serve this special population include matching client with religious, educational, and professional organizations, and ongoing development and counseling around the impact of serving in a religious vocation across the lifespan. Career counseling for persons working in religious vocations will effectively support the client through person-centered, culturally sensitive interventions that will bring honor to God and direction to the call to serve in religious vocations (Frame & Shehan, 2005).

THERAPEUTIC FOUNDATION WITHIN A FAITH FRAMEWORK

To foster a culturally sensitive, client-centered approach to counseling persons in this unique population, the career counselor will seek to examine how employment is viewed in the client's faith. Within this awareness, the framework for the counseling process is developed.

The counseling process will guide the client from exploration to determination of a career path within a religious or nonreligious vocation (Bloch, 2004). The counselor's role would include approaching career development viewing client faith as a part of the whole, not just an isolated part. Because the basis of traditional career counseling is rationally based, it does not address human complexities. Qualities such as consciousness, spirit, and purpose are not included in science; therefore, the whole person is not addressed but rather a part of the person (Savickas, 1997). Because these human qualities may drive the career choice with more direction in this population, the career counselor should employ techniques such as narrative approaches to vet career development. The effective career counselor will utilize the clients' spiritual views and understand that the client's beliefs about being called to a particular vocation may supersede their decision-making.

"I therefore, the prisoner of the Lord, beseech you that ye walk worthy of the vocation wherewith ye are called, With all lowliness and meekness, with longsuffering, forbearing one another in love; Endeavoring to keep the unity of the Spirit in the bond of peace" (Ephesians 4:1–3, KJV). This scripture written by the Apostle Paul to the church at Ephesus encourages believers to follow God's call to a vocation in an honorable manner. He highlights that being placed in a vocation is due to a calling, and that calling comes from the Lord Jesus Christ. Persons who are exploring or have chosen careers in religious vocations may do so because of a conviction that they have been called (O'Neil, 2010). Listening to their inner voice is how the manifestation of that call is realized because "our vocation marks the convergence of God's design and our discernment of the gift" (O'Neil, 2010, p.19). In career counseling, the influence of God's voice within career choice and development can begin with the exploration of a calling, vocation, and a job.

"A CALL" OR "A JOB": EXPLORING PERCEPTIONS ABOUT VOCATION

In career counseling, assessing the client's perceptions about a calling, a vocation, and a job can be used to guide the therapeutic process. Dik, Eldridge and Duffy (2009) explored perceptions of calling and vocation of clients so counselors can understand how their perceptions impact career development. Processing perceptions, however, can be challenging because of the overlapping dimension of a calling, a vocation and a job. The career counselor's initial task when working with people in religious vocations is to provide the client with definitional lines as a foundation of what is meant by someone's call, their vocation, and their job.

O'Neil (2010) utilizes the New Shorter Oxford English Dictionary to provide definitions in his exploration of career development in theological education. One common perspective in research is that calling and vocation are similar and spiritual by definition. This study shares that vocation is defined as "the fact or feeling of being called by God to undertake a specific (esp. religious) career function or occupation; a divine call to do certain work; a strong feeling of fitness or suitability for a particular career" (O'Neil, 2010, p. 18). Dik et al. (2009) provide a view which "conceptualized calling as consisting of three overlapping dimensions: (a) 'a transcendent summons, experienced as originating beyond the self'; (b) 'to approach a particular life role in a manner oriented toward demonstrating or deriving a sense of purpose or meaningfulness'; [and] (c) 'that holds other-oriented values and goals as primary sources of motivation'" (Dik et al., 2009, p. 6). In this view, vocation can be separated from calling only if the person doing the work does not attribute their motivation to the work as being prompted by an outside source that is usually spiritual.

Since the 16th century, various discourses have explored the concept of calling and the impact of cultural values (Eastern or Western) on the dynamics of calling and vocation (Dik et al., 2009). The use of these terms by clients has been thought to express the need to assign meaning to one's career. When meaning is ascribed to career choice, individuals are truer to their career choices (Dik et al., 2009). Research confirms that although some individuals consider the idea of calling irrelevant, the vast majority of career- seeking persons share its importance (Dik et al., 2009). Career counselors therefore cannot ignore this component of career development.

Calling or vocation can impact desired career outcomes and overall wellness (Dik et al., 2009). In their review of research of college students, Dik et al. (2009) share that students who identified their career as a calling also displayed a clear sense of their path resulting in being comfortable and secure in their career choices, and able to utilize adaptive coping skills. As revealed in a study conducted by Duffy and Sedlacek (2007), calling and vocation are linked to satisfaction in life or work along with staying committed to one's occupation. Having a clear sense of a call or vocation aids in the development of one's career, supporting the work of career counseling. The spiritual overshadowing with the dynamic of call and vocation cannot be ignored (Dik et al., 2009). Spiritual values and religiosity can influence career choices, development, and satisfaction. It can also be the foundation of meaning for the client.

The career calling can be motivated by meaningfulness and purpose (Dik et al., 2009). When exploring careers, the counselor should discuss what the client's career will mean to their life holistically. Dik et al. (2009) share a literature review highlighting the importance of purpose even above occupational prestige and income. Furthermore, people following a career call are more satisfied in their roles than those who do not consider their careers as a call. When work has meaning through missions and is pro-social or focuses on others, employees may be more productive, and be psychologically and physically preserved from burn out (Dik et al., 2009).

Unlike calling or vocations, client perceptions of a job may impact career development as well. O'Neil (2010, p. 18) defines the term job as "a piece of work." Dik et al. (2009) suggest that everyone does not relate to their careers through their beliefs about being called. While researchers believe values impact career choice, the individual who does not perceive a call or vocation can still be successful and dedicated to their career (Dik et al., 2009). People who refer to their career choice as a job will still exhibit some connectedness between their thoughts and their heart, passion, and job satisfaction (O'Neil, 2010).

Similar to person-environment matches, people can have person-job connections. Nillsen, Earl, Elizondo, Wadlington (2014) highlight the theory that some individuals will prosper in a particular career not because of a call but because their other abilities fit the job. The religious client's ideas of calling or vocation have seemingly developed into strength-based approaches where calling is denoted by internal skills as opposed to external influences (Nillsen et al., 2014). In this theory, people do not excel at a job because of a special motivation but because of inherent skills and characteristics to do so (Nillsen et al., 2014). This ideology has given rise to the development of vocational matching models and assessments. The dynamics of a job opposed to a call or vocation would suggest that the individual is in control of finding a career path instead of the path being inevitable because of life or spiritual influence and purpose.

People engage with a career counselor with the expectation of developing their career while clarifying their life mission. The career counselor should prepare to integrate in their discussion with their client how personality, calling, or vocation may impact their career choice. According to Nillsen et al. (2014), characteristics and personality are correlated to job satisfaction similarly to but not as strong as calling. In their study, they found that clergy reported higher work satisfaction than other occupations, including sales engineers, graphic designers, and teachers. (Nillsen et al., 2014). Further analysis suggests that clergy have higher professional satisfaction and longevity compared to other professions such as a teacher or sales engineer. The analysis further reveals that calling among clergy has a significant impact on the meaning of work.

In career counseling, initial exploration will include the clients' perceptions about career. Regardless of the stage of career development, client perceptions of calling, vocation, and job can influence how the counselor will address client needs. This foundation of a client's motivation toward a particular career can change and is open for continual inspection. Once the counselor and client have explored vocation and a religious vocation is the chosen career path, the client will need information about the field of religious vocation and employment possibilities. Since organizations that employ people in religious vocations do not employ a single or consistent model for vetting employees, the career counselor should conduct assessments to support matching abilities to available occupations (Booney & Park, 2012).

ASSESSMENT OF SPIRITUAL AND NATURAL GIFTS

In counseling this special population, the career counselor can utilize spiritual and natural assessments to explore areas of gifts that might be used in career development. Deng, Armstrong, and Rounds (2007) share the usefulness of the Holland's RIASEC model for career assessments because of the model's type classification system relation to most occupations in the United States. They further share that for clergy, results of this personality type indicator reveal which of the person's characteristics were similar to other clergypersons (Frame & Shehan, 2005). This assessment would help the client discover and decide what path in the religious vocation they will be best fit for. In addition, to explore if interests and values align with their profession, career counselors can utilize computerized career development tools. (Frame & Shehan, 2005). Two such tools are ChoicePlanner and SIGI Plus. When exploring other characteristics that are aligned with this vocation, the career counselor can discuss conflict management styles with the client. Beebe (2007) shares how exploring these styles may give insight into a prospective clergyperson's ability to manage the stress of the job. A clergyperson who possesses an avoidant conflict management style will exhibit more interpersonal conflict (Beebe, 2007). Career preparation may include exploring personality characteristics along with spiritual gifts.

An assessment of spiritual gifts can help the client outline which path they would like to complete in their quest to fulfill their call. Clayton (2014) shares the value of enneagrams, which delineate spiritual formation, personality types, and personality temperaments. Career counselors can use assessment results to determine job roles best suited for their clients entering ministerial vocations. According to Malony and Majovski (1986), psychological assessments for ministers are numerous and varying in characteristics. Schuller, Strommen, and Brekke (1980) developed the Ministerial Effectiveness Inventory (MEI) after reviewing characteristics utilized to determine who would be most successful as ministers in the United Methodist Church. This inventory can be used by the career counselor to explore personality traits that might be congruent with those needed in ministerial duties. This supports career matching as the career counselor works with their client to develop their career plan.

RELIGIOUS VOCATIONS: IDENTIFIED, DEFINED, AND UNDEFINED VOCATIONS

There are many fields of work a person in a religious vocation can enter. The career counselor can engage clients in a creative process of exploring the development of their career. To start, one might choose a specific religious vocation like a pastor, youth pastor, worship leader, children's church leader, teacher, missionary, doctor, or chaplain.

When conducting career counseling with a client, open-ended questions may be utilized to ascertain the heart of the client, their personal goals, and which aspect of ministry they would like to work in. A client may not be aware of the numerous employment sites, such as prisons, schools and hospitals, where clergy may be accepted. According to Wake Forest University (2016) a little over one third of their divinity school graduates enter congregational ministry, a little lower than one third work in various fields, and the middle third work in ministry, counseling, schools, and nonprofits. For the client, options may even include the development of a small business, which may not follow the traditional career path of persons working in religious vocations or ministry.

Educational Requirements for Religious Vocations

People in religious vocations should explore the educational requirements of being in the field during career development and counseling. According to the Educational Standards of the Association of Theological School Commission on Accrediting (2015), degrees that are recommended for persons who are seeking to work in ministerial leadership include master's degrees in divinity, religious education, arts, and sacred music or doctoral degrees in ministry, educational ministry, or musical arts. Furthermore, the Association of Theological Schools has established guidelines concerning educational experience that is deemed necessary for the prospective minister. These experiences include a residency in which the prospective minister will have an opportunity to be mentored and guided by persons already experienced in the field. The residency experience also should be discussed with the career counselor, who may be able to help the client see this opportunity as a way of experiencing different aspects of working in ministry.

To support the career development process, the career counselor needs to be equipped with this knowledge in order support with the client's planning of their education. When working with this specialized population, the career counselor should also work with the client to seek out their specific denominational requirements so after they are complete their degree, they will be accepted into the career path they are feeling called to. The educational experience should equip the person entering in the religious vocation.

Working in the Field

In career counseling with persons in religious vocations, the client and counselor, within the context of the counseling sessions, will set goals to complete the mission of the one called to the field. Jesus shared "I must work the works of him that sent me, while it is day: the night cometh, when no man can work" (John 9:4, KJV) to express the importance of completing the work while opportunities are present. Working in the field of ministry carries unique dynamics that may not be present in other vocations, and counselors-in-training should be aware of this. Ministry work includes job stressors such as feelings of reduced effectiveness because of emotional exhaustion that may be experienced (Booney and Park, 2012). When counselors utilize knowledge about the field in assessment with prospective candidates for ministry careers, treatment planning can support the development of goals which can highlight important factors that may impede career success (Booney and Park, 2012).

Salary Analysis: Is This Enough?

"And said unto them; Go ye also into the vineyard and whatsoever is right I will give you. And they went their way" (Matthew 20:4, KJV). Career counseling includes addressing concerns about income and financial stability within a career. For persons in religious vocations, the area of salary may be taboo because of perceptions of being called to work for the Lord. In the Gospel, according to Matthew, Jesus shared a parable about men called into labor and promised a salary that is appropriate. In the career counseling process, salary expectations and goals should be explored.

Despite salary not generally being the main focus for most entering this field, career counseling with people in ministry should explore the topic of salary (Bikos, Dykhouse, Boutin, Gowen, & Rodney, 2013). Bikos et al. express the impact of being a missionary and how it sometimes impacts financial stability. Since missionaries may travel around the world to remote, impoverished parts of cities, they can experience financial strain (Bikos et al.). This strain can be coupled by constant moving, and the ability to develop financial stability through having a home, car, and other property may not occur. If the client is considering engaging in missionary work, and may do so internationally, the career counselor should support explorations and planning around what this might entail.

Persons in religious vocations are compensated according to the income of the host religious organization. According to Briggs (2016), clergy are not as financially well-compensated as are doctors, lawyers, or financial managers. While respecting the power of being called to the field of ministry, career counselors should include financial planning as a part of career development because it can impact career longevity. Brigg's (2016) 20-year review confirmed that non-Catholic clergy members earned at least one third less than other Americans with college degrees except those in the top third of professional money makers. While the salary gap did decrease to 26% by 2002, there still remains a major earning gap between clerical vocations and secular vocations even though people in both vocations may possess college degrees. These improvements, however, do not benefit everyone; clergypersons serving in smaller urban or rural communities receive less than those in larger cities or at megaministries. Career counselors will need to explore with their client the misperceptions of clergy salaries. In addition, other benefits such as housing provisions have also decreased (Briggs, 2016).

Briggs (2016) still offers hope for this profession because the salary gap has decreased. In the process of improvements, work hours have decreased from 52 hours, which was common in the 1970s, to around 41 hours per week today. These dynamics have led to the exploration of religious vocations outside of the church and into mainstream institutions such as hospitals, schools, and other large organizations (Briggs, 2016). While transitions to nonreligious vocations may yield an increase in salary, clients may struggle with the psychological guilt of disappointing God and people (Briggs, 2016). These concerns may be explored in career counseling as clients make career transitions. Career counselors should note that while six out of 10 clergypersons report happiness and satisfaction in their work, financially they may lose about 15% in salary (Briggs, 2016). Higher satisfaction among clergy is greater than other people, but is this enough? The career counselor should explore all concerns with their clients as the perceived fluidity of careers may be a difficult transition for the client. Job satisfaction may not be enough for the transitioning career person.

STRATEGIES IN CAREER DEVELOPMENT

Career development with persons in ministry will require strategies which may not apply to other professions. The deep connection with a spiritual call should be explored as this may have great impact (Dik et al., 2009). During the initial stages of counseling, clients' perspectives of calling can build the foundation of clinical work.

Integration of Spirituality in the Counseling Process

The field of career counseling has continually explored the impact of spirituality on career development (Dik et al., 2009). The exploration of calling and vocation is not a new concept and is manifested in the views of many cultures. Nillsen et al. (2014) found a significant correlation between the concept of calling, job satisfaction, and the likelihood of a person staying on a job. In this study, persons in religious vocations (clergy) aligned with more traditional and spiritual views of calling in comparison to teachers, for example, who were more aligned with sales engineers who did not strongly express being called to their careers (Nillsen et al., 2014).

John G. Cullen (2011) shared that client-centered career counseling and development should include values of the client. He further recommends that clients be encouraged to explore vocation because this can shift their career paradigm Cullen explores the impact of spirituality and religion on the historical evolution of career development. During the medieval period, calling held religious connotations. Protestant views leans more toward productivity while Catholic views leaned more toward social responsibility as related to a spiritual call (Cullen, 2011). Career counseling has continually swayed between theories and interventions that have either ignored the importance of spirituality in career development or focused on it exclusively. As Western culture shifts to an increased interest in spirituality, so has the interest in concepts of vocation (Cullen, 2011) and the techniques of career counseling.

Modern techniques in career development and research are designed to address not only productivity but satisfaction and longevity in a field of work that is closely correlated to the idea of vocation (Cullen, 2011). Mitroff and Denton (1999) highlight that when managers' employees consider their own beliefs along with their personalities, they have more productive workers.

As a career counselor, supporting the individual in looking for a job may be an easier task than defining a call. Career success carries immediate outcomes such as completing tasks, while exploring a vocation suggests lifelong development, the outcome of which may be more psychosocial than tangible (Cullen, 2011). Career counselors should also remember that while some may hold values related to their faith tradition, expressing beliefs may not appear profitable in the workplace. Cullen shared that in our post-secular world where people are nonreligious, faith is not necessarily considered a key component of progress in a career. Because vocation is perceived as a religious concept, it is not remembered during occupational exploration.

For the client in religious vocations, the career counselor will foster self-exploration to build self-awareness, ethics, and values around what career path will be taken (Cullen, 2011). In the career counseling process, administration of career assessment and subsequent discussions about assessment scores will help the client gain clarity about which careers match their personality type. As the call becomes clearer, the career counselor can help the client by highlighting the value of the work as opposed to the salary, prestige, or perks of a career in religious vocation, which may be vastly different from other vocations. Cullen (2011) suggests that the career counselor explore why a client has decided on a particular career path. As the counseling process continues, the career counselor can connect clients with organizations that can support them throughout their career.

Professional Organizations and Ethics for Religious Vocations

There are numerous professional organizations that guide religious professionals on a local, national, and international level. Each organization can provide the person in ministry with support and guidance for education and professional development. In career counseling, the client should be introduced to these organizations for exploration in their benefits. The Association of Theological Schools, the American Association of Christian Counselors, and the American Association of Pastoral Counselors are examples of organizations that can support people working in a religious vocation.

Association of Theological Schools. This organization oversees the educational process for clergy with Christian and Jewish faiths in the United States and Canada (Association of Theological Schools in the United States and Canada, The Commission on Accrediting, 2016). The mission of the organization is "to promote the improvement and enhancement of theological schools to the benefit of communities of faith and the broader public" (Association of Theological Schools, 2016). The career counselor should be aware of this organization when the client needs information about where to explore educational degrees according to career interest. Most major schools in the United States, including Harvard University, are accredited by this body.

American Association of Christian Counselors and American Association of Pastoral Counselors. Christian organizations such as the American Association of Christian Counselors and the American Association of Pastoral Counselors provide support and ethical guidance to those who enter the ministry and fulfil their call as counselors. The career counselor should provide the client information about these national organizations if they apply. In addition, by sharing alternative options for ministry opportunities, the client may not feel that he/she is boxed into a particular role in ministry.

Impact of Careers in Religious Vocations Across the Life Span

For persons who work in religious vocations, unique considerations should be given concerning career impact across the life span. First, the denominational standards of religious careers may impact how long personnel may remain in a position. Frame and Shehan (2005) highlight the number of job tasks for which ministers may be responsible. In addition, there are blurred work boundaries, such as expectations or hours, that may place clergy at a higher risk for stress. In the United Methodist Church, for example, clergy may be often relocated through appointments by the church leadership (Frame & Shehan, 2005). This possibility should be fully disclosed to the potential clergyperson. In the Frame and Shehan (2005) study of women clergy in the United Methodist Church, participants reported an average of 11-plus years in service, an average 53 hours worked each week with a mean salary of $29,668; and pastoring local church ministries of about 500 members. The women in this study earned master's degrees in divinity in order to obtain their position. This highlights the fact that despite the high standards of education and service, religious vocations do not provide large monetary compensation.

Since religious vocations emphasize service, persons entering these careers may experience high levels of stress. Frame and Shehan (2005) share how not setting boundaries and exercising poor time management skills can be barriers that impact stress. In their study, 25% of the participants agreed that balancing time between work, family, free personal time, and spiritual development along with cultivating a professional support system are areas that weigh on their psychological well-being. Developing coping strategies are important for the worker to maintain mental wellness across the career; thus, career counselors should foster plans to address possible stress-reducing strategies that may help.

Impact of careers in religious vocations and the family. People working in religious vocations have a unique lifestyle. Their work is often driven by social needs; therefore, stability can be questionable (Frame & Shehan, 2005). Depending on appointment of some organizations, families may need to be very mobile and not live in one place for an extended period of time. Career counselors should prompt consideration of this in career development. A study of women pastors found that they believed their gender is an asset to their role because it leans them to nurture and be sensitive, but also that gender can cause conflict and internal feelings of guilt around balancing time between church, spouse, and children (Frame & Shehan, 2005).

Impact of ministry on children. In counseling people in ministry, counselors should consider the impact of ministry on children. For missionary kids (MK), living with parents who are missionaries presents specific challenges of which a career counselor should be aware (Bikos et al., 2013). As the adult client is exploring ministry as a vocation, counselors should explore the impact living in a country or culture different from where they were raised might impact career choice and the life of their families (Bikos et al., 2013). The stress experience of children of ministers may include adjustments to new locations, cultures, and overall stability (Bikos et al., 2013). The career counselor should share this information with the client as part of their decision making process.

In their study of MKs ranging in age from 18 to 25 years, Bikos et al. (2013) highlighted some key factors MKs noted in their experience that could be utilized in the career development process. According to MKs, a high level of support was received from extended family, friends, and the church community. In career development, the counselor may help the client develop a support system. Support systems may provide emotional, financial, and transitional help when the ministry family is moving. According to this study, the MKs shared that this help was provided when moving from location to location, and by providing a place to stay during holidays (Bikos et al., 2013). When parents were in financial challenges, this group also provided some financial support to help the family. The benefit of a strong support system for ministry families is a key component of career decision-making and, subsequently, career development. The career counselor can support the client in their exploration of how they will prepare for work in ministry to supplement family needs when they are at work.

Ministry and divorce. When a clergyperson divorces, the change in relational status is impactful. Career counselors may be charged with supporting a divorced clergyperson whose career can be hindered by a change in marital status. According to Hutchison and Hutchison (1979), divorce was positively correlated to a higher number of job changes. This may be due to the perceived or actual impact of the clergyperson's marital dissatisfaction on their congregation, which may be resistant toward that person remaining. Career development with a person after a divorce may include seeking another work location, a different religious vocation, or a nonreligious vocation (Hutchison & Hutchison, 1979).

Changing Over from Careers in Religious Vocations to Alternative Careers

Persons in ministry may choose to change from religious to nonreligious vocations for many reasons. According to Briggs (2016), clergy who move to nonreligious vocations may experience an increase in salary. Furthermore, the person in ministry may choose to leave working at a specific church to explore employment at a larger company or work in the nonprofit sector (Briggs, 2016). Career counselors should develop and expand a resource base of employment opportunities for persons in ministry who may choose to change careers or work locations. In the early stages of educational and career development, the counselor and client should make career plans and forecasts, as this unique career does not necessarily have a retirement age. Special considerations should be utilized when counseling the person in ministry.

Special Considerations for Career Development in Religious Vocations

Frame and Shehan (2005) suggest that career counselors take a more deliberate approach when working with people who may want a religious vocation. Frame and Shehan suggest making connections at local universities which offer theological education within denominational organizations. They also share that because of the unique nature of religious vocations, having counselors with specific knowledge about religious vocations can be helpful for those considering this career. The utilization of career assessments such as the Myers-Brigg Type Indicator and the Self-Directed Search as well as specific religious assessments such as the Enneagram or Spiritual Gift Assessment may help identify personality traits and help when attempting to match the potential employee to a specific religious vocational path (Frame & Shehan, 2005). These assessment tools can also be used to provide insight into clients' giftedness, the unique talents and personality traits which could be congruent with tasks and duties in ministry.

When a client is considering a religious vocation, the career counselor can share information to prepare the client for the demands of this career, whether anticipated or unexpected (Frame & Shehan, 2005). Career counseling sessions also can be utilized to brainstorm with the potential employee to develop coping strategies. For women, it is suggested that career counseling can help to address concerns through the development of strategies to create and maintain personal boundaries, stress management, self-care, life-balance, and time management.

CONCLUSION

Career counseling with persons thinking about a religious vocation or ministry requires special skills, knowledge, and awareness. With the vast number of available assessment tools, educational requirements, and varying desired characteristics that may differ depending on the organization, working with this unique population has challenges (Booney & Park, 2012). The foundation of the career development for this population will explore the difference between call, vocation, and job. The client's perception may impact their career choice and future career satisfaction. The influence of spirituality is an important component of career counseling with persons exploring religious vocations; therefore, career exploration can be effective once a solid clinical foundation is established.

In the exploration process, the skilled career counselor will conduct assessment to highlight the client's natural and spiritual gifts. Results of assessment tools will be used to match the client's interests, personality, and call to occupations. After identification of possible career paths is discovered, the career counselor should review the educational requirements for the ministry area the client desires to be employed in. Since ministry careers are unique, the educational expectations may include theological school as opposed to secular universities. In addition, career development should include discussions about work environment and possible work salary. Through assessment and the exploration of work environment and salary, a viable career path can be developed, as the client is now informed about their direction and the requirements to reach their goals. The career development process will include integration of spirituality, as this drives career choice and how people feel about their jobs.

For the counseling process to be effective, the counselor should remind the client about how ministry occupations may differ other professions in role, stress, and work longevity. Specific professional organization skills and ethics should be reviewed. Further movement into the field of ministry should include the client gaining an awareness of how their unique career choice will impact their family, children, and marriage. For the person working in ministry, their family may have to adjust to moving to different locations, splitting time between their children or spouse and their work, or the stress of working for an employer that may not be able to provide high salaries. A career counselor who supports their client through evaluating their thoughts about these dynamics may help them enter the field of ministry with a greater understanding of the possible barriers they might face. If the client is in counseling because they are at an impasse and exploring leaving ministry as a career, the counselor should be equipped to discuss feelings of remorse, regret, and guilt. The counseling of persons seeking religious vocations is unique work, and with proper training, the career counselor can effectively support the exploration and development of their clients.

KEY TERMS

Call: consists of three overlapping dimensions: (a) "a transcendent summons, experienced as originating beyond the self," (b) "to approach a particular life role in a manner oriented toward demonstrating or deriving a sense of purpose or meaningfulness," and (c) "that holds other-oriented values and goals as primary sources of motivation" (Dik et al., 2009)

Clergyperson: a member of the clergy (M-V, 2017)

Job: a piece of work (M-V, 2017)

Minister: a clergyman or clergywoman, especially of a Protestant communion (M-V, 2017)

Ministry: the office, duties, or functions of a minister (M-V, 2017)

Missionary: a person undertaking a mission, especially a religious mission (M-V, 2017)

Pastor: a clergyman serving a local church or parish (M-V, 2017)

Religious vocation: the work in which a person is employed which is relating to or manifesting faithful devotion to an acknowledged ultimate reality or deity (M-V, 2017)

Spirituality: sensitivity or attachment to religious values (M-V, 2017)

Vocation: "the fact or feeling of being called by God to undertake a specific (esp. religious) career function or occupation; a divine call to do certain work; a strong feeling of fitness or suitability for a particular career" (Dik et al., 2009)

REFLECTION AND DISCUSSION

1. How can career assessments be utilized for this population?
2. Explain how spirituality impacts decision-making in career development with persons in religious vocations?
3. Explain how work may impact life and family for persons in religious vocations?
4. What are the sacrifices a person in ministry might have to make?
5. What psychological coping skills could best prepare someone considering this field?

ADDITIONAL READINGS, RESOURCES, AND WEBSITES

- American Association of Christian Counselors; www.aacc.org
- American Association of Pastoral Counselors; www.aapc.org
- Wake Forest University School of Divinity; wfu.edu
- Association of Theological Schools; www.ats.org

TRADITIONAL ACTIVITY

Envision

1. When reading this story, students should consider the need for the career counselor to encourage ongoing career development for persons in religious vocations.

2. When reading this story, students should consider what possible interventions can be utilized to help foster transition from a religious vocation to a secular vocation.

Case Study/Intervention

Joe, now 60 years old, has been the pastor of the largest church in his city for over 30 years. He was a key asset for the large growth experienced in the church, which now has over 10,000 members. Joe provided mentoring for young men and pastoral counseling, and was the director of the church's nonprofit organization, which provides job employment services. After his recent divorce, his church voted to remove Joe from his role as pastor because of a bylaw that states that pastors who divorce cannot maintain their position. Joe comes to you for career counseling because he still needs to work to support his children, who are 15 and 17 and live with their mother, to whom he is required to pay child support. Joe has a master's degree in divinity and pastoral counseling. Prior to his entering the ministry, Joe worked in business finance for 10 years.

Respond

1. What options for career transition can you offer Joe?

2. What will be the benefits of Joe accepting a secular job or another ministry position?

SPIRITUAL ACTIVITY

Envision

1. When reading this story, the student should envision how to support someone transitioning from a secular career to ministry.

2. When reading this story, the student should envision how education can promote career development.

"As Jesus was walking beside the Sea of Galilee, He saw two brothers, Simon called Peter and his brother Andrew. They were casting a net into the sea, for they were fishermen. 'Come, follow Me,' Jesus said, 'and I will make you fishers of men.' And at once they left their nets and followed Him" (Matthew 4:18–19, KJV).

When Jesus called his disciples Peter and Andrew from their secular business of fishing, He told them to come, and they came. After coming and following the call, they were trained before being sent out.

1. If you were with Peter and Andrew, what would you tell them about their career change leaving the fishing job and following Christ?
2. Share how Jesus used education to prepare his disciples for the work he called them to.

REFERENCES

Association of Theological Schools in the United States and Canada The Commission on Accrediting. Retrieved from http://www.ats.edu/.

Beebe, R. S. (2007). Predicting burnout, conflict management style, and turnover among clergy. Journal of Career Assessment, 15(2), 257–275. doi:10.1177/1069072706298157

Bikos, L. H., Dykhouse, E. C., Boutin, S. K., Gowen, M. J., & Rodney, H. E. (2013). Practice and research in career counseling and Development—2012. The Career Development Quarterly, 61(4), 290–329. doi:10.1002/j.2161-0045.2013.00058.x

Bloch, D. P. (2004). Spirituality, Complexity, and Career Counseling. Professional School Counseling, 7(5), 343–350.

Booney, Lewis A, Park, Hae Seong (2012). Appraisal of applicants for ministry careers. Mental Health, Religion & Culture, 15(7), 721–739.

Briggs, D. (2016). Long-term study shows wage gap for clergy is being narrowed. Christian Century, 133(19), 16–17.

Clayton, T. L. (2014). Clergy spiritual assessment using the enneagram (Order No. 3624532). Available from ProQuest Central; ProQuest Dissertations & Theses Global. (1553234188). Retrieved from http://eres.regent.edu:2048/login?url=https://search-proquest- com.ezproxy.regent.edu/docview/1553234188?accountid=13479

Cullen, John G. (2011). Differentiating between Vocations and Careers. National University of Ireland. Retrieved from https://ssrn.com/abstract=1943566 or http://dx.doi.org/10.2139/ssrn.1943566

Deng, Chi-Ping, Patrick Ian Armstrong, James Rounds (2007). The fit of Holland's RIASEC model to US occupations. Journal of Vocational Behavior, 71(1), 1–22. Retrieved from https://doi.org/10.1016/j.jvb.2007.04.002.

Dik, B. J., Eldridge, B. M., & Duffy, R. D. (2009). Calling and Vocation in Career Counseling: Recommendations for Promoting Meaningful Work. Professional Psychology: Research & Practice, 40(6), 625–632. doi:10.1037/a0015547

Duffy, R. D., & Sedlacek, W. E. (2007). The presence of and search for a calling: Connections to career development. Journal of Vocational Behavior, 70, 590–601.

Frame, M. W., & Shehan, C. L. (2005). The record between work and well-being in clergywomen: implication for career counseling. Journal Of Employment Counseling, 42(1), 10–19.

Hutchison, I. W., & Hutchison, K. R. (1979). The Impact of Divorce Upon Clergy Career Mobility. Journal of Marriage & Family, 41(4), 847.

Malony, H., & Majovski, L. (1986). The Role of Psychological Assessment in Predicting Ministerial Effectiveness. Review of Religious Research, 28(1), 29–39. doi:10.2307/3511335

Merriam-Webster. (n.d.) Merriam-Webster.com. Retrieved from https://www.merriamwebster.com/dictionary/

Mitroff, I. I., & Denton, E. A. (1999). A Study of Spirituality in the Workplace. Sloan Management Review, 40(4), 83–92.

Nillsen, C., J.K., Elizondo, E, F. & Wadlington, P.L. (2014). Do Birds of a Feather Flock Together? An Examination of Calling, Congruence, Job Design and Personality as Predictors of Job Satisfaction and Tenure. Journal of Beliefs & Values: Studies In Religion & Education 35(1), 10–24.

O'Neil, K. (2010). Job, Career, Profession, Vocation: What Exactly Am I Doing in Theological Education?. Seminary Journal, 16(3), 18–23.

Savickas, M.L. (1997). The spirit in career counseling: Fostering self-completion through work. In D. P. Bloch & L.J. Richmonds (Eds.), Connections between spirit and work in career development: New approaches and practical perspectives (pp. 3–35). Palo Alto, CA: Davies-Black.

Schuller, D.S., Strommen, M.P. and Brekke, M.L.(1980) Ministry in America. San Francisco: Harper and Row.

The Association of Theological Schools: The commission on accrediting. (2015). Standards of accreditation. Retrieved from http://www.ats.edu/uploads/accrediting/documents/standards-of-accreditation.pdf

Appendix

The ASCA Mindsets & Behaviors for Student Success: K-12 College- and Career-Readiness Standards for Every Student

Each of the following standards can be applied to the academic, career and social/emotional domains.

Category 1: Mindset Standards
School counselors encourage the following mindsets for all students.

M 1. Belief in development of whole self, including a healthy balance of mental, social/emotional and physical well-being

M 2. Self-confidence in ability to succeed

M 3. Sense of belonging in the school environment

M 4. Understanding that postsecondary education and life-long learning are necessary for long-term career success

M 5. Belief in using abilities to their fullest to achieve high-quality results and outcomes

M 6. Positive attitude toward work and learning

Category 2: Behavior Standards
Students will demonstrate the following standards through classroom lessons, activities and/or individual/small-group counseling.

Learning Strategies		Self-Management Skills		Social Skills	
B-LS 1.	Demonstrate critical-thinking skills to make informed decisions	**B-SMS 1.**	Demonstrate ability to assume responsibility	**B-SS 1.**	Use effective oral and written communication skills and listening skills
B-LS 2.	Demonstrate creativity	**B-SMS 2.**	Demonstrate self-discipline and self-control	**B-SS 2.**	Create positive and supportive relationships with other students
B-LS 3.	Use time-management, organizational and study skills	**B-SMS 3.**	Demonstrate ability to work independently	**B-SS 3.**	Create relationships with adults that support success
B-LS 4.	Apply self-motivation and self-direction to learning	**B-SMS 4.**	Demonstrate ability to delay immediate gratification for long-term rewards	**B-SS 4.**	Demonstrate empathy
B-LS 5.	Apply media and technology skills	**B-SMS 5.**	Demonstrate perseverance to achieve long- and short-term goals	**B-SS 5.**	Demonstrate ethical decision-making and social responsibility
B-LS 6.	Set high standards of quality	**B-SMS 6.**	Demonstrate ability to overcome barriers to learning	**B-SS 6.**	Use effective collaboration and cooperation skills
B-LS 7.	Identify long- and short-term academic, career and social/emotional goals	**B-SMS 7.**	Demonstrate effective coping skills when faced with a problem	**B-SS 7.**	Use leadership and teamwork skills to work effectively in diverse teams
B-LS 8.	Actively engage in challenging coursework	**B-SMS 8.**	Demonstrate the ability to balance school, home and community activities	**B-SS 8.**	Demonstrate advocacy skills and ability to assert self, when necessary
B-LS 9.	Gather evidence and consider multiple perspectives to make informed decisions	**B-SMS 9.**	Demonstrate personal safety skills	**B-SS 9.**	Demonstrate social maturity and behaviors appropriate to the situation and environment
B-LS 10.	Participate in enrichment and extracurricular activities	**B-SMS 10.**	Demonstrate ability to manage transitions and ability to adapt to changing situations and responsibilities		

CPSIA information can be obtained
at www.ICGtesting.com
Printed in the USA
LVHW062203280519
619375LV00004B/324/P

9 781516 510474